SHERIDAN'S

D0254484

# RICHARD BRINSLEY SHERIDAN

Christened, Dublin, 4 November 1751
Died, London, 7 July 1816

# SHERIDAN'S PLAYS

*Edited with an introduction by*

CECIL PRICE

OXFORD UNIVERSITY PRESS

LONDON   OXFORD   NEW YORK

1975

*Oxford University Press*

LONDON  OXFORD  NEW YORK

GLASGOW  TORONTO  MELBOURNE  WELLINGTON

CAPE TOWN  IBADAN  NAIROBI  DAR ES SALAAM  LUSAKA  ADDIS ABABA

DELHI  BOMBAY  CALCUTTA  MADRAS  KARACHI  LAHORE  DACCA

KUALA LUMPUR  SINGAPORE  HONG KONG  TOKYO


Hardbound edition   ISBN 0 19 254169 2
Paperback edition   ISBN 0 19 281158 4


Introduction and Notes
© Oxford University Press 1975


First published as an Oxford University Press paperback,
by Oxford University Press, London, 1975

Printed in Great Britain by
Fletcher & Son Ltd, Norwich

# CONTENTS

# FOREWORD

THE texts printed here are based on those given in my edition, *The Dramatic Works of Richard Brinsley Sheridan* (1973), published in two volumes by the Clarendon Press as part of the Oxford English Texts series. Readers who seek a critical apparatus or further information on the composition, reception, and printing of the plays, are referred to that work.

CECIL PRICE

# INTRODUCTION

LIKE a number of other eighteenth-century dramatists, Sheridan was born in Ireland but made his name in England. His father, Thomas Sheridan, was an actor, teacher of elocution, and author of a popular farce. His mother, Frances Sheridan, was a successful novelist and dramatist.

When he was eight, Richard Brinsley Sheridan was brought to England and he never afterwards returned to Ireland. He spent five undistinguished years at Harrow School, and passed through a moody adolescent phase before he joined his father in London. In September 1770 when he was almost twenty, he moved with him to Bath, the fashionable centre of the day. Many years later he claimed to have 'danced with all the women' there, written 'sonnets and verses in praise of some, satires and lampoons upon others', and become 'the established wit and fashion of the place'. The gloss of recollection may give us an exaggerated idea of his position at Bath, but he certainly enjoyed his twenty-two months there developing his satirical talents. To posterity the most interesting of his ephemeral verses is 'Hymen and Hirco', a mordant comment on the broken engagement between the sixteen-year-old singer, Elizabeth Linley, and an elderly Wiltshire squire, Walter Long. The truth about the situation is not completely known but Long was described as being lustful and importunate, ready to take advantage of the girl's innocence. The wider world became interested in the subject when Samuel Foote made it the theme of his satirical play, *The Maid of Bath*. Eventually Long handed over three thousand pounds to Elizabeth's father for breach of promise, and part of it became her dowry when she married Sheridan on 13 April 1773.

Before this date, however, she had been involved in other adventures that delighted the scandalmongers. In the spring of 1772 she had been so annoyed by advances made to her by one Thomas Mathews that she had decided to leave home and enter a French convent. Sheridan accompanied her, in romantic style, as her cavalier, and they reached Lille before her father caught up with them and persuaded her to return home. Sheridan came back to England to fight two duels with Mathews, and in the second of them he was thought to be so badly wounded as to be in danger of dying. He recovered and was despatched by his exasperated father to Waltham Abbey to read for the bar with a tutor.

This plan came to an abrupt end when Sheridan defied his father and married. Since he thought it undignified for his wife to continue her career as a professional singer, he set about trying to earn a living by writing.

On 17 November 1774 he told his father-in-law that there would be a comedy of his in rehearsal at Covent Garden within a few days, and added proudly that he had not written a line of it two months before, 'except a scene or two, which I believe you have seen in an odd act of a little farce'. He also mentioned that he had 'done it at Mr. Harris's (the manager's) own request, it is now complete in his hands'. Thomas Harris helped Sheridan to cut it down, but when it was first presented (17 January 1775), it was still too long and was not well received. Criticism was directed chiefly at the bad performances of John Lee as Sir Lucius and Shuter as Sir Anthony, but the play was also thought to be too coarse as well as too wordy. Harris still had faith in it and strongly encouraged Sheridan to set about a revision. In ten days the plot was tightened and the language and characterization were made less extravagant. The alterations were so successful that the *Critical Review* exaggerated only a little when it called it a new play. Sheridan himself is said to have remarked, 'I have now got the last, and it shall be my fault if I don't make the shoe to fit next time'.

The remark is a characteristic one, and in a sense it is amplified by a sentence in the preface to the first edition of *The Rivals*: 'For my own part I see no reason why the Author of a Play should not regard a First Night's Audience, as a candid and judicious Friend attending in behalf of the Public, at his last Rehearsal.' This was to become his normal outlook, though we have to wait for over twenty years before we find him giving another of his plays (*Pizarro*) such a drastic revision.

It is worth looking at some of the changes in detail because they indicate how necessary it is for a dramatist to have critical as well as creative powers, and to be able to perceive either in rehearsal or at a first night the means of improving his play. Sheridan now makes Sir Lucius and Sir Anthony appear more attractive characters by altering the phrasing as well as the positioning of some of their speeches. No one was antagonized when Acres called Sir Lucius 'Old Bulls and Blunders' for self-contradiction was a commonly accepted trait of the stage Irishman, but Sir Lucius also seemed a bullying fortune hunter. For example, he cries, 'My pretensions are to the Person and Fortune of Miss Lydia Languish and I'll cut any man's throat that stands in my way.' These lines were in the last act and may well have affected the audience when a verdict on the comedy had to be given on the first night. So, in his revision, Sheridan eliminated passages like this one and took care to make complimentary allusions to Sir Lucius in the curtain lines of Acts I and II, where they would have considerable effect. Sir Lucius remains a peremptory man of honour, but his manners are more courteous and some of the old bluster and hectoring are gone. Besides his humour is attractively Irish when he says, 'I am so poor that I can't afford to do a dirty action. If I did not want money I'd steal your mistress and her fortune with a great deal of pleasure.'

The model for Sir Anthony seems to be that side of Sir Sampson (in Congreve's *Love for Love*) that is represented in the complaint, 'What, I warrant my Son thought nothing belong'd to a Father, but Forgiveness and Affection; no Authority, no Correction, no Arbitrary Power . . .', and his later reply, 'Oons whose Son are you? how were you engendered Muckworm?' Domineering abruptness is a trait of Sir Anthony in both versions of *The Rivals*, but the hint of lechery to be found in the text sent to the Lord Chamberlain is carefully toned down. All that remains in the later versions is Sir Anthony's rapture over Lydia's beauty and the reference to his once being a bold intriguer who had married for love.

Sheridan showed an acute theatrical sense in these changes, but obviously needed to observe an audience's reactions and to read the critics' reports before he discerned that alterations were required. Even then he did not always accept the advice given him. A writer in the *Public Ledger* of 18 January 1775, declared that 'the author seems to have considered puns, witticisms, similes and metaphors, as admirable substitutes for polished diction'. Sheridan took out some of the more unusual of them and confined the malapropisms to Mrs. Malaprop, but he retained whatever he thought racy or genuinely humorous. Acres loses some of his oaths but still has plenty. Julia and Faulkland indulge themselves freely in over-emotional exchanges.

At this point it is worth examining the character relationships. Julia and Faulkland present us with the greatest difficulty because they belong so much to a period that had an intense admiration for delicacy of mind and sensitivity of feeling. Vibrations of sympathy indicated nobility of soul. Tears were never idle but demonstrated a tender responsiveness.

Sheridan's own temperament was an uneasy mixture of the satirical and the sentimental: he laughed at Faulkland but also luxuriated in his feverish sensibility. He took considerable trouble to draw the character in detail and, as elsewhere, to emphasize certain phrases. Early in the play, Julia defends him by saying, 'he is too proud, too noble to be jealous; if he is captious, 'tis without dissembling; if fretful, without rudeness'. His pride and nobleness of mind need to be stressed to counter the emphasis placed on his foibles. Jack reproaches him for being the 'most teasing, captious, incorrigible lover'. Faulkland refers to his own 'captious, unsatisfied temper', and Julia mentions his 'teasing, minute caprice'. To Jack Absolute these are womanish traits but Faulkland's defence lies in his cry from the heart, 'O! Jack, when delicate and feeling souls are separated, there is not . . . an aspiration of the breeze, but hints some cause for a lover's apprehension!' Romantic lovers are commonly hypersensitive. They are also very possessive, so we forgive his petulant outbursts at the report that Julia has been enjoying life in the country. From the point of view of delicacy of feeling this is understandable, but Jack speaks for many in the audience (then as now) when he cries, 'You have been confoundedly stupid indeed.' All this we can make allowances for, but not for the strained rhetoric that Faulkland employs. Some eighteenth-century spectators felt differently, and the *Morning Post* of 24 January 1775 noted that 'the exquisite refinement in his disposition, opposed to the noble simplicity, tenderness, and candour of Julia's, give rise to some of the most affecting sentimental scenes'.

We certainly find Julia a more sympathetic character. She knows that Faulkland is not over-accustomed to affairs of the heart and that he is sincere even in his fluctuating moods, so she does her best to give this imperious and egotistic lover a feeling that her 'every thought and emotion . . . move in unison' with his own. She is also clear-sighted enough to see that capriciousness is not confined to Faulkland, when she comments on Lydia's refusal to love any man who can delay marriage and, later, warns her against letting 'a man who loves you with sincerity, suffer that unhappiness from your caprice, which I know too well caprice can inflict'.

In fact the relationship between Faulkland and Julia is nicely balanced against that of Jack and Lydia. Jack is in love with 'a lady of a very singular taste: a lady who likes him better as a *half pay Ensign* than if she knew he was son and heir to Sir Anthony Absolute, a baronet of three thousand a-year'. Off-stage Jack is a suitably romantic lover, as we learn from Lydia's reports: 'Then would he kneel to me in the snow, and sneeze, and cough so pathetically! he shivering with cold, and I with apprehension.' He tells his father, too, that his heart 'is engaged to an angel', but generally he is preoccupied with his schemes for persuading Lydia to accept him with financial blessings on both sides. He pretends to be Beverley to bring her round to his way of thinking, but circumstances are too much for him and he has to lament that he is 'a poor industrious devil' who has 'toiled, and drudged, and plotted' to gain his ends and is 'at last disappointed by other people's folly'. In the same strain he cries out, 'A noble reward for all my schemes, upon my soul!— A little gypsy!—I did not think her romance could have made her so d—n'd absurd either.' She has set her heart on an elopement and a 'surprise to Mrs. Malaprop'. Her delicacy of feeling is evident in her contempt for an arranged match and her generosity towards the beggarly Beverley, but they are so exaggerated as to appear silly. When she learns the truth, she charges Jack with a 'mean, unmanly imposition'. The audience acquits him of this and of Sir Anthony's complaint that he played the hypocrite, because it realizes that Jack dissimulates not for dissimulation's sake but in the cause of commonsense. He believes that adequate money on both sides will make their marriage happier, and sees it as his duty to rescue Lydia from her singular fantasies.

The warmest relationship in the play is between father and son. Their scenes have a rich comic quality that is unequalled in *The Rivals*, except perhaps in a few brief passages of dialogue involving David and Acres. Sir Anthony demands implicit obedience but is far from pleased when Jack agrees to marry niece or aunt:

SIR ANTHONY. . . . The aunt, indeed! Odds life! when I ran away with your mother, I would not have touched anything old or ugly to gain an empire.
ABSOLUTE. Not to please your father, sir?

This ability to turn the situation with a nice irony is one of Sheridan's gifts as a playwright, and in this example and a few others, the reversals spring from character. Jack owes his father a certain duty; Sir Anthony demands far more. The struggle between them is an enduring one, presented with rueful humour.

The comedy exhibits the vitality and exaggerations of youth, yet its theme clearly favours a balanced view of life, rational and sensible. People like Lydia and Faulkland, who try to live in a world of their own devising, have to come to terms with the accepted conventions and must give up their constant search for proof of their power over their prospective partners.

The self-satisfaction of Acres and Mrs. Malaprop is treated with indulgence. Acres is a country booby and a coward but there is something attractive in his openness. Mrs. Malaprop's use of language has a bumptious assertiveness that makes the contrast between her vanity and her howlers very amusing. 'Antistrophe' for 'catastrophe' and 'allegory' for 'alligator' seem strained when we read them, but delight an audience because of the air of superiority with which they are pronounced. Sometimes she blunders into an Irish 'bull'; at others she pleases us with an unexpectedly neat phrase like 'soft impeachment' or the oddity of 'the pineapple of politeness', just as 'my oracular tongue' and 'you forfeit my malevolence' have a curious irony.

Sheridan undoubtedly had particular players in mind when fashioning some of these parts. Five of them had already acted in Goldsmith's *She Stoops to Conquer*. Edward Shuter took droll old gentlemen so was cast as Mr. Hardcastle and Sir Anthony. John Quick acted young, countrified squires, and was a natural Tony Lumpkin as well as Bob Acres. Lee Lewes was good at the arrogant or pert, and was therefore chosen to create Young Marlow and Fag. Mrs. Green shone as the would-be gentlewoman full of her own importance, so was both Mrs. Hardcastle and Mrs. Malaprop. Mrs. Bulkeley excelled as a pleasing young woman, and took Kate Hardcastle and Julia.

John Lee was so bad as Sir Lucius at the first performance that he was replaced by Clinch. Sheridan seems to have felt that he owed a debt to the substitute for his clever acting and agreed to make a short play available for Clinch's benefit night. On 2 May 1775 *St. Patrick's Day* was presented for the first time.

Nothing much was expected. As the *London Magazine* remarked, 'Whatever pieces are presented on a benefit night, are in no degree fair objects of public criticism, from being intended chiefly for the entertainment of the actor or actress's particular friends. It is perhaps as well for the author of *St. Patrick's Day* that such is the public idea; for his canvas is certainly filled with the likeness of no one human creature in existence.' Other opinions were more generous: the *Morning Chronicle* thought some of the jests 'too low and vulgar', but found Rosy and Credulous 'laughable instances of the extravagant in dramatic portrait painting', and believed that the entertainment had more 'humour, satire and observation in it than most of the afterpieces lately produced'. The *Morning Post* concurred: 'it contains some truly farcical situations, and though the humour is here and there extravagant, it is not too strong for what is called farce'. Quick and Lee Lewes, as Dr. Rosy and Justice Credulous, were again picked out for praise.

*St. Patrick's Day*, written very much for the moment, is still revived. Its central figure is a young officer who (as in *The Rivals*) is highly inventive in schemes and stratagems to win a wilful young woman. From its opening the play strikes a humorous note that is sustained throughout, and that softens the Lieutenant's indignant refusal at the close, when he dismisses Credulous's demand that he 'forswear' his country (Ireland) and quit the army. The hardships of a soldier's life are lightly described and even mutilation in a far distant American war is jestingly mentioned in the idea of a campaigner's returning home with 'one leg in Boston, and the other in Chelsea Hospital'.

There is little development of character, but Dr. Rosy remains a comic figure. His mind keeps leaving the matter in hand for recollections of his long-dead wife. He praises her in the language of the dispensary, phrases as bewildering to the Lieutenant as the idea that the doctor could possibly mourn 'an old fat hag'. Snuff alone puts him into a sufficiently comfortable frame of mind to help O'Connor deceive the magistrate.

The action moves rapidly within the normal conventions of farce. For example, we notice that when the Lieutenant's first disguise proves ineffective, he tries another means of penetrating the magistrate's guard by pretending to be a quack doctor. An occasional situation belongs more to satirical comedy: when the Sergeant recruits the disguised Lieutenant, the reversal of roles leads to some amusing irony. When Justice Credulous needs the attention of his wife and daughter, they are too busy arguing to bother with him. Of course this farce is far more entertaining when seen than when read. Sheridan's feeling for the theatre is pretty sure and even those effects that seem implausible, succeed on the stage. A contemporary remarked that he was 'deep read in the whole catalogue of forgotten farces', and he had obviously learned much from them. At the same time, *St. Patrick's Day* shows some characteristics that were to be more fully developed later: neatly organized jests at the expense of women's fashions or witty ridicule like the line on make-up—'in my mind, there is nothing on Earth so impudent as an everlasting blush'.

*St. Patrick's Day*, like the second version of *The Rivals*, was quite well received, but *The Duenna* (presented for the first time in November of the same remarkable year) was wildly successful and did more to establish Sheridan in the theatre than any of his other achievements.

The circumstances in which the libretto was written were unusual. On 22 September, Thomas Linley mentioned in a letter to a friend that he had 'engaged to assist my son-in-law Sheridan in composing an opera, which he is to bring out at Covent Garden this winter . . . for it is a matter of absolute necessity that he should endeavour to get money by this means, as he will not be prevailed upon to let his wife sing'. Six days later, Linley mentioned their progress in a letter to Garrick: 'I have already sett some Airs which he has given me, and he intends writing new Words to some other Tunes of mine. My Son has likewise written some Tunes for him, and I understand, he is to have others from Mr. Jackson of Exeter. This is a mode of proceeding in regard to his Composition I do not by any means approve of; I think he ought first to have finish'd his Opera with the Songs he intends to introduce in it: no Musician can set a Song properly unless he understands the Characters and knows the Performer who is to exhibit it.' Sheridan had no knowledge of music but he knew the effects he wished to achieve and, with his wife's advice, tried to make them clear. He procrastinated as usual and infuriated his father-in-law, who complained of his neglect and extravagance. Fortunately Thomas Harris was once again full of enthusiasm for the project, and 'extravagantly sanguine of its success as to plot and dialogue'. Eventually the work was completed and the comic opera given its first production at Covent Garden on 21 November.

Harris's judgement was shown to be sound. The newspaper critics commended the variety of incidents and neatness of dialogue. The *London Packet* thought it was a better comedy than any since *The Clandestine Marriage* (1766). The *Morning Chronicle* praised Sheridan's 'fertile imagination, great ability, and real genius'. In the chorus of praise there were also a few inharmonious notes: the plot was a little forced and the play was too long. Sheridan was so anxious to get away from the proverbial phraseology and staid situations of sentimental comedy that he sometimes sank into farce. The main objections, however, were to the 'churchy' music, and there was even a suggestion that this comic opera 'would deserve more approbation if it was freed from its musical appendage and performed as a comedy'.

In spite of these criticisms, *The Duenna* had an astonishing run and enjoyed an applause that lasted until the early decades of the nineteenth century, when Hazlitt proclaimed it 'a perfect work of art'. More recent judges have sometimes thought it a perfect piece of artifice: its skilful structure with one situation or character or theme nicely balanced against another, suggests a work of merely formal beauty and not much real imaginative power, one that is stagey and contrived rather than fresh and striking. Clearly the later eighteenth century did not think so, since it took delight in an original like Isaac as well as in lyrics that had 'meaning, sense, and poetry'. It liked, too, the general gaiety which the *London Packet* described as 'rescuing the stage from that state of lethargy, and melancholy madness, into which Cumberland and his sentimental compeers had lulled it'. Justice lies somewhere between the extremes: there is some artifice and over-complication, but the general design presents us with a delightfully comic view of life.

The first act carefully reveals Louisa's plight: she is in love with Antonio but her domineering father wishes her to marry the obnoxious Isaac Mendoza. Louisa takes matters into her own hands by plotting with her duenna, Margaret, to escape from home and allow Margaret to trap Isaac into marriage. Isaac's overbearing vanity makes him 'the dupe of his own art' and leads to the highly amusing situation in which he first encounters Margaret. Jerome had led him to expect youth and beauty and Isaac can only attribute the charms so described to a father's blind partiality. When Margaret says that she is willing to elope with him, he readily agrees because he will then secure her supposed fortune without making any settlement in return. His aims in marriage are unashamedly mercenary, but so too are Margaret's and Jerome's. Margaret declares, 'Now I shall try whether I can't play the fine lady as well as my mistress, and if I succeed, I may be a fine lady for the rest of my life.' Jerome is no less calculating: 'Why I must confess I had a great affection for your mother's ducats, but . . . I married her for her fortune.'

The younger people vary in their cynicism. Though Antonio is 'a gay, dissipated rake who has squandered his patrimony', Louisa does not think any the less of him:

> Thou can'st not boast of fortune's store,
> My love, while me they wealthy call,
> For I was glad to find thee poor,
> For with my heart I'd give thee all.

She realizes that her money will be useful: 'there is a chilling air around poverty that often kills affection. . . . If we would make love our household god, we had better secure him a comfortable roof.' In her scheming and her common sense she is a female Jack Absolute.

Clara is more romantic in attitude, and her delicacy is offended when Ferdinand gets into her bedroom at two in the morning. His abrupt dismissal bewilders him as much as Antonio:

FERD.  . . . I was forced to leave the house as I came in.

ANT.  And you did nothing to offend her?

FERD.  Nothing, as I hope to be saved—I believe I might snatch a dozen or two kisses.

ANT.  Was that all? Well, I think I never heard of such assurance.

FERD.  Zounds! I tell you I behaved with the utmost respect.

ANT.  O lord! I don't mean you, but in her. (I. iii)

When she describes this incident, Clara admits that she feared her 'treacherous heart might grant him more', and so decides to seek security in the convent of St. Catherine. Louisa then pokes fun at Clara's romantic notion of taking the veil: 'The character of a nun is a very becoming one— at a masquerade—but no pretty woman in her senses ever thought of taking the veil for above a night.' Louisa, too, is responsible for pointing out that 'in religion, as in friendship, they who profess most are ever the least sincere', a suspicion that is amply justified by the behaviour of Father Paul and his brethren. All this is intended to put Clara on her guard against trusting in appearances or professions. She must learn, like Lydia Languish, that over-romantic love is foolish since it springs from a refusal to see life as it really is.

The characters (apart from Isaac) are lightly sketched in and some of the speeches might be made by any one of the leading figures. The best example of this is to be found in Louisa's comment on Isaac's conversion to Christianity: he 'stands like a dead wall between church and synagogue, or like the blank leaves between the Old and New Testament'. This seems rather forced, as is the reference to Egyptian embalmers' practice of extracting the brain through the ears, a direct borrowing from Goldsmith's *Citizen of the World*.

Yet if the allusions are occasionally too literary, the songs of *The Duenna* admirably serve to illustrate character or enhance a situation. Jerome is unpleasant when he asks the duenna what she has pilfered, but regains our goodwill when he plaintively cries 'O what a plague is an obstinate daughter', and remembers a glorious past in 'O the days when I was young'. The cleverest use of a song to turn a situation is to be found at the end of the second act, when Carlos's lyric has a sweetness of romance that is contrasted humorously with the pair of lovers (Margaret and Isaac) it celebrates. This provides the kind of irony so often to be seen in Sheridan's work, associated as it is with situation and delighting the audience with its ambiguities of meaning.

If the words of most of the songs serve to strengthen the romantic side of *The Duenna*, the misunderstandings and mistaken identities that abound in the libretto suggest, like the friars' scene, the world of farce. The more thoughtful nature of the dramatist is indicated in isolated remarks like Ferdinand's, 'We never mean that others shou'd act to our sisters and wives as we do to theirs'. On the whole, it is unlikely that

Sheridan intended any more forceful conclusion than the idea that cynics will take all they can get and that they can be challenged successfully only by those who have the intelligence and good sense to outwit them. The tone of the libretto remains genial, even accommodating. With John Quick playing the part of Isaac, how could it be otherwise?

The enormous success of the comic opera brought Sheridan considerable sums of money, and his collaboration with Thomas Linley had an unexpected consequence. It interested David Garrick, who wished to retire from the management of Drury Lane Theatre but to retain some of his investments in the building. Approaches were made and in due course Sheridan bought a share in Garrick's playhouse. He was joined by Linley, who took over the musical direction, and by a physician named James Ford, who put money into the venture merely as a sleeping partner.

The new management opened in September 1776, under Sheridan's superintendence. His contributions to the repertoire included revised texts of Congreve's *The Old Bachelor* and *Love for Love* that were meant to be more suitable for the delicate ears of his audiences than the seventeenth-century versions.

On 8 February 1777, the *Morning Chronicle* reported that two comedies by Sheridan were being prepared for representation. One of them was *A Trip to Scarborough*. In spite of the fact that it was advertised as an alteration of Sir John Vanbrugh's *The Relapse* (1696), some members of the audience seem to have expected an entirely new play and were irritated to find before them an old favourite in a new shape. Sheridan improved the structure and toned down some of the language and situations. He took particular pains to make the Berinthia–Loveless and Coupler–Fashion scenes acceptable by turning Coupler into a professional matchmaker (Mrs. Coupler) and by making Berinthia an intriguer whose motives are really above suspicion. Little harm is meant; little offence given, but the scenes concerning Foppington, Sir Tunbelly, and Miss Hoyden are retained almost in their entirety. Foppington's lines on the dullness of Sunday are omitted, and the subject of his sneering is changed from church-going to opera-going. Sir Tunbelly is made a little less blustering. When Townly takes over the part of Worthy and some of the functions of Coupler, he links the Foppington–Fashion and Foppington–Tunbelly scenes more closely. The Berinthia–Loveless–Amanda scenes are carefully cut, and unity of place is achieved by setting the action at Scarborough. The empty verse of the first scene and Loveless's long soliloquy (III. 2) are both eliminated. These alterations were so effective that the revision ousted the original from the repertoire for very many years. Sheridan, however, knew that some of the vigour of the original had been lost, and confessed to Thomas Moore that the dialogue of Vanbrugh was quite inimitable. He laughed at his own handiwork when he commented in *The Critic* on contemporary taste: 'I think the worst alteration is in the nicety of the audience.—No double entendre, no smart innuendo admitted; even Vanbrugh and Congreve obliged to undergo a bungling reformation.'

*The Duenna* had been such a success at Covent Garden that the Drury Lane audiences expected something really new and exciting from this promising young author. He had disappointed them with *A Trip to Scarborough*, so now had to meet once again the challenge of their expectations.

This time he made no mistake. For a couple of months he worked desperately to bind together certain themes that had struck his imagination. The Teazle story and the scandalmongers may have been suggested by the wooing of Elizabeth Linley by Walter Long. For the contrast between two brothers he does not need to have read *Tom Jones*, for *The Duenna* itself contains a foreshadowing of one of them. Jerome says of Antonio, 'Is he not a gay, dissipated rake who has squander'd his patrimony?' Ferdinand replies, 'Sir, he has inherited but little; and that his generosity, more than his profuseness, have stript him of—but he has never sullied his honor.' Charles Surface stands for these characteristics and is not greatly developed beyond them. The eighteenth century was as sentimental about the generous-hearted rake as the twentieth century is about the good-natured prostitute, and with better reason. Charles is frank, genial, quixotic, and he is balanced against his prudent brother, Joseph, who embodies all that Sheridan found detestable in Chesterfield's letters to his son. The contrast is such a common one in the century that perhaps it goes back to cavalier and roundhead. Its explicit meaning is revealed in *Tristram Shandy* (I. ii): 'In the naked temper which a merry heart discovers he would say, there was no danger,—but to itself:— whereas the very essence of gravity was design, and consequently deceit.' The usurer Sheridan found close at hand in one called Moses in real life, and the play was given topicality by references to the Annuity Bill and its damned register.

Sheridan's methods of composition were probably much the same as those he mentioned to his wife at a much later date: 'When I have fix'd my characters and the Construction of my Plot, I can go on with the Dialogue, travelling, visiting, walking, anyhow and anywhere.' I read this as meaning that he applied himself with determination to plotting and construction, and that once these difficulties were overcome dialogue flowed easily, perhaps too easily for we find him in the different versions of *The Rivals* and *The School for Scandal* frequently tightening it to satisfy his sense of balance or altering it for the sake of a greater propriety.

After a number of revisions the text of *The School for Scandal* was handed to the prompter for copying, and the actors prepared for their task. The full resources of the company were made ready for the occasion for nearly every member of the cast was a specialist in the kind of role he performed. King and Mrs. Abington were renowned for the way in which they brought out the best in each other, particularly in pointing humorous situations. John Palmer was perfectly suited to Joseph Surface because he possessed 'a sort of elaborate grace and stately superiority . . . with an accompaniment of the most plausible politeness'. Charles was given to the elegant William Smith, while La Mash was Trip; Dodd, Sir Benjamin; and Jane Pope was Mrs. Candour. Sheridan took no chances as Charles Lamb noted when he said that 'no piece was ever so completely cast as this Manager's Comedy'.

At its first performance on 8 May 1777, *The School for Scandal* was extraordinarily successful, and the newspaper critics were warm in their praise. The *Morning Chronicle* admired the satire on detraction and hypocrisy, 'which are the prevailing vices of times'. The fable was well conducted and 'there hardly ever was a better dramatic situation than occurs in the fourth act'. The *Morning Post* declared that the principal excellence of the piece lay in the wit and elegance of the dialogue, though it criticized 'the chain of wit traps in the second act' as too studiously laid. The *St. James's Chronicle* contained a notice that was probably by David Garrick. Part of it read: 'If *Dialogue* replete with Wit, yet as easy and natural as if there were none, and if that Wit, by being unaffected, is sub-servient to the Character, be the true Conversation of Comedy, Mr. Sheridan is most happy in that Part of the Drama. If *Characters* happily, but not too artfully contrasted, and distinguished by those nice Shadow-ings, which fly from common Observation, are Marks of true Genius, they will be found in *The School for Scandal*. If a *Fable* new and probable, clear, yet complicated in the Incidents, rising from Scene to Scene and Act to Act in Interest and Entertainment, employing in its Operations and unfolding the peculiar Humours and Passions of each Character, with an Art that not only occasions Bursts of Laughter, but an uncommon Agitation of Spirit in the Audience; if this I say, is the grand Arcanum, the Philosopher's Stone of Dramatic Poetry, who bids more fair to find Gold at the bottom of the Crucible, than our young Alchymist? The *Moral* is obvious, but not by throwing *Speeches, Observations*, and trite *Sentiments* among the Spectators, but it comes forth from *a certain Impression* made upon the Minds of the Audience, which arises from the Actions.' The great actor mentioned in passing some 'Errors and Negli-gences, some few Wants and Exuberances (ever attendant upon Genius)' but was otherwise very delighted with the play.

In the general applause the severer critics were hardly heard or were looked upon as merely jealous. As far as we can tell, Sheridan made no substantial changes in his text after the first night or after the fortieth, yet he refused to publish the work. He may well have resisted offers because he could make much more money from performances at Drury Lane than from the sale of a copyright or because, as one writer claimed, he wished 'to preserve his language from mutilation'. Towards the end of the century

Ridgway, the publisher, reproached him with his tardiness, and Sheridan retorted that he had been trying to satisfy his own taste in correcting the play for some nineteen years, but that he had not succeeded yet. The dialogue had been frequently altered before the first performance, and in manuscript for sometime afterwards, but there is no real evidence to show that he worked at the text for nineteen years. The probability is that he looked at it from time to time and jotted down a few phrases with the intention of thoroughly correcting it later. In spite of several approaches by publishers he did not complete a revision before he died.

As it stands his phrasing is well suited to his purposes. Snake's compliment to Lady Sneerwell on her 'delicacy of Hint—and mellowness of sneer' is ironically apt. Lady Teazle's forceful rebuke to Joseph remains within the limits of fashionable politeness: 'You seem to adopt a very tender method of reasoning—do you usually argue on your knees?' When the language takes on a highly literary flavour, the reason is often to be found in the self-importance of the speaker. Lady Sneerwell's measured explanation of her own maliciousness is a case in point: 'wounded myself, in the early Part of my Life by the envenom'd Tongue of Slander I confess I have since known no Pleasure equal to the reducing others, to the Level of my own injured Reputation'. The warmth of her haughty resentment is obvious, and distinguishes her at once from her accomplice. Joseph's soulful statements are the product of cold calculation, but sound so stylish and sincere that they dignify him and give him a cover for his schemes.

As in *The Rivals*, Sheridan repeats certain words to fix a type in the minds of the audience. Sir Peter is 'peevish' and Premium is 'prudent', but there are ironical inflections here, too. Sir Peter's soliloquy at the end of Act II, Scene 1, is more humorously rueful. Sir Oliver hates to see prudence in youth because the grown man may well become over-reaching, and this justifies his suspicious attitude towards Joseph's behaviour. Careless extends the argument by saying, 'usury is *prudence* and industry and deserves to succeed'. So we gather that prudence may well be more characteristic of rogues than of people with good hearts.

Some of the witty lines were criticized as not being characteristic of the speaker. The objection is a familiar one, for while wit may be malicious, genial or airy, it lacks the individualizing power of humour. Sheridan was inventive enough but he disliked wasting his fancies, and in the course of revising he was guilty sometimes of redistributing witty speeches without too much regard for the character delivering them. The *London Evening Post* noted the foible: 'If the piece has any fault, it is the same which was attributed to Congreve, that his wit flashed too often and sometimes from characters that it could not be expected from.' The gossip of worthless people could be, and was, transferred without difficulty from one generalized type like Spatter (in an early draft) to another like Crabtree, but it is not so easy to reconcile the sedate Rowley with some of his bright remarks. Any defence of Sheridan's practice must rest on the fact that high spirits and ready responsiveness appear to invigorate everyone in the play from time to time, and that wit is their natural consequence. 'I am not for making slavish distinctions,' said Puff, 'and giving all the fine language to the upper sort of people.'

Some of the changes were very effective. A striking one is to be seen in the positioning of the speech, 'For my Part I profess Scandal merely for amusement—I never feel any malice against the people I abuse—and take it for granted they all speak in the same manner of me.' This was originally uttered in an early version of the play, by a nondescript character called Verjuice, but in giving it to Lady Teazle, Sheridan made it an important disclosure of her outlook.

He took plenty of trouble over her lines, and there are some superb runs of dialogue whenever she is involved. What could be more pleasing than the last part of Joseph's attempt to seduce her? His subtle insinuations are contrasted with her mocking banter:

SURFACE.   O certainly madam your understanding *should* be convinced—yes—yes—Heav'n forbid I should perswade you to do any thing you *thought* wrong—no—no—I have too much honor to desire it—

LADY TEAZLE.   Don't—you think we may as well leave Honor out of the Argument?

SURFACE.   Ah—the ill effects of your country education I see still remain with you.

This is infinitely more imaginative than the way in which the slanderers cap jests, because it is strictly tied to character and in its rhythms and pointing shows the wheedling nature of Joseph's advances.

The later developments are also happily conceived. Lady Teazle repents because she discovers that Sir Peter is as good-natured as she thought he was when he wooed her. The scandalmongers had led her astray and she had been so dazzled by the opportunity of cutting a dash that she had not appreciated their malice to the full. Now their petty spite and credulousness become as apparent as Joseph's cunning. Her change of heart is not sentimental but properly shows the growth of character in particular circumstances.

Even Joseph is allowed to speak in his own defence. As in *The Rivals*, Sheridan uses curtain lines to give the audience a special insight, and in this case they take the form of a soliloquy revealing Joseph's motives: 'I wanted at first only to ingratiate myself with Lady Teazle that she might not be my enemy with Maria—and I have I don't know how—become her serious Lover.—Sincerely I begin to wish I had never made such a Point of gaining so very good a Character—for it has led me into so many curs'd Rogueries that I doubt I shall be exposed at last!' The appeal to the audience's charity is clear, and so is the fact that his hypocrisy sprang from an excessive desire to please. What distinguishes the bad from the good is the degree of heartlessness in their behaviour. Sheridan wanted this to be recognized rather than strongly reproved. Good nature could not cure all the ills of society, but real generosity of spirit might enhance the life of an extravagantly competitive and fashionable set of people.

While all this is implicit in the play, Sheridan also used Maria and Rowley to guide the audience's reactions. Both are paragons, hardly developed at all as characters, but they have the important function of being moral touchstones. In the early scenes Maria condemns male scandalmongers even more than female, and also declares that she cannot respect wit when she sees it in company with malice. Rowley, who is right about everything else, must be believed when he says that Charles 'will retrieve his errors yet' and forecasts that he will follow his father's example, who was 'at his years nearly as wild a spark—yet when he died, he did not leave a more benevolent heart to lament his loss.' Rowley, too, brings Sir Peter and Lady Teazle together again, and produces Snake to confound Joseph's last machinations.

In general, Sheridan subordinated character-drawing to theatrical necessity, though not to mere stage effect. This is not surprising for plays in their very economy need only well-defined types; 'round' characters are more appropriately found in the diffuseness of the novel.

Beauty of form was surely one of his aims but his achievement had its critics. Some were carping, like the contemporary who said that he wished the chatter of the opening scenes would stop so that the play could begin, forgetting that the gossip was essential to bring out a main theme—the contrast between truth and rumour. Others found the comedy too long. Sheridan's skill in creating brilliant theatrical situations is seen at its best in Act IV, Scene 3, where the destinies of the four main characters are affected when the screen falls, but it is so striking that the last scenes then appear unduly protracted. Act V, Scene 2 in *The School for Scandal* (as in *The Rivals*) is interesting in itself but holds up the action.

Critics were easily outnumbered by eulogists, and Garrick's opinion of the play's worth pretty closely represented the general outlook. Sheridan's complicated plot undoubtedly had a clear line of development. His exposure of the selfishness, envy, and hypocrisy of contemporary society was humorous enough to delight audiences and to make them think. He had also captured the current forms of fashionable speech and heightened them with fine phrases and sustained wit.

The intense labour that Sheridan had put into *The School for Scandal* was not required for his next piece, the libretto of a musical entertainment called *The Camp*. The summer of 1778 had seen great public interest in the defence of England against an invader and in the establishment of camps for the volunteer recruits. The most important of them was situated at Coxheath, near Maidstone, and was visited by Georgiana, Duchess of Devonshire, and other fashionable ladies. The painter, Philippe de Loutherbourgh, was engaged by Drury Lane Theatre to go there and design scenes that might be employed in a topical piece on the subject, and Thomas Linley was called upon to supply the music. The urgency of the request may be seen in the fact that he had little time for originality and made use of tunes that he had composed for an earlier entertainment. Sheridan himself paid particular attention to the stage business, and when the drill sergeant gave the commands in intelligible terms, he rebuked him saying, 'That won't do at all, Mr. Bannister; it is very unsoldierlike—you speak to be understood; they never do that on the parade.'

In its notice of the first night, the *Morning Post*, 16 October 1778, said, 'This petit piece is said to be the production of Mr. Sheridan, who tacked the dialogue part of it together, in order to introduce Mr. Loutherbourgh's scenic spectacle of Coxheath Camp, with a kind of dramatic propriety; and in which he has been very successful.' The other newspapers agreed with this but the *St. James's Chronicle* was rather more spleenish in its comments: 'The Dialogue appears to be the Work of Mr. Sheridan, junior. It has the Excellencies and Blemishes of that Writer. It is sprightly, ornamental, and yet level to the tinselled or untinselled Vulgar; but the witty Passages are indiscriminately dispersed; and held out too ostentatiously for Persons of Judgment and Taste. The Characters are drawn from Fancy more than Observation.'

It was taken for granted that the piece was by Sheridan until 1795, when Tate Wilkinson declared that he 'never wrote a line or espoused it'. More recently it has been suggested that *The Camp* was partly written by General Burgoyne or by Sheridan's brother-in-law, Richard Tickell. Since the prologue appeared under Tickell's name and a manuscript copy of the play in his hand is in existence, a case for the attribution to him has some basis. Yet the evidence in general indicates that Sheridan himself was mainly responsible for this trifle, and that his associates provided only ideas or minor assistance. The satirical passages on the follies of the day, the military madness and the camp fashions, are all in his vein. The soldiers and the country lads belong to the same breed as those in *St. Patrick's Day*. Gauge, broken attorney turned exciseman, has a namesake in *The Rivals* in the exciseman from the Coachman's village. The entertainment is probably a good example of what Sheridan could achieve on the spur of the moment and without having to exert himself.

His next composition was also occasional. On 11 March 1779 he produced 'A Monody' in memory of Garrick, who had died in January. Since it was afterwards published as 'Verses to the Memory of Mr. Garrick', it is worth looking at the way in which it was performed at Drury Lane Theatre. The *Morning Chronicle* reported: 'The Monody is divided into three parts, between each of which, and at the conclusion, solemn airs are sung by Mr. Webster, Mr. Gaudry, a Young Lady [Miss Wright], and Mrs. Wrighten, supported by a band of choristers. . . . In the center of the perspective, amidst a thick grove of bays and cypress, stands a monumental pyramid representing the funeral pile of Mr. Garrick. The figures of tragedy and comedy appear as if in basso relievo, in positions expressive of their loss, while fame is mounting the skies with a medallion of Mr. Garrick, and the little Cupids are weeping over his urn beneath. . . . Before the pyramid Mrs. Yates with dishevelled hair and in a flowing robe of purple sattin, speaks the Monody.' *The Gazetteer* was so impressed by it that it recommended that in future Sheridan should give most of his time to 'poetical composition, as it seems reserved for him to give the last polish to harmony, force, and elegance of English verse'. The other newspaper notices were less enthusiastic: the *Morning Chronicle* criticized 'the apparent artifice of composition throughout', while the *St. James's Chronicle* severely castigated the lines as 'destitute of all poetical Merit except Versification'. Nowadays 'the Monody' makes little appeal to us, but we have to remember that it was greatly admired by Byron and that Mrs. Siddons said she could never read it without weeping.

On 30 October of the same year, Sheridan brought out *The Critic*, a piece that was also partly occasional. Fear of invasion had recurred in August and September, and letters under Roman pseudonyms appeared in the newspapers, drawing attention to the common danger. Some periodicals printed Queen Elizabeth's speech to her troops at Tilbury, and many allusions were heard to the days of the Armada. By October the fever had died down and people were inclined to laugh at themselves and at the phantom fleet of invaders. *The Critic* caught this mood as is evident in the famous lines:

> Hold daughter! peace! this love hath turn'd thy brain;
> The Spanish fleet thou *canst* not see—because
> —It is not yet in sight.

The rehearsing a mock-tragedy followed the model of Buckingham's popular burlesque *The Rehearsal* (1671), and allowed Sheridan to poke fun at some of the political figures of the day and, also, at the absurdities in some theatrical conventions. Puff's long interpretation of Burleigh's expressive silence was (as the *Morning Post* said) not 'by any means an ill-timed stroke of political satire', clearly at the expense of the current Prime Minister. At the same time, 'the manner of bringing Burleigh on, and Puff discovering so much anxiety for the performer being perfect in a character that had not a syllable to utter, is an excellent conceit'. The same reviewer correctly suggested that the principal excellence of the mock-tragedy 'must naturally consist in dumb shew, extravagant gestures, or the dullest of all tragic rhapsodies'. Stage business came into its own. In the discovery scene, father, mother, and son 'faint alternately into each other's arms'. Death cuts short the broken utterance of Whiskerandos, and the Beefeater obligingly completes the sentence. The audience's delight in a desperate situation was fully gratified by the 'heroic group!—I have them all at a deadlock', and the prayer to the gods that they will sanctify whatever means the participants use to gain their ends is followed by their all springing off with a glance at the pit. The tragic rhapsodies, however, were not dull but absurd in their inconsequentiality.

The players also seized the opportunity of having some fun at the expense of their fellows. Miss Pope, as Tilburina, took off the well-known tragic actress, Mrs. Crawford, and Bannister, as Whiskerandos, amused everyone by imitating William Smith's 'flounder-like death' as Gloster in *Richard III*.

Personal satire of a severer kind is to be found in the first act of *The Critic*, which precedes the rehearsal. Sheridan declared he 'valued it . . . more than any thing he ever wrote' and admitted that the masterly portrait of Sir Fretful Plagiary was based on the dramatist and critic, Richard Cumberland, who had abused him in the *St. James's Chronicle*. It is uncertain just what Sheridan had in mind in this accusation but possibly he believed that Cumberland was responsible for the unkind notices of *The Camp* and *The Monody*, quoted above from the newspaper. What gives the portrait satiric depth, however, is the fact that it could be applied to the envious author of any period or even to Sheridan himself.

Other well-known people of the day were also ridiculed. Thomas Vaughan was a green-room gossip or 'dangler', and is laughed at in Dangle. The flowery phrases of the auctioneer, Robert Langford, were parodied by Puff and 'threw the whole house into convulsions of laughter'. References to George Colman the elder and others were also to be found in the text, but are not now readily divined.

Puff is a much less personal portrait. The *Public Advertiser* made clear his significance to contemporaries: 'This Character is undoubtedly taken from Nature, and is peculiar to the present times. It is not however the Portrait of any single *Individual* but the display of the whole *Species*, whose ridiculous Abuse of the Liberty of the Press, though too low an Offence for serious Severity, was of all others the properest Theme for the Author of The School for Scandal; the News-Papers having of late super-seded the more contracted Practice of private Defamation, by giving a wider Circulation to secret Malice, and becoming the open Registers of anonymous Detraction. With the liveliest display of this Science, the first Act of *The Critic* closes.'

Once again Sheridan had amalgamated two themes. The consequence was that the piece was found at its first performance to be far too long, and the section concerning the long-lost son had to be omitted. For the second night twenty minutes' playing time was cut from the first act, while 'The Tragedy rehearsed' had the author's 'pruning knife applied to it, as well as that of the comedians'. The long-lost son episode was not presented until 1 January 1780. As time passed other changes were made in the acting text, and it grew shorter and shorter. When the topical jests lost their point, Sheridan allowed his company to bring in new ones. This process went on for so many years that, by 1888, the prompt book was 'a strange mass of absurd incongruity'. Sheridan, like Puff, had to resign himself to seeing his play hacked by the players, and to find the same consolation in 'printing it every word'. He brought out a corrected version in August 1781.

This is obviously more elaborate than the playhouse texts and it makes delightful reading. What could be better phrased than the lines, 'Is this the time for maudlin tenderness? And Cupid's baby woes?' What more comic than the unintelligible interpreter? There is a splendid absurdity in the confidante who is 'always to do whatever her mistress does; weep when she weeps, smile when she smiles, go mad when she goes mad'. In fact, the humour of the piece is even more striking than its wit, though that is telling enough in such lines as Puff's 'the number of those who go thro' the fatigue of judging for themselves is very small indeed.' Read or seen, *The Critic* is hilarious.

In four years Sheridan had produced six plays, and three of them had been rapturously applauded. He had tried his hand at farce, comedy of manners, and burlesque, and his wit was so appreciated that he had become known as 'the modern Congreve'. He now sought a new outlet for his talents and in September 1780, was elected Member of Parliament for Stafford. He tried to rid himself of his theatrical management and shares, but negotiations came to nothing and he had to divide his time between the playhouse and the Commons. He gave more attention to politics than his company would have wished, but did not completely forsake the affairs of the theatre. His livelihood lay there and he had to subsidize his political work from the takings of Drury Lane.

With his wife Sheridan read plays submitted for his consideration. Some received little correction, but he added new dialogue to others. More frequently he jotted down some production notes.

T. L. O'Beirne's *The Generous Impostor* (1780) appears to have been prepared for the stage by Sheridan. For *Fortunatus* (1780) and *Robinson Crusoe* (1781) he wrote naval songs that became popular: 'Chearly, my hearts' and 'Come, come, my jolly lads'. He may have contributed more but it is now difficult to assess the full share he had in these mediocre entertainments. To *The Statesman* (due for presentation in 1782) he added some amusing dialogue, but the farce was never acted. He also wrote some ironical lines on slave-trading for a translation of the libretto of Grétry's *La Caravan du Caire* (1783), but did not go on with the work.

*The Glorious First of June* (1794) is interesting in a different way. It was put together very rapidly to provide a means of obtaining money for the widows of sailors killed in the famous battle at sea. Sheridan undoubtedly drafted a scenario to be filled in by the hack-dramatist, James Cobb, but he was dissatisfied with the result and issued to the actors during rehearsal scraps of paper containing new dialogue. Once again it is impossible to tell how thorough his revisions were.

The same is true of his share in *The Stranger* (1798), a translation by Benjamin Thompson of Kotzebue's *Menschenhass und Reue*. Samuel Rogers said that Sheridan claimed on two occasions that he had·written every sentence in the play as it was acted. The last phrase may be the key to the puzzle concerning the authorship of *The Stranger*. Sheridan may have rewritten all the lines for production, but have allowed the translator to print his own text, as far as he wished to do so. The theory is an attractive one, even if it is not yet completely acceptable. What is certain is that a lithographed copy of a manuscript translation of two scenes in the fifth act of *The Stranger* is extant, and that it contains many corrections in Sheridan's hand. They indicate that *The Times* was justified in writing of the first night's performance, 'for the ultimate polish and mechanism of the Piece, the Public are indebted to the taste and discrimination of Mr. Sheridan'.

Much of the success of *The Stranger* was due to the inspired acting of Mrs. Siddons and John Philip Kemble. Sheridan therefore sought another play that would give them further scope and also rescue Drury Lane Theatre from bankruptcy. *Pizarro*, drawn from Kotzebue's *Die Spanier in Peru*, achieved the first of these aims and almost the second.

Sheridan knew no German so he depended on translations for his knowledge of Kotzebue's text. One of those he used was (and remained) anonymous. Another was by the celebrated Matthew ('Monk') Lewis, who complained bitterly to Byron that Sheridan had taken over some of his ideas without acknowledgement. Anne Plumptre was responsible for the third one, and Drury Lane paid her fees amounting to fifty pounds for its use.

Thomas Moore was of the opinion that Sheridan revised only part of the text: 'A few speeches, and a few short scenes, re-written constitute almost the whole of the contribution he has furnished to it.' Mrs. Bouverie, a close friend of the Sheridans, stated that Sheridan had 'completely written it over again'. The *Morning Herald* corrected its own report that the manager had made only 'such variations in the translation as will give it quite a new cast', to read 'the entire is written by Mr. Sheridan'. He may have thought Anne Plumptre's lines too staccato and have paraphrased them to give a more highly wrought oratorical effect, one that is elevated, balanced, and moving towards the poetical. Daniel Stuart's description of him at a performance absorbed in counting the beats of the syllables on his fingers provides a very good reason for believing that the words and the iambic rhythms were Sheridan's own. There is no mention of the translators on the title-page of *Pizarro*: it merely records that the play was taken from the German drama of Kotzebue and 'adapted to the English stage by Richard Brinsley Sheridan'. The 'Advertisement', however, mentioned two translations that had been generally read and left it to the public to decide on the merits and defects of Sheridan's own version. He was very satisfied with it and dedicated it, though not by name, to his wife.

The difference between Anne Plumptre's lines and his is sometimes marked in the heightening of histrionic effect:

| *Plumptre* | *Sheridan* |
|---|---|
| CORA.  He is very like you. | CORA.  Now confess, does he resemble thee, or not? |
| ALONZO.  No, like you. | ALONZO.  Indeed he is liker thee—thy rosy softness, thy smiling gentleness. |

Look also at their versions of a speech by Las-Casas:

| | |
|---|---|
| I can go no farther;—my efforts are exhausted: but the charms of a woman may prove more powerful than the eloquence of an old man. Perhaps you may be elevated as the guardian angel, of these unfortunate Peruvians. | I alone am useless here. Perhaps thy loveliness may persuade to pity, where reason and religion plead in vain. Oh! save thy innocent fellow creatures if thou canst; then shall thy frailty be redeemed and thou wilt share the mercy thou bestowest. |

Sheridan's version was meant to be declaimed. Kotzebue's few lines on 'sacred nature' gave an opportunity for a long panegyric beginning 'O holy nature!' Fear of invasion, now no laughing matter, was worked up in a patriotic speech comparing, by implication, Pizarro with Buonaparte and it drew ecstatic applause. Thomas Moore coldly pointed out that Sheridan had delivered many of the sentiments in Parliament a year earlier, and that the image of the Vulture and the Lamb was introduced from his speech at the trial of Hastings. In Parliament or theatre Sheridan did not rise above what was commonly regarded as the language of high passion, one that was derived ultimately from heroic tragedy. Moore mentioned its defects: 'in order to give pomp to the language, inversion is substituted for metre; and one of the worst faults of poetry, a superfluity of epithets is adopted, without that harmony which alone makes it venial or tolerable'. An over-exclamatory style was exhausting. Eloquence too easily became grandiloquence. Even the stage directions had a more exalted tone: Plumptre's 'open space in the forest' became Sheridan's 'wild retreat among stupendous rocks'.

At its first showing on 24 May 1799 the play ran for nearly five hours, and was not really successful. Once again Sheridan had treated an opening night as another dress rehearsal. Spectacular effects were bungled by the stage hands, the comic scene was disliked, and Mrs. Siddons drew unexpected laughter. Discipline and cutting were required: on the second night the playing time was reduced by an hour, and on the fourth, by a further twenty minutes. The comic relief was deleted; the tragic effect, concentrated. As in *The Stranger* Sheridan improved 'the mechanism of the Piece to exploit the situation to the full'.

He aimed at, and for many of his contemporaries achieved, the sublime. In this he was undoubtedly aided by the reputation he had gained as an orator who had eloquently supported the noblest causes, freedom and justice, the deliverance of the oppressed. Sentiments of this kind were not mere clap-trap but expressed Sheridan's sincere convictions, and led Byron to call him 'the delegated voice of God'. In Rolla he portrayed the true nobility of feeling of the natural man or child of nature, as contrasted with the ruthlessness of the civilized but corrupt Pizarro. Rolla's virtue was so great that it awed even the tyrant, but just when it seemed possible that he might escape the doom that was the prerogative of the romantic hero, chance brought about the fulfilment of his death-wish. The theme was to be repeated in one way or another for many years but never in quite so exalted a way as this: heroes like Sidney Carton lack Rolla's grandeur.

Kemble was very shrewdly cast in this part. The *Morning Post* mentioned his 'awful pauses between each weighty sentence . . . the forceful interest of every line, clothed with all the sacred dignity of truth'. *The Times* (5 October 1804) went further, saying that the play was 'the production of a poet profoundly skilled in dramatic effect; and every line that is put into the mouth of the Peruvian hero, and every situation in which he is placed, is written and concerted to produce it. The part of Rolla, in the language of the profession, plays itself.' After her faltering start Mrs. Siddons, as Elvira, had gained rapidly in public favour and 'made a heroine of a soldier's trull'. Even when these great performers retired, the play went on being given with success, and records show that it was still being acted in 1878. As far as I know, it is never produced now, and meets with little appreciation from readers.

Sheridan lived for seventeen years after the remarkable success of *Pizarro* but achieved no further theatrical triumphs. He retained some share in the management of Drury Lane Theatre and occasionally tinkered with plays or sketched out a plan for a new one, but most of his time was given to politics. Then, in 1809, the playhouse was burned down and he was ousted from the control of the theatre that took its place. He also lost his seat in the Commons and was subjected to arrest for debt. His last four years were rather miserable ones. When he died on 7 July 1816, the public suddenly realized what it had lost. He was given an elaborate funeral and buried in Poets' Corner.

In the years that followed many tributes were paid to his skill as a playwright. Hazlitt praised the comedies highly for 'brilliant fancy, for vivacity of description, for animation, for acuteness, for wit, for good sense and real discrimination'. Lockhart admired his 'exquisite knowledge of stage-effect and consummate ease and elegance of idiomatic language'. Byron was even more enthusiastic, remarking that '*his* very dregs are better than the first sprightly runnings of others', and specifying his great achievements in a famous eulogy: 'He has written the *best* comedy (School for Scandal), the best opera (The Duenna—in my mind far before that St. Giles' lampoon, The Beggar's Opera), the *best* farce (The Critic—it is only too good for an afterpiece) . . .' Clearly some of the finest critics of the period thought very highly of his work.

Their main points are still valid, and Sheridan holds his place as one of the greatest comic writers in the English theatre, so that plays that belong essentially to the society and stage of his own day continue to give delight to audiences throughout the English-speaking world. We are sentimental about other things, question the value of the upper-class code, fear any hint of prudishness, but we have to acknowledge that in the playhouse, Sheridan's comedies banish our doubts and hold our full attention because they are histrionically brilliant. The interviews between Jack Absolute and Lydia or the screen and auction scenes in *The School for Scandal* are written with such splendid craftsmanship that no one can resist them. Stage types are given real freshness, and originals like Isaac Mendoza, the soul of self-satisfaction, or the thin-skinned Sir Fretful, are held up to our inspection with unerring skill. Dialogue came easily to Sheridan once character and situation were fixed in his mind, and there is plenty of evidence to suggest that Puff spoke for him when he said, 'I know I am luxuriant'. Pruning and cutting of the text went on even after the first performance, till every word counted, for as Hazlitt said, 'This is the merit of Sheridan's comedies, that everything in them tells.' The pointing is superb, bringing out satiric wit, flights of fancy, comic logic, or warm humour with equal effect. The slight exaggerations of the printed page become really natural in the playhouse, language and character are unified, and the dialogue has an edge that can only be fully appreciated from the lips of professionals.

# SOME DATES IN SHERIDAN'S LIFE

4 November 1751. Christened 'Thos. Brinsley Sheridan' at St. Mary's Church, Dublin.

1762–*c*. 1767–8. At Harrow School.

September 1770–August 1772. At Bath.

August 1772–March 1773. At Waltham Abbey.

13 April 1773. Married Elizabeth Linley at Marylebone Church.

17 and 28 January 1775. *The Rivals* acted at Covent Garden Theatre.

2 May 1775. *St. Patrick's Day* acted at Covent Garden Theatre.

21 November 1775. *The Duenna* acted at Covent Garden Theatre.

21 September 1776. Opened Drury Lane Theatre as principal manager.

24 February 1777. *A Trip to Scarborough* acted at Drury Lane Theatre.

March 1777. Elected a member of the Literary Club on the motion of Samuel Johnson.

8 May 1777. *The School for Scandal* acted at Drury Lane Theatre.

15 October 1778. *The Camp* acted at Drury Lane Theatre.

12 September 1780. Elected M.P. for Stafford.

27 March–1 July 1782. Under-Secretary of State for Foreign Affairs.

21 February–18 December 1783. Secretary to the Treasury.

7 February 1787. Made a celebrated speech on the Begums of Oude in the proceedings against Warren Hastings, and others (3–13 June 1788) on his impeachment.

November–December 1788. Confidential adviser to the Prince of Wales in the Regency crisis.

28 June 1792. Death of his first wife at Bristol Wells.

21 April 1794. Opened the rebuilt Drury Lane Theatre.

27 April 1795. Married Esther Ogle, daughter of the Dean of Winchester.

24 May 1799. *Pizarro* acted at Drury Lane Theatre.

November 1806. Succeeded Charles James Fox as M.P. for Westminster.

May 1807. Defeated in the Westminster election but became M.P. for Ilchester.

24 February 1809. Drury Lane Theatre destroyed by fire.

Autumn 1812. Defeated at the Stafford election, so losing a seat in Parliament.

7 July 1816. Died at Savile Row.

13 July 1816. Buried in Westminster Abbey.

# THE RIVALS

# THE

# RIVALS,

A

# COMEDY.

As it is ACTED at the

Theatre-Royal in Covent-Garden.

LONDON:

Printed for JOHN WILKIE, No. 71, St. Paul's Church-Yard.
M DCC LXXV.

The title-page of the first edition of *The Rivals*

# PREFACE[1]

A PREFACE to a Play seems generally to be considered as a kind of Closet-prologue, in which—if his Piece has been successful—the Author solicits that indulgence from the Reader which he had before experienced from the Audience: But as the scope and immediate object of a Play is to please a mixed assembly in *Representation* (whose judgment in the Theatre at least is decisive) its degree of reputation is usually as determined as public, before it can be prepared for the cooler tribunal of the Study. Thus any farther solicitude on the part of the Writer becomes unnecessary at least, if not an intrusion: and if the Piece has been condemned in the Performance, I fear an Address to the Closet, like an Appeal to Posterity, is constantly regarded as the procrastination of a suit, from a consciousness of the weakness of the cause. From these considerations, the following Comedy would certainly have been submitted to the Reader, without any further introduction than what it had in the Representation, but that its success has probably been founded on a circumstance which the Author is informed has not before attended a theatrical trial, and which consequently ought not to pass unnoticed.

I need scarcely add, that the circumstance alluded to, was the withdrawing of the Piece, to remove those imperfections in the first Representation which were too obvious to escape reprehension, and too numerous to admit of a hasty correction. There are few writers, I believe, who, even in the fullest consciousness of error, do not wish to palliate the faults which they acknowledge; and, however trifling the performance, to second their confession of its deficiencies, by whatever plea seems least disgraceful to their ability. In the present instance, it cannot be said to amount either to candour or modesty in me, to acknowledge an extreme inexperience and want of judgment on matters, in which, without guidance from practice, or spur from success, a young man should scarcely boast of being an adept. If it be said, that under such disadvantages no one should attempt to write a play—I must beg leave to dissent from the position, while the first point of experience that I have gained on the subject is, a knowledge of the candour and judgment with which an impartial Public distinguishes between the errors of inexperience and incapacity, and the indulgence which it shews even to a disposition to remedy the defects of either.

It were unnecessary to enter into any farther extenuation of what was thought exceptionable in this Play, but that it has been said, that the Managers should have prevented some of the defects before its appearance to the Public—and in particular the uncommon length of the piece as represented the first night.—It were an ill return for the most liberal

[1] This is printed in the first and second editions only.

and gentlemanly conduct on their side, to suffer any censure to rest where none was deserved. Hurry in writing has long been exploded as an excuse for an Author;—however, in the dramatic line, it may happen, that both an Author and a Manager may wish to fill a chasm in the entertainment of the Public with a hastiness not altogether culpable. The season was advanced when I first put the play into Mr. Harris's hands:—it was at that time at least double the length of any acting comedy.—I profited by his judgment and experience in the curtailing of it—'till, I believe, his feeling for the vanity of a young Author got the better of his desire for correctness, and he left many excrescences remaining, because he had assisted in pruning so many more. Hence, though I was not uninformed that the Acts were still too long, I flatter'd myself that, after the first trial, I might with safer judgment proceed to remove what should appear to have been most dissatisfactory.—Many other errors there were, which might in part have arisen from my being by no means conversant with plays in general, either in reading or at the theatre.—Yet I own that, in one respect, I did not regret my ignorance: for as my first wish in attempting a Play, was to avoid every appearance of plagiary, I thought I should stand a better chance of effecting this from being in a walk which I had not frequented, and where consequently the progress of invention was less likely to be interrupted by starts of recollection: for on subjects on which the mind has been much informed, invention is slow of exerting itself.—Faded ideas float in the fancy like half-forgotten dreams; and the imagination in its fullest enjoyments becomes suspicious of its offspring, and doubts whether it has created or adopted.

With regard to some particular passages which on the First Night's Representation seemed generally disliked, I confess, that if I felt any emotion of surprise at the disapprobation, it was not that they were disapproved of, but that I had not before perceived that they deserved it. As some part of the attack on the Piece was begun too early to pass for the sentence of *Judgment*, which is ever tardy in condemning, it has been suggested to me, that much of the disapprobation must have arisen from virulence of Malice, rather than severity of Criticism: But as I was more apprehensive of there being just grounds to excite the latter, than conscious of having deserved the former, I continue not to believe that probable, which I am sure must have been unprovoked. However, if it was so, and I could even mark the quarter from whence it came, it would be ungenerous to retort; for no passion suffers more than malice from disappointment. For my own part, I see no reason why the Author of a Play should not regard a First Night's Audience, as a candid and judicious friend attending, in behalf of the Public, at his last Rehearsal. If he can dispense with flattery, he is sure at least of sincerity, and even though the annotation be rude, he may rely upon the justness of the comment. Considered in this light, that Audience, whose *fiat* is essential to the Poet's claim, whether his object be Fame or Profit, has surely a right to expect some deference to its opinion, from principles of Politeness at least, if not from Gratitude.

As for the little puny Critics, who scatter their peevish strictures in private circles, and scribble at every Author who has the eminence of being unconnected with them, as they are usually spleen-swoln from a vain idea of increasing their consequence, there will always be found a petulance and illiberality in their remarks, which should place them as far beneath the notice of a Gentleman, as their original dulness had sunk them from the level of the most unsuccessful Author.

It is not without pleasure that I catch at an opportunity of justifying myself from the charge of intending any national reflection in the character of Sir *Lucius O'Trigger*. If any Gentlemen opposed the Piece from that idea, I thank them sincerely for their opposition; and if the condemnation of this Comedy (however misconceived the provocation,) could have added one spark to the decaying flame of national attachment to the country supposed to be reflected on, I should have been happy in its fate; and might with truth have boasted, that it had done more real service in its failure, than the successful morality of a thousand stage-novels will ever effect.

It is usual, I believe, to thank the Performers in a new Play, for the exertion of their several abilities. But where (as in this instance) their merit has been so striking and uncontroverted, as to call for the warmest and truest applause from a number of judicious Audiences, the Poet's after-praise comes like the feeble acclamation of a child to close the shouts of a multitude. The conduct, however, of the Principals in a Theatre cannot be so apparent to the Public.—I think it therefore but justice to declare, that from this Theatre (the only one I can speak of from experience,) those Writers who wish to try the Dramatic Line, will meet with that candour and liberal attention, which are generally allowed to be better calculated to lead genius into excellence, than either the precepts of judgment, or the guidance of experience.

THE AUTHOR

# PROLOGUE

BY THE AUTHOR

Spoken by Mr. WOODWARD and
Mr. QUICK

*Enter* SERJEANT AT LAW, *and* ATTORNEY *following, and giving a Paper.*

SERJ. What's here—a vile cramp hand! I cannot see
Without my spectacles. ATT. He means his fee.
Nay, Mr. Serjeant, good Sir, try again.        [*Gives Money.*
SERJ. The scrawl improves [*more*] O come, 'tis pretty plain.
Hey! how's this?—*Dibble!*—sure it cannot be!
A Poet's Brief! A Poet and a Fee!
ATT. Yea Sir!—tho' *you* without Reward, I know,
Would gladly plead the muses cause—[SERJ.] So—So!
And if the Fee offends—your wrath should fall
On me—[SERJ.] Dear *Dibble* no offence at all—                10
ATT. Some Sons of Phœbus—in the Courts we meet,
SERJ. And fifty Sons of Phœbus in the Fleet!
ATT. Nor pleads he worse, who with a decent sprig
Of Bays—adorns his legal waste of wig.
SERJ. Full-bottom'd Heroes thus, on signs, unfurl
A leaf of laurel—in a grove of curl!
Yet tell your Client, that, in adverse days,
This Wig is warmer than a bush of Bays.
ATT. Do you then, Sir, my Client's place supply,
Profuse of robe, and prodigal of tye—                           20
Do you, with all those blushing pow'rs of face,
And wonted bashful hesitating grace,
Rise in the Court, and flourish on the Case.

                                             [*Exit.*

SERJ. For practice then suppose—this Brief will shew it,——
Me, Serjeant *Woodward*,—Counsel for the Poet.
Us'd to the ground—I know 'tis hard to deal
With this dread *Court*, from whence there's *no appeal*;
No *Tricking* here, to blunt the edge of *Law*,
Or, damn'd in *Equity*—escape by *Flaw*:

But *Judgment* given—*your Sentence* must remain;                    30
—No *Writ of Error* lies—to *Drury-lane*!
Yet when so kind you seem—'tis past dispute
We gain some favour, if not *Costs of Suit*.
No spleen is here! I see no hoarded fury;
—I think I never fac'd a milder Jury!
Sad else our plight!—where frowns are transportation,
A hiss the gallows,—and a groan, damnation!
But such the public candour, without fear
My Client waves all *right of challenge* here.
No Newsman from *our* Session is dismiss'd,                           40
Nor Wit nor Critic *we* scratch off the list;
His faults can never hurt another's ease,
His crime at worst—a *bad attempt* to please:
Thus, all respecting, he appeals to all,
And by the general voice will *stand* or *fall*.

# PROLOGUE

## BY THE AUTHOR

Spoken on the Tenth Night, by Mrs.
BULKLEY

Granted our Cause, our suit and trial o'er,
The worthy Serjeant need appear no more:
In pleasing I a different Client chuse,
He serv'd the Poet,—I would serve the Muse:
Like him, I'll try to merit your applause,
A female counsel in a female's cause.
   Look on this form,[1]—where Humour quaint and fly,
Dimples the cheek, and points the beaming eye;
Where gay Invention seems to boast its wiles
In amorous hint, and half-triumphant smiles;       10
While her light masks or[2] covers Satire's strokes,
All hides the conscious blush, her wit provokes.
—Look on her well—does she seem form'd to teach?
Shou'd you *expect* to hear this lady—preach?
Is grey experience suited to her youth?
Do solemn sentiments become that mouth?
Bid her be grave, those lips should rebel prove
To every theme that slanders mirth or love.
   Yet thus adorn'd with every graceful art
To charm the fancy and yet reach the heart——      20
Must we displace her? And instead advance
The Goddess of the woeful countenance—
The sentimental Muse!—Her emblems view
The Pilgrim's progress, and a sprig of rue!
View her—too chaste to look like flesh and blood—
Primly portray'd on emblematic wood!
There fix'd in usurpation shou'd she stand,
She'll snatch the dagger from her sister's hand:
And having made her votaries *weep a flood*
Good Heav'n! she'll end her Comedies in blood—      30

---

[1] 'Pointing to the Figure of Comedy.' It was shown on one side of the stage and Tragedy appeared on the other.
[2] O'er?

Bid *Harry Woodward* break poor *Dunstall*'s crown!
Imprison *Quick*—and knock *Ned Shuter* down;
While sad *Barsanti*—weeping o'er the scene,
Shall stab herself—or poison Mrs. *Green.*——
    Such dire encroachments to prevent in time,
Demands the Critic's voice—the Poet's rhyme.
Can our light scenes add strength to holy laws!
Such puny patronage but hurts the cause:
Fair Virtue scorns our feeble aid to ask;
And moral Truth disdains the trickster's mask.
For here their fav'rite stands,[1] whose brow—severe
And sad—claims Youth's respect, and Pity's tear;
Who—when oppress'd by foes her worth creates—
Can point a poignard at the Guilt she hates.

[1] 'Pointing to Tragedy.'

# DRAMATIS PERSONÆ

## MEN

| | |
|---|---|
| SIR ANTHONY ABSOLUTE | Mr. Shuter |
| CAPT. ABSOLUTE | Mr. Woodward |
| FAULKLAND | Mr. Lewes |
| ACRES | Mr. Quick |
| SIR LUCIUS O'TRIGGER | Mr. Clinch |
| FAG | Mr. Lee-Lewes |
| DAVID | Mr. Dunstal[l] |
| COACHMAN | Mr. Fearon |

## WOMEN

| | |
|---|---|
| MRS. MALAPROP | Mrs. Green |
| LYDIA LANGUISH | Miss Barsanti |
| JULIA | Mrs. Bulkley |
| LUCY | Mrs. Lessingham |

MAID, BOY, SERVANTS, &c.

SCENE, *Bath*
Time of Action, *within One Day*

# THE RIVALS

## ACT I

### SCENE I[1]

#### *A* STREET *in* Bath

COACHMAN *crosses the stage.—Enter* FAG, *looking after him.*

FAG. What!—Thomas!—Sure 'tis he?—What!—Thomas!—Thomas!

COACH. Hay!—Odd's life!—Mr. Fag!—give us your hand, my old fellow-servant.

FAG. Excuse my glove, Thomas:—I'm dev'lish glad to see you, my lad: why, my prince of charioteers, you look as hearty!—but who the deuce thought of seeing you in Bath!

COACH. Sure, Master, Madam Julia, Harry, Mrs. Kate, and the postillion be all come!

FAG. Indeed!

COACH. Aye! Master thought another fit of the gout was coming to  10 make him a visit:—so he'd a mind to gi't the slip, and whip we were all off at an hour's warning.

FAG. Aye, aye! hasty in every thing, or it would not be Sir Anthony Absolute!

COACH. But tell us, Mr. Fag, how does young Master? Odd! Sir Anthony will stare to see the Captain here!

FAG. I do not serve Capt. Absolute now.—

COACH. Why sure!

FAG. At present I am employ'd by Ensign Beverley.

COACH. I doubt, Mr. Fag, you ha'n't changed for the better.  20

FAG. I have not changed, Thomas.

COACH. No! why didn't you say you had left young Master?

FAG. No——Well, honest Thomas, I must puzzle you no farther:— briefly then—Capt. Absolute and Ensign Beverley are one and the same person.

COACH. The devil they are!

FAG. So it is indeed, Thomas; and the *Ensign* half of my master being on guard at present—the *Captain* has nothing to do with me.

---

[1] An interleaved, early nineteenth-century prompt copy of *The Rivals* (. . . Dublin, Printed for R. Moncrieffe, 1775), now in the Bodleian Library, as Vet A. 5 e. 1849, contains a note, opposite p. 17 and reading, 'This Scene is generally left out.'

COACH. So, so!—what, this is some freak, I warrant!—Do, tell us, Mr. Fag, the meaning o't—you know I ha' trusted you.          30

FAG. You'll be secret, Thomas.

COACH. As a coach-horse.

FAG. Why then the cause of all this is—LOVE,—Love, Thomas, who (as you may get read to you) has been a masquerader ever since the days of Jupiter.

COACH. Aye, aye;—I guessed there was a lady in the case:—but pray, why does your Master pass only for *Ensign*?—now if he had shamm'd *General* indeed——

FAG. Ah! Thomas, there lies the mystery o' the matter.—Hark'ee, Thomas, my Master is in love with a lady of a very singular taste:          40 a lady who likes him better as a *half-pay Ensign* than if she knew he was son and heir to Sir Anthony Absolute, a baronet with three thousand a-year!

COACH. That is an odd taste indeed!—but has she got the stuff, Mr. Fag; is she rich, hey?

FAG. Rich!—why, I believe she owns half the stocks!—Z——ds! Thomas, she could pay the national debt as easy as I could my washer-woman!—She has a lap-dog that eats out of gold,—she feeds her parrot with small pearls,—and all her thread-papers are made of bank-notes!

COACH. Bravo!—faith!——Odd! I warrant she has a set of thousands at          50 least:—but does she draw kindly with the Captain?

FAG. As fond as pigeons.

COACH. May one hear her name?

FAG. Miss Lydia Languish—But there is an old tough aunt in the way; —though by the bye—she has never seen my Master—for he got acquainted with Miss while on a visit in Gloucestershire.

COACH. Well—I wish they were once harness'd together in matrimony. —But pray, Mr. Fag, what kind of a place is this Bath?—I ha' heard a deal of it—here's a mort o'merry-making—hey?

FAG. Pretty well, Thomas, pretty well—'tis a good lounge; in the morning          60 we go to the pump-room (though neither my Master nor I drink the waters); after breakfast we saunter on the parades or play a game at billiards; at night we dance: but d—n the place, I'm tired of it: their regular hours stupify me—not a fiddle nor a card after eleven!—however Mr. Faulkland's gentleman and I keep it up a little in private parties; —I'll introduce you there, Thomas—you'll like him much.

COACH. Sure I know Mr. Du-Peigne—you know his Master is to marry Madam Julia.

FAG. I had forgot.—But Thomas, you must polish a little—indeed you must:—here now—this wig!—what the devil do you do with a *wig*,          70 Thomas?—none of the London whips of any degree of Ton wear *wigs* now.

COACH. More's the pity! more's the pity, I say.—Odd's life! when I heard how the lawyers and doctors had took to their own hair,[1] I thought how 'twould go next:—Odd rabbit it! when the fashion had got foot on the Bar, I guess'd 'twould mount to the Box!—but 'tis all out of character, believe me, Mr. Fag: and look'ee, I'll never gi' up mine—the lawyers and doctors may do as they will.

FAG. Well, Thomas, we'll not quarrel about that.

COACH. Why, bless you, the gentlemen of they professions ben't all of 80 a mind—for in our village now tho'ff[2] *Jack Gauge* the *exciseman*,[3] has ta'en to his carrots, there's little Dick the farrier swears he'll never forsake his *bob*, tho' all the college should appear with their own heads!

FAG. Indeed! well said Dick! but hold—mark! mark! Thomas.

COACH. Zooks! 'tis the Captain—Is that the lady with him?

FAG. No! no! that is Madam Lucy—my Master's mistress's maid.— They lodge at that house—but I must after him to tell him the news.

COACH. Odd! he's giving her money!—well, Mr. Fag——

FAG. Good bye, Thomas.—I have an appointment in Gyde's Porch[4] this evening at eight; meet me there, and we'll make a little party.          90

*[Exeunt severally.*


## SCENE II

*A Dressing-room in Mrs. MALAPROP's lodgings*
LYDIA *sitting on a sopha with a book in her hand.—*
LUCY,[5] *as just returned from a message.*

LUCY. Indeed, Ma'am, I transferr'd half the town in search of it:—I don't believe there's a circulating library[6] in Bath I ha'n't been at.

LYD. And could not you get '*The Reward of Constancy*?'[7]

LUCY. No, indeed, Ma'am.

LYD. Nor '*The Fatal Connection*?'[8]

LUCY. No, indeed, Ma'am.

LYD. Nor '*The Mistakes of the Heart*'?[9]

---

[1] Cf. the prologue to *A Trip to Scarborough*, lines 21–4.

[2] This appears to suggest a vulgar pronunciation. Cf. Win Jenkins's 'thof' in Smollett's *Humphry Clinker* (ed. L. M. Knapp, 1966), pp. 42, 107, 220, 338, 352.

[3] 'Mr. Gage the Exciseman' is mentioned in *The Beaux' Stratagem*, V. i.

[4] Gyde kept the old (or lower) assembly rooms on the Lower Walks.

[5] Lucy is also the maid in Congreve's *The Old Batchelor*.

[6] 'Where we read novels, plays, pamphlets, and news-papers, for so small a subscription as a crown a quarter' (Smollett, *Humphry Clinker*, ed. cit., p. 40).

[7] Possibly *The Happy Pair, or, Virtue and Constancy Rewarded* (1771).

[8] A novel by Mrs. Fogerty in two volumes (1773).

[9] A novel in French, dedicated to Rousseau and probably by Pierre Treyssac de Vergy. It appeared in English in three volumes in 1769, with the subsidiary title of 'Memoirs of Lady Caroline Pelham and Lady Victoria Nevil. In a Series of Letters'.

LUCY. Ma'am, as ill-luck would have it, Mr. Bull[1] said Miss Sukey Saunter had just fetch'd it away.

LYD. Heigh-ho!—Did you inquire for '*The Delicate Distress*'?[2]——    10

LUCY. ——Or '*The Memoirs of Lady Woodford*?'[3] Yes indeed, Ma'am.— I ask'd every where for it; and I might have brought it from Mr. Frederick's,[4] but Lady Slattern Lounger, who had just sent it home, had so soiled and dog's-ear'd it, it wa'n't fit for a christian to read.

LYD. Heigh-ho![5]—Yes, I always know when Lady Slattern has been before me.—She has a most observing thumb; and I believe cherishes her nails for the convenience of making marginal notes.—Well, child, what *have* you brought me?

LUCY. Oh! here Ma'am.

    [*Taking books from under her cloke, and from her pockets.*]
This is '*The Gordian Knot*,'—and this '*Peregrine Pickle*.' Here are  20 '*The Tears of Sensibility*'[6] and '*Humphry Clinker*.' This is '*The Memoirs of a Lady of Quality, written by herself*,'—and here the second volume of '*The Sentimental Journey*.'

LYD. Heigh-ho!—What are those books by the glass?

LUCY. The great one is only '*The whole Duty of Man*'[7]—where I press a few blonds, Ma'am.

LYD. Very well—give me the *sal volatile*.[8]

LUCY. Is it in a blue cover, Ma'am?

LYD. My smelling-bottle, you simpleton!

LUCY. O, the drops![9]—here Ma'am.    30

---

[1] Lewis Bull, bookseller at Bath.

[2] *The Delicate Distress and The Gordian Knot* (1769–70). The first was by Elizabeth Griffith (d. 1793), and the second by her husband, Richard Griffith (d. 1788).

[3] Anonymous (1771).

[4] William Frederick, Bath bookseller. In the *Bath Journal*, 24 Sept. 1770, he announced that he was giving up his circulating library.

[5] Cf. *The Beaux' Stratagem*, V. ii:
*Mrs. Sullen.* I don't know what to do? hey-hoe.
*Dor.* That's a desiring Sigh, Sister.
*Mrs. Sullen.* This is a languishing Hour, Sister.

[6] Baculard D'Arnaud's *Les Épreuves du Sentiment*, translated into English by J. Murdoch, as *The Tears of Sensibility* (2 vols., 1773).

[7] *The Whole Duty of Man* (1659), by Richard Allestree (1618–91). Possibly Lucy meant the folio *Works of the learned and pious Author of The Whole Duty of Man*, published in 1704 and 1723.

[8] Cf. Mrs. Tryfort, in Frances Sheridan's *A Journey to Bath*, II, ii: 'I am so low every morning, ha, ha, ha, I protest I use almost an ounce of sal volatile constantly in my tea.'

[9] *Lady Rusport.* Give me the drops; I'm all in a flutter.
*Major.* Hark'e sweetheart, what are those same drops? . . .
*Lucy.* Oh! Sir, they are called the cordial restorative elixir, or the nervous golden drops; they are only for ladies cases.
(R. Cumberland, *The West Indian* (1771), II. xi.)

LYD. Hold!—here's some one coming—quick, see who it is.——

[*Exit* LUCY.

Surely I heard my cousin Julia's voice! [*Re-enter* LUCY.

LUCY. Lud! Ma'am, here is Miss Melville.

LYD. Is it possible!——

*Enter* JULIA.

LYD. My dearest Julia, how delighted am I!—[*Embrace*] How unexpected
was this happiness!

JUL. True, Lydia—and our pleasure is the greater;—but what has been
the matter?—you were denied to me at first!

LYD. Ah! Julia, I have a thousand things to tell you!—but first inform
me, what has conjur'd you to Bath?—Is Sir Anthony here? 40

JUL. He is—we are arrived within this hour—and I suppose he will be
here to wait on Mrs. Malaprop as soon as he is dress'd.

LYD. Then before we are interrupted, let me impart to you some of my
distress!—I know your gentle nature will sympathize with me, tho'
your prudence may condemn me!—My letters have inform'd you of my
whole connexion with Beverley;—but I have lost him, Julia!—my aunt
has discover'd our intercourse by a note she intercepted, and has confin'd me ever since!——Yet, would you believe it? she has fallen
absolutely in love with a tall Irish baronet she met one night since we
have been here, at Lady Macshuffle's rout. 50

JUL. You jest, Lydia!

LYD. No, upon my word.—She really carries on a kind of correspondence
with him, under a feigned name though, till she chuses to be known to
him;——but it is a *Delia* or a *Celia*, I assure you.

JUL. Then, surely, she is now more indulgent to her niece.

LYD. Quite the contrary. Since she has discovered her own frailty, she
is become more suspicious of mine. Then I must inform you of another
plague!—That odious Acres is to be in Bath to-day; so that I protest
I shall be teased out of all spirits!

JUL. Come, come, Lydia, hope the best.—Sir Anthony shall use his 60
interest with Mrs. Malaprop.

LYD. But you have not heard the worst. Unfortunately I had quar-
rell'd with my poor Beverley, just before my aunt made the discovery,
and I have not seen him since, to make it up.

JUL. What was his offence?

LYD. Nothing at all!—But, I don't know how it was, as often as we had
been together, we had never had a quarrel!—And, somehow I was
afraid he would never give me an opportunity.—So, last Thursday,
I wrote a letter to myself, to inform myself that Beverley was at that
time paying his addresses to another woman.—I sign'd it *your Friend* 70
*unknown*, shew'd it to Beverley, charg'd him with his falsehood, put

myself in a violent passion, and vow'd I'd never see him more.

JUL. And you let him depart so, and have not seen him since?

LYD. 'Twas the next day my aunt found the matter out. I intended only
to have teased him three days and a half, and now I've lost him for ever.

JUL. If he is as deserving and sincere as you have represented him to me,
he will never give you up so. Yet consider, Lydia, you tell me he is but
an ensign, and you have thirty thousand pounds!

LYD. But you know I lose most of my fortune, if I marry without my
aunt's consent, till of age; and that is what I have determin'd to do, ever 80
since I knew the penalty.—Nor could I love the man, who would wish
to wait a day for the alternative.

JUL. Nay, this is caprice!

LYD. What, does Julia tax me with caprice?—I thought her lover Faulkland had enured her to it.

JUL. I do not love even *his* faults.

LYD. But a-propos—you have sent to him, I suppose?

JUL. Not yet, upon my word—nor has he the least idea of my being in
Bath.—Sir Anthony's resolution was so sudden, I could not inform
him of it.                                                               90

LYD. Well, Julia, you are your own mistress, (though under the protection of Sir Anthony) yet have you, for this long year, been a slave to the
caprice, the whim, the jealousy of this ungrateful Faulkland,[1] who will
ever delay assuming the right of a husband, while you suffer him to be
equally imperious as a lover.

JUL. Nay, you are wrong entirely.—We were contracted before my
father's death.—*That*, and some consequent embarrassments, have
delay'd what I know to be my Faulkland's most ardent wish.—He is too
generous to trifle on such a point.—And for his character, you wrong
him there too.—No, Lydia, he is too proud, too noble to be jealous; 100
if he is captious, 'tis without dissembling; if fretful, without rudeness.
—Unus'd to the fopperies of love, he is negligent of the little duties
expected from a lover—but being unhackney'd in the passion, his
affection is ardent and sincere; and as it engrosses his whole soul, he
expects every thought and emotion of his mistress to move in unison
with his.—Yet, though his pride calls for this full return—his humility
makes him undervalue those qualities in him, which would entitle him to
it; and not feeling why he should be lov'd to the degree he wishes, he still
suspects that he is not lov'd enough:—This temper, I must own, has cost
me many unhappy hours; but I have learn'd to think myself his debtor, 110
for those imperfections which arise from the ardour of his attachment.

[1] 'His [Faulkland's] ideas of love, honour, generosity, and gratitude, are so refined,
that no hero in romance ever went beyond him' (Frances Sheridan, *Memoirs of Miss
Sidney Bidulph*, 1761, p. 23).

LYD. Well, I cannot blame you for defending him.—But tell me candidly, Julia, had he never sav'd your life, do you think you should have been attach'd to him as you are?—Believe me, the rude blast that overset your boat was a prosperous gale of love to him.

JUL. Gratitude may have strengthened my attachment to Mr. Faulkland, but I lov'd him before he had preserv'd me; yet surely that alone were an obligation sufficient.

LYD. Obligation!—Why a water-spaniel would have done as much.— Well, I should never think of giving my heart to a man because he 120 could swim!

JUL. Come, Lydia, you are too inconsiderate.

LYD. Nay, I do but jest.——What's here?

*Enter* LUCY *in a hurry.*

LUCY. O Ma'am, here is Sir Anthony Absolute just come home with your aunt.

LYD. They'll not come here.—Lucy do you watch. [*Exit* LUCY.

JUL. Yet I must go.—Sir Anthony does not know I am here, and if we meet, he'll detain me, to shew me the town.—I'll take another opportunity of paying my respects to Mrs. Malaprop, when she shall treat me, as long as she chooses, with her select words so ingeniously *mis-* 130 *applied*, without being *mispronounced*.[1]

*Re-enter* LUCY.

LUCY. O Lud! Ma'am, they are both coming up stairs.

LYD. Well, I'll not detain you Coz.—Adieu, my dear Julia, I'm sure you are in haste to send to Faulkland.——There—through my room you'll find another stair-case.

JUL. Adieu.—[*Embrace.*] [*Exit* JULIA.

LYD. Here, my dear Lucy, hide these books.—Quick, quick.—Fling *Peregrine Pickle* under the toilet—throw *Roderick Random* into the closet—put *the Innocent Adultery*[2] into *The Whole Duty of Man*— thrust *Lord Aimworth*[3] under the sopha—cram *Ovid* behind the bolster 140 —there—put *the Man of Feeling*[4] into your pocket—so, so, now lay

[1] Cf. Lady Filmot's description of Mrs. Tryfort in Frances Sheridan's *A Journey to Bath*. I. v: 'the vainest poor creature, and the fondest of hard words, which without *miscalling*, she always takes care to misapply.'

[2] Paul Scarron's *L'Adultère innocente*, translated by Samuel Croxall, in 1722. In Congreve's *The Old Batchelor*, IV. ii, Bellmour remarks, 'I have out-fac'd Suspicion, and even dar'd Discovery—This Cloak my Sanctity, and trusty *Scarron's* Novels my Prayer-Book.'

[3] *The History of Lord Aimsworth, and the Honourable Charles Hartford, Esq., in a Series of Letters.* By the author of *Dorinda Catsby*, and *Ermina, or the Fair Recluse*, 3 vols. (1773).

[4] Henry Mackenzie, *The Man of Feeling* (1771).

*Mrs. Chapone*[1] in sight, and leave *Fordyce's Sermons*[2] open on the table.

LUCY. O burn it, Ma'am, the hair-dresser has torn away as far as *Proper Pride*.

LYD. Never mind—open at *Sobriety*.—Fling me *Lord Chesterfield's Letters*.[3]——Now for 'em.

*Enter Mrs.* MALAPROP *and Sir* ANTHONY ABSOLUTE.

MRS. MAL. There, Sir Anthony, there sits the deliberate Simpleton, who wants to disgrace her family, and lavish herself on a fellow not worth a shilling!

LYD. Madam, I thought you once——                                   150

MRS. MAL. You thought, Miss!—I don't know any business you have to think at all—thought does not become a young woman. But the point we would request of you is, that you will promise to forget this fellow—to illiterate him, I say, quite from your memory.

LYD. Ah! Madam! our memories are independent of our wills.—It is not so easy to forget.

MRS. MAL. But I say it is, Miss; there is nothing on earth so easy as to *forget*, if a person chooses to set about it.—I'm sure I have as much forgot your poor dear uncle as if he had never existed—and I thought it my duty so to do; and let me tell you, Lydia, these violent memories   160 don't become a young woman.

SIR ANTH. Why sure she won't pretend to remember what she's order'd not!—aye, this comes of her reading!

LYD. What crime, Madam, have I committed to be treated thus?

MRS. MAL. Now don't attempt to extirpate yourself from the matter; you know I have proof controvertible of it.—But tell me, will you promise to do as you're bid?—Will you take a husband of your friend's choosing?

LYD. Madam, I must tell you plainly, that had I no preference for any one else, the choice you have made would be my aversion.           170

MRS. MAL. What business have you, Miss, with *preference* and *aversion*? They don't become a young woman; and you ought to know, that as both always wear off, 'tis safest in matrimony to begin with a little *aversion*. I am sure I hated your poor dear uncle before marriage as if he'd been a black-a-moor—and yet, Miss, you are sensible what a wife I made!—and when it pleas'd Heav'n to release me from him, 'tis unknown what tears I shed!—But suppose we were going to give you another choice, will you promise us to give up this Beverley?

[1] *Letters on the Improvement of the Mind. Addressed to a Young Lady* (1773).
[2] *Sermons to Young Women* (1765; 7th edn., 1771), by James Fordyce (1720–96).
[3] *Letters . . . to his Son* (2 vols., 1774) by Philip Dormer Stanhope, 4th Earl of Chesterfield (1694–1773).

LYD. Could I belie my thoughts so far, as to give that promise, my
actions would certainly as far belie my words.                                   180
MRS. MAL. Take yourself to your room.—You are fit company for
nothing but your own ill-humours.
LYD. Willingly, Ma'am—I cannot change for the worse.    [Exit LYDIA.
MRS. MAL. There's a little intricate hussy for you!
SIR ANTH. It is not to be wonder'd at, Ma'am—all this is the natural
consequence of teaching girls to read.—Had I a thousand daughters,
by Heaven! I'd as soon have them taught the black-art as their
alphabet!
MRS. MAL. Nay, nay, Sir Anthony, you are an absolute misanthropy.
SIR ANTH. In my way hither, Mrs. Malaprop, I observed your niece's  190
maid coming forth from a circulating library!—She had a book in each
hand—they were half-bound volumes, with marble covers!—From that
moment I guess'd how full of duty I should see her mistress!
MRS. MAL. Those are vile places, indeed!
SIR ANTH. Madam, a circulating library in a town is, as an ever-green
tree, of diabolical knowledge!—It blossoms through the year!—And
depend on it, Mrs. Malaprop, that they who are so fond of handling
the leaves, will long for the fruit at last.
MRS. MAL. Fie, fie, Sir Anthony, you surely speak laconically!
SIR ANTH. Why, Mrs. Malaprop, in moderation, now, what would you  200
have a woman know?
MRS. MAL. Observe me, Sir Anthony.—I would by no means wish a
daughter of mine to be a progeny[1] of learning; I don't think so much
learning becomes a young woman; for instance—I would never let her
meddle with Greek, or Hebrew, or Algebra, or Simony, or Fluxions,
or Paradoxes,[2] or such inflammatory branches of learning—neither
would it be necessary for her to handle any of your mathematical,
astronomical, diabolical instruments;—But, Sir Anthony, I would send
her, at nine years old, to a boarding-school, in order to learn a little
ingenuity and artifice.—Then, Sir, she should have a supercilious  210
knowledge in accounts;—and as she grew up, I would have her instructed in geometry, that she might know something of the contagious[3]
countries;—but above all, Sir Anthony, she should be mistress of
orthodoxy, that she might not mis-spell, and mis-pronounce words so
shamefully as girls usually do; and likewise that she might reprehend
the true meaning of what she is saying.—This, Sir Anthony, is what

---

[1] Mrs. Tryfort (in *A Journey to Bath*) calls Lord Stewkly 'a progeny! a perfect
progeny!'
[2] Cyclometry, or fluxions, or parallax?
[3] Mrs. Tryfort adds, 'Oh if you were to hear him describe contagious countries as I
have done, it would astonish you.'

I would have a woman know;—and I don't think there is a superstitious article in it.

SIR ANTH. Well, well, Mrs. Malaprop, I will dispute the point no further with you; though I must confess, that you are a truly moderate and polite arguer, for almost every third word you say is on my side of the question.—But, Mrs. Malaprop, to the more important point in debate, —you say, you have no objection to my proposal.

MRS. MAL. None, I assure you.—I am under no positive engagement with Mr. Acres, and as Lydia is so obstinate against him, perhaps your son may have better success.

SIR ANTH. Well, Madam, I will write for the boy directly.—He knows not a syllable of this yet, though I have for some time had the proposal in my head. He is at present with his regiment.

MRS. MAL. We have never seen your son, Sir Anthony; but I hope no objection on his side.

SIR ANTH. Objection!—let him object if he dare!—No, no, Mrs. Malaprop, Jack knows that the least demur puts me in a frenzy directly. —My process was always very simple—in their younger days, 'twas 'Jack, do this;'—if he demur'd—I knock'd him down—and if he grumbled at that—I always sent him out of the room.

MRS. MAL. Aye, and the properest way, o' my conscience!—nothing is so conciliating to young people as severity.—Well, Sir Anthony, I shall give Mr. Acres his discharge, and prepare Lydia to receive your son's invocations;—and I hope you will represent *her* to the Captain as an object not altogether illegible.

SIR ANTH. Madam, I will handle the subject prudently.—Well, I must leave you—and let me beg you, Mrs. Malaprop, to enforce this matter roundly to the girl;—take my advice—keep a tight hand—if she rejects this proposal—clap her under lock and key:—and if you were just to let the servants forget to bring her dinner for three or four days, you can't conceive how she'd come about!                    [*Exit Sir* ANTH.

MRS. MAL. Well, at any rate I shall be glad to get her from under my intuition.—She has somehow discovered my partiality for Sir Lucius O'Trigger—sure, Lucy can't have betray'd me!—No, the girl is such a simpleton, I should have made her confess it.—Lucy!—Lucy!— [*calls*] Had she been one of your artificial ones, I should never have trusted her.

*Enter* LUCY.

LUCY. Did you call, Ma'am?

MRS. MAL. Yes, girl—Did you see Sir Lucius while you was out?

LUCY. No, indeed, Ma'am, not a glimpse of him.

MRS. MAL. You are sure, Lucy, that you never mention'd——

LUCY. O Gemini! I'd sooner cut my tongue out.

MRS. MAL. Well, don't let your simplicity be impos'd on.

LUCY. No. Ma'am.                                                            260

MRS. MAL. So, come to me presently, and I'll give you another letter to Sir Lucius;—but mind Lucy—if ever you betray what you are entrusted with—(unless it be other people's secrets to me) you forfeit my malevolence for ever:—and your being a simpleton shall be no excuse for your locality.                        [*Exit Mrs.* MALAPROP.

LUCY. Ha! ha! ha!—So, my dear *simplicity*, let me give you a little respite—[*altering her manner*]—let girls in my station be as fond as they please of appearing expert, and knowing in their trusts;—commend me to a mask of *silliness*, and a pair of sharp eyes for my own interest under it!—Let me see to what account I have turn'd my *simplicity*   270 lately—                                                     [*looks at a paper*]
For *abetting Miss Lydia Languish in a design of running away with an Ensign!—in money—sundry times—twelve pound twelve—gowns, five —hats, ruffles, caps,* etc. etc.—*numberless!—From the said Ensign, within this last month, six guineas and a half.*—About a quarter's pay!—Item, *from Mrs. Malaprop, for betraying the young people to her*—when I found matters were likely to be discovered—*two guineas, and a black paduasoy.*—Item, *from Mr. Acres, for carrying divers letters*—which I never deliver'd—*two guineas, and a pair of buckles.*—Item, *from Sir Lucius O'Trigger—three crowns—two gold pocket-pieces*[1]—*and a silver*   280 *snuff-box!*——Well done, *simplicity!*—yet I was forced to make my Hibernian believe, that he was corresponding, not with the *Aunt*, but with the *Niece*: for, though not over rich, I found he had too much pride and delicacy to sacrifice the feelings of a gentleman to the necessities of his fortune.                                                    [*Exit.*

END OF THE FIRST ACT

# ACT II

## SCENE I

*Captain* ABSOLUTE's *Lodgings*

*Captain* ABSOLUTE *and* FAG

FAG. Sir, while I was there, Sir Anthony came in: I told him, you had sent me to inquire after his health, and to know if he was at leisure to see you.

---

[1] Coins carried as lucky charms, or medallions: cf. S. Foote, *The Maid of Bath* (1771), II. i:
  *Flint.* Here is a Porto-Bello pocket piece of Admiral Varnon, with his image on one side, and six men of war only, all in full sail, on the other—
  *L. Cath.* That's a curious medallion!

ABS. And what did he say, on hearing I was at Bath?

FAG. Sir, in my life I never saw an elderly gentleman more astonished! He started back two or three paces, rapt out a dozen interjectoral oaths, and asked, what the devil had brought you here!

ABS. Well, Sir, and what did you say?

FAG. O, I lied, Sir—I forget the precise lie, but you may depend on't; he got no truth from me. Yet, with submission, for fear of blunders in future, I should be glad to fix what *has* brought us to Bath: in order that we may lie a little consistently.—Sir Anthony's servants were curious, Sir, very curious indeed.

ABS. You have said nothing to them——?

FAG. O, not a word, Sir—not a word.—Mr. Thomas, indeed, the coachman (whom I take to be the discreetest of whips)—

ABS. S'death!—you rascal! you have not trusted him!

FAG. O, *no*, Sir—no—no—not a syllable, upon my veracity!—He was, indeed, a little inquisitive; but I was sly, Sir—devilish sly!—My Master (said I) honest Thomas (you know, Sir, one says *honest* to one's inferiors) is come to Bath to *recruit*—Yes, Sir—I said, *to recruit*—and whether for men, money, or constitution, you know, Sir, is nothing to him, nor any one else.

ABS. Well—*recruit* will do—let it be so—

FAG. O, Sir, recruit will do surprisingly—indeed, to give the thing an air, I told Thomas, that your Honour had already inlisted, five disbanded chairmen, seven minority waiters,[1] and thirteen billiard markers.

ABS. You blockhead, never say more than is necessary.

FAG. I beg pardon, Sir—I beg pardon—But with submission, a lie is nothing unless one supports it.—Sir, whenever I draw on my invention for a good current lie, I always forge *indorsements*, as well as the bill.

ABS. Well, take care you don't hurt your credit, by offering too much security.—Is Mr. Faulkland returned?

FAG. He is above, Sir, changing his dress.

ABS. Can you tell whether he has been informed of Sir Anthony's and Miss Melville's arrival?

FAG. I fancy not, Sir; he has seen no one since he came in, but his gentleman, who was with him at Bristol.—I think, Sir, I hear Mr. Faulkland coming down—

ABS. Go, tell him I am here.

FAG. Yes, Sir—[*going*] I beg pardon, Sir, but should Sir Anthony call, you will do me the favour to remember, that we are *recruiting*, if you please.

ABS. Well, well.

[1] Young waiters? Philip B. Daghlian suggests, in *Modern Language Quarterly*, vi (1945), 421-2, that it bears some reference to Robert Mackreth (?1725-1819), once a waiter but M.P. for Castle Rising from 1774.

FAG. And in tenderness to my character, if your Honour could bring in
the chairmen and waiters, I shall esteem it as an obligation;—for
though I never scruple a lie to serve my Master, yet it *hurts* one's
conscience, to be found out.                                    [*Exit.*

ABS. Now for my whimsical friend—if he does not know that his
mistress is here, I'll tease him a little before I tell him——          50

*Enter* FAULKLAND.

Faulkland, you're welcome to Bath again; you are punctual in your
return.

FAULK. Yes; I had nothing to detain me, when I had finished the business I went on. Well, what news since I left you? How stand matters
between you and Lydia?

ABS. Faith, much as they were; I have not seen her since our quarrel,
however I expect to be recalled every hour.

FAULK. Why don't you persuade her to go off with you at once?

ABS. What, and lose two thirds of her fortune? You forget that my friend.
—No, no, I could have brought her to that long ago.                    60

FAULK. Nay then, you trifle too long—if you are sure of *her*, propose to
the aunt *in your own character*, and write to Sir Anthony for his consent.

ABS. Softly, softly, for though I am convinced my little Lydia would
elope with me as Ensign Beverley, yet am I by no means certain that
she would take me with the impediment of our friend's consent, a
regular humdrum wedding, and the reversion of a good fortune on my
side; no, no, I must prepare her gradually for the discovery, and make
myself necessary to her, before I risk it.—Well, but Faulkland, you'll
dine with us to-day at the Hotel?

FAULK. Indeed I cannot: I am not in spirits to be of such a party.          70

ABS. By Heavens! I shall forswear your company. You are the most
teasing, captious, incorrigible lover!—Do love like a man.

FAULK. I own I am unfit for company.

ABS. Am not *I* a lover; aye, and a romantic one too? Yet do I carry every
where with me such a confounded farago of doubts, fears, hopes, wishes,
and all the flimsy furniture of a country Miss's brain!

FAULK. Ah! Jack, your heart and soul are not, like mine, fixed immutably
on one only object.—You throw for a large stake, but losing—you could
stake, and throw again:—but I have set my sum of happiness on this
cast, and not to succeed, were to be stript of all.                      80

ABS. But for Heaven's sake! what grounds for apprehension can your
whimsical brain conjure up at present?

FAULK. What grounds for apprehension did you say? Heavens! are there
not a thousand! I fear for her spirits—her health—her life.—My
absence may fret her; her anxiety for my return, her fears for me, may
oppress her gentle temper. And for her health—does not every hour

bring me cause to be alarmed? If it rains, some shower may even then have chilled her delicate frame!—If the wind be keen, some rude blast may have affected her! The heat of noon, the dews of the evening, may endanger the life of her, for whom only I value mine. O! Jack, when delicate and feeling souls are separated, there is not a feature in the sky, not a movement of the elements; not an aspiration of the breeze, but hints some cause for a lover's apprehension!

ABS. Aye, but we may choose whether we will take the hint or not.— So then, Faulkland, if you were convinced that Julia were well and in spirits, you would be entirely content.

FAULK. I should be happy beyond measure—I am anxious only for that.

ABS. Then to cure your anxiety at once—Miss Melville is in perfect health, and is at this moment in Bath.

FAULK. Nay Jack—don't trifle with me.

ABS. She is arrived here with my father within this hour.

FAULK. Can you be serious?

ABS. I thought you knew Sir Anthony better than to be surprised at a sudden whim of this kind.—Seriously then, it is as I tell you—upon my honour.

FAULK. My dear friend!——Hollo, Du-Peigne! my hat—my dear Jack—*now nothing on earth can give me a moment's uneasiness.*

*Enter* FAG.

FAG. Sir, Mr. Acres just arrived is below.

ABS. Stay, Faulkland, this Acres lives within a mile of Sir Anthony, and he shall tell you how your mistress has been ever since you left her.— Fag, shew the gentleman up. [*Exit* FAG.

FAULK. What, is he much acquainted in the family?

ABS. O, very intimate: I insist on your not going: besides, his character will divert you.

FAULK. Well, I should like to ask him a few questions.

ABS. He is likewise a rival of mine—that is of my *other self's*, for he does not think his friend Capt. Absolute ever saw the lady in question;—and it is ridiculous enough to hear him complain to me of *one Beverley*, a concealed sculking rival, who——

FAULK. Hush!—He's here.

*Enter* ACRES.

ACRES. Hah! my dear friend, noble captain, and honest Jack, how do'st thou? just arrived faith, as you see.—Sir, your humble servant. Warm work on the roads Jack—Odds whips and wheels, I've travelled like a Comet, with a tail of dust all the way as long as the Mall.

ABS. Ah! Bob, you are indeed an excentric Planet, but we know your attraction hither—give me leave to introduce Mr. Faulkland to you; Mr. Faulkland, Mr. Acres.

ACRES. Sir, I am most heartily glad to see you: Sir, I solicit your connections.—Hey Jack—what this is Mr. Faulkland, who——

ABS. Aye, Bob, Miss Melville's Mr. Faulkland. 130

ACRES. Od'so! she and your father can be but just arrived before me—I suppose you have seen them.——Ah! Mr. Faulkland, you are indeed a happy man.

FAULK. I have not seen Miss Melville yet, Sir—I hope she enjoyed full health and spirits in Devonshire?

ACRES. Never knew her better in my life, Sir,—never better.—Odd's Blushes and Blooms! she has been as healthy as the German Spa.

FAULK. Indeed!—I did hear that she had been a little indisposed.

ACRES. False, false, Sir—only said to vex you: quite the reverse I assure you. 140

FAULK. There, Jack, you see she has the advantage of me; I had almost fretted myself ill.

ABS. Now are you angry with your mistress for not having been sick.

FAULK. No, no, you misunderstand me:—yet surely a little trifling indisposition is not an unnatural consequence of absence from those we love.—Now confess—isn't there something unkind in this violent, robust, unfeeling health?

ABS. O, it was very unkind of her to be well in your absence to be sure!

ACRES. Good apartments, Jack.

FAULK. Well, Sir, but you were saying that Miss Melville has been so 150 *exceedingly* well—what then she has been merry and gay I suppose?—Always in spirits—hey?

ACRES. Merry, Odds Crickets! she has been the bell and spirit of the company wherever she has been—so lively and entertaining! so full of wit and humour!

FAULK. There, Jack, there.—O, by my soul! there is an innate levity in woman, that nothing can overcome.—What! happy and I away!

ABS. Have done: how foolish this is! just now you were only apprehensive for your mistress's *spirits*.

FAULK. Why, Jack, have I been the joy and spirit of the company? 160

ABS. No, indeed, you have not.

FAULK. Have I been lively and entertaining?

ABS. O, upon my word, I acquit you.

FAULK. Have I been full of wit and humour?

ABS. No, faith, to do you justice, you have been confoundedly stupid indeed.

ACRES. What's the matter with the gentleman?

ABS. He is only expressing his great satisfaction at hearing that Julia has been so well and happy—that's all—hey, Faulkland?

FAULK. Oh! I am rejoiced to hear it—yes, yes, she has a *happy* disposition! 170

ACRES. That she has indeed—then she is so accomplished—so sweet a voice—so expert at her Harpsichord—such a mistress of flat and sharp, squallante, rumblante, and quiverante!—there was this time month—Odds Minnums and Crotchets! how she did chir[r]up at Mrs. Piano's Concert.

FAULK. There again, what say you to this? you see she has been all mirth and song—not a thought of me!

ABS. Pho! man, is not music the food of love?[1]

FAULK. Well, well, it may be so.—Pray Mr. —— what's his d—d name? —Do you remember what songs Miss Melville sung?                    180

ACRES. Not I, indeed.

ABS. Stay now, they were some pretty, melancholy, purling stream airs, I warrant; perhaps you may recollect:—did she sing—'*When absent from my soul's delight?*'[2]

ACRES. No, that wa'n't it.

ABS. Or—'*Go, gentle Gales!*'[3]——'*Go, gentle Gales!*' [sings]

ACRES. O no! nothing like it.—Odds! now I recollect one of them— '*My heart's my own, my will is free.*'[4] [sings]

---

[1] *Twelfth Night*, I. i. 'If music be the food of love, play on.'

[2] The sixth of *Twelve Songs set to Music by William Jackson of Exeter: Opera Quarta*. (n.d.), pp. 14–19. The first of the three stanzas reads:

> When absent from my Soul's Delight,
> What terrors fill my troubled Breast,
> Once more return'd to thy lov'd sight,
> Hope too returns, my Fears have rest.

[3] The fifth of the same set of songs by Jackson, pp. 10–14. The words are from Pope, 'Autumn: the third Pastoral', ll. 17–22. The first two stanzas (of four) read:

> Go, gentle Gales, go gentle Gales
> And bear my sighs away
> To Delia's Ear, to Delia's Ear,
> The tender Notes convey.

> As some sad Turtle his long lost Love deplores
> And with deep Murmurs fills the sounding Shores,
> Thus far from Delia to the Wood I mourn,
> Alike unheard, unpitied, and forlorn.

[4] From Isaac Bickerstaff's *Love in a Village* (1762), Act I:

> My heart's my own, my will is free,
> And so shall be my voice;
> No mortal man shall wed with me,
> Till first he's made my choice.

> Let parents rule, cry nature's laws;
> And children still obey;
> And is there then no saving clause
> Against tyrannic sway.

'Charles', writing in *The Gazetteer*, 21 Sept. 1771, remarks that the 'ill-effects, which romance and novel-reading, has upon the minds of the fair sex has been often and justly exposed; but there is another part of their study, which, is in my opinion, of a similar nature . . . I mean the fashionable songs and airs which young ladies are taught from

FAULK. Fool! fool that I am! to fix all my happiness on such a trifler!
S'death! to make herself the pipe and ballad-monger of a circle! to sooth   190
her light heart with catches and glees!—What can you say to this, Sir?

ABS. Why, that I should be glad to hear my mistress had been so
merry, *Sir*.

FAULK. Nay, nay, nay—I am not sorry that she has been happy—no, no,
I am glad of that—I would not have had her sad or sick—yet surely
a sympathetic heart would have shewn itself even in the choice of a
song—she might have been temperately healthy, and somehow,
plaintively gay;—but she has been dancing too, I doubt not!

ACRES. What does the gentleman say about dancing?

ABS. He says the lady we speak of dances as well as she sings.             200

ACRES. Aye truly, does she—there was at our last race-ball——

FAULK. Hell and the devil!—There! there!I— told you so! I told you so!
Oh! she thrives in my absence!—Dancing!—but her whole feelings
have been in opposition with mine!—I have been anxious, silent,
pensive, sedentary—my days have been hours of care, my nights of
watchfulness.—She has been all Health! Spirit! Laugh! Song! Dance!
—Oh! d—n'd, d—n'd levity!

ABS. For Heaven's sake! Faulkland, don't expose yourself so.—Suppose
she has danced, what then?—does not the ceremony of society often
oblige——                                                                  210

FAULK. Well, well, I'll contain myself—perhaps, as you say—for form
sake.—What, Mr. Acres, you were praising Miss Melville's manner of
dancing a *minuet*—hey?

ACRES. O I dare insure her for that—but what I was going to speak of was
her *country dancing*:—Odds swimmings! she has such an air with her!—

FAULK. Now disappointment on her!—defend this, Absolute, why don't
you defend this?—Country-dances! jiggs, and reels! am I to blame now?
A Minuet I could have forgiven—I should not have minded that—I
say I should not have regarded a Minuet—but *Country-dances*! Z——ds!
had she made one in a *Cotillon*—I believe I could have forgiven even   220
that—but to be monkey-led for a night!—to run the gauntlet thro'
a string of amorous palming puppies!—to shew paces like a managed[1]
filly!—O Jack, there never can be but *one* man in the world, whom a
truly modest and delicate woman ought to pair with in a *Country-dance*;
and even then, the rest of the couples should be her great uncles and
aunts!

ABS. Aye, to be sure!—grand-fathers and grand-mothers!

---

their childhood to sing, and get by heart.' He mentions 'My heart's my own' as among
the fifteen that seem to him to be 'extravagant' and 'inflammatory'.

[1] Taught the 'manège', stepping and moving according to the strict practice of the
riding school.

FAULK. If there be but one vicious mind in the Set, 'twill spread like a contagion—the action of their pulse beats to the lascivious movement of the jigg—their quivering, warm-breath'd sighs impregnate the very 230 air—the atmosphere becomes electrical to love, and each amorous spark[1] darts thro' every link of the chain!—I must leave you—I own I am somewhat flurried—and that confounded looby has perceived it. [*Going.*

ABS. Nay, but stay Faulkland, and thank Mr. Acres for his good news.

FAULK. D—n his news! [*Exit* FAULKLAND.

ABS. Ha! ha! ha! poor Faulkland five minutes since—'nothing on earth could give him a moment's uneasiness!'

ACRES. The gentleman wa'n't angry at my praising his mistress, was he?

ABS. A little jealous, I believe, Bob. 240

ACRES. You don't say so? Ha! ha! jealous of me—that's a good joke.

ABS. There's nothing strange in that, Bob: let me tell you, that sprightly grace and insinuating manner of your's will do some mischief among the girls here.

ACRES. Ah! you joke—ha! ha! mischief—ha! ha! but you know I am not my own property, my dear Lydia, has forestalled me.——She could never abide me in the country, because I used to dress so badly —but odds frogs and tambours! I shan't take matters so here—now ancient Madam has no voice in it—I'll make my old clothes know who's master—I shall straitway cashier the hunting-frock—and render 250 my leather breeches incapable—My hair has been in training some time.

ABS. Indeed!

ACRES. Aye—and tho'ff[2] the side-curls are a little restive, my hind-part takes to it very kindly.

ABS. O, you'll polish, I doubt not.

ACRES. Absolutely I propose so—then if I can find out this Ensign Beverley, odds triggers and flints! I'll make him know the difference o't.

ABS. Spoke like a man——but pray, Bob, I observe you have got an odd kind of a new method of swearing——

ACRES. Ha! ha! you've taken notice of it—'tis genteel, isn't *it*?—I didn't 260 invent it myself though; but a commander in our militia—a great scholar, I assure you—says that there is no meaning in the common oaths, and that nothing but their antiquity makes them respectable;— because, he says, the ancients would never stick to an oath or two, but would say By Jove! or by Bacchus! or by Mars! or by Venus! or by Pallas! according to the sentiment—so that to swear with propriety,

---

[1] 'These exhalations, or subtle effluvia, constitute electricity . . . They seem to adhere to the extremities of the bodies which they surround, and from which they recede, in the form of sparks' (*A New and Complete Dictionary of Arts and Sciences* (2nd edn., 1763), p. 1050).

[2] See p. 15, n. 2.

says my little Major, the 'oath should be an echo to the sense;'[1] and
this we call the *oath referential,* or *sentimental swearing*[2]—ha! ha! ha!
'tis genteel, isn't it?

ABS. Very genteel, and very new indeed—and I dare say will supplant    270
all other figures of imprecation.

ACRES. Aye, aye, the best terms will grow obsolete——D—ns have had
their day.

*Enter* FAG.

FAG. Sir, there is a gentleman below, desires to see you—shall I shew
him into the parlour?

ABS. Aye—you may.

ACRES. Well, I must be gone——

ABS. Stay; who is it, Fag?

FAG. Your father, Sir.

ABS. You puppy, why didn't you shew him up directly?      [*Exit* FAG.    280

ACRES. You have business with Sir Anthony.—I expect a message from
Mrs. Malaprop at my lodgings—I have sent also to my dear friend Sir
Lucius O'Trigger.—Adieu, Jack, we must meet at night, when you
shall give me a dozen bumpers to little Lydia.

ABS. That I will with all my heart.                       [*Exit* ACRES.
Now for a parental lecture—I hope he has heard nothing of the
business that has brought me here.—I wish the gout had held him fast
in Devonshire, with all my soul!

*Enter Sir* ANTHONY.

ABS. Sir, I am delighted to see you here; and looking so well!—your
sudden arrival at Bath made me apprehensive for your health.          290

SIR ANTH. Very apprehensive, I dare say, Jack.—What, you are recruiting here, hey?

ABS. Yes, Sir, I am on duty.

SIR ANTH. Well, Jack, I am glad to see you, tho' I did not expect it, for
I was going to write to you on a little matter of business.—Jack, I have
been considering that I grow old and infirm, and shall probably not
trouble you long.

ABS. Pardon me, Sir, I never saw you look more strong and hearty; and
I pray frequently that you may continue so.

SIR ANTH. I hope your prayers may be heard with all my heart. Well    300
then, Jack, I have been considering that I am so strong and hearty,
I may continue to plague you a long time.—Now, Jack, I am sensible

---

[1] A. Pope, *An Essay in Criticism* (1711), ll. 364–5:
> 'Tis not enough no harshness gives offence,
> The sound must seem an echo to the sense.

[2] Cf. L. Sterne, *Tristam Shandy*, 3. 12: 'I declare I object only to a connoisseur in
swearing.'

that the income of your commission, and what I have hitherto allowed you, is but a small pittance for a lad of your spirit.

ABS. Sir, you are very good.

SIR ANTH. And it is my wish, while yet I live, to have my Boy make some figure in the world.—I have resolved, therefore, to fix you at once in a noble independence.

ABS. Sir, your kindness overpowers me—such generosity makes the gratitude of reason more lively than the sensations even of filial affection. 310

SIR ANTH. I am glad you are so sensible of my attention—and you shall be master of a large estate in a few weeks.

ABS. Let my future life, Sir, speak my gratitude: I cannot express the sense I have of your munificence.——Yet, Sir, I presume you would not wish me to quit the army?

SIR ANTH. O, that shall be as your wife chooses.

ABS. My wife, Sir!

SIR ANTH. Aye, aye, settle that between you—settle that between you.

ABS. A *wife*, Sir, did you say?

SIR ANTH. Aye, a wife—why; did not I mention her before? 320

ABS. Not a word of her, Sir.

SIR ANTH. Odd so!—I mustn't forget *her* tho'.—Yes, Jack, the independence I was talking of is by a marriage—the fortune is saddled with a wife—but I suppose that makes no difference.

ABS. Sir! Sir!—you amaze me!

SIR ANTH. Why, what the d——l's the matter with the fool? Just now you were all gratitude and duty.

ABS. I was, Sir,—you talked to me of independence and a fortune, but not a word of a wife.

SIR ANTH. Why—what difference does that make? Odd's life, Sir! if you 330 have the estate, you must take it with the live stock on it, as it stands.

ABS. If my happiness is to be the price, I must beg leave to decline the purchase.——Pray, Sir, who is the lady?

SIR ANTH. What's that to you, Sir?—Come, give me your promise to love, and to marry her directly.

ABS. Sure, Sir, this is not very reasonable, to summon my affections for a lady I know nothing of!

SIR ANTH. I am sure, Sir, 'tis more unreasonable in you to *object* to a lady you know nothing of.

ABS. Then, Sir, I must tell you plainly, that my inclinations are fix'd on 340 another—my heart is engaged to an Angel.

SIR ANTH. Then pray let it send an excuse.——It is very sorry—but *business* prevents its waiting on her.

ABS. But my vows are pledged to her.

SIR ANTH. Let her foreclose, Jack; let her foreclose; they are not worth redeeming: besides, you have the Angel's vows in exchange, I suppose; so there can be no loss there.

ABS. You must excuse me, Sir, if I tell you, once for all, that in this point I cannot obey you.

SIR ANTH. Hark'ee Jack;—I have heard you for some time with patience  350
—I have been cool,—quite cool;—but take care—you know I am compliance itself—when I am not thwarted;—no one more easily led—when I have my own way;—but don't put me in a phrenzy.

ABS. Sir, I must repeat it—in this I cannot obey you.

SIR ANTH. Now, d—n me! if ever I call you *Jack* again while I live!

ABS. Nay, Sir, but hear me.

SIR ANTH. Sir, I won't hear a word—not a word! not one word! so give me your promise by a nod—and I'll tell you what, Jack—I mean, you Dog—if you don't, by——

ABS. What, Sir, promise to link myself to some mass of ugliness! to——  360

SIR ANTH. Z——ds! sirrah! the lady shall be as ugly as I choose: she shall have a hump on each shoulder; she shall be as crooked as the Crescent; her one eye shall roll like the Bull's in Cox's musæum[1]—she shall have a skin like a mummy, and the beard of a Jew—she shall be all this, sirrah!—yet I'll make you ogle her all day, and sit up all night to write sonnets on her beauty.

ABS. This is reason and moderation indeed!

SIR ANTH. None of your sneering, puppy! no grinning, jackanapes!

ABS. Indeed, Sir, I never was in a worse humour for mirth in my life.

SIR ANTH. 'Tis false, Sir! I know you are laughing in your sleeve: I know  370
you'll grin when I am gone, sirrah!

ABS. Sir, I hope I know my duty better.

SIR ANTH. None of your passion, Sir! none of your violence! if you please.—It won't do with me, I promise you.

ABS. ·Indeed, Sir, I never was cooler in my life.

SIR ANTH. 'Tis a confounded lie!—I know you are in a passion in your heart; I know you are, you hypocritical young dog! but it won't do.

ABS. Nay, Sir, upon my word.

SIR ANTH. So you will fly out! can't you be cool, like me? What the devil good can *Passion* do!—*Passion* is of no service, you impudent,  380
insolent, over-bearing Reprobate!—There you sneer again!—don't provoke me!—but you rely upon the mildness of my temper—you do, you Dog! you play upon the meekness of my disposition! Yet take care
—the patience of a saint may be overcome at last!—but mark! I give you six hours and a half to consider of this: if you then agree, without

___

[1] James Cox exhibited mechanical 'toys'—singing birds, chronoscopes, costly and jewelled ornaments—in Spring Gardens. One of them was described as 'a curious bull', and another was 'a pedestal of four bulls'. See the *Hibernian Magazine*, Feb. 1772, pp. 205-10.

any condition, to do every thing on earth that I choose, why—confound
you! I may in time forgive you——If not, z——ds! don't enter the same
hemisphere with me! don't dare to breathe the same air, or use the
same light with me; but get an atmosphere and a sun of your own!
I'll strip you of your commission; I'll lodge a five-and-threepence in    390
the hands of trustees, and you shall live on the interest.—I'll disown
you, I'll disinherit you, I'll unget you![1] and—d—n me, if ever I call
you Jack again!                                   [*Exit* SIR ANTHONY.

ABSOLUTE, *solus.*

ABS. Mild, gentle, considerate father—I kiss your hands.—What a
   tender method of giving his opinion in these matters Sir Anthony has!
   I dare not trust him with the truth.—I wonder what old, wealthy Hag
   it is that he wants to bestow on me!—yet he married himself for love!
   and was in his youth a bold Intriguer, and a gay Companion!

*Enter* FAG.

FAG. Assuredly, Sir, our Father is wrath to a degree; he comes down
   stairs eight or ten steps at a time—muttering, growling, and thumping    400
   the bannisters all the way: I, and the Cook's dog, stand bowing at the
   door—rap! he gives me a stroke on the head with his cane; bids me
   carry that to my master, then kicking the poor Turnspit into the area,
   d—ns us all, for a puppy triumvirate!——Upon my credit, Sir, were
   I in your place, and found my father such very bad company, I should
   certainly drop his acquaintance.
ABS. Cease your impertinence, Sir, at present.—Did you come in for
   nothing more?——Stand out of the way!
                                   [*Pushes him aside, and Exit.*

FAG, *solus.*

FAG. Soh! Sir Anthony trims my Master; He is afraid to reply to his
   Father—then vents his spleen on poor Fag!——When one is vexed by    410
   one person, to revenge one's self on another, who happens to come in
   the way—is the vilest injustice! Ah! it shews the worst temper—the
   basest——

*Enter* ERRAND-BOY.

BOY. Mr. Fag! Mr. Fag! your Master calls you.
FAG. Well, you little, dirty puppy, you need not baul so!——The
   meanest disposition! the——
BOY. Quick, quick, Mr. Fag.

---

[1] Cf. Sir Sampson (Congreve, *Love for Love*, II. i): 'Are you not my Slave? Did I
not beget you? And might I not have chosen whether I would have begot you or no?'

FAG. *Quick, quick*, you impudent Jackanapes! am I to be commanded by you too? you little, impertinent, insolent, kitchen-bred——

*[Exit, kicking and beating him.*

## SCENE II

### *The* North Parade

#### *Enter* LUCY.

LUCY. So—I shall have another Rival to add to my mistress's list—Captain Absolute.——However, I shall not enter his name till my purse has received notice in form. Poor Acres is dismissed!—Well, I have done him a last friendly office, in letting him know that Beverley was here before him.—Sir Lucius is generally more punctual, when he expects to hear from his *dear Dalia*,[1] as he calls her: —I wonder he's not here!—I have a little scruple of conscience from this deceit; tho' I should not be paid so well, if my hero knew that *Delia* was near fifty, and her own mistress.

#### *Enter* SIR LUCIUS O'TRIGGER.

SIR LUC. Hah! my little embassadress—upon my conscience I have been looking for you; I have been on the South Parade this half-hour.                10

LUCY. (*Speaking simply*) O gemini! and I have been waiting for your worship here on the North.

SIR LUC. Faith!—may be, that was the reason we did not meet; and it is very comical too, how you could go out and I not see you—for I was only taking a nap at the Parade-Coffee-house, and I chose the *window* on purpose that I might not miss you.

LUCY. My stars! Now I'd wager a six-pence I went by while you were asleep.

SIR LUC. Sure enough it must have been so——and I never dreamt it was so late, till I waked. Well, but my little girl, have you got nothing for me?    20

LUCY. Yes, but I have:——I've got a letter for you in my pocket.

SIR LUC. O faith! I guessed you weren't come empty-handed—well—let me see what the dear creature says.

LUCY. There, Sir Lucius.                                    *[Gives him a letter.*

---

[1] Cf. 'The Bath Toast', a glee for three voices, by Henry Harrington (1727–1816):

> To Delia fill the sprightly wine,
> The health's engaging and divine;
> O'er ev'ry heart this toast shall reign,
> Whose eyes out-sparkle bright Champaign.
> Let purest odours scent the air,
> And wreaths of roses bind our hair,
> In her chaste lips these blushing lie,
> And those her gentle sighs supply.

[J. Bowen], *A Selection of Favourite Catches, Glees, &c., as sung at the Meetings of the Harmonic Society in the City of Bath* (Bath, 1798), pp. 33–4.

SIR LUC. (Reads) '*Sir—there is often a sudden incentive impulse in love,
that has a greater induction than years of domestic combination: such was
the commotion I felt at the first superfluous view of Sir Lucius O'Trigger.*'
Very pretty, upon my word. '*Female punctuation forbids me to say more;
yet let me add, that it will give me joy infallible to find Sir Lucius worthy
the last criterion of my affections.*——DELIA.' Upon my conscience!    30
Lucy, your lady is a great mistress of language.—Faith, she's quite the
queen of the dictionary!—for the devil a word dare refuse coming at
her call—tho' one would think it was quite out of hearing.

LUCY. Aye, Sir, a lady of her experience.

SIR LUC. Experience! what, at seventeen?

LUCY. O true, Sir—but then she reads so——my stars! how she will
read off-hand!

SIR LUC. Faith, she must be very deep read to write this way—tho' she
is rather an arbitrary writer too—for here are a great many poor words
pressed into the service of this note, that would get their *habeas corpus*    40
from any court in Christendom.

LUCY. Ah! Sir Lucius, if you were to hear how she talks of you!

SIR LUC. O tell her, I'll make her the best husband in the world, and
Lady O'Trigger into the bargain!—But we must get the old gentlewoman's consent—and do every thing fairly.

LUCY. Nay, Sir Lucius, I thought you wa'n't rich enough to be so nice!

SIR LUC. Upon my word, young woman, you have hit it:—I am so poor
that I can't afford to do a dirty action.—If I did not want money I'd
steal your mistress and her fortune with a great deal of pleasure.—
However, my pretty girl, (*gives her money*) here's a little something to    50
buy you a ribband; and meet me in the evening, and I'll give you an
answer to this. So, hussy, take a kiss before-hand, to put you in mind.
                                                      [*Kisses her.*

LUCY. O lud! Sir Lucius—I never seed such a gemman! My lady won't
like you if you're so impudent.

SIR LUC. Faith she will, Lucy——that same——pho! what's the name
of it?——*Modesty*!——is a quality in a lover more praised by the
women than liked; so, if your mistress asks you whether Sir Lucius
ever gave you a kiss, tell her *fifty*—my dear.

LUCY. What, would you have me tell her a lie?

SIR LUC. Ah then, you baggage! I'll make it a truth presently.    60

LUCY. For shame now; here is some one coming.

SIR LUC. O faith, I'll quiet your conscience!
                        [*Sees* FAG.—*Exit, humming a Tune.*


*Enter* FAG.

FAG. So, so, Ma'am. I humbly beg pardon.

LUCY. O lud!—now, Mr. Fag—you flurry one so.

FAG. Come, come, Lucy, here's no one bye—so a little less simplicity,
with a grain or two more sincerity, if you please.——You play false
with us, Madam.——I saw you give the Baronet a letter.——My
Master shall know this—and if he don't call him out—I will.

LUCY. Ha! ha! ha! you gentlemen's gentlemen are so hasty.——That
letter was from Mrs. Malaprop, simpleton.——She is taken with Sir 70
Lucius's address.

FAG. How! what tastes some people have!——Why I suppose I have
walked by her window an hundred times.——But what says our young
lady? Any message to my master?

LUCY. Sad news! Mr. Fag.—A worse Rival than Acres!—Sir Anthony
Absolute has proposed his son.

FAG. What, Captain Absolute?

LUCY. Even so.—I overheard it all.

FAG. Ha! ha! ha!—very good, faith.—Goodbye, Lucy, I must away
with this news.                                                                        80

LUCY. Well—you may laugh—but it is true, I assure you. [*Going.*] But
—Mr. Fag—tell your master not to be cast down by this.

FAG. O, he'll be so disconsolate!

LUCY. And charge him not to think of quarrelling with young Absolute.

FAG. Never fear!—never fear!

LUCY. Be sure—bid him keep up his spirits.

FAG. We will—we will.                                    [*Exeunt severally.*

END OF THE SECOND ACT


# ACT III

## SCENE I

### *The* North Parade

#### *Enter* ABSOLUTE.

'Tis just as Fag told me, indeed.—Whimsical enough, faith! My
Father wants to *force* me to marry the very girl I am plotting to run
away with!——He must not know of my connection with her yet
a-while.——He has too summary a method of proceeding in these
matters.——However, I'll read my recantation instantly.——My conversion is something sudden, indeed—but I can assure him it is very
*sincere.*——So, so—here he comes.—He looks plaguy gruff.

[*Steps aside.*

*Enter Sir* ANTHONY.

SIR ANTH. No—I'll die sooner than forgive him.—*Die*, did I say? I'll live
these fifty years to plague him.——At our last meeting, his impudence
had almost put me out of temper.—An obstinate, passionate, self-willed 10
boy!—Who can he take after? This is my return for getting him before
all his brothers and sisters!—for putting him, at twelve years old, into
a marching regiment, and allowing him fifty pounds a year, beside his
pay ever since!—But I have done with him;—he's any body's son for
me.——I never will see him more,—never—never—never—never.[1]

ABS. Now for a penitential face.

SIR ANTH. Fellow, get out of my way.

ABS. Sir, you see a penitent before you.

SIR ANTH. I see an impudent scoundrel before me.

ABS. A sincere penitent.——I am come, Sir, to acknowledge my error, 20
and to submit entirely to your will.

SIR ANTH. What's that?

ABS. I have been revolving, and reflecting, and considering on your past
goodness, and kindness, and condescension to me.

SIR ANTH. Well, Sir?

ABS. I have been likewise weighing and balancing what you were pleased
to mention concerning duty, and obedience, and authority.

SIR ANTH. Well, Puppy?

ABS. Why then, Sir, the result of my reflections is—a resolution to sacrifice every inclination of my own to your satisfaction. 30

SIR ANTH. Why now, you talk sense—absolute sense—I never heard
any thing more sensible in my life.————Confound you; you shall be
*Jack* again.

ABS. I am happy in the appellation.

SIR ANTH. Why, then, Jack, my dear Jack, I will now inform you—who
the lady really is.——Nothing but your passion and violence, you silly
fellow, prevented my telling you at first. Prepare, Jack, for wonder and
rapture—prepare.——What think you of Miss Lydia Languish?

ABS. Languish! What, the Languishes of Worcestershire?

SIR ANTH. Worcestershire! No. Did you never meet Mrs. Malaprop 40
and her Niece, Miss Languish, who came into our country just before
you were last ordered to your regiment?

ABS. Malaprop! Languish! I don't remember ever to have heard the
names before. Yet, stay—I think I do recollect something.——
*Languish! Languish!* She squints, don't she?——A little, red-haired
girl?

---

[1] Cf. *King Lear*, v. iii:

> Thou'lt come no more
> Never, never, never, never, never.

SIR ANTH. Squints?——A red-haired girl!——Z——ds, no.

ABS. Then I must have forgot; it can't be the same person.

SIR ANTH. Jack! Jack! what think you of blooming, love-breathing seventeen? 50

ABS. As to that, Sir, I am quite indifferent.—If I can please you in the matter, 'tis all I desire.

SIR ANTH. Nay, but Jack, such eyes! such eyes! so innocently wild! so bashfully irresolute! Not a glance but speaks and kindles some thought of love! Then, Jack, her cheeks! her cheeks, Jack! so deeply blushing at the insinuations of her tell-tale eyes! Then, Jack, her lips! —O Jack, lips smiling at their own discretion; and if not smiling, more sweetly pouting; more lovely in sullenness!

ABS. That's she indeed.—Well done, old gentleman!

SIR ANTH. Then, Jack, her neck.——O Jack! Jack! 60

ABS. And which is to be mine, Sir, the Niece or the Aunt?

SIR ANTH. Why, you unfeeling, insensible Puppy, I despise you. When I was of your age, such a description would have made me fly like a rocket! The *Aunt*, indeed!—Odds life! when I ran away with your mother, I would not have touched any thing old or ugly to gain an empire.

ABS. Not to please your father, Sir?

SIR ANTH. To please my father!——Z——ds! not to please——O my father!——Oddso!——yes—yes! if my father indeed had desired—— that's quite another matter.——Tho' he wa'n't the indulgent father 70 that I am, Jack.

ABS. I dare say not, Sir.

SIR ANTH. But, Jack, you are not sorry to find your mistress is so beautiful.

ABS. Sir, I repeat it; if I please you in this affair, 'tis all I desire. Not that I think a woman the worse for being handsome; but, Sir, if you please to recollect, you before hinted something about a hump or two, one eye, and a few more graces of that kind—now, without being very nice, I own I should rather chuse a wife of mine to have the usual number of limbs, and a limited quantity of back: and tho' *one* eye may 80 be very agreeable, yet as the prejudice has always run in favour of *two*, I would not wish to affect a singularity in that article.

SIR ANTH. What a phlegmatic sot it is! Why, sirrah, you're an anchorite! —a vile insensible stock.—You a soldier!—you're a walking block, fit only to dust the company's regimentals on!——Odds life! I've a great mind to marry the girl myself!

ABS. I am entirely at your disposal, Sir; if you should think of addressing Miss Languish yourself, I suppose you would have me marry the *Aunt*; or if you should change your mind, and take the old lady—'tis the same to me—I'll marry the *Niece*. 90

SIR ANTH. Upon my word, Jack, thou'rt either a very great hypocrite, or——but, come, I know your indifference on such a subject must be all a lie—I'm sure it must—come, now—d—n your demure face!—come, confess, Jack—you have been lying—ha'n't you? You have been playing the hypocrite, hey—I'll never forgive you, if you ha'n't been lying and playing the hypocrite.

ABS. I'm sorry, Sir, that the respect and duty which I bear to you should be so mistaken.

SIR ANTH. Hang your respect and duty! But, come along with me, I'll write a note to Mrs. Malaprop, and you shall visit the lady directly. 100

ABS. Where does she lodge, Sir?

SIR ANTH. What a dull question!—only on the Grove here.

ABS. O! then I can call on her in my way to the coffee-house.

SIR ANTH. In your way to the coffee-house! You'll set your heart down in your way to the coffee-house, hey? Ah! you leaden-nerv'd, wooden-hearted dolt! But come along, you shall see her directly; her eyes shall be the Promethian torch to you—come along, I'll never forgive you, if you don't come back, stark mad with rapture and impatience—if you don't, egad, I'll marry the girl myself! [*Exeunt.*

## SCENE II

### JULIA'*s Dressing-room*

#### FAULKLAND, *solus.*

FAULK. They told me Julia would return directly; I wonder she is not yet come!—How mean does this captious, unsatisfied temper of mine appear to my cooler judgment! Yet I know not that I indulge it in any other point:—but on this one subject, and to this one subject, whom I think I love beyond my life, I am ever ungenerously fretful, and madly capricious!—I am conscious of it—yet I cannot correct myself! What tender, honest joy sparkled in her eyes when we met!—How delicate was the warmth of her expressions!——I was ashamed to appear less happy—though I had come resolved to wear a face of cool-ness and upbraiding. Sir Anthony's presence prevented my proposed 10 expostulations:—yet I must be satisfied that she has not been so *very* happy in my absence.—She is coming!—Yes!—I know the nimbleness of her tread, when she thinks her impatient Faulkland counts the moments of her stay.

#### *Enter* JULIA.

JUL. I had not hop'd to see you again so soon.

FAULK. Could I, Julia, be contented with my first welcome—restrained as we were by the presence of a third person?

JUL. O Faulkland, when your kindness can make me thus happy, let me not think that I discovered something of coldness in your first salutation. 20

FAULK. 'Twas but your fancy, Julia.—I *was* rejoiced to see you—to see you in such health—Sure I had no cause for coldness?

JUL. Nay then, I see you have taken something ill.—You must not conceal from me what it is.

FAULK. Well then—shall I own to you that my joy at hearing of your health and arrival here, by your neighbour Acres, was somewhat damped, by his dwelling much on the high spirits you had enjoyed in Devonshire—on your mirth—your singing—dancing, and I know not what!—For such is my temper, Julia, that I should regard every mirthful moment in your absence as a treason to constancy:—The mutual 30 tear that steals down the cheek of parting lovers is a compact, that no smile shall live there till they meet again.

JUL. Must I never cease to tax my Faulkland with this teasing minute caprice?—Can the idle reports of a silly boor weigh in your breast against my tried affection?

FAULK. They have no weight with me, Julia: no, no—I am happy if you have been so—yet only say, that you did not sing with *mirth*—say that you *thought* of Faulkland in the dance.

JUL. I never can be happy, in your absence.——If I wear a countenance of content, it is to shew that my mind holds no doubt of my Faulk- 40 land's truth.——If I seem'd sad—it were to make malice triumph; and say, that I had fixed my heart on one, who left me to lament his roving, and my own credulity.——Believe me, Faulkland, I mean not to upbraid you, when I say, that I have often dressed sorrow in smiles, lest my friends should guess whose unkindness had caused my tears.

FAULK. You were ever all goodness to me.—O, I am a brute, when I but admit a doubt of your true constancy!

JUL. If ever, without such cause from you, as I will not suppose possible, you find my affections veering but a point, may I become a proverbial 50 scoff for levity, and base ingratitude.

FAULK. Ah! Julia, that *last* word is grating to me. I would I had no title to your *gratitude*! Search your heart, Julia; perhaps what you have mistaken for Love, is but the warm effusion of a too thankful heart!

JUL. For what quality must I love you?

FAULK. For no quality! To regard me for any quality of mind or understanding, were only to *esteem* me. And for person—I have often wish'd myself deformed, to be convinced that I owed no obligation *there* for any part of your affection.

JUL. Where Nature has bestowed a shew of nice attention in the features 60 of a man, he should laugh at it, as misplaced. I have seen men, who in *this* vain article perhaps might rank above you; but my heart has never asked my eyes if it were so or not.

FAULK. Now this is not well from *you*, Julia—I despise person in a man ——Yet if you lov'd me as I wish, though I were an Æthiop, you'd think none so fair.

JUL. I see you are determined to be unkind.—The *contract* which my poor father bound us in gives you more than a lover's privilege.

FAULK. Again, Julia, you raise ideas that feed and justify my doubts. ——I would not have been more free—no—I am proud of my restraint.——Yet—yet—perhaps your high respect alone for this solemn compact has fettered your inclinations, which else had made a worthier choice.—How shall I be sure, had you remained unbound in thought and promise, that I should still have been the object of your persevering love?

JUL. Then try me now.—Let us be free as strangers as to what is past: —*my* heart will not feel more liberty!

FAULK. There now! so hasty, Julia! so anxious to be free!—If your love for me were fixed and ardent, you would not loose your hold, even tho' I wish'd it!

JUL. O, you torture me to the heart!—I cannot bear it.

FAULK. I do not mean to distress you.—If I lov'd you less, I should never give you an uneasy moment.—But hear me.—All my fretful doubts arise from this—Women are not used to weigh, and separate the motives of their affections:—the cold dictates of prudence, gratitude, or filial duty, may sometimes be mistaken for the pleadings of the heart. ——I would not boast—yet let me say, that I have neither age, person, or character, to found dislike on;—my fortune such as few ladies could be charged with *indiscretion* in the match.—O Julia! when *Love* receives such countenance from *Prudence*, nice minds will be suspicious of its birth.

JUL. I know not whither your insinuations would tend:—But as they seem pressing to insult me—I will spare you the regret of having done so.—I have given you no cause for this! [*Exit in Tears.*

FAULK. In Tears! stay, Julia: stay but for a moment.——The door is fastened!—Julia!—my soul—but for one moment:—I hear her sobbing!—'Sdeath! what a brute am I to use her thus! Yet stay.—Aye— she is coming now:—how little resolution there is in woman!—how a few soft words can turn them!——No, faith!—she is *not* coming either.——Why, Julia—my love—say but that you forgive me—come but to tell me that—now, this is being *too* resentful:—stay! she *is* coming too—I thought she would—no *steadiness* in any thing! her going away must have been a mere trick then—she sha'n't see that I was hurt by it.—I'll affect indifference——[*hums a tune: then listens*]——No— Z—ds! she's *not* coming!—nor don't intend it, I suppose.—This is not *steadiness,* but *obstinacy!* Yet I deserve it.—What, after so long an absence, to quarrel with her tenderness!—'twas barbarous and unmanly!——I should be ashamed to see her now.—I'll wait till her just resentment is abated—and when I distress her so again, may I lose her for ever! and be linked instead to some antique virago, whose knawing 110 passions, and long-hoarded spleen, shall make me curse my folly half the day, and all the night!                                        [*Exit.*

<br>

## SCENE III

*Mrs.* MALAPROP's *Lodgings*

*Mrs.* MALAPROP, *with a letter in her hand, and Captain* ABSOLUTE.

MRS. MAL. Your being Sir Anthony's son, Captain, would itself be a sufficient accommodation;—but from the ingenuity of your appearance, I am convinced you deserve the character here given of you.

ABS. Permit me to say, Madam, that as I never yet have had the pleasure of seeing Miss Languish, my principal inducement in this affair at present, is the honour of being allied to Mrs. Malaprop; of whose intellectual accomplishments, elegant manners, and unaffected learning, no tongue is silent.

MRS. MAL. Sir, you do me infinite honour!—I beg, Captain, you'll be seated.—(*Sit*)—Ah! few gentlemen, now a days, know how to value 10 the ineffectual qualities in a woman! few think how a little knowledge becomes a gentlewoman! Men have no sense now but for the worthless flower of beauty!

ABS. It is but too true indeed, Ma'am;—yet I fear our ladies should share the blame—they think our admiration of *beauty* so great, that *knowledge* in *them* would be superfluous. Thus, like garden-trees, they seldom shew fruit, till time has robb'd them of the more specious blossom.—Few, like Mrs. Malaprop and the Orange-tree, are rich in both at once!

MRS. MAL. Sir—you overpower me with good-breeding.—He is the very Pine-apple of politeness! You are not ignorant, Captain, that this giddy 20 girl has somehow contrived to fix her affections on a beggarly, strolling, eves-dropping Ensign, whom none of us have seen, and nobody knows any thing of.

ABS. O, I have heard the silly affair before.—I'm not at all prejudiced against her on *that* account.

MRS. MAL. You are very good, and very considerate, Captain.—I am sure I have done every thing in my power since I exploded the affair! long ago I laid my positive conjunctions on her never to think on the fellow again;—I have since laid Sir Anthony's preposition before her;

—but I'm sorry to say she seems resolved to decline every particle that 30
I enjoin her.

ABS. It must be very distressing indeed, Ma'am.

MRS. MAL. Oh! it gives me the hydrostatics to such a degree!—I thought
she had persisted from corresponding with him; but behold this very
day, I have interceded another letter from the fellow! I believe I have
it in my pocket.

ABS. O the devil! my last note.                                   [*Aside.*

MRS. MAL. Aye, here it is.

ABS. Aye, my note indeed! O the little traitress Lucy.            [*Aside.*

MRS. MAL. There, perhaps you may know the writing.                      40
                                            [*Gives him the letter.*

ABS. I think I have seen the hand before—yes, I *certainly must* have seen
this hand before:——

MRS. MAL. Nay, but read it, Captain.

ABS. [*Reads*] '*My soul's idol, my ador'd Lydia!*'—Very tender indeed!

MRS. MAL. Tender! aye, and prophane too, o' my conscience!

ABS. '*I am excessively alarmed at the intelligence you send me, the more so
as my new rival*'——

MRS. MAL. That's *you*, Sir.

ABS. '*has universally the character of being an accomplished gentleman, and
a man of honour.*'——Well, that's handsome enough.                      50

MRS. MAL. O, the fellow has some design in writing so——

ABS. That he had, I'll answer for him, Ma'am.

MRS. MAL. But go on, Sir—you'll see presently.

ABS. '*As for the old weather-beaten she-dragon who guards you,*'—Who can
he mean by that?

MRS. MAL. *Me*, Sir—*me*—he means *me* there—what do you think now?
—but go on a little further.

ABS. Impudent scoundrel!—'*it shall go hard but I will elude her vigilance,
as I am told that the same ridiculous vanity, which makes her dress up her
coarse features, and deck her dull chat with hard words which she don't* 60
*understand*'——

MRS. MAL. There, Sir! an attack upon my language! what do you think
of that?—an aspersion upon my parts of speech! was ever such a
brute! Sure if I reprehend any thing in this world, it is the use of my
oracular tongue, and a nice derangement of epitaphs!

ABS. He deserves to be hang'd and quartered! let me see—'*same ridiculous
vanity*'——

MRS. MAL. You need not read it again, Sir.

ABS. I beg pardon, Ma'am '*does also lay her open to the grossest deceptions from
flattery and pretended admiration*'—an impudent coxcomb! '*so that I* 70
*have a scheme to see you shortly with the old Harridan's consent, and even
to make her a go between in our interviews.*'——Was ever such assurance.

MRS. MAL. Did you ever hear any thing like it?—he'll elude my vigilance, will he?—yes, yes! ha! ha! he's very likely to enter these doors!—
we'll try who can plot best!

ABS. So we will Ma'am—so we will.—Ha! ha! ha! a conceited puppy,
ha! ha! ha!——Well, but Mrs. Malaprop, as the girl seems so infatuated
by this fellow, suppose you were to wink at her corresponding with him
for a little time—let her even plot an elopement with him—then do you
connive at her escape—while *I*, just in the nick, will have the fellow 80
laid by the heels, and fairly contrive to carry her off in his stead.

MRS. MAL. I am delighted with the scheme, never was any thing better
perpetrated!

ABS. But, pray, could not I see the lady for a few minutes now?—I
should like to try her temper a little.

MRS. MAL. Why, I don't know——I doubt she is not prepared for a
visit of this kind.——There is a decorum in these matters.

ABS. O Lord! she won't mind *me*—only tell her Beverley——

MRS. MAL. Sir!——

ABS. Gently, good tongue. [*Aside.* 90

MRS. MAL. What did you say of Beverley?

ABS. O, I was going to propose that you should tell her, by way of jest,
that it was Beverley who was below—she'd come down fast enough
then—ha! ha! ha!

MRS. MAL. 'Twould be a trick she well-deserves—besides you know the
fellow tells her he'll get my consent to see her—ha! ha!—Let him if he
can, I say again.—Lydia, come down here! [*Calling.*
—He'll make me a *go-between in their interviews*!—ha! ha! ha! Come
down, I say, Lydia!—I don't wonder at your laughing, ha! ha! ha! his
impudence is truly ridiculous. 100

ABS. 'Tis very ridiculous, upon my soul, Ma'am, ha! ha! ha!

MRS. MAL. The little hussy won't hear.—Well, I'll go and tell her at
once who it is—she shall know that Capt. Absolute is come to wait on
her.—And I'll make her behave as becomes a young woman.

ABS. As you please, Ma'am.

MRS. MAL. For the present, Captain, your servant—Ah! you've not done
laughing yet, I see—*elude my vigilance*! yes, yes, ha! ha! ha! [*Exit.*

ABS. Ha! ha! ha! one would think now that I might throw off all disguise
at once, and seize my prize with security—but such is Lydia's caprice,
that to undeceive were probably to lose her.—I'll see whether she 110
knows me. [*Walks aside, and seems engaged*
*in looking at the pictures.*

*Enter* LYDIA.

LYD. What a scene am I now to go thro'! surely nothing can be more
dreadful than to be obliged to listen to the loathsome addresses of a

stranger to one's heart.—I have heard of girls persecuted as I am, who have appealed in behalf of their favoured lover to the generosity of his rival: suppose I were to try it—there stands the hated rival—an officer too!—but O how unlike my Beverley!—I wonder he don't begin— truly he seems a very negligent wooer!—quite at his ease, upon my word! I'll speak first—Mr. Absolute.

ABS. Madam. [*Turns round.* 120

LYD. O Heav'ns! Beverley!

ABS. Hush!—hush, my life!—softly! be not surprised!

LYD. I am so astonished! and so terrified! and so overjoy'd!—for Heav'n's sake! how came you here?

ABS. Briefly—I have deceived your Aunt—I was informed that my new rival was to visit here this evening, and contriving to have him kept away, have passed myself on *her* for Capt. Absolute.

LYD. O, charming!—And she really takes you for young Absolute?

ABS. O, she's convinced of it.

LYD. Ha! ha! ha! I can't forbear laughing to think how her sagacity is 130 over-reached!

ABS. But we trifle with our precious moments—such another opportunity may not occur—then let me now conjure my kind, my condescending angel, to fix the time when I may rescue her from undeserved persecution, and with a licensed warmth plead for my reward.

LYD. Will you then, Beverley, consent to forfeit that portion of my paltry wealth?—that burthen on the wings of love?

ABS. O come to me—rich only thus—in loveliness—Bring no portion to me but thy love—'twill be generous in you, Lydia—for well you know, it is the only dower your poor Beverley can repay. 140

LYD. How persuasive are his words!—how charming will poverty be with him!

ABS. Ah! my soul, what a life will we then live? Love shall be our idol and support! we will worship him with a monastic strictness; abjuring all worldly toys, to center every thought and action there.—Proud of calamity, we will enjoy the wreck of wealth; while the surrounding gloom of adversity shall make the flame of our pure love show doubly bright.—By Heav'ns! I would fling all goods of fortune from me with a prodigal hand to enjoy the scene where I might clasp my Lydia to my bosom, and say, the world affords no smile to me—but here—— 150

[*Embracing her.*

If she holds out now the devil is in it! [*Aside.*

LYD. Now could I fly with him to the Antipodes! but my persecution is not yet come to a crisis.

*Enter Mrs.* MALAPROP, *listening.*

MRS. MAL. I'm impatient to know how the little huzzy deports herself.
[*Aside*.

ABS. So pensive, Lydia!—is then your warmth abated?

MRS. MAL. *Warmth abated*!—so!—she has been in a passion, I suppose.

LYD. No—nor ever can while I have life.

MRS. MAL. An ill-temper'd little devil!—She'll be *in a passion all her life* —will she? 160

LYD. Think not the idle threats of my ridiculous aunt can ever have any weight with me.

MRS. MAL. Very dutiful, upon my word!

LYD. Let her choice be *Capt. Absolute*, but Beverley is mine.

MRS MAL. I am astonished at her assurance!—*to his face—this is to his face!*

ABS. Thus then let me enforce my suit. [*Kneeling*.

MRS. MAL. Aye—poor young man!—down on his knees entreating for pity!—I can contain no longer.——Why, thou vixen!—I have overheard you. 170

ABS. O confound her vigilance! [*Aside*.

MRS. MAL. Capt. Absolute—I know not how to apologize for her shocking rudeness.

ABS. So—all's safe, I find. [*Aside*.
I have hopes, Madam, that time will bring the young lady——

MRS. MAL. O, there's nothing to be hoped for from her! she's as headstrong as an allegory on the banks of Nile.

LYD. Nay, Madam, what do you charge me with now?

MRS. MAL. Why, thou unblushing rebel—didn't you tell this gentleman to his face that you loved another better?—didn't you say you never 180 would be his?

LYD. No, Madam—I did not.

MRS. MAL. Good Heav'ns! what assurance!—Lydia, Lydia, you ought to know that lying don't become a young woman!—Didn't you boast that Beverley—that stroller Beverley, possessed your heart?—Tell me that, I say.

LYD. 'Tis true, Ma'am, and none but Beverley—

MRS. MAL. Hold;—hold Assurance!—you shall not be so rude.

ABS. Nay, pray Mrs. Malaprop, don't stop the young lady's speech:— she's very welcome to talk thus—it does not hurt *me* in the least, I 190 assure you.

MRS. MAL. You are *too* good, Captain—*too* amiably patient—but come with me, Miss—let us see you again soon, Captain—remember what we have fixed.

ABS. I shall, Ma'am.

MRS. MAL. Come, take a graceful leave of the gentleman.

LYD. May every blessing wait on my Beverley, my lov'd Bev——

MRS. MAL. Huzzy! I'll choak the word in your throat!—come along—
come along.                                              [*Exeunt severally.*

[BEVERLEY *kissing his hand to* LYDIA—*Mrs.*
MALAPROP *stopping her from speaking.*

## SCENE IV. ACRES'S *lodgings*

### ACRES *and* DAVID

### ACRES *as just dress'd.*

ACRES. Indeed, David—do you think I become it so?

DAVID. You are quite another creature, believe me Master, by the Mass!
an' we've any luck we shall see the Devon monkeyrony[1] in all the
print-shops in Bath!

ACRES. Dress *does* make a difference, David.

DAVID. 'Tis all in all, I think—difference! why, an' you were to go now
to Clod-Hall, I am certain the old lady wouldn't know you: Master
Butler wouldn't believe his own eyes, and Mrs. Pickle would cry,
'Lard presarve me!' our dairy-maid would come giggling to the door,
and I warrant Dolly Tester, your Honour's favourite, would blush   10
like my waistcoat.—Oons! I'll hold a gallon, there an't a dog in the
house but would bark, and I question whether *Phillis* would wag a hair
of her tail!

ACRES. Aye, David, there's nothing like *polishing*.

DAVID. So I says of your Honour's boots; but the boy never heeds me!

ACRES. But, David, has Mr. De-la-Grace been here? I must rub up
my balancing, and chasing, and boring.[2]

DAVID. I'll call again, Sir.

ACRES. Do—and see if there are any letters for me at the post-office.

DAVID. I will.——By the Mass, I can't help looking at your head!—if   20
I hadn't been by at the cooking, I wish I may die if I should have known
the dish again myself!                                   [*Exit.*

[ACRES *comes forward, practising a dancing step.*

ACRES. Sink, slide—coupee—Confound the first inventors of cotillons!
say I—they are as bad as algebra to us country gentlemen—I can walk
a Minuet easy enough when I'm forced!—and I have been accounted

---

[1] A macaroni, between 1772 and 1775, was a fop affecting Italian fashions. John
Quick, who created the part of Acres, gave 'A Dissertation on Macaronies' at his benefit
night in Bristol: see *Felix Farley's Bristol Journal*, 2 Sept. 1775. 'Monkey' was used
more generally for a fop. Cf. 'A slim beast made for shew | Which the men call a
monkey, but ladies a beau!' (Anthony Pasquin, *A Postscript to the New Bath Guide*
(1790), p. 62.)

[2] Dance movements: 'boring' is from the French 'bourrée', and 'chasing' from
'chassée'. 'Balancing' is to move in the opposite direction from one's partner.

a good stick in a Country-dance.—Odd's jigs and tabors!—I never
valued your cross-over to couple—figure in—right and left—and I'd
foot it with e'er a captain in the county!—but these outlandish heathen
Allemandes and Cotillons are quite beyond me!—I shall never prosper
at 'em, that's sure—mine are true-born English legs—they don't 30
understand their curst French lingo!—their *Pas* this, and *Pas* that,
and *Pas* t'other!—d—n me, my feet don't like to be called Paws! no,
'tis certain I have most Antigallican Toes!

*Enter* SERVANT.

SERV. Here is Sir Lucius O'Trigger to wait on you, Sir.
ACRES. Shew him in.

*Enter Sir* LUCIUS.

SIR LUC. Mr. Acres, I am delighted to embrace you.
ACRES. My dear Sir Lucius, I kiss your hands.
SIR LUC. Pray, my friend, what has brought you so suddenly to Bath?
ACRES. Faith! I have followed Cupid's Jack-a-Lantern, and find myself
   in a quagmire at last.—In short, I have been very ill-used, Sir Lucius. 40
   —I don't choose to mention names, but look on me as a very ill-used
   gentleman.
SIR LUC. Pray, what is the case?—I ask no names.
ACRES. Mark me, Sir Lucius, I fall as deep as need be in love with a
   young lady——her friends take my part—I follow her to Bath—send
   word of my arrival; and receive answer, that the lady is to be otherwise
   disposed of.—This, Sir Lucius, I call being ill-used.
SIR LUC. Very ill, upon my conscience—Pray, can you divine the cause
   of it?
ACRES. Why, there's the matter: she has another lover, *one* Beverley, 50
   who, I am told, is now in Bath.—Odds slanders and lies! he must be
   at the bottom of it.
SIR LUC. A rival in the case, is there?—and you think he has supplanted
   you unfairly.
ACRES. *Unfairly!*—to be sure he has.—He never could have done it
   fairly.
SIR LUC. Then sure you know what is to be done!
ACRES. Not I, upon my soul!
SIR LUC. We wear no swords here,[1] but you understand me.
ACRES. What! fight him!                                      60
SIR LUC. Aye, to be sure: what can I mean else?
ACRES. But he has given me no provocation.

---

[1] Beau Nash, Master of Ceremonies at Bath, forbade the wearing of swords 'as
they often tore the ladies' clothes'.

SIR LUC. Now, I think he has given you the greatest provocation in the
world.——Can a man commit a more heinous offence against another
than to fall in love with the same woman? O, by my soul, it is the most
unpardonable breach of friendship!

ACRES. Breach of *friendship*! Aye, aye; but I have no acquaintance with
this man. I never saw him in my life.

SIR LUC. That's no argument at all—he has the less right then to take
such a liberty.                                                                          70

ACRES. 'Gad that's true—I grow full of anger, Sir Lucius!—I fire apace!
Odds hilts and blades![1] I find a man may have a deal of valour in him,
and not know it! But couldn't I contrive to have a little right of my
side?

SIR LUC. What the d——l signifies *right*, when your *honour* is concerned?
Do you think *Achilles*, or my little *Alexander the Great* ever inquired
where the right lay? No, by my soul, they drew their broad-swords,
and left the lazy sons of peace to settle the justice of it.

ACRES. Your words are a grenadier's[2] march to my heart! I believe
courage must be catching!—I certainly do feel a kind of valour rising     80
as it were——a kind of courage, as I may say——Odds flints, pans, and
triggers! I'll challenge him directly.

SIR LUC. Ah, my little friend! if we had *Blunderbuss-Hall* here[3]—I could
shew you a range of ancestry, in the O'Trigger line, that would furnish
the new room;[4] every one of whom had killed his man!——For though
the mansion-house and dirty acres have slipt through my fingers,
I thank Heav'n our honour, and the family-pictures, are as fresh as
ever.

ACRES. O Sir Lucius! I have had ancestors too! every man of 'em colonel
or captain in the militia!——Odds balls and barrels! say no more—I'm     90
brac'd for it—The thunder of your words has soured the milk of human
kindness in my breast![5]——Z—ds! as the man in the play says, 'I could
do such deeds!'[6]

---

[1] Cf. Sir Joseph Wittol's oath in Congreve's *The Old Batchelor* (1693), II. i: 'Gads-
Daggers-Belts-Blades-and Scabbards'.

[2] Acres connects Achilles and Alexander with the first line of 'The British Grenadiers':
'Some talk of Alexander, and some of Achilles'. For recent research on the wording
of the song, see *The Times*, 22 Jan. 1969.

[3] See Sir Jeremy's lines in *A Journey to Bath*:
*Sir Jeremy.* If I had your ladyship at Bull-hall, I cou'd shew you a line of ancestry,
that wou'd convince you we are not a people of yesterday.
*Edward.* Pray Uncle how came it, you never shewd them to me.
*Sir Jeremy.* Why the land and the Mansion house has slipp'd thro' our fingers boy;
but thank heaven the family pictures are still extant.

[4] The Upper Assembly rooms at Bath, built by John Wood (d. 1782), and opened in
1771.

[5] *Macbeth*, I. v.

[6] Possibly misquoting Lear's 'I will do such things' (II. iv).

SIR LUC. Come, come, there must be no passion at all in the case—these things should always be done civilly.

ACRES. I must be in a passion, Sir Lucius——I must be in a rage——Dear Sir Lucius let me be in a rage, if you love me.——Come, here's pen and paper. [*Sits down to write*] I would the ink were red!——Indite, I say, indite!—How shall I begin? Odds bullets and blades! I'll write a good *bold hand*, however.  100

SIR LUC. Pray compose yourself.

ACRES. Come—now shall I begin with an oath? Do, Sir Lucius, let me begin with a damme.

SIR LUC. Pho! pho! do the thing *decently* and like a Christian. Begin now,——'*Sir*'——

ACRES. That's too civil by half.

SIR LUC. '*To prevent the confusion that might arise.*'

ACRES. Well——

SIR LUC. '*From our both addressing the same lady.*'

ACRES. Aye—there's the reason—'*same lady*'—Well——  110

SIR LUC. '*I shall expect the honour of your company*'——

ACRES. Z——ds! I'm not asking him to dinner.

SIR LUC. Pray be easy.

ACRES. Well then, 'honour of your company'

SIR LUC. '*To settle our pretensions.*'

ACRES. Well.

SIR LUC. Let me see, aye, *King's Mead-fields* will do.——'*In King's Mead fields.*'

ACRES. So that's done.——Well, I'll fold it up presently; my own crest—a hand and dagger shall be the seal.  120

SIR LUC. You see now this little explanation will put a stop at once to all confusion or misunderstanding that might arise between you.

ACRES. Aye, we fight to prevent any misunderstanding.

SIR LUC. Now, I'll leave you to fix your own time.—take my advice, and you'll decide it this evening if you can; then let the worst come of it, 'twill be off your mind to-morrow.

ACRES. Very true.

SIR LUC. So I shall see nothing more of you, unless it be by letter, till the evening.——I would do myself the honour to carry your message; but, to tell you a secret, I believe I shall have just such another affair  130 on my own hands. There is a gay captain here, who put a jest on me lately, at the expence of my country, and I only want to fall in with the gentleman, to call him out.

ACRES. By my valour, I should like to see you fight first! Odds life! I should like to see you kill him, if it was only to get a little lesson.

SIR LUC. I shall be very proud of instructing you.——Well for the present——but remember now, when you meet your antagonist, do every

thing in a mild and agreeable manner.——Let your courage be as keen,
but at the same time as polished as your sword.      [*Exeunt severally.*

END OF THE THIRD ACT

# ACT IV

## SCENE I

### ACRES's *Lodgings*

#### ACRES *and* DAVID.

DAVID. Then, by the Mass, Sir! I would do no such thing—ne'er a Sir
Lucius O'Trigger in the kingdom should make me fight, when I
wa'n't so minded. Oons! what will the old lady say, when she hears o't!

ACRES. Ah! David, if you had heard Sir Lucius!—Odds sparks and
flames! he would have rous'd your valour.

DAVID. Not he, indeed. I hates such bloodthirsty cormorants. Look'ee,
Master, if you'd wanted a bout at boxing, quarter-staff, or short-staff,
I should never be the man to bid you cry off: But for your curst sharps[1]
and snaps,[2] I never knew any good come of 'em.

ACRES. But my *honour*, David, my *honour*! I must be very careful of my   10
honour.

DAVID. Aye, by the Mass! and I would be very careful of it; and I think
in return my *honour* couldn't do less than to be very careful of *me*.

ACRES. Odds blades! David, no gentleman will ever risk the loss of his
honour!

DAVID. I say then, it would be but civil in *honour* never to risk the loss
of a *gentleman*.——Lookee, Master, this *honour* seems to me to be a
marvellous false friend; aye, truly, a very courtier-like servant.——Put
the case, I was a gentleman (which, thank God, no one can say of me);
well—my honour makes me quarrel with another gentleman of my   20
acquaintance.—So—we fight. (Pleasant enough that) Boh!—I kill him—
(the more's my luck.) Now, pray who gets the profit of it?—Why, my
*honour*.——But put the case that he kills me!——by the Mass! I go to
the worms, and my honour whips over to my enemy!

ACRES. No, David—in that case!—Odds crowns and laurels! your honour
follows you to the grave.

----

[1] Swords. Cf. Farquhar, *The Recruiting Officer*, v. vi: *Brazen*: Look'e, my dear, I do
not care for pistols. Pray oblige me and let us have a bout at sharps.
[2] Pistols.

DAVID. Now, that's just the place where I could make a shift to do without it.

ACRES. Z——ds, David! you're a coward!—It doesn't become my valour to listen to you.——What, shall I disgrace my ancestors?— 30 Think of that, David—think what it would be to disgrace my ancestors!

DAVID. Under favour, the surest way of not disgracing them, is to keep as long as you can out of their company. Look'ee now, Master, to go to them in such haste—with an ounce of lead in your brains—I should think might as well be let alone. Our ancestors are very good kind of folks; but they are the last people I should choose to have a visiting acquaintance with.

ACRES. But David, now, you don't think there is such very, very, *very* great danger, hey?——Odds life! people often fight without any mischief done! 40

DAVID. By the Mass, I think 'tis ten to one against you!——Oons! here to meet some lion-headed fellow, I warrant, with his d——n'd double-barrell'd swords, and cut and thrust pistols! Lord bless us! it makes me tremble to think o't!——Those be such desperate bloody-minded weapons! Well, I never could abide 'em!—from a child I never could fancy 'em!—I suppose there a'n't so merciless a beast in the world as your loaded pistol!

ACRES. Z——ds! I *won't* be afraid—Odds fire and fury! you shan't make me afraid.——Here is the challenge, and I have sent for my dear friend Jack Absolute to carry it for me. 50

DAVID. Aye, I'the name of mischief, let *him* be the messenger.—For my part, I wouldn't lend a hand to it for the best horse in your stable. By the Mass! it don't look like another letter!—It is, as I may say, a designing and malicious-looking letter!—and I warrant smells of gun-powder like a soldier's pouch!—Oons! I wouldn't swear it mayn't go off!

ACRES. Out, you poltroon!—you ha'n't the valour of a grass-hopper.

DAVID. Well, I say no more—'twill be sad news, to be sure, at Clod-Hall!—but I ha'done.—How Phyllis will howl when she hears of it! —Aye, poor bitch, she little thinks what shooting her Master's going 60 after!—And I warrant old Crop, who has carried your honour, field and road, these ten years, will curse the hour he was born.

[*Whimpering.*]

ACRES. It won't do, David—I am determined to fight—so get along, you Coward, while I'm in the mind.

*Enter* SERVANT.

SERV. Captain Absolute, Sir.

ACRES. O! shew him up. [*Exit* SERVANT.

DAVID. Well, Heaven send we be all alive this time to-morrow.

ACRES. What's that!—Don't provoke me, David!

DAVID. Good bye, Master.                    [*Whimpering.*]

ACRES. Get along, you cowardly, dastardly, croaking raven.    70

                                 [*Exit* DAVID.

*Enter* ABSOLUTE.

*need not in mss.*

ABS. What's the matter, Bob?

ACRES. A vile, sheep-hearted blockhead!—If I hadn't the valour of St. George and the dragon to boot——

ABS. But what did you want with me, Bob?

ACRES. O!—There—          [*Gives him the challenge.*]

ABS. 'To Ensign Beverley.' So—what's going on now!    [*Aside.* Well, what's this?

ACRES. A challenge!

ABS. Indeed!—Why, you won't fight him; will you Bob?

ACRES. 'Egad but I will, Jack.—Sir Lucius has wrought me to it. He 80 has left me full of rage—and I'll fight this evening, that so much good passion mayn't be wasted.

ABS. But what have I to do with this?

ACRES. Why, as I think you know something of this fellow, I want you to find him out for me, and give him this mortal *defiance*.

ABS. Well, give it to me, and trust me he gets it.

ACRES. Thank you, my dear friend, my dear Jack; but it is giving you a great deal of trouble.

ABS. Not in the least—I beg you won't mention it.—No trouble in the world, I assure you.    90

ACRES. You are very kind.——What it is to have a friend!——You couldn't be my second—could you, Jack?

ABS. Why no, Bob—not in *this* affair—it would not be quite so proper.

ACRES. Well then I must get my friend Sir Lucius. I shall have your good wishes, however, Jack.

ABS. Whenever he meets you, believe me.

*Enter* SERVANT.

SERV. Sir Anthony Absolute is below, inquiring for the Captain.

ABS. I'll come instantly.——Well, my little hero, success attend you.

                                 [*Going.*

ACRES. Stay—stay, Jack.——If Beverley should ask you what kind of a man your friend Acres is, do tell him I am a devil of a fellow—will 100 you, Jack?

ABS. To be sure I shall.——I'll say you are a determined dog—hey, Bob!

ACRES. Aye, do, do—and if that frightens him, 'egad perhaps he mayn't come. So tell him I generally kill a man a week; will you, Jack!

ABS. I will, I will; I'll say you are call'd in the country '*Fighting Bob!*'

ACRES. Right, right—'tis all to prevent mischief; for I don't want to take his life if I clear my honour.

ABS. No!—that's very kind of you.

ACRES. Why, you don't wish me to kill him—do you, Jack?

ABS. No, upon my soul, I do not.—But a devil of a fellow, hey? [*Going.* 110

ACRES. True, true—but stay—stay, Jack—you may add that you never saw me in such a rage before—a most devouring rage!

ABS. I will, I will.

ACRES. Remember, Jack——a determined dog!

ABS. Aye, aye, '*Fighting Bob!*'                    [*Exeunt severally.*

## SCENE II

*Mrs.* MALAPROP's *Lodgings*

*Mrs.* MALAPROP *and* LYDIA.

MRS. MAL. Why, thou perverse one!—tell me what you can object to him?——Isn't he a handsome man?—tell me that.—A genteel man? a pretty figure of a man?

LYD. She little thinks whom she is praising! [*aside*]—So is Beverley, Ma'am.

MRS. MAL. No caparisons, Miss, if you please!—Caparisons don't become a young woman.—No! Captain Absolute is indeed a fine gentleman!

LYD. Aye, the Captain Absolute *you* have seen.                    [*Aside.*

MRS. MAL. Then he's *so* well bred;—*so* full of alacrity, and adulation! 10 —and has *so much* to say for himself:—in such good language too!— His physiognomy so grammatical!—Then his presence is so noble!— I protest, when I saw him, I thought of what Hamlet says in the Play: —'Hesperian curls!—the front of *Job* himself!—an eye, like *March*, to threaten at command!—a Station, like Harry Mercury, new—' Something about kissing—on a hill—however, the similitude struck me directly.[1]

LYD. How enraged she'll be presently when she discovers her mistake!
                    [*Aside.*

*Enter* SERVANT.

SERV. Sir Anthony, and Captain Absolute are below Ma'am.

MRS. MAL. Shew them up here.                    [*Exit* SERV. 20

Now, Lydia, I insist on you behaving as becomes a young woman.— Shew your good breeding at least, though you have forgot your duty.

---

[1] From *Hamlet*, III. iv:
> Hyperion's curls; the front of Jove himself;
> An eye like Mars to threaten and command;
> A station like the herald Mercury
> New-lighted on a heaven-kissing hill.

LYD. Madam, I have told you my resolution;—I shall not only give him no encouragement, but I won't even speak to, or look at him.

[*Flings herself into a chair, with her face from the door.*

*Enter* SIR ANTHONY *and* ABSOLUTE.

SIR ANTH. Here we are, Mrs. Malaprop; come to mitigate the frowns of unrelenting beauty—and difficulty enough I had to bring this fellow. —I don't know what's the matter; but if I hadn't held him by force, he'd have given me the slip.

MRS. MAL. You have infinite trouble, Sir Anthony, in the affair.—I am ashamed for the cause! Lydia, Lydia, rise I beseech you!—pay your respects! [*Aside to her.* 30

SIR ANTH. I hope, Madam, that Miss Languish has reflected on the worth of this gentleman, and the regard due to her Aunt's choice, and *my* alliance.—Now, Jack, speak to her! [*Aside to him.*

ABS. What the d—l shall I do!—[*Aside*]—You see, Sir, she won't even look at me, whilst you are here.—I knew she wouldn't!—I told you so— Let me intreat you, Sir, to leave us together!

[ABSOLUTE *seems to expostulate with his Father.*

LYD. [*aside.*] I wonder I ha'n't heard my Aunt exclaim yet! sure she can't have look'd at him!—perhaps their regimentals are alike, and she is something blind. 40

SIR ANTH. I say, Sir, I won't stir a foot yet.

MRS. MAL. I am sorry to say, Sir Anthony, that my affluence over my Niece is very small.—Turn round Lydia, I blush for you!

[*Aside to her.*

SIR ANTH. May I not flatter myself that Miss Languish will assign what cause of dislike she can have to my son!—Why don't you begin, Jack? —Speak, you puppy—speak! [*Aside to him.*

MRS. MAL. It is impossible, Sir Anthony, she can have any.—She will not *say* she has.——Answer, hussy! why don't you answer? [*Aside to her.*

SIR ANTH. Then, Madam, I trust that a childish and hasty predilection will be no bar to Jack's happiness.—Z—ds! sirrah! why don't you speak? [*Aside to him.* 50

LYD. [*aside*] I think my lover seems as little inclined to conversation as myself.—How strangely blind my Aunt must be!

ABS. Hem! hem!—Madam—hem! [Absolute *attempts to speak, then returns to Sir* Anthony]—Faith! Sir, I am so confounded!—and so—so —confused!—I told you I should be so, Sir,—I knew it.—The—the— tremor of my passion, entirely takes away my presence of mind.

SIR ANTH. But it don't take away your voice, fool, does it?—Go up, and speak to her directly! [ABS. *makes signs to Mrs.* MAL. *to leave them together.*]

MRS. MAL. Sir Anthony, shall we leave them together?—Ah! you 60
stubborn, little vixen!                              [*Aside to her.*

SIR ANTH. Not yet, Ma'am, not yet!—what the d—l are you at? unlock
your jaws, sirrah, or—                              [*Aside to him.*


[ABSOLUTE *draws near* LYDIA.]

ABS. Now Heav'n send she may be too sullen to look round!—I must
disguise my voice—[*Aside*]—            [*Speaks in a low hoarse tone.*
—Will not Miss Languish lend an ear to the mild accents of true love?
—Will not——

SIR ANTH. What the d—l ails the fellow?—Why don't you speak out?
—not stand croaking like a frog in a quinsey!

ABS. The—the—excess of my awe, and my—my—my modesty, quite choak 70
me!

SIR ANTH. Ah! your *modesty* again!—I'll tell you what, Jack; if you don't
speak out directly, and glibly too, I shall be in such a rage!—Mrs.
Malaprop, I wish the lady would favour us with something more than
a side-front!
                          [*Mrs.* MALAPROP *seems to chide* LYDIA.

ABS. So!—all will out I see!
                          [*Goes up to* LYDIA, *speaks softly.*
Be not surprised, my Lydia, suppress all surprise at present.

LYD. [*Aside*] Heav'ns! 'tis Beverley's voice!—Sure he can't have impos'd
on Sir Anthony too!—          [*Looks round by degrees, then starts up.*
Is this possible!—my Beverley!—how can this be?—my Beverley? 80

ABS. Ah! 'tis all over.                                [*Aside.*

SIR ANTH. Beverley!—the devil—Beverley!——What can the girl mean?
—This is my son, Jack Absolute!

MRS. MAL. For shame, hussy! for shame!—your head runs so on that
fellow, that you have him always in your eyes!—beg Captain Absolute's
pardon directly.

LYD. I see no Captain Absolute, but my lov'd Beverley!

SIR ANTH. Z—ds! the girl's mad!—her brain's turn'd by reading!

MRS. MAL. O' my conscience, I believe so!—what do you mean by
Beverley, hussy?—You saw Captain Absolute before to-day; there he is 90
—your husband that shall be.

LYD. With all my soul, Ma'am—when I refuse my Beverley——

SIR ANTH. O! she's as mad as Bedlam!—or has this fellow been playing
us a rogue's trick!—Come here, sirrah! who the d—l are you?

ABS. Faith, Sir, I am not quite clear myself; but I'll endeavour to
recollect.

SIR ANTH. Are you my son, or not?—answer for your mother, you dog,
if you won't for me.

MRS. MAL. Aye, Sir, who are you? O mercy! I begin to suspect!—

ABS. Ye Powers of Impudence befriend me! [*aside*] Sir Anthony, most 100
assuredly I am your wife's son; and that I sincerely believe myself to
be *your's* also, I hope my duty has always shewn.—Mrs. Malaprop,
I am your most respectful admirer—and shall be proud to add *affectionate
nephew*.—I need not tell my Lydia, that she sees her faithful Beverley,
who, knowing the singular generosity of her temper, assum'd that name,
and a station, which has proved a test of the most disinterested love,
which he now hopes to enjoy in a more elevated character.

LYD. So!—there will be no elopement after all!                [*sullenly.*]

SIR ANTH. Upon my soul, Jack, thou art a very impudent fellow![1] to do
you justice, I think I never saw a piece of more consummate assurance! 110

ABS. O, you flatter me, Sir—you compliment—'tis my *modesty* you know,
Sir—my *modesty* that has stood in my way.

SIR ANTH. Well, I am glad you are not the dull, insensible varlet you
pretended to be, however!—I'm glad you have made a fool of your
father, you dog—I am.——So this was your *penitence*, your *duty*, and
*obedience*!—I thought it was d—n'd sudden!—You *never heard their
names before*, not you!—*What, Languishes of Worcestershire*, hey?—*if
you could please me in the affair, 'twas all you desired*!—Ah! you dissembling villain!—What! (*pointing to* Lydia) *she squints, don't she?*—*a
little red-hair'd girl*!—hey?—Why, you hypocritical young rascal—I 120
wonder you a'n't asham'd to hold up your head!

ABS. 'Tis with difficulty, Sir—I *am* confus'd—very much confus'd, as
you must perceive.

MRS. MAL. O Lud! Sir Anthony!—a new light breaks in upon me!—
hey! how! what! Captain, did *you* write the letters then?—What!—am
I to thank *you* for the elegant compilation of '*an old weather-beaten she-
dragon*'—hey?—O mercy!—was it *you* that reflected on my parts of
speech?

ABS. Dear Sir! my modesty will be overpower'd at last, if you don't assist
me.—I shall certainly not be able to stand it!                        130

SIR ANTH. Come, come, Mrs. Malaprop, we must forget and forgive;
—odds' life! matters have taken so clever a turn all of a sudden, that
I could find in my heart, to be so good-humour'd! and so gallant!—
hey! Mrs. Malaprop!

MRS. MAL. Well, Sir Anthony, since *you* desire it, we will not anticipate
the past;—so mind young people—our retrospection will now be all to
the future.

SIR ANTH. Come, we must leave them together; Mrs. Malaprop, they
long to fly into each other's arms, I warrant!—Jack—is'n't the *cheek*

---

[1] Cf. Lord Foppington's line in Vanbrugh's *The Relapse*, IV. vi: 'Strike me dumb,
Tam, thou art a very impudent fellow.'

as I said, hey?—and the eye, you rogue!—and the lip—hey? Come,  140
Mrs. Malaprop, we'll not disturb their tenderness—their's is the time
of life for happiness!——'*Youth's the season made for joy*'¹—[sings]—
hey!—Odds'life! I'm in such spirits,—I don't know what I couldn't
do!—Permit me, Ma'am—[*gives his hand to Mrs. Mal.*] [*sings*] Tol-de-
rol—'gad I should like a little fooling myself—Tol-de-rol! de-rol!

> [*Exit singing, and handing Mrs.* MAL.

> [LYDIA *sits sullenly in her chair.*]

ABS. So much thought bodes me no good [*aside*]—So grave, Lydia!

LYD. Sir!

ABS. So!—egad! I thought as much!—that d—n'd monosyllable has
froze me! [*aside*]—What, Lydia, now that we are as happy in our *friends
consent*, as in our *mutual vows*——                              150

LYD. *Friends consent*, indeed! [*peevishly*]

ABS. Come, come, we must lay aside some of our romance—a little
*wealth* and *comfort* may be endur'd after all. And for your fortune, the
lawyers shall make such settlements as——

LYD. *Lawyers*! I *hate* lawyers!

ABS. Nay then, we will not wait for their lingering forms, but instantly
procure the licence, and—

LYD. The *licence*!—I *hate* licence!

ABS. O my Love! *be* not so unkind!—thus let me intreat—— [*Kneeling.*

LYD. Pshaw!—what signifies kneeling, when you know I *must* have you?  160

ABS. [*rising*] Nay, Madam, there shall be no constraint upon your inclinations, I promise you.—If I have lost your *heart*,—I resign the rest.—
'Gad, I must try what a little *spirit* will do.                 [*Aside.*

LYD. [*rising*] Then, Sir, let me tell you, the interest you had there was
acquired by a mean, unmanly imposition, and deserves the punishment
of fraud.—What, you have been treating *me* like a *child*!—humouring
my romance! and laughing, I suppose, at your success!

¹ J. Gay, *The Beggar's Opera* (1728), II. iv:

> Youth's the season made for joys,
> Love is then our duty;
> She alone who that employs,
> Well deserves her beauty.
>> Let's be gay,
>> While we may,
> Beauty's a flower, despised in decay.

> Let us drink and sport today,
> Ours is not tomorrow.
> Love with youth flies swift away,
> Age is nought but sorrow,
>> Dance and sing,
>> Time's on the wing,
> Life never knows the return of spring.

ABS. You wrong me, Lydia, you wrong me—only hear——

LYD. So, while *I* fondly imagined we were deceiving my relations, and flatter'd myself that I should outwit and incense them *all*—behold! 170 my hopes are to be crush'd at once, by my Aunt's consent and approbation!—and *I* am *myself*, the only dupe at last!

[*Walking about in heat.*

—But here, Sir, here is the picture—Beverley's picture! [*taking a miniature from her bosom*] which I have worn, night and day, in spite of threats and entreaties!—There, Sir, [*flings it to him*] and be assured I throw the original from my heart as easily!

ABS. Nay, nay, Ma'am, we will not differ as to that.—Here, [*taking out a picture*] *here* is Miss Lydia Languish.—What a difference!—aye, *there* is the heav'nly assenting smile, that first gave soul and spirit to my hopes!—those are the lips which seal'd a vow, as yet scarce dry in 180 Cupid's calendar!—and *there* the *half* resentful blush, that *would* have check'd the ardour of my thanks—Well, all that's past!—all over indeed! —There, Madam—in *beauty*, that copy is not equal to you, but in my mind its merit over the original, in being still the same, is such—that —I cannot find in my heart to *part with* it.          [*Puts it up again.*

LYD. [*Softening*] 'Tis *your own* doing, Sir—I, I, I suppose you are perfectly satisfied.

ABS. O, most certainly—sure now this is much better than being in love! —ha! ha! ha!—there's some spirit in *this!*—What signifies breaking some scores of solemn promises:—all that's of no consequence you 190 know.—To be sure people will say, that Miss didn't know her own mind—but never mind that:—or perhaps they may be ill-natured enough to hint, that the gentleman grew tired of the lady and forsook her—but don't let that fret you.

LYD. There's no bearing his insolence.          [*Bursts into tears.*

*Enter Mrs.* MALAPROP *and Sir* ANTHONY.

MRS. MAL. [*Entering*] Come, we must interrupt your billing and cooing a while.

LYD. *This* is *worse* than your treachery and deceit, you base ingrate!

[*Sobbing.*

SIR ANTH. What the devil's the matter now!—Z—ds! Mrs. Malaprop, this is the *oddest billing* and *cooing* I ever heard!—but what the deuce 200 is the meaning of it?—I'm quite astonish'd!

ABS. Ask the lady, Sir.

MRS. MAL. O mercy!—I'm quite analys'd for my part!—why, Lydia, what is the reason of this?

LYD. Ask the *gentleman*, Ma'am.

SIR ANTH. Z—ds! I shall be in a phrenzy!—why Jack, you are not come out to be any one else, are you?

MRS. MAL. Aye, Sir, there's no more *trick*, is there?—you are not like Cerberus, *three* Gentlemen[1] at once, are you?

ABS. You'll not let me speak—I say the *lady* can account for *this* much 210 better than I can.

LYD. Ma'am, you once commanded me never to think of Beverley again —*there* is the man—I now obey you:—for, from this moment, I renounce him for ever.                                         [*Exit* LYDIA.

MRS. MAL. O mercy! and miracles! what a turn here is—why sure, Captain, you haven't behaved disrespectfully to my Niece.

SIR ANTH. Ha! ha! ha!—ha! ha! ha!—now I see it—Ha! ha! ha!—now I see it—you have been too lively, Jack.

ABS. Nay, Sir, upon my word——

SIR ANTH. Come, no lying, Jack—I'm sure '*twas* so.                    220

MRS. MAL. O Lud! Sir Anthony!——O fie, Captain!

ABS. Upon my soul, Ma'am——

SIR ANTH. Come, no excuses, Jack;—why, your father, you rogue, was so before you:—the blood of the Absolutes was always impatient.—Ha! ha! ha! poor little Lydia!—why, you've frighten'd her, you Dog, you have.

ABS. By all that's good, Sir——

SIR ANTH. Z—ds! say no more, I tell you.—Mrs. Malaprop shall make your peace.—You must make his peace, Mrs. Malaprop;—you must tell her 'tis Jack's way—tell her 'tis all our ways—it runs in the blood of our family!—Come, get on, Jack—ha! ha! ha! Mrs. Malaprop—a 230 young villain!                                    [*Pushes him out.*

MRS. MAL. O! Sir Anthony!—O fie, Captain!        [*Exeunt severally.*


## SCENE III[2]

### *The* North-Parade

#### *Enter* SIR LUCIUS O'TRIGGER.

SIR LUC. I wonder where this Capt. Absolute hides himself.—Upon my conscience!—these officers are always in one's way in love-affairs:— I remember I might have married Lady Dorothy Carmine, if it had not been for a little rogue of a Major, who ran away with her before she could get a sight of me!—And I wonder too what it is the ladies can see in them to be so fond of them—unless it be a touch of the old serpent in 'em, that makes the little creatures be caught, like vipers with

[1] In Garrick's *A Peep behind the Curtain* (1767), pp. 15-17, Glib claims that a stroke of genius to fill the boxes for a month, is the use of Cerberus to guard the entrance to Hades. 'Author' then remarks, 'You know, I suppose, that Cerberus is a dog and has three heads? . . . I make the three heads sing a *trio*.'

[2] This is mistakenly numbered 'IV' in all early editions from the Larpent MS. onwards.

a bit of red cloth.—Hah!—isn't this the Captain coming?—faith it is!
—There is a probability of succeeding about that fellow, that is mighty
provoking!—Who the devil is he talking to?                    [*Steps aside.*  10

*Enter* CAPT. ABSOLUTE.

ABS. To what fine purpose I have been plotting! a noble reward for all
   my schemes, upon my soul!—a little gypsey!—I did not think her
   romance could have made her so d—nd absurd either—S'death, I
   never was in a worse humour in my life—I could cut my own throat,
   or any other person's, with the greatest pleasure in the world!

SIR LUC. O, faith! I'm in the luck of it—I never could have found him
   in a sweeter temper for my purpose—to be sure I'm just come in the
   nick! now to enter into conversation with him, and so quarrel genteelly.
   [SIR LUCIUS *goes up to* ABSOLUTE.]——With regard to that matter,
   Captain, I must beg leave to differ in opinion with you.               20

ABS. Upon my word then, you must be a very subtle disputant:—
   because, Sir, I happen'd just then to be giving no opinion at all.

SIR LUC. That's no reason.—For give me leave to tell you, a man may
   *think* an untruth as well as *speak* one.

ABS. Very true, Sir, but if the man never utters his thoughts,[1] I should
   think they *might* stand a *chance* of escaping controversy.

SIR LUC. Then, Sir, you differ in opinion with me, which amounts to the
   same thing.

ABS. Hark'ee, Sir Lucius,—if I had not before known you to be a gentleman, upon my soul, I should not have discovered it at this interview:—  30
   for what you can drive at, unless you mean to quarrel with me, I
   cannot conceive!

SIR LUC. I humbly thank you, Sir, for the quickness of your apprehension,                                                     [*Bowing.*
   —you have nam'd the very thing I would be at.

ABS. Very well, Sir—I shall certainly not baulk your inclinations:——
   but I should be glad you would please to explain your motives.

SIR LUC. Pray, Sir, be easy—the quarrel is a very pretty quarrel as it
   stands—we should only spoil it, by trying to explain it.—However, your
   memory is very short—or you could not have forgot an affront pass'd you  40
   on me within this week.—So no more, but name your time and place.

ABS. Well, Sir, since you are so bent on it, the sooner the better;—let it
   be this evening—here, by the Spring Gardens.[2]—We shall scarcely
   be interrupted.

---

[1] Cf. Buckingham's *The Rehearsal* (1671), II. iv:
   *Smith*: That's very complaisant, I swear, Mr. Bayes, to be of another man's opinion,
   before he knows what it is.

[2] A summer meeting-place for public breakfasts, teas, concerts, and fireworks. It
lay on the Bathwick side of the Pulteney Bridge.

SIR LUC. Faith! that same interruption in affairs of this nature, shews very great ill-breeding.——I don't know what's the reason, but in England, if a thing of this kind gets wind, people make such a pother, that a gentleman can never fight in peace and quietness.—However, if it's the same to you, Captain, I should take it as a particular kindness, if you'd let us meet in King's-Mead-Fields,[1] as a little business will call me there about six o'clock, and I may dispatch both matters at once. 50

ABS. 'Tis the same to me exactly.—A little after six, then we will discuss this matter more seriously.

SIR LUC. If you please, Sir, there will be very pretty small-sword light, tho' it won't do for a long shot.—So that matter's settled! and my mind's at ease.                                    [*Exit* SIR LUCIUS.

*Enter* FAULKLAND, *meeting* ABSOLUTE.

ABS. Well met.—I was going to look for you.—O, Faulkland! all the Dæmons of spite and disappointment have conspired against me! I'm so vex'd, that if I had not the prospect of a resource in being knock'd o'the head by and bye, I should scarce have spirits to tell you the cause. 60

FAULK. What can you mean?——Has Lydia chang'd her mind?—I should have thought her duty and inclination would now have pointed to the same object.

ABS. Aye, just as the eyes do of a person who squints[2]:—when her *love eye* was fix'd on *me*——t'other—her *eye* of *duty*, was finely obliqued:—but when duty bid her point *that* the same way—off t'other turn'd on a swivel, and secured its retreat with a frown!

FAULK. But what's the resource you——

ABS. O, to wind up the whole, a good natured Irishman here has (*mimicking* SIR LUCIUS) beg'd leave to have the pleasure of cutting my 70 throat—and I mean to indulge him—that's all.

FAULK. Prithee, be serious.

ABS. 'Tis fact, upon my soul.——Sir Lucius O'Trigger—you know him by sight—for some affront, which I am sure I never intended, has obliged me to meet him this evening at six o'clock:—'tis on that account I wish'd to see you—you must go with me.

FAULK. Nay, there must be some mistake, sure.—Sir Lucius shall explain himself—and I dare say matters may be accommodated:—but this evening, did you say?—I wish it had been any other time.

ABS. Why?—there will be light enough:——there will (as Sir Lucius 80

---

[1] Sheridan himself had lived in Kingsmead Street. Open fields lay beyond it.

[2] Was the comparison prompted by the following exchange in Wycherley's *The Plain Dealer* (1676), II. i?

*Olivia.* First, can any one be call'd beautiful that squints?

*Lord Plausible.* Her eyes languish a little, I own.

*Novel.* Languish! ha, ha.

says) 'be very pretty small-sword light, tho' it won't do for a long shot.'
—Confound his long shots!

FAULK. But I am myself a good deal ruffled, by a difference I have had
with Julia—my vile tormenting temper has made me treat her so
cruelly, that I shall not be myself till we are reconciled.

ABS. By Heav'ns, Faulkland, you don't deserve her.

*Enter* SERVANT, *gives* FAULKLAND *a letter.*

FAULK. O Jack! this is from Julia—I dread to open it—I fear it may
be to take a last leave—perhaps to bid me return her letters—and restore
——O! how I suffer for my folly!

ABS. Here—let me see.                    [*Takes the letter and opens it.* 90
Aye, a final sentence indeed!—'tis all over with you, faith!

FAULK. Nay, Jack—don't keep me in suspence.

ABS. Hear then.—'*As I am convinced that my dear* Faulkland's *own
reflections have already upbraided him for his last unkindness to me, I will
not add a word on the subject.—I wish to speak with you as soon as possible.
—Your's ever and truly,* Julia.'—There's stubborness and resentment
for you!                                        [*Gives him the letter.*
Why, man, you don't seem one whit the happier at this.

FAULK. O, yes, I am—but—but——

ABS. Confound your *buts.*—You never hear any thing that would make 100
another man bless himself, but you immediately d—n it with a *but.*

FAULK. Now, Jack, as you are my friend, own honestly—don't you think
there is something forward—something indelicate in this haste to forgive?—Women should never sue for reconciliation:—*that* should *always*
come from us.—*They* should retain their coldness till *woo'd* to kindness
—and their *pardon,* like their *love,* should 'not unsought be won.'[1]

ABS. I have not patience to listen to you:—thou'rt incorrigible!—so say
no more on the subject.—I must go to settle a few matters—let me see
you before six—remember—at my lodgings.——A poor industrious
devil like me, who have toil'd, and drudg'd, and plotted to gain my 110
ends, and am at last disappointed by other people's folly—may in pity
be allowed to swear and grumble a little;—but a captious sceptic in
love,—a slave to fretfulness and whim—who has no difficulties but of
*his own* creating—is a subject more fit for ridicule than compassion!
                                                [*Exit* ABSOLUTE.

FAULK. I feel his reproaches!—yet I would not change this too exquisite
nicety, for the gross content with which *he* trandples on the thorns of
love.—His engaging me in this duel, has started an idea in my head,
which I will instantly pursue.—I'll use it as the touch-stone of Julia's

---

[1] From *Paradise Lost,* viii. 502–3:
        Her virtue, and the conscience of her worth,
        That would be wooed, and not unsought be won.

sincerity and disinterestedness—if her love prove pure and sterling
ore—my name will rest on it with honour!—and once I've stamp'd it   120
there, I lay aside my doubts for ever:—but if the dross of selfishness, the
allay of pride predominate—'twill be best to leave her as a toy for some
less cautious Fool to sigh for.                          [*Exit* FAULKLAND.

END OF THE FOURTH ACT

# ACT V

## SCENE I

JULIA's *Dressing-Room*

JULIA, *sola.*

How this message has alarmed me! what dreadful accident can he
mean! why such charge to be alone?——O Faulkland!—how many
unhappy moments!—how many tears have you cost me!

*Enter* FAULKLAND, *muffled up in a Riding-coat.*

JUL. What means this?——why this caution, Faulkland?

FAULK. Alas! Julia, I am come to take a long farewell.

JUL. Heav'ns! what do you mean?

FAULK. You see before you a wretch, whose life is forfeited.—Nay, start
not!—the infirmity of my temper has drawn all this misery on me.—
I left you fretful and passionate—an untoward accident drew me into
a quarrel—the event is, that I must fly this kingdom instantly.—O Julia,   10
had I been so fortunate as to have call'd you mine intirely, before
this mischance had fallen on me, I should not so deeply dread my
banishment!——

JUL. My soul is oppress'd with sorrow at the *nature* of your misfortune:
had these adverse circumstances arisen from a less fatal cause, I should
have felt strong comfort in the thought that I could *now* chase from
your bosom every doubt of the warm sincerity of my love.——My heart
has long known no other guardian—I now entrust my person to your
honour—we will fly together.—When safe from pursuit, my Father's
will may be fulfilled—and I receive a legal claim to be the partner of   20
your sorrows, and tenderest comforter. Then on the bosom of your
wedded Julia, you may lull your keen regret to slumbering; while
virtuous love, with a Cherub's hand, shall smooth the brow of upbraiding thought, and pluck the thorn from compunction.

FAULK. O Julia! I am bankrupt in gratitude! but the time is so pressing, it calls on you for so hasty a resolution.—Would you not wish some hours to weigh the advantages you forego, and what little compensation poor Faulkland can make you beside his solitary love?

JUL. I ask not a moment.—No, Faulkland, I have lov'd you for yourself: and if I now, more than ever, prize the solemn engagement which so 30 long has pledged us to each other, it is because it leaves no room for hard aspersions on my fame, and puts the seal of duty to an act of love.—But let us not linger.—Perhaps this delay——

FAULK. 'Twill be better I should not venture out again till dark.—Yet am I griev'd to think what numberless distresses will press heavy on your gentle disposition!

JUL. Perhaps your fortune may be forfeited by this unhappy act.—I know not whether 'tis so—but sure that alone can never make us unhappy.— The little I have will be sufficient to *support* us; and *exile* never should be splendid. 40

FAULK. Aye, but in such an abject state of life, my wounded pride perhaps may increase the natural fretfulness of my temper, till I become a rude, morose companion, beyond your patience to endure. Perhaps the recollection of a deed, my conscience cannot justify, may haunt me in such gloomy and unsocial fits, that I shall hate the tenderness that would relieve me, break from your arms, and quarrel with your fondness!

JUL. If your thoughts should assume so unhappy a bent, you will the more want some mild and affectionate spirit to watch over and console you:—One who, by bearing *your* infirmities with gentleness 50 and resignation, may teach you *so* to bear the evils of your fortune.

FAULK. Julia, I have proved you to the quick! and with this useless device I throw away all my doubts. How shall I plead to be forgiven this last unworthy effect of my restless, unsatisfied disposition?

JUL. Has no such disaster happened as you related?

FAULK. I am ashamed to own that it was all pretended; yet in pity, Julia, do not kill me with resenting a fault which never can be repeated: But sealing, this once, my pardon, let me to-morrow, in the face of Heaven, receive my future guide and monitress, and expiate my past folly, by 60 years of tender adoration.

JUL. Hold, Faulkland!—that you are free from a crime, which I before fear'd to name, Heaven knows how sincerely I rejoice!—These are tears of thankfulness for that! But that your cruel doubts should have urged you to an imposition that has wrung my heart, gives me now a pang, more keen than I can express!

FAULK. By Heav'ns! Julia——

JUL. Yet hear me.——My Father lov'd you, Faulkland! and you preserv'd the life that tender parent gave me; in his presence I pledged my hand—*joyfully* pledged it—where before I had given my heart. When, 70 soon after, I lost that parent, it seem'd to me that Providence had, in Faulkland, shewn me whither to transfer, without a pause, my grateful duty, as well as my affection: Hence I have been content to bear from you what pride and delicacy would have forbid me from another.—I will not upbraid you, by repeating how you have trifled with my sincerity.——

FAULK. I confess it all! yet hear——

JUL. After such a year of trial—I might have flattered myself that I should not have been insulted with a new probation of my sincerity, as cruel as unnecessary! I now see it is not in your nature to be content, 80 or confident in love. With this conviction—I never will be yours. While I had hopes that my persevering attention, and unreproaching kindness might in time reform your temper, I should have been happy to have gain'd a dearer influence over you; but I will not furnish you with a licensed power to keep alive an incorrigible fault, at the expence of one who never would contend with you.

FAULK. Nay, but Julia, by my soul and honour, if after this——

JUL. But one word more.—As my faith has once been given to you, I never will barter it with another.—I shall pray for your happiness with the truest sincerity; and the dearest blessing I can ask of Heaven to 90 send you, will be to charm you from that unhappy temper, which alone has prevented the performance of our solemn engagement.—All I request of *you* is, that you will yourself reflect upon this infirmity, and when you number up the many true delights it has deprived you of—let it not be your *least* regret, that it lost you the love of one—who would have follow'd you in beggary through the world! [*Exit.*

FAULK. She's gone!—for ever!—There was an awful resolution in her manner, that rivetted me to my place.——O Fool!—Dolt!—Barbarian! —Curst as I am, with more imperfections than my fellow-wretches, kind Fortune sent a heaven-gifted cherub to my aid, and, like a ruffian, 100 I have driven her from my side!—I must now haste to my appointment.—Well my mind is tuned for such a scene.—I shall wish only to become a principal in it, and reverse the tale my cursed folly put me upon forging here.——O Love!—Tormentor!—Fiend!—whose influence, like the Moon's, acting on men of dull souls, makes idiots of them, but meeting subtler spirits, betrays their course, and urges sensibility to madness! [*Exit.*

*Enter* MAID *and* LYDIA.

MAID. My Mistress, Ma'am, I know, was here just now—perhaps she is only in the next room. [*Exit* MAID.

LYD. Heigh ho!—Though he has used me so, this fellow runs strangely 110
in my head. I believe one lecture from my grave Cousin will make me
recall him.

*Enter* JULIA.

LYD. O Julia, I am come to you with such an appetite for consolation.
—Lud! Child, what's the matter with you?—You have been crying!
—I'll be hanged, if that Faulkland has not been tormenting you!

JUL. You mistake the cause of my uneasiness.—Something *has* flurried
me a little.—Nothing that you can guess at.——I would not accuse
Faulkland to a Sister!                                        [*Aside.*

LYD. Ah! whatever vexations you may have, I can assure you mine
surpass them.——You know who Beverley proves to be?              120

JUL. I will now own to you, Lydia, that Mr. Faulkland had before
inform'd me of the whole affair. Had young Absolute been the person
you took him for, I should not have accepted your confidence on the
subject, without a serious endeavour to counteract your caprice.

LYD. So, then, I see I have been deceived by every one!—but I don't
care—I'll never have him.

JUL. Nay, Lydia——

LYD. Why, is it not provoking; when I thought we were coming to the
prettiest distress imaginable, to find myself made a mere Smithfield
bargain[1] of at last——There had I projected one of the most sentimental 130
elopements!—so becoming a disguise!—so amiable a ladder of Ropes!
—Conscious Moon—four horses—Scotch parson—with such surprise
to Mrs. Malaprop—and such paragraphs in the News-papers!——O,
I shall die with disappointment.

JUL. I don't wonder at it!

LYD. Now—sad reverse!—what have I to expect, but, after a deal of
flimsy preparation with a bishop's licence, and my Aunt's blessing, to
go simpering up to the Altar; or perhaps be cried three times in a
country-church, and have an unmannerly fat clerk ask the consent of
every butcher in the parish to join John Absolute and Lydia Languish, 140
*Spinster*! O, that I should live to hear myself called Spinster!

JUL. Melancholy, indeed!

LYD. How mortifying, to remember the dear delicious shifts I used to
be put to, to gain half a minute's conversation with this fellow!——
How often have I stole forth, in the coldest night in January, and found
him in the garden, stuck like a dripping statue!—There would he kneel
to me in the snow, and sneeze and cough so pathetically! he shivering
with cold, and I with apprehension! and while the freezing blast

---

[1] A marriage of interest, in which money is the chief consideration (*O.E.D.*).

numb'd our joints, how warmly would he press me to pity his flame, and
glow with mutual ardour!——Ah, Julia! that was something like being  150
in love.

JUL. If I were in spirits, Lydia, I should chide you only by laughing
heartily at you: but it suits more the situation of my mind, at present,
earnestly to entreat you, not to let a man, who loves you with sincerity,
suffer that unhappiness from your *caprice*, which I know too well
caprice can inflict.

LYD. O Lud! what has brought my Aunt here!

*Enter* MRS. MALAPROP, FAG, *and* DAVID.

MRS. MAL. So! so! here's fine work!—here's fine suicide, paracide, and
simulation going on in the fields! and Sir Anthony not to be found to
prevent the antistrophe!                                         160

JUL. For Heaven's sake, Madam, what's the meaning of this?

MRS. MAL. That gentleman can tell you—'twas he enveloped the affair
to me.

LYD. Do, Sir, will you inform us.                    [*To* FAG.

FAG. Ma'am, I should hold myself very deficient in every requisite that
forms the man of breeding, if I delay'd a moment to give all the information in my power to a lady so deeply interested in the affair as you are.

LYD. But quick! quick, Sir!

FAG. True, Ma'am, as you say, one should be quick in divulging matters
of this nature; for should we be tedious, perhaps while we are flourish-  170
ing on the subject, two or three lives may be lost!

LYD. O patience!—Do, Ma'am, for Heaven's sake! tell us what is the
matter?

MRS. MAL. Why, murder's the matter! slaughter's the matter! killing's
the matter!—but he can tell you the perpendiculars.

LYD. Then, prythee, Sir, be brief.

FAG. Why then, Ma'am—as to murder—I cannot take upon me to say
—and as to slaughter, or man-slaughter, that will be as the jury finds it.

LYD. But who, Sir—who are engaged in this?

FAG. Faith, Ma'am, one is a young gentleman whom I should be very  180
sorry any thing was to happen to—a very pretty behaved gentleman!—
We have lived much together, and always on terms.

LYD. But who is this? who! who! who!

FAG. My Master, Ma'am—my Master—I speak of my Master.

LYD. Heavens! What, Captain Absolute!

MRS. MAL. O, to be sure, you are frightened now!

JUL. But who are with him, Sir?

FAG. As to the rest, Ma'am, this gentleman can inform you better than I.

JUL. Do speak, friend.                              [*To* DAVID.

DAVID. Look'ee, my Lady——by the Mass! there's mischief going on.  190

——Folks don't use to meet for amusement with fire-arms, firelocks,
fire-engines, fire-screens, fire-office,[1] and the devil knows what other
crackers besides!——This, my Lady, I say, has an angry favour.

JUL. But who is there beside Captain Absolute, friend?

DAVID. My poor Master—under favour, for mentioning him first.—You
know me, my Lady—I am David—and my Master of course is, or *was*,
Squire Acres.—Then comes Squire Faulkland.

JUL. Do, Ma'am, let us instantly endeavour to prevent mischief.

MRS. MAL. O fie—it would be very inelegant in us:—we should only
participate things.                                                    200

DAVID. Ah! do, Mrs. Aunt, save a few lives—they are desperately given,
believe me.—Above all, there is that blood-thirsty Philistine, Sir Lucius
O'Trigger.

MRS. MAL. Sir Lucius O'Trigger!—O mercy! have they drawn poor little
dear Sir Lucius into the scrape?—why, how, how you stand, girl!
you have no more feeling than one of the Derbyshire Putrefactions![2]

LYD. What are we to do, Madam?

MRS. MAL. Why, fly with the utmost felicity to be sure, to prevent
mischief:—here, friend—you can shew us the place?

FAG. If you please, Ma'am, I will conduct you.—David, do you look for   210
Sir Anthony.                                           [*Exit* DAVID.

MRS. MAL. Come, girls!—this gentleman will exhort us.—Come, Sir,
you're our envoy—lead the way, and we'll precede.

FAG. Not a step before the ladies for the world!

MRS. MAL. You're sure you know the spot.

FAG. I think I can find it, Ma'am; and one good thing is, we shall hear
the report of the pistols as we draw near, so we can't well miss them;
never fear, Ma'am, never fear.                    [*Exeunt, he talking.*


## SCENE II

### South-Parade

*Enter* ABSOLUTE, *putting his sword under his greatcoat.*

ABS. A sword seen in the streets of Bath[3] would raise as great an alarm
as a mad-dog.—How provoking this is in Faulkland!—never punctual!

---

[1] Office of an insurance company dealing with fires.

[2] The 'wonders of the Peak' were often described, and R. Brookes's *General Gazetteer*
(10th edn., 1797) says of Pool's Hole, near Buxton, that it 'contains many stalactitious
concretions, and several curious representations both of art and nature, produced by
the petrifying water continually dropping from the rock'.

[3] Beau Nash had both parties arrested whenever he heard of a challenge to a duel
at Bath.

I shall be obliged to go without him at last.—O, the devil! here's Sir Anthony!——how shall I escape him? *[Muffles up his, face, and [takes a circle to go off.*

*Enter* SIR ANTHONY.

SIR ANTH. How one may be deceived at a little distance! only that I see he don't know me, I could have sworn that was Jack!—Hey!—'Gad's life; it is.—Why, Jack,—what are you afraid of?—hey! sure I'm right. —Why, Jack—Jack Absolute! *[Goes up to him.*

ABS. Really, Sir, you have the advantage of me:—I don't remember ever to have had the honour——my name is Saunderson, at your 10 service.

SIR ANTH. Sir, I beg your pardon—I took you—hey!—why, z—ds! it is——Stay—— *[Looks up to his face.* So, so—your humble servant, Mr. Saunderson!—Why, you scoundrel, what tricks are you after now?

ABS. O! a joke, Sir, a joke!—I came here on purpose to look for you, Sir.

SIR ANTH. You did! well, I am glad you were so lucky:—but what are you muffled up so for?—what's this for?—hey?

ABS. 'Tis cool, Sir; isn't it?—rather chilly somehow:—but I shall be late—I have a particular engagement. 20

SIR ANTH. Stay.—why, I thought you were looking for me?—Pray, Jack, where is't you are going?

ABS. Going, Sir!

SIR ANTH. Aye—where are you going?

ABS. Where am I going?

SIR ANTH. You unmannerly puppy!

ABS. I was going, Sir, to—to—to—to Lydia—Sir to Lydia—to make matters up if I could;—and I was looking for you, Sir, to—to——

SIR ANTH. To go with you, I suppose—Well, come along.

ABS. O! z—ds! no, Sir, not for the world!—I wish'd to meet with you, 30 Sir, to—to—to—— You find it cool, I'm sure, Sir—you'd better not stay out.

SIR ANTH. Cool!—not at all—Well, Jack—and what will you say to Lydia?

ABS. O, Sir, beg her pardon, humour her—promise and vow:—but I detain you, Sir—consider the cold air on your gout.

SIR ANTH. O, not at all!—not at all!—I'm in no hurry.—Ah! Jack, you youngsters when once you are wounded here. *[Putting his hand to ABSOLUTE's breast.* Hey! what the deuce have you got here?

ABS. Nothing, Sir—nothing. 40

SIR ANTH. What's this?—here's something d—d hard!

ABS. O, trinkets, Sir! trinkets—a bauble for Lydia!

SIR ANTH. Nay, let me see your taste.

> [*Pulls his coat open, the sword falls.*

Trinkets!—a bauble for Lydia!—z—ds! sirrah, you are not going to
cut her throat, are you?

ABS. Ha! ha! ha!—I thought it would divert you, Sir, tho' I didn't mean
to tell you till afterwards.

SIR ANTH. You didn't?—Yes, this is a very diverting trinket, truly.

ABS. Sir, I'll explain to you.—You know, Sir, Lydia is romantic—dev'lish
romantic, and very absurd of course:—now, Sir, I intend, if she refuses 50
to forgive me—to unsheath this sword—and swear—I'll fall upon its
point, and expire at her feet!

SIR ANTH. Fall upon a fiddle-stick's end!—why, I suppose it is the very
thing that would please her—Get along, you Fool.—

ABS. Well, Sir, you shall hear of my success—you shall hear.—'O,
Lydia!—forgive me, or this pointed steel'—says I.

SIR ANTH. 'O, Booby! stab away, and welcome'—says she—Get along!
—and d—n your trinkets!                                    [*Exit* ABSOLUTE.

### *Enter* DAVID, *running.*

DAVID. Stop him! stop him! Murder! Thief! Fire!—Stop fire! Stop fire!
—O! Sir Anthony—call! call! bid 'em stop! Murder! Fire!            60

SIR ANTH. Fire! Murder! where?

DAVID. Oons! he's out of sight! and I'm out of breath, for my part! O,
Sir Anthony, why didn't you stop him? why didn't you stop him?

SIR ANTH. Z—ds! the fellow's mad!—Stop whom? stop Jack?

DAVID. Aye, the Captain, Sir!—there's murder and slaughter——

SIR ANTH. Murder!

DAVID. Aye, please you, Sir Anthony, there's all kinds of murder, all
sorts of slaughter to be seen in the fields: there's fighting going on,
Sir—bloody sword-and-gun fighting!

SIR ANTH. Who are going to fight, Dunce?                            70

DAVID. Every body that I know of, Sir Anthony:—every body is going to
fight, my poor Master, Sir Lucius O'Trigger, your son, the Captain——

SIR ANTH. O, the Dog!—I see his tricks:—do you know the place?

DAVID. King's-Mead-Fields.

SIR ANTH. You know the way?

DAVID. Not an inch;—but I'll call the Mayor—Aldermen—Constables—
Church-wardens—and Beadles—we can't be too many to part them.

SIR ANTH. Come along—give me your shoulder! we'll get assistance as
we go—the lying villain!—Well, I shall be in such a phrenzy—So—
this was the history of his d—d trinkets! I'll bauble him!      [*Exeunt.* 80

## SCENE III
### King's-Mead-Fields

SIR LUCIUS *and* ACRES, *with pistols.*

ACRES. By my valour! then, Sir Lucius, forty yards is a good distance—
Odds levels and aims!—I say it is a good distance.

SIR LUC. Is it for muskets or small field-pieces? upon my conscience,
Mr. Acres, you must leave those things to me.—Stay now—I'll shew
you.                                          [*Measures paces along the stage.*
there now, that is a very pretty distance—a pretty gentleman's distance.

ACRES. Z—ds! we might as well fight in a sentry-box!—I tell you, Sir
Lucius, the farther he is off, the cooler I shall take my aim.

SIR LUC. Faith! then I suppose you would aim at him best of all if he was
out of sight!                                                                    10

ACRES. No, Sir Lucius—but I should think forty or eight and thirty
yards——

SIR LUC. Pho! pho! nonsense! three or four feet between the mouths of
your pistols is as good as a mile.

ACRES. Odds bullets, no!—by my valour! there is no merit in killing
him so near:—no, my dear Sir Lucius, let me bring him down at a long
shot:—a long shot, Sir Lucius, if you love me!

SIR LUC. Well—the gentleman's friend and I must settle that.—But tell
me now, Mr. Acres, in case of an accident, is there any little will or
commission I could execute for you?                                             20

ACRES. I am much obliged to you, Sir Lucius—but I don't understand——

SIR LUC. Why, you may think there's no being shot at without a
little risk—and if an unlucky bullet should carry a *Quietus* with it—
I say it will be no time then to be bothering you about family
matters.

ACRES. A *Quietus*!

SIR LUC. For instance, now—if that should be the case—would you
chuse to be pickled and sent home?—or would it be the same to you
to lie here in the Abbey?—I'm told there is very snug lying in the   30
Abbey.

ACRES. Pickled!—Snug lying in the Abbey!—Odds tremors! Sir Lucius,
don't talk so!

SIR LUC. I suppose, Mr. Acres, you never were engaged in an affair of
this kind before?

ACRES. No, Sir Lucius, never before.

SIR LUC. Ah! that's a pity!—there's nothing like being used to a thing.
—Pray now, how would you receive the gentleman's shot?

ACRES. Odds files!¹—I've practised that—there, Sir Lucius—there

[*Puts himself in an attitude.*

——a side-front, hey?—Odd! I'll make myself small enough:—I'll 40
stand edge-ways.

SIR LUC. Now—you're quite out—for if you stand so when I take my
aim—— [*Levelling at him.*

ACRES. Z—ds! Sir Lucius—are you sure it is not cock'd?

SIR LUC. Never fear.

ACRES. But—but—you don't know—it may go off of its own head!

SIR LUC. Pho! be easy—Well, now if I hit you in the body, my bullet
has a double chance—for if it misses a vital part on your right side—
'twill be very hard if it don't succeed on the left!

ACRES. A vital part! 50

SIR LUC. But, there—fix yourself so— [*Placing him.*
let him see the broad side of your full front—there—now a ball or two
may pass clean thro' your body, and never do any harm at all.

ACRES. Clean thro' me!—a ball or two clean thro' me!

SIR LUC. Aye—may they—and it is much the genteelest attitude into the
bargain.

ACRES. Look'ee! Sir Lucius—I'd just as leive be shot in an aukward
posture as a genteel one—so, by my valour! I will stand edge-ways.

SIR LUC. [*Looking at his watch.*] Sure they don't mean to disappoint us.
—Hah?—no faith—I think I see them coming. 60

ACRES. Hey!—what!—coming!——

SIR LUC. Aye—Who are those yonder getting over the stile?

ACRES. There are two of them, indeed!—well—let them come—hey,
Sir Lucius!—we—we—we—we—won't run—

SIR LUC. Run!

ACRES. No—I say—we *won't* run, by my valour!

SIR LUC. What the devil's the matter with you?

ACRES. Nothing—nothing—my dear friend——my dear Sir Lucius—
but—I—I—I don't feel quite so bold, somehow—as I did.

SIR LUC. O fie!—consider your honour. 70

ACRES. Aye—true—my honour——Do, Sir Lucius, edge in a word or
two every now and then about my honour.

SIR LUC. Well, here they're coming. [*Looking.*

ACRES. Sir Lucius—if I wa'n't with you, I should almost think I was
afraid—if my valour should leave me!—Valour will come and go.

SIR LUC. Then, pray keep it fast, while you have it.

ACRES. Sir Lucius—I doubt it is going—yes—my valour is certainly
going!—it is sneaking off!—I feel it oozing out as it were at the palms
of my hands!

¹ A file was a sword used in fencing.

SIR LUC. Your honour—your honour——Here they are.                                    80

ACRES. O mercy!—now—that I were safe at *Clod-hall!* or could be shot
before I was aware!

*Enter* FAULKLAND *and* ABSOLUTE.

SIR LUC. Gentlemen, your most obedient—hah!—what Captain Absolute!—So, I suppose, Sir, you are come here, just like myself—to do
a kind office, first for your friend—then to proceed to business on your
own account.

ACRES. What, Jack!—my dear Jack!—my dear friend!

ABS. Heark'ee, Bob, Beverley's at hand.

SIR LUC. Well, Mr. Acres—I don't blame your saluting the gentleman
civilly.—So, Mr. Beverley, [*to* FAULKLAND] if you'll chuse your   90
weapons, the Captain and I will measure the ground.

FAULK. *My* weapons, Sir.

ACRES. Odds life! Sir Lucius, I'm not going to fight Mr. Faulkland; these
are my particular friends.

SIR LUC. What, Sir, did not you come here to fight Mr. Acres?

FAULK. Not I, upon my word, Sir.

SIR LUC. Well, now, that's mighty provoking! But I hope, Mr. Faulkland, as there are three of us come on purpose for the game—you won't
be so cantanckerous as to spoil the party by sitting out.

ABS. O pray, Faulkland, fight to oblige Sir Lucius.                                    100

FAULK. Nay, if Mr. Acres is so bent on the matter.

ACRES. No, no, Mr. Faulkland—I'll bear my disappointment like a
Christian—Look'ee, Sir Lucius, there's no occasion at all for me to
fight; and if it is the same to you, I'd as lieve let it alone.

SIR LUC. Observe me, Mr. Acres—I must not be trifled with. You have
certainly challenged somebody—and you came here to fight him—Now,
if that gentleman is willing to represent him—I can't see, for my soul,
why it isn't just the same thing.

ACRES. Why no—Sir Lucius—I tell you, 'tis one Beverley I've challenged
—a fellow, you see, that dare not shew his face! If *he* were here, I'd   110
make him give up his pretensions directly!——

ABS. Hold, Bob—let me set you right—there is no such man as Beverley
in the case.—The person who assumed that name is before you; and
as his pretensions are the same in both characters, he is ready to support
them in whatever way you please.

SIR LUC. Well, this is lucky—Now you have an opportunity—

ACRES. What, quarrel with my dear friend Jack Absolute—not if he were
fifty Beverleys! Z—ds! Sir Lucius, you would not have me be so
unnatural.

SIR LUC. Upon my conscience, Mr. Acres, your valour has *oozed* away   120
with a vengeance!

ACRES. Not in the least! Odds Backs[1] and Abettors! I'll be your second with all my heart—and if you should get a *Quietus*, you may command me entirely. I'll get you a *snug lying* in the *Abbey here*; or *pickle* you, and send you over to Blunderbuss-hall, or any thing of the kind with the greatest pleasure.

SIR LUC. Pho! pho! you are little better than a coward.

ACRES. Mind, gentlemen, he calls me a *Coward*; Coward was the word, by my valour!

SIR LUC. Well, Sir?                                                    130

ACRES. Look'ee, Sir Lucius, 'tisn't that I mind the word Coward—*Coward* may be said in joke.—But if you had call'd me a *Poltroon*, Odds Daggers and Balls!

SIR LUC. Well, Sir?

ACRES. ——I should have thought you a very ill-bred man.

SIR LUC. Pho! you are beneath my notice.

ABS. Nay, Sir Lucius, you can't have a better second than my friend, Acres—He is a most *determined dog*—call'd in the country, *Fighting Bob*.—He generally *kills a man a week*; don't you, Bob?

ACRES. Aye—at home!                                                   140

SIR LUC. Well then, Captain, 'tis we must begin—so come out, my little counsellor,                                          [*draws his sword.*
and ask the gentleman, whether he will resign the lady, without forcing you to proceed against him?

ABS. Come on then, Sir; (*draws*) since you won't let it be an amicable suit, here's *my reply*.

*Enter Sir* ANTHONY, DAVID, *and the* WOMEN.

DAVID. Knock 'em all down, sweet Sir Anthony, knock down my Master in particular—and bind his hands over to their good behaviour!

SIR ANTH. Put up, Jack, put up, or I shall be in a frenzy—how came you 150 in a duel, Sir?

ABS. Faith, Sir, that gentleman can tell you better than I; 'twas he call'd on me, and you know, Sir, I serve his Majesty.

SIR ANTH. Here's a pretty fellow; I catch him going to cut a man's throat, and he tells me, he serves his Majesty!——Zounds! sirrah, then how durst you draw the King's sword against one of his subjects?

ABS. Sir, I tell you! That gentleman call'd me out, without explaining his reasons.

SIR ANTH. Gad! Sir, how came you to call my son out, without explaining your reasons?                                                      160

---

[1] Cf. Congreve, *The Old Batchelor*, II. i: 'Ah my Hector of *Troy*, welcome my Bully, my Back.'

SIR LUC. Your son, Sir, insulted me in a manner which my honour could not brook.

SIR ANTH. Zounds! Jack, how durst you insult the gentleman in a manner which his honour could not brook?

MRS. MAL. Come, come, let's have no Honour before ladies—Captain Absolute, come here—How could you intimidate us so?—Here's Lydia has been terrified to death for you.

ABS. For fear I should be kill'd, or escape, Ma'am?

MRS. MAL. Nay, no delusions to the past—Lydia is convinc'd; speak child.                                                                                    170

SIR LUC. With your leave, Ma'am, I must put in a word here—I believe I could interpret the young lady's silence—Now mark—

LYD. What is it you mean, Sir?

SIR LUC. Come, come, Delia, we must be serious now—this is no time for trifling.

LYD. 'Tis true, Sir; and your reproof bids me offer this gentleman my hand, and solicit the return of his affections.

ABS. O! my little angel, say you so?—Sir Lucius—I perceive there must be some mistake here—with regard to the affront, which you affirm I have given you—I can only say, that it could not have been intentional. 180 —And as you must be convinced, that I should not fear to support a real injury—you shall now see that I am not ashamed to atone for an inadvertency—I ask your pardon.—But for this lady, while honour'd with her approbation, I will support my claim against any man whatever.

SIR ANTH. Well said, Jack, and I'll stand by you, my Boy.

ACRES. Mind, I give up all my claim—I make no pretensions to any thing in the world—and if I can't get a wife, without fighting for her, by my Valour! I'll live a bachelor.

SIR LUC. Captain, give me your hand—an affront handsomely acknow- 190 ledged becomes an obligation—and as for the Lady—if she chuses to deny her own hand writing here—                                   [*Takes out letters.*

MRS. MAL. O, he will dissolve my mystery!—Sir Lucius, perhaps there's some mistake—perhaps, I can illuminate—

SIR LUC. Pray, old gentlewoman, don't interfere, where you have no business.—Miss Languish, are you my Delia, or not?

LYD. Indeed, Sir Lucius, I am not.

[*LYDIA and* ABSOLUTE *walk aside.*

MRS MAL. Sir Lucius O'Trigger—ungrateful as you are—I own the soft impeachment—pardon my blushes, I am Delia.

SIR LUC. You Delia—pho! pho! be easy.[1]                                    200

MRS. MAL. Why, thou barbarous Vandyke—those letters are mine—

---

[1] Don't be sought after: a sense still used on the Stock Exchange.

When you are more sensible of my benignity—perhaps I may be brought to encourage your addresses.

SIR LUC. Mrs. Malaprop ,I am extremely sensible of your condescension; and whether you or Lucy have put this trick upon me, I am equally beholden to you.—And to shew you I'm not ungrateful, Captain Absolute! since you have taken that lady from me, I'll give you my Delia into the bargain.

ABS. I am much obliged to you, Sir Lucius; but here's our friend, fighting Bob, unprovided for. 210

SIR LUC. Hah! little Valour—here, will you make your fortune?

ACRES. Odds Wrinkles! No.—But give me your hand, Sir Lucius, forget and forgive; but if ever I give you a chance of *pickling* me again, say Bob Acres is a Dunce, that's all.

SIR ANTH. Come, Mrs. Malaprop, don't be cast down—you are in your bloom yet.

MRS. MAL. O Sir Anthony!—men are all barbarians—
                              [*All retire but* JULIA *and* FAULKLAND.

JUL. He seems dejected and unhappy—not sullen—there was some foundation, however, for the tale he told me—O woman! how true should be your judgment, when your resolution is so weak! 220

FAULK. Julia!—how can I sue for what I so little deserve? I dare not presume—yet Hope is the child of Penitence.

JUL. Oh! Faulkland, you have not been more faulty in your unkind treatment of me, than I am now in wanting inclination to resent it. As my heart honestly bids me place my weakness to the account of love, I should be ungenerous not to admit the same plea for your's.

FAULK. Now I shall be blest indeed! [SIR ANTHONY *comes forward.*

SIR ANTH. What's going on here?—So you have been quarrelling too, I warrant.——Come, Julia, I never interfered before; but let me have a hand in the matter at last.—All the faults I have ever seen in my 230 friend Faulkland, seemed to proceed from what he calls the *delicacy* and *warmth* of his affection for you——There, marry him directly, Julia, you'll find he'll mend surprisingly! [*The rest come forward.*

SIR LUC. Come now, I hope there is no dissatisfied person, but what is content; for as I have been disappointed myself, it will be very hard if I have not the satisfaction of seeing other people succeed better—

ACRES. You are right, Sir Lucius.—So, Jack, I wish you joy—Mr. Faulkland the same.—Ladies,—come now, to shew you I'm neither vex'd nor angry, Odds Tabors and Pipes! I'll order the fiddles in half an hour, to the New Rooms[1]—and I insist on your all meeting me there. 240

SIR ANTH. Gad! Sir, I like your spirit; and at night we single lads will drink a health to the young couples, and a husband to Mrs. Malaprop.

---

[1] Built by John Wood the younger, and opened in 1771.

FAULK. Our partners are stolen from us, Jack—I hope to be congratu-
lated by each other—yours for having checked in time, the errors of an
ill-directed Imagination, which might have betray'd an innocent heart;
and mine, for having, by her gentleness and candour, reformed the
unhappy temper of one, who by it made wretched whom he loved most,
and tortured the heart he ought to have ador'd.

ABS. Well, Faulkland, we have both tasted the Bitters, as well as the
Sweets of Love—with this difference only, that *you* always prepared the   250
bitter cup for yourself, while *I*——

LYD. Was always obliged to *me* for it, hey! Mr. Modesty?——But come,
no more of that—our happiness is now as unallay'd as general.

JUL. Then let us study to preserve it so: and while Hope pictures to us
a flattering scene of future Bliss, let us deny its pencil those colours
which are too bright to be lasting.—When Hearts deserving Happiness
would unite their fortunes, Virtue would crown them with an unfading
garland of modest, hurtless flowers; but ill-judging Passion will force
the gaudier Rose into the wreath, whose thorn offends them, when
its Leaves are dropt!                                                      260

Finis

# EPILOGUE

## BY THE AUTHOR

### Spoken by Mrs. BULKLEY

Ladies for *You*—I heard our Poet say—
He'd try to coax some *Moral* from his Play:
'One moral's plain'—cried I—'without more fuss;
Man's social happiness all rests on Us—
Thro' all the Drama—whether damn'd or not—
*Love* gilds the *Scene*, and *Women* guide the *plot*.
From ev'ry rank—obedience is our due—
D'ye doubt?—The world's great stage shall prove it true.'

    The Cit—well skill'd to shun domestic strife—
Will sup abroad;—but first—he'll ask his *wife*:          10
*John Trot*, his friend for once, will do the same,
But then—he'll just *step home to tell his dame*.—

    The *surly 'Squire*—at noon resolves to rule,
And half the day—Zounds! Madam is a fool!
Convinc'd at night—the vanquish'd Victor[1] says,
Ah! Kate! *you women have such coaxing ways!*——

    The *jolly Toper* chides each tardy blade,—
Till reeling Bacchus calls on Love for aid:
Then with each Toast, he sees fair bumpers swim,
And kisses Chloe on the sparkling Brim!          20

    Nay, I have heard that Statesmen—great and wise—
Will *sometimes* counsel with a Lady's eyes;
The servile suitors—watch her various face,
She smiles preferment—or she frowns disgrace,
Curtsies a pension here—there nods a place.

[1] Dryden, 'Alexander's Feast', 114–15:
> At length, with Love and Wine at once oppress'd,
> The vanquish'd Victor sunk upon her Breast.

Nor with less awe, in scenes of humbler life,
Is *view'd* the *mistress,* or is *heard* the *wife.*
The poorest Peasant of the poorest soil,
The child of Poverty, and heir to Toil—
Early from radiant Love's impartial light,                         30
Steals one small spark, to cheer his world of night:
Dear spark!—that oft thro' winter's chilling woes,
Is all the warmth his little cottage knows!

    The wand'ring *Tar*—who, not for *years,* has press'd
The widow'd partner of his *day* of rest—
On the cold deck—far from her arms remov'd—
Still hums the ditty[1] which his Susan lov'd:
And while around the cadence rude is blown,
The Boatswain whistles in a softer tone.

    The *Soldier,* fairly proud of wounds and toil,          40
Pants for the *triumph* of his Nancy's smile;
But ere the battle, should he list' her cries,
The Lover trembles—and the Hero dies!
That heart, by war and honour steel'd to fear,
Droops on a sigh, and sickens at a tear!

    But Ye more cautious—ye nice judging few,
Who give to Beauty only Beauty's due,
Tho' friends to Love—*Ye* view with deep regret
Our conquests marr'd—and triumphs incomplete,
'Till polish'd Wit more lasting charms disclose,                  50
And Judgment fix the darts which Beauty throws!
—In female breasts did Sense and Merit rule,
The Lover's mind would ask no other school;
Sham'd into sense—the Scholars of our eyes,
Our Beaux from *Gallantry* would soon be wise;
Would gladly light, their homage to improve,
The Lamp of Knowledge at the Torch of Love!

---

[1] Gay's ballad, 'Sweet William's Farewell to Black-eyed Susan'. Stanza six runs:

> If to far India's coast we sail,
>    Thy eyes are seen in di'monds bright,
> Thy breath is Africk's spicy gale,
>    Thy skin is ivory, so white.
> Thus ev'ry beauteous object that I view,
> Wakes in my soul some charm of lovely Sue.

# ST. PATRICK'S DAY

## OR

## THE SCHEMING LIEUTENANT

*A Farce*

# St PATRICK's DAY;

OR, THE

# SCHEMING LIEUTENANT.

A

# COMIC OPERA:

AS IT IS ACTED

AT THE

*THEATRE-ROYAL,*

SMOKE-ALLEY.

———

PRINTED FOR THE BOOKSELLERS.

M,DCC,LXXXVIII.

The title-page of the first (pirated) edition of
*St. Patrick's Day*

# DRAMATIS PERSONÆ[1]

| | |
|---|---|
| JUSTICE CREDULOUS | Mr. Lee Lewes |
| LIEUTENANT O'CONNOR | Mr. Clinch |
| DOCTOR ROSY | Mr. Quick |
| SERJEANT TROUNCE | Mr. Dunstall |
| CORPORAL FLINT | Mr. Fox |
| SOLDIERS, AND COUNTRYMEN | |
| BRIDGET | Mrs. Pitt |
| LAURETTA | Miss Brown |

[1] The names of the actors and actresses are taken from the *Morning Chronicle*, 3 May 1775. It mentions that Davies, Wewitzer, and Chaplin performed the parts of soldiers. *The London Stage*, p. 1889, lists a further five names: Fearon (probably the blacksmith: cf. p. 1913), Thompson, Cushing, Bates, and Hollingsworth. When the farce was given at Bristol Theatre on 17 Apr. 1779 the cast included 'Steward—Mr. Brookes': see *Felix Farley's Bristol Journal*, 17 Apr. 1779.

# PROLOGUE

In this gay Month when thro' the sultry Hour
The vernal Sun denies the wonted Shower
When youthful Spring usurps maturer sway—
And pal[l]id April Steals the Blush of May
How joys the rustic Tribe to view display'd
The Lib'ral Blossom and the early Shade!
—But Ah! far other Air our Soil delights!
—Here 'Charming Weather' is the worst of Blights!
No genial Beams rejoice our rustic Train
Their Harvest's still the better for the Rain!                    10
To Summer Suns our Groves no tribute owe
They thrive in Frost, and flourish best in Snow!
When other Woods resound the feather'd throng
Our Groves, our Woods, are destitute of Song.
The Thrush—the Lark—all leave our mimic Vale
—No more we boast the Christmas Nightingale—
Poor Ros[s]ignol[1]—The Wonder of his Day—
Sung thro the Winter—but is mute in May.
Then boastful Spring that gilds fair Nature's Scene
O'ercasts our Lawns—and deadens ev'ry Green                       20
Obscures our Sky, embrowns the wooden Shade
And dries the Channel of each tin Cascade!
O hapless We whom such ill fate Betides!
Hurt by the Beam, which chears the World besides!
Who love the ling'ring Frost, nice, chilling Showers
While Nature's BENEFIT—is Death to ours
Who, Witch-like, best in noxious Mists perform,
Thrive in the Tempest and enjoy the Storm.
O hapless We—unless your generous care
Bids us no more lament that Spring is fair,                       30
But plenteous glean from the dramatic Soil,
The Vernal Harvest of our Winter's Toil.

[1] Signor Rossignol, bird-imitator, gave his last performance of the season at Covent Garden Theatre on 16 Mar. 1775. A contemporary was impressed by his 'most amazing imitations of singing Birds, which He does to that perfection that it is impossible to distinguish them from the finest notes of the Nightingale, Canary Bird, Goldfinch, Linnet, etc., for all appearance of the human voice is entirely lost' (*Sir Joshua's Nephew*, ed. S. M. Radcliffe, 1930, p. 83).

For April Suns to us no pleasure bring
Your Presence here is all we feel of Spring
May's Riper Beauties here no Bloom display
Your fostering Smile alone to Us is May.

# ST. PATRICK'S DAY

## OR

## THE SCHEMING LIEUTENANT

*Act 1st—Scene 1st*

*A walk near the* JUSTICE's *house*

*Enter* SERJEANT TROUNCE, CORPORAL FLINT,—*and several Soldiers,—
Some with Shambrogues[1] in their Hats.*

1ST SOLDIER. I say you're wrong—We should all speak together—each
for himself—and all at once—that we may be heard the better.

2ND SOLDIER. Right, Jack, we'll argue in Platoons.

3RD SOLDIER. Aye, aye, let him have our Grievances in a Volley:—or
if we be to have a Spokesman,—there's our Corporal is the Lieutenant's
Countryman, and knows his humour.

CORPORAL. Let me alone for that—I sarv'd three years within a little
bit, under his Honour in the Royal Inniskillins; and I never will see
a sweeter timper'd officer, nor one more free with his Purse—I put
a great Shambrogue in his hat this Morning, and I'll be bound for him    10
he'll wear it, if it was as big as Stephen's Green.

4TH SOLDIER. I say again then, ye talk like Youngsters—like Militia
Striplings.—There is a Discipline—lookee, in all things—whereof the
Serjeant must be our Man.—Besides, he is a Gentleman of Words.
—He understands your foreign Lingo—your Figures—and such
Auxiliaries in scoring—confess now, for a reckoning—whether in
Chalk or writing,—ben't he your only Interpreter?

CORPORAL. Why the Serjeant is a Scholar, to be sure, and has the Gift
of Reading.

SERJEANT. Good Soldiers, and fellow Gentlemen, if ye will make me    20
your Spokesman—So—ye will shew the more Judgment: and let me
alone for the Argument, I'll be as loud as a Drum—and point blank
from the Purpose.

ALL SOLDIERS. Agreed! agreed!

CORPORAL. O faith, here comes the Lieutenant—Now, Serjeant.

---

[1] Cf. Samuel Whyte, *The Shamrock* (1772), p. vii: 'The old *Milesians* contend for
original orthography, and write *Shambrogue, Shamrogue,* or *Shamrog*; *Spenser* and
Dr. *S. Johnson* authorize our spelling, conformably to the established idiom of pronunciation, the rational way of writing all words. . . .'

SERJEANT. So then—to order—look out your mutiny looks—let every man grumble a little to himself—and some of you hum the Deserter's march.[1]

*Enter* LIEUTENANT O'CONNOR.

LIEUT. Well, honest Lads, what is it ye have to complain of?

SERJEANT. Ahem!—hem!—hem! 30

4TH SOLDIER. There—damme!—did you ever hear a better hem! to begin with?—The Lieutenant's stagger'd already.

SERJEANT. So please your Honour,—the Grievance of the matter is this—Ever since your Honour has differ'd with Justice Credulous, here, our Inn-keepers use us most scurvily—by my Halbert, their treatment is such, that if our Spirit was willing to put up with it, Flesh and Blood would by no means agree—So we humbly petition, that your Honour would make an end of the matter, by running away with the Justice's Daughter at once, or else get us fresh Quarters—hem!—hem! 40

LIEUT. Indeed! pray which of the Houses use you ill?

1ST SOLDIER. There's the red Lion ha'n't half the civility as the old red Lion had.

2ND SOLDIER. Aye, and there's the White horse, if he wa'n't case hardened, ought to be asham'd to shew his face.

LIEUT. Very well, the Horse and Lion shall answer for it at the Quarter Sessions.

SERJEANT. The two Magpies are civil enough, but the Angel uses us like devils,[2] and the rising Sun refuses us light to go to bed by.

LIEUT. Indeed! then upon my word I'll have the rising Sun put down, 50 and the Angel shall give Security for his good behavior—but are you sure you do nothing to quit Scores with them?

CORPORAL. Nothing at all, your Honour, unless now and then we happen to fling a Cartridge into the Kitchen fire, or put a Spatterdash or so into the Soup—and sometimes Ned drums a little up and down Stairs of a night.

LIEUT. Oh that's all fair—Well, harkee, Lads, I must have no grumbling on St. Patrick's day so, here, take this, and divide it amongst you. But observe me now, Shew yourselves Men of Spirit, and don't spend a Sixpence of it in Drink. 60

[1] *Le Déserteur*, with music by P. A. Monsigny and text by J. M. Sédaine, was presented in Paris on 6 Mar. 1769, and proved very popular. It was adapted for production at Drury Lane Theatre on 2 Nov. 1773, by Charles Dibdin. The British Museum Music Catalogue lists a single sheet folio, *c.* 1775, as 'March in the Desertore' and describes it as 'from the Overture to *Le Déserteur*'.

[2] The plot summary in the *Morning Chronicle*, 4 May 1775, records that the Serjeant 'says they are very ill-treated at their several quarters; that at the Angel they are used *devilish* bad. . . .'

SERJEANT. Nay, hang it, Soldiers shouldn't bear Malice—We must drink St. Patrick, and your Honour's health.

ALL SOLDIERS. Oh! damn Malice! St. Patrick and his Honour, by all means.

CORPORAL. Come away then, Lads—And first we'll parade round the Market Cross, for the honour of King William.

ALL SOLDIERS. Thank your Honour—Come along—His honour, St. Patrick, and strong beer for ever.          [*Exeunt all but* LIEUTENANT.

LIEUT. Get along ye thoughtless Vagabonds—Yet, upon my Conscience, 'tis very hard, that these poor Fellows should scarcely have bread from 70 the Soil they would die to defend.

*Enter* DR. ROSY.

Ah! my little Doctor Rosy, my Galen abridg'd, what's the News?

DOCTOR. All things are as they were, my Alexander,—the Justice is as violent as ever.—I felt his Pulse on the matter again, and thinking his Rage began to intermit, I wanted to throw in the Bark[1] of good Advice—but it would not do—he says, you and your Cut throats have a Plot upon his Life, and swears he had rather see his Daughter in a scarlet Fever, than in the arms of a Soldier.

LIEUT. Upon my word, the Army is very much obliged to him—Well then I must marry the Girl first, and ask his Consent afterwards.          80

DOCTOR. So then the case of her Fortune is desperate, that's given over, hey?

LIEUT. O hang the Fortune, let that take its chance—There is a beauty in Lauretta's Manner, so pure a bloom upon her Charms,—something so interesting in her Simplicity.—

DOCTOR. So there is—So there is—I understand you—You are for Loveliness as Nature made her, hey?—No artificial Graces—no Cosmetic Varnish—no Beauty in Grain, hey, Lieutenant?

LIEUT. Upon my word, Doctor, you're right—The London Ladies were always too handsome for me—Then they are so defended—Such a 90 Circumvallation of Hoop—with a breast work of whalebone, that would turn a Pistol bullét—much less Cupid's Arrows—. Then Turret on Turret on top, with store of conceal'd weapons, under pretence of black pins—and above all, a Standard of Feathers, that would do Honour to a Knight of the Bath![2]—Upon my Conscience, I could as soon embrace an Amazon, arm'd at all Points.

DOCTOR. Right, right, my Alexander—my Taste to a tittle.

---

[1] Peruvian bark or quinine, used for reducing fever.

[2] 'The town ladies . . . are surrounded by a circumvallation of hoop, six feet in circumference; a breast work of whalebone, which would turn a pistol bullet; a plume of feathers, large enough for the cap of a Knight of the Bath. . . .' (*Morning Chronicle*, 4 May 1775.)

LIEUT. Then, Doctor, tho' I admire Modesty in Women,—yet I like
to see their faces—I'm for the changeable Rose—but with one of these
Quality Amazons,—if their Midnight Dissipations had left them blood    100
enough, to raise a blush—they haven't room on their Cheeks to shew
it.—To be sure, Bashfullness is a very pretty thing,—but in my mind,
there is nothing on Earth so impudent as an everlasting blush.[1]

DOCTOR. My taste, my taste, Lieutenant!—Well, Lauretta is none of
these—Ah! I never see her, but she reminds me of my poor dear Wife.

LIEUT. Aye!—Faith, and in my Opinion, she can't do a worse thing—
Now he's going to bother me about an old fat Hag, who has been dead
these six years—[aside]

DOCTOR. Ah! poor Dolly!—I never shall see her like again!—such an
arm for a Bandage—Veins that seem'd to invite the Lancet—then her    110
Skin—smooth and white as a Gallypot—her Mouth round, and not
larger than the mouth of a penny Phial!—Her lips!—Conserve of
Roses!—then her Teeth!—none of your sturdy Fixtures—ach[e], as
they would—'twas but a Pull, and out they came—I beleive I've drawn
half a score of her poor dear Pearls—[weeps]—but what avails her
Beauty,—Death has no Consideration—one must die as well as another.

LIEUT. O! if he begins to moralize—[takes out his snuff box]

DOCTOR. Fair or ugly—Crooked or straight—Rich or Poor—Flesh is
Grass[2]—Flowers fade.

LIEUT. Here, Doctor, take a Pinch, and keep up your Spirits.    120

DOCTOR. True—true, my Friend—Grief can't mend the matter—All's
for the best—but such a Woman was a great loss, Lieutenant.

LIEUT. To be sure, for doubtless she had mental Accomplishments
equal to her Beauty.

DOCTOR. Mental Accomplishments!—She should have stuff'd an
Alligator,—or pickled a Lizard, with any Apothecary's wife in the
Kingdom!—Why, she could decypher a prescription, and invent the
Ingredients[3] almost as well as myself—Then she was such a hand at
making foreign waters—for Seltzer[4]—Pyrmont[5]—Islington[6]—or Chaly-

---

[1] Walter Sichel, *Sheridan* (1909), i. 565 n., shows that a similar thought appeared in a
very early draft sheet of dialogue called 'The Slanderers—A *Pump-Room* Scene': 'The
most intrepid Blush;—I've known her complexion stand fire for an hour together.' Cf.
Thomas Moore, *Memoirs of . . . Sheridan* (2nd edn., 1825), i. 211.

[2] Isaiah 40: 6.

[3] 'She could spread a plaister, prepare a bolus, compound a draught, aye, and
*invent ingredients*, as well as ever an apothecary's wife in the country.' (*Morning
Chronicle*, 4 May 1775.)

[4] 'Seltzer Nieder . . . 10 miles from Francfort on the Maine; celebrated for a spring
of mineral water, which is exported, in great quantities, to other countries.' (R. Brookes,
*The General Gazetteer*, 10th edn., 1797.)

[5] 'Pyrmont, a town of Westphalia. . . . Near it are mineral waters, well known to all
Europe, and often frequented by persons of the highest rank.' (R. Brookes, op. cit.)

[6] 'Islington, a large village, N of London, to which it is now contiguous. The New

beate, she had not her equal—And her Bath and Bristol Springs[1] 130
exceeded the Originals.—King Bladud[2] never dipt his toe in better—
Ah! poor Dolly!—She fell a Martyr to her Discoveries.

LIEUT. How so pray?

DOCTOR. Poor Soul, her Illness was all occasioned by her zeal in trying
an improvement on her Spaw water, by an infusion of Rum and Acid.

LIEUT. Aye, aye, Spirits never agree with Water Drinkers.

DOCTOR. No!—no—you mistake—The Rum agreed with her well
enough—'twas the water that kill'd the dear Creature—for she died
of a Dropsy—Well! She's gone!—Never to return!—and has left no
Pledge of our Loves behind—No little Baby, to hang like a labell 140
round Papa's neck—well—we're all mortal—sooner or later—Flesh is
Grass—Flowers fade!—

LIEUT. O! the Devil! again—

DOCTOR. Life's a Shadow![3]—The World's a Stage![4]—we strut our hour.

LIEUT. Here, Doctor.                              [*gives snuff.*

DOCTOR. True, true, my Friend—well—Grief can't mend it—All's for
the best—hey, my Alexander!

LIEUT. Right! right!—An apothecary should never be out of Spirits,—
But, come,—Faith 'tis time honest Humphry, should wait on the
Justice—that must be our first Scheme.                        150

DOCTOR. True—true—you should be ready—The Clothes are at my
House—and I have given you such a Character, that he is impatient
to have you—He swears you shall be his Body Guard—Well, I honour
the Army—or I should never do so much to serve you.

LIEUT. Indeed I'm bound to you for ever, Doctor, and when once I'm
possessed of my Dear Lauretta, I'll endeavour to make work for you
as fast as possible.

DOCTOR. Now you put me in mind of my poor wife again.

LIEUT. Ah! pray forget her a little,—faith, we shall be too late.

DOCTOR. Poor Dolly!                              160

LIEUT. 'Tis past twelve.

DOCTOR. Inhuman Dropsy!

LIEUT. The Justice will wait.

DOCTOR. Cropt in her Prime.

LIEUT. For Heaven's sake, come.

---

River is received at the SW end of it, into a large reservoir, called the New River Head,
whence its water is conveyed, in pipes, to all parts of the metropolis. Near this, is a
famous spring of Chalybeate water. . . .' (R. Brookes, op. cit.)

[1] Of Clifton Wells.
[2] The mythical discoverer of the mineral springs at Bath.
[3] 'Life's but a walking shadow.' (*Macbeth*, V. v.)
[4] 'All the world's a stage.' (*As You Like It*, II. vii.)

DOCTOR. Well, Flesh is Grass.

LIEUT. Oh, the Deuce!—come, come along.

DOCTOR. Flowers fade!     [*Exeunt, the* LIEUTENANT *hawls him out.*

*Scene 2nd*

*A Room in the* JUSTICE's *house*

*Enter* LAURETTA *and* BRIDGET.

LAUR. I repeat it again, Mama,—officers are the prettiest men in the World—and Lieutenant O'Connor, the prettiest Officer I ever saw.

BRID. For shame, Laury, how can you talk so,—or if you must have a Military Man—there's Lieutenant Plough—or Captain Haycock—or Major Dray, the Brewer—Are all your Admirers—and tho' they are peaceable, good kind of Men, they have as large Cockades, and become Scarlet, as well as the fighting Folks.

LAUR. Psha! Mama! you know I hate the Militia—officers indeed!—a set of Dunghill cocks with spurs on—Heroes scratch'd off a church door—Clowns in Military masquerade—wearing the Dress without 10 supporting the Character—No, give me the bold, upright, noble Youth, —who makes love one day, and has his head shot off the next— Dear!—to think how the sweet Fellows sleep on the Ground, and fight in silk Stockings and lac'd Ruffles.

BRID. O barbarous! to want a husband, who may wed you in the morning, and be sent the Lord knows where, before Night.—Then in a Twelve month, perhaps, to have him come home like a Colossus, with one leg at Boston, and the other in Chelsea Hospital.

LAUR. Then I would be his Crutch, Mama.

BRID. No, give me a husband who knows where his limbs are—tho' 20 he hasn't the use of 'em;—or, if he should take you with him, Child, —what a Scene!—to sleep in a Baggage Cart—and stroll about the Camp like a Gypsey, with a Knapsack, and two Children at your back— then by way of Entertainment in the Evening, to make a Party with the Serjeant's wife, to drink Bohea Tea, and play at all fours[1] on a Drum top,—O! 'tis a precious life, to be sure.

LAUR. Nay, Mama, you should not be against my Lieutenant,—for I heard him say you were the best natur'd, and best looking woman that cou'd be.

BRID. Why, Child, I never said but that Lieutenant O'Connor was a 30 very well bred discerning young man—'Tis your Papa is so violent against him.

LAUR. Why, Mama, Cousin Sophy married an Officer.

---

[1] A card game, described in C. Cotton, *The Compleat Gamester* (1709), p. 81, as 'very much played in Kent'.

BRID. Ay, Laury, an Officer in the Militia.

LAUR. No, indeed, Mama, he was in a Marching regiment.

BRID. No, Child, I tell you he was a Major of Militia.

LAUR. Indeed, Mama, he wa'n't.

*Enter* JUSTICE CREDULOUS.

JUS. Bridget, my lovee, I've had a message.

LAUR. It was Cousin Sophy, Mama, told me so.

JUS. I have had a message, my Love.                              40

BRID. Pho, Child, she could say no such thing.

JUS. A message, I say—

LAUR. How could he be in the Militia, when he was order'd abroad?

JUS. Why, Laury—

BRID. Aye, Girl, hold your Tongue—Well, my Dear?

JUS. I have had a message I say, from Doctor Rosy.

BRID. He wasn't order'd abroad, Miss, he went for his health.

JUS. Why, Bridget—

BRID. Well, Dearee,—now hold your tongue, miss.

JUS. A message I say from Doctor Rosy, and Doctor Rosy says—    50

LAUR. I am sure, Mama, his Regimentals—

JUS. Damn his Regimentals, why don't you listen hussy.

BRID. Aye, Girl, how durst you interrupt your Papa?

LAUR. Well, Papa.

JUS. Doctor Rosy says that he will bring—

LAUR. Were blue turn'd up with red, Mama.

JUS. Laury!—says that he will bring the young man—

BRID. Red and yellow, if you please.

JUS. Bridget!—the young man to be hired.

BRID. Besides, Miss, it is very unbecoming of you to want to have the   60
last word with your Mama—you ought to know—

JUS. Why, zounds! will you hear me, or no?

BRID. I'm listening, my love—I'm listening—but what signifies my
silence,—what good is my not speaking a word, if this Girl will
interrupt, and let her tongue run, and try for the last word—and let
nobody speak but herself—I don't wonder, my Life, at your impatience—your poor dear lips quiver to speak,—but I suppose she'll
run on, and not let you put in a word—Aye, Lovee, you may well be
angry, there is nothing to be sure so provoking, as a chattering talking—

LAUR. Nay, Mama, I'm sure 'tis you won't let Papa speak now.        70

BRID. Why you little provoking Minx—

JUS. Get out of the Room directly, both of ye get out.

BRID. Ay, go, Girl.

JUS. Go, Bridget, you're worse than she, you old Mag[1]—and I wish you

---

[1] Scold or magpie.

were both up to your necks in the Canal—to argue there, 'till I took you out.

*Enter a* SERVANT.

SER. Doctor Rosy, Sir.

JUS. Shew him up.                                          [*Exit* SERVANT.

LAUR. Then, Mama, you own he was in a marching Regiment.

BRID. You're an obstinate Fool—for, if that had been the case—      80

JUS. You won't go?

BRID. We're going, Mr. Surly—if that had been the Case, I say, how could—

LAUR. Nay, Mama, one Proof—

BRID. How could Major—

LAUR. And a full proof—      [*Exit* BRIDGET *and* LAURETTA—*arguing.*

JUS. There they go, ding dong, in for the Day—Good lack! a fluent tongue is the only thing a mother don't like her Daughter to resemble her in.

*Enter* DOCTOR ROSY.

Well, Doctor, where's the Lad!—where's Trusty?                    90

DOCTOR. At hand—He'll be here in a minute—I'll answer for't, he's such a one as you ha'n't met with—brave as a Lion, and at the same time as gentle as a saline Draught.

JUS. Ah! he comes in the place of a Rogue! a Dog! that was corrupted by the Lieutenant.—But this is a sturdy fellow, is he?

DOCTOR. A very Hercules—and the best back sword[1] in the County—he'll make the red coats keep their distance.

JUS. Ah! the Villain!—this is St. Patrick's day,—and the Rascals have been parading round my house, all the morning—I know they have a design on me—but I have taken all precautions,—I have Magazines  100 of Arms—and if this Fellow proves faithful, I shall be more at ease.

DOCTOR. Doubtless, he'll be a Comfort to you.

*Enter a* SERVANT.

SER. There is a Man below, Sir, enquiring for Doctor Rosy.

DOCTOR. Shew him up here.

JUS. Hold—hold—a little caution.—How does he look?

SER. A Country looking Fellow, your Worship.

JUS. O well—well—for Doctor, the Rascals try all ways to get in here.

SER. Aye, please your Worship, there was one here this morning, would ha' spoke to you, who said A's name was Corporal Break-bones.

---

[1] Best at single-stick: a contest with staves, in which victory usually went to the player who made his opponent's head bleed first. But see, too, the *Sporting Magazine*, xliv (1814), 129: 'The Hampshire man saved his head, but received so much beating on his arm, that he could not raise his stick, which obliged him to quit the stage.'

JUS. Corporal Break-bones—there, you see.—

SER. And there was Drummer Crack-skull come again.

DOCTOR. Drummer Crack-skull!

JUS. Aye! did you ever hear of such a damn'd confounded Crew? well bring the lad here.                              [*Exit* SERVANT.

DOCTOR. Aye! he'll be your Porter, he'll give such Rogues their answer.

*Re-enter the* SERVANT, *introducing the* LIEUTENANT
*in a Countryman's dress.*

JUS. So—a tall fellow—i'faith!—what, has he lost an eye?

DOCTOR. Only a bruise he got one day in taking seven or eight Highway-men.

JUS. Hey!—but he has a damn'd wicked leer somehow with t'other.

DOCTOR. Oh! no! he's bashful—a sheepish look.                    120

JUS. Well, my lad, what's your name?

LIEUT. Humphry¹ Hum.

JUS. Humphry Hum!—I don't like Hum!²

LIEUT. But I be mostly call'd Honest Humphry.

DOCTOR. There, I told you so—of noted Honesty.

JUS. Honest Humphry—well—the Doctor has told you my terms,— you're willing to serve? hey?

LIEUT. An't please your Worship, I shall be well content.

JUS. Well then, hearkee, honest Humphry, you're sure now you'll never be a Rogue—never be brib'd?—hey, honest Humphry?            130

LIEUT. Brib'd! what's that?

JUS. A very ignorant Fellow indeed.

DOCTOR. His Worship hopes you will never part with your honesty for money, Humphry?

LIEUT. O Noa!—noa!—

JUS. Well, honest Humphry,—my chief business for you is to watch the motions of a Rake helly fellow here, one Lieutenant O'Connor.

DOCTOR. Aye!—you don't value the Soldiers, do you, Humphry?

LIEUT. Not I—they are but Swaggerers—and you'll see they will be as much afraid of me, as they would of their Captain.            140

JUS. And, i'faith, Humphry, you have a pretty Cudgel there.

LIEUT. Aye—the Switch is better than nothing, but I should be glad of a Stouter—ha' ye got such a thing in the house as an old Coach pole, or a spare Bed post?

JUS. Ouns! what a Dragon it is!—Well, Humphry, come with me, I'll just shew him to Bridget, Doctor, and then we'll agree—Come, honest Humphry.                                      [*Exit.*

¹ 'Humphry' was suitable for 'awkward country clowns': Lady Willit describes one of that name in this phrase in Gay's *The Distress'd Wife*, IV.
² A hoax.

LIEUT. My dear Doctor—now remember to bring the Justice presently to the walk—I've a Scheme to get into his Confidence at once.

DOCTOR. I will, I will.                                                                            150

### Re-enter JUSTICE CREDULOUS.

JUS. Why, Humphry, Humphry—what the devil are you at?

DOCTOR. I was just giving him a little advice.—Well, I must go for the present—good morning to your Worship—you need not fear the Lieutenant, while he's in your house.

JUS. Well—get on, Humphry—good-bye, Doctor—Come along, Humphry—Now I think I'm a match for the Lieutenant. Ha! ha! ha!—

[*Exeunt.*

### END OF THE FIRST ACT

### Act 2d. Scene 1st

#### *Enter* SERJEANT, *some* SOLDIERS, *and a* DRUMMER.

SERJ. Come, silence your Drum, There is no valour stirring today,— I had hoped St. Patrick would have given us a Recruit or two.

1ST SOLDIER. Mark, Serjeant!—

#### *Enter a* BLACKSMITH,[1] *and an* IRISHMAN, *drunk.*

SERJ. Hah! my fine fellows—Come, now for the honour of St. Patrick,— will ye be after serving his Majesty?—and instead of drowsy[2] beer, have Seas of Punch, and Shambrogue Islands, all your lives after.

IRISH. Come, Neighbour, what say you? shall we make a Friend of his Majesty? I feel as if I could handle a Musket.

2ND MAN. Taddy,[3] you're drunk—but I who am sober, know better— sometimes when I'm merry, I thinks how I could make a Soldier, but   10 when I'm sober, I knows that I am fit for nothing but a civil employment.

IRISH. Aye! Neighbour, but I feel bould at all times.

2ND MAN. Taddy, you're a Fool, I tell ye, You're brave only when you are drunk; and if you were a General, 'twould cost his Majesty five Shillings a day to keep you in Courage, so, come along—Good liquor and a whole Skin to put it in for ever—

[*Exeunt* IRISHMAN *and* BLACKSMITH.

SERJ. Poltroons, by my halbert.

---

[1] Farquhar's *The Recruiting Officer*, IV. ii, introduces a smith who is recruited.

[2] Possibly warm beer, described in the *Weekly Journal*, 22 Feb. 1724: 'beer, so qualified, is far more wholesome than that which is drank cold'. See *The Poetical Works of Richard Savage*, ed. C. Tracy (Cambridge, 1962), p. 70.

[3] The late J. O. Bartley suggested that this meant 'Thady', not 'Paddy'. Cf. Teady Shagnessy in Thomas Sheridan's *The Brave Irishman* (1737).

*Enter 2 Countrymen.*

Oh! here are the Lads I was looking for, these have the looks of
gentlemen—A'n't you single, my Lads?                                    20

1ST CLOWN. Yes, an't please you, I be quite single,—Thank God, my
Relations be all dead, more or less; I have but one poor Mother left
in the world, and She's a helpless Woman.

SERJ. Indeed. A very extraordinary Case; quite your own Master then—
the fitter to serve his Majesty—Can you read?

1ST CLOWN. Noa—I was always too lively to take to my Larning.

SERJ. A good Quality in a Soldier;—look for Preferment.

1ST CLOWN. But Jan here is main Clever at it.

SERJ. So,—what you are a Scholar, friend?

2ND CLOWN. I was born so, Master—Fayther taught Grammar School.  30

SERJ. Lucky man!—In a Campaign or two, put yourself down Chaplain
to the Regiment—and I warrant you have read of Warriors, and
Hero's.

2ND CLOWN. Yes, that I have—I ha' read of Jack the Giant killer, and
the Dragon of Wantley[1]—and the—Noa—I believe that's all in the
Hero way—except once a little about a Comet.[2]

SERJ. Wonderful Knowledge!—Well, my Warriors, I'll write word to
the King directly of your good Intentions, and meet me in half an hour
at the two Magpies.

BOTH. We wull, your honour, we wull.

SERJ. But stay—for fear I shou'dn't know ye again in the Croud, clap  40
these little bits of Ribband into your Hats.

1ST CLOWN. Our hats are none of the best.

SERJ. Well, stay at the Magpies, and I'll fetch ye money to buy new ones.

BOTH. Bless your Honour.

[1ST CLOWN.] Come, Jan,                          [*Exeunt* CLOWNS.

SERJ. Jack! [*to the Soldiers, who go off after the Clowns*]. Soh!—here
comes one would make a Grenadier.

*Enter* LIEUTENANT.

Stop, Friend, will ye list?

LIEUT. Who shall I serve under?

SERJ. Under me to be sure.                                              50

LIEUT. Isn't Lieutenant O'Connor, your Officer?

SERJ. He is, and I am Commander over him.

LIEUT. What be you Serjeants greater than Captains?

---

[1] The monster, killed by More of More Hall, is the centre of a favourite chap-book
story. Henry Carey's musical burlesque of this theme, *The Dragon of Wantly*, was
first performed at the Haymarket on 16 May 1737, and was revived in 1774.

[2] We can read in the article on comets in E. Chambers, *Cyclopaedia* (5th edn., 1741),
of the 'popular division of comets into three kinds, viz. *bearded, tailed,* and *hairy*'.

SERJ. To be sure we are—'Tis our business to keep them in Order—
For instance—The General writes to me—Dear Serjeant—or Dear
Trounce—or Dear Serjeant Trounce (according to his hurry) if your
Lieutenant does not demean himself accordingly, let me know—Yours
to Command—General Deluge.

LIEUT. And do you complain of him often?

SERJ. Why, know, the lad is good natur'd at bottom,—so I pass over   60
small things—but hearkee, between ourselves—he is confoundedly
given to wenching.[1]

*Enter* CORPORAL.

CORP. Please your Honour, the Doctor is coming with his worship, we
are all ready, and have our Cues.

LIEUT. Then, my dear Serjeant—or dear Trounce—or dear Serjeant
Trounce—take yourself away.

SERJ. Ouns! 'tis the Lieutenant!—I smell the black hole[2] already.

CORP. Come away—Quick—            [*Exeunt* SERJEANT *and* CORPORAL.

LIEUT. [*walks about, whistling*]

*Enter the* JUSTICE *and* DOCTOR.

JUST. I thought I saw some of the Cut throats.

DOCTOR. I fancy not—there's no one but honest Humphry—Ha! Odds-   70
life! here are some of them—We'll stay by these Trees, and let them
pass.

JUST. Oh the bloody looking dogs.                        [*Stands aside*

*Enter* CORPORAL, *and 2* SOLDIERS.

CORP. Hollo, Friend, do you serve Justice Credulous?

LIEUT. I do.

CORP. Are you rich?

LIEUT. No.

CORP. Nor ever will be with that old stingy Booby—look here take it.—
[*Shews a Purse*]

LIEUT. What must I do for this?

CORP. Mark me—Our Lieutenant is in love with the old Rogue's   80
Daughter—help us to break his Worship's bones—and carry off the Girl,
and you are a made man.

LIEUT. I'll see you hang'd first ye pack of scurvy Villains—[*flings down
the purse*]

CORP. What, Sirrah!—mutinous—lay hold of him.

LIEUT. Nay then—I'll try your Armour for you.            [*beats them*

---

[1] 'Their Lieutenant is an arrant whore-master.' (*Morning Chronicle*, 4 May 1775.)

[2] Cell. Cf. the *Public Advertiser*, 6 July 1779: five 'impressed men . . . confined in
Covent Garden Watch-house, having forced their way up from the Black Hole, in
which they had been thrown' pelted glass at the constables.

SOLDIERS. Oh!—oh!—Quarter! Quarter! [*Lieutenant beats them off*]
[JUSTICE *and* DOCTOR *come forward.*

JUST. Trim 'em!—trounce 'em, Humphry—break me all their bones,
honest Humphry—what a Spirit he has, Doctor.

DOCTOR. Aqua fortis.

LIEUT. Betray my Master, indeed!—                                          90

DOCTOR. What a Miracle of fidelity.

JUST. Ay, and it sha'n't go unrewarded—I'll give him Sixpence on the
Spot—here, honest Humphry—there's for yourself. As for this base
Bribe, such trash is best in the hands of Justice[1]—[*picks up the purse*]—
Now then, Doctor, I think I may trust him to guard the Women—
While he is with them, I may go out with Safety.

DOCTOR. Doubtless, you may—I'll answer for the Lieutenant's good
behavior, while honest Humphry is with your Daughter.

JUST. Aye,—aye—She shall go nowhere without him—Come follow,
honest Humphry—how rare it is to meet with such a Servant.—          100
[*Exeunt, the* DOCTOR *and* LIEUTENANT *making signs to each other.*

*Scene 2nd. The Garden. A Summer house near*
LAURETTA—*Sitting with a Guittar*[2]
*Song*[3]

*Enter* JUSTICE *and* LIEUTENANT.

JUST. Why, you little Truant, how durst you leave the House without
my leave?—Do you want to invite that Scoundrel Lieutenant to scale
the walls, and carry you off?

LAUR. Lud Papa, you are so apprehensive about nothing—

JUST. What, Hussy!

LAUR. Well then, I can't bear to be shut up so all day long, like a Nun!—
I'm sure 'tis enough to make one wish to be run away with—and I
wish I was run away with,—I do—and I wish the Lieutenant knew
it.

---

[1] 'Such bribes are safest in the hands of justice.' (*Morning Chronicle*, 4 May 1775.)

[2] 'His daughter . . . is discovered seated in a garden and singing.' (ibid.)

[3] The text is missing. Mr. F. W. Bateson tells me that though the song was a regular
item in the playbills until 1783, he has not been able to find a copy. Since Sheridan
referred to two songs by Jackson of Exeter in *The Rivals*, I wonder if he had in mind
for performance here, yet another from Jackson's *Opera Quarta*? Song X would be
suitable in theme:

> Ah! what avails this sweetly solemn Bow'r,
> That silent Stream where dimpling Eddies play.
> Yon' thymy Bank bedekt with many a Flow'r,
> Where branching Trees exclude the Beam of Day.
> Far from my Love Ah! how can these delight
> Tho' lavish Spring her smiles around has cast.
> Despair alas that whelms the Soul in Night,
> Dims the sad Eye and deadens ev'ry Taste.

JUST. You do—do you, Hussy?—well, I think I'll take pretty good care 10 to prevent that—Here, Humphry—I leave this Lady in care to you—Now you may walk about the Garden, Miss Pert—but Humphry shall go with you where ever you go—So mind honest Humphry—I am obliged to go abroad for a little while—Let no one but yourself come near her—Don't be shame fac'd you Booby—but keep close to her.—And now, Miss, let your Lieutenant, or any of his Crew come near you, if they can.                                [*Exit* JUSTICE.

LAUR. How the Looby gapes after him—            [*sits down, and Sings*

LIEUT. Lauretta!

LAUR. Not so free, Fellow—[*sings*]                                      20

LIEUT. Lauretta, look on me.

LAUR. Don't interrupt me, Booby, [*sings*]

LIEUT. No recollection!

LAUR. Honest Humphry, be quiet. [*sings*]

LIEUT. Have you forgot your faithful Soldier?

LAUR. Oh! preserve me!

LIEUT. 'Tis I—my Soul—your truest Slave—passing in this disguise—

LAUR. Well—now I declare this is charming—You are so disguised, my dear Lieutenant,—and you do look so delightfully ugly—I'm sure no one will find you out—Ha! ha! ha!—You know I'm under 30 your Protection—ha! ha! ha!—Papa charg'd you to keep close to me.

LIEUT. True, my angel,—and thus let me fulfil—

LAUR. O pray now—Dear Humphry—

LIEUT. Nay, 'tis but what old Mittimus[1] commanded

[*strug[g]ling to kiss her*].

*Enter the* JUSTICE.

JUST. Stay, Laury—my—Hey! what the Devil's here?

LAUR. Well now, one kiss, and be quiet—O Mercy!

JUST. Your humble Servant, honest Humphry—don't mind me—pray don't let me interrupt you.

LAUR. Lud, Papa—now that's so good-natur'd—indeed there's no 40 harm—you didn't mean any rudeness, did you, Humphry?

LIEUT. No, indeed, Miss—His Worship knows it isn't in me.

JUST. I know that you are a lying, canting Hypocritical Scoundrel—and if you don't take yourself out of my Sight—

LAUR. Indeed, Papa, now I'll tell you how it was—I was somehow taken with a sudden Giddyness—and Humphry seeing me begin to totter, ran to my assistance—quite frighted poor Fellow—and got me in his Arms.

JUST. O, poor Fellow, was that all—nothing but a little giddyness, hey?

---

[1] A magistrate's warrant, but used here to denote the magistrate himself.

LIEUT. That's all, indeed your Worship—for seeing Miss change colour—
I ran up instantly.                                                          50
JUST. O! 'twas very kind in you.
LIEUT. And luckily recover'd her.
JUST. And who made you a Doctor, you impudent Scoundrel, hey?—
Get out, I say, this instant—or by all the Statutes—
LAUR. O now, Papa, you frighten me, and I'm giddy again—oh! help!—
LIEUT. O dear Lady—she'll fall!—                    [catches her in his arms
JUST. Zounds! what, before my face!—why, thou mirrour of Impu-
dence!— [lays hold of his hair, his wig comes off, and discovers him]
Mercy on me! who have we here?—Murder! Robbery—Fire—Rape—
John,—Susan—Bridget—                                                        60
LIEUT. Good sir, don't be so alarm'd, I intend you no harm.
JUST. Thieves—Robbers—Soldiers—
LIEUT. You know my Love for your Daughter—
JUST. Fire—Cut throats—
LIEUT. And that alone—
JUST. Treason—Gun Powder.

*Enter* SERVANTS *with Arms.*

*The* JUSTICE *takes a Blunderbuss.*

Now, you Scoundrel, let her go this Instant.
LAUR. Oh! Papa, you'll kill me.
JUST. Honest Humphry, be advis'd—aye, miss, this way, if you please.
LIEUT. Nay, Sir, but hear me—                                              70
JUST. I'll shoot.
LIEUT. And you'll be convinc'd—
JUST. I'll shoot.
LIEUT. How very injurious—
JUST. I'll shoot—take her along [*to a* SERVANT]. And so, your humble
Servant, honest Humphry Hum.                        [*Exeunt severally.*

*Scene 3d. The Walk*

*Enter Dr.* ROSY.

DOCTOR. Well, I think my Friend is now in a fair way of succeeding—.
Ah!—I warrant he's full of hope—and doubt,—and fear—and
Anxiety—Truly he has the fever of Love strong upon him—Faint—
Peevish—Languishing all day—with burning restless Nights.—Ah!
just my Case—when first I pined for my poor Dear Dolly—when she
used to have daily Cholics, that her little Doctor might be sent for—
then would I interpret the language of the Pulse—declare my own
sufferings in my Recipes for hers—Send her a pearl necklace in a Pill

box, or a Cordial Draught with an acrostic on the Labell! well those
days are over,—No happiness lasting! all's Vanity! now Sunshine!    10
now Clouded!—we are as we were made—King and Peasant! then
what avails—

*Enter* LIEUTENANT.

LIEUT. O Doctor! ruined and undone!

DOCTOR. The Pride of Beauty—

LIEUT. I'm discovered, and—

DOCTOR. The gaudy Palace—

LIEUT. The Justice is—

DOCTOR. The pompous wig—

LIEUT. More enrag'd than ever.

DOCTOR. The gilded Cane[1]—                                        20

LIEUT. Why, Doctor.

DOCTOR. Hey!

LIEUT. Confound your morals! I tell you I'm discovered! discomfited!
disappointed! ruined!

DOCTOR. Indeed! Good lack! to think of the Instability of human
Affairs!—nothing certain in this world! most deceiv'd when most
confident!—Fools of Fortune all!—

LIEUT. My dear Doctor, I want at present a little practical Wisdom!—
I am resolved this instant, to try the Scheme we were going to put into
Execution last week—The present event will give probability to the    30
Plan—I have the Letter ready written, and only want your assistance
to recover my Ground.

DOCTOR. With all my heart, I warrant I'll bear my part in it—but how
the deuce were you discovered?

LIEUT. I'll tell you as we go—there's not a moment to be lost.

DOCTOR. Heaven send we succeed better at present—but there's no
knowing.

LIEUT. Very true.

DOCTOR. We may, and we may not.

LIEUT. Right.                                                      40

DOCTOR. Time must shew.

LIEUT. Certainly.

DOCTOR. We are but blind Guessers.

LIEUT. Nothing more.

DOCTOR. Thick sighted mortals.

LIEUT. Remarkably.

DOCTOR. Wand'ring in error.

LIEUT. Even so.

DOCTOR. Futurity is dark.

[1] The cane of John Radcliffe (1650–1741), the symbol of a successful physician.

LIEUT. As a Cellar.                                                        50
DOCTOR. Men are Moles—            [*Exeunt; the* DOCTOR *pondering.*

### *Scene 4th. The* JUSTICE'S *house*

#### *Enter the* JUSTICE *and* BRIDGET.

JUST. Addslife, Bridget, you are enough to make one mad,—I tell you
he would have deceived a Chief Justice—The dog seem'd as ignorant
as my Clerk—and talk'd of Honesty as if he had been a Church Warden.

BRID. Pho! Nonsense! Honesty indeed! what had you to do, pray with
Honesty!—a fine business indeed, you have made of it, with your
Humphry Hum, truly.—And Miss too, she must have been privy to
it—Lauretta!—aye, you would have her called so—but for my part, I
never knew any good come of giving Girls these Heathen Christian
Names. If you had call'd her Deborah—or Tabitha—or Ruth—or
Rebecca—nothing of this would have happened—but I always knew   10
Lauretta was a run away name.

JUST. Pshaw! you're a fool.

BRID. No, Mr. Credulous, 'tis you are the fool, and no one but such a
Simpleton, would have been so imposed on.

JUST. Why zounds, Madam, how durst you talk so? If you have no
respect for your Husband—I should think Unus Quorum[1] might
command a little Deference.

BRID. Don't tell me—Unus Fiddlestick!—you ought to be asham'd to
shew your Face at the Sessions—You'll be the laughing stock of the
Bench, and a bye word with all the Pigtail'd Lawyers and Bobwig   20
Attornies.

JUST. Is this Language to his Majesty's Representative? By the Statutes
'tis High Treason, and Petty Treason both at once.

#### *Enter a* SERVANT.

SERV. A Letter for your Worship.

JUST. Who brought it?

SERV. A Soldier, your Worship.                                    [*Exit.*

JUST. Take it away—and bury it—Combustible Stuff, I warrant it—
a threatening letter—Put ten pounds under a Stone—with damn'd
inflammatory Spelling—and the bloody hands of a dozen rogues at
bottom.                                                           30

BRID. Stay now—you're in such a hurry—'tis some canting Scrawl from
the Lieutenant, I suppose—here—let me see.—Aye, 'tis signed
Lieutenant O'Connor—[*taking the letter*]

JUST. Well, come read it out.

---

[1] One of the justices constituting a bench.

BRID. [*Reads*] 'Revenge is sweet.'[1]

JUST. It begins so, does it?—I'm glad of that—and I'll let the dog know I'm of his Opinion.

BRID. [*reads*] 'And tho' disappointed in my Designs on your Daughter, I have still the Satisfaction of knowing that I am reveng'd on her unnatural Father—for this morning, in your Chocolate, I had the 40 pleasure of Administ[e]ring to you a Dose of Poison.'—Mercy on us.

JUST. No Tricks, Bridget, come now you know 'tis not so—you know 'tis a lie.

BRID. Read it yourself—[*crying*]

JUST. [*Reads*] 'Pleasure of administering a dose of Poison.'—O horrible!— Cut throat Villain!—Bridget—

BRID. Lovee!—stay here's a Postscript—'N.B. 'tis not in the power of Medicine to save you!'—Oh! oh!

JUST. Odds life, Bridget, why don't you call for help?—I've lost my Voice—my Brain's giddy—I shall burst—and no assistance—John! 50 Laury! John!

BRID. Oh! oh!—you see, my Lovee, what you have brought on yourself.

*Enter* JOHN.

JOHN. Your Worship!

JUST. Stay, John!—did you perceive any thing in my Chocolate cup, this morning?

JOHN. Nothing your Worship, unless it was a little Grounds.

JUST. Aye, Arsenick—Arsenick!—'tis plain enough—why don't you run for Doctor Rosy, you Rascal.

JOHN. Now, your Worship?

BRID. Oh! Lovee! you may be sure 'tis in vain—Let him go for the 60 Lawyer, to witness your will, my Life.

JUST. Zounds! go for the Doctor, you Scoundrel—you are all confederate murderers.

JOHN. O! here he is, your Worship!

JUST. Now Bridget—hold your tongue—let me see if my horrid situation is apparent.

*Enter* DOCTOR ROSY.

DOCTOR. I have but just call'd in to inform—hey!—bless me, what's the matter with your Worship?

JUST. There—he sees it already—Poison in my face in Capitals—Yes, yes, I am a sure job for the Undertakers indeed! 70

BRID. Oh! oh!—alas, Doctor!

JUST. Peace, Bridget—why Doctor—my dear old Friend—do you really—see any change in me—hey?

[1] Cf. Jonson, *The Silent Woman*, IV. v: 'O revenge, how sweet art thou'.

DOCTOR. Change?—Never was man so alter'd—how came those black Spots on your nose?

JUST. Spots on my nose.

DOCTOR. And that wild stare in your right eye?

JUST. In my right eye?

DOCTOR. Aye—and—O! lack! O! lack! how you're swell'd.

JUST. Swell'd! 80

DOCTOR. Aye—don't you think he is Madam?

BRID. Oh! 'tis in vain to conceal it—indeed, Lovee, you are as big again as you were in the morning.

JUST. Yes—I feel it now—I'm poison'd, Doctor—help me for the love of Justice—give me life to see my murderer hang'd.

DOCTOR. What?

JUST. I'm poison'd, I say.

DOCTOR. Speak out.

JUST. What, can't you hear me?

DOCTOR. Your voice—is so low and hollow, as it were, I can't hear a 90 word you say.

JUST. I am gone then—Hic Jacet—many years one of His Majesty's Justices.

BRID. Read that, Doctor.—Ah!—Lovee, the Will—Consider, my life, how soon you'll be dead.

JUST. No, Bridget, I shall die by inches—

BRID. Well, Lovee, and at twelve inches a day, and that's good slow dying—you'll be gone in five days and a half.

JUST. 'Tis false, Cockatrice!—I'm five foot eight.

DOCTOR. I never heard of such a monstrous Iniquity—Ah! you are gone indeed, my Friend—The mortgage of your little bit of clay is up— 100 and the Sexton has nothing to do but foreclose—we must all go— Sooner or later—High or Low—Death's a Debt—his Mandamus[1] binds all alike—no Bail—no Demurrer—

JUST. Silence, Doctor Croaker[2]—will you cure me, or will you not?

DOCTOR. Alas, my Friend—it isn't in my power—but I'll certainly see justice done on your Murderer.

JUST. I thank you, my dear Friend—but I had rather see it myself.

DOCTOR. Aye, but if you recover, the Villain will escape.

BRID. Will he?—then indeed Lovee, 'twould be a pity you should recover—I'm so enraged against the Villain, that I can't bear the 110 thought of his escaping the halter.

JUST. That's very kind, my Dear—but if it is the same to you, I had as lieve recover, notwithstanding.—Doctor, no assistance?

DOCTOR. Efacks—I can do nothing—but here is the German Quack,

---

[1] Command from a superior court to an inferior one.

[2] Croaker in Goldsmith's *The Good Natur'd Man* (1768) thinks all life is vanity but Sheridan is probably using the name more generally to suggest utter despair.

whom you wanted to send from the Town,—I met him at the next door,—I know that he has Antidotes for all Poisons.

JUST. Fetch him, my dear Friend, fetch him—I'll get him a Diploma if he cures me.

DOCTOR. Well, there's no time to be lost—you continue to swell immensely.                                                    [*Exit.* 120

BRID. What, my Dear, will you submit to be cur'd by a Quack ? a Nostrummonger?—For my part, as much as I love you, I had rather follow you to the Grave, than see you owe your life to any one but a regular bred Physician.

JUST. I'm sensible of your affection, Dearest—and believe me nothing consoles me in my present melancholy situation, so much as the thought of leaving you behind, my Angel.

*Enter* DOCTOR ROSY, *and the* LIEUTENANT.

*The* LIEUTENANT *dress'd in a wig and Cloak, as a Physician.*

DOCTOR. Great luck—I met him passing by the door—      [*they salute*

LIEUT. Metto—dowsci pulseum.

DOCTOR. He desires to feel your pulse.

JUST. Can't he speak English.                                      130

DOCTOR. Not a word.

LIEUT. Palio-vivem-mortem-soonem.[1]

DOCTOR. He says you have not six hours to live.

JUST. O mercy! does he know my Distemper ?

DOCTOR. I beleive not.

JUST. Tell him 'tis Arsenick they have given me.

DOCTOR. Geneabant illi Arseneca.[2]

LIEUT. Poisonatus.

JUST. What does he say ?

DOCTOR. He says then, that you are poison'd!                       140

JUST. We know that—but what will be the Effect?

DOCTOR. Quid Effectum ?

LIEUT. Diabet toutalar.[3]

DOCTOR. He says you'll die presently.

JUST. O Horrible! what no Antidote ?

LIEUT. Curum—Benakere—bono—Fullum.

DOCTOR. He says he'll undertake to cure you for three thousand pounds.[4]

---

[1] 'At length Dosy returns, introducing the Lieutenant disguised as Doctor; the latter talks gibberish on first seeing Credulous, which Dosy interprets, declaring that the German Doctor, after having felt his pulse, is of opinion that he'll be a dead man in less than an hour.' (*Morning Chronicle*, 4 May 1775.)

[2] Mr. F. W. Bateson has suggested that 'the sentence must originally have run "Giveabant illi Arsenica", i.e. they gave him arsenic.'

[3] Mr. Bateson suggests 'Diabit toutalar', i.e. he will die presently (*tout à l'heure*).

[4] 'He'll cure him for 3000 guineas.' (*Morning Chronicle*, 4 May 1775.)

BRID. Three thousand halters—No, Lovee, you shall never submit to such an imposition.—Die at once my Life, and be a Customer to none of them.

JUST. I will not die, Bridget—I do not like death.                               150

BRID. Pshaw! there's nothing in it—a moment and it is over.

JUST. Ay, but it leaves a numbness behind, that lasts for a plaguy long time.

*Enter* LAURETTA.

LAUR. O! my Father! what is it I hear?

LIEUT. Quiddum seeo miram Deos tollam Rosum.

DOCTOR. The Doctor is astonished at the sight of your Daughter.

JUST. How so?

LIEUT. Damsellum—Luvum—even—vislebani—

DOCTOR. He says, that he has long lost his heart to her—and that if you will give him leave to pay his Addresses to the young Lady, and   160 promise your consent to their union, if he should gain her affections, he will, on those Conditions, cure you instantly without Fee, or Reward.

JUST. The devil! did he say all that in so few words? what a fine Language it is!—well, I agree—if he can prevail on the girl—and that I am sure he never will—                                        [*aside*

DOCTOR. Greeat.

LIEUT. Writum Bothum.

DOCTOR. He says you must give this under your hand, while he writes you a miraculous Recipe.—                     [*Both write at the Table*

LAUR. Do, Mama, tell me the meaning of all this.                    170

BRID. Don't speak to me, Girl, unnatural Parasite.

JUST. There, Doctor, that's what he requires.

DOCTOR. And here's your Recipe, read it yourself.

JUST. Hey!—what's here? plain English?

DOCTOR. Read it out—a wondrous Nostrum, I'll answer for't. [*While the Justice reads, the Lieutenant throws off his disguise, and kneels with Lauretta.*]

JUST. [*Reads*] 'On reading this, you are Cured by your affectionate Son in law, O'Connor.'

JUST. What the deuce is the meaning of all this?

BRID. Oh! monstrous imposition.

JUST. In the name of Belzebub, who have we here?                    180

LIEUT. Lieutenant O'Connor, at your Service, and your faithful Servant, honest Humphry.

BRID. So, so, another Trick.

JUST. Out of my Sight, Varlet. I'll be off the bargain, I'll be poison'd again—and you shall be hang'd.

DOCTOR. Come, come, my Dear Friend, don't put yourself in a Passion— a man just escap'd from the Jaws of Death shou'dn't be so violent—

Come, make a merit of Necessity, and let your Blessing join those,
whom nothing on Earth can keep asunder.

JUST. I'll not  do it—I'd sooner die, and leave my Fortune to Bridget.  190

BRID. To be sure—O' my Conscience, I'd rather you should die, and
leave me ten Estates, than consent to such a thing.

JUST. You had, had you.—Harkee, Bridget, you behaved so affectionately
just now, that I'll never follow your advice again, while I live—so,
Mr. Lieutenant—

LIEUT. Sir!

JUST. You're an Irishman, and an officer, ar'n't you?

LIEUT. I am, and proud of both.

JUST. The two things in the world I hate most—So mark me—Forswear
your Country, and quit the Army—and I'll receive you as my Son in  200
law.

LIEUT. You, Mr. Justice, if you were not the father of your Daughter
there, I'd pull your nose for mentioning the first, and break your bones
for proposing the latter.[1]

DOCTOR. You're right, Lieutenant.

JUST. Is he?—why then I must be wrong—here, Lauretta, you're a sly
tricking little Baggage, and I believe no one so fit to manage you,
as my honest friend here, who is the most impudent dog, I ever saw.

LIEUT. With such a Gift, every word is a Compliment.

BRID. Come, then, since everything's settled, I give my Consent, and  210
this day's Adventure, Lovee, will be a good scolding Subject for you
and me these ten years.

JUST. So it will, my Dear—tho' we are never much at a loss.

DOCTOR. Come, I insist on one day without wrangling—The Captain
shall give us a Dinner at the two Magpies, and your Worship shall
put every man in the Stocks, who is sober at Eight o'clock—So, joy
to you, my little Favourite [to Lauretta]—And I wish you may make
just such a Wife, as my poor Dear Dolly—

FINIS[2]

---

[1] 'Mentioning the first . . . proposing the second.' (*Morning Chronicle*, 4 May 1775.)

[2] Sichel, i. 503 n., notes that in the Frampton Court MS. 'the whole is signed "S"
with a flourish, and a triumphant "Finis" afterwards'. Rae, p. 96, says that the manuscript ends '&c. &c.' and 'Finis', and that 'an L. is written between "&c." and "Finis" '.
Rhodes, i. 170 n., interpreted this 'as meaning that "L." (Lauretta or Lieutenant)
spoke a final tag, possibly in rhyme'. I think it is just possible that Lauretta recited a
verse, but there is no mention of an epilogue in the newspaper reports.

# THE DUENNA

THE

# DUENNA:

## *A COMIC OPERA.*

### IN THREE ACTS.

AS PERFORMED AT THE

## THEATRE ROYAL,

## *COVENT GARDEN:*

WITH UNIVERSAL APPLAUSE.

By R. B. SHERIDAN, Esǫ

𝕃 𝔇 𝔫 𝔇 𝔇 𝔫.

Printed for T. N. LONGMAN, No. 39, Pater Noster Row.

[ PRICE EIGHTEEN-PENCE ]

1794.

The title-page of the first authorized edition
of *The Duenna*

# DRAMATIS PERSONÆ

## ORIGINAL CAST OF CHARACTERS, 1775[1]

| | |
|---|---|
| DON JEROME | Mr. Wilson |
| FERDINAND | Mr. Mattocks |
| ANTONIO | Mr. Du Bellamy |
| CARLOS | Mr. Leoni |
| ISAAC MENDOZA | Mr. Quick |
| FATHER PAUL | Mr. Mahon |
| LOPEZ | Mr. Wewitzer |
| LEWIS | Mr. Castevens |
| LOUISA | Mrs. Mattocks |
| CLARA | Miss Brown |
| MARGARET (*the Duenna*) | Mrs. Green |

[1] To this list of performers at the first representation at Covent Garden Theatre on 21 Nov. 1775, we may add 'Augustin', Mr. Baker; 'Francis', Mr. Fox; 'Porter', Mr. Besford; as well as 'Friars, Servants, Masks'. Folger MS. D.a. 48 describes the extra characters as Francis and Augustine, fathers of the Convent of St. Catherine, Lay Brother, four other fathers, a nun, a maid servant to Louisa, 1st and 2nd Masks, and other Masks.

# THE DUENNA:

## AN OPERA

## ACT I

### SCENE I—A STREET

*Enter LOPEZ, with a dark Lanthorn.*

LOPEZ. Past three o'clock! soh! a notable hour for one of my regular disposition to be strolling like a bravo thro' the streets of Seville; well, of all services, to serve a young lover is the hardest—not that I am an enemy to love; but my love and my master's differ strangely—Don Ferdinand is much too gallant to eat, drink or sleep—now, my love gives me an appetite—then I am fond of dreaming of my mistress, and I love dearly to toast her—This cannot be done without good sleep, and good liquor, hence my partiality to a feather bed, and a bottle—what a pity now, that I have not further time for reflections; but thy master expects thee, honest Lopez, to secure his retreat from Donna Clara's 10 window, as I guess [*Music without*] hey! sure I heard music! so! so! who have we here? Oh, Don Antonio, my master's friend, come from the Masquerade to serenade my young mistress, Donna Louisa, I suppose! soh! we shall have the old gentleman up presently—lest he shou'd miss his son, I had best lose no time in getting to my post.

[*Exit.*

*Enter ANTONIO, with Masks and Music.*
ANTONIO.—SONG.—[*Soft Sym.*]
    Tell me, my lute, can thy fond strain
    So gently speak thy master's pain;
So softly sing, so humbly sigh,
    That tho' my sleeping love shall know
    Who sings—who sighs below.           20
Her rosy slumbers shall not fly?
    Thus may some vision whisper more
    Than ever I dare speak before.

IST MASK. Antonio, your mistress will never wake while you sing so dolefully; love, like a cradled infant, is lull'd by a sad melody.
ANTONIO. I do not wish to disturb her rest.

1ST MASK. The reason is, because you know she does not regard you
enough, to appear if you waked her.
ANTONIO. Nay, then I'll convince you.

### SINGS

The breath of morn bids hence the night,    30
Unveil those beauteous eyes, my fair,
For till the dawn of love is there,
    I feel no day, I own no light.

LOUISA *replies from a Window.*

Waking I heard thy numbers chide,
    Waking, the dawn did bless my sight,
'Tis Phœbus sure that woos, I cried,
    Who speaks in song, who moves in light.

DON JEROME *from a Window.*

What vagabonds are these I hear
Fid[d]ling, fluting, rhyming, ranting,
Piping, scraping, whining, canting,    40
    Fly, scurvy minstrels, fly.

### TRIO

LOUISA. Nay, prythee, father, why so rough,
ANT. An humble lover I,
JER. How durst you daughter lend an ear
    To such deceitful stuff?
        Quick from the window fly.
LOUISA. Adieu, Antonio!
ANT.    Must you go?
LOUISA.⎫    We soon perhaps, may meet again
ANT.  ⎬        For tho' hard fortune is our foe,    50
        The god of love will fight for us.
JER. Reach me the Blunderbuss.
ANT. & LOU. The god of love, who knows our pain,
JER. Hence, or these slugs are thro' your brain.    [*Exeunt severally.*

## SCENE II.—*A* PIAZZA

*Enter* FERDINAND *and* LOPEZ.

LOPEZ. Truly, sir, I think that a little sleep once in a week or so.
FERD. Peace fool, don't mention sleep to me.

LOPEZ. No, no, sir, I don't mention your low-bred, vulgar, sound sleep; but I can't help thinking that a genteel slumber, or half an hour's dozing, if it were only for the novelty of the thing.

FERD. Peace, booby, I say. O Clara, dear, cruel disturber of my rest.

LOPEZ. And of mine too.

FERD. S'death! to trifle with me at such a juncture as this—now to stand on punctilios—love me! I don't believe she ever did.

LOPEZ. Nor I either. 10

FERD. Or is it that her sex never know their desires for an hour together.

LOPEZ. Ah, they know them oftner than they'll own them.

FERD. Is there in the world so inconsistent a creature as Clara?

LOPEZ. I cou'd name one.

FERD. Yes; the tame fool who submits to her caprice.

LOPEZ. I thought he couldn't miss it.

FERD. Is she not capricious, teizing, tyrannical, obstinate, perverse, absurd, ay, a wilderness of faults and follies, her looks are scorn, and her very smiles—s'death! I wish I hadn't mention'd her smiles; for she does smile such beaming loveliness, and fascinating brightness—O 20 death and madness, I shall die if I lose her.

LOPEZ. O those damn'd smiles have undone all.

### AIR

FERDINAND.

Could I her faults remember,
Forgetting ev'ry charm,
Soon would impartial reason
The tyrant love disarm.
But when enraged I number
Each failing of her mind,
Love still suggests her beauty,
And sees—while reason's blind. 30

LOPEZ. Here comes Don Antonio, sir.

FERD. Well, go you home—I shall be there presently.

LOPEZ. Ah those curst smiles. [*Exit.*

*Enter* ANTONIO.

FERD. Antonio, Lopez tells me he left you chaunting before our door—was my father wak'd?

ANT. Yes, yes; he has a singular affection for music, so I left him roaring at his barr'd window like the print of Bajazet in the cage. And what brings you out so early?

FERD. I believe I told you that to-morrow was the day fix'd by Don Pedro and Clara's unnatural step-mother, for her to enter a Convent, 40 in order that her brat might possess her fortune, made desperate by this,

I procur'd a key to the door, and brib'd Clara's maid to leave it unbolted; at two this morning I entered, unperceived, and stole to her chamber—I found her waking and weeping.

ANT. Happy Ferdinand!

FERD. S'death, hear the conclusion—I was rated as the most confident ruffian, for daring to approach her room at that hour of night.

ANT. Ay, ay, this was at first.

FERD. No such thing! she wou'd not hear a word from me, but threat'ned to raise her father if I did not instantly leave her.          50

ANT. Well; but at last?—

FERD. At last! why, I was forced to leave the house as I came in.

ANT. And did you do nothing to offend her?

FERD. Nothing, as I hope to be saved—I believe I might snatch a dozen or two kisses.

ANT. Was that all? well, I think I never heard of such assurance.

FERD. Zounds! I tell you I behaved with the utmost respect.

ANT. O lord! I dont mean you, but in her—but, hark'y, Ferdinand, did you leave your key with them?

FERD. Yes; the maid who saw me out took it from the door.          60

ANT. Then my life for it, her mistress elopes after you.

FERD. Ay, to bless some rival perhaps—I am in a humour to suspect everybody—you lov'd her once, and thought her an angel, as I do now.

ANT. Yes, I loved her till I found she wou'dn't love me, and then I discovered that she hadn't a good feature in her face.

*AIR*

I ne'er could any lustre see[1]
In eyes that wou'd not look on me:
I ne'er saw nectar on a lip,
But where my own did hope to sip.
Has the maid who seeks my heart          70
Cheeks of rose untouch'd by art?
I will own the colour true,
When yielding blushes aid their hue.

[1] A comic poem originally. Two stanzas in a Yale MS. in Sheridan's hand, read:

I ne'er could any Lustre see
In Eyes that would not look on me—
And when a Glance aversion hints
I always think the Lady squints—

I ne'er saw Nectar on a Lip
But where my own did hope to sip.
No pearly Teeth rejoice my view
Unless a Yes displays their hue.

Is her hand so soft and pure?
I must press it to be sure:
Nor can I be certain then
Till it grateful press again:
Must I with attentive eye
Watch her heaving bosom sigh?
I will do so when I see          80
That heaving bosom sigh for me.

Besides, Ferdinand, you have full security in my love for your sister, help me there, and I can never disturb you with Clara.

FERD. As far as I can consistently with the honor of our family, you know I will; but there must be no eloping.

ANT. And yet now, you wou'd carry off Clara.

FERD. Ay, that's a different case—we never mean that others shou'd act to our sisters and wives as we do to theirs—But to-morrow Clara is to be forc'd into a convent.

ANT. Well: and am not I as unfortunately circumstanc'd? To-morrow  90 your father forces Louisa to marry Isaac, the Portugueze—but come with me, and we'll devise something, I warrant.

FERD. I must go home.

ANT. Well, adieu.

FERD. But, Antonio, if you did not love my sister, you have too much honor and friendship to think of supplanting me with Clara.

### AIR

#### ANTONIO.

Friendship is the bond of reason,
   But if beauty disapprove,
Heaven absolves all other treason
   In the heart that's true to love.      100

The faith which to my friend I swore
   As a civil oath I view,
But to the charms which I adore,
   'Tis religion to be true.

Then if to one I false must be;
   Can I doubt which to prefer—
A breach of social faith with thee,
   Or sacrilege to love and her.    [*Exit* ANTONIO.

FERD. There is always a levity in Antonio's manner of replying to me on

this subject, that is very alarming—S'death, if Clara shou'd love him   110
after all.

*AIR*

> Tho' cause for suspicion appears,
>   Yet proofs of her love too are strong;
> I'm a wretch if I'm right in my fears,
>   And unworthy of bliss if I'm wrong.
> What heart-breaking torments from jealousy flow,
> Ah, none but the jealous, the jealous can know.
>
> When blest with the smiles of my fair,
>   I know not how much I adore;
> Those smiles let another but share,                    120
>   And I wonder I priz'd them no more.
> Then whence can I hope a relief from my woe,
> When the falser she seems still the fonder I grow.   [*Exit.*

## SCENE III. *A Room in Don Jerome's house*

### Enter LOUISA *and* DUENNA.

LOUISA. But my dear Margaret, my charming Duenna, do you think we
shall succeed?

DUENNA. I tell you again I have no doubt on't; but it must be instantly
put to the trial—Every thing is prepared in your room, and for the rest
we must trust to fortune.

LOUISA. My father's oath was never to see me till I had consented to—

DUENNA. 'Twas thus I overheard him say to his friend, Don Guzman,
'I will demand of her to-morrow, once for all, whether she will consent
to marry Isaac Mendoza—If she hesitates, I will make a solemn oath
never to see or speak to her till she returns to her duty'—these were his   10
very words.

LOUISA. And on his known obstinate adherence to what he has once said,
you have form'd this plan for my escape—But have you secured my
maid in our interest.

DUENNA. She is a party in the whole—but remember, if we succeed, you
resign all right and title in little Isaac the Jew, over to me.

LOUISA. That I do with all my soul, get him if you can, and I shall wish
you joy most heartily. He is twenty times as rich as my poor Antonio.

*AIR*

> Thou cans't not boast of fortune's store,
>   My love, while me they wealthy call,                  20
> But I was glad to find thee poor,
>   For with my heart I'd give thee all.

And then the grateful youth shall own,
   I lov'd him for himself alone.

But when his worth my hand shall gain,
   No word or look of mine shall shew,
That I, the smallest thought retain
   Of what my bounty did bestow.
      Yet still his grateful heart shall own,
      I lov'd him for himself alone.                    30

DUENNA. I hear Don Jerome coming—Quick, give me the last letter I
   brought you from Antonio—you know that is to be the ground of my
   dismission—I must slip out to seal it up as undelivered.        [*Exit.*

*Enter* DON JEROME *and* FERDINAND.

JEROME. What, I suppose you have been serenading too! Eh, disturbing
   some peaceable neighbourhood with villainous catgut and lascivious
   piping, out on't! you set your sister here a vile example—but I come
   to tell you, madam, that I'll suffer no more of these midnight incanta-
   tions, these amorous orgies that steal the senses in the hearing, as they
   say Egyptian Embalmers serve mummies, extracting the brain thro'
   the ears; however, there's an end of your frolics—Isaac Mendoza will   40
   be here presently, and to-morrow you shall marry him.

LOUISA. Never while I have life.

FERD. Indeed, Sir, I wonder how you can think of such a man for a
   son-in-law.

JEROME. Sir, you are very kind to favour me with your sentiments—and
   pray, what is your objection to him.

FERD. He is a Portugueze in the first place.

JEROME. No such thing, boy, he has forsworn his country.

LOUISA. He is a Jew.

JEROME. Another mistake: he has been a christian these six weeks.        50

FERD. Ay, he left his old religion for an estate, and has not had time to
   get a new one.

LOUISA. But stands like a dead wall between church and synagogue, or
   like the blank leaves between the Old and New Testament.

JEROME. Any thing more?

FERD. But the most remarkable part of his character, is his passion for
   deceit, and tricks of cunning.

LOUISA. Tho' at the same time, the fool predominates so much over the
   knave, that I am told he is generally the dupe of his own art.

FERD. True, like an unskilful gunner, he usually misses his aim, and is   60
   hurt by the recoil of his own piece.

JEROME. Any thing more?

LOUISA. To sum up all, he has the worst fault a husband can have—he's not my choice.

JEROME. But you are his; and choice on one side is sufficient—two lovers shou'd never meet in marriage—be you sour as you please, he is sweet temper'd, and for your good fruit, there's nothing like ingrafting on a crab.

LOUISA. I detest him as a lover, and shall ten times more as a husband.

JEROME. I don't know that—marriage generally makes a great change— 70 but to cut the matter short, will you have him or not?

LOUISA. There is nothing else I could disobey you in.

JEROME. Do you value your father's peace?

LOUISA. So much, that I will not fasten on him the regret of making an only daughter wretched.

JEROME. Very well, ma'am, then mark me—never more will I see or converse with you till you return to your duty—no reply—this and your chamber shall be your appartments, I never will stir out without leaving you under lock and key, and when I'm at home no creature can approach you but thro' my library—we'll try who can be most obstinate 80 —out of my sight—There remain till you know your duty.

[*Pushes her out.*

FERD. Surely, Sir, my sister's inclinations should be consulted in a matter of this kind, and some regard paid to Don Antonio, being my particular friend.

JEROME. That, doubtless, is a very great recommendation—I certainly have not paid sufficient respect to it.

FERD. There is not a man living I wou'd sooner chuse for a brother-in-law.

JEROME. Very possible; and if you happen to have e'er a sister, who is not at the same time a daughter of mine, I'm sure I shall have no objec- 90 tion to the relationship—but at present, if you please, we'll drop the subject.

FERD. Nay, sir, 'tis only my regard for my sister makes me speak.

JEROME. Then, pray, sir, in future, let your regard for your father make you hold your tongue.

FERD. I have done, sir—I shall only add a wish that you wou'd reflect what at our age you wou'd have felt, had you been crost in your affection for the mother of her you are so severe to.

JEROME. Why I must confess I had a great affection for your mother's ducats, but that was all, boy—I married her for her fortune, and she 100 took me in obedience to her father, and a very happy couple we were —we never expected any love from one another, and so we were never disappointed—If we grumbled a little now and then, it was soon over, for we were never fond enough to quarrel, and when the good woman died, why, why—I had as lieve she had lived, and I wish every widower

in Seville cou'd say the same—I shall now go and get the key of this
dressing room—So, good son, if you have any lecture in support of
disobedience to give your sister, it must be brief; so make the best of
your time d'ye hear.                                    [*Exit* JEROME.

FERD. I fear indeed, my friend Antonio, has little to hope for—however 110
Louisa has firmness, and my father's anger will probably only increase
her affection—In our intercourse with the world, it is natural for us to
dislike those who are innocently the cause of our distress; but in the
heart's attachment, a woman never likes a man with ardor till she has
suffer'd for his sake [*Noise.*] soh! what bustle is here! between my
father and the Duenna too—I'll e'en get out of the way.         [*Exit.*

*Enter* DON JEROME (*with a Letter*) *pulling in the* DUENNA.

JEROME. I'm astonished! I'm thunder struck! here's treachery and
conspiracy with a vengeance! you, Antonio's creature, and chief
manager of this plot for my daughter's eloping! you that I placed here
as a scare-crow.                                        120

DUENNA. What?

JEROME. A scare-crow—To prove a decoy duck—what have you to say
for yourself?

DUENNA. Well, sir, since you have forced that letter from me, and discover'd my real sentiments, I scorn to renounce 'em—I am Antonio's
friend, and it was my intention that your daughter shou'd have serv'd
you as all such old tyrannical sots shou'd be serv'd—I delight in the
tender passions, and would befriend all under their influence.

JEROME. The tender passions! yes, they wou'd become those impenetrable features—why, thou deceitful hag! I plac'd thee as a guard to the 130
rich blos[s]oms of my daughter's beauty—I thought that dragon's front
of thine wou'd cry aloof to the sons of gallantry—steel traps and spring
guns seem'd writ in every wrinkle of it—but you shall quit my house
this instant—the tender passions, indeed! go thou wanton sybil, thou
amorous woman of Endor,[1] go!

DUENNA. You base, scurrilous, old—but I wont demean myself by
naming what you are—yes, Savage, I'll leave your den, but I suppose
you don't mean to detain my apparel—I may have my things I presume.

JEROME. I took you, mistress, with your wardrobe on—what have you
pilfer'd, heh?                                          140

DUENNA. Sir, I must take leave of my mistress, she has valuables of
mine, besides, my cardinal and veil are in her room.

JEROME. Your veil for sooth! what do you dread being gazed at? or are
you afraid of your complexion? well, go take your leave, and get your
veil and cardinal! soh! you quit the house within these five minutes—

---

[1] The witch consulted by Saul before the battle of Gilboa: see 1 Samuel 28: 7.

In—in—quick.                                            [*Exit* DUENNA.
Here was a precious plot of mischief—! these are the comforts daughters
bring us.

*AIR*

If a daughter you have, she's the plague of your life,
No peace shall you know, tho' you've buried your wife,          150
At twenty she mocks at the duty you taught her,
O, what a plague is an obstinate daughter.
   Sighing and whining,
   Dying and pining,
O what a plague is an obstinate daughter.
When scarce in their teens, they have wit to perplex us,
With letters and lovers for ever they vex us,
While each still rejects the fair suitor you've brought her,
O what a plague is an obstinate daughter.
   Wrangling and jangling,          160
   Flouting and pouting,
O what a plague is an obstinate daughter.

*Enter* LOUISA, *dress'd as the* DUENNA, *with Cardinal and
Veil, seeming to cry.*

JEROME. This way, mistress, this way—what, I warrant, a tender parting soh! tears of turpentine down those deal cheeks—Aye, you may
well hide your head—yes, whine till your heart breaks, but I'll not hear
one word of excuse—so you are right to be dumb, this way—this way.
                [*Exeunt.*

*Enter* DUENNA.

DUENNA. So speed you well, sagacious Don Jerome! O, rare effects of
passion and obstinacy—now shall I try whether I can't play the fine
lady as well as my mistress, and if I succeed, I may be a fine lady for the
rest of my life—I'll lose no time to equip myself.          [*Exit.* 170

SCENE IV. *The Court before* DON JEROME'*s house*

*Enter* DON JEROME *and* LOUISA.

JEROME. Come, mistress, there is your way—The world lies before you,
so troop, thou antiquated Eve, thou original sin—hold, yonder is some
fellow skulking, perhaps it is Antonio—go to him, d'ye hear, and tell
him to make you amends, and as he has got you turn'd away, tell him I
say it is but just he shou'd take you himself, go.          [*Exit* LOUISA.
Soh! I am rid of her, thank heaven! and now I shall be able to keep my
oath, and confine my daughter with better security.          [*Exit.*

## SCENE V.—*The* PIAZZA

*Enter* CLARA, *and her Maid.*

MAID. But where madam, is it you intend to go?

CLARA. Any where to avoid the selfish violence of my mother-in-law, and Ferdinand's insolent importunity.

MAID. Indeed, ma'am, since we have profited by Don Ferdinand's key in making our escape, I think we had best find him, if it were only to thank him.

CLARA. No—he has offended me exceedingly.          [*Retire.*

*Enter* LOUISA.

LOUISA. So, I have succeeded in being turn'd out of doors—but how shall I find Antonio? I dare not enquire for him for fear of being discovered; I would send to my friend Clara, but that I doubt her prudery 10 wou'd condemn me.

MAID. Then suppose, ma'am, you were to try if your friend Donna Louisa would not receive you.

CLARA. No, her notions of filial duty are so severe, she would certainly betray me.

LOUISA. Clara is of a cold temper, and would think this step of mine highly forward.

CLARA. Louisa's respect for her father is so great, she would not credit the unkindness of mine.     [LOUISA *turns, and sees* CLARA *and* MAID.

LOUISA. Ha! who are those? sure one is Clara—if it be, I'll trust her— 20 Clara!                                     [*Advances.*

CLARA. Louisa! and in Masquerade too!

LOUISA. You will be more surprized when I tell you that I have run away from my father.

CLARA. Surprized indeed! and I should certainly chide you most horridly, only that I have just run away from mine.

LOUISA. My dear Clara!                              [*Embrace.*

CLARA. Dear sister truant! and whither are you going?

LOUISA. To find the man I love to be sure—And I presume you wou'd have no aversion to meet with my brother.                    30

CLARA. Indeed I should—he has behaved so ill to me, I don't believe I shall ever forgive him.

### *AIR*

#### CLARA.

When sable night, each drooping plant restoring,
    Wept o'er the flowers her breath did cheer,
As some sad widow o'er her babe deploring,
    Wakes its beauty with a tear;

When all did sleep, whose weary hearts did borrow
   One hour from love and care to rest,
Lo! as I prest my couch in silent sorrow,
   My lover caught me to his breast;                    40
      He vowed he came to save me
      From those who would enslave me!
        Then kneeling,
        Kisses stealing
Endless faith he swore,
      But soon I chid him thence,
      For had his fond pretence,
      Obtain'd one favour then,
      And he had press'd again
I fear'd my treacherous heart might grant him more.        50

LOUISA. Well, for all this, I would have sent him to plead his pardon, but that I would not yet awhile have him know of my flight. And where do you hope to find protection?

CLARA. The lady Abbess of the convent of St. Catherine is a relation and kind friend of mine—I shall be secure with her, and you had best go thither with me.

LOUISA. No; I am determined to find Antonio first, and as I live, here comes the very man I will employ to seek him for me.

CLARA. Who is he? he's a strange figure!

LOUISA. Yes, that sweet creature is the man whom my father has fixed  60
on for my husband.

CLARA. And will you speak to him? are you mad?

LOUISA. He is the fittest man in the world for my purpose—for, tho' I was to have married him to-morrow, he is the only man in Seville, who I am sure never saw me in his life.

CLARA. And how do you know him?

LOUISA. He arrived but yesterday, and he was shewn me from the window as he visited my father.

CLARA. Well, I'll be gone.

LOUISA. Hold, my dear Clara—a thought has struck me, will you give  70
me leave to borrow your name as I see occasion.

CLARA. It will but disgrace you—but use it as you please—I dare not stay [*going*] but, Louisa, if you shou'd see your brother, be sure you don't inform him that I have taken refuge with the Dame Prior of the convent of St. Catherine, on the left hand side of the Piazza which leads to the church of St. Anthony.

LOUISA. Ha, ha, ha! I'll be very particular in my directions where he may not find you.                    [*Exeunt* CLARA *and* MAID.
So! my swain yonder has done admiring himself and draws nearer.
                                [*Retires.*

*Enter* ISAAC *and* CARLOS, ISAAC *with a pocket glass.*

ISAAC. [*Looking in the glass.*] I tell you, friend Carlos, I will please 80
myself in the habit of my chin.

CARLOS. But, my dear friend, how can you think to please a lady with
such a face.

ISAAC. Why, what's the matter with the face? I think it is a very engaging
face; and I am sure a lady must have very little taste, who could
dislike my beard [*Sees* LOUISA.] See now—I'll die if here is not a little
damsel struck with it already.

LOUISA. Signor, are you disposed to oblige a lady who greatly wants
your assistance. [*Unveils.*]

ISAAC. Egad, a very pretty black-eyed girl; she has certainly taken a 90
fancy to me, Carlos—first ma'am, I must beg the favour of your name.

LOUISA. Soh! it's well I am provided. [*Aside*] My name, sir, is Donna
Clara D'Almanza.

ISAAC. What!—Don Guzman's daughter? I'faith, I just now heard she
was missing.

LOUISA. But, sure sir, you have too much gallantry and honor to betray
me, whose fault is love.

ISAAC. So! a passion for me! poor girl! why, ma'am, as for betraying you,
I don't see how I cou'd get any thing by it; so you may rely on my
honour; but as for your love, I am sorry your case is so desperate. 100

LOUISA. Why so Signor?

ISAAC. Because I'm positively engaged to another—an't I Carlos?

LOUISA. Nay, but hear me.

ISAAC. No, no; what should I hear for? It is impossible for me to court you
in an honourable way; and for any thing else, if I were to comply now, I
suppose you have some ungrateful brother, or cousin, who would want to
cut my throat for my civility—so, truly you had best go home again.

LOUISA. Odious wretch! [*aside*] But, good Signor, it is Antonio
d'Ercilla, on whose account I have eloped.

ISAAC. How! what! it is not with me then, that you are in love? 110

LOUISA. No indeed it is not.

ISAAC. Then you are a forward, impertinent simpleton! and I shall
certainly acquaint your father.

LOUISA. Is this your gallantry.

ISAAC. Yet hold—Antonio d'Ercilla did you say? egad, I may make
something of this—Antonio d'Ercilla?

LOUISA. Yes, and if ever you hope to prosper in love, you will bring me
to him.

ISAAC. By St. Iago, and I will too—Carlos, this Antonio is one who rivals
me (as I have heard) with Louisa—now, if I could hamper him with 120
this girl, I should have the field to myself, hey, Carlos! A lucky thought,
isn't it?—

CARLOS. Yes, very good—very good—

ISAAC. Ah! this little brain is never at a loss—cunning Isaac! cunning rogue! Donna Clara, will you trust yourself a while to my friend's direction.

LOUISA. May I rely on you good Signor?

CARLOS. Lady, it is impossible I should deceive you.

*AIR*

> Had I a heart for falsehood framed,
>    I ne'er could injure you;                                    130
> For tho' your tongue no promise claimed,
>    Your charms wou'd make me true.
> To you no soul shall bear deceit,
>    No stranger offer wrong,
> But friends in all the aged you'll meet;
>    And lovers in the young.
>
> But when they learn that you have blest
>    Another with your heart,
> They'll bid aspiring passion rest,
>    And act a brother's part;                                   140
> Then, lady, dread not here deceit,
>    Nor fear to suffer wrong;
> For friends in all the aged you'll meet,
>    And brothers in the young.

ISAAC. Conduct the lady to my lodgings, Carlos; I must haste to Don Jerome—perhaps you know Louisa, ma'am. She is divinely handsome—isn't she?

LOUISA. You must excuse me not joining with you.

ISAAC. Why, I have heard it on all hands.

LOUISA. Her father is uncommonly partial to her, but I believe you will   150
find she has rather a matronly air.

ISAAC. Carlos, this is all envy—you pretty girls never speak well of one another—[*To Don Carlos*] hark'y, find out Antonio, and I'll saddle him with this scrape, I warrant! oh, 'twas the luckiest thought—Donna Clara, your very obedient—Carlos, to your post.

*DUETT*

ISAAC.          My mistress expects me, and I must go to her,
                   Or how can I hope for a smile?
LOUISA.         Soon may you return a prosperous wooer,
                   But think what I suffer the while:
                Alone and away from the man whom I love,      160
                   In strangers I'm forced to confide,

ISAAC.        Dear lady, my friend you may trust, and he'll prove,
                    Your servant, protector, and guide.

                              *AIR*
                            CARLOS.

                    Gentle maid, ah! why suspect me?
                    Let me serve thee—then reject me,
                    Can'st thou trust, and I deceive thee?
                    Art thou sad, and shall I grieve thee?
                    Gentle maid, Ah! why suspect me?
                    Let me serve thee—then reject me.

                              *TRIO*
LOUISA.        Never may'st thou happy be,                          170
                    If in ought thou'rt false to me.
ISAAC.         Never may he happy be,
                    If in ought he's false to thee.
CARLOS.        Never may I happy be,
                    If in ought I'm false to thee.
LOUISA.        Never may'st thou &c.
ISAAC.         Never may he &c.
CARLOS.        Never may I &c.

                                                        [*Exeunt.*


                         END OF ACT I


                         ACT II

                    SCENE I.—*A Library in* JEROME's *House*

                         *Enter* DON JEROME *and* ISAAC.

JEROME. Ha, ha, ha! run away from her father, has she? given him the
slip! Ha, ha, ha! poor Don Guzman!
ISAAC. Ay; and I am to conduct her to Antonio; by which means you
see I shall hamper him so that he can give me no disturbance with your
daughter—this is a trap, isn't it? a nice stroke of cunning, heh!
JEROME. Excellent! Excellent! yes, yes, carry her to him, hamper him
by all means, ha, ha, ha! poor Don Guzman! an old fool! imposed on
by a girl!
ISAAC. Nay, they have the cunning of serpents, that's the truth on't.
JEROME. Psha! they are cunning only when they have fools to deal with  10
—why don't my girl play me such a trick—let her cunning over-reach
my caution, I say—heh little Isaac!

ISAAC. True, true; or let me see any of the sex make a fool of me—No, no,
egad, little Solomon, (as my aunt used to call me) understands tricking
a little too well.

JEROME. Ay, but such a driveller as Don Guzman.

ISAAC. And such a dupe as Antonio.

JEROME. True; sure never were seen such a couple of credulous simple-
tons, but come, 'tis time you should see my daughter—you must carry
on the siege by yourself, friend Isaac,                                          20

ISAAC. Sure, you'll introduce me—

JEROME. No—I have sworn a solemn oath not to see or speak to her till
she renounces her disobedience; win her to that, and she gains a father
and a husband at once.

ISAAC. Gad, I shall never be able to deal with her alone; nothing keeps
me in such awe as perfect beauty—now there is something consoling
and encouraging in ugliness.


### SONG

Give Isaac the nymph who no beauty can boast;
But health and good humour to make her his toast,
If strait, I dont mind whether slender or fat,                                   30
And six feet or four—we'll ne'er quarrel for that.

Whate'er her complexion, I vow I don't care,
If brown it is lasting, more pleasing if fair;
And tho' in her cheeks I no dimples shou'd see,
Let her smile, and each dell is a dimple to me.

Let her locks be the reddest that ever were seen,
And her eyes may be e'en any colour but green,
For in eyes, tho' so various in lustre and hue,
I swear I've no choice, only let her have two.

'Tis true I'd dispense with a throne on her back,                                40
And white teeth I own, are genteeler than black,
A little round chin too's a beauty I've heard,
But I only desire she mayn't have a beard.

JEROME. You will change your note, my friend, when you've seen Louisa.

ISAAC. O Don Jerome, the honour of your alliance—

JEROME. Aye, but her beauty will affect you—she is, tho' I say it, who
am her father, a very prodigy—there you will see Features with an eye
like mine—yes I'faith, there is a kind of wicked sparkling—something
of a roguish brightness that shews her to be my own.

ISAAC. Pretty rogue!                                            50
JEROME. Then, when she smiles, you'll see a little dimple in one cheek
  only; a beauty it is certainly, yet you shall not say which is prettiest,
  the cheek with the dimple, or the cheek without.
ISAAC. Pretty rogue!
JEROME. Then the roses on those cheeks are shaded with a sort of velvet
  down, that gives a delicacy to the glow of health.
ISAAC. Pretty rogue!
JEROME. Her skin pure dimity, yet more fair, being spangled here and
  there with a golden freckle.
ISAAC. Charming pretty rogue!                                   60

*DUET*

JEROME.     Dominion was given
              To Beauty from Heav'n
              Pleasing Bondage to the Mind!—
              Will *you* then alone
              Its Worship disown?—
ISAAC.      Never!—could I favour find
              But when for my Pain
              I meet with Disdain
JEROME. Coax her, kiss her, till she's kind.

JEROME. Come courage man—you must not be dismay'd if you find 70
  Louisa a little haughty at first.
ISAAC. Pray how is the tone of her voice?
JEROME. Remarkably pleasing—but if you cou'd prevail on her to sing
  you would be enchanted—she is a nightingale—a Virginia nightingale[1]
  —but come, come, her maid shall conduct you to her Antichamber.
ISAAC. Well, egad, I'll pluck up resolution and meet her frowns intrepidly.
JEROME. Aye! woo her briskly—win her and give me a proof of your
  address, my little Solomon.
ISAAC. But hold—I expect my friend Carlos to call on me here—If he
  comes will you send him to me?                               80
JEROME. I will—Lauretta, come—she'll shew you to the room—what!
  do you droop? here's a mournful face to make love with.

*SONG*

When the maid whom we love
No entreaties can move,

---

[1] The cardinal. Cf. Christopher Smart's 'Ode to a Virginia Nightingale' (1754):
      O let us fellow warblers join,
      Our patroness to crown.

Who'd lead a life of pining?
If her charms will excuse
The fond rashness we use,
—Away with idle whining!

Never stand like a fool
With looks sheepish and cool—                                    90
Such bashful love is tiezing:
But with spirit address
And you're sure of success
—For honest warmth is pleasing.

Nay tho' wedlock's your view,
Like a rake if you'll woo,
Girls sooner quit their coldness:
They know beauty inspires
Less respect than desires
—Hence love is prov'd by boldness.          [*Exeunt.*  100

### SCENE II.—LOUISA's *Dressing Room*
#### *Enter* MAID *and* ISAAC.

MAID. Sir, my mistress will wait on you presently.     [*Goes to the door.*
ISAAC. When she's at leisure—don't hurry her.          [*Exit* MAID.
   I wish I had ever practised a love-scene—I doubt I shall make a poor
   figure—I cou'd'nt be more afraid if I was going before the Inquisition[1]
   —so! the door opens—yes, she's coming—the very rustling of her silks
   has a disdainful sound.

#### *Enter* DUENNA (*drest as* LOUISA.)

   Now dar'n't I look round for the soul of me—her beauty will certainly
   strike me dumb if I do. I wish she'd speak first.
DUENNA. Sir, I attend your pleasure.
ISAAC. So! the ice is broke, and a pretty civil beginning too! [*aside*]  10
   hem! madam—Miss—I'm all attention.
DUENNA. Nay, Sir, 'tis I who shou'd listen, and you propose.
ISAAC. Egad, this is'nt so disdainful neither—I believe I may venture to
   look—No—I dar'n't—one glance of those roguish sparklers wou'd fix
   me again.
DUENNA. You seem thoughtful, Sir—let me persuade you to sit down.
ISAAC. So, so; she mol[l]ifies apace—she's struck with my figure, this
   attitude has had its effect.                               [*aside.*
DUENNA. Come, Sir, here's a chair.

---

[1] It lasted in Spain from the Middle Ages to 1835.

ISAAC. Madam, the greatness of your goodness overpowers me—that 20
a lady so lovely shou'd deign to turn her beauteous eyes on one so.
                        [*She takes his hand, he turns and sees her.*

DUENNA. You seem surpriz'd at my condescension.

ISAAC. Why, yes, madam, I am a little surprized at—at—zounds! this
can never be Louisa—she's as old as my mother.        [*aside.*

DUENNA. But former prepossessions give way to my father's commands.

ISAAC. [*aside,*] Her father! Yes, 'tis she then—Lord, lord; how blind
some parents are!

DUENNA. Signor Isaac.

ISAAC. Truely, the little damsel was right—she has rather a matronly
air indeed! ah! 'tis well my affections are fixed on her fortune and not 30
her person.

DUENNA. Signor Isaac, wont you sit?        [*she sits.*

ISAAC. Pardon me, madam, I have scarce recover'd my astonishment at
—your condescension, madam—she has the devil's own dimples to be
sure.        [*aside.*

DUENNA. Nay, you shall not stand [*he sits*] I do not wonder, Sir, that you
are su[r]priz'd at my affability—I own Signor, that I was vastly pre-
possessed against you, and being teiz'd by my father, I did give some
encouragement to Antonio, But then, Sir, you were described to me as
a quite different person.        40

ISAAC. Aye, and so you were to me upon my soul, madam.

DUENNA. But when I saw you, I was never more struck in my life.

ISAAC. That was just my case too, madam; I was struck all of a heap for
my part.

DUENNA. Well, Sir, I see our misapprehension has been mutual—you
expected to find me haughty and averse, and I was taught to believe
you a little black snub-nosed fellow, without person, manners or address.

ISAAC. Egad, I wish she had answer'd her picture as well.        [*aside.*

DUENNA. But, Sir, your air is noble—something so liberal in your carriage, with so penetrating an eye, and so bewitching a smile.        50

ISAAC. Efaith, now I look at her again, I dont think she is so ugly. [*aside.*

DUENNA. So little like a jew, and so much like a gentleman.

ISAAC. Well, there certainly *is* something pleasing in the tone of her voice.

DUENNA. You will pardon this breach of decorum in my praising you
thus, but my joy at being so agreeably deceiv'd has given me such a flow
of spirits.

ISAAC. O dear lady, may I thank those sweet lips for this goodness
[*kisses her*] why, she has a pretty sort of velvet down, that's the truth
on't.        [*aside.*

DUENNA. O Sir, you have the most insinuating manner, but indeed you 60
shou'd get rid of that odious beard—one might as well kiss a hedge-hog.

ISAAC. Yes ma'am—the razor wou'd'nt be amiss for either of us [*aside*].

Could you favour me with a song?

DUENNA. Willingly, Sir, tho' I am rather hoarse—Ahem!

[*Begins to sing.*

ISAAC. Very like a Virginia nightingale—ma'am, I perceive you're hoarse
—I beg you will not distress—

DUENNA. O not in the least distressed;—now, Sir.

*SONG*

When a tender maid
Is first essayed,
By some admiring swain.                                70
How her blushes rise,
If she meets his eyes,
While he unfolds his pain;
If he takes her hand, she trembles quite,
Touch her lips, and she swoons outright,
While a pit a pat, &c.
Her heart avows her fright.

But in time appear,
Fewer signs of fear,
The youth she boldly views,                            80
If her hand he grasp,
Or her bosom clasp,
No mantling blush ensues.
Then to church well pleas'd the lovers move,
While her smiles her contentment prove,
And a pit a pat, &c.
Her heart avows her love.

ISAAC. Charming, ma'am! Enchanting! and truely your notes put me in
mind of one that's very dear to me, a lady indeed, whom you greatly
resemble.                                              90

DUENNA. How! is there then another so dear to you?

ISAAC. O, no, ma'am, you mistake me—

DUENNA. No—no you offer me your hand—then another has your
Heart—

ISAAC. Oh Lud! no ma'am—'twas my Mother I meant as I hop'd to be
saved.

DUENNA. What—Sir—am I like your Mother?

ISAAC. Stay, dear ma'am, I meant that you put me in mind of what my
mother was when a Girl!—Yes—yes—ma'am my Mother was formerly
a great Beauty I assure you—and when she married my Father about  100
thirty years ago—as you may perhaps remember Ma'am—

DUENNA. I Sir—I remember thirty years ago?

ISAAC. O good lack—no ma'am—thirty years! No—no Ma'am it was thirty months I said—yes—yes Ma'am thirty months ago on her marriage with my Father who was as I was saying a great Beauty—but catching cold the year afterwards in Child Bed of your humble Servant.

DUENNA. Of *you* Sir—and married within these thirty months?

ISAAC. O the Devil I've made myself out but a year old!

DUENNA. Come, Sir, I see you are amazed and confounded at my condescension and know not what to say.                                   110

ISAAC. It is very true indeed, ma'am—but it is a judgment, I look on it as a judgment on me for delaying to urge the time when you'll permit me to compleat my happiness, by acquainting Don Jerome with your condescension.

DUENNA. Sir, I must frankly own to you that I can never be yours with my father's consent.

ISAAC. Good lack! how so?

DUENNA. When my father in his passion swore he would not see me again 'till I acquiesced in his will—I also made a vow that I would never take a husband from his hand—nothing shall make me break that oath   120 —but if you have spirit and contrivance enough to carry me off without his knowledge, I'm yours.

ISAAC. Hum!

DUENNA. Nay, Sir, if you hesitate—

ISAAC. I'faith no bad whim this—if I take her at her word, I shall secure her fortune, and avoid making any settlement in return; thus I shall not only cheat the lover but the father too, Oh! cunning rogue, Isaac! Ay, ay, let this little brain alone—Egad, I'll take her in the mind.   [*aside*.

DUENNA. Well, Sir, what's your determination?

ISAAC. Madam, I was dumb only from rapture—I applaud your spirit,  130 and joyfully close with your proposal; for which, thus let me on this lilly hand express my gratitude.                    [*Kisses her hand*.

DUENNA. Well, Sir, you must get my father's consent to walk with me in the garden. But by no means inform him of my kindness to you.

ISAAC. No, to be sure—that wou'd spoil all—But trust me when tricking is the word—let me alone for a piece of cunning; this very day you shall be out of his power.

DUENNA. Well, I leave the management of it all to you, I perceive plainly, Sir, that you are not one that can be easily outwitted.

ISAAC. Egad, you're right, madam—you're right I'faith.                140

ENTER MAID. Here's a gentleman at the door, who begs permission to speak with Signor Isaac.

ISAAC. O, a friend of mine ma'am, and a trusty friend—Let him come in.                                                        [*Exit* MAID.

He is one to be depended on, ma'am.

ENTER CARLOS. So, coz.                                        [*aside*.

CARLOS. I have left Donna Clara safe at your lodgings; but can no
where find Antonio.

ISAAC. Well I will search him out myself anon—Carlos, you rogue,
I thrive, I prosper.                                                    150

CARLOS. Where is your mistress?

ISAAC. There, you booby, there she stands.

CARLOS. Why she's dam'd ugly.

ISAAC. Hush!                                          [*Stops his mouth.*

DUENNA. What is your friend saying, Signor?

ISAAC. O ma'am, he is expressing his raptures at such charms as he never
saw before, hey Carlos?

CARLOS. Aye, such as I never saw before, indeed.

DUENNA. You are a very obliging Gentleman—well, Signor Isaac, I
believe we had better part for the present. Remember our plan.          160

ISAAC. O, ma'am, it is written in my heart, fixed as the image of those
divine beauties—adieu, Idol of my soul—yet, once more permit me.—
                                                       [*kisses her.*

DUENNA. Sweet, courteous Sir, adieu.

ISAAC. Your slave eternally—come Carlos, say something civil at taking
leave.

CARLOS. I'faith, Isaac, she is the hardest woman to compliment I ever
saw, however, I'll try something I had studied for the occasion.

### SONG

Ah! sure a pair was never seen,
So justly form'd to meet by nature.
The youth excelling so in mien,                                          170
The maid in ev'ry grace of feature.
O how happy are such lovers,
When kindred beauties each discovers.
For surely she
Was made for thee,
And thou to bless this lovely creature.

So mild your looks, your children thence,
Will early learn the task of duty,
The boys with all their father's sense,
The girls with all their mother's beauty.                               180
Oh! how charming to inherit,
At once such graces and such spirit.
Thus while you live
May fortune give,
Each blessing equal to your merit.

[*Exeunt* ISAAC, CARLOS, *and* DUENNA.

## SCENE III—*A Library*

JEROME *and* FERDINAND *discovered.*

JEROME. Object to Antonio? I have said it! his poverty, can you acquit him of that?

FERD. Sir, I own he is not over rich—but he is of as antient and as reputable a family as any in the kingdom.

JEROME. Yes, I know the beggars are a very ancient family in most kingdoms; but never in any great repute, boy.

FERD. Antonio, Sir, has many amiable qualities.

JEROME. But he is poor, can you clear him of that, I say—is he not a gay, dissipated rake, who has squander'd his patrimony?

FERD. Sir, he inherited but little; and that his generosity, more than his profuseness, has stript him of—but he has never sullied his honor, which, with his title, has outlived his means.

JEROME. Psha! you talk like a blockhead! nobility without an estate is as ridiculous as gold-lace on a frize-coat.

FERD. This language, Sir, wou'd better become a Dutch or English trader, than a Spaniard.

JEROME. Yes; and those Dutch and English traders, as you call them, are the wiser people. Why, booby, in England they were formerly as nice as to birth and family as we are—but they have long discover'd what a wonderful purifier gold is—and now no one there regards pedigree in any thing but a horse.

FERD. True Sir, and the consequence is, that a nobleman is surer of the breed of his poney than the legitimacy of his heir.

JEROME. Ferdinand—I insist on it that this subject be dropt once for all.—O, here comes Isaac! I hope he has prosper'd in his suit.

FERD. Doubtless, that agreeable figure of his must have help'd his cause surprizingly.

JEROME. How now?                    [FERD. *walks aside.*

### *Enter* ISAAC.

Well, my friend, have you soften'd her?

ISAAC. O yes; I have soften'd her.

JEROME. What, does she come to?

ISAAC. Why, truely, she was kinder than I expected to find her.

JEROME. And the dear pretty little Angel was civil, hey!

ISAAC. Yes, the pretty little Angel was very civil.

JEROME. I'm transported to hear it, well, and you were astonished at her beauty, hey?

ISAAC. I was astonished indeed! pray, how old is miss?

JEROME. How old? let me see—eight and twelve—she is just twenty.

ISAAC. Twenty?

JEROME. Aye, to a month.                                                        40

ISAAC. Then, upon my soul, she is the oldest looking girl of her age in
Christendom.

JEROME. Do you think so? but I believe you will not see a prettier girl.

ISAAC. Here and there one.

JEROME. Louisa has the family face.

ISAAC. Yes, egad, I shou'd have taken it for a family face, and one that
has been in the family some time too.                         [*half aside.*

JEROME. She has her father's eyes.

ISAAC. Truely I shou'd have guess'd them to have been so—and if she
had her mother's spectacles I believe she would not see the worse. [*aside.* 50

JEROME. Her aunt Ursula's nose, and her grandmother's forehead to a hair.

ISAAC. Ay, faith, and her grandfather's chin to a hair.            [*aside.*

JEROME. Well, if she was but as dutiful as she's handsome—and harky,
friend Isaac, she is none of your made up beauties—her charms are of
the lasting kind.

ISAAC. I'faith, so they shou'd—for if she be but twenty now, she may
double her age, before her years will overtake her face.

JEROME. Why, zounds, master Isaac, you are not sneering, are you?

ISAAC. Why, now seriously, Don Jerome, do you think your daughter
handsome?                                                                      60

JEROME. By this light, she's as handsome a girl as any in Seville.

ISAAC. Then, by these eyes, I think her as plain a woman as ever I beheld.

JEROME. By St. Iago you must be blind.

ISAAC. No, no; 'tis you are partial.

JEROME. How! have I neither sense nor taste? If a fair skin, fine eyes,
teeth of ivory, with a lovely bloom, and a delicate shape—if these,
with a heavenly voice, and a world of grace, are not charms, I know
not what you call beautiful.

ISAAC. Good lack, with what eyes a father sees! As I have life, she is
the very reverse of all this, as for the dimity skin you told me of, I  70
swear 'tis a thorough nankeen as ever I saw; for her eyes, their utmost
merit is in not squinting—for her teeth, where there is one of ivory,
its neighbour is pure ebony, black and white alternately, just like the
keys of an harpsicord. Then as to her singing, and heavenly voice—
by this hand, she has a shrill crack'd pipe, that sounds for all the world
like a child's trumpet.

JEROME. Why, you little Hebrew scoundrel, do you mean to insult me?
out of my house, out, I say.

FERD. Dear Sir, what's the matter?

JEROME. Why, this Israelite here, has the impudence to say your sister's  80
ugly.

FERD. He must be either blind or insolent.

ISAAC. So, I find they are all in a story. Egad, I believe I have gone too far.                                                           [*aside.*

FERD. Sure, Sir, there must be some mistake—It can't be my sister whom he has seen.

JEROME. S'death! you are as great a fool as he, what mistake can there be? did not I lock up Louisa myself, and hav'n't I the key in my own pocket? And didn't her maid shew him into the dressing room? and yet you talk of a mistake, no, the Portugueze meant to insult me— 90 and, but that this roof protects him, old as I am, this sword shou'd do me justice.

ISAAC. I must get off as well as I can—her fortune is not the less handsome.                                                            [*aside.*

### DUET

ISAAC.    Believe me, good Sir, I ne'er meant to offend,
          My mistress I love, and I value my friend:
          To win her, and wed her, is still my request,
          For better, for worse, and I swear I don't jest.

JEROME. Zounds! you'd best not provoke me, my rage is so high.

ISAAC.    Hold him fast, I beseech you, his rage is so high,         100
          Good Sir, you're too hot and this place I must fly.

JEROME. You're a knave and a sot, and this place you'd best fly.

ISAAC. Don Jerome, come now, let us lay aside all joking and be serious.

JEROME. How?

ISAAC. Ha, ha, ha! I'll be hang'd if you hav'n't taken my abuse of your daughter seriously.

JEROME. You meant it so, did not you?

ISAAC. O mercy, no! a joke—just to try how angry it wou'd make you.

JEROME. Was that all I'faith! I did'n't know you had been such a wag; ha, ha, ha! By St. Iago, you made me very angry tho', well, and you 110 do think Louisa handsome?

ISAAC. Handsome! Venus de Medicis was a sybil to her.

JEROME. Give me your hand, you little jocose rogue—Egad, I thought we had been all off.

FERD. So! I was in hopes this would have been a quarrel; but I find the Jew is too cunning.

JEROME. Aye, this gust of passion has made me dry—I am but seldom ruffled; order some wine in the next room—let us drink the girl's health—poor Louisa! ugly, heh! Ha, ha, ha! 'Twas a very good joke indeed.                                                               120

ISAAC. And a very true one for all that.                          [*aside.*

JEROME. And, Ferdinand, I insist upon your drinking success to my friend.

FERD. Sir, I will drink success to my friend with all my heart.

JEROME. Come, little Solomon, if any sparks of anger had remain'd, this would be the only way to quench them.

### TRIO

A bumper of good liquor,
Will end a contest quicker,
Than justice, judge or vicar.
 So fill a cheerful glass,    130
 And let good humour pass.

But if more deep the quarrel,
Why, sooner drain the barrel,
Than be the hateful fellow,
That's crabbed when he is mellow.
 A bumper, &c.    [*Exeunt.*

### SCENE IV—ISAAC's *Lodgings*

#### *Enter* LOUISA.

LOUISA. Was ever truant daughter so whimsically circumstanced as I am! I have sent my intended husband to look after my lover—the man of my father's choice is gone to bring me the man of my own, but how dispiriting is this interval of expectation?

### SONG

What bard, O time discover,
 With wings first made thee move;
Ah! sure he was some lover,
 Who ne'er had left his love.

For who that once did prove,
 The pangs which absence brings,    10
  Tho' but one day,
  He were away,
Could picture thee with wings.

#### *Enter* CARLOS.

So, friend, is Antonio found?

CARLOS. I could not meet with him, lady; but I doubt not my friend Isaac will be here with him presently.

LOUISA. O shame! you have used no diligence—Is this your courtesy to a lady who has trusted herself to your protection?

CARLOS. Indeed, madam, I have not been remiss.

LOUISA. Well, well; but if either of you had known how each moment  20

of delay weighs upon the heart of her who loves, and waits the object
of her love, O, ye wou'd not then have trifled thus.

CARLOS. Alas! I know it well.

LOUISA. Were you ever in love then?

CARLOS. I was, lady: but while I have life will never be again.

LOUISA. Was your mistress so cruel?

CARLOS. If she had always been so, I shou'd have been happier.

*SONG*

> O had my love ne'er smil'd on me,
>   I ne'er had known such anguish;
> But think how false, how cruel she,       30
>   To bid me cease to languish.
> To bid me hope her hand to gain,
>   Breathe on a flame half perish'd,
> And then with cold and fix'd disdain,
>   To kill the hope she cherish'd.
>
> Not worse his fate, who on a wreck,
>   That drove as winds did blow it,
> Silent had left the shatter'd deck,
>   To find a grave below it.
> Then land was cried—no more resign'd,       40
>   He glow'd with joy to hear it,
> Not worse his fate, his woe to find,
>   The wreck must sink ere near it.

LOUISA. As I live, here is your friend coming with Antonio—I'll retire
for a moment to surprize him.       [*Exit.*

*Enter* ISAAC *and* ANTONIO.

ANTONIO. Indeed, my friend Isaac, you must be mistaken. Clara
D'Almanza in love with me, and employ you to bring me to meet her!
It is impossible!

ISAAC. That you shall see in an instant—Carlos, where is the lady?
[CARLOS *points to the doors*] In the next room is she?       50

ANTONIO. Nay, if that lady is really here, she certainly wants me to
conduct her to a dear friend of mine, who has long been her lover.

ISAAC. Psha! I tell you 'tis no such thing—you are the man she wants,
and nobody but you. Here's, ado to persuade you to take a pretty girl
that's dying for you.

ANTONIO. But I have no affection for this lady.

ISAAC. And you have for Louisa, hey? but take my word for it, Antonio,
you have no chance there—so you may as well secure the good that
offers itself to you.

ANTONIO. And could you reconcile it to your conscience, to supplant 60 your friend?

ISAAC. Pish! Conscience has no more to do with gallantry than it has with politicks—why, you are no honest fellow, if love can't make a rogue of you—so come,—do go in and speak to her at least.

ANTONIO. Well, I have no objection to that,

ISAAC. [opens the door]. There—there she is—yonder by the window— get in, do [pushes him in, and half shuts the door] now, Carlos, now I shall hamper him I warrant—stay—I'll peep how they go on—egad, he looks confoundedly posed—now she's coaxing him—see, Carlos, he begins to come to—aye, aye, he'll soon forget his conscience.     70

CARLOS. Look! now they are both laughing.

ISAAC. Aye! so they are both laughing—yes, yes, they are laughing at that dear friend he talked of—aye poor devil, they have outwitted him.

CARLOS. Now he's kissing her hand.

ISAAC. Yes, yes, faith, they're agreed—he's caught, he's entangled— my dear Carlos, we have brought it about. O, this little cunning head! I'm a Machiavel, a very Machieval.

CARLOS. I hear somebody enquiring for you—I'll see who it is.

[Exit CARLOS.

*Enter* ANTONIO *and* LOUISA.

ANTONIO. Well, my good friend, this lady has so entirely convinc'd me of the certainty of your success at Don Jerome's, that I now resign 80 my pretensions there.

ISAAC. You never did a wiser thing, believe me—and as for deceiving your friend, that's nothing at all—tricking is all fair in love, isn't it, ma'am?

LOUISA. Certainly, Sir, and I am particularly glad to find you are of that opinion.

ISAAC. O lud, yes, ma'am—let any one outwit me that can, I say— but here let me join your hands—there you lucky rogue, I wish you happily married from the bottom of my soul.

LOUISA. And I am sure, if you wish it, no one else shou'd prevent it.

ISAAC. Now, Antonio, we are rivals no more, so let us be friends, will 90 you.

ANTONIO. With all my heart, Isaac.

ISAAC. It is not every man, let me tell you, that wou'd have taken such pains, or been so generous to a rival.

ANTONIO. No, faith, I don't believe there's another beside yourself in Spain.

ISAAC. Well, but you resign all pretensions to the other lady?

ANTONIO. That I do most sincerely.

ISAAC. I doubt you have a little hankering there still.

ANTONIO. None in the least, upon my soul.     100

ISAAC. I mean after her fortune?

ANTONIO. No, believe me. You are heartily welcome to every thing she has.

ISAAC. Well, I'faith, you have the best of the bargain as to beauty, twenty to one—now I'll tell you a secret—I am to carry off Louisa this very evening.

LOUISA. Indeed!

ISAAC. Yes, she has sworn not to take a husband from her father's hand— so, I've persuaded him to trust her to walk with me in the garden, and then we shall give him the slip.                                          110

LOUISA. And is Don Jerome to know nothing of this?

ISAAC. O lud no: there lies the jest! Don't you see that, by this step, I over-reach him, I shall be intitled to the girl's fortune without settling a ducat on her, ha, ha, ha! I'm a cunning dog, a'n't I? A sly little villain, heh?

ANTONIO. Ha, ha, ha! you are indeed!

ISAAC. Roguish you'll say—but keen hey?—devilish keen!

ANTONIO. So you are indeed—keen—very keen.

ISAAC. And what a laugh we shall have at Don Jerome's, when the truth comes out, hey?                                                            120

LOUISA. Yes, I'll answer for't, we shall have a good laugh when the truth comes out, ha, ha, ha!

*Enter* CARLOS.

CARLOS. Here are the dancers come to practice the fandango[1] you in- tended to have honor'd Donna Louisa with.

ISAAC. O, I sha'n't want them, but as I must pay them, I'll see a caper for my money—will you excuse me?

LOUISA. Willingly.

ISAAC. Here's my friend, whom you may command for any services, Madam, your most obedient—Antonio, I wish you all happiness. O the easy blockhead! what a fool I have made of him?—This was a   130 master-piece.                                              [*Exit* ISAAC.

LOUISA. Carlos, will you be my guard again, and conduct me to the Convent of St. Catherine?

ANTONIO. Why, Louisa, why shou'd you go thither?

LOUISA. I have my reasons, and you must not be seen to go with me, I shall write from thence to my father, perhaps, when he finds what he has driven me to, he may relent.

ANTONIO. I have no hope from him—O Louisa, in these arms should be your sanctuary.

---

[1] 'End of Act II—a new Spanish Dance by Signor and Signora Zucelli, Mr. Dague- ville, Signora Vidini, etc.' (*The Gazetteer*, 21 Nov. 1775). It was given fourteen per- formances, then dropped. After this, Isaac was probably given the present lines 125-6.

LOUISA. Be patient but for a little while—my father cannot force me thence.    140
But let me see you there before evening, and I will explain myself.
ANTONIO. I shall obey.
LOUISA. Come friend—Antonio, Carlos has been a lover himself.
ANTONIO. Then he knows the value of his trust.
CARLOS. You shall not find me unfaithful.

### TRIO

Soft pity never leaves the gentle breast,
Where love has been received a welcome guest,
As wand'ring saints poor huts have sacred made,
He hallows ev'ry heart he once has sway'd;
And when his presence we no longer share,    150
Still leaves compassion as a relic there.

[*Exeunt* CARLOS, LOUISA, *and* ANTONIO.

END OF ACT II

# ACT III

## SCENE I.—*A Library*

*Enter* JEROME, *and* SERVANT.

JEROME. Why, I never was so amazed in my life! Louisa gone off
with Isaac Mendoza! what, steal away with the very man whom I
wanted her to marry—elope with her own husband as it were—it is
impossible.
SERVANT. Her maid says, Sir, they had your leave to walk in the garden
while you was abroad: The door by the shrubbery was found open,
and they have not been heard of since.    [*Exit.*
JEROME. Well, it is the most unaccountable affair! s'death, there is
certainly some infernal mystery in it, I can't comprehend.

*Enter* 2D SERVANT, *with a Letter.*

SERVANT. Here is a letter, Sir, from Signor Isaac.    [*Exit.*    10
JEROME. So, so, this will explain—ay, 'Isaac Mendoza,' let me see.
[*Reads*] 'Dearest Sir, you must, doubtless, be much surprized at my
flight with your daughter'—Yes, faith and well I may. 'I had the
happiness to gain her heart at our first interview'—The devil you had!
'But she having unfortunately made a vow not to receive a husband
from your hands, I was obliged to comply with her whim' So, so!

'We shall shortly throw ourselves at your feet, and I hope you will have
a blessing ready for one who will then be

Your son-in-law,

ISAAC MENDOZA.'    20

A whim, heigh? Why, the devil's in the girl, I think—This morning
she wou'd die sooner than have him, and before evening she runs
away with him. Well, well, my will's accomplished—let the motive
be what it will—and the Portugueze, sure, will never deny to fulfill
the rest of the article.

Re-enter SERVANT with another letter.

SERVANT. Sir, here's a man below who says he brought this from my
    young lady, Donna Louisa,                    [*Exit.*

JEROME. How! yes, it is my daughter's hand indeed! lord, there was
    no occasion for them both to write; well, let's see what she says:
    [*reads*] 'My dearest father, how shall I intreat your pardon for the rash   30
    step I have taken, how confess the motive?' Pish! hasn't Isaac just
    told me the motive—one would think they weren't together, when they
    wrote. 'If I have a spirit too resentful of ill usage, I have also a heart as
    easily affected by kindness'—So, so, here the whole matter comes out,
    her resentment for Antonio's ill usage, has made her sensible of Isaac's
    kindness—yes, yes, it is all plain enough—well 'I am not married yet,
    tho' with a man I am convinced adores me'—Yes, yes, I dare say
    Isaac is very fond of her—'but I shall anxiously expect your answer,
    in which, should I be so fortunate as to receive your consent, you
    will make compleatly happy,                    40

Your ever affectionate daughter,

LOUISA.'

My consent! to be sure she shall have it; egad, I was never better
pleased—I have fulfilled my resolution—I knew I should—O there's
nothing like obstinacy—Lewis!                    [*Calls.*

Enter SERVANT.

Let the man who brought the last letter wait, and get me a pen and
ink below. (*Exit* SERVANT) I am impatient to set poor Louisa's heart
at rest, holloa! Lewis! Sancho!

Enter SERVANTS.

See that there be a noble supper provided in the Saloon to-night—
  serve up my best wines, and let me have music, d'ye hear?                    50

SERVANTS. Yes, sir.                    [*Exeunt.*

JEROME. And order all my doors to be thrown open—admit all guests
    with masks or without masks—I'faith, we'll have a night of it—And
    I'll let 'em see how merry an old man can be.

## SONG

O the days when I was young,
   When I laugh't in fortune's spight,
Talk'd of love the whole day long,
   And with nectar crown'd the night,
Then it was old father Care,
   Little reck'd I of thy frown,         60
Half thy malice youth could bear,
   And the rest a bumper drown.

Truth they say lies in a well,
   Why I vow I ne'er could see,
Let the water-drinkers tell,
   There it always lay for me.
For when sparkling wine went round,
   Never saw I falsehood's mask,
But still honest truth I found,
   In the bottom of each flask.         70

True, at length my vigour's flown,
   I have years to bring decay;
Few the locks that now I own,
   And the few I have, are grey.
Yet, old Jerome, thou may'st boast,
   While thy spirits do not tire,
Still beneath thy age's frost;
   Glows a spark of youthful fire.     *[Exit.*

### SCENE II.—*The New Piazza*

*Enter* FERDINAND, *and* LOPEZ.

FERD. What, cou'd you gather no tidings of her? Nor guess where she
was gone? O Clara! Clara!

LOPEZ. In truth, Sir, I could not—that she was run away from her father,
was in every body's mouth,—and that Don Guzman was in pursuit
of her, was also a very common report—where she was gone, or what
was become of her, no one could take upon 'em to say.

FERD. S'death and fury, you blockhead, she cant be out of Seville.

LOPEZ. So I said to myself, Sir! S'death and fury, you blockhead, says
I, she can't be out of Seville—then some said, she had hang'd herself
for love, and others have it, Don Antonio had carried her off.     10

FERD. 'Tis false, scoundrel! no one said that.

LOPEZ. Then I misunderstood 'em, Sir.

FERD. Go, fool, get home, and never let me see you again, till you bring me news of her.                                             [*Exit* LOPEZ.

O! how my fondness for this ungrateful girl, has hurt my disposition!

### SONG

Ah, cruel maid, how hast thou changed
  The temper of my mind?
My heart by thee from mirth estrang'd
  Becomes, like thee, unkind.
By fortune favour'd, clear in fame                           20
  I once ambitious was;
And friends I had, that fann'd the flame,
  And gave my youth applause.

But now my weakness all abuse,
  Yet vain their taunts on me,
Friends, fortune, fame itself I'd lose;
  To gain one smile from thee.
Yet, only thou shouldst not despise
  My folly, or my woe;
If I am mad in others eyes,                                  30
  'Tis thou hast made me so.

But days like these, with doubting curst
  I will not long endure;
Am I despised, I know the worst,
  And also know my cure.
If false, her vows she dare renounce,
  She instant ends my pain,
For, Oh, that heart must break at once;
  Which cannot hate again.

*Enter* ISAAC.

ISAAC. So, I have her safe—and have only to find a priest to marry us, 40 Antonio now may marry Clara, or not, if he pleases.

FERD. What? what was that you said of Clara?

ISAAC. O Ferdinand! my brother-in-law that shall be, who thought of meeting you.

FERD. But what of Clara?

ISAAC. I'faith, you shall hear.—This morning as I was coming down, I met a pretty damsel, who told me her name was Clara d'Almanza, and begg'd my protection.

FERD. How?

ISAAC. She said she had eloped from her father, Don Guzman, but  50
   that love for a young gentleman in Seville, was the cause.

FERD. O heavens! did she confess it?

ISAAC. O yes, she confess'd at once—but then, says she, my lover is
   not inform'd of my flight, nor suspects my intention.

FERD. Dear creature! no more I did indeed! O, I am the happiest
   fellow—well, Isaac!                                    [aside.

ISAAC. Why, then she intreated me to find him out for her, and bring
   him to her.

FERD. Good heavens, how lucky! well, come along, lets lose no time,
                                                   [pulling him.

ISAAC. Zooks! where are we to go?                                   60

FERD. Why, did any thing more pass?

ISAAC. Any thing more!—yes, the end on't was, that I was moved by
   her speeches, and complied with her desires.

FERD. Well, and where is she?

ISAAC. Where is she? why, dont I tell you I complied with her request,
   and left her safe in the arms of her lover.

FERD. S'death! you trifle with me—I have never seen her.

ISAAC. You! O lud, no! How the devil shou'd you? 'Twas Antonio she
   wanted, and with Antonio I left her.

FERD. Hell and madness [aside] what Antonio d'Ercilla?                70

ISAAC. Aye, aye, the very man; and the best part of it was, he was shy
   of taking her at first—He talk'd a good deal about honor and conscience,
   and deceiving some dear friend; but, lord, we soon over ruled that.

FERD. You did?

ISAAC. O yes, presently—such deceit, says he—Pish! says the lady,
   tricking is all fair in love—but then, my friend, says he—Psha! damn
   your friend, says I—so, poor wretch, he has no chance—no, no—he
   may hang himself as soon as he pleases.

FERD. I must go, or I shall betray myself.                          [aside.

ISAAC. But stay, Ferdinand, you han't heard the best of the joke.    80

FERD. Curse on your joke.

ISAAC. Goodlack! what's the matter now? I thought to have diverted
   you.

FERD. Be rack'd, tortur'd, damn'd—

ISAAC. Why, sure you're not the poor devil of a lover are you? I'faith,
   as sure as can be, he is—this is a better joke than t'other, ha, ha, ha!

FERD. What do you laugh, you vile, mischievous varlet [collars him] but
   that you're beneath my anger, I'd tear your heart out.
                                          [Throws him from him.

ISAAC. O mercy! here's usage for a brother-in-law!

FERD. But, harky, rascal! tell me directly where these false friends are  90
   gone, or by my soul [draws.]

ISAAC. For heavens sake, now, my dear Brother-in-law don't be in a rage—I'll recollect as well as I can.

FERD. Be quick then!

ISAAC. I will, I will—but people's memories differ—some have a treacherous memory—now mine is a cowardly memory—it takes to its heels at sight of a drawn sword, it does I'faith—and I could as soon fight as recollect.

FERD. Zounds, tell me the truth, and I won't hurt you.

ISAAC. No, no; I know you won't, my dear brother-in-law—but that 100 ill looking thing there.

FERD. What, then, you won't tell me?

ISAAC. Yes, yes, I will—I'll tell you all upon my soul, but why need you listen sword in hand.

FERD. Well, there [*puts up*] now.

ISAAC. Why then, I believe they are gone to—that is my friend, Carlos, told me he had léft Donna Clara—dear Ferdinand keep your hand off—at the Convent of St. Catherine.

FERD. St. Catherine!

ISAAC. Yes; and that Antonio was to come to her there.          110

FERD. Is this the truth?

ISAAC. It is indeed; and all I know, as I hope for life.

FERD. Well, coward, take your life—'tis that false, dishonourable Antonio, who shall feel my vengeance.

ISAAC. Ay, ay, kill him—cut his throat and welcome.

FERD. But for Clara—infamy on her—she is not worth my resentment.

ISAAC. No more she is, my dear brother-in-law, I'faith I would not be angry about her—she is not worth it indeed.

FERD. 'Tis false—she is worth the enmity of princes.

ISAAC. True, true; so she is, and I pity you exceedingly for having lost 120 her.

FERD. S'death, you rascal! how durst you talk of pitying me.

ISAAC. O dear brother-in-law, I beg pardon—I don't pity you in the least, upon my soul.

FERD. Get hence, fool, and provoke me no further—Nothing but your insignificance saves you.

ISAAC. (*Aside*) I'faith, then my insignificance is the best friend I have—I'm going, dear Ferdinand—What a curst, hot-headed bully it is! [*Exit.*

FERD. From this hour, I disclaim all trust in man, or love for woman, but does Antonio think to triumph with impunity, when he has left 130 me no hope of joy on earth, but in revenge.

### SONG

Sharp is the woe, that wounds the jealous mind,
When treachery two fond hearts would rend,

But oh, how keener far, the pang to find
That traitor is our bosom friend.                    [*Exit.*

### SCENE III.—*The Garden of the Convent*

*Enter* LOUISA *and* CLARA.

LOUISA. And you really wish my brother may not find you out.

CLARA. Why else, have I conceal'd myself under this disguise?

LOUISA. Why, perhaps, because the dress becomes you, for you certainly don't intend to be a nun for life.

CLARA. If, indeed, Ferdinand had not offended me so, last night.

LOUISA. Come, come, it was his fear of losing you, made him so rash.

CLARA. Well, you may think me cruel—but I swear if he were here this instant, I believe I shou'd forgive him.

### SONG

#### CLARA

By him we love offended,
　　How soon our anger flies,
One day apart, 'tis ended,
　　Behold him and it dies,                    10

Last night, your roving brother,
　　Enrag'd I bade depart,
And sure his rude presumption,
　　Deserv'd to lose my heart.

Yet, were he now before me,
　　In spite of injured pride,
I fear my eyes wou'd pardon,
　　Before my tongue cou'd chide.                    20

With truth, the bold deceiver,
　　To me thus oft has said,
'In vain wou'd Clara slight me,
　　In vain wou'd she upbraid;
No scorn those lips discover,
　　Where dimples laugh the while,
No frowns appear resentful,
　　Where Heaven has stampt a smile.'

LOUISA. I protest Clara, I shall begin to think you are seriously resolved to enter on your probation.                    30

CLARA. And, seriously, I very much doubt whether the character of a nun wou'd not become me best.

LOUISA. Why, to be sure, the character of a nun is a very becoming one—at a masquerade—but no pretty woman in her senses ever thought of taking the veil for above a night.

CLARA. Yonder I see your Antonio is returned—I shall only interrupt you; ah, Louisa, with what happy eagerness you turn to look for him!

[*Exit.*

*Enter* ANTONIO.

ANTONIO. Well, my Louisa, any news since I left you?

LOUISA. None—The messenger is not returned from my father.

ANTONIO. Well, I confess, I do not perceive what we are to expect 40 from him.

LOUISA. I shall be easier however, in having made the trial, I do not doubt your sincerity, Antonio: but there is a chilling air around poverty that often kills affection, that was not nurs'd in it—If we would make love our household god, we had best secure him a comfortable roof.

*SONG*

How oft Louisa hast thou said
    (Nor wilt thou the fond boast disown)
Thou wouldst not lose Antonio's love
    To reign the partner of a throne.                    50

And by those lips that spoke so kind,
    And by this hand, I press'd to mine;
To be the lord of wealth and power,
    I swear, I would not part with thine.

Then how, my soul, can we be poor
    Who own what kingdoms could not buy?
Of this true heart, thou shalt be queen,
    And serving thee, a monarch I.

Thus uncontroul'd in mutual bliss,
    And rich in love's exhaustless mine;                 60
Do thou snatch treasures from my lips,
    And I'll take kingdoms back from thine.
            [*Enter* MAID, *with a letter to* LOUISA *and Exit.*

My father's answer I suppose.

ANTONIO. My dearest Louisa, you may be assured that it contains nothing but threats and reproaches.

LOUISA. Let us see however [*reads*] 'Dearest daughter, make your lover happy, you have my full consent to marry as your whim has chosen, but be sure come home to sup with your affectionate father'.

ANTONIO. You jest, Louisa.

LOUISA. [*Gives him the Letter*] Read—read.                                70

ANTONIO. 'Tis so, by heavens! sure there must be some mistake; but that's none of our business—now, Louisa, you have no excuse for delay.

LOUISA. Shall we not then return and thank my father?

ANTONIO. But first let the priest put it out of his power to recall his word.—I'll fly to procure one.

LOUISA. Nay, if you part with me again, perhaps you may lose me.

ANTONIO. Come then—there is a friar of a neighbouring convent is my friend; you have already been diverted by the manners of a nunnery—let us see, whether there is less hypocrisy among the holy fathers.                                                                  80

LOUISA. I'm afraid not, Antonio—for in religion, as in friendship, they who profess most are ever the least sincere.                    [*Exeunt.*

*Enter* CLARA.

CLARA. So, yonder they go, as happy as a mutual and confess'd affection can make them; while I am left in solitude. Heigho! love may perhaps excuse the rashness of an elopement from one's friend; but I am sure; nothing but the presence of the man we love can support it—Ha! what do I see; Ferdinand as I live, how cou'd he gain admission—by potent gold I suppose, as Antonio did—how eager and disturbed he seems—he shall not know me as yet.                              [*Lets down her veil.*]

*Enter* FERDINAND.

FERD. Yes, those were certainly they—my information was right.     90
                                                                  [*going.*

CLARA. [*Stops him*] Pray, Signor, what is your business here.

FERD. No matter—no matter—Oh, they stop—[*looks out*] yes, that is the perfidious Clara indeed.

CLARA. So, a jealous error—I'm glad to see him so mov'd.     [*aside.*

FERD. Her disguise can't conceal her—No, no, I know her too well.

CLARA. Wonderful discernment! but Signor—

FERD. Be quiet, good nun, don't teize me—by heavens she leans upon his arm, hangs fondly on it! O woman! woman!

CLARA. But, Signor, who is it you want?

FERD. Not you, not you, so, prythee don't torment me. Yet pray stay—   100
gentle nun, was it not Donna Clara d'Almanza just parted from you?

CLARA. Clara d'Almanza, Signor, is not yet out of the garden.

FERD. Aye, aye, I knew I was right—and pray, is not that gentleman now at the porch with her, Antonio d'Ercilla?

CLARA. It is indeed, Signor.

FERD. So, so, now but one question more—can you inform me for what purpose they have gone away?

CLARA. They are gone to be married, I believe.

FERD. Very well—enough—now if I don't marr their wedding.     [*Exit.*

CLARA. [*unveils*] I thought jealousy had made lovers quick-sighted, but 110 it has made mine blind—Louisa's story accounts to me for this error, and I am glad to find I have power enough over him to make him so unhappy—but why should not I be present at his surprize when undeceived? When he's thro' the porch I'll follow him, and, perhaps, Louisa shall not singly be a bride.


### SONG

Adieu, thou dreary pile, where never dies,
The sullen echo of repentant sighs:
Ye sister mourners of each lonely cell,
Inured to hymns and sorrow, fare ye well;
For happier scenes I fly this darksome grove,          120
To saints a prison, but a tomb to love.          [*Exit.*


### SCENE IV—*A Court before the Priory*

*Enter* ISAAC, *crossing the Stage.*

*Enter* ANTONIO.

ANTONIO. What, my friend Isaac:

ISAAC. What, Antonio! wish me joy! I have Louisa safe.

ANTONIO. Have you? I wish you joy with all my soul.

ISAAC. Yes, I am come here to procure a priest to marry us.

ANTONIO. So, then we are both on the same errand, I am come to look for father Paul.

ISAAC. Hah! I am glad on't—but I'faith he must tack me first, my love is waiting.

ANTONIO. So is mine—I left her in the porch.

ISAAC. Aye, but I am in haste to get back to Don Jerome.          10

ANTONIO. And so am I too.

ISAAC. Well, perhaps he'll save time and marry us both together— or I'll be your father and you shall be mine—Come along—but you're oblig'd to me for all this.

ANTONIO. Yes, yes.          [*Exeunt.*

## SCENE V.¹—*A Room in the Priory*
### *Friars at a Table drinking*
#### *GLEE and CHORUS*

This bottle's the sun of our Table,
His beams are rosy wine;
We, Planets that are not able,
Without his help to shine,
Let mirth and glee abound,
You'll soon grow bright,
With borrow'd light;
And shine as he goes round.

PAUL. Brother Francis, toss the bottle about, and give me your toast.
FRANCIS. Have we drank the abbess of St. Ursuline?                    10
AUG. Yes, yes; she was the last.
FRANCIS. Then I'll give you the blue-ey'd nun of St. Catherine's.
PAUL. With all my heart [*drinks*]. Pray brother, Augustine, were there
     any benefactions left in my absence?
FRANCIS. Don Juan Corduba has left an hundred ducats to remember
     him in our masses.
PAUL. Has he! let them be paid to our wine merchant, and we'll remem-
     ber him in our cups, which will do just as well. Any thing more?
AUG. Yes, Baptista, the rich miser, who died last week, has bequeath'd
     us a thousand Pistoles, and the silver lamp he used in his own chamber, 20
     to burn before the image of St. Anthony.
PAUL. 'Twas well meant; but we'll employ his money better—Baptista's
     bounty shall light the living, not the dead—St. Anthony is not afraid
     to be left in the dark, tho' he was—see who's there.
          [*A knocking*, FRANCIS *goes to the door, and opens it.*

#### *Enter* PORTER.

PORTER. Here's one without in pressing haste to speak with father
     Paul.
AUG. Brother Paul!
          [PAUL *comes from behind a curtain with a glass of wine,*
                         *and in his hand a piece of cake.*
PAUL. Here! how durst you, fellow, thus abruptly break in upon our
     devotions?
PORTER. I thought they were finished.                              30
PAUL. No they were not—were they brother Francis?

¹ R. C. Rhodes, *The Plays and Poems of . . . Sheridan* (Oxford, 1928), ii. 265–7, prints
this scene as it appeared in the *European Magazine*, iii (1783), 335–6, and suggests that
the version is a reconstruction from memory.

AUG. Not by a bottle each.

PAUL. But neither you nor your fellows mark how the hours go—no, you mind nothing but the gratifying of your appetites; ye eat and swill, and sleep, and gormandize, and thrive while we are wasting in mortification.

PORTER. We ask no more than nature craves.

PAUL. 'Tis false, ye have more appetites than hairs, and your flush'd, sleek, and pampered appearance is the disgrace of our order—out on't—if you are hungry, can't you be content with the wholesome roots of the earth, and if you are dry, isn't there the crystal spring [*drinks*]? 40 Put this away [*gives a glass*] and shew me where I'm wanted. [PORTER *drains the glass*—PAUL *going, turns*]—so, you wou'd have drunk it, if there had been any left. Ah, glutton! glutton!                [*Exeunt.*

### SCENE VI. *The Court before the Priory*

#### *Enter* ISAAC *and* ANTONIO.

ISAAC. A plaguy while coming this same father Paul—He's detain'd at vespers I suppose, poor fellow.

ANTONIO. No, here he comes.

Good father Paul, [*Enter* PAUL] I crave your blessing.

ISAAC. Yes good father Paul, we are come to beg a favour.

PAUL. What is it pray?

ISAAC. To marry us, good father Paul; and in truth, thou do'st look the very priest of Hymen.

PAUL. In short I may be called so; for I deal in repentance and mortification.                                                                          10

ISAAC. No, no, thou seem'st an officer of Hymen, because thy presence speaks content and good humour.

PAUL. Alas! my appearance is deceitful. Bloated I am, indeed, for fasting is a windy recreation, and it hath swoln me like a bladder.[1]

ANTONIO. But thou hast a good fresh colour in thy face father, rosy I'faith.

PAUL. Yes, I have blush'd for mankind, till the hue of my shame is as fixed as their vices.

ISAAC. Good man!

PAUL. And I have labour'd too—but to what purpose, they continue to sin under my very nose.                                                            20

ISAAC. Efecks, father, I shou'd have guess'd as much, for your nose seems to be put to the blush more than any other part of your face.

PAUL. Go, you're a wag.

ANTONIO. But to the purpose, father—will you officiate for us?

PAUL. To join young people thus clandestinely is not safe, and indeed, I have in my heart many weighty reasons against it.

---

[1] Gomez in Dryden's *Spanish Friar* is carbuncled and bloated, 'which he attributes to abstinence and fasting. . . . Paul says almost the same'. (*More Kotzebue* (1799), p. 13 n.)

ANTONIO. And I have in my hand many weighty reasons for it—Isaac, hav'n't you an argument or two in our favour about you?

ISAAC. Yes, yes; here is a most unanswerable purse.

PAUL. For shame, you make me angry; you forget that I am a Jacobin,[1]    30 and when importunate people have forced their trash—aye, into this pocket here—or into this—why, then the sin was theirs [*they put money into his pockets*] fie! now you distress me!—I wou'd return it, but that I must touch it that way, and so wrong my oath.

ANTONIO. Now then, come with us.

ISAAC. Aye, now give us our title to joy and rapture.

FRIAR. Well, when your hour of repentance comes, don't blame me.

ANTONIO. No bad caution to my friend Isaac [*aside*]. Well, well, father, do you do your part and I'll abide the consequence.

ISAAC. Aye, and so will I [*they are going.*]    40

*Enter* LOUISA [*running.*]

LOUISA. O, Antonio, Ferdinand is at the porch and enquiring for us.

ISAAC. Who? Don Ferdinand! he's not enquiring for me I hope.

ANTONIO. Fear not, my love, I'll soon pacify him.

ISAAC. Egad, you won't—Antonio, take my advice and run away; this Ferdinand is the most unmerciful dog! and has the cursedest long sword! and upon my soul he comes on purpose to cut your throat.

ANTONIO. Never fear, never fear.

ISAAC. Well, you may stay if you will—but I'll get some body else to marry me, for by St. Iago, he shall never meet me again, while I am master of a pair of heels. [*Runs out*—DONNA LOUISA *lets down her veil.*    50

*Enter* FERDINAND.

FERD. So, Sir, I have met with you at last.

ANTONIO. Well, Sir?

FERD. Base treacherous man! whence can a false, deceitful soul like yours borrow confidence to look so steadily on the man you've injured?

ANTONIO. Ferdinand, you are too warm—'tis true you find me on the point of wedding one I love beyond my life, but no argument of mine prevail'd on her to elope—I scorn deceit as much as you—by heav'n, I knew not she had left her father's till I saw her.

FERD. What a mean excuse! you have wrong'd your friend then, for one,    whose wanton forwardness anticipated your treachery—of this indeed,    60 your Jew pander inform'd me; but let your conduct be consistent, and since you have dar'd to do a wrong, follow me, and shew you have spirit to avow it.

---

[1] 'Any one the least conversant in Ecclesiastical Reading or that has ever landed on the Continent, must be sensible that the Jacobins, or Friars, are never dressed in blue; the former wearing a black Habit mixed with white on the fore part . . .' ('Spectator' in *St. James's Chronicle*, 12–14 Dec. 1775).

LOUISA. Antonio, I perceive his mistake—leave him to me.

PAUL. Friend, you are rude to interrupt the union of two willing hearts.

FERD. No, meddling priest, the hand he seeks is mine.

PAUL. If so, I'll proceed no further—lady, did you ever promise this youth your hand? [*To* LOUISA, *who shakes her head.*]

FERD. Clara, I thank you for your silence—I would not have heard your tongue avow such falsity—be't your punishment to remember I have not reproached you.                                                          70

*Enter* CLARA

CLARA. What mockery is this?

FERD. Antonio, you are protected now, but we shall meet.

[*Going,* CLARA *holds one arm and* LOUISA *the other.*]

*DUET*

| LOUISA. | Turn thee round I pray thee, |
| | Calm awhile thy rage, |
| CLARA. | I must help to stay thee, |
| | And thy wrath assuage. |
| LOUISA. | Could'st thou not discover |
| | One so dear to thee? |
| CLARA. | Can'st thou be a lover, |
| | And thus fly from me?          [*both unveil.* |

(line 80)

FERD. How's this! my sister! Clara too—I'm confounded.

LOUISA. 'Tis even so, good brother.

PAUL. How! what impiety! Did the man want to marry his own sister?

LOUISA. And arn't you asham'd of yourself not to know your own sister?

CLARA. To drive away your own mistress—

LOUISA. Don't you see how jealousy blinds people?

CLARA. Aye, and will you ever be jealous again?                      90

FERD. Never—never—you, sister, I know will forgive me—but how, Clara, shall I presume——

CLARA. No, no, just now you told me not to tieze you 'Who do you want, good Signor?' 'not you, not you.' O you blind wretch! but swear never to be jealous again, and I'll forgive you.

FERD. By all—

CLARA. There, that will do—you'll keep the oath just as well.

[*gives her hand.*

LOUISA. But, brother, here is one, to whom some apology is due.

FERD. Antonio, I am asham'd to think—

ANTONIO. Not a word of excuse, Ferdinand—I have not been in love       100

myself, without learning that a lover's anger shou'd never be resented—
but come—let us retire with this good father, and we'll explain to you
the cause of your error.

*GLEE and CHORUS*

Oft' does Hymen smile to hear,
  Wordy vows of feign'd regard;
Well he knows when they're sincere.
  Never slow to give reward:
For his glory is to prove,
  Kind to those who wed for love.          [*Exeunt.*

## SCENE VII.—*and Last. A Grand Saloon*

*Enter* DON JEROME, LOPEZ, *and* SERVANTS.

JEROME. Be sure now let every thing be in the best order—let all my
  Servants have on their merriest faces—but tell 'em to get as little
  drunk as possible till after supper. So, Lopez, where's your master?
  sha'n't we have him at supper.

LOPEZ. Indeed, I believe not, Sir—he's mad, I doubt; I'm sure he has
  frighted me from him.

JEROME. Aye, aye, he's after some wench, I suppose, a young rake!
  Well, well, we'll be merry without him.

*Enter a* SERVANT.

SERVANT. Sir, here is Signor Isaac.

*Enter* ISAAC.

JEROME. So, my dear son-in-law—there, take my blessing and forgive-  10
  ness, but where's my daughter? where's Louisa?

ISAAC. She's without impatient for a blessing, but almost afraid to enter.

JEROME. O fly and bring her in.          [*Exit* ISAAC.
  Poor girl, I long to see her pretty face.

ISAAC. [*without*] Come, my charmer! my trembling Angel!

*Enter* ISAAC *and* DUENNA, DON JEROME *runs to meet them* [*she kneels.*]

JEROME. Come to my arms, my—[*starts back*] why who the devil have
  we here?

ISAAC. Nay, Don Jerome, you promised her forgiveness; see how the
  dear creature droops.

JEROME. Droops indeed! Why, gad take me, this is old Margaret—  20
  but where's my daughter, where's Louisa?

ISAAC. Why here, before your eyes—nay, don't be abashed, my sweet
  wife!

JEROME. Wife with a vengeance! Why, zounds you have not married
  the Duenna!

MARGARET. [*kneeling*] O dear papa! you'll not disown me sure!

JEROME. Papa! dear papa! Why, zounds, your impudence is as great as your ugliness.

ISAAC. Rise, my charmer, go throw your snowy arms about his neck, and convince him you are—— 30

DUENNA. O Sir, forgive me!                                        [*Embraces him.*

JEROME. Help! murder!                                   [*Servants come forward.*

SERVANTS. What's the matter, Sir?

JEROME. Why here, this damn'd Jew, has brought an old Harridan to strangle me.

ISAAC. Lord, it is his own daughter, and he is so hard hearted he won't forgive her.

*Enter* ANTONIO *and* LOUISA, *they kneel.*

JEROME. Zounds and fury what's here now? who sent for you, Sir, and who the devil are you?

ANTONIO. This lady's husband, Sir.                                      40

ISAAC. Aye, that he is I'll be sworn; for I left 'em with the Priest, and was to have given her away.

JEROME. You were?

ISAAC. Aye; that's my honest friend, Antonio; and that's the little girl I told you I had hamper'd him with.

JEROME. Why, you are either drunk or mad—this is my daughter.

ISAAC. No, no; 'tis you are both drunk and mad, I think—here's your daughter.

JEROME. Hark'ee, old iniquity, will you explain all this or not?

DUENNA. Come then, Don Jerome, I will—tho' our habits might inform 50 you all—look on your daughter, there and on me.

ISAAC. What's this I hear?

DUENNA. The truth is, that in your passion this morning, you made a small mistake, for you turn'd your daughter out of doors, and lock'd up your humble servant.

ISAAC. O lud! O lud! here's a pretty fellow! to turn his daughter out of doors instead of an old Duenna.

JEROME. And, O lud! O lud! here's a pretty fellow to marry an old Duenna instead of my daughter—but how came the rest about?

DUENNA. I have only to add, that I remain'd in your daughter's place, and 60 had the good fortune to engage the affections of my sweet husband here.

ISAAC. Her husband! why, you old witch, do you think I'll be your husband now! this is a trick, a cheat, and you ought all to be asham'd of yourselves.

ANTONIO. Hark'ee, Isaac, do you dare to complain of tricking—Don Jerome, I give you my word, this cunning Portugueze has brought all this upon himself, by endeavouring to over-reach you by getting your daughter's fortune, without making any settlement in return.

JEROME. Over-reach me!

ANTONIO. 'Tis so indeed, Sir, and we can prove it to you.

JEROME. Why, gad take me, it must be so, or he cou'd never have put 70
up with such a face as Margaret's—so, little Solomon, I wish you
joy of your wife with all my soul.

LOUISA. Isaac, tricking is all fair in love—let you alone for the plot

ANTONIO. A cunning dog ar'n't you? A sly little villain, heh!

LOUISA. Roguish, perhaps; but keen, devilish keen.

JEROME. Yes, yes, his aunt always call'd him little Solomon.

ISAAC. Why, the plagues of Egypt upon you all—but do you think I'll
submit to such an imposition?

ANTONIO. Isaac, one serious word—you'd better be content as you are,
for believe me, you will find, that in the opinion of the world, there 80
is not a fairer subject for contempt and ridicule, than a knave become
the dupe of his own art.

ISAAC. I don't care—I'll not endure this—Don Jerome 'tis you have done
it—you wou'd be so curst positive about the beauty of her you lock'd
up, and all the time, I told you she was as old as my mother, and as
ugly as the Devil.

DUENNA. Why you little insignificant reptile.

JEROME. That's right—attack him, Margaret.

DUENNA. Dares such a thing as you pretend to talk of beauty—a walking
rouleau—a body that seems to owe all its consequence to the dropsy— 90
a pair of eyes like two dead beetles in a wad of brown dough. A beard
like an artichoke, with dry shrivell'd jaws that wou'd disgrace the
mummy of a monkey.

JEROME. Well done, Margaret.

DUENNA. But you shall know that I have a brother who wears a sword,
and if you don't do me justice—

ISAAC. Fire seize your brother, and you too—I'll fly to Jerusalem to
avoid you.

DUENNA. Fly where you will, I'll follow you.

JEROME. Throw your snowy arms about him, Margaret. 100

[*Exeunt* ISAAC *and* DUENNA.

But Louisa, are you really married to this modest gentleman?

LOUISA. Sir, in obedience to your commands I gave him my hand within
this hour.

JEROME. My commands!

ANTONIO. Yes, Sir, here is your consent under your own hand.

JEROME. How? wou'd you rob me of my child by a trick, a false pretence,
and do you think to get her fortune by the same means? why s'life,
you are as great a rogue as Isaac.

ANTONIO. No, Don Jerome, tho' I have profited by this paper in gaining
your daughter's hand, I scorn to obtain her fortune by deceit, there 110

Sir, [*Gives a letter*] now give her your blessing for a dower, and all
the little I possess, shall be settled on her in return. Had you wedded
her to a prince, he could do no more.

JEROME. Why, gad take me, but you are a very extraordinary fellow,
but have you the impudence to suppose no one can do a generous
action but yourself? Here Louisa, tell this proud fool of yours, that
he's the only man I know that wou'd renounce your fortune; and by
my soul, he's the only man in Spain that's worthy of it—there, bless
you both, I'm an obstinate old fellow when I am in the wrong; but
you shall now find me as steady in the right.                    120

*Enter* FERDINAND *and* CLARA

Another wonder still! why, Sirrah! Ferdinand, you have not stole a
nun, have you?

FERD. She is a nun in nothing but her habit, Sir—look nearer, and you
will perceive 'tis Clara d'Almanza, Don Guzman's daughter, and with
pardon for stealing a wedding, she is also my wife.

JEROME. Gadsbud,[1] and a great fortune—Ferdinand, you are a prudent
young rogue and I forgive you; and ifecks you are a pretty little damsel.
Give your father-in-law a kiss, you smiling rogue.

CLARA. There old gentleman, and now mind you behave well to us.

JEROME. Efecks, those lips ha'n't been chill'd by kissing beads—Egad,   130
I believe I shall grow the best humour'd fellow in Spain—Lewis,
Sancho, Carlos, d'ye hear, are all my doors thrown open? Our childrens
weddings are the only hollidays that age can boast, and then we drain
with pleasure, the little stock of spirits time has left us. [*Music within*]
But see, here come our friends and neighbours.

*Enter* MASQUERADERS.

And I'faith we'll make a night on't, with wine and dance, and catches—
then old and young shall join us.

*FINALE*

JEROME.              Come now for jest and smiling,
                     Both old and young beguiling,
                     Let us laugh and play, so blyth and gay,        140
                     Till we banish care away.


LOUISA.              Thus crown'd with dance and song,
                     The hours shall glide along,
                     With a heart at ease, merry, merry glees,
                     Can never fail to please,

---

[1] The oath associated with Sir Paul Plyant, 'an uxorious, Foolish, old Knight', in
Congreve's *The Double Dealer*.

FERDINAND.          Each bride with blushes glowing,
                    Our wine as rosy flowing,
                        Let us laugh and play, so blythe and gay,
                        Till we banish care away,—


ANTONIO.            Then, healths to every friend,                    150
                    The night's repast shall end,
                        With a heart at ease, merry, merry, glees,
                        Can never fail to please.


CLARA.              Nor while we are so joyous,
                    Shall anxious fear annoy us,
                        Let us laugh and play, so blythe and gay,
                        Till we banish care away.


JEROME.             For generous guests like these,
                    Accept the wish to please,
                        So we'll laugh and play, so blithe and gay,    160
                        Your smiles drive care away.        [*Exeunt omnes.*

# A TRIP TO SCARBOROUGH

# A
# TRIP
## TO
# SCARBOROUGH.

### A
## COMEDY.

AS PERFORMED AT THE

## THEATRE ROYAL

IN

## DRURY LANE.

ALTERED FROM

*Vanbrugh's Relapse*; *or*, *Virtue in Danger.*

By RICHARD BRINSLEY SHERIDAN, Esq.

LONDON.

Printed for G. WILKIE, No. 71, St. Paul's Church-yard.

MDCCLXXXI.

The title-page of the first edition of
*A Trip to Scarborough*

# PROLOGUE.

Written by DAVID GARRICK, Esq.
Spoken by Mr. KING.

WHAT various transformations we remark,
From East Whitechapel to the West Hyde-park!
Men, women, children, houses, signs, and fashions,
State, stage, trade, taste, the humours and the passions;
Th' Exchange, 'Change alley, wheresoe'er you're ranging,
Court, city, country, all are chang'd, or changing;
The streets sometime ago, were pav'd with stones,
Which, aided by a hackney coach, half broke your bones.
The purest lovers then indulg'd no bliss;
They run great hazard if they stole a kiss—                    10
*One chaste salute*—the Damsel cry'd, *O fye!*
As they approach'd, slap went the coach awry,
—Poor Sylvia got a bump, and Damon a black eye.
But now weak nerves in hackney coaches roam,
And the cramm'd glutton snores unjolted home:
Of former times that polish'd thing a *Beau*,
Is metamorphos'd now, from top to toe;
Then the full flaxen wig, spread o'er the shoulders,
Conceal'd the shallow head from the beholders!
But now the whole's revers'd—each fop appears,          20
Cropp'd, and trimm'd up—exposing head and ears;
The buckle then its modest limits knew—
Now, like the ocean, dreadful to the view,
Hath broke its bounds, and swallows up the shoe;
The wearer's foot, like his once fine estate,
Is almost lost, th' *incumbrance* is so great.
Ladies may smile—are they not in the plot?
The bounds of nature have not they forgot?
Were they design'd to be, when put together,
Made up, like shuttlecocks, of cork and feather?          30
Their pale fac'd grand-mama's appear'd with grace,
When dawning blushes rose upon the face;
No blushes now their once lov'd station seek,
The foe is in possession of the cheek!

No head of old, too high in feather'd state,
Hinder'd the fair to pass the lowest gate;
A church to enter now, they must be bent,
If ev'n they should try th' experiment.

As change thus circulates throughout the nation,
Some plays may justly call for alteration; 40
At least to draw some slender cov'ring o'er
That graceless wit,[1] which was too bare before:
Those writers well and wisely use their pens,
Who turn our Wantons into Magdalens;
And howsoever wicked wits revile 'em,
We hope to find in you, their Stage Asylum.

---

[1] 'And Van wants Grace, who never wanted Wit' ('The First Epistle of the Second Book of Horace, Imitated', *Imitations of Horace* in *The Poems of Alexander Pope*, ed. J. Butt (repr. edn., 1961), IV. 219, l. 289).

# DRAMATIS PERSONÆ.[1]

| | |
|---|---|
| Lord FOPPINGTON, | Mr. Dodd. |
| YOUNG FASHION, | Mr. Reddish. |
| LOVELESS, | Mr. Smith. |
| Colonel TOWNLY, | Mr. Brereton. |
| Sir TUNBELLY CLUMSEY, | Mr. Moody. |
| PROBE, | Mr. Parsons. |
| LORY, | Mr. Baddeley. |
| LA VAROLE, | Mr. Burton. |
| SHOEMAKER, | Mr. Carpenter. |
| TAYLOR, | Mr. Baker. |
| HOSIER, | Mr. Norris. |
| JEWELLER, | Mr. La Mash. |
| SERVANTS, etc. | Mr. Wrighten, Mr. Everard. |
| | |
| BERINTHIA, | Mrs. Yates. |
| AMANDA, | Mrs. Robinson. |
| MRS. COUPLER, | Mrs. Booth. |
| NURSE, | Mrs. Bradshaw. |
| MISS HOYDEN, | Mrs. Abington. |
| SERVANTS, etc. | Miss Platt, Mrs. Smith. |

[1] The leading parts (Foppington, Fashion, Loveless, Clumsey, Probe, Lory, Berinthia, Amanda, and Hoyden) are noted in the *London Evening Post*, 22–25 Feb. 1777. The players who took the shoemaker, tailor, and nurse, are named in the manuscript sent to the Lord Chamberlin (Larpent MS. 426 in the Huntington Library, California). The remainder are taken from the general list printed in the playbill of the second performance, and are allocated by following the Dramatis Personæ printed with the text of 1781.

# A TRIP TO SCARBOROUGH

## A COMEDY

## ACT I

### SCENE I, *the Hall of an Inn*

*Enter* YOUNG FASHION *and* LORY—Postillion *following with a Portmanteau.*

Y. FASHION. Lory, pay the post-boy, and take the portmanteau.

LORY. Faith, sir, we had better let the post-boy take the portmanteau and pay himself.

Y. FASHION. Why sure there's something left in it.

LORY. Not a rag, upon my honour, sir—we eat the last of your wardrobe at Newmalton[1]—and if we had had twenty miles farther to go, our next meal must have been off the cloak-bag.

Y. FASHION. Why 'sdeath it appears full.

LORY. Yes, sir—I made bold to stuff it with hay, to save appearances, and look like baggage. 10

Y. FASHION. What the devil shall I do!—harkee, boy, what's the chaise?

BOY. Thirteen shillings, please your honour.

Y. FASHION. Can you give me change for a guinea?

BOY. O yes, sir.

LORY. Soh, what will he do now?—Lord, sir, you had better let the boy be paid below.

Y. FASHION. Why, as you say, Lory, I believe it will be as well.

LORY. Yes, yes; tell them to discharge you below, honest friend.

BOY. Please your honour, there are the turnpikes too.

Y. FASHION. Aye, aye; the turnpikes by all means. 20

BOY. And I hope your honour will order me something for myself.

Y. FASHION. To be sure, bid them give you a crown.

LORY. Yes, yes—my master doesn't care what you charge them—so get along you——

BOY. Your honour promised to send the hostler——

LORY. P'shaw! damn the hostler—would you impose upon the gentleman's generosity?—[*Pushes him out*]—A rascal, to be so curst ready with his change!

Y. FASHION. Why faith, Lory, he had near pos'd me.

---

[1] Or Malton, a market town twenty-two miles from Scarborough.

LORY. Well, sir, we are arrived at Scarborough, not worth a guinea!—I 30
hope you'll own yourself a happy man—You have outliv'd all your cares.

Y. FASHION. How so, sir?

LORY. Why you have nothing left to take care of.

Y. FASHION. Yes, sirrah, I have myself and you to take care of still.

LORY. Sir, if you could prevail with some-body else to do that for you, I
fancy we might both fare the better for't—But now, sir, for my Lord
Foppington, your elder brother.

Y. FASHION. Damn my elder brother!

LORY. With all my heart; but get him to redeem your annuity however.—
Look you, sir, you must wheedle him, or you must starve.                    40

Y. FASHION. Look you, sir, I will neither wheedle him nor starve.

LORY. Why what will you do then?

Y. FASHION. Cut his throat, or get some one to do it for me.

LORY. Gad-so, sir, I'm glad to find I was not so well acquainted with the
strength of your conscience as with the weakness of your purse.

Y. FASHION. Why, art thou so impenetrable a blockhead as to believe
he'll help me with a farthing?

LORY. Not if you treat him *de haut en bas* as you used to do.

Y. FASHION. Why how would'st have me treat him?

LORY. Like a trout—tickle him.                                              50

Y. FASHION. I can't flatter.

LORY. Can you starve?

Y. FASHION. Yes.

LORY. I can't—Good-bye t'ye, sir.

Y. FASHION. Stay—thou'lt distract me. But who comes here—my old
friend, Colonel Townly?

*Enter* COLONEL TOWNLY.

My dear Colonel, I am rejoiced to meet you here.

TOWNLY. Dear Tom, this is an unexpected pleasure—what, are you
come to Scarbro' to be present at your brother's wedding?

LORY. Ah, sir, if it had been his funeral, we should have come with 60
pleasure.

TOWNLY. What, honest Lory, are you with your master still?

LORY. Yes, sir, I have been starving with him ever since I saw your
honour last.

Y. FASHION. Why, Lory is an attach'd rogue; there's no getting rid of
him.

LORY. True, sir, as my master says, there's no seducing me from his
service, 'till he's able to pay me my wages.                    [*Aside.*

Y. FASHION. Go, go, sir—and take care of the baggage.

LORY. Yes, sir—the baggage!—O Lord!—I suppose, sir, I must charge 70
the landlord to be very particular where he stows this.

Y. FASHION. Get along, you rascal. [*Exit* LORY, *with the Portmanteau.*
But, Colonel, are you acquainted with my proposed sister-in-law?

TOWNLY. Only by character—her father, Sir Tunbelly Clumsey, lives
within a quarter of a mile of this place, in a lonely old house, which
nobody comes near. She never goes abroad, nor sees company at home;
to prevent all misfortunes, she has her breeding within doors; the
parson of the parish teaches her to play upon the dulcimer; the clerk to
sing, her nurse to dress, and her father to dance:—in short, nobody has
free admission there but our old acquaintance, Mother Coupler, who   80
has procured your brother this match, and is, I believe, a distant
relation of Sir Tunbelly's.

Y. FASHION. But is her fortune so considerable?

TOWNLY. Three thousand a year, and a good sum of money independent
of her father beside.

Y. FASHION. 'Sdeath! that my old acquaintance, dame Coupler, could
not have thought of me as well as my brother for such a prize.

TOWNLY. Egad I wouldn't swear that you are too late—his Lordship, I
know, hasn't yet seen the lady, and, I believe, has quarrelled with his
patroness.                                                          90

Y. FASHION. My dear Colonel, what an idea have you started?

TOWNLY. Pursue it if you can, and I promise you you shall have my
assistance; for besides my natural contempt for his Lordship, I have at
present the enmity of a rival towards him.

Y. FASHION. What, has he been addressing your old flame, the sprightly
widow Berinthia?

TOWNLY. Faith, Tom, I am at present most whimsically circumstanced
—I came here near a month ago to meet the lady you mention; but she
failing in her promise, I, partly from pique, and partly from idleness,
have been diverting my chagrin by offering up chaste incense to the  100
beauties of Amanda, our friend Loveless's wife.

Y. FASHION. I have never seen her, but have heard her spoken of as a
youthful wonder of beauty and prudence.

TOWNLY. She is so indeed; and Loveless being too careless and insensible of the treasure he possesses—my lodging in the same house has
given me a thousand opportunities of making my assiduities acceptable;
so that in less than a fortnight, I began to bear my disappointment from
the widow, with the most Christian resignation.

Y. FASHION. And Berinthia has never appear'd?

TOWNLY. O there's the perplexity; for just as I began not to care whether  110
I ever saw her again or not, last night she arrived.

Y. FASHION. And instantly reassumed her empire.

TOWNLY. No faith—we met—but the lady not condescending to give
me any serious reasons for having fool'd me for a month, I left her in a
huff.

Y. FASHION. Well, well, I'll answer for't, she'll soon resume her power, especially as friendship will prevent your pursuing the other too far—but my coxcomb of a brother is an admirer of Amanda's too, is he?

TOWNLY. Yes; and I believe is most heartily despised by her—but come with me, and you shall see her and your old friend Loveless.       120

Y. FASHION. I must pay my respects to his Lordship—perhaps you can direct me to his lodgings.

TOWNLY. Come with me, I shall pass by it.

Y. FASHION. I wish you could pay the visit for me; or could tell me what I should say to him.

TOWNLY. Say nothing to him—apply yourself to his bag, his sword, his feather, his snuff-box; and when you are well with them, desire him to lend you a thousand pounds, and I'll engage you prosper.

Y. FASHION. 'Sdeath and furies! why was that coxcomb thrust into the world before me? O Fortune! Fortune! thou art a jilt, by Gad. [*Exit.* 130

### SCENE II, *a Dressing Room*

#### LORD FOPPINGTON, *in his Night Gown, and* LA VAROLE.

LD. FOPPINGTON. Well, 'tis an unspeakable pleasure to be a man of quality—strike me dumb!—even the boors of this Northern spa have learn'd the respect due to a title—La Varole!

LA VAROLE. Mi Lor——

LD. FOPPINGTON. You han't yet been at Muddy-Moat-Hall to announce my arrival, have you?

LA VAROLE. Not yet, mi Lor.

LD. FOPPINGTON. Then you need not go till Saturday.

[*Exit* LA VA.

as I am in no particular haste to view my intended Sposa—I shall sacrifice a day or two more to the pursuit of my friend Loveless's wife—      10 Amanda is a charming creature—strike me ugly; and if I have any discernment in the world, she thinks no less of my Lord Foppington.

#### *Enter* LA VAROLE.

LA VAROLE. Mi Lor, de shoemaker, de taylor, de hosier, de sempstress, de peru, be all ready, if your lordship please to dress.

LD. FOPPINGTON. 'Tis well, admit them.

LA VAROLE. Hey, Messieurs, entrez.

#### *Enter* TAYLOR, *&c. &c.*

LD. FOPPINGTON. So, gentlemen, I hope you have all taken pains to shew yourselves masters in your professions.

TAYLOR. I think I may presume to say, Sir——

LA VAROLE. My Lor, you clown you!    20

TAYLOR. My Lord, I ask your Lordship's pardon, my Lord. I hope, my Lord, your Lordship will please to own, I have brought your Lordship as accomplished a suit of clothes as ever Peer of England wore, my Lord—will your Lordship please to try 'em now?

LD. FOPPINGTON. Ay; but let my people dispose the glasses so, that I may see myself before and behind; for I love to see myself all round.

*Whilst he puts on his clothes, enter* YOUNG FASHION *and* LORY.

Y. FASHION. Hey-day! What the devil have we here?—Sure my gentleman's grown a favourite at court, he has got so many people at his levee.

LORY. Sir, these people come in order to make him a favourite at court—they are to establish him with the ladies.    30

Y. FASHION. Good Heav'n! to what an ebb of taste are women fallen, that it should be in the power of a laced coat to recommend a gallant to them!

LORY. Sir, Taylors and Hair-dressers are now become the bawds of the nation—'tis they that debauch all the women.

Y. FASHION. Thou say'st true; for there's that fop now has not, by nature, wherewithal to move a cook maid: and by the time these fellows have done with him, egad he shall melt down a Countess—but now for my reception.

LD. FOPPINGTON. Death and eternal tartures! Sir—I say the coat is too    40 wide here by a foot.

TAYLOR. My Lord, if it had been tighter, 'twould neither have hook'd nor button'd.

LD. FOPPINGTON. Rat the hooks and buttons, Sir, can any thing be worse than this?—As Gad shall jedge me! it hangs on my shoulders like a chairman's surtout.

TAYLOR. 'Tis not for me to dispute your Lordship's fancy.

LORY. There, Sir, observe what respect does.

Y. FASHION. Respect!—D—m him for a coxcomb—but let's accost him. —Brother, I'm your humble servant.    50

LD. FOPPINGTON. O Lard, Tam, I did not expect you in England—Brother, I'm glad to see you—but what has brought you to Scarbro' Tam?—Look you, Sir, [*to the Taylor*] I shall never be reconciled to this nauseous wrapping gown; therefore, pray get me another suit with all possible expedition; for this is my eternal aversion—Well, but Tam, you don't tell me what has driven you to Scarbro'?—Mrs. Callicoe, are not you of my mind?

SEMPSTRESS. Directly, my Lord.—I hope your Lordship is pleased with your ruffles?

LD. FOPPINGTON. In love with them, stap my vitals!—Bring my bill,    60 you shall be paid to-morrow.

SEMPSTRESS. I humbly thank your Lordship.                    [*Exit* SEMP.

LD. FOPPINGTON. Heark thee, shoemaker, these shoes a'nt ugly, but they don't fit me.

SHOEMAKER. My Lord, I think they fit you very well.

LD. FOPPINGTON. They hurt me just below the instep.

SHOEMAKER. [*feeling his foot*] No, my Lord, they don't hurt you there.

LD. FOPPINGTON. I tell thee they pinch me execrably.

SHOEMAKER. Why then, my Lord, if those shoes pinch you I'll be d—n'd.

LD. FOPPINGTON. Why wilt thou undertake to persuade me I cannot feel! 70

SHOEMAKER. Your Lordship may please to feel what you think fit, but that shoe does not hurt you—I think I understand my trade.

LD. FOPPINGTON. Now by all that's great and powerful, thou art an incomprehensible coxcomb—but thou makest good shoes, and so I'll bear with thee.

SHOEMAKER. My Lord, I have work'd for half the people of quality in this town these twenty years, and 'tis very hard I shoudn't know when a shoe hurts, and when it don't.

LD. FOPPINGTON. Well, prithee be gone about thy business. [*Exit* SHOE. Mr. Mendlegs, a word with you. The calves of these stockings are 80 thicken'd a little too much; they make my legs look like a porter's.

MENDLEGS. My Lord, methinks they look mighty well.

LD. FOPPINGTON. Aye, but you are not so good a judge of those things as I am—I have study'd them all my life—therefore pray let the next be the thickness of a crown piece less.

MENDLEGS. Indeed, my Lord, they are the same kind I had the honour to furnish your Lordship with in town.

LD. FOPPINGTON. Very possibly, Mr. Mendlegs; but *that* was in the beginning of the winter; and you should always remember, Mr. Hosier, that if you make a Nobleman's spring legs as robust as his 90 autumnal calves, you commit a manstrous impropriety, and make no allowance for the fatigues of the winter.

JEW. I hope, my Lord, those buckles have had the unspeakable satisfaction of being honoured with your Lordship's approbation?

LD. FOPPINGTON. Why they are of a pretty fancy; but don't you think them rather of the smallest?

JEW. My Lord, they could not well be larger to keep on your Lordship's shoe.

LD. FOPPINGTON. My good Sir, you forget that these matters are not as they used to be: formerly, indeed, the buckle was a sort of machine, 100 intended to keep on the shoe; but the case is now quite reversed, and the shoe is of no earthly use, but to keep on the buckle.—Now give me my watches, and the business of the morning will be pretty well over.

Y. FASHION. Well, Lory, what dost think on't?—a very friendly reception from a brother after three years absence!

LORY. Why, Sir, 'tis your own fault—here you have stood ever since you
came in, and have not commended any one thing that belongs to him.

Y. FASHION. Nor ever shall, while they belong to a coxcomb.—Now your
people of business are gone, brother, I hope I may obtain a quarter of
an hour's audience of you?                                                   110

LD. FOPPINGTON. Faith, Tam, I must beg you'll excuse me at this time,
for I have an engagement which I would not break for the salvation of
mankind. Hey!—there!—is my carriage at the door?—You'll excuse me,
brother.                                                          [Going.

Y. FASHION. Shall you be back to dinner?

LD. FOPPINGTON. As Gad shall jedge me, I can't tell, for it is passible I
may dine with some friends at Donner's.[1]

Y. FASHION. Shall I meet you there? for I must needs talk with you.

LD. FOPPINGTON. That I'm afraid may'nt be quite so praper;—for those
I commonly eat with are a people of nice conversation; and you know,   120
Tam, your education has been a little at large—but there are other
ordinaries in the town—very good beef ordinaries—I suppose, Tam,
you can eat beef?—However, dear Tam, I'm glad to see thee in England,
stap my vitals!                                                    [Exit.

Y. FASHION. Hell and furies! Is this to be borne?

LORY. Faith, Sir, I could almost have given him a knock o' the pate
myself.

Y. FASHION. 'Tis enough; I will now shew you the excess of my passion,
by being very calm.—Come, Lory, lay your loggerhead to mine, and,
in cold blood, let us contrive his destruction.                         130

LORY. Here comes a head, Sir, would contrive it better than us both, if
she would but join in the confederacy.

Y. FASHION. By this light, Madam Coupler; she seems dissatisfied at
something: let us observe her.

*Enter* COUPLER.

COUPLER. Soh! I am likely to be well rewarded for my services, truly;
my suspicions, I find, were but too just—What! refuse to advance me a
paltry sum, when I am upon the point of making him master of a
Galloon![2] But let him look to the consequences, an ungrateful, narrow-
minded coxcomb.

Y. FASHION. So he is, upon my soul, old lady: it must be my brother you   140
speak of.

COUPLER. Hah!—stripling, how came you here? What, hast spent all,
hey? And art thou come to dun his Lordship for assistance?

[1] The Assembly Rooms at Scarborough: see R. C. Rhodes, *The Plays and Poems of . . .
Sheridan* (Oxford, 1928), i. 284 n. 1.
[2] 'A ribbon of gold, silver or silk thread' (*O.E.D.*). Or 'galleon': cf. the next page,
l. 181.

Y. FASHION. No;—I want somebody's assistance to cut his Lordship's throat, without the risque of being hang'd for him.

COUPLER. Egad, sirrah, I could help thee to do him almost as good a turn without the danger of being burnt in the hand for't.

Y. FASHION. How—how, old Mischief?

COUPLER. Why you must know I have done you the kindness to make up a match for your brother.　　　　　　　150

Y. FASHION. I'm very much beholden to you, truly.

COUPLER. You may be before the wedding-day yet: the lady is a great heiress, the match is concluded, the writings are drawn, and his lordship is come hither to put the finishing hand to the business.

Y. FASHION. I understand as much.

COUPLER. Now you must know, stripling, your brother's a knave.

Y. FASHION. Good.

COUPLER. He has given me a bond of a thousand pounds for helping him to this fortune, and has promised me as much more in ready money upon the day of the marriage; which, I understand by a friend, he 160 never designs to pay me; and his just now refusing to pay me a part, is a proof of it. If, therefore, you will be a generous young rogue and secure me five thousand pounds, I'll help you to the lady.

Y. FASHION. And how the devil wilt thou do that?

COUPLER. Without the devil's aid, I warrant thee. Thy brother's face not one of the family ever saw; the whole business has been managed by me, and all the letters go thro' my hands. Sir Tunbelly Clumsey, my relation, (for that's the old gentleman's name) is apprized of his lord-ship's being down here, and expects him to morrow to receive his daughter's hand; but the Peer, I find, means to bait here a few days 170 longer, to recover the fatigue of his journey, I suppose. Now you shall go to Muddymoat-hall in his place. I'll give you a letter of introduction; and if you don't marry the girl before sun-set, you deserve to be hang'd before morning.

Y. FASHION. Agreed, agreed; and for thy reward——

COUPLER. Well, well;—tho' I warrant thou hast not a farthing of money in thy pocket now—no—one may see it in thy face.

Y. FASHION. Not a souse, by Jupiter.

COUPLER. Must I advance then?—well, be at my lodgings next door this evening, and I'll see what may be done—We'll sign and seal, and when 180 I have given thee some farther instructions, thou shalt hoist sail and be gone.　　　　　　　[*Exit* COUP.

Y. FASHION. So, Lory; Providence thou seest at last takes care of merit: we are in a fair way to be great people.

LORY. Aye, sir, if the devil don't step between the cup and the lip, as he uses to do.

Y. FASHION. Why, faith, he has play'd me many a damn'd trick to spoil

my fortune; and, egad, I'm almost afraid he's at work about it again
now; but if I should tell thee how, thou'dst wonder at me.

LORY. Indeed, sir, I should not.                              190

Y. FASHION. How dost know?

LORY. Because, sir, I have wondered at you so often, I can wonder at you
no more.

Y. FASHION. No! what wouldst thou say if a qualm of conscience should
spoil my design?

LORY. I would eat my words, and wonder more than ever!

Y. FASHION. Why faith, Lory, tho' I am a young Rake-hell, and have
play'd many a rogueish trick, this is so full-grown a cheat, I find I must
take pains to come up to't——I have scruples.

LORY. They are strong symptoms of death. If you find they encrease, sir,  200
pray make your will.

Y. FASHION. No, my conscience shan't starve me neither, but thus far
I'll listen to it. Before I execute this project, I'll try my brother to the
bottom. If he has yet so much humanity about him as to assist me (tho'
with a moderate aid) I'll drop my project at his feet, and shew him how
I can do for him much more than what I'd ask he'd do for me. This one
conclusive trial of him I resolve to make.—
Succeed or fail, still victory's my lot,
If I subdue his heart, 'tis well—if not
I will subdue my conscience to my plot.                   [*Exeunt.*  210

END OF THE FIRST ACT


# ACT II

## SCENE I

### *Enter* LOVELESS *and* AMANDA.

LOVELESS. How do you like these lodgings, my dear? For my part, I am
so well pleas'd with them, I shall hardly remove whilst we stay here, if
you are satisfied.

AMANDA. I am satisfied with every thing that pleases you, else I had not
come to Scarbro' at all.

LOVELESS. O! a little of the noise and folly of this place will sweeten the
pleasures of our retreat; we shall find the charms of our retirement
doubled when we return to it.

AMANDA. That pleasing prospect will be my chiefest entertainment,
whilst, much against my will, I engage in those empty pleasures which  10
'tis so much the fashion to be fond of.

LOVELESS. I own most of them are, indeed, but empty; yet there are
delights, of which a private life is destitute, which may divert an
honest man, and be a harmless entertainment to a virtuous woman:
good musick is one; and truly, (with some small allowance) the plays,
I think, may be esteemed another.

AMANDA. Plays, I must confess, have some small charms, and would
have more, would they restrain that loose encouragement to vice,
which shocks, if not the virtue of some women, at least the modesty of
all. 20

LOVELESS. But, 'till that reformation can be wholly made, 'twould surely
be a pity to exclude the productions of some of our best writers for
want of a little wholesome pruning; which might be effected by any
one who possessed modesty enough to believe that we should preserve
all we can of our deceased authors, at least 'till they are outdone by the
living ones.

AMANDA. What do you think of that you saw last night?

LOVELESS. To say truth, I did not mind it much; my attention was for
some time taken off to admire the workmanship of Nature, in the face
of a young lady who sat some distance from me, she was so exquisitely 30
handsome!

AMANDA. So exquisitely handsome!

LOVELESS. Why do you repeat my words, my dear?

AMANDA. Because you seem'd to speak them with such pleasure, I
thought I might oblige you with their echo.

LOVELESS. Then you are alarm'd, Amanda?

AMANDA. It is my duty to be so when you are in danger.

LOVELESS. You are too quick in apprehending for me. I view'd her with
a world of admiration, but not one glance of love.

AMANDA. Take heed of trusting to such nice distinctions. But were your 40
eyes the only things that were inquisitive? Had I been in your place,
my tongue, I fancy, had been curious too. I should have ask'd her,
where she liv'd (yet still without design) who was she pray?

LOVELESS. Indeed, I cannot tell.

AMANDA. You will not tell.

LOVELESS. By all that's sacred then, I did not ask.

AMANDA. Nor do you know what company was with her?

LOVELESS. I do not; but why are you so earnest?

AMANDA. I thought I had cause.

LOVELESS. But you thought wrong, Amanda; for turn the case, and let it 50
be your story; should you come home and tell me you had seen a
handsome man, should I grow jealous because you had eyes?

AMANDA. But should I tell you he was *exquisitely* so, and that I had gazed
on him with admiration, should you not think 'twere possible I might
go one step further, and enquire his name?

LOVELESS. [*Aside.*] She has reason on her side, I have talk'd too much; but I must turn off another way. [*To her.*] Will you then make no difference, Amanda, between the language of our sex and yours? There is a modesty restrains your tongues, which makes you speak by halves when you commend, but roving flattery gives a loose to ours, which 60 makes us still speak double what we think. You should not, therefore, in so strict a sense, take what I said to her advantage.

AMANDA. Those flights of flattery, sir, are to our faces only; when women are once out of hearing, you are as modest in your commendations as we are; but I shan't put you to the trouble of farther excuses;——if you please, this business shall rest here, only give me leave to wish, both for your peace and mine, that you may never meet this miracle of beauty more.

LOVELESS. I am content.

*Enter* SERVANT.

SERVANT. Madam, there is a lady at the door in a chair, desires to know 70 whether your Ladyship sees company? her name is Berinthia.

AMANDA. O dear!—'tis a relation I have not seen these five years, pray her to walk in. [*Exit* SERV.] Here's another beauty for you; she was, when I saw her last, reckoned extremely handsome.

LOVELESS. Don't be jealous now, for I shall gaze upon her too.

*Enter* BERINTHIA.

LOVELESS. [*Aside.*] Ha!—by Heav'ns the very woman!

BERINTHIA. [*Saluting* AMANDA.] Dear Amanda, I did not expect to meet with you in Scarbro'.

AMANDA. Sweet cousin, I'm overjoy'd to see you. [*To* LOV.] Mr. Loveless, here's a relation and a friend of mine, I desire you'll be better 80 acquainted with.

LOVELESS. [*Saluting* BERINTHIA.] If my wife never desires a harder thing, Madam, her request will be easily granted.

*Enter* SERVANT.

SERVANT. Sir, my Lord Foppington presents his humble service to you, and desires to know how you do. He's at the next door, and if it be not inconvenient to you, he'll come and wait upon you.

LOVELESS. Give my compliments to his Lordship, and I shall be glad to see him. [*Exit* SERV.] If you are not acquainted with his Lordship, Madam, you will be entertained with his character.

AMANDA. Now it moves my pity more than my mirth, to see a man whom 90 Nature has made no fool, be so very industrious to pass for an ass.

LOVELESS. No, there you are wrong, Amanda; you should never bestow your pity upon those who take pains for your contempt; pity those whom Nature abuses, never those who abuse Nature.

*Enter* LORD FOPPINGTON.

LD. FOPPINGTON. Dear Loveless, I am your most humble servant.

LOVELESS. My Lord, I'm your's.

LD. FOPPINGTON. Madam, your Ladyship's very humble slave.

LOVELESS. My Lord, this lady is a relation of my wife's.

LD. FOPPINGTON. [*Saluting her.*] The beautifullest race of people upon earth, rat me. Dear Loveless, I am overjoyed that you think of continu- 100 ing here. I am, stap my vitals. [*To* AMANDA.] For Gad's sake, Madam, how has your ladyship been able to subsist thus long, under the fatigue of a country life?

AMANDA. My life has been very far from that, my Lord, it has been a very quiet one.

LD. FOPPINGTON. Why that's the fatigue I speak of, Madam; for 'tis impossible to be quiet, without thinking; now thinking is to me the greatest fatigue in the world.

AMANDA. Does not your lordship love reading then?

LD. FOPPINGTON. Oh, passionately, Madam, but I never think of what 110 I read.

BERINTHIA. Why, can your lordship read without thinking?

LD. FOPPINGTON. O Lard, can your ladyship pray without devotion, Madam?

AMANDA. Well, I must own, I think books the best entertainment in the world.

LD. FOPPINGTON. I am so much of your ladyship's mind, Madam, that I have a private gallery in town, where I walk sometimes, which is furnished with nothing but books and looking glasses. Madam, I have gilded them, and ranged them so prettily, before Gad, it is the most 120 entertaining thing in the world, to walk and look at them.

AMANDA. Nay, I love a neat library too, but 'tis, I think, the inside of a book should recommend it most to us.

LD. FOPPINGTON. That, I must confess, I am not altogether so fand of, far to my mind, the inside of a book is to entertain one's self with the forced product of another man's brain. Now I think a man of quality and breeding may be much more diverted with the natural sprauts of his own; but to say the truth, Madam, let a man love reading never so well, when once he comes to know the tawn, he finds so many better ways of passing away the four-and-twenty hours, that it were ten thou- 130 sand pities he should consume his time in that. Far example, Madam, now my life, my life, Madam, is a perpetual stream of pleasure, that glides through with such a variety of entertainments, I believe the wisest of our ancestors never had the least conception of any of 'em. I rise, Madam, when in town, about twelve o'clock. I don't rise sooner, because it is the worst thing in the world for the complexion; nat that I pretend to be a beau, but a man must endeavour to look decent, lest he

makes so odious a figure in the side-box, the ladies should be compelled
to turn their eyes upon the play; so, at twelve o'clock I say I rise. Naw,
if I find it a good day, I resalve to take the exercise of riding, so drink 140
my chocolate, and draw on my boots by two. On my return, I dress;
and after dinner, lounge, perhaps to the Opera.

BERINTHIA. Your lordship, I suppose, is fond of music?

LD. FOPPINGTON. O, passionately, on Tuesdays and Saturdays, provided there is good company, and one is not expected to undergo the
fatigue of listening.

AMANDA. Does your lordship think that the case at the Opera?

LD. FOPPINGTON. Most certainly, Madam; there is my Lady Tattle,
my Lady Prate, my Lady Titter, my Lady Sneer, my Lady Giggle, and
my Lady Grin,—these have boxes in the front, and while any favourite 150
air is singing, are the prettiest company in the waurld, stap my vitals!
May'nt we hope for the honour to see you added to our society, Madam?

AMANDA. Alas, my Lord, I am the worst company in the world at a
concert, I'm so apt to attend to the music.

LD. FOPPINGTON. Why, Madam, that is very pardonable in the country,
or at church; but a monstrous inattention in a polite assembly. But I am
afraid I tire the company?

LOVELESS. Not at all; pray go on.

LD. FOPPINGTON. Why then, ladies, there only remains to add, that I
generally conclude the evening at one or other of the Clubs, nat that I 160
ever play deep; indeed I have been for some time tied up from losing
above five thousand pawnds at a sitting.

LOVELESS. But is'nt your Lordship sometimes obliged to attend the
weighty affairs of the nation?

LD. FOPPINGTON. Sir, as to weighty affairs, I leave them to weighty
heads; I never intend mine shall be a burthen to my body.

BERINTHIA. Nay, my Lord, but you are a pillar of the state.

LD. FOPPINGTON. An ornamental pillar, Madam; for sooner than
undergo any part of the burthen, rat me, but the whole building should
fall to the ground.                                                      170

AMANDA. But, my Lord, a fine gentleman spends a great deal of his time
in his intrigues; you have given us no account of them yet.

LD. FOPPINGTON. [Aside.] Soh! She would enquire into my amours,
that's jealousy; poor soul! I see she's in love with me. [To her.] Why,
Madam, I should have mentioned my intrigues, but I am really afraid
I begin to be troublesome with the length of my visit.

AMANDA. Your lordship is too entertaining to grow troublesome any
where.

LD. FOPPINGTON. [Aside.] That now was as much as if she had said pray
make love to me. I'll let her see I'm quick of apprehension. [To her.] 180
O Lard, Madam, I had like to have forgot a secret I must needs tell your

ladyship. [*To* LOV.] Ned, you must not be so jealous now as to listen.

LOVELESS. Not I, my Lord, I am too fashionable a husband to pry into the secrets of my wife.

LD. FOPPINGTON. [*To* AMAN. *squeezing her hand.*] I am in love with you to desperation, strike me speechless!

AMANDA. [*Giving him a box o' the ear.*] Then thus I return your passion,— an impudent fool!

LD. FOPPINGTON. Gad's curse, Madam, I'm a Peer of the Realm.

LOVELESS. Hey, what the Devil do you affront my wife, Sir? Nay then—— [*Draws and fights.* 190

AMANDA. Ah! What has my folly done?—Help! murder! help! Part them, for Heaven's sake.

LD. FOPPINGTON. [*Falling back, and leaning on his sword.*] Ah! quite through the body, stap my vitals!

*Enter* SERVANTS.

LOVELESS. [*Running to him.*] I hope I han't killed the fool, however— bear him up—where's your wound?

LD. FOPPINGTON. Just thro' the guts.

LOVELESS. Call a surgeon, there—unbutton him quickly.

LD. FOPPINGTON. Ay, pray make haste. 200

LOVELESS. This mischief you may thank yourself for.

LD. FOPPINGTON. I may so, love's the Devil, indeed, Ned.

*Enter* PROBE *and* SERVANT.

SERVANT. Here's Mr. Probe, sir, was just going by the door.

LD. FOPPINGTON. He's the welcomest man alive.

PROBE. Stand by, stand by, stand by; pray, Gentlemen, stand by; Lord have mercy upon us! did you never see a man run through the body before? Pray stand by.

LD. FOPPINGTON. Ah! Mr. Probe, I'm a dead man.

PROBE. A dead man, and I by! I should laugh to see that, egad.

LOVELESS. Prithee, don't stand prating, but look upon his wound. 210

PROBE. Why, what if I won't look upon his wound this hour, sir?

LOVELESS. Why then he'll bleed to death, sir.

PROBE. Why then I'll fetch him to life again, sir.

LOVELESS. 'Slife! he's run thro' the guts, I tell thee.

PROBE. I wish he was run thro' the heart, and I should get the more credit by his cure.—Now I hope you are satisfied?—Come, now let me come at him—now let me come at him—[*viewing his wound*] Oons! what a gash is here!—Why, sir, a man may drive a coach and six horses into your body!

LD. FOPPINGTON. Oh!

PROBE. Why, what the devil have you run the gentleman thro' with a 220 scythe?—[*aside*] A little scratch between the skin and the ribs, that's all.

LOVELESS. Let me see his wound.

PROBE. Then you shall dress it, Sir—for if any body looks upon it I won't.

LOVELESS. Why thou art the veriest coxcomb I ever saw.

PROBE. Sir, I am not master of my trade for nothing.

LD. FOPPINGTON. Surgeon!

PROBE. Sir?

LD. FOPPINGTON. Are there any hopes?

PROBE. Hopes! I can't tell—What are you willing to give for a cure?

LD. FOPPINGTON. Five hundred paunds with pleasure.                    230

PROBE. Why then perhaps there may be hopes; but we must avoid a further delay—here—help the gentleman into a chair, and carry him to my house presently—that's the properest place—[aside] to bubble him out of his money.——Come, a chair—a chair quickly—there, in with him.—[they put him into a chair]

LD. FOPPINGTON. Dear Loveless, adieu: if I die, I forgive thee; and if I live, I hope thou wilt do as much by me.—I am sorry you and I should quarrel, but I hope here's an end on't; for if you are satisfied, I am.

LOVELESS. I shall hardly think it worth my prosecuting any farther, so   240
you may be at rest, sir.

LD. FOPPINGTON. Thou art a generous fellow, strike me dumb!— [aside] but thou hast an impertinent wife, stap my vitals!

PROBE. So—carry him off—carry him off—we shall have him prate himself into a fever by and by—carry him off.

[Exit with LD. FOPPINGTON and PROBE.

AMANDA. Now on my knees, my dear, let me ask your pardon for my indiscretion—my own I never shall obtain.

LOVELESS. Oh, there's no harm done—you serv'd him well.

AMANDA. He did indeed deserve it; but I tremble to think how dear my indiscreet resentment might have cost you.                    250

LOVELESS. O, no matter—never trouble yourself about that.

*Enter* COLONEL TOWNLY.

TOWNLY. So, so, I'm glad to find you all alive—I met a wounded Peer carrying off—for Heav'ns sake what was the matter?

LOVELESS. O, a trifle—he would have made love to my wife before my face, so she obliged him with a box o'the ear, and I run him through the body, that was all.

TOWNLY. Bagatelle on all sides—but pray, Madam, how long has this noble Lord been an humble servant of your's?

AMANDA. This is the first I have heard on't—so I suppose 'tis his quality   260
more than his love has brought him into this adventure. He thinks his title an authentic passport to every woman's heart, below the degree of a Peeress.

TOWNLY. He's coxcomb enough to think any thing; but I would not have you brought into trouble for him.—I hope there's no danger of his life?

LOVELESS. None at all—he's fallen into the hands of a roguish surgeon, who, I perceive, designs to frighten a little money out of him—but I saw his wound—'tis nothing—he may go to the ball tonight if he pleases.

TOWNLY. I am glad you have corrected him without farther mischief, or you might have deprived me of the pleasure of executing a plot against his Lordship, which I have been contriving with an old acquaintance of  270 yours.

LOVELESS. Explain——

TOWNLY. His brother, Tom Fashion, is come down here, and we have it in contemplation to save him the trouble of his intended wedding; but we want your assistance. Tom would have called, but he is preparing for his enterprize, so I promised to bring you to him—so, sir, if these ladies can spare you—

LOVELESS. I'll go with you with all my heart—[aside]—tho' I could wish, methinks, to stay and gaze a little longer on that creature—Good Gods! how engaging she is—but what have I to do with beauty?—I have  280 already had my portion, and must not covet more.—[To TOWNLY] Come, sir, when you please.

TOWNLY. Ladies, your servant.

AMANDA. Mr. Loveless, pray one word with you before you go.

LOVELESS. [to TOWNLY.] I'll overtake you, Colonel. [Exit TOWNLY]. What would my dear?

AMANDA. Only a woman's foolish question, how do you like my cousin here?

LOVELESS. Jealous already, Amanda?

AMANDA. Not at all—I ask you for another reason.  290

LOVELESS. [Aside.] Whate'er her reason be, I must not tell her true. [to her]. Why, I confess she's handsome—but you must not think I slight your kinswoman, if I own to you, of all the women who may claim that character, she is the last would triumph in my heart.

AMANDA. I'm satisfied.

LOVELESS. Now tell me why you ask'd?

AMANDA. At night I will—Adieu.—

LOVELESS. [Kissing her.] I'm yours——                    [Exit.

AMANDA. [Aside.] I'm glad to find he does not like her, for I have a great mind to persuade her to come and live with me.  300

BERINTHIA. [Aside.] Soh! I find my Colonel continues in his airs; there must be something more at the bottom of this than the provocation he pretends from me.

AMANDA. For Heav'ns sake, Berinthia, tell me what way I shall take to persuade you to come and live with me?

BERINTHIA. Why one way in the world there is—and but one.

AMANDA. And pray what is that?

BERINTHIA. It is to assure me—I shall be very welcome.

AMANDA. If that be all, you shall e'en sleep here tonight.

BERINTHIA. To-night!                                                        310

AMANDA. Yes, to-night.

BERINTHIA. Why the people where I lodge will think me mad.

AMANDA. Let 'em think what they please.

BERINTHIA. Say you so, Amanda?—Why then they shall think what they
please—for I'm a young widow, and I care not what any body thinks.
——Ah, Amanda, it's a delicious thing to be a young widow.

AMANDA. You'll hardly make me think so.

BERINTHIA. Puh! because you are in love with your husband—but that is
not every woman's case.

AMANDA. I hope 'twas yours at least.                                        320

BERINTHIA. Mine, say you?—Now I have a great mind to tell you a lye,
but I shall do it so aukwardly, you'd find me out.

AMANDA. Then e'en speak the truth.

BERINTHIA. Shall I?—then, after all, I did love him, Amanda, as a
Nun does penance.

AMANDA. How did you live together?

BERINTHIA. Like man and wife—asunder—he lov'd the country—I the
town.—He hawks and hounds—I coaches and equipage.—He eating
and drinking—I carding and playing.—He the sound of a horn—I the
squeek of a fiddle.—We were dull company at table—worse a-bed:        330
whenever we met we gave one another the spleen, and never agreed but
once, which was about lying alone.

AMANDA. But tell me one thing truly and sincerely—notwithstanding all
these jars, did not his death at last extremely trouble you?

BERINTHIA. O yes.—I was forced to wear an odious Widow's band a
twelve-month for't.

AMANDA. Women, I find, have different inclinations:—prithee,
Berinthia, instruct me a little farther—for I'm so great a novice,
I'm almost asham'd on't.—Not Heav'n knows that what you call
intrigues have any charms for me—the practical part of all unlawful    340
love is——

BERINTHIA. O 'tis abominable—but for the speculative, that we must all
confess is entertaining enough.

AMANDA. Pray, be so just then to me, to believe, 'tis with a world of
innocence I would enquire whether you think those, we call Women of
Reputation, do really escape all other men, as they do those shadows of
'em the beaus?

BERINTHIA. O no, Amanda—there are a sort of men make dreadful
work amongst 'em—men that may be called the beaus' Antipathy—
for they agree in nothing but walking upon two legs. These have brains  350

—the beau has none.—These are in love with their mistress—the beau with himself.—They take care of her reputation—he's industrious to destroy it—They are decent—he's a fop. They are men—he's an ass.

AMANDA. If this be their character, I fancy we had here e'en now a pattern of 'em both.

BERINTHIA. His Lordship and Colonel Townly?

AMANDA. The same.

BERINTHIA. As for the Lord, he's eminently so; and for the other, I can assure you there's not a man in town who has a better interest with the women, that are worth having an interest with. 360

AMANDA. He answers then the opinion I had ever of him—Heav'ns! what a difference there is between a man like him, and that vain nauseous fop, Lord Foppington—[*taking her hand*] I must acquaint you with a secret, cousin—'tis not that fool alone has talked to me of love.— Townly has been tampering too.

BERINTHIA. [*Aside.*] So, so!—here the mystery comes out!—Colonel Townly!—impossible, my dear!

AMANDA. 'Tis true, indeed!—tho' he has done it in vain; nor do I think that all the merit of mankind combined, could shake the tender love I bear my husband; yet I will own to you, Berinthia, I did not start at his 370 addresses, as when they came from one whom I contemned.

BERINTHIA. [*Aside.*] O this is better and better—well said innocence!— and you really think, my dear, that nothing could abate your constancy and attachment to your husband?

AMANDA. Nothing, I am convinced.

BERINTHIA. What if you found he lov'd another woman better?

AMANDA. Well!

BERINTHIA. Well!—why were I that thing they call a slighted wife; somebody should run the risk of being that thing they call—a husband.

AMANDA. O fie, Berinthia, no revenge should ever be taken against a hus- 380 band—but to wrong his bed is a vengeance, which of all vengeance——

BERINTHIA. Is the sweetest!—ha! ha! ha!—don't I talk madly?

AMANDA. Madly indeed!

BERINTHIA. Yet I'm very innocent.

AMANDA. That I dare swear you are.—I know how to make allowances for your humour—but you resolve then never to marry again?

BERINTHIA. O no!—I resolve I will.

AMANDA. How so?

BERINTHIA. That I never may.

AMANDA. You banter me. 390

BERINTHIA. Indeed I don't—but I consider I'm a woman, and form my resolutions accordingly.

AMANDA. Well, my opinion is, form what resolution you will, matrimony will be the end on't.

BERINTHIA. I doubt it—but A Heav'ns!—I have business at home, and
am half an hour too late.

AMANDA. As you are to return with me, I'll just give some orders, and
walk with you.

BERINTHIA. Well, make haste, and we'll finish this subject as we go.
[*Exit* AMANDA.

Ah! poor Amanda, you have led a country life! Well, this discovery is   400
lucky!—base Townly!—at once false to me, and treacherous to his
friend! and my innocent, demure, cousin, too!—I have it in my power
to be revenged on her, however. Her husband, if I have any skill in
countenance, would be as happy in my smiles, as Townly can hope to
be in her's.—I'll make the experiment, come what will on't.—The
woman who can forgive the being robb'd of a favour'd lover, must be
either an ideot or a wanton.

### END OF ACT THE SECOND

# ACT III

## SCENE I

*Enter* LORD FOPPINGTON *and* LA VAROLE.

LD. FOPPINGTON. Hey, fellow—let my vis-a-vis[1] come to the door.

LA VAROLE. Will your lordship venture so soon to expose yourself to
the weather?

LD. FOPPINGTON. Sir, I will venture as soon as I can to expose myself
to the ladies.

LA VAROLE. I wish your lordship would please to keep house a little
longer; I'm affraid your honour does not well consider your wound.

LD. FOPPINGTON. My wound!—I would not be in eclipse another day,
tho' I had as many wounds in my body as I have had in my heart. So
mind, Varole, let these cards be left as directed. For this evening I shall   10
wait on my father-in-law, Sir Tunbelly, and I mean to commence my
devoirs to the lady, by giving an entertainment at her father's expence;
and heark thee, tell Mr. Loveless I request he and his company will
honour me with their presence, or I shall think we are not friends.

LA VAROLE. I will be sure.                                        [*Exit.*

*Enter* YOUNG FASHION.

[1] 'A light carriage for two persons sitting face to face' (*O.E.D.*). In *The Relapse*
Lord Foppington refers to 'the coach'.

Y. FASHION. Brother, your servant, how do you find yourself to day?

LD. FOPPINGTON. So well, that I have ardered my carriage to the door;
—so there's no great danger of death this baut, Tam.

Y. FASHION. I'm very glad of it.

LD. FOPPINGTON. [*Aside.*] That I believe's a lye.—Prithee, Tam, tell    20
me one thing—did not your heart cut a caper up to your mauth, when
you heard I was run thro' the bady?

Y. FASHION. Why do you think it should?

LD. FOPPINGTON. Because I remember mine did so when I heard my
uncle was shot thro' the head.

Y. FASHION. It then did very ill.

LD. FOPPINGTON. Prithee, why so?

Y. FASHION. Because he used you very well.

LD. FOPPINGTON. Well!—Naw, strike me dumb, he starv'd me—he
has let me want a thausand women, for want of a thausand pound.    30

Y. FASHION. Then he hinder'd you from making a great many ill
bargains—for I think no woman worth money that will take money.

LD. FOPPINGTON. If I was a younger brother, I should think so too.

Y. FASHION. Then you are seldom much in love?

LD. FOPPINGTON. Never, stap my vitals.

Y. FASHION. Why then did you make all this bustle about Amanda?

LD. FOPPINGTON. Because she was a woman of an insolent virtue—and
I thought myself piqu'd in honour to debauch her.

Y. FASHION. [*Aside.*] Very well. Here's a rare fellow for you, to have the
spending of five thousand pounds a year. But now for my business with    40
him.—Brother, tho' I know to talk of business (especially of money) is a
theme not quite so entertaining to you as that of the ladies, my necessities are such, I hope you'll have patience to hear me.

LD. FOPPINGTON. The greatness of your necessities, Tam, is the worst
argument in the warld for your being patiently heard. I do believe you
are going to make a very good speech, but strike me dumb, it has the
worst beginning of any speech I have heard this twelvemonth.

Y. FASHION. I'm sorry you think so.

LD. FOPPINGTON. I do believe thou art—but come, let's know the affair
quickly.    50

Y. FASHION. Why then, my case in a word is this.—The necessary
expences of my travels have so much exceeded the wretched income of
my annuity, that I have been forced to mortgage it for five hundred
pounds, which is spent. So unless you are so kind as to assist me in
redeeming it, I know no remedy but to take a purse.

LD. FOPPINGTON. Why, faith, Tam, to give you my sense of the thing,
I do think taking a purse the best remedy in the warld—for if you
succeed you are relieved that way, if you are taken—you are relieved
t'other.

Y. FASHION. I'm glad to see you are in so pleasant a humour; I hope I  60
shall find the effects on't.

LD. FOPPINGTON. Why, do you then really think it a reasonable thing
that I should give you five hundred pawnds?

Y. FASHION. I do not ask it as a due, brother, I am willing to receive it as
a favour.

LD. FOPPINGTON. Then thou art willing to receive it any how, strike
me speechless.—But these are d——n'd times to give money in; taxes
are so great, repairs so exorbitant, tenants such rogues, and bouquets[1]
so dear, that the Devil take me, I am reduced to that extremity in my
cash, I have been forced to retrench in that one article of sweet pawder,[2]  70
till I have brought it dawn to five guineas a maunth—now judge, Tam,
whether I can spare you five hundred pawnds?

Y. FASHION. If you can't I must starve, that's all.          [*Aside.*
Damn him.

LD. FOPPINGTON. All I can say is, you should have been a better husband.[3]

Y. FASHION. Ouns!—If you can't live upon ten thousand a-year, how do
you think I should do't upon two hundred?

LD. FOPPINGTON. Don't be in a passion, Tam, for passion is the most
unbecoming thing in the warld—to the face. Look you, I don't love to
say any thing to you to make you melancholy, but upon this occasion I  80
must take leave to put you in mind, that a running-horse does require
more attendance than a coach-horse.—Nature has made some difference
'twixt you and me.

Y. FASHION. Yes.—She has made you older. [*Aside.*] Plague take her.

LD. FOPPINGTON. That is not all, Tam.

Y. FASHION. Why, what is there else?

LD. FOPPINGTON. [*Looking first upon himself and then upon his brother.*]
Ask the ladies.

Y. FASHION. Why, thou Essence-bottle, thou Musk Cat,—dost thou
then think thou hast any advantage over me but what fortune has given
thee?                                                                 90

LD. FOPPINGTON. I do, stap my vitals.

Y. FASHION. Now, by all that's great and powerful thou art the Prince of
Coxcombs.

LD. FOPPINGTON. Sir, I am praud at being at the head of so prevailing
a party.

Y. FASHION. Will nothing then provoke thee?—Draw, Coward.

LD. FOPPINGTON. Look you, Tam, you know I have always taken you
for a mighty dull fellow, and here is one of the foolishest plats broke out,
that I have seen a lang time. Your poverty makes life so burthensome to

[1] See p. 258, n. 2.
[2] 'Perfumed powder used as a cosmetic' (*O.E.D.*).          [3] Manager.

you, you would provoke me to a quarrel, in hopes either to slip through 100
my lungs into my estate, or to get yourself run thro' the guts, to put an
end to your pain, but I will disappoint you in both your designs; far
with the temper of a Philasapher, and the discretion of a statesman—I
shall leave the room with my sword in the scabbard. [*Exit.*

Y. FASHION. So! farewell brother; and now conscience I defy thee.——
Lory!

*Enter* LORY.

LORY. Sir?

Y. FASHION. Here's rare news, Lory, his Lordship has given me a pill
has purged off all my scruples.

LORY. Then my heart's at ease again. For I have been in a lamentable 110
fright, sir, ever since your conscience had the impudence to intrude into
your company.

Y. FASHION. Be at peace; it will come there no more, my brother has
given it a wring by the nose, and I have kick'd it down stairs. So run
away to the inn, get the chaise ready quickly, and bring it to dame
Coupler's without a moment's delay.

LORY. Then, sir, you are going straight about the fortune?

Y. FASHION. I am.—Away—fly, Lory.

LORY. The happiest day I ever saw. I'm upon the wing already.

[*Exeunt severally.*

SCENE II, A GARDEN

*Enter* LOVELESS *and* SERVANT.

LOVELESS. Is my wife within?

SERVANT. No, sir, she has been gone out this half hour.

LOVELESS. Well, leave me. [*Exit* SERVANT.] How strangely does my
mind run on this widow—never was my heart so suddenly seiz'd on
before—that my wife should pick out her, of all woman-kind, to be her
playfellow.—But what fate does, let fate answer for—I sought it not—
soh!—by heav'ns!—here she comes.

*Enter* BERINTHIA.

BERINTHIA. What makes you look so thoughtful, Sir? I hope you are not
ill.

LOVELESS. I was debating, madam, whether I was so or not, and that was 10
it which made me look so thoughtful.

BERINTHIA. Is it then so hard a matter to decide?—I thought all
people were acquainted with their own bodies, tho' few people know
their own minds.

LOVELESS. What if the distemper I suspect be in the mind?

BERINTHIA. Why then I'll undertake to prescribe you a cure.

LOVELESS. Alas! you undertake you know not what.

BERINTHIA. So far at least then you allow me to be a Physician.

LOVELESS. Nay, I'll allow you to be so yet farther, for I have reason to believe, should I put myself into your hands, you would increase my distemper. 20

BERINTHIA. How?

LOVELESS. Oh, you might betray my complaints to my wife.

BERINTHIA. And so lose all my practice.

LOVELESS. Will you then keep my secret?

BERINTHIA. I will.

LOVELESS. I'm satisfied. Now hear my symptoms, and give me your advice. The first were these when I saw you at the play; a random glance you threw, at first alarm'd me. I could not turn my eyes from whence the danger came—I gaz'd upon you till my heart began to pant 30 —nay, even now on your approaching me, my illness is so increas'd, that if you do not help me I shall, whilst you look on, consume to Ashes.
                                        [*Taking her hand.*

BERINTHIA. [*Breaking from him.*] O Lord let me go, 'tis the plague, and we shall be infected.

LOVELESS. Then we'll die together, my charming angel.

BERINTHIA. O Gad! the devil's in you. Lord, let me go—here's somebody coming.

*Enter* SERVANT.

SERVANT. Sir, my lady's come home, and desires to speak with you.

LOVELESS. Tell her I'm coming. [*Exit* SERVANT.]——[*To* BERINTHIA] But before I go, one glass of nectar to drink her health. 40

BERINTHIA. Stand off, or I shall hate you, by heavens.

LOVELESS. [*Kissing her.*] In matters of love, a woman's oath is no more to be minded than a man's.                    [*Exit* LOV.

BERINTHIA. Um!

*Enter* TOWNLY.

TOWNLY. Soh! what's here—Berinthia and Loveless—and in such *close* conversation!—I cannot now wonder at her indifference in excusing herself to me!—O rare woman,—well then, let Loveless look to his wife, 'twill be but the retort courteous on both sides.—[*To* BERINTHIA.] Your servant, Madam, I need not ask you how you do, you have got so good a colour. 50

BERINTHIA. No better than I used to have, I suppose.

TOWNLY. A little more blood in your cheeks.

BERINTHIA. I have been walking!

TOWNLY. Is that all? Pray was it Mr. Loveless went from here just now?

BERINTHIA. O yes—he has been walking with me.

TOWNLY. He has!

BERINTHIA. Upon my word I think he is a very agreeable man!—and there is certainly something particularly insinuating in his address!

TOWNLY. So! so! she hasn't even the modesty to dissemble! Pray, madam, may I, without impertinence, trouble you with a few serious 60 questions?

BERINTHIA. As many as you please; but pray let them be as little serious as possible.

TOWNLY. Is it not near two years since I have presumed to address you?

BERINTHIA. I don't know exactly—but it has been a tedious long time.

TOWNLY. Have I not, during that period, had every reason to believe that my assiduities were far from being unacceptable?

BERINTHIA. Why, to do you justice, you have been extremely trouble-some—and I confess I have been more civil to you than you deserved.

TOWNLY. Did I not come to this place at your express desire? and for no 70 purpose but the honour of meeting you?—and after waiting a month in disappointment, have you condescended to explain, or in the slightest way apologize, for your conduct?

BERINTHIA. O heav'ns! apologize for my conduct!—apologise to you!— O you barbarian!—But pray now, my good serious Colonel, have you any thing more to add?

TOWNLY. Nothing, madam, but that after such behaviour I am less surpris'd at what I saw just now; it is not very wonderful that the woman who can trifle with the delicate addresses of an honourable lover, should be found coquetting with the husband of her friend. 80

BERINTHIA. Very true—no more wonderful than it was for this *honour-able* lover to divert himself in the absence of this coquet, with endeavour-ing to seduce his friend's wife! O Colonel, Colonel, don't talk of honor or your friend, for heav'ns sake.

TOWNLY. S'death! how came she to suspect this!—Really madam, I don't understand you.

BERINTHIA. Nay—nay—you saw I did not pretend to misunderstand you.—But here comes the Lady—perhaps you would be glad to be left with her for an explanation.

TOWNLY. O madam, this recrimination is a poor resource, and to 90 convince you how much you are mistaken, I beg leave to decline the happiness you propose me.—Madam, your servant.

*Enter* AMANDA. [TOWNLY *whispers* AMANDA, *and exit.*]

BERINTHIA. He carries it off well however—upon my word—very well! —how tenderly they part!——So, cousin—I hope you have not been

chiding your admirer for being with me—I assure you we have been
talking of you.

AMANDA. Fie, Berinthia!—my admirer—will you never learn to talk in
earnest of any thing?

BERINTHIA. Why this shall be in earnest, if you please; for my part I
only tell you matter of fact.                                        100

AMANDA. I'm sure there's so much jest and earnest in what you say to
me on this subject, I scarce know how to take it.—I have just parted
with Mr. Loveless—perhaps it is my fancy, but I think there is an
alteration in his manner, which alarms me.

BERINTHIA. And so you are jealous? is that all?

AMANDA. That all!—is jealousy then nothing?

BERINTHIA. It should be nothing, if I were in your case.

AMANDA. Why what would you do?

BERINTHIA. I'd cure myself.

AMANDA. How?                                                          110

BERINTHIA. Care as little for my husband as he did for me. Look you,
Amanda, you may build castles in the air, and fume, and fret, and grow
thin, and lean, and pale, and ugly, if you please, but I tell you, no man
worth having is true to his wife, or ever was, or ever will be so.

AMANDA. Do you then really think he's false to me? for I did not suspect
him.

BERINTHIA. Think so!—I am sure of it.

AMANDA. You are sure on't?

BERINTHIA. Positively—he fell in love at the play.

AMANDA. Right—the very same—but who could have told you this?       120

BERINTHIA. Um——O—Townly!——I suppose your husband has
made him his confidant.

AMANDA. O base Loveless!—and what did Townly say on't?

BERINTHIA. So, so—why should she ask that?——[aside]——say!—
why he abused Loveless extremely, and said all the tender things of you
in the world.

AMANDA. Did he?—Oh! my heart!—I'm very ill—I must go to my
chamber—dear Berinthia, don't leave me a moment.          [Exit.

BERINTHIA. No—don't fear.——So—there is certainly some affection
on her side at least, towards Townly. If it prove so, and her agreeable  130
husband perseveres—Heav'n send me resolution!—well—how this
business will end I know not—but I seem to be in as fair a way to lose
my gallant Colonel, as a boy is to be a rogue, when he's put clerk to an
attorney.                                                    [Exit.

### SCENE III, *a Country House*

*Enter* YOUNG FASHION *and* LORY.

Y. FASHION. So—here's our inheritance, Lory, if we can but get into possession—but methinks the seat of our family looks like Noah's ark, as if the chief part on't were designed for the fowls of the air, and the beasts of the field.

LORY. Pray, sir, don't let your head run upon the orders of building here—get but the heiress, let the devil take the house.

Y. FASHION. Get but the house! let the devil take the heiress, I say—but come, we have no time to squander, knock at the door—

[LORY *knocks two or three times.*

What the devil have they got no ears in this house?—knock harder.

LORY. I'gad, sir, this will prove some inchanted castle—we shall have 10 the giant come out by and by with his club, and beat our brains out.

[*knocks again.*

Y. FASHION. Hush—they come—[*from within*] who is there?

LORY. Open the door and see—is that your country breeding?—

SERVANT. [*within*] Ay, but two words to that bargain—Tummas, is the blunderbuss prim'd?

Y. FASHION. Ouns! give 'em good words Lory—or we shall be shot here a fortune catching.

LORY. Egad sir, I think you're in the right on't—ho!—Mr. what d'ye callum—will you please to let us in? or are we to be left to grow like willows by your moat side? 20

[SERVANT *appears at the window with a blunderbuss.*

SERVANT. Weel naw, what's ya're business?

Y. FASHION. Nothing, sir, but to wait upon Sir Tunbelly, with your leave.

SERVANT. To weat upon Sir Tunbelly?—why you'll find that's just as Sir Tunbelly pleases.

Y. FASHION. But will you do me the favour, sir, to know whether Sir Tunbelly pleases or not?

SERVANT. Why look you d'ye see, with good words much may be done.— Ralph, go thy waes, and ask Sir Tunbelly if he pleases to be waited upon —and dost hear? call to nurse that she may lock up Miss Hoyden before the geats open. 30

Y. FASHION. D'ye hear that Lory?

*Enter* SIR TUNBELLY, *with Servants, armed with guns, clubs, pitchforks, &c.*

LORY. O (*Running behind his master*) O Lord, O Lord, Lord, we are both dead men.

Y. FASHION. Take heed fool, thy fear will ruin us.

LORY. My fear, sir, 'sdeath, sir, I fear nothing—[*aside*] would I were well up to the chin in a horse pond.

SIR TUNBELLY. Who is it here has any business with me?

Y. FASHION. Sir, 'tis I, if your name be Sir Tunbelly Clumsey?

SIR TUNBELLY. Sir, my name is Sir Tunbelly Clumsy, whether you have any business with me or not—so you see I am not asham'd of my 40 name, nor my face either.

Y. FASHION. Sir, you have no cause that I know of.

SIR TUNBELLY. Sir, if you have no cause either, I desire to know who you are; for 'till I know your name, I shan't ask you to come into my house: and when I do know your name, 'tis six to four I don't ask you then.

Y. FASHION. [Giving him a Letter] Sir, I hope you'll find this letter an authentic passport.

SIR TUNBELLY. Cod's my life, from Mrs. Coupler.—I ask your Lordship's pardon ten thousand times—[to his Servant]—Here, run in a doors quickly; get a Scotch coal fire in the great parlour—set all the Turkey 50 work chairs in their places; get the brass candlesticks out, and be sure stick the socket full of laurel, run—[turning to YOUNG FASHION] My Lord, I ask your Lordship's pardon—[to SERVANT] and do you hear, run away to nurse, bid her let Miss Hoyden loose again. [Exit SERVANT. [To YOUNG FASHION] I hope your honour will excuse the disorder of my family—we are not used to receive men of your Lordship's great quality every day—pray where are your coaches and servants, my Lord?

Y. FASHION. Sir, that I might give you and your fair daughter a proof how impatient I am to be nearer akin to you, I left my equipage to follow me, and came away post with only one servant.                    60

SIR TUNBELLY. Your Lordship does me too much honour—It was exposing your person to too much fatigue and danger, I protest it was— but my daughter shall endeavour to make you what amends she can— and tho' I say it, that should not say it, Hoyden has charms.

Y. FASHION. Sir, I am not a stranger to them, tho' I am to her: common fame has done her justice.

SIR TUNBELLY. My Lord, I am common Fame's very grateful humble servant.—My Lord, my girl's young—Hoyden is young, my Lord; but this I must say for her, what she wants in art, she has by nature— what she wants in experience, she has in breeding—and what's wanting 70 in her age, is made good in her constitution—so pray, my Lord, walk in; pray, my Lord, walk in.

Y. FASHION. Sir, I wait upon you.                    [Exeunt thro' the gate.


MISS HOYDEN sola.

MISS. Sure, nobody was ever used as I am. I know well enough what other girls do, for all they think to make a fool of me. It's well I have a husband a-coming, or I'cod I'd marry the baker, I would so.—Nobody can knock at the gate, but presently I must be lock'd up—and here's the

young greyhound can run loose about the house all the day long, so she  25
can.—'Tis very well——

[NURSE, *without opening the door.*]

NURSE. Miss Hoyden, Miss, Miss, Miss, Miss Hoyden!  80

*Enter* NURSE.

MISS. Well, what do you make such a noise for, ha?—what do you din a
body's ears for?—can't one be at quiet for you?

NURSE. What do I din your ears for?—here's one come will din your ears
for you.

MISS. What care I who's come?—I care not a fig who comes, nor who
goes, as long as I must be lock'd up like the ale cellar.

NURSE. That, Miss, is for fear you should be drank before you are ripe.

MISS. O don't you trouble your head about that, I'm as ripe as you,
though not so mellow.

NURSE. Very well—now I have a good mind to lock you up again, and  90
not let you see my Lord tonight.

MISS. My Lord! why is my husband come?

NURSE. Yes, marry is he, and a goodly person too.

MISS. [*Hugging* NURSE] O my dear nurse, forgive me this once, and I'll
never misuse you again; no, if I do, you shall give me three thumps on
the back, and a great pinch by the cheek.

NURSE. Ah! the poor thing, see how it melts, it's as full of good nature as
an egg's full of meat.

MISS. But my dear Nurse, don't lie now, is he come by your troth?

NURSE. Yes, by my truly is he.  100

MISS. O Lord! I'll go and put on my laced tucker, tho' I'm lock'd up a
month for't.  [*Exit running.*

END OF THE THIRD ACT

# ACT IV

## SCENE I

*Enter* MISS HOYDEN *and* NURSE.

NURSE. Well, Miss, how do you like your husband that is to be?

MISS. O Lord, Nurse, I'm so overjoy'd, I can scarce contain myself.

NURSE. O but you must have a care of being too fond, for men now-a-
days, hate a woman that loves 'em.

MISS. Love him! Why do you think I love him, Nurse? I'cod, I would
not care if he was hang'd, so I were but once married to him.—No, that
which pleases me, is to think what work I'll make when I get to London;
for when I am a wife and a Lady both, I'cod I'll flaunt it with the best of
'em. Aye, and I shall have money enough to do so too, Nurse.

NURSE. Ah! there's no knowing that Miss, for though these Lords have  10
a power of wealth, indeed, yet, as I have heard say, they give it all to
their sluts and their trulls, who joggle it about in their coaches, with a
murrain to 'em, whilst poor Madam sits sighing and wishing, and has
not a spare half crown to buy her a Practice of Piety.[1]

MISS. O, but for that, don't deceive yourself, Nurse, for this I must say
of my Lord, he's as free as an open house at Christmas. For this very
morning he told me, I should have six hundred a year to buy pins.
Now, Nurse, if he gives me six hundred a year to buy pins, what do you
think he'll give me to buy fine petticoats?

NURSE. Ah, my dearest, he deceives thee foul[l]y, and he's no better than  20
a rogue for his pains. These Londoners have got a gibberage with 'em,
would confound a gipsey. That which they call pin-money, is to buy
their wives every thing in the versal world, down to their very shoc-
knots.—Nay, I have heard folks say, that some ladies, if they will have
gallants, as they call 'em, are forced to find them out of their pin-money
too. But, look, look, if his Honor be not coming to you.—Now, if I
were sure you would behave yourself handsomely, and not disgrace me
that have brought you up, I'd leave you alone together.

MISS. That's my best Nurse, do as you'd be done by—trust us together
this once, and if I don't shew my breeding, may I never be married but  30
die an old maid.

NURSE. Well, this once I'll venture you.—But if you disparage me——

MISS. Never fear.                                    [*Exit* NURSE.

*Enter* Y. FASHION.

Y. FASHION. Your servant, Madam, I'm glad to find you alone, for I
have something of importance to speak to you about.

MISS. Sir, (my Lord, I meant) you may speak to me about what you
please, I shall give you a civil answer.

Y. FASHION. You give me so obliging a one, it encourages me to tell you
in a few words, what I think both for your interest and mine. Your
father, I suppose you know, has resolved to make me happy in being  40
your husband, and I hope I may depend on your consent to perform
what he desires.

MISS. Sir, I never disobey my father in any thing but eating green
gooseberries.

---

[1] By Lewis Bayly, Bishop of Bangor (d. 1631).

Y. FASHION. So good a daughter must needs be an admirable wife.—I am therefore impatient till you are mine, and hope you will so far consider the violence of my love, that you won't have the cruelty to defer my happiness so long as your father designs it.

MISS. Pray, my Lord, how long is that?

Y. FASHION. Madam—a thousand years—a whole week.                    50

MISS. A week!—Why I shall be an old woman by that time.

Y. FASHION. And I an old man.

MISS. Why I thought it was to be to-morrow morning, as soon as I was up. I'm sure nurse told me so.

Y. FASHION. And it shall be to-morrow morning, if you'll consent?

MISS. If I'll consent! Why I thought I was to obey you as my husband?

Y. FASHION. That's when we are married. Till then I'm to obey you

MISS. Why then if we are to take it by turns, it's the same thing. I'll obey you now, and when we are married you shall obey me.

Y. FASHION. With all my heart. But I doubt we must get Nurse on our 60 side, or we shall hardly prevail with the Chaplain.

MISS. No more we shan't indeed, for he loves her better than he loves his pulpit, and would always be a-preaching to her by his good will.

Y. FASHION. Why then, my dear, if you'll call her hither, we'll try to persuade her presently.

MISS. O Lord, I can tell you a way how to perswade her to any thing.

Y. FASHION. How's that?

MISS. Why tell her she's a handsome, comely woman, and give her half-a-crown.

Y. FASHION. Nay, if that will do, she shall have half a score of them.    70

MISS. O Gemini, for half that she'd marry you herself.—I'll run and call her.                                                        [*Exit.*

Y. FASHION. Soh, matters go swimmingly. This is a rare girl I'faith. I shall have a fine time on't with her at London. But no matter—she brings me an estate will afford me a separate maintenance.

*Enter* LORY.

Y. FASHION. So, Lory, what's the matter?

LORY. Here, Sir; an intercepted packet from the enemy—your brother's postillion brought it—I knew the livery, pretended to be a servant of Sir Tunbelly's, and so got possession of the letter.

Y. FASHION. [*Looking at it.*] Ouns!—He tells Sir Tunbelly here, that he 80 will be with him this evening, with a large party to supper,—'egad! I must marry the girl directly.

LORY. O Zounds, Sir, directly to be sure! Here she comes.

[*Exit* LORY.

Y. FASHION. And the old Jesabel with her. She has a thorough procuring countenance, however.

*Enter* MISS HOYDEN *and* NURSE.

Y. FASHION. How do you do, Mrs. Nurse?—I desired your young lady
would give me leave to see you, that I might thank you for your extraordinary care and conduct in her education; pray accept of this small
acknowledgement for it at present, and depend upon my farther
kindness when I shall be that happy thing her husband.          90

NURSE. [*Aside.*] Gold by Maakins!—Your Honour's goodness is too
great. Alas! all I can boast of is, I gave her pure good milk, and so your
Honour would have said, an you had seen how the poor thing thrived—
and how it would look up in my face—and crow and laugh it would!

MISS. [*To* NURSE, *taking her angrily aside.*] Pray one word with you·
Prithee, Nurse, don't stand ripping up old stories, to make one ashamed
before one's love; do you think such a fine, proper gentleman as he is,
cares for a fiddle-come tale of a child? If you have a mind to make him
have a good opinion of a woman, don't tell him what one did then, tell
him what one can do now. [*To him*]. I hope your Honour will excuse my          100
miss-manners, to whisper before you, it was only to give some orders
about the family.

Y. FASHION. O every thing, Madam, is to give way to business; besides,
good housewifery is a very commendable quality in a young lady.

MISS. Pray, Sir, are young ladies good housewives at London town? Do
they darn their own linnen.

Y. FASHION. O no;—they study how to spend money, not to save it.

MISS. I'cod, I don't know but that may be better sport, ha', Nurse!

Y. FASHION. Well, you shall have your choice when you come there.

MISS. Shall I?—then by my troth I'll get there as fast as I can. [*To*          110
NURSE.] His Honour desires you'll be so kind, as to let us be married
to-morrow.

NURSE. To-morrow, my dear Madam?

Y. FASHION. Aye faith, Nurse, you may well be surprised at Miss's
wanting to put it off so long—to-morrow! no, no,—'tis now, this very
hour, I would have the ceremony perform'd.

MISS. I'cod with all my heart.

NURSE. O mercy, worse and worse.

Y. FASHION. Yes, sweet Nurse, now, and privately. For all things being
signed and sealed, why should Sir Tunbelly make us stay a week for a          120
wedding dinner?

NURSE. But if you should be married now, what will you do when Sir
Tunbelly calls for you to be wedded?

MISS. Why then we will be married again.

NURSE. What twice, my child!

MISS. I'cod, I don't care how often I'm married, not I.

NURSE. Well—I'm such a tender hearted fool, I find I can refuse you
nothing. So you shall e'en follow your own inventions.

MISS. Shall I?—[*Aside.*] O Lord I could leap over the Moon.

Y. FASHION. Dear Nurse, this goodness of yours shall be still more 130 rewarded. But now you must employ your power with the Chaplain, that he may do his friendly office too, and then we shall be all happy. Do you think you can prevail with him?

NURSE. Prevail with him!—Or he shall never prevail with me, I can tell him that.

Y. FASHION. I'm glad to hear it; however, to strengthen your interest with him, you may let him know, I have several fat livings in my gift, and that the first that falls shall be in your disposal.

NURSE. Nay then, I'll make him marry more folks than one, I'll promise him. 140

MISS. Faith do, Nurse, make him marry you too, I'm sure he'll do't for a fat living.

Y. FASHION. Well, Nurse, while you go and settle matters with him, your lady and I will go and take a walk in the garden. [*Exit* NURSE.

Y. FASHION. [*Giving her his hand.*] Come, Madam, dare you venture yourself alone with me?

MISS. O dear, yes, Sir, I don't think you'll do any thing to me I need be afraid on. [*Exeunt.*

## SCENE II

*Enter* AMANDA, *her* WOMAN *following.*

MAID. If you please, Madam, only to say whether you'll have me buy them or not?

AMANDA. Yes—no—go—Teazer!—I care not what you do—prithee leave me. [*Exit* MAID.

*Enter* BERINTHIA.

BERINTHIA. What, in the name of Jove's the matter with you?

AMANDA. The matter, Berinthia? I'm almost mad; I'm plagued to death.

BERINTHIA. Who is it that plagues you?

AMANDA. Who do you think should plague a wife, but her husband?

BERINTHIA. O ho! is it come to that?—we shall have you with yourself a widow, by and bye. 10

AMANDA. Would I were any thing but what I am!—a base, ungrateful man, to use me thus!

BERINTHIA. What, has he given you fresh reason to suspect his wandering?

AMANDA. Every hour gives me reason.

BERINTHIA. And yet, Amanda, you perhaps at this moment cause in another's breast the same tormenting doubts and jealousies which you feel so sensibly yourself.

AMANDA. Heaven knows I would not!

BERINTHIA. Why, you can't tell but there may be some one as tenderly 20 attached to Townly, whom you boast of as your conquest, as you can be to your husband.

AMANDA. I'm sure I never encouraged his pretensions.

BERINTHIA. Pshaw! Pshaw!—No sensible man ever perseveres to love, without encouragement. Why have you not treated him as you have Lord Foppington?

AMANDA. Because he has not presum'd so far. But let us drop the subject. Men, not women, are riddles. Mr. Loveless now follows some flirt for variety, whom I'm sure he does not like so well as he does me.

BERINTHIA. That's more than you know, Madam.                    30

AMANDA. Why, do you know the ugly thing?

BERINTHIA. I think I can guess at the person—but she's no such ugly thing neither.

AMANDA. Is she very handsome?

BERINTHIA. Truly I think so.

AMANDA. Whate'er she be, I'm sure he does not like her well enough to bestow any thing more than a little outward gallantry upon her.

BERINTHIA. [*Aside.*] Outward gallantry.—I can't bear this.—Come, come, don't you be too secure, Amanda; while you suffer Townly to imagine that you do not detest him for his designs on you, you have no 40 right to complain that your husband is engaged elsewhere. But here comes the person we were speaking of.

*Enter* TOWNLY.

TOWNLY. Ladies, as I come uninvited, I beg, if I intrude you will use the same freedom in turning me out again.

AMANDA. I believe, sir, it is near the time Mr. Loveless said he would be at home. He talked of accepting Lord Foppington's invitation to sup at Sir Tunbelly Clumsey's.

TOWNLY. His Lordship has done me the honor to invite me also. If you'll let me escort you, I'll let you into a mystery as we go, in which you must play a part when we arrive.                                   50

AMANDA. But we have two hours yet to spare—the carriages are not ordered 'till eight—and it is not a five minutes drive. So, Cousin, let us keep the Colonel to play piquet with us, till Mr. Loveless comes home.

BERINTHIA. As you please, Madam, but you know I have letters to write.

TOWNLY. Madam, you know you may command me, tho' I'm a very wretched gamester.

AMANDA. O, you play well enough to lose your money, and that's all the

ladies require—and so without any more ceremony, let us go into the
next room and call for cards and candles.                    [*Exeunt.*  60

## SCENE III

BERINTHIA'*s Dressing-Room*

*Enter* LOVELESS.

LOVELESS. So—thus far all's well—I have got into her dressing-room,
and it being dusk, I think nobody has perceived me steal into the house.
I heard Berinthia tell my wife she had some particular letters to write
this evening, before we went to Sir Tunbelly's, and here are the imple-
ments for correspondence—how shall I muster up assurance to shew
myself when she comes?—I think she has given me encouragement—
and to do my impudence justice, I have made the most of it.—I hear a
door open and some one coming; if it should be my wife, what the Devil
should I say?—I believe she mistrusts me, and by my life I don't
deserve her tenderness; however I am determined to reform, tho' not  10
yet. Hah!—Berinthia—so I'll step in here till I see what sort of humour
she is in.                                    [*Goes into the Closet.*

*Enter* BERINTHIA.

BERINTHIA. Was ever so provoking a situation!—To think I should sit
and hear him compliment Amanda to my face!—I have lost all patience
with them both. I would not for something have Loveless know what
temper of mind they have piqued me into, yet I can't bear to leave them
together. No—I'll put my papers away, and return, to disappoint them.
[*Goes to the closet.*] O Lord! a ghost! a ghost! a ghost!

*Enter* LOVELESS.

LOVELESS. Peace, my Angel—it's no ghost—but one worth a hundred
spirits.                                                         20
BERINTHIA. How, sir, have you had the insolence to presume to——run
in again—here's somebody coming.

*Enter* MAID.

MAID. O Lord, Ma'am, what's the matter?
BERINTHIA. O Heav'ns I'm almost frightened out of my wits!—I
thought verily I had seen a ghost, and 'twas nothing but a black hood
pin'd against the wall.—You may go again, I am the fearfullest fool!
                                                           [*Exit* MAID.

*Re-enter* LOVELESS.

LOVELESS. Is the coast clear?

BERINTHIA. The coast clear!—Upon my word I wonder at your assurance!

LOVELESS. Why then you wonder before I have given you a proof of it. 30 But where's my wife?

BERINTHIA. At cards.

LOVELESS. With whom?

BERINTHIA. With Townly.

LOVELESS. Then we are safe enough.

BERINTHIA. You are so!—Some husbands would be of another mind were he at cards with their wives.

LOVELESS. And they'd be in the right on't too—but I dare trust mine.

BERINTHIA. Indeed!—And she, I doubt not, has the same confidence in you. Yet do you think she'd be content to come and find you here? 40

LOVELESS. 'Egad, as you say, that's true—then for fear she should come, hadn't we better go into the next room out of her way?

BERINTHIA. What—in the dark?

LOVELESS. Aye—or with a light, which you please.

BERINTHIA. You are certainly very impudent.

LOVELESS. Nay then—let me conduct you, my Angel.

BERINTHIA. Hold, hold, you are mistaken in your Angel, I assure you.

LOVELESS. I hope not, for by this hand I swear.

BERINTHIA. Come, come, let go my hand, or I shall hate you, I'll cry out as I live. 50

LOVELESS. Impossible!—you cannot be so cruel.

BERINTHIA. Ha!—here's some one coming—be gone instantly.

LOVELESS. Will you promise to return if I remain here?

BERINTHIA. Never trust myself in a room with you again while I live.

LOVELESS. But I have something particular to communicate to you.

BERINTHIA. Well, well, before we go to Sir Tunbelly's I'll walk upon the lawn. If you are fond of a Moon-light evening, you will find me there.

LOVELESS. E'faith, they're coming here now.—I take you at your word.

[*Exit* LOVELESS *into the Closet.*

BERINTHIA. 'Tis Amanda, as I live—I hope she has not heard his voice. 60 Tho' I mean she should have her share of jealousy in turn.

*Enter* AMANDA.

AMANDA. Berinthia, why did you leave me?

BERINTHIA. I thought I only spoil'd your party.

AMANDA. Since you have been gone, Townly has attempted to renew his importunities.——I must break with him—for I cannot venture to acquaint Mr. Loveless with his conduct.

BERINTHIA. O no—Mr. Loveless mustn't know of it by any means.

AMANDA. O not for the world.——I wish, Berinthia, you would undertake to speak to Townly on the subject.

BERINTHIA. Upon my word it would be a very pleasant subject for me to 70
talk to him on.—But come—let us go back,—and you may depend on't
I'll not leave you together again, if I can help it.           [*Exeunt.*

*Enter* LOVELESS.

LOVELESS. Soh—so!—a pretty piece of business I have over-heard—
Townly makes love to my wife—and I'm not to know it for the world—
I must enquire into this—and, by Heav'n, if I find that Amanda has in
the smallest degree——Yet what have I been at here?—O s'death!
that's no rule.

> That wife alone, unsullied credit wins,
> Whose virtues can atone her husband's sins;
> Thus while the man has other nymphs in view,                    80
> It suits the woman to be doubly true.           [*Exit.*

### END OF THE FOURTH ACT

# ACT V

## SCENE I

*A Garden—Moon Light*

*Enter* LOVELESS.

LOVELESS. Now, does she mean to make a fool of me, or not?—I shan't
wait much longer, for my wife will soon be enquiring for me to set out
on our supping party.—Suspence is at all times the devil—but of all
modes of suspence, the watching for a loitering mistress is the worst—
but let me accuse her no longer—she approaches with one smile to
o'erpay the anxiety of a year.

*Enter* BERINTHIA.

O Berinthia, what a world of kindness are you in my debt!—had you
staid five minutes longer—

BERINTHIA. You would have been gone, I suppose.

LOVELESS. [*Aside.*] Egad she's right enough.                    10

BERINTHIA. And I assure you 'twas ten to one that I came at all. In
short, I begin to think you are too dangerous a Being to trifle with; and

as I shall probably only make a fool of you at last, I believe we had better let matters rest as they are.

LOVELESS. You cannot mean it sure?

BERINTHIA. No!—why do you think you are really so irresistable, and master of so much address, as to deprive a woman of her senses in a few days acquaintance?

LOVELESS. O, no, Madam; 'tis only by your preserving your senses that I can hope to be admitted into your favour—your taste, judgment, and 20 discernment, are what I build my hopes on.

BERINTHIA. Very modest upon my word—and it certainly follows, that the greatest proof I can give of my possessing those qualities, would be my admiring Mr. Loveless!

LOVELESS. O that were so cold a proof—

BERINTHIA. What shall I do more?—esteem you?

LOVELESS. O, no—worse and worse.—Can you behold a man, whose every faculty your attractions have engrossed—whose whole soul, as by enchantment, you have seiz'd on—can you see him tremble at your feet, and talk of so poor a return as your esteem!                              30

BERINTHIA. What more would you have me give to a married man?

LOVELESS. How doubly cruel to remind me of misfortunes!

BERINTHIA. A misfortune to be married to so charming a woman as Amanda!

LOVELESS. I grant all her merit, but—'sdeath, now see what you have done by talking of her—she's here by all that's unlucky.

BERINTHIA. O Ged, we had both better get out of the way, for I should feel as aukward to meet her as you.

LOVELESS. Aye—but if I mistake not, I see Townly coming this way also —I must see a little into this matter. [*Steps aside*]                       40

BERINTHIA. O, if that's your intention—I am no woman if I suffer myself to be outdone in curiosity.                              [*goes on the other side.*

*Enter* AMANDA.

AMANDA. Mr. Loveless come home and walking on the lawn!—I will not suffer him to walk so late, tho' perhaps it is to shew his neglect of me ——Mr. Loveless—ha!—Townly again!—how I am persecuted!

*Enter* TOWNLY.

TOWNLY. Madam, you seem disturbed!

AMANDA. Sir, I have reason.

TOWNLY. Whatever be the cause, I would to Heaven it were in my power to bear the pain, or to remove the malady.

AMANDA. Your interference can only add to my distress.                        50

TOWNLY. Ah! Madam, if it be the sting of unrequited love you suffer from, seek for your remedy in revenge—weigh well the strength and beauty of your charms, and rouse up that spirit a woman ought to bear —disdain the false embraces of a husband—see at your feet a real lover —his zeal may give him title to your pity, altho' his merit cannot claim your love!

LOVELESS. [*Aside*] So, so, very fine, e'faith!

AMANDA. Why do you presume to talk to me thus?—is this your friend-ship to Mr. Loveless?—I perceive you will compel me at last to acquaint him with your treachery. 60

TOWNLY. He could not upbraid me if you were—he deserves it from me —for he has not been more false to you, than faithless to me.

AMANDA. To you!

TOWNLY. Yes, Madam; the lady for whom he now deserts those charms which he was never worthy of, was mine by right; and I imagined too, by inclination—Yes, Madam, Berinthia, who now——

AMANDA. Berinthia!—impossible!—

TOWNLY. 'Tis true, or may I never merit your attention.—She is the deceitful sorceress who now holds your husband's heart in bondage.

AMANDA. I will not believe it. 70

TOWNLY. By the faith of a true lover, I speak from conviction.—This very day I saw them together, and overheard——

AMANDA. Peace, Sir, I will not even listen to such slander—this is a poor device to work on my resentment, to listen to your insidious addresses. No, Sir; though Mr. Loveless may be capable of error, I am convinced I cannot be deceived so grossly in him, as to believe what you now report; and for Berinthia, you should have fixed on some more probable person for my rival, than she who is my relation, and my friend: for while I am myself free from guilt, I will never believe that love can beget injury, or confidence create ingratitude. 80

TOWNLY. If I do not prove this to you——

AMANDA. You never shall have an opportunity—from the artful manner in which you first shew'd yourself attentive to me, I might have been led, as far as virtue permitted, to have thought you less criminal than unhappy—but this last unmanly artifice merits at once my resentment and contempt. [*Exit.*

TOWNLY. Sure there's divinity about her; and she has dispensed some portion of honor's light to me: yet can I bear to lose Berinthia without revenge or compensation?—Perhaps she is not so culpable as I thought her. I was mistaken when I began to think lightly of Amanda's virtue, 90 and may be in my censure of my Berinthia.—Surely I love her still; for I feel I should be happy to find myself in the wrong. [*Exit.*

*Enter* LOVELESS *and* BERINTHIA.

BERINTHIA. Your servant, Mr. Loveless.

LOVELESS. Your servant, Madam.

BERINTHIA. Pray, what do you think of this?

LOVELESS. Truly, I don't know what to say.

BERINTHIA. Don't you think we steal forth two very contemptible creatures?

LOVELESS. Why tolerably so I must confess.

BERINTHIA. And do you conceive it possible for you ever to give Amanda 100 the least uneasiness again?

LOVELESS. No, I think we never should, indeed.

BERINTHIA. We!—why, monster, you don't pretend that I ever entertain'd a thought.

LOVELESS. Why then, sincerely, and honestly, Berinthia, there is something in my wife's conduct which strikes me so forcibly, that if it were not for shame, and the fear of hurting you in her opinion, I swear I would follow her, confess my error, and trust to her generosity for forgiveness.

BERINTHIA. Nay, prithee don't let your respect for me prevent you; for 110 as my object in trifling with you was nothing more than to pique Townly; and as I perceive he has been actuated by a similar motive, you may depend on't I shall make no mystery of the matter to him.

LOVELESS. By no means inform him—for tho' I may chuse to pass by his conduct without resentment, how will he presume to look me in the face again!

BERINTHIA. How will you presume to look him in the face again?

LOVELESS. He—who has dared to attempt the honour of my wife!

BERINTHIA. You—who have dared to attempt the honour of his mistress!—Come, come, be ruled by me who affect more levity than I have, 120 and don't think of anger in this cause. A Readiness to resent injuries, is a virtue only in those who are slow to injure.

LOVELESS. Then I will be ruled by you—and when you shall think proper to undeceive Townly, may your good qualities make as sincere a convert of him, as Amanda's have of me. When truth's extorted from us, then we own the robe of virtue is a graceful habit.

> Could women but our secret counsels scan—
> Could they but read the deep reserve of man—
> To keep our love—they'd rate their virtue high—
> They'd live together, and together die!            [*Exit.* 130

## SCENE II—Sir Tunbelly's House

*Enter* MISS HOYDEN, NURSE, *and* Y. FASHION.

Y. FASHION. This quick dispatch of the chaplain's I take so kindly, it shall give him claim to my favour as long as I live, I assure you.

MISS. And to mine too, I promise you.

NURSE. I most humbly thank your honors; and may your children swarm about you, like bees about a honey-comb.

MISS. I'cod with all my heart—the more the merrier, I say—ha Nurse?

*Enter* LORY, *taking* Y. FASHION *hastily aside.*

LORY. One word with you, for Heav'ns sake.

Y. FASHION. What the Devil's the matter?

LORY. Sir, your fortune's ruin'd, if you are not married—yonder's your brother, arrived with two coaches and six horses, twenty footmen, and 10 a coat worth fourscore pounds—so judge what will become of your Lady's heart.

Y. FASHION. Is he in the house yet?

LORY. No—they are capitulating with him at the gate—Sir Tunbelly luckily takes him for an impostor, and I have told him that we had heard of this plot before.

Y. FASHION. That's right: [*to* MISS] my dear, here's a troublesome business my man tells me of, but don't be frighten'd, we shall be too hard for the rogue.—Here's an impudent fellow at the gate (not knowing I was come hither incognito) has taken my name upon him, 20 in hopes to run away with you.

MISS. O the brazen-faced varlet, it's well we are married, or may be we might never have been so.

Y. FASHION. [*Aside.*] Egad like enough.—Prithee, Nurse, run to Sir Tunbelly, and stop him from going to the gate before I speak with him.

NURSE. An't please your honour, my Lady and I had best lock ourselves up till the danger be over.

Y. FASHION. Do so, if you please.

MISS. Not so fast—I won't be lock'd up any more, now I'm married.

Y. FASHION. Yes, pray, my dear do, till we have seiz'd this rascal. 30

MISS. Nay, if you'll pray me, I'll do any thing. [*Exit* MISS *and* NURSE.

Y. FASHION. [*To* LORY.] Hark you, sirrah, things are better than you imagine. The wedding's over.

LORY. [*Aside.*] The Devil it is, Sir!

Y. FASHION. Not a word—all's safe—but Sir Tunbelly don't know it, nor must not, yet. So I am resolved to brazen the business out, and have the pleasure of turning the imposture upon his Lordship, which I believe may easily be done.

*Enter* SIR TUNBELLY, *and* SERVANTS, *armed with clubs, pitch-forks, &c.*

Y. FASHION. Did you ever hear, Sir, of so impudent an undertaking?

SIR TUNBELLY. Never, by the Mass—but we'll tickle him, I'll warrant 40
you.

Y. FASHION. They tell me, Sir, he has a great many people with him,
disguised like servants.

SIR TUNBELLY. Ay, ay, rogues enow—but we have master'd them.—
We only fired a few shot over their heads, and the regiment scower'd
in an instant.—Here, Tommas, bring in your prisoner.

Y. FASHION. If you please, Sir Tunbelly, it will be best for me not to
confront the fellow yet, till you have heard how far his impudence will
carry him.

SIR TUNBELLY. 'Egad, your Lordship is an ingenious person. Your 50
Lordship then will please to step aside.

LORY. [*Aside.*] 'Fore Heaven I applaud my master's modesty.

[*Exe.* YOUNG FASHION *and* LORY.

*Enter* SERVANTS, *with* LORD FOPPINGTON, *disarmed.*

SIR TUNBELLY. Come—bring him along, bring him along.

LD. FOPPINGTON. What the pax do you mean, gentlemen, is it fair time
that you are all drunk before supper?

SIR TUNBELLY. Drunk, sirrah!—here's an impudent rogue for you.
Drunk, or sober, bully, I'm a Justice of the Peace, and know how to
deal with strollers.

LD. FOPPINGTON. Strollers!

SIR TUNBELLY. Aye, strollers.—Come, give an account of yourself.— 60
What's your name? Where do you live? Do you pay scot and lot?
Come, are you a freeholder or a copyholder?

LD. FOPPINGTON. And why dost thou ask me so many impertinent
questions?

SIR TUNBELLY. Because I'll make you answer 'em before I have done
with you, you rascal, you.

LD. FOPPINGTON. Before Gad, all the answer I can make to 'em, is,
that thou art a very extraordinary old fellow, stap my vitals!

SIR TUNBELLY. Nay, if you are for joking with Deputy Lieutenants,
we know how to deal with you.—Here, draw a warrant for him 70
immediately.

LD. FOPPINGTON. A warrant!—What the Devil is't thou would'st be at,
old gentleman?

SIR TUNBELLY. I would be at you, sirrah, (if my hands were not tied as
a Magistrate) and with these two double fists beat your teeth down your
throat you dog you.

LD. FOPPINGTON. And why would'st thou spoil my face at that rate?

SIR TUNBELLY. For your design to rob me of my daughter, villain.

LD. FOPPINGTON. Rab thee of thy daughter! Now do I begin to
believe I am in bed and asleep, and that all this is but a dream. Prithee, 80
old father, wilt thou give me leave to ask thee one question?

SIR TUNBELLY. I can't tell whether I will or not, till I know what it is.

LD. FOPPINGTON. Why then it is, whether thou didst not write to my
Lord Foppington to come down and marry thy daughter?

SIR TUNBELLY. Yes, marry did I, and my Lord Foppington is come
down, and shall marry my daughter before she's a day older.

LD. FOPPINGTON. Now give me thy hand, old dad, I thought we should
understand one another at last.

SIR TUNBELLY. This fellow's mad—here, bind him hand and foot.

[*They bind him.*

LD. FOPPINGTON. Nay, prithee Knight, leave fooling, thy jest begins to 90
grow dull.

SIR TUNBELLY. Bind him, I say—he's mad—bread and water, a dark
room, and a whip, may bring him to his senses again.

LD. FOPPINGTON. Prithee, Sir Tunbelly, why should you take such an
aversion to the freedom of my address, as to suffer the rascals thus to
skewer down my arms like a rabbit? 'Egad, if I don't waken quickly,
by all that I can see, this is like to prove one of the most impertinent
dreams that ever I dreamt in my life.                                   [*Aside.*

*Enter* MISS HOYDEN *and* NURSE.

MISS. [*Going up to him.*] Is this he that would have run away with me?
Fough! how he stinks of sweets![1]—Pray, father, let him be dragged 100
thro' the horse-pond.

LD. FOPPINGTON. [*Aside.*] This must be my wife, by her natural
inclination to her husband.

MISS. Pray, father, what do you intend to do with him—hang him?

SIR TUNBELLY. That, at least, child.

NURSE. Aye, and it's e'en too good for him too.

LD. FOPPINGTON. [*Aside.*] Madame la Governante, I presume;
hitherto this appears to me one of the most extraordinary families that
ever man of quality match'd into.

SIR TUNBELLY. What's become of my Lord, daughter?                      110

MISS. He's just coming, Sir.

LD. FOPPINGTON. [*Aside.*] My Lord!—What does he mean by that,
now?

*Enter* YOUNG FASHION *and* LORY.

LD. FOPPINGTON. Stap my vitals, Tam, now the dream's out.

Y. FASHION. Is this the fellow, Sir, that design'd to trick me of your
daughter?

---

¹ Scent.

SIR TUNBELLY. This is he, my Lord; how do you like him? is not he a pretty fellow to get a fortune?

Y. FASHION. I find by his dress, he thought your daughter might be taken with a beau.                                                                        120

MISS. O gemini! Is this a beau? Let me see him again. Ha! I find a beau is no such ugly thing, neither.

Y. FASHION. 'Egad, she'll be in love with him presently.—I'll e'en have him sent away to gaol. [*To* LORD FOP.] Sir, tho' your undertaking shews you a person of no extraordinary modesty, I suppose you ha'n't confidence enough to expect much favour from me.

LD. FOPPINGTON. Strike me dumb, Tam, thou art a very impudent fellow.

NURSE. Look; if the varlot has not the frontery to call his Lordship, plain Thomas.                                                                          130

SIR TUNBELLY. Come, is the warrant writ?

CHAPLAIN. Yes, Sir.

LD. FOPPINGTON. Hold, one moment.—Pray gentlemen—my Lord Foppington, shall I beg one word with your Lordship?

NURSE. O, ho, it's my Lord, with him now; see how afflictions will humble folks.

MISS. Pray, my Lord, don't let him whisper too close, lest he bite your ear off.

LD. FOPPINGTON. I am not altogether so hungry as your Ladyship is pleased to imagine. [*To* Y. FASHION.] Look you, Tam, I am sensible I  140 have not been so kind to you as I ought, but I hope you'll forgive what's past, and accept of the five thousand pounds I offer. Thou may'st live in extreme splendor with it, stap my vitals!

Y. FASHION. It's a much easier matter to prevent a disease, than to cure it. A quarter of that sum would have secured your mistress, twice as much won't redeem her.                                         [*Leaving him.*

SIR TUNBELLY. Well, what says he?

Y. FASHION. Only the rascal offered me a bribe to let him go.

SIR TUNBELLY. Aye, he shall go, with a halter to him—lead on, Constable.                                                                                     150

*Enter* SERVANT.

SERVANT. Sir, here is Muster Loveless, and Muster Colonel Townly, and some ladies, to wait on you.

LORY. [*Aside.*] So, Sir, What will you do now?

Y. FASHION. Be quiet—they are in the plot. [*To* SIR TUNBELLY.] Only a few friends, Sir Tunbelly, whom I wish'd to introduce to you.

LD. FOPPINGTON. Thou art the most impudent fellow, Tam, that ever Nature yet brought into the world. Sir Tunbelly, strike me speechless, but these are my friends and my guests, and they will soon inform thee, whether I am the true Lord Foppington or not.

*Enter* LOVELESS, TOWNLY, AMANDA, *and* BERINTHIA.

Y. FASHION. So, gentlemen, this is friendly; I rejoice to see you.　160

TOWNLY. My Lord, we are fortunate to be the witnesses of your Lordship's happiness.

LOVELESS. But your Lordship will do us the honour to introduce us to Sir Tunbelly Clumsey?

AMANDA. And us to your Lady.

LD. FOPPINGTON. Ged take me, but they are all in a story.

SIR TUNBELLY. Gentlemen, you do me great honour; my Lord Foppington's friends will ever be welcome to me and mine.

Y. FASHION. My love, let me introduce you to these ladies.

MISS. By goles,[1] they look so fine and so stiff, I am almost asham'd to　170 come nigh 'em.

AMANDA. A most engaging young lady, indeed!

MISS. Thank ye, Ma'am!

BERINTHIA. And I doubt not will soon distinguish herself in the Beau Monde.

MISS. Where is that?

Y. FASHION. You'll soon learn, my dear.

LOVELESS. But, Lord Foppington——

LD. FOPPINGTON. Sir!

LOVELESS. Sir! I was not addressing myself to you, Sir; pray who is this　180 gentlemen? He seems rather in a singular predicament.

SIR TUNBELLY. Ha, ha, ha!—So, these are your friends and your guests, ha, my adventurer?

LD. FOPPINGTON. I am struck dumb with their impudence, and cannot positively say whether I shall ever speak again or not.

SIR TUNBELLY. Why, Sir, this modest gentleman wanted to pass himself upon me for Lord Foppington, and carry off my daughter.

LOVELESS. A likely plot to succeed, truly, ha, ha!

LD. FOPPINGTON. As Gad shall judge me, Loveless, I did not expect this from thee; come, prithee confess the joke; tell Sir Tunbelly that I　190 am the real Lord Foppington, who yesterday made love to thy wife; was honour'd by her with a slap on the face, and afterward pink'd thro' the bady by thee.

SIR TUNBELLY. A likely story, truly, that a Peer wou'd behave thus!

LOVELESS. A curious fellow indeed! that wou'd scandalize the character he wants to assume; but what will you do with him, Sir Tunbelly?

---

[1] By God. Lucy, in a similar situation to Miss Hoyden's, says 'Then I'll have Mr. Thomas, by goles', in Fielding's *Old Man Taught Wisdom*.

SIR TUNBELLY. Commit him certainly, unless the bride and bridegroom chuse to pardon him.

LD. FOPPINGTON. Bride and bridegroom! For Gad's sake, Sir Tunbelly, 'tis tarture to me to hear you call 'em so. 200

MISS. Why, you ugly thing, what would you have him call us? dog and cat!

LD. FOPPINGTON. By no means, Miss; for that sounds ten times more like man and wife, than t'other.

SIR TUNBELLY. A precious rogue this, to come a wooing!

*Enter* SERVANT.

SERVANT. There are some more gentlefolks below, to wait upon Lord Foppington.

TOWNLY. S'death, Tom, what will you do now?

LD. FOPPINGTON. Now, Sir Tunbelly, here are witnesses, who I believe are not corrupted. 210

SIR TUNBELLY. Peace, fellow!—Wou'd your Lordship chuse to have your guests shewn here, or shall they wait till we come to 'em?

Y. FASHION. I believe, Sir Tunbelly, we had better not have these visitors here yet; 'egad, all must out! [*Aside.*

LOVELESS. Confess, confess, we'll stand by you.

LD. FOPPINGTON. Nay, Sir Tunbelly, I insist on your calling evidence on both sides, and if I do not prove that fellow an impostor——

Y. FASHION. Brother, I will save you the trouble, by now confessing, that I am not what I have passed myself for;—Sir Tunbelly, I am a gentleman, and I flatter myself a man of character; but 'tis with great pride I 220 assure you, I am not Lord Foppington.

SIR TUNBELLY. Oun's!—what's this!—an impostor!—a cheat!—fire and faggots, Sir!—if you are not Lord Foppington, who the Devil are you?

Y. FASHION. Sir, the best of my condition is, I am your son-in-law, and the worst of it is, I am brother to that noble Peer.

LD. FOPPINGTON. Impudent to the last!

SIR TUNBELLY. My son-in-law! Not yet, I hope?

Y. FASHION. Pardon me, Sir, I am, thanks to the goodness of your Chaplain, and the kind offices of this old gentlewoman. 230

LORY. 'Tis true, indeed, Sir; I gave your daughter away, and Mrs. Nurse, here, was clerk.

SIR TUNBELLY. Knock that rascal down!—But speak, Jezabel, how's this?

NURSE. Alas, your honour, forgive me!—I have been overreach'd in this business as well as you; your Worship knows, if the wedding dinner had been ready, you would have given her away with your own hands.

SIR TUNBELLY. But how durst you do this without acquainting me!

NURSE. Alas, if your Worship had seen how the poor thing begg'd and pray'd, and clung and twin'd about me like ivy round an old wall, you wou'd say I who had nurs'd it and rear'd it, must have had a heart of stone to refuse it. 240

SIR TUNBELLY. Ouns! I shall go mad! Unloose my Lord there, you scoundrels!

LD. FOPPINGTON. Why, when these gentlemen are at leisure, I shou'd be glad to congratulate you on your son-in-law, with a little more freedom of address.

MISS. 'Egad, tho'—I don't see which is to be my husband, after all.

LOVELESS. Come, come, Sir Tunbelly, a man of your understanding must perceive, that an affair of this kind is not to be mended by anger and reproaches. 250

TOWNLY. Take my word for it, Sir Tunbelly, you are only tricked into a son-in-law you may be proud of; my friend, Tom Fashion, is as honest a fellow as ever breath'd.

LOVELESS. That he is, depend on't, and will hunt or drink with you most affectionately; be generous, old boy, and forgive them.

SIR TUNBELLY. Never—the hussey.—when I had set my heart on getting her a title!

LD. FOPPINGTON. Now, Sir Tunbelly, that I am untruss'd, give me leave to thank thee for the very extraordinary reception I have met with in thy damn'd, execrable mansion, and at the same time to assure thee, that of all the bumpkins and blockheads I have had the misfortune to meet with, thou art the most obstinate and egregious, strike me ugly! 260

SIR TUNBELLY. What's this!—Ouns! I believe you are both rogues alike!

LD. FOPPINGTON. No, Sir Tunbelly, thou wilt find to thy unspeakable mortification, that I am the real Lord Foppington, who was to have disgraced myself by an alliance with a clod; and that thou hast match'd thy girl to a beggarly younger brother of mine, whose title deeds might be contain'd in thy tobacco-box. 270

SIR TUNBELLY. Puppy, puppy!—I might prevent their being beggars if I chose it;—for I cou'd give 'em as good a rent-roll as your Lordship.

TOWNLY. Well said, Sir Tunbelly.

LD. FOPPINGTON. Aye, old fellow, but you will not do it; for that would be acting like a Christian, and thou art a thorough barbarian, stap my vitals.

SIR TUNBELLY. Udzookers! Now six such words more, and I'll forgive them directly.

LOVELESS. 'Slife, Sir Tunbelly, you shou'd do it, and bless yourself; ladies what say you?

AMANDA. Good Sir Tunbelly, you must consent. 280

BERINTHIA. Come, you have been young yourself, Sir Tunbelly.

SIR TUNBELLY. Well, then, if I must, I must;—but turn that sneering

Lord out, however; and let me be revenged on somebody; but first, look whether I am a barbarian, or not; there, children, I join your hands, and when I'm in a better humour, I'll give you my blessing.

LOVELESS. Nobly done, Sir Tunbelly; and we shall see you dance at a grandson's wedding, yet.

MISS. By goles tho', I don't understand this; what, an't I to be a lady after all? only plain Mrs.— What's my husband's name, Nurse?

NURSE. 'Squire Fashion.                                              290

MISS. 'Squire, is he?—Well, that's better than nothing.

LD. FOPPINGTON. Now will I put on a Philosophic air, and shew these people, that it is not possible to put a man of my quality out of countenance. Dear Tam, since things are thus fallen out, prythee give me leave to wish thee joy; I do it *de bon coeur*, strike me dumb! You have married into a family of great politeness and uncommon elegance of manners; and your bride appears to be a lady beautiful in her person, modest in her deportment, refined in her sentiments, and of a nice morality, split my windpipe!

MISS. By goles, husband, break his bones, if he calls me names.      300

Y. FASHION. Your Lordship may keep up your spirits with your grimace, if you please, I shall support mine by Sir Tunbelly's favour, with this lady, and three thousand pounds a year.

LD. FOPPINGTON. Well, adieu, Tam; ladies, I kiss your hands; Sir Tunbelly, I shall now quit thy den, but while I retain my arms, I shall remember thou art a savage, stap my vitals!            [*Exit.*

SIR TUNBELLY. By the mass, 'tis well he's gone, for I shou'd ha' been provok'd by and by, to ha' dun'un a mischief;—Well, if this is a Lord, I think Hoyden has luck o' her side, in troth!

TOWNLY. She has, indeed, Sir Tunbelly, but I hear the fiddles; his   310
Lordship, I know, had provided 'em.

LOVELESS. O, a dance, and a bottle, Sir Tunbelly, by all means.

SIR TUNBELLY. I had forgot the company below; well, what—we must be merry then, ha?—and dance and drink, ha?—Well, 'fore George, you shan't say I do things by halves; son-in-law there looks like a hearty rogue, so we'll have a night of it; and which of these gay ladies will be the old man's partner, ha?—Ecod, I don't know how I came to be in so good a humour.

BERINTHIA. Well, Sir Tunbelly, my friend and I both will endeavour to keep you so; you have done a generous action, and are entitled to our   320
attention; and if you shou'd be at a loss to divert your new guests, we will assist you to relate to them the plot of your daughter's marriage, and his Lordship's deserved mortification, a subject which, perhaps, may afford no bad evening's entertainment.

SIR TUNBELLY. 'Ecod, with all my heart; tho' I am a main bungler at a long story.

# THE SCHOOL FOR SCANDAL

*A Comedy*

THE

# SCHOOL FOR SCANDAL,

A

# C O M E D Y;

AS IT IS PERFORMED AT THE

*T H E A T R E S-R O Y A L,*

IN

# L O N D O N

AND

# D U B L I N.

———————————
———————————

D U B L I N:

PRINTED IN THE YEAR, M,DCC,LXXX.

The title-page of the first published (pirated) edition of
*The School for Scandal*

# DRAMATIS PERSONÆ

As acted at Drury Lane Theatre, May 1777[1]

| | |
|---|---|
| SIR PETER TEAZLE | Mr. King |
| SIR OLIVER SURFACE | Mr. Yates |
| JOSEPH SURFACE | Mr. Palmer |
| CHARLES SURFACE | Mr. Smith |
| CRABTREE | Mr. Parsons |
| SIR BENJAMIN BACKBITE | Mr. Dodd |
| ROWLEY | Mr. Aickin |
| MOSES | Mr. Baddeley |
| TRIP | Mr. La Mash |
| SNAKE | Mr. Packer |
| CARELESS | Mr. Farren |
| SIR TOBY BUMPER | Mr. Gaudry |
| LADY TEAZLE | Mrs. Abington |
| MARIA | Miss P. Hopkins |
| LADY SNEERWELL | Miss Sherry |
| MRS. CANDOUR | Miss Pope |

[1] A report of the first performance, in the *Public Advertiser*, 9 May, noted that the 'gentlemen' (i.e. Charles's friends) were played by R. Palmer, Norris, and Chaplin. 'Sir Harry Bumper' was taken by J. S. Gaudry.

# A PORTRAIT

## Address'd to a Lady[1] with the Comedy of the School for Scandal

Tell me, ye prim Adepts in Scandal's School
Who rail by Precept, and detract by Rule,
Lives there no Character so tried—so known
So deck'd with Grace—and so unlike your own—
That even *you* assist her Fame to raise,
Approve by Envy, and by Silence praise?

Attend!—a model shall attract your view—
Daughters of Calumny[2]:—I summon YOU:—
*You* shall decide if this a *Portrait* prove,
Or fond Creation of the Muse and Love.                    10

Attend!—Ye Virgin Critics shrewd and sage,
Ye Matron Censors of this Childish age,—
Whose peering Eye, and wrinkled Front declare
A fix'd Antipathy to *Young* and *Fair*:
By Cunning cautious, or by Nature cold,
In maiden Malice virulently bold—

Attend—Ye skill'd to coin the precious Tale,
Creating Proof—where Innuendos fail!
Whose practic'd Mem'ries—cruelly exact—
Omit no Circumstance—except the Fact!                     20
Attend!—All ye who boast—or Old or Young—
The living Libel of a Sland'rous Tongue!
So shall my Theme as far contrasted be
As Saints by Fiends—or Hymns by Calumny.

Come, gentle *Amoret*,[3] (—for 'neath that Name
In worthier Verse[4] is sung thy Beauty's Fame)

---

[1] Frances Anne Crewe (1748–1818), wife of John, later first Lord Crewe (1742–1829). *The Critic* was dedicated to her mother, Frances Greville.

[2] Harlan W. Hamilton, *Doctor Syntax, A Silhouette of William Combe, Esq., 1742–1823* (1969), pp. 58, 286, notes that in the *Morning Post*, 25 Feb., 31 Mar. 1777, the play was called *The School for Slander*. He suggests that Sheridan changed the title to achieve greater accuracy.

[3] Frances Crewe. She was on very friendly terms with the Sheridans for many years.

[4] See R. C. Rhodes, *The Plays and Poems of . . . Sheridan*, iii. 199–200, for the sug-

Come—for but *thee* whom seeks the Muse?—and while
Celestial Blushes check thy conscious Smile,—
With timid Grace, and hesitating Eye—
The perfect Model which I boast—supply!                    30
Vain Muse,—could'st Thou the humblest Sketch create
Of *Her*—or slightest Charm could'st imitate,—
Could thy blest Strain, in kindred Colours, trace
The faintest Wonder of her Form, or Face—
Poets would study the immortal Line,
And *Reynolds*[1] own his *Art* subdued by *thine*!
That Art!—which well might added Lustre give
To Nature's best!—and Heaven's superlative!—
On *Granby's*[2] Cheek might bid new Glories rise,
Or point a purer Beam from *Devon's*[3] Eyes!—           40

Hard is the Task to shape that Beauty's Praise,
Whose Judgment scorns the Homage—Flatt'ry pays!
But praising *Amoret*—we cannot err:—
No Tongue o'ervalues Heav'n—or flatters *Her*!
Yet *She*—by Fate's Perverseness!—She alone
Would doubt our Truth—nor deem such Praise her *own*.

Adorning Fashion—unadorn'd by Dress—
Simple from Taste—and not from Carelessness.
Discreet in Gesture, in Deportment mild,
Not stiff with Prudence, nor uncouthly wild—             50
No State has *Amoret*!—no studied Mien!
She apes no·*Goddess*!—and she *moves* no *Queen*!
The softer Charm that in her Manner lies
Is fram'd to captivate, yet not surprise;
It justly suits th'Expression of her Face,—
'Tis less than Dignity—and more than Grace!

---

gestion that Sheridan's first wife gave the name of Amoret to Mrs. Crewe in her poem 'Laura to Silvio', praising her 'gentle step and hesitating grace'. He adds that this poem is the 'worthier verse', and that Sheridan replied to it and echoed some phrases in 'A Portrait'. Charles Fox, however, also wrote verses to 'Amoret', which are mentioned by Horace Walpole in a letter of 27 May 1775, to William Mason.

[1] Sir Joshua Reynolds (1723–92) painted three portraits of Mrs. Crewe.

[2] Mary Isabella (Somerset), wife of Charles Manners, Marquis of Granby, and afterwards fourth Duke of Rutland. Cf. 'To Silvio' (T. Moore, *Memoirs of . . . Sheridan*, i. 204).

[3] Georgiana (Spencer), first wife of William Cavendish, fifth Duke of Devonshire. The beauty of her eyes was constantly mentioned: cf. 'To Silvio' (Moore, op. cit., i. 204). Iris Palmer, *The Face without a Frown* (1944), p. 85, mentions that the Devonshires were thought to be the originals of Sir Peter and Lady Teazle.

On her pure Cheek the native Hue is such,
That form'd by Heav'n to be admir'd so much,
The Hand that made her with such partial Care,
Might well have fix'd a fainter Crimson there,                    60
And bade the gentle Inmate of her Breast,
Inshrined Modesty!—supply the Rest.


But Who the Peril of her Lips shall paint?—
Strip them of smiles—still, still all words were faint!
But moving—Love himself appears to teach
Their *Action*—tho' denied to rule her *Speech*!
And Thou,—who *seest* her speak—and dost not *hear*,
Mourn not her distant Accents 'scape thine ear,
*Viewing* those Lips—thou still may'st make pretence
To judge of what she says—and swear 'tis Sense;                  70
Cloath'd with such Grace, with such Expression fraught,
They move in meaning, and they pause in Thought!
But do'st thou further watch, with charm'd Surprise,
The mild Irresolution of her Eyes?
Curious to mark—how frequent they repose
In brief Eclipse, and momentary close?
Ah!—see'st Thou not!—an ambush'd Cupid there—
Too tim'rous of his Charge!—with jealous care
Veils, and unveils those Beams of heav'nly Light,
Too full—too fatal else for mortal Sight!                        80
Nor yet—such pleasing Vengeance fond to meet—
In pard'ning Dimples hope a safe retreat,
What tho' her peaceful Breast should ne'er allow
Subduing Frowns to arm her alter'd Brow,
By Love! I swear—and by his gentler wiles!—
More fatal still—the Mercy of her Smiles!


Thus lovely!—thus adorn'd!—possessing all
Of bright, or fair—that can to woman fall,
The Height of Vanity might well be thought
Prerogative in her,—and Nature's Fault;                          90
Yet gentle *Amoret*—in mind supreme
As well as Charms—rejects the vainer Theme;
And half mistrustful of her Beauty's store
She barbs with Wit—those Darts too keen before.


Grac'd by those signs—which Truth delights to own,
The timid Blush,—and mild submitted Tone—

Whate'er she says—tho' Sense appear throughout—
Bears the unartful Hue of female Doubt.
Deck'd with that Charm, how lovely *Wit* appears.
How graceful *Science* when that Robe she wears!          100
Such too her Talents, and her Bent of Mind
As speak a sprightly Heart—by Thought refin'd:
A Taste for Mirth—by Contemplation school'd;
A Turn for Ridicule—by Candour rul'd;
A Scorn of Folly—which she tries to hide;
An awe of Talent—which she owns with Pride.

Peace idle Muse!—no more thy Strain prolong,
But yield a Theme, thy warmest Praises wrong,
Just to her Merit tho' thou canst not raise
Thy feeble Verse—behold th'acknowledg'd Praise          110
Has spread Conviction thro' the envious Train,
And cast a fatal Gloom o'er Scandal's Reign!
And Lo! each pallid Hag, with blister'd Tongue,
Mutters Assent to all thy Zeal has sung,
Owns all the Colours just—the Outline true,
*Thee* my Inspirer—and my *Model*—CREWE!

# PROLOGUE

*Spoken by Mr. King*
*Written by D. Garrick, Esqr.*


*A School for Scandal*! tell me I beseech you
Needs there a School this modish art to teach you?
No need of lessons *now* the knowing think:
We might as well be taught to Eat, and drink:
Caus'd by a Dearth of Scandal, should the Vapours
Distress our Fair ones,—let 'Em read the Papers—
Their pow'rful Mixtures such disorders hit
Crave what they will, there's *quantum Sufficit.*


  'Lud' cries *my Lady Wormwood*, who loves Tattle,
And puts much Salt and pepper in her prattle;         10
Just ris'n at Noon, all Night at Cards when threshing;
Strong Tea and Scandal, 'bless me how refreshing!
Give me the Papers *Lisp*—how bold, and free—*(sips)*
Last Night Lord *L—* *(sips)* was caught with Lady *D—*
For aching heads what charming Sal Volatile! *(sips)*
If Mrs. B: will still continue flirting,
We hope she'll *draw*, or we'll *un-*draw the Curtain.
Fine Satire poz—in publick all abuse it—
But by Ourselves,—*(sips)* our praise we can't refuse it.
Now Lisp read *you*—there at that dash and Star'—*(sips)*    20
'Yes Ma'am—a certain Lord had best beware,
Who lives not twenty Miles from Grosv'nor Square
For should he *Lady W* find willing,
*Wormwood is bitter'*—'O that's me the villain
Throw it behind the fire, and never more,
Let that vile paper come within my door.'
Thus at our friends we laugh, who feel the Dart—
To reach *our* feelings, we ourselves must Smart.


Is our Young Bard so young to think that He
Can Stop *the full Spring-tide* of Calumny—         30
Knows he the World so little and Its trade?
Alas, the Devil is sooner *rais'd*, than *laid*—

So strong, so swift, the Monster there's no gagging;
Cut Scandal's head off—still the tongue is wagging.
Proud of your Smiles once lavishly bestow'd
Again our young Don Quixote takes the road:
To shew his Gratitude—he draws his pen,
And seeks this Hydra—Scandal in Its den
From his fell gripe the frighted fair to save
Tho he should fall—th'attempt must please the brave.          40
For your applause, all perils he would through,
He'll *fight*, that's *write*, a Cavalliero true,
Till Ev'ry drop of Blood, that's Ink, is spilt for *You*.

# THE SCHOOL FOR SCANDAL

*Act 1st*

*Scene 1st*

LADY SNEERWELL'S[1] *House*

LADY SNEERWELL *at the dressing Table*

SNAKE *drinking Chocolate.*

LADY SNEERWELL. The Paragraphs you say, Mr. Snake, were all inserted?

SNAKE. They were Madam—and as I copied them myself in a feign'd Hand there can be no suspicion whence they came.—

LADY SNEER. Did you circulate the Report of Lady Brittle's Intrigue with Captain Boastall?

SNAKE. That is in as fine a Train as your Ladyship could wish.—In the common course of Things, I think it must reach Mrs. Clackit's[2] Ears within four and twenty Hours and then you know the Business is as good as done. 10

LADY SNEER. Why truly Mrs. Clackit has a very pretty Talent, and a great deal of industry.

SNAKE. True madam and has been tolerably successful in her day. To my Knowledge—she has been the cause of six matches being broken off, and three sons being disinherited, of four forced Elopements, as many close confinements, nine separate maintenances, and two Divorces.—nay, I have more than once traced her causing a Tête-à-Tête in the Town and Country Magazine[3]—when the Parties perhaps have never seen each other's Faces before in the course of their Lives.

---

[1] There is a critic named Sneerwell in Fielding's *Pasquin* (1736), but he seems like Lady Sneerwell only when he says, 'Consider, sir, I am my own enemy.'

[2] Mrs. Clackit is a character in Gay's *The Distress'd Wife*. The name is also used in a story in the *Town and Country Magazine*, iii (1771), 242.

[3] This monthly periodical began in Jan. 1769, and in its first number declared, 'we flatter ourselves that the anecdotes we shall be able to furnish, will be the means of handing down to posterity a lively idea of the prevailing beauties, and their most zealous admirers, of this aera'. These were the basis of the Tête-à-Tête, in which a scandalous intrigue between a man and woman in fashionable life was described in plausible detail, and illustrated with portraits of the parties concerned. Their identities were also suggested by pseudonyms or initials. The authors of these pieces were apparently men named Beaufort and Caracioli: see E. H. W. Meyerstein, *A Life of Thomas Chatterton* (1930), p. 404.

LADY SNEER. She certainly has Talents, but her manner is gross.          20

SNAKE. 'Tis very true—she generally designs well—has a free tongue
and a bold invention—but her colouring is too dark and her outline
often extravagant. She wants that delicacy of Hint—and mellowness of
sneer which distinguish your Ladyship's Scandal.

LADY SNEER. Ah! you are Partial Snake.

SNAKE. Not in the least—everybody allows that Lady Sneerwell can do
more with a word or a Look, than many can with the most labour'd
Detail even when they happen to have a little truth on their side to
support it.

LADY SNEER. Yes my dear Snake, and I am no Hypocrite to deny the          30
satisfaction I reap from the Success of my Efforts—wounded myself
in the early Part of my Life by the envenom'd Tongue of Slander
I confess I have since known no Pleasure equal to the reducing others,
to the Level of my own injured Reputation—.

SNAKE. Nothing can be more natural—But Lady Sneerwell—There is
one affair in which you have lately employ'd me wherein I confess
I am at a Loss to guess your motives.

LADY SNEER. I conceive you mean with respect to my neighbour Sir
Peter Teazle and his Family?

SNAKE. I do; here are two young men, to whom Sir Peter has acted as          40
a kind of Guardian since their Father's death, the elder possessing the
most amiable Character and universally well spoken of, the other the
most dissipated and extravagant young Fellow in the Kingdom without Friends or Character—the former an avow'd Admirer of your
Ladyship, and apparently your Favourite; the latter attached to Maria,
Sir Peter's ward—and confessedly belov'd by her—now on the face of
these circumstances it is utterly unaccountable to me why you, the
Widow of a City Knight with a good Jointure—should not close with the
Passion of a man of such character and expectations as Mr. Surface—
and more so why you should be so uncommonly earnest to destroy the          50
mutual Attachment—subsisting between his brother Charles, and Maria.

LADY SNEER. Then at once to unravel this mystery—I must inform
you that Love has no share whatever in the intercourse between Mr.
Surface and me.

SNAKE. No!

LADY SNEER. His real attachment is to Maria or her Fortune—but
finding in his Brother a favour'd Rival He has been obliged to mask
his Pretensions—and profit by my Assistance.

SNAKE. Yet still I am more puzzled why you should interest yourself
in his Success—          60

LADY SNEER. Heav'ns! how dull you are!,—cannot you surmise the
weakness which I hitherto thro' shame have conceal'd even from you?
—must I confess that Charles—that Libertine, that extravagant—that

Bankrupt in Fortune and Reputation—that He it is for whom I am
thus anxious and malicious and to gain whom I would sacrifice—
everything?[1]

SNAKE. Now indeed—your conduct appears consistent—but how came
you and Mr. Surface so confidential—

LADY SNEER. For our mutual interest; I have found him out a long time
since—I know him to be artful selfish and malicious—in short, a   70
Sentimental[2] Knave.

SNAKE. Yet, Sir Peter vows He has not his equal in England—and above
all—he praises him as a *man of Sentiment*—

LADY SNEER. True and with the assistance of his Sentiments and
Hypocrisy he has brought him entirely into his Interest with regard to
Maria.

*Enter* SERVANT.

SERVANT. Mr. Surface.

LADY SNEER. Shew him up.                              [*Exit* SERVANT.
He generally calls about this Time—I don't wonder at People's giving
him to me for a Lover—                                           80

*Enter* SURFACE.

SURFACE. My dear Lady Sneerwell—how do you do—to Day? Mr.
Snake your most Obedient.

LADY SNEER. Snake has just been arraigning me on our mutual attachment but I have informed him of our real views—you know how useful
he has been to us—and believe me the confidence is not ill placed.

SURFACE. Madam it is impossible for me to suspect a man of Mr.
Snake's sensibility and discernment—

LADY SNEER. Well—well—no compliments now—but tell me when you
saw your Mistress Maria, or what is more material to me your Brother—

SURFACE. I have not seen either since I left you—but I can inform you  90
that they never meet—some of your Stories have taken a good effect
on Maria.

LADY SNEER. Ah! my dear Snake the merit of this belongs to you—but
do your Brother's Distresses encrease—?

SURFACE. Every—hour—I am told He has had another execution in the
House yesterday—in short his Dissipation and extravagance exceed
any thing I ever heard of—

---

[1] Cf. Mellefont's lines in Congreve's *The Double-Dealer* (1694), I. i: 'None besides
you, and *Maskwell*, are acquainted with the Secret of my Aunt *Touchwood's* violent
Passion for me. Since my first refusal of her Addresses, she has endeavour'd to do me
all ill Offices with my Uncle. . . .'

[2] Given to moral reflections. See Erik Erämetsä, *A Study of the Word 'Sentimental'
and of other Linguistic Characteristics of Eighteenth Century Sentimentalism in England*
(Helsinki, 1951), pp. 27–39; and [Samuel Richardson] *A Collection of Moral Sentiments*
(1755).

LADY SNEER. Poor Charles!

SURFACE. True Madam—notwithstanding his Vices one can't help feeling for him—aye, poor Charles! I'm sure I wish it was in my Power 100 to be of any essential Service to him—for the man who does not share in the Distresses of a Brother, even tho' merited by his own misconduct —deserves—

LADY SNEER. O Lud you are going to be moral and forget that you are among Friends—

SURFACE. Egad that's true—I'll keep that sentiment 'till I see Sir Peter, however it is certainly a charity to rescue Maria from such a Libertine —who if He is to be reclaim'd can be so only by a Person of your Ladyship's superior accomplishments and understanding.—

SNAKE. I believe Lady Sneerwell here's Company coming, I'll go and 110 Copy the Letter I mentioned to you.—Mr. Surface your most Obedient. [*Exit* SNAKE.

SURFACE. Sir, your very devoted.—Lady Sneerwell, I am very sorry you have put any further confidence in that Fellow.

LADY SNEER. Why so?

SURFACE. I have lately detected him in frequent Conference with old Rowley who was formerly my Father's Steward, and has never, you know, been a Friend of mine.

LADY SNEER. And do you think he would betray us?

SURFACE. Nothing more likely: take my word for't Lady Sneerwell, 120 that Fellow hasn't Virtue enough to be faithful even to his own Villainy.—hah! Maria!

*Enter* MARIA.

LADY SNEER. Maria, my dear—how do you do—what's the matter?

MARIA. O there is that disagreeable Lover of mine Sir Benjamin Backbite has just call'd at my Guardian's, with his Odious Uncle Crabtree— so I slipt out and run hither to avoid them.

LADY SNEER. Is that all—?

SURFACE. If my Brother Charles had been of the Party, Ma'am, perhaps you would not have been so much alarmed.

LADY SNEER. Nay now—you are severe for I dare swear the Truth of 130 the matter is Maria heard *you* were here;—but—my dear—what has Sir Benjamin done that you should avoid him so—

MARIA. Oh He has done nothing—but tis for what he has said—his conversation is a perpetual Libel on all his Acquaintance.

SURFACE. Aye and the worst of it is there is no advantage in not knowing him; for He'll abuse a Stranger just as soon as his best Friend—and his Uncle's as bad.

LADY SNEER. Nay but we should make allowance, Sir Benjamin is a Wit and a Poet.

MARIA. For my part—I own madam—Wit loses its respect with me when  140
  I see it in company with malice.[1]—what do you think Mr. Surface?
SURFACE. Certainly, Madam, to smile at the jest which plants a Thorn in
  another's Breast is to become a principal in the Mischief.
LADY SNEER. Pshaw!—there's no possibility of being witty—without a
  little ill nature—the malice of a good thing is the Barb that makes it
  stick—what's your opinion, Mr. Surface?
SURFACE. To be sure madam—that conversation where the Spirit of
  Raillery is suppress'd will ever appear tedious and insipid—
LADY SNEER. Well I'll not debate how far Scandal may be allowable—but
  in a man I am sure it is always contemptible;—we have Pride, envy,  150
  Rivalship, and a Thousand motives to depreciate each other—but the
  male-Slanderer—must have the cowardice of a woman before He can
  traduce one.

*Enter* SERVANT.

SERVANT. Madam Mrs. Candour is below and if your Ladyship's at
  leisure will leave her carriage—
LADY SNEER. Beg her to walk in—Now Maria however here is a Character to your Taste for tho' Mrs. Candour is a little talkative Everybody
  allows her to be the best natured and best sort of Woman—
MARIA. Yes with a very gross affectation of good Nature and Benevolence—she does more Mischief than the Direct malice of old Crabtree.—  160
SURFACE. 'Efaith 'tis very true Lady Sneerwell. Whenever—I hear the
  current running against the Characters of my Friends I never think
  them in such Danger as when Candour undertakes their Defence.
LADY SNEER. Hush here she is—

*Enter* MRS. CANDOUR.

MRS. CANDOUR. My dear Lady Sneerwell, how have you been this
  Century—Mr. Surface, what News do you hear? tho' indeed it is no
  matter, for I think one hears nothing else but Scandal—
SURFACE. Just so, indeed Madam—.
MRS. CANDOUR. Ah! Maria Child—what is the whole affair off between
  you and Charles—His extravagance I presume—The Town talks of  170
  nothing else—
MARIA. I am very sorry Ma'am, the Town has so little to do.
MRS. CANDOUR. True—true Child but there is no stopping People's
  Tongues. I own I was hurt to hear it—as indeed I was to learn from
  the same quarter that your Guardian Sir Peter and Lady Teazle have
  not agreed lately so well as could be wish'd.
MARIA. 'Tis strangely impertinent for People to busy themselves so—

[1] Cf. Steele's statement, 'I abhor . . . that kind of Wit which betrays hardness of
Heart' (*Richard Steele's Periodical Journalism*, ed. R. Blanchard (Oxford, 1959), p. 35).

MRS. CANDOUR. Very true Child but what's to be done? People will talk—there's no preventing it.—why it was but yesterday, I was told that Miss Gadabout had eloped with Sir Filagree Flirt—but Lord! 180 there is no minding what one hears—tho' to be sure I had this from very good Authority.—

MARIA. Such Reports are highly scandalous—

MRS. CANDOUR. So they are Child—shameful! shameful! but the world is so censorious, no character escapes—Lud now!—who would have suspected your Friend Miss Prim of an Indiscretion yet such is the ill nature of People that they say her Uckle stopt her last Week just as she was stepping into the York Diligence with her Dancing master.

MARIA. I'll answer for't there are no grounds for the Report—

MRS. CANDOUR. Oh no foundation in the world I dare swear, no more 190 probably than for the story circulated last month—of Mrs. Festino's[1] affair with Colonel Cassino—tho' to be sure that matter was never rightly clear'd up.

SURFACE. The Licence of invention some People take is monstrous indeed.

MARIA. 'Tis so—but in my opinion those who report such things are equally culpable.

MRS. CANDOUR. To be sure they are—Tale Bearers are as bad as the Tale makers—'tis an old observation and a very true one—but what's to be done as I said before—how will you prevent People from talking? 200 —to Day Mrs. Clackit assur'd me Mr. and Mrs. Honeymoon—were at last become mere man and wife like the rest of their acquaintances —she likewise hinted that a certain widow in the next street had got rid of her Dropsy and recover'd her shape in a most surprising manner —and at the same time Miss Tattle who was bye affirm'd that Lord Buffalo had discover'd his Lady at a house of no extraordinary Fame— and that Sir Harry Bouquet[2] and Tom Saunter were to measure swords on a similar Provocation, but Lord! do you think I would report these Things? No—no Tale Bearers as I said before are just as bad as tale-makers. 210

SURFACE. Ah! Mrs. Candour—if everybody had your Forbearance and Good nature!

MRS. CANDOUR. I confess Mr. Surface I cannot bear to hear People Attack'd behind their Backs and when ugly circumstances come out against one's acquaintances I own I always love to think the best—by the bye I hope 'tis not true;—that your Brother is absolutely ruin'd—

SURFACE. I am afraid his circumstances are very bad indeed—Ma'am.

---

[1] The seventh meeting of the 'Subscription Festinos' (Italianate entertainments) in Hanover Square, were advertised in the *Public Advertiser*, 25 Apr. 1776.

[2] He appears again in *The Camp*.

MRS. CANDOUR. Ah! I heard so—but you must tell him to keep up his Spirits—every body almost is in the same way—Lord Spindle,[1] Sir Thomas Splint, Captain Quinze, and Mr. Nickit[2]—all up I hear within 220 this Week! so if Charles is undone He'll find half his Acquaintances ruin'd too—and that you know is a consolation—

SURFACE. Doubtless Ma'am—a very great one—

*Enter* SERVANT.

SERVANT. Mr. Crabtree and Sir Benjamin Backbite.    [*Exit* SERVANT.

LADY SNEER. Soh! Maria, You see your Lover pursues you. Positively you shan't escape—

*Enter* CRABTREE, *and* SIR BENJAMIN BACKBITE.

CRABTREE. Lady Sneerwell—I kiss your hands—Mrs. Candour I don't believe you are acquainted with my Nephew Sir Benjamin Backbite— egad Ma'am—He has a pretty Wit—and is a pretty Poet too isn't He Lady Sneerwell?—                                                    230

SIR BENJ. O fie Uncle—

CRABTREE. Nay egad it's true. I'll back him at a Rebus[3] or a Charade[4] against the best Rhymer in the Kingdom—has your Ladyship heard the Epigram He wrote last week on Lady Frizzle's Feather catching Fire? do Benjamin repeat it—or the Charade you made last Night extempore at Mrs. Drowzy's conversazione—come now your first is the Name of a Fish, your second a great Naval Commander—and

SIR BENJ. Uncle—now—prithee—

CRABTREE. Efaith Ma'am—'twould surprise you to hear how ready He is at these Things.—                                                  240

LADY SNEER. I wonder Sir Benjamin you never publish any-thing.

SIR BENJ. To say truth Ma'am 'tis very vulgar to Print, and as my little Productions are mostly Satires and Lampoons on particular people I find they circulate more by giving copies[5] in confidence to the Friends

---

[1] 'Lord Spindle' was one of the figures in a puppet-show play called *The Auction Room*, given in the Grand Saloon of Exeter 'Change on 23 December 1776.

[2] 'Nick' was a winning throw at dice. To 'nick it' was to guess correctly.

[3] Condemned by Addison in one of his papers on 'false wit': 'I find likewise among the Ancients that ingenious Kind of Conceit, which the Moderns distinguish by the Name of a Rebus, that does not sink a Letter but a whole Word, by substituting a Picture in its place' (*The Spectator*, ed. D. F. Bond (Oxford, 1965), i. 250).

[4] Cf. R. Tickell, *The Wreath of Fashion* (1777), p. 7:
> With *chips* of wit, and mutilated lays,
> See *Palmerston* fineer his *Bout's Rhimées*.
> Fav'rite of ev'ry Muse, elect of Phoebus,
> To string Charades, or fabricate a Rebus.

[5] Cf. *Poetical Amusements at a Villa near Bath* (2nd edn., 1776), i. p. v: 'The Editor does not apprehend private confidence wounded in the present publication, as the greatest part of these poems were acknowledged by their Authors in numerous assemblies, and with their approbation copied and dispersed through every quarter of England.'

of the Parties—however I have some love-Elegies[1] which when favour'd
—with this Lady's smiles I mean to give to the Public.

CRABTREE. 'Fore Heav'n Ma'am they'll immortalise you—you'll be
handed down to Posterity like Petrarch's Laura or Waller's Sacharissa.[2]

SIR BENJ. Yes Madam I think you will like them—when you shall see
them on a beautiful Quarto page where a neat rivulet of Text shall    250
murmur thro' a meadow of margin.—'fore Gad they will be the most
elegant Things of their Kind.

CRABTREE. But Ladies that's true have you heard the news?—

MRS. CANDOUR. What Sir, do you mean the Report of—

CRABTREE. No ma'am that's not it.—Miss Nicely is going to be married
to her own Footman.

MRS. CANDOUR. Impossible!

CRABTREE. Ask Sir Benjamin.

SIR BENJ. 'Tis very true Ma'am—everything is fix'd and the Wedding
Livery bespoke.                                                       260

CRABTREE. Yes and they *do* say there were pressing Reasons for't.

LADY SNEER. Why I *have* heard something of this before.

MRS. CANDOUR. It can't be—and I wonder any one should believe such
a story of so prudent a Lady as Miss Nicely.

SIR BENJ. O Lud ma'am that's the very reason 'twas believed at once,—
she has always been so cautious and so reserved that every Body was
sure there was some reason for it at bottom.

MRS. CANDOUR. Why to be sure a Tale of Scandal is as fatal to the Credit
of a prudent Lady of her Stamp as a Fever is generally to those of the
strongest Constitutions, but there is a sort of puny sickly Reputation    270
that is always ailing yet will outlive the robuster Characters of a hundred
Prudes.

SIR BENJ. True Madam there are Valetudinarians in Reputation as well
as constitution—who being conscious of their weak Part avoid the
least breath of air and supply their want of Stamina by care and
circumspection.

MRS. CANDOUR. Well but this may be all a mistake—you know Sir
Benjamin very trifling circumstances often give rise to the most
injurious Tales—

---

[1] The *Love Elegies* (1743) of James Hammond (1710–42) were very well known,
but Sheridan may have intended a more personal jest at the expense of the author of
*Nuptial Elegies* (1774). A copy of this work is listed in Sotheby's Catalogue of 15 July
1929, item 288, as follows: '*Nuptial Elegies*, vignette on title, two leaves containing a
manuscript poem, "Sonnet to Mrs. Sheridan with *Nuptial Elegies*," in six six-line
stanzas, bound before title, on verso of the second leaf (facing the title) "From the
Author" in a contemporary hand. . . .'

[2] Edmund Waller (1606–87) wrote verses to 'Sacharissa', Lady Dorothy Sidney
(1617–84), afterwards Countess of Sunderland.

CRABTREE. That they do I'll be sworn Ma'am—did you ever hear how 280
Miss Piper came to lose her Lover and her Character last Summer at
Tunbridge?—Sir Benjamin you remember it—

SIR BENJ. O to be sure the most whimsical Circumstance—

LADY SNEER. How was it Pray?

CRABTREE. Why one Evening at Mrs. Ponto's Assembly the conversation
happen'd to turn on the difficulty of breeding Nova-Scotia Sheep in
this Country—says a young Lady in company, 'I have known instances
of it for Miss Letitia Piper, a first cousin of mine, had a Nova-Scotia
Sheep that produc'd her Twins.'—'what!' cries the old Dowager Lady
Dundizzy (who you know is as deaf as a Post) 'has Miss Piper had 290
twins?' this Mistake as you may imagine threw the whole company
into a fit of Laughing;—however 'twas the next morning everywhere
reported and in a few Days believ'd by the whole Town, that Miss
Letitia Piper had actually been brought to Bed of a fine Boy and a Girl
—and in less than a Week there were People who could name the Father,
and the Farm House where the Babies were put out to Nurse.

LADY SNEER. Strange indeed!

CRABTREE. Matter of Fact I assure you—O Lud Mr. Surface pray is it
true that your Unkle Sir Oliver is coming home—

SURFACE. Not that I know of indeed Sir.                              300

CRABTREE. He has been in the east Indies a long time—you can
Scarcely remember him—I believe—sad comfort whenever he returns
to hear how your Brother has gone on.—

SURFACE. Charles has been imprudent Sir to be sure but I hope no Busy
People have already prejudiced Sir Oliver against him—he may
reform—

SIR BENJ. To be sure He may—for my Part I never believed him to be
so utterly void of Principle as People say—and tho' He has lost all his
Friends I am told no body is better spoken of—by the Jews.

CRABTREE. That's true egad nephew—if the old Jewry were a Ward 310
I believe Charles would be an alderman—no man more popular there
—foregad I hear He pays as many annuities[1] as the Irish Tontine[2]

---

[1] 'My Lord Winterbottom . . . though he is little more than thirty years of age,
pays to Jew Annuitants the moderate sum of 5700 l. only out of an estate of 9000 l.
per Annum.' (Robert Bage, *Barham Downs* (1784), i. 119.)

[2] Lorenzo Tonti, a seventeenth-century Neapolitan banker, invented the scheme
named after him, by which contributors to a loan were paid an annuity during their
lifetime and it grew in size as the number of subscribers died. The last to remain took
the whole. The Irish government set up a tontine to help pay off its debts. An advertisement of the 'English Tontine Annuities' in the *London Evening Post*, 28–30 Sept. 1775,
claimed that its benefits were greater than those of the 'Irish Tontine': 'A subscription
of 100 l. in the Irish Tontine (which filled with such rapidity) produced only 100 l. a
year, and 883 lives must drop before that sum could be obtained; whereas, in this
Tontine, five guineas will produce 100 l. a year, or fifty guineas 1000 l. a year, after the
fall of 499 lives only.'

and that whenever He's sick they have Prayers for the recovery of his Health in the Synagogue—

SIR BENJ. Yet no man lives in greater Splendour:—they tell me when He entertains his Friends—He can sit down to dinner with a dozen of his own Securities, have a score Tradesmen waiting in the Anti-Chamber and an Officer behind every Guest's Chair.

SURFACE. This may be entertainment to you Gentlemen but you pay very little regard to the Feelings of a Brother.                              320

MARIA. Their Malice is intollerable.—Lady Sneerwell I must wish you a good morning—I'm not very well—                    [*Exit* MARIA.

MRS. CANDOUR. O dear she chang'd colour very much—!

LADY SNEER. Do Mrs. Candour follow her—she may want assistance.

MRS. CANDOUR. That I will with all my soul. Ma'am—poor dear Girl— who knows—what her situation may be!        [*Exit* MRS. CANDOUR.

LADY SNEER. 'Twas nothing but that she could not bear to hear Charles reflected on notwithstanding their difference.

SIR BENJ. The young Lady's Penchant is obvious.

CRABTREE. But Benjamin—you mustn't give up the Pursuit for that—  330 follow her and put her into good humour—repeat her some of your own Verses—come I'll assist you.

SIR BENJ. Mr. Surface I did not mean to hurt you—but depend upon't your Brother is utterly undone—                    [*going.*

CRABTREE. O Lud! aye—undone as ever man was—can't raise a guinea.
                                                            [*going.*

SIR BENJ. And every thing sold—I'm told that was moveable.—
                                                            [*going.*

CRABTREE. I have seen one that was at his house—not a thing left but some empty Bottles that were over-look'd, and the Family Pictures which I believe are framed in the Wainscoat.—        [*going.*

SIR BENJ. And I'm very sorry to hear also some bad stories against him.  340
                                                            [*going.*

CRABTREE. O He has done many mean things—that's certain!

SIR BENJ. But however as He's your Brother—            [*going.*

CRABTREE. We'll tell you all another opportunity.

                            [*Exeunt* CRABTREE *and* SIR BENJAMIN.

LADY SNEER. Ha, ha! ha! 'tis very hard for them to leave a subject they have not quite run down.

SURFACE. And I believe the Abuse was no more acceptable to your Ladyship than to Maria.

LADY SNEER. I doubt her Affections are farther engaged than we imagin'd but the Family are to be here this Evening so you may as well dine where you are and we shall have an opportunity of observing  350 farther, in the meantime I'll go and Plot mischief and you shall study Sentiments—                                        [*Exeunt.*

*Scene 2d*

SIR PETER's *House*

*Enter* SIR PETER.

SIR PETER. When an Old Bachelor takes a young Wife—what is he to expect!—'Tis now Six Months since Lady Teazle made me the happiest of Men—and I have been the miserablest Dog ever since that ever committed wedlock:—we tift a little going to church—and came to a Quarrel before the Bells were done ringing—I was more than once nearly choak'd with gall during the Honeymoon—and had lost all comfort in Life before my Friends had done wishing me Joy—yet I chose with caution—a Girl bred whol[l]y in the country—who never knew Luxury beyond one silk Gown nor Dissipation above the annual Gala of a Race-Ball—yet now she plays her Part in all the extravagant 10 Fopperies of the Fashion and the Town with as ready a Grace as if she had never seen a Bush nor a grass Plat out of Grosvenor-Square—! I am sneer'd at by my old acquaintance—paragraph'd—in the news-Papers—She dissipate[s] my Fortune, and contradicts all my Humours: —Yet the worst of it is I doubt I love her or I should never bear all this —However I'll never be weak enough to own it.

*Enter* ROWLEY.

ROWLEY. Oh, Sir Peter your Servant—how is it with you Sir—

SIR PETER. Very bad—Master Rowley—very bad. I meet with nothing but crosses and vexations—

ROWLEY. What can have happen'd to trouble you since yesterday?          20

SIR PETER. A good—question to a married man.—

ROWLEY. Nay I'm sure your Lady Sir Peter can't be the cause of your uneasiness.

SIR PETER. Why has anyone told you she was dead?

ROWLEY. Come—come Sir Peter you love her notwithstanding your tempers do not exactly agree.

SIR PETER. But the Fault is entirely hers Master Rowley—I am myself the sweetest temper'd Man alive and hate a teizing Temper—and so I tell her a hundred Times—a day—

ROWLEY. Indeed!                                                          30

SIR PETER. Aye and what is very extraordinary in all our disputes she is always in the wrong! but Lady Sneerwell and the Set she meets at her House encourage the perverseness of her Disposition—then to complete my vex[a]tions—Maria—my Ward—whom I ought to have the Power of a Father over—is determined to turn Rebel too—and absolutely refuses the man whom I have long resolved on for her husband—meaning I suppose to bestow herself on his profligate Brother.

ROWLEY. You know Sir Peter I have always taken the Liberty to differ
with you on the subject of these two young Gentlemen.—I only wish   40
you may not be deceiv'd in your opinion of the elder—for Charles—my
life on't—He will retrieve his Errors yet—their worthy Father, once
my honour'd master, was at his years nearly as wild a Spark—yet when
he died, he did not leave a more benevolent heart to lament his
loss.

SIR PETER. You are wrong Master Rowley—on their Father's Death
you know I acted as a kind of Guardian to them both—'till their unk[l]e
Sir Oliver's eastern liberality gave them an early independance—of
course no Person could have more opportunities of judging of their
Hearts, and I was never mistaken in my Life. Joseph is indeed a model   50
for the young men of the Age. He is a man of Sentiment—and acts up
to the Sentiments he professes—but for the other take my word for't
if he had any grains of Virtue by descent—he has dissipated them with
the rest of his inheritance.—Ah! my old Friend Sir Oliver will be deeply
mortified when he finds how Part of his Bounty has been misapplied—!

ROWLEY. I am sorry to find you so violent against the young man because
this may be the most critical Period of his Fortune—I came hither
with news that will surprise you.

SIR PETER. What!—let me hear—

ROWLEY. Sir Oliver *is* arrived and at this moment in Town.   60

SIR PETER. How!—you astonish me. I thought you did not expect him
this month!—

ROWLEY. I did not—but his Passage has been remarkably quick.

SIR PETER. 'Egad I shall rejoice to see my old Friend—'tis Sixteen Years
since we met—we have had many a Day together, but does He still
enjoin us not to inform his Nephews of his Arrival—?

ROWLEY. Most—strictly—he means before it is known to make some
trial of their Dispositions.—

SIR PETER. Ah there needs no art to discover their merits—! however
he shall have his way—but pray does he know I am married?   70

ROWLEY. Yes and will soon wish you joy.

SIR PETER. What as we drink health to a Friend in a Consumption—ah
Oliver will laugh at me—we used to rail at matrimony together—but
He has been steady to his Text.—well He must be at my house tho'
—I'll instantly give orders for his Reception—but Master Rowley—
don't drop a word that Lady Teazle and I ever disagree.

ROWLEY. By no means—

SIR PETER. For I should never be able to stand Noll's Jokes—so I'd have
him think, Lord Forgive me, that we are a very happy couple.

ROWLEY. I—understand you—but then you must be very careful not to   80
differ while He's in the House with you.

SIR PETER. 'Egad—and so we must—and that's impossible—ah!

Master Rowley when an old Batchelor marries a young wife—He
deserves—no the Crime carries the Punishment along with it—
                                                      [*Exeunt.*

END OF ACT 1ST


*Act 2d*

*Scene 1st.*—SIR PETER TEAZLE's *House*

*Enter* SIR PETER *and* LADY TEAZLE.

SIR PETER. Lady Teazle—Lady Teazle I'll not bear it.

LADY TEAZLE. Sir Peter—Sir Peter you—may bear it or not as you please,
   but I ought to have my own way in every thing, and what's more I will
   too—what! tho' I was educated in the country I know very well that
   women of Fashion in London are accountable to nobody after they are
   married.

SIR PETER. Very well!—Ma'am very well! so a husband is to have no
   influence, no authority?

LADY TEAZLE. Authority! no to be sure—if you wanted authority over
   me you should have adopted me and not married me I am sure you   10
   were Old enough.

SIR PETER. Old enough!—aye there it is—well—well—Lady Teazle
   tho' my Life may be made unhappy by your Temper—I'll not be
   ruin'd by your extravagance.

LADY TEAZLE. My extravagance!—I'm sure I'm not more extravagant
   than a woman of Fashion ought to be.—

SIR PETER. No no Madam you shall throw away no more sums on such
   unmeaning Luxury—'slife to spend as much to furnish your Dressing
   Room with Flow'rs in winter, as would suffice to turn the Pantheon[1]
   into a Green-house and give a Fête-Champêtre at Christmas!        20

LADY TEAZLE. Lord! Sir Peter am I to blame because Flow'rs are dear
   in cold weather? you should find fault with the Climate and not with
   me. For my part I am sure I wish it was Spring all the year round—and
   that Roses grew under one's feet!—

SIR PETER. Oons! Madam—if you had been born to this I shouldn't
   Wonder at your talking thus.—but you forget what your situation was
   when I married you.

---

[1] 'The much-talked-of Receptacle of fashionable Pleasure the Pantheon. . . . The
whole Building is composed of a Suite of 14 Rooms, . . . each affording a striking
Instance of the Splendour and Profusion of modern Times' (*The Public Advertiser*,
29 Jan. 1772). See the view of the interior by C. Brandoin included in *Johnson's England*,
ed. A. S. Turberville (Oxford, 1933), i. 344; and compare the supper room at The Oaks
erected by Robert Adam for the *fête-champêtre* there, ii. 112.

LADY TEAZLE. No—no—I don't—'twas a very disagreeable one or I should never have married you—

SIR PETER. Yes—yes madam you were then in somewhat an humbler 30 Style—the Daughter of a plain country Squire—recollect Lady Teazle when I saw you first—sitting at your tambour in a pretty figured Linnen gown—with a Bunch of Keys by your side, your hair comb'd smooth over a Roll, and your apartment hung round with Fruits in worsted of your own working—

LADY TEAZLE. O Yes, I remember it very well, and a Curious life I led! My daily occupation to inspect the Dairy, superintend the Poultry, make extracts from the Family Receipt book and Comb my aunt Deborah's Lap-Dog.

SIR PETER. Yes, yes, Ma'am, 'twas so indeed.                               40

LADY TEAZLE. And then you know my evening amusements—to draw Patterns for Ruffles which I had not the Materials to make—to play Pope Joan with the Curate—to read a Novel to my Aunt—or to be stuck down to an old Spinnet—to strum my Father to sleep after a Fox chase.

SIR PETER. I am glad you have so good a Memory,—Yes—Madam— These were the Recreations I took you from.—But now you must have your Coach, Vis-à-Vis,[1] and three powder'd Footmen before your Chair —and in summer a pair of white Cats[2] to draw you to Kensington gardens—no Recollection I suppose when you were content to ride double behind the Butler on a dock'd Coach Horse.                          50

LADY TEAZLE. No—I swear I never did that—I deny the Butler, and the Coach Horse.

SIR PETER. This madam was your Situation—and what have I not done for you?-I have made you a woman of Fashion, of Fortune, of Rank —in short I have made you my Wife—

LADY TEAZLE. Well then and there is but one thing more you can make me to add to the obligation—and that is—

SIR PETER. My widow I suppose?

LADY TEAZLE. Hem! hem!

SIR PETER. Thank-you Madam—but don't flatter yourself for—tho' 60 your ill conduct may disturb my Peace it shall never break my Heart I promise you:—however I am equally oblig'd to you for the Hint.

LADY TEAZLE. Then why will you endeavour to make yourself so disagreeable to me, and thwart me in every little elegant expence?

[1] Cf. p. 187, n. 1, below.
[2] Short for 'cattle'? Or possibly suggested by Colman's prologue to Garrick's *Bon Ton* (1775):

> Nature it [*Bon Ton*] thwarts, and contradicts all reason;
> 'Tis stiff French stays, and fruit when out of season;
> A rose, when half a guinea is the price;
> A set of bays, scarce bigger than six mice.

SIR PETER. 'Slife—Madam I say had you any of these Elegant expences when you married me?

LADY TEAZLE. Lud Sir Peter would you have me be out of the Fashion—?

SIR PETER. The Fashion indeed!—what had you to do with the Fashion before you married me?                                                    70

LADY TEAZLE. For my Part—I should think you would like to have your Wife thought a Woman of Taste.

SIR PETER. Aye, there again—Taste!—zounds Madam you had no Taste when you married me—

LADY TEAZLE. That's very true indeed Sir Peter and after having married you I am sure I should never pretend to Taste again!—But now Sir Peter if we have finish'd our daily Jangle I presume I may go to my Engagement at Lady Sneerwell's—

SIR PETER. Aye—there's another Precious circumstance, a charming set of acquaintance—you have made there.                                    80

LADY TEAZLE. Nay Sir Peter They are People of Rank and Fortune—and remarkably tenacious of Reputation.

SIR PETER. Yes 'egad they are tenacious of Reputation with a vengeance, for they don't chuse any body should have a Character—but themselves —such a crew! ah! many a wretch has rid on a hurdle[1] who has done less mischief than those utterers of forg'd Tales, coiners of Scandal, —and clippers of Reputation.

LADY TEAZLE. What would you restrain the freedom of speech?

SIR PETER. O! they have made you just as bad as any one of the Society.                                                                    90

LADY TEAZLE. Why—I believe I do bear a Part with a tolerable Grace— —But I vow I have no malice against the People I abuse, when I say an ill natured thing 'tis out of pure Good-Humour—and I take it for granted they deal exactly in the same manner with me but Sir Peter you know you promised to come to Lady Sneerwell's too.

SIR PETER. Well well I'll call in just to look after my own character.

LADY TEAZLE. Then indeed you must make Haste after me or you'll be too late—so good bye to ye.                    [*Exit* LADY TEAZLE.

SIR PETER. So—I have gain'd much by my intended expostulations[2]— yet with what a charming air she contradicts every thing I say—and   100 how pleasingly she shews her contempt of my authority—well tho' I can't make her love me there is a great Satisfaction in quar[r]elling with her and I think she never appear[s] to such advantage as when she's doing every thing in her Power to plague me.               [*Exit*.

---

[1] Criminals were drawn on a rough sledge to the place of execution.

[2] Cf. Clerimont Senior in Steele's *The Tender Husband* (1705), I. i: 'Now I can neither Mortify her Vanity, that I may Live at ease with her, or quite discard her, till have catched her a little enlarging her Innocent Freedoms, as she calls 'em.'

*Scene 2d.* LADY SNEERWELL'*s*

LADY SNEERWELL—MRS. CANDOUR—CRABTREE—SIR BENJAMIN
—*and* SURFACE.

LADY SNEERWELL. Nay positively we will hear it—

SURFACE. Yes—yes the Epigram[1] by all means.—

SIR BENJ. Plague on't Unkle—'tis mere nonsense.

CRABTREE. No no—'fore gad very clever for an extempore—

SIR BENJ. But Ladies you should be acquainted with the circumstance,
you must know that one day last week as Lady Betty Curricle—was
taking the Dust in Hyde Park, in a sort of duodecimo Phaeton—She
desir'd me to write some verses on her Ponies—upon which I took out
my Pocket-Book—and in one moment produc'd—the following[2]—

> Sure never were seen two such beautiful Ponies          10
> Other Horses are Clowns—and these—macaronies.
> Nay to give 'em this Title I'm sure isn't wrong—
> —Their Legs are so slim—and their Tails are so long.[3]

CRABTREE. There—Ladies—done in the smack of a whip—and on
Horseback too—

SURFACE. A very Phœbus mounted—indeed, Sir Benjamin.

SIR BENJ. O dear Sir Trifles—Trifles!—

*Enter* LADY TEAZLE *and* MARIA.

MRS. CANDOUR. I must have a Copy.

LADY SNEERWELL. Lady Teazle—I hope we shall see Sir Peter—

LADY TEAZLE. I believe He'll wait on your La'ship—presently.          20

LADY SNEERWELL. Maria my Love you look grave—come you shall sit
down to Cards with Mr. Surface—

MARIA. I take very little Pleasure in Cards—however I'll do as your
Ladyship pleases.

LADY TEAZLE. I am surprised Mr. Surface should sit down with her—I

---

[1] 'Wherever the spirit of the salon appears, evidence of its presence is seen in the
production and general esteem of such trifles: rebuses, anagrams, madrigals, enigmas,
charades, and *bouts rimés*. The explanation of it all goes back, perhaps, to the Italian
Renaissance, when, as Burckhardt has shown, an epigram could lay the foundation of a
scholar's celebrity' (C. B. Tinker, *The Salon and English Letters*, New York, 1915,
p. 117).

[2] For an earlier form of these lines, see W. Fraser Rae, *Sheridan* (1896), i. 330–1.

[3] Cf. the article on macaronis in the *Town and Country Magazine*, iv (1772), 243:
'They do indeed make a most ridiculous figure . . . with about two pounds of fictitious
hair, formed into what is called a club, hanging down their shoulders as white as a
baker's sack. . . . Their legs are at times covered with all the colours of the rainbow;
even flesh-coloured and green silk stockings are not excluded.'

thought He would have embraced this opportunity of speaking to me before Sir Peter came—

MRS. CANDOUR. [*Coming forward*] Now I'll die but you are so scandalous I'll forswear your society.—

LADY TEAZLE. What's the matter Mrs. Candour—? 30

MRS. CANDOUR. They'll not allow our Friend Miss Vermillion to be handsome.

LADY SNEERWELL. O surely she's a pretty woman—

CRABTREE. I am very glad you think so Ma'am—

MRS. CANDOUR. She has a charming fresh Colour—

LADY TEAZLE. Yes when it is fresh put on—

MRS. CANDOUR. O fie I'll swear her Colour is natural—I have seen it come and go—

LADY TEAZLE. I dare swear you have, ma'am—it goes of a Night and comes again in the morning. 40

MRS. CANDOUR. Ha! ha! ha! how I hate to hear you talk so—but surely now her Sister is or was very Handsome.

CRABTREE. Who, Mrs. Evergreen?—O Lud she's six and fifty if she's an hour—

MRS. CANDOUR. Now positively you wrong her fifty-two or fifty-three is the utmost—and I don't think she looks more—

SIR BENJ. Ah there is no judging by her Looks unless one could see her Face.

LADY SNEERWELL. Well—well—if Mrs. Evergreen does take some pains to repair the Ravages of Time—you must allow she effects it with great 50 ingenuity—and surely that's better than the careless manner in which the Widow Ocre—caulks her wrinkles.

SIR BENJ. Nay now Lady Sneerwell—you are severe upon the Widow —come—come it is not that she paints so ill—but when she has finish'd her Face she joins it on so badly to her Neck that she looks like a mended Statue in which the Connoisseur sees at once that the Head's modern tho' the Trunk's antique.—

CRABTREE. Ha! ha! ha! well said Nephew!

MRS. CANDOUR. Ha! ha! ha! well you make me laugh but I vow I hate you for't—what do you think of Miss Simper? 60

SIR BENJ. Why she has very pretty Teeth.

LADY TEAZLE. Yes and on that account when she is neither speaking nor laughing (which very seldom happens)—she never absolutely shuts her mouth, but leaves it always on a Jar as it were.

MRS. CANDOUR. How can you be so ill natur'd?

LADY TEAZLE. Nay I allow even that's better than the Pains Mrs. Prim takes to conceal her losses in Front. She draws her mouth 'till it positively resembles the aperture of a Poor's-Box, and all her words appear to slide out edgeways.

LADY SNEERWELL. Very well Lady Teazle I see you can be a little 70
severe—

LADY TEAZLE. In defence of a Friend it is but justice but here comes Sir
Peter to spoil our Pleasantry—!

*Enter* SIR PETER TEAZLE.

SIR PETER. Ladies your most obedient—Mercy on me, here is the
whole set! a character dead at every word[1] I suppose. [*aside*]

MRS. CANDOUR. I am rejoic'd you are come Sir Peter—they have been
so censorious—they will allow good Qualities to nobody—not even
good-nature to our Friend Mrs. Pursy.—

LADY TEAZLE. What the Fat Dowager—who was at Mrs. Codille's
last Night.— 80

MRS. CANDOUR. Nay—her bulk is her misfortune and when she takes
such Pains to get rid of it you ought not to reflect on her.

LADY SNEERWELL. That's very true indeed.

LADY TEAZLE. Yes I know she almost lives on acids and small whey—
laces herself by pullies and often in the hottest noon of summer you
may see her on a little squat Poney with her hair platted up behind
like a Drummer's—and puffing round the Ring[2] on a full Trot.

MRS. CANDOUR. I thank you Lady Teazle for defending her.

SIR PETER. Yes a good Defence truly.

MRS. CANDOUR. But Sir Benjamin is as Censorious as Miss Sallow. 90

CRABTREE. Yes and she is a curious Being to pretend to be censorious
—an aukward Gawky without any one good Point under Heaven!

MRS. CANDOUR. Positively you shall not be so very severe. Miss Sallow
is a Relation of mine by marriage and as for her Person great allowance
is to be made—for let me tell you a woman labours under many disadvantages who tries to pass for a girl at six and thirty.

LADY SNEERWELL. Tho' surely she is handsome still—and for the weakness in her eyes considering how much she reads by candle light it is
not to be wonder'd at.

MRS. CANDOUR. True, and then as to her manner—upon my word I 100
think it is particularly graceful considering she never had the least
Education for you know her Mother was a Welch millener and her
Father a Sugar-Baker at Bristow.—

SIR BENJ. Ah! you are both of you too good natur'd!

SIR PETER. Yes damn'd good natur'd!—this their own Relation!—
mercy on me! [*aside*]

SIR BENJ. And Mrs. Candour is of so moral a turn—she can sit for an
hour to hear Lady Stucco talk Sentiment.

[1] Cf. A. Pope, *The Rape of the Lock*, iii. 16: 'At ev'ry word a reputation dies.'
[2] The fashionable drive in Hyde Park, shut in by railings and fine trees.

LADY TEAZLE. Nay, I vow Lady Stucco is very well with the Des[s]ert after dinner for she's just like the French Fruit one cracks for mottos[1]  110 —made up of Paint and Proverb.—

MRS. CANDOUR. Well I never will Join in ridiculing a Friend—and so I constantly tell my Cousin Ogle—and you all know what pretentions She has to be critical in Beauty—

CRABTREE. O to be sure she has herself the oddest countenance that ever was seen—'tis a collection of Features from all the different Countries of the Globe.

SIR BENJ. So she has indeed.—An Irish front

CRABTREE. Caledonian Locks—

SIR BENJ. Dutch nose—                                                  120

CRABTREE. Austrian lip—

SIR BENJ. Complexion of a Spaniard—

CRABTREE. And Teeth à la Chinoise[2]—

SIR BENJ. In short her Face resembles a Table d'hôte at Spaw where no two guests are of a nation—

CRABTREE. Or a Congress at the close of a general War—wherein all the members even to her eyes appear to have a different interest and her Nose and Chin are the only Parties likely to join issue.

MRS. CANDOUR. Ha! ha! ha!

SIR PETER. Mercy on my life! a Person they dine with twice a Week.  130 [aside]

MRS. CANDOUR. Nay but I vow you shall not carry the Laugh off so—for give me leave to say that Mrs. Ogle—

SIR PETER. Madam—madam—I beg your Pardon—There's no stopping these good Gentlemen's Tongues—but when I tell you Mrs. Candour that the Lady they are abusing is a particular Friend of mine—I hope you'll not take her Part.

LADY SNEERWELL. Well said Sir Peter, but you are a cruel creature—too Phlegmatic yourself for a jest and too peevish to allow wit on others.

SIR PETER. Ah! Madam true wit is more nearly allied to good Nature  140 than your Ladyship is aware of.

LADY TEAZLE. True Sir Peter I believe they are so near akin that they can never be united—

SIR BENJ. Or rather Madam suppose them man and wife because one so seldom sees them together.

---

[1] Cf. Horace Walpole to Lady Ossory: 'Paragraphs of news . . . are like mottoes too wrapped in sugar, which everybody breaks, finds nothing worth reading, and yet goes on cracking' (Walpole Corr. xxxiii (1965), 213).

[2] Cf. The Citizen of the World: 'And first the beauties of China appeared . . . Their black teeth and plucked eye-brows were however alleged by the Genius against them' (Collected Works of Oliver Goldsmith, ed. A. Friedman (Oxford, 1966), ii. 442).

LADY TEAZLE. But Sir Peter is such an Enemy to Scandal I believe He would have it put down by Parliament.

SIR PETER. 'Fore Heaven! Madam if they were to Consider—the Sporting with Reputation of as much importance as poaching on manors[1]—and pass An Act for the Preservation of Fame—I believe there are many would thank them for the Bill.    150

LADY SNEERWELL. O Lud! Sir Peter would you deprive us of our Privileges—

SIR PETER. Aye Madam—and then no Person should be permitted to kill characters, or run down Reputations but qualified old Maids and disap[p]ointed Widows.—

LADY SNEERWELL. Go—you Monster—

MRS. CANDOUR. But sure you would not be quite so severe on those who only report what they hear.

SIR PETER. Yes Madam I would have Law Merchant[2] for them—too—    160
and in all cases of Slander currency whenever the Drawer of the Lie was not to be found the injured Party should have a right to come on any of the indorsers.

CRABTREE. Well for my Part I believe there never was a Scandalous Tale without some foundation—

LADY SNEERWELL. Come Ladies shall we sit down to Cards in the next Room—

*Enter* SERVANT *and Whispers* SIR PETER.

SIR PETER. I'll be with them directly!—[*Exeunt*]—I'll get away unperceiv'd.

LADY SNEERWELL. Sir Peter you are not leaving us?    170

SIR PETER. Your Ladyship must excuse me—I'm called away by particular Business—but I leave my Character behind me.—

[*Exit* SIR PETER.

SIR BENJ. Well certainly Lady Teazle that Lord of yours is a strange being—I could tell you some stories of him would make you laugh heartily if he wasn't your Husband—

---

[1] Cf. Miss Walsingham's speech in Hugh Kelly's *The School for Wives*, 4th edn. (1774), p. 63: 'And yet if the laws against it [duelling], were as well enforced as the laws against destroying the game, perhaps it would be equally for the benefit of the kingdom.' See, also, the *Public Advertiser*, 22 Apr. 1776: 'The Noblemen and Gentlemen of the Association for the Preservation of Game all over England, are desired to meet To-morrow at Eleven o'Clock, at the St. Alban's Tavern in St. Alban's-street: WHEREAS the said Noblemen and Gentlemen have prosecuted and convicted several Poulterers, Higlers, Carriers, Stage Coachmen, Masters of Vessels, Night Netters, Snarers and others, for destroying the Game and carrying and selling the same. . . .'

[2] Privileges peculiar to merchants, differing from Common Law but the same as the Law of the Staple.

LADY TEAZLE. O pray don't mind that.—come do let's hear 'em.

[*They join the rest of the Company all talking as they are going into the next room.*

SURFACE. [*rising with* MARIA] Maria I see you have no satisfaction in this society.

MARIA. How is it possible I should?—if to raise malicious smiles at the infirmities and misfortunes—of those who have never injured us be the 180 province of wit or Humour Heav'n grant me a double Portion of Dullness—

SURFACE. Yet they appear more ill natur'd than they are—They have no malice at heart—

MARIA. Then is their conduct still more contemptible for in my opinion —nothing could—excuse the intemperance of their tongues but a natural and ungovernable bitterness of Mind.

SURFACE. But can you Maria feel thus for others and be unkind to me alone—is hope to be denied the tenderest Passion?—

MARIA. Why will you distress me by renewing this subject—          190

SURFACE. Ah! Maria you would not treat me thus and oppose your Guardian's Sir Peter's wishes—but that I see that profligate Charles is still a favour'd Rival.

MARIA. Ungenerously urged—but whatever my sentiments of that Unfortunate young man are—be assured I shall not feel more bound to give him up because his Distresses have lost him the regard even of a Brother.—                                        [LADY TEAZLE *returns.*

SURFACE. Nay but Maria do not leave me with a Frown—by all that's honest I swear—Gad's life here's Lady Teazle. [*aside*]—you must not— no you shall not—for tho' I have the greatest Regard for Lady Teazle— 200

MARIA. Lady Teazle—!

SURFACE. Yet were Sir Peter to suspect—

LADY TEAZLE. [*Coming forward*] What's this Pray—do you take her for me!—Child you are wanted in the next Room—          [*Exit* MARIA. what is all this pray—

SURFACE. O the most unlucky circumstance in Nature. Maria has somehow suspected the tender concern which I have for your happiness and threaten'd to acquaint Sir Peter with her suspicions—and I was just endeavouring to reason with her when you came.

LADY TEAZLE. Indeed but you seem'd to adopt—a very tender method 210 of reasoning—do you usually argue on your knees—?

SURFACE. O she's a Child—and I thought a little Bombast—but Lady Teazle when are you to give me your Judgment on my Library as you promised?

LADY TEAZLE. No—no I begin to think it would be imprudent—and you know I admit you as a Lover no further than Fashion requires.—

SURFACE. True—a mere Platonic Cicisbeo[1]—what every London wife is
entitled too.

LADY TEAZLE. Certainly one must not be out of the Fashion—however I    220
have so much of my country Prejudices left—that—tho' Sir Peter's ill
humour may vex me ever so—it never shall provoke me to—

SURFACE. The only revenge in your Power—well I applaud your
moderation.

LADY TEAZLE. Go—you are an insinuating Wretch—but we shall be
miss'd—let us join the company.

SURFACE. But we had best not return together.

LADY TEAZLE. Well don't stay—for Maria shan't come to hear any more
of your Reasoning I promise you—                    [Exit LADY TEAZLE.

SURFACE. A curious Dilemma truly my Politics have run me into.—I    230
wanted at first only to ingratiate myself with Lady Teazle that she
might not be my enemy with Maria—and I have I don't know how—
become her serious Lover.—Sincerely I begin to wish I had never made
such a Point of gaining so very good a character—for it has led me into
so many curs'd Rogueries that I doubt I shall be exposed at last.

[Exit.

### Scene 3d. SIR PETER's

#### Enter SIR OLIVER and ROWLEY.

SIR OLIVER. Ha! ha! ha! and so my old Friend is married hey?—a
young Wife out of the Country!—ha! ha! ha!—that he should have
stood Bluff[2] to old Batchelor so long and sink into a Husband at last!—

ROWLEY. But you must not rally him on the subject Sir Oliver—'tis a
tender Point I assure you tho He has been married only seven months.

---

[1] The privileges of the cicisbeo are described in Frances Sheridan's *A Journey
to Bath*: see Rae, pp. 296–7: 'I may come in when you are dressing. I am to put essence
into your handkerchief, reach you your combs, your pins . . . I am never to be from
your elbow if you command me. I am to help you tea, coffee, and fruit before any
other lady in the company, and give it you on my knee. . . . I am to attend you to all
publick places and home again, and to see you up to your chamber door.'

[2] Sheridan may have picked up the phrase from some satirical verses on him by
'Philo-Musa', that appeared in the *Morning Chronicle*, 2 Apr. 1777:

> Between us we'll monopolize,
> Monopolies are now the fashion,
> *Your* [Thomas Linley's] care our *harmony* supplies,
> And *Van's* [Vanbrugh's] old scenes I now am slashing.

> No matter whether new or stale,
> I'll furnish *Comedy* enough,
> The *whoreson authors* may turn pale,
> 'Gainst their intrusion we'll stand bluff.

*The School for Scandal* reference is the earliest usage given in the *O.E.D.*

SIR OLIVER. Then He has been just half a year on the stool of Repentance—Poor Peter! But you say he has entirely given up Charles? never sees him hey?

ROWLEY. His Prejudice against him is astonishing—and I am sure greatly encreas'd by a Jealousy of him with Lady Teazle—which He has been industriously led into by a scandalous Society in the neighbourhood—who have contributed not a little to Charles's ill name. Whereas the truth is I believe if the Lady is partial to either of them his Brother is the Favourite.

SIR OLIVER. Aye—I know—there are a set of malicious prating prudent Gossips both male and Female, who murder characters to kill time and will rob a young Fellow of his good name before He has years to know the value of it.—but I am not to be prejudic'd—against my nephew by such I promise you. No! no—if Charles has done nothing false or mean[1] I shall compound for his extravagance.

ROWLEY. Then my life on't you will reclaim him. Ah Sir—it gives me new life to find that your heart is not turned against him—and that the son of my good old master has one friend however left.

SIR OLIVER. What! shall I forget Master Rowley—when I was at his years my self?—egad my Brother and I were neither of us very prudent youths—and yet I believe you have not seen many better Men than your old master was.

ROWLEY. Sir, 'tis this reflection gives me assurance that Charles may yet be a Credit to his Family—but here comes Sir Peter—

SIR OLIVER. 'Egad so He does—mercy on me—He's greatly alter'd— and seems to have a settled Married look—one may read husband in his Face at this Distance.—

*Enter* SIR PETER TEAZLE.

SIR PETER. Hah! Sir Oliver—my Old Friend:—welcome to England— a thousand Times!

SIR OLIVER. Thank you—thank—you Sir Peter—and—'efaith—I am as glad to find you well, believe me—

SIR PETER. Ah! 'tis a long time since we met—sixteen years I doubt, Sir Oliver—and many a cross accident in the Time—

SIR OLIVER. Aye I have had my share—but what I find you are married —hey my old Boy—well—well it can't be help'd—and so I wish you joy with all my heart.—

SIR PETER. Thank—you—thank you Sir Oliver—yes I have enter'd into the happy state but we'll not talk of that now.

[1] Cf. Marvell's 'Horatian Ode Upon Cromwell's Return from Ireland', stanza 15, of Charles I:

> He nothing common did or mean
> Upon that memorable scene.

SIR OLIVER. True true Sir Peter, Old Friends should not begin on
Grievances—at first meeting—no—no—no.

ROWLEY. [*to* SIR OLIVER] Take Care pray Sir—

SIR OLIVER. Well—so one of my Nephews I find is a wild Rogue—hey?

SIR PETER. Wild!—ah! my old Friend—I grieve for your disap[p]oint-
ment there—He's a lost Young Man indeed—however his Brother will
make you amends. Joseph is indeed what a youth should be—every 50
body in the world speaks well of him—

SIR OLIVER. I am sorry to hear it—he has too good a character to be an
honest Fellow.—Every body speaks well of him! Psha! then He has
bow'd as low to Knaves and Fools—as to the honest dignity of Genius
or Virtue.

SIR PETER. What Sir Oliver do you blame him for not making
Enemies—?

SIR OLIVER. Yes—if He has merit enough to deserve them.

SIR PETER. Well—well—you'll be convinc'd when you know him—'tis
edification to hear him converse—he professes the noblest—Sentiments. 60

SIR OLIVER. Ah plague on his Sentiments—if He salutes me with a
Scrap of morality in his mouth I shall be sick directly.—but however
don't mistake me Sir Peter—I don't mean to defend Charles' Errors—
but before I form my judgement of either of them I intend to make a
trial of their Hearts—and my Friend Rowley and I have plann'd
something for the Purpose—

ROWLEY. And Sir Peter shall own he has been for once mistaken.

SIR PETER. O—my Life on Joseph's Honour!

SIR OLIVER. Well come give us a bottle of good wine—and we'll drink
the Lads Healths and tell you our scheme.— 70

SIR PETER. Al[l]ons then—

SIR OLIVER. And don't Sir Peter be so severe against your old Friend's
son—Odds—my Life—I am not sorry that He has run out of the
course a little—for my Part I hate to see Prudence clinging to the green
Succours of Youth—'tis like Ivy round a sapling and spoils the Growth
of the Tree.                                        [*Exeunt.*

END OF ACT 2

## Act 3d

### Scene 1st.—SIR PETER's

SIR PETER—SIR OLIVER—*and* ROWLEY.

SIR PETER. Well then—we will see this Fellow first and have our wine afterwards.—but how is this—Master Rowley—I don't see the Jet[1] of your Scheme—?

ROWLEY. Why Sir—this Mr. Stanley whom I was speaking of—is nearly related to them by their mother. He was once a merchant in Dublin—but has been ruined by a series of undeserved misfortunes— He has applied by Letter since his confinement both to Mr. Surface and Charles.—from the former—He has received nothing but evasive promises of future Service—while Charles has done all that his extravagance has left him power to do—and He is at this time endeavour- 10 ing to raise a sum of money—part of which in the midst of his own distresses I know he intends for the service of poor Stanley.

SIR OLIVER. Ah! He is my Brother's Son—

SIR PETER. Well—but how is Sir Oliver personally to—

ROWLEY. Why Sir I will inform Charles—and his Brother that Stanley has obtain'd Permission to apply in Person to his Friends—and as they have neither of them ever seen him let Sir Oliver assume his Character —and he will have a fair opportunity of judging at least of the Benevolence of their Dispositions, and believe me Sir, you will find in the youngest Brother—one who in the midst of Folly and Dissipation 20 —has still as our immortal Bard expresses it—'a Tear for Pity and a Hand open as Day for melting Charity.'[2]

SIR PETER. Pshaw! what signifies his having an open Hand or Purse either when He has nothing left to give!—Well—well—make the Trial if you please—but where is the Fellow whom you brought for Sir Oliver to Examine relative to Charles's Affairs?

ROWLEY. Below, waiting his commands, and no one can give him better intelligence;—This Sir Oliver is a friendly Jew who to do him justice has done every thing in his power to bring your Nephew to a proper sense of his Extravagance.                                                  30

SIR PETER. Pray let us have him in—

ROWLEY. Desire Mr. Moses to walk upstairs.—

SIR PETER. But why should you suppose He will speak the Truth.

ROWLEY. O I have convinced him that he has no chance of recovering Certain Sums advanced to Charles, but thro' the Bounty of Sir Oliver, who he knows is arriv'd; so that you may depend on his fidelity to his Interest; I have also another Evidence in my power, one Snake—whom I have detected in a Matter little short of Forgery, and shall shortly produce to remove some of your prejudices Sir Peter, relative to Charles and Lady Teazle.                                              40

SIR PETER. I have heard too much on that Subject.

ROWLEY. Here comes the honest Israelite.

---

[1] Cf. R. Cumberland, *The West Indian* (1771), III. x: 'the jet of the story is . . . .' The sense is 'gist'.

[2] *2 Henry IV*, IV. iv.

*Enter* MOSES.

This is Sir Oliver—

SIR OLIVER. Sir—I—understand you have lately had great dealings with
my Nephew Charles.

MOSES. Yes Sir Oliver—I have done all I could for him, but He was
ruin'd before He came to me for Assistance.

SIR OLIVER. That was unlucky truly—for you have had no opportunity
of shewing your Talents.—

MOSES. None at all—I hadn't the Pleasure of knowing his Distresses—    50
'till He was some thousands worse than nothing.

SIR OLIVER. Unfortunate indeed! but I suppose you have done all in
your Power for him honest Moses?

MOSES. Yes he knows that.—This very Evening I was to have brought
him a Gentleman from the city who doesn't know him and will I
believe advance him some money.

SIR PETER. What one Charles has never had money from before?

MOSES. Yes Mr. Premium of Crutched-Friars[1]—formerly a Broker.

SIR PETER. Egad Sir Oliver a Thought strikes me—Charles you say
doesn't know Mr.—Premium—    60

MOSES. Not at all.—

SIR PETER. Now then Sir Oliver you may have a better opportunity of
satisfying yourself than by an old romancing tale of a poor Relation.—
go with my Friend Moses and Represent Mr. Premium and then I'll
answer for't, you will see your Nephew in all his Glory.—

SIR OLIVER. Egad I like this Idea better than the other and I may visit
Joseph afterwards as old Stanley.

SIR PETER. True so you may—

ROWLEY. Well this is taking Charles rather at a disadvantage to be sure
—however Moses—you understand Sir Peter and will be faithful.—    70

MOSES. You may depend upon me—this is near the Time I was to have gone.

SIR OLIVER. I'll accompany you as soon as you please, Moses, but hold
—I have forgot one thing—how the Plague shall I be able to pass for a
Jew?

MOSES. There's no need—the Principal is Christian.

SIR OLIVER. Is He—I'm sorry to hear it—but then again—an't I rather
too smartly dress'd to look like a money-Lender?—

SIR PETER. Not at all—'twould not be out of character if you went in
your own carriage—would it Moses—?

MOSES. Not in the least.    80

SIR OLIVER. Well—but—how must I talk? there's certainly some cant
of usury—and mode of treating that I ought to know—

[1] A continuation of Jewry Street, running from Aldgate to Mark Lane.

SIR PETER. O there's not much to learn—the great point as I take it is
to be exorbitant enough in your Demands, hey Moses?

MOSES. Yes, that's a very great Point—

SIR OLIVER. I'll answer for't I'll not be wanting in that—I'll ask him
eight or ten per cent on the loan—at least.

MOSES. If you ask him no more than that, you'll be discovered
immediately.

SIR OLIVER. Hey—what the Plague! how much then?                    90

MOSES. That depends upon the Circumstances, if he appears not very
anxious for the supply—you should require only forty or fifty per cent
—but if you find him in great Distress and want the monies very bad—
you may ask double.

SIR PETER. A good Honest Trade you're learning Sir Oliver—

SIR OLIVER. Truly I think so—and not unprofitable—

MOSES. Then you know—you haven't the monies yourself—but are
forced—to borrow them for him of a Friend.

SIR OLIVER. Oh I borrow it of a Friend do I?

MOSES. Yes—and your friend is an unconscionable Dog,—but you can't   100
help it.—

SIR OLIVER. My Friend is an unconscionable Dog is he?

MOSES. Yes—and He himself hasn't the moneys by him—but is forced
to sell stock at a great Loss—

SIR OLIVER. He is forced to sell stock is he—at a great loss is he—well
that's very kind of him.

SIR PETER. Efaith Sir Oliver, Mr. Premium, I mean, you'll soon be
Master of the Trade—but Moses—wouldn't you have him run out a little
against the annuity Bill[1] that would be in character I should think—

MOSES. Very much—                                                   110

ROWLEY. And lament that a young man now must be at years of discretion before He is suffered to ruin himself—

MOSES. Aye—great Pity!

SIR PETER. And abuse—the Public—for allowing merit to an act whose
only object—is to snatch Misfortune and imprudence—from the
rapacious Relief of usury! and give the minor a chance of inheriting
his estate, without being undone by coming into Possession.—

SIR OLIVER. So—so—Moses shall give me further instructions as we go
together—

SIR PETER. You will not have much time for your Nephew lives hard   120
bye—

SIR OLIVER. O Never fear—my Tutor appears so able that tho' Charles
lived in the next street it must be my own Fault if I am not a compleat

---

[1] By its terms anyone who took more than ten shillings per hundred pounds lent as
annuities, was liable to imprisonment or a fine. The Annuity Bill was passed on 12 May
1777, four days after the first performance of *The School for Scandal*.

Rogue before I turn the corner.— [*Exeunt* SIR OLIVER *and* MOSES.

SIR PETER. So—now I think Sir Oliver will be convinced—you are partial Rowley—and would have prepared Charles for the other Plot.

ROWLEY. No upon my Word Sir Peter—

SIR PETER. Well go bring me this Snake, and I'll hear what he has to say presently—I see Maria and want to Speak with her—[*Exit* ROWLEY] I should be glad to be convinced, my Suspicions of Lady Teazle and 130 Charles were unjust—I have never yet open'd my mind on this subject to my—Friend Joseph—I'm determined I will do it—He will give me his Opinion Sincerely.—

*Enter* MARIA.

So—child—has Mr. Surface returned with you?

MARIA. No Sir—He was engaged—

SIR PETER. Well—Maria—do you not reflect the more you converse with that amiable young man, what return his Partiality for you deserves?

MARIA. Indeed Sir Peter—your frequent importunity on this subject—distresses me extremely—you compel me to Declare that I know no man who has ever paid me a particular attention whom I would not 140 prefer to Mr. Surface.

SIR PETER. Soh! Here's Perverseness!—no—no—Maria—'tis Charles—only whom you would prefer—'tis evident his Vices and Follies have won your Heart.

MARIA. This is unkind Sir—you know I have obey'd you in neither seeing nor corresponding with him—I have heard enough to convince me that He is unworthy my regard—Yet I cannot think it culpable—if while my understanding severely condemns his Vices—my Heart suggests some Pity for his Distresses.—

SIR PETER. Well well Pity him as much as you please but give your 150 Heart and Hand—to a worthier object.

MARIA. Never to his Brother—

SIR PETER. Go—perverse and obstinate! but take care Madam—you have never yet known what the authority of a Guardian is—don't compel me to inform you of it.—

MARIA. I can only say you shall not have just reason—'tis true by my Father's will I am for a short period bound to regard you as his substitute, but must cease to think you so, when you would compel me to be miserable.                                        [*Exit* MARIA.

SIR PETER. Was ever Man so cross'd as I am!—everything conspiring to 160 fret me!—I hadn't been involv'd in matrimony a fortnight before her Father—a hale and hearty man—died on purpose I believe—for the Pleasure of plaguing me with the care of his Daughter.—but here comes my Helpmate!—She appears—in great good-humour—how happy I should be if I could teaze her into loving me tho' but a little.—

*Enter* LADY TEAZLE.

LADY TEAZLE. Lud! Sir Peter—I hope you haven't been quarrelling with Maria—it isn't using me well to be ill-humour'd when I am not bye—!

SIR PETER. Ah! Lady Teazle you might have the Power to make me good humour'd at all times.—                                                           170

LADY TEAZLE. I am sure—I wish I had—for I want you to be in charming sweet Temper at this moment—do be good humour'd now—and let me have two hundred Pounds will you?

SIR PETER. Two hundred-Pounds—! what an't I to be in a good humour without paying for it—but speak to me thus—and efaith there's nothing I could refuse you. You shall have it—but seal me a bond for the repayment—

LADY TEAZLE. O no—there my Note of Hand will do as well—

SIR PETER. [*kissing her hand*] And you shall no longer reproach me with not giving you an independent settlement—I mean shortly to surprise   180
you—but shall we always live thus—hey?

LADY TEAZLE. If you—please—I'm sure I don't care how soon we leave off quarrelling provided you'll own you were tired first—

SIR PETER. Well—then let our future contest be who shall be most obliging.

LADY TEAZLE. I assure you Sir Peter Good Nature becomes you—you look now as you did before we were married!—when you us'd to walk with me under the Elms and tell me stories of what a Gallant you were in your youth and chuck me under the Chin—you would—and ask me if I thought I could love an Old Fellow who would deny me nothing—   190
didn't you?

SIR PETER. Yes—yes—and you were as kind and attentive.

LADY TEAZLE. Aye so I was—and would always take your Part when my acquaintance used to abuse you and turn you into ridicule—

SIR PETER. Indeed—!

LADY TEAZLE. Aye—and when my cousin Sophy[1] has call'd you a stiff peevish old batchelor and laugh'd at me for thinking of marrying one who might be my Father—I have always defended you—and said I didn't think you so ugly by any means and that I dared say you'd make a very good sort of a Husband.                                                   200

SIR PETER. And you prophesied right—and we shall certainly now be the happiest couple.

LADY TEAZLE. And never differ again—

SIR PETER. No never—tho' at the same time—indeed my dear Lady Teazle—you must watch your Temper very narrowly—for in all our little Quarrels—my dear—if you recollect my Love you always began first—

---

[1] Cousin Sophy in *St. Patrick's Day*, I. ii, 'married an officer'.

LADY TEAZLE. I beg your Pardon—my dear Sir Peter—indeed you always gave the provocation.

SIR PETER. Now—see my—Angel take care—contradicting isn't the way to keep Friends.                                                                                           210

LADY TEAZLE. Then don't you begin it, my Love!

SIR PETER. There now—you—you are going on—you don't perceive my Life that you are just doing the very thing which you know always makes me angry.

LADY TEAZLE. Nay—you know if you will be angry without any reason—

SIR PETER. There now you want to quarrel again—

LADY TEAZLE. No—I am sure I don't—but if you will be so peevish—

SIR PETER. There—now who begins first—

LADY TEAZLE. Why you to be sure. I said nothing but—there's no bearing—your Temper—                                                                                    220

SIR PETER. No—no—Madam—the Fault's in your own temper—

LADY TEAZLE. Aye you are just what my cousin Sophy said you would be.

SIR PETER. Your cousin Sophy—is a forward impertinent Gypsey—

LADY TEAZLE. You are a great Bear I'm sure to abuse my Relations[1]—

SIR PETER. Now may all the Plagues of marriage be doubled on me if ever I try to be Friends with you any more—

LADY TEAZLE. So much the Better—

SIR PETER. No—no madam 'tis evident you—never cared a Pin for me—and I was a madman to marry you—a Pert rural Coquet that had refused half the honest Squires in the neighbourhood.                                                       230

LADY TEAZLE. And I am sure I was a Fool to marry you—an Old dangling Batchelor who was single at fifty only because He never could meet with any one who would have him.

SIR PETER. Aye—aye—Madam—but you were pleased enough—to listen to me—you never had such an Offer before.

LADY TEAZLE. No! didn't I refuse Sir Twivy Tarrier—who every body said would have been a better Match—for his Estate is just as good as yours—and He has broke his Neck[2] since we have been married!

SIR PETER. I have done with you Madam—you are an unfeeling—ungrateful—but there's an end of every thing—I believe you capable of 240 anything that's bad—yes Madam—I now believe the Reports relative

---

[1] Charles Reade's mother related that Sheridan stopped Mrs. Abington in rehearsal and said: 'No, no, that won't do at all. It mustn't be *pettish*. That's shallow—shallow. You must go up stage with, "You are just what my cousin Sophy said you would be," and then turn and sweep down on him like a volcano. "You are a great bear to abuse my relations! How *dare* you abuse my relations!"' See Ellen Terry, *The Story of my Life*, 2nd edn. (1908), p. 49.

[2] Cf. Garrick's *Bon Ton*, Act I: '*Lady Minikin*: He's a colonel: his elder brother, Sir Tan Tivy, will certainly break his neck, and then my friend will be a happy man.' See also 'the famous Tantwivy mare' in Colman's *The Jealous Wife*, II. i.

to you and Charles—Madam—yes Madam you and—Charles are not
without Grounds—

LADY TEAZLE. Take—care Sir Peter—you had better not insinuate any
such thing! I'll not be suspected without cause I promise you.—

SIR PETER. Very—well, Madam—very well—a separate maintenance—
as soon as you Please—yes Madam or a Divorce—I'll make an example
of myself for the benefit of all old Batchelors. Let us separate Madam—

LADY TEAZLE. Agreed—agreed—and now—my Dear Sir Peter we are
of a Mind once more we may be the happiest Couple—and never differ    250
again you know; ha! ha!—well you are going to be in a Passion I see—
and I shall only interrupt you—so, bye, bye!                [*Exit.*

SIR PETER. Plagues and Tortures! can't I make her Angry neither!
O I am the miserablest Fellow—But I'll not bear her presuming to keep
her Temper—No she may break my Heart but she shan't keep her
Temper.                                                     [*Exit.*


### Scene 2d. CHARLES's *House*

#### *Enter* TRIP—MOSES *and* SIR OLIVER.

TRIP. Here Master Moses—if you'll stay a moment—I'll try whether
Mr.—what's the Gentleman's Name?

SIR OLIVER. Mr.——. Moses—what *is* my name? [*aside*]

MOSES. Mr. Premium—

TRIP. Premium—very well.                        [*Exit* TRIP *taking snuff.*

SIR OLIVER. To Judge by the Servants—one wouldn't believe the master
was ruin'd—but what—sure this was my Brother's House?

MOSES. Yes Sir Mr. Charles bought it of Mr. Joseph with the Furniture
Pictures—etc.—just as the old Gentleman left—it—Sir Peter thought
it a great Piece of Extravagance in him!                             10

SIR OLIVER. In my mind the other's œconomy in selling it to him was
more reprehensible by half.—

#### *Re-enter* TRIP.

TRIP. My Master says you must wait Gentlemen. He has Company and
can't Speak with you yet.—

SIR OLIVER. If He knew who it was wanted to see him perhaps He
wouldn't have sent such a Message.

TRIP. Yes—yes—Sir—He knows you are here—I didn't forget little
Premium—no, no, no—

SIR OLIVER. Very well—and I pray Sir what may be your Name?—

TRIP. Trip Sir—my Name is Trip at your Service.                     20

SIR OLIVER. Well then Mr. Trip—you have a pleasant sort of a place
here I guess.

TRIP. Why yes—here are three or four of us pass our time agreeably enough—but then our wages are sometimes a little in arrear—and not very great either—but fifty Pounds a year and find our own Bags[1] and Bouquets[2]—

SIR OLIVER. [*Aside*] Bags and Bouquets!—Halters and Bastinadoes!—

TRIP. But à propos Moses—have you been able to get me that little Bill discounted?

SIR OLIVER. Wants to raise Money too!—mercy on me—has his 30 distresses I warrant like a Lord—and affects Creditors and Duns!

MOSES. 'Twas not to be done indeed Mr. Trip—[*gives the Note.*]

TRIP. Good lack—you surprize me—my Friend Brush has indorsed it and I thought when he put his Mark on the Back of a Bill 'twas as good as cash—

MOSES. No 'twouldn't do—

TRIP. A small—sum—but twenty Pounds—hearkee Moses do you think you couldn't get it me by way of annuity?

SIR OLIVER. An annuity! ha! ha! ha! a Footman raise Money by annuity—well done Luxury egad!                                                40

MOSES. But you must ensure your Place.

TRIP. O with all my Heart—I'll ensure my Place and my Life too if you Please—

SIR OLIVER. It's more than I would your neck.

TRIP. But then, Moses, it must be done before this d——d register[3] takes place—one wouldn't like to have one's Name made public you know.

MOSES. No certainly, But is there nothing you could deposit.

TRIP. Why, nothing capital of my master's wardrobe has dropp'd lately— but I could give you a mortgage on some of his winter Cloaths with 50 equity of redemption before November—or—you shall have the reversion—of the French Velvet—or a post Obit on the Blue and Silver —These I should think Moses—with a few Pair of Point Ruffles as a collateral security—hey my little Fellow—?

MOSES. Well, well.                                        [*bell rings.*

TRIP. Gad I heard the Bell—I believe Gentlemen I can now introduce you—don't forget the annuity little Moses; this way Gentlemen, ensure my place! you know—

SIR OLIVER. If the man be a shadow of his Master—this is the Temple of Dissipation indeed!                                    [*Exeunt.* 60

---

[1] A pouch of silk for the tail of a bag-wig.

[2] The English fop in Paris 'tops the mode with a white feather, red heels, and an immense *bouquet*' (*Town and Country Magazine*, v (1773), 261).

[3] The Annuity Bill required all grants of life annuities to be registered.

*Scene 3d*

CHARLES—CARELESS—*etc. etc.*

*at a Table with Wine etc.*

CHARLES. 'Fore heaven, 'tis true—there's the great Degeneracy of the age—many of our acquaintance have Taste, spirit, and Politeness—but plague on't they won't drink.

CARELESS. It is so indeed Charles—they give into all the Substantial Luxuries of the Table—and abstain from nothing but wine and wit—

CHARLES. O certainly Society suffers by it intolerably—for now instead of the social spirit of Raillery that used to mantle over a glass of bright Burgundy their conversation is become just like the Spa water they drink which has all the Pertness and flatulence of Champaine without its Spirit or Flavour.—                                                          10

1ST. GENT. But what are they to do who love Play better than wine?

CARELESS. True—there's Harry diets himself—for Gaming and is now under a Hazard—Regimen—

CHARLES. Then He'll have the worst of it—what you wouldn't train a horse for the course by keeping him from corn—for my Part egad I am now—never so successful as when I am a little—merry—let me throw on a Bottle of Champaine and I never lose—at least I never feel my losses which is exactly the same thing.

2D. GENT. Aye—that I believe.

CHARLES. And then what man can pretend to be a Believer in Love who   20 is an abjuror of Wine—tis the Test by which the Lover knows his own Heart, fill a dozen Bumpers to a dozen Beauties—and she that floats at top is the Maid that has bewitch'd you—

CARELESS. Now then Charles—be honest and give us your real favorite—

CHARLES. Why I have withheld her only in compassion to you—if I toast her you must give a round of her Peers which is impossible! on earth!

CARELESS. O then we'll find some canonized Vestals or heathen Goddesses that will do I warrant—

CHARLES. Here then—Bumpers—you Rogues—Bumpers!—Maria——Maria—[*drink*]                                                            30

1ST. GENT. Maria who?

CHARLES. O damn the Surname! 'tis too formal to be register'd in Love's Calendar.—but now Sir Toby Bumper beware—we must have Beauty superlative.

CARELESS. Nay never Study Sir Toby—we'll Stand to The toast—tho' your mistress should want an Eye—and you know you have a song will excuse you—

SIR TOBY. Egad so I have—and I'll give him the Song instead of the Lady.—

### Song[1] and Chorus

Here's to the maiden of Bashful fifteen                    40
  Here's to the Widow of Fifty
Here's to the flaunting, Extravagant Quean,
  And here's to the House Wife that's thrifty.
CHORUS.      Let the toast pass—
          Drink to the Lass—
I'll warrant She'll prove an Excuse for the Glass!

#### 2d.

Here's to the Charmer whose Dimples we Prize!
  Now to the Maid who has none Sir;
Here's to the Girl with a pair of blue Eyes,
  —And Here's to the Nymph with but one Sir!          50
CHORUS.      Let the Toast pass etc.

#### 3d.

Here's to the Maid with a Bosom of Snow,
  Now to her that's as brown as a berry:
Here's to the Wife with a face full of Woe,
  And now for the Damsel that's Merry.
CHORUS.      Let the Toast pass etc.

#### 4th.

For let 'Em be Clumsy or let 'Em be Slim
  Young or Ancient, I care not a Feather:
—So fill a Pint Bumper Quite up to the Brim
  —And let us E'en toast 'Em together!                60
CHORUS.      Let the Toast pass etc.
ALL.—Bravo. Bravo!

### Enter TRIP and Whispers CHARLES.

CHARLES. Gentlemen you must excuse me a little—Careless take the
Chair will you?
CARELESS. Nay prithee Charles—what now—this is one of your Peerless
Beauties I suppose—has dropt in by chance.

---

[1] W. Sichel, *Sheridan* (1909), i. 576, denies that its source was a song in *The Goblins*:
           A health to the nut-brown lass,
           With the hazle eyes, let it pass,
              She that has good eyes
              Has good thighs:
           Let it pass, . . . let it pass.
(*The Works of Sir John Suckling* (1770), ii. 313.)

CHARLES. No—Faith—to tell you the Truth 'tis a Jew—and a broker
who are come—by appointment.

CARELESS. O damn it let's have the Jew in—

1ST. GENT. Aye and the Broker too by all means—                    70

2ND. GENT. Yes yes the Jew and the Broker.

CHARLES. Egad with all my Heart—Trip—bid the Gentlemen walk in—
tho' there's one of them a Stranger I can tell you—

CARELESS. Charles—let us Give them some generous Burgundy—and
perhaps they'll grow conscientious.

CHARLES. O Hang 'em—no—wine does but draw forth a man's natural
qualities and to make them drink would only be to whet their Knavery.—

*Enter* TRIP—SIR OLIVER *and* MOSES.

CHARLES. So—honest Moses—walk in—walk in, pray Mr. Premium—
that's the Gentleman's name isn't it Moses?

MOSES. Yes Sir.                                                    80

CHARLES. Set Chairs—Trip—sit down Mr. Premium—Glasses Trip—
Sit down Moses.—come Mr. Premium I'll give you a sentiment[1]—
Here's Success to Usury—Moses fill the Gentleman a Bumper.

MOSES. Success to Usury—

CARELESS. Right Moses—Usury is Prudence and industry and deserves
to succeed—

SIR OLIVER. Then Here is all the success it deserves.

CARELESS. No, no—that won't do Mr. Premium, you have demur'd to
the Toast, and must Drink it in a Pint Bumper.

1ST. GENT. A Pint Bumper at least.                                 90

MOSES. O Pray Sir consider Mr. Premium's a Gentleman.

CARELESS. And therefore loves good Wine.

2D. GENT Give Moses a Quart Glass—this is Mutiny, and a High
contempt of the Chair.

CARELESS. Here—now for't—I'll see Justice done to the last drop of my
Bottle.

SIR OLIVER. Nay pray Gentlemen—I did not Expect this Usage.

CHARLES. No—hang it—Careless—you Shan't: Mr. Premium's a
Stranger.

SIR OLIVER. Odd—I wish I was well out of this Company.             100

CARELESS. Plague on 'Em then—if they won't Drink—we'll not Sit down
with 'em; come Harry the Dice are in the next Room; Charles you'll
Join us—when you have finish'd your Business with these Gentlemen—

CHARLES. I will. I will.—[*Exeunt*] Careless—!

CARELESS. Well—

CHARLES. Perhaps I may want you.

[1] Cf. Edward Bull's statement in Frances Sheridan's *A Journey to Bath*: 'I have
drunk sentiments very often, we give them for toasts' (Rae, p. 281).

CARELESS. O you know I am always ready—Word, Note—or Bond 'tis all the same to me.                                                    [*Exit.*

MOSES. Sir—this is Mr. Premium, a Gentleman of the Strictest honour and Secrecy—and always performs what he undertakes—Mr. Premium 110 this is—

CHARLES. Pshaw have done!—Sir, my Friend Moses is a very honest fellow, but a little Slow at Expression, he'll be an Hour giving us our Titles—Mr. Premium—the Plain State of the Matter is this—I am an Extravagant young Fellow, who want[s] Money to Borrow,[1] you I take to be a Prudent old Fellow, who has got Money to lend—I am Blockhead enough to give Fifty per Cent. sooner than not have it, and you I presume are Rogue Enough to take a hundred if you could get it,—Now Sir, you See we are acquainted at once, and may proceed to Business without farther Ceremony.                                          120

SIR OLIVER. Exceeding frank upon my Word—I see Sir, you are not a Man of many Compliments.

CHARLES. O No Sir—plain Dealing in Business I always think best.

SIR OLIVER. Sir—I like you the better for't—however you are Mistaken in one thing—I have no Money to lend. But I believe I could procure some of a Friend; but then he's an unconscionable Dog isn't he Moses? and must sell Stock to accom[m]odate you—mustn't he Moses?

MOSES. Yes indeed!—you know I always speak the truth, and Scorn to tell a lie.                                                            130

CHARLES. Right! People that Expect truth Generally do—but these are Trifles Mr. Premium—What—I know money isn't to be bought without paying for't.

SIR OLIVER. Well but what Security could you give—you have no Land I suppose?

CHARLES. Not a Mole-hill—nor a Twig, but what's in beau pots out at the Window.

SIR OLIVER. Nor any Stock I presume.

CHARLES. Nothing but live stock—and that's only a few Pointers and Ponies. But pray Mr. Premium are you acquainted at all with any of 140 my connections—

SIR OLIVER. Why to say truth I am.

CHARLES. Then you must know that I have a devilish rich Uncle in the East Indies—Sir Oliver Surface—from whom I have the greatest Expectations.

SIR OLIVER. That you have a Wealthy Uncle I have heard—but how your Expectations will turn out is more I believe than you can tell.

---

[1] 'Thespis' in *The Oracle*, 17 Sept. 1792, asked 'Why in such polished dialogue as *The School for Scandal* have we such blots as "I am an extravagant young fellow who want money to borrow?" an uncouth phrase!'

CHARLES. O no—there can be no doubt of it—they tell me I'm a prodigious Favorite—and that he talks of leaving me every thing.

SIR OLIVER. Indeed this is the first I've heard on't. 150

CHARLES. Yes, yes—tis just so—Moses knows 'tis true—don't you Moses?

MOSES. O yes—I'll swear to't—

SIR OLIVER. Egad they'll persuade me presently I'm at Bengal.

CHARLES. Now I propose Mr. Premium if it's agreeable to you to Grant you a Post Obit on Sir Oliver's Life tho' at the same time the Old Fellow has been so liberal to me that I give you my word I should be very Sorry to hear any thing had happen'd to him.

SIR OLIVER. Not more than I should I assure you; But the bond you mention happens to be Just the worst Security you could Offer me— for I might Live to a hundred and never recover the Principal. 160

CHARLES. O yes you would—the moment Sir Oliver dies you know you'd come on me for the Money.

SIR OLIVER. Then I believe I should be the most unwelcome Dun you Ever had in your Life.

CHARLES. What I suppose you are afraid now that Sir Oliver is too good a Life.

SIR OLIVER. No indeed I am not—tho' I have heard he is as hale and healthy as any Man of his years in Christendom.

CHARLES. There again you are misinformed—No, no, the Climate has hurt him considerably—Poor uncle Oliver—yes he breaks apace I'm 170 told—and so much alter'd lately that his nearest Relations don't know him—

SIR OLIVER. No!—ha! ha! ha! so much altered lately that his Relations don't know him, ha! ha! ha! that's droll egad—ha! ha! ha!—

CHARLES. Ha! ha! you're glad to hear that little Premium.

SIR OLIVER. No—no—I'm not.

CHARLES. Yes, yes, you are—ha! ha! ha!—you know that mends your Chance.

SIR OLIVER. But I'm told Sir Oliver is coming over—nay some say he is Actually Arrived. 180

CHARLES. Pshaw! Sure I must know better than you whether He's come or not—no, no, rely on't, he is at this Moment at Calcutta, isn't he Moses?

MOSES. O yes certainly.

SIR OLIVER. Very true, as you Say—you must know better than I; tho' I have it from pretty good Authority—hav'nt I Moses?

MOSES. Yes—most undoubted—

SIR OLIVER. But Sir—as I understand you want a few hundreds immediately—is there nothing you would dispose of?

CHARLES. How do you mean?

SIR OLIVER. For instance now—I have heard—that your Father left 190 behind him a Great Quantity of Massy old Plate—

CHARLES. O Lud that's gone, long ago—Moses can tell you how better than I can—

SIR OLIVER. Good lack! all the Family Race cups and Corporation Bowls! [*aside*]—then it was also Suppos'd that his Library was one of the most Valuable and compleat—

CHARLES. Yes—yes. So it was—vastly too much so for a private Gentleman—for my part I was always of a Communicative disposition, So I thought it a Shame to keep so much knowledge to myself—

SIR OLIVER. Mercy on me! Learning that had run in the Family like an 200 Heir Loom! Pray what are become of the Books?[1]

CHARLES. You must Enquire of the Auctioneer, Master Premium, for I don't believe Even Moses can direct you there.

MOSES. I never Meddle with Books.

SIR OLIVER. So—so—nothing of the Family Property left I suppose.

CHARLES. Not much Indeed, unless you have a mind to the Family Pictures[2]—I have got a Room full of Ancestors above—and if you have a Taste for old Paintings Egad, you shall have 'Em a Bargain.

SIR OLIVER. Hey! and the Devil! Sure you wouldn't Sell your Forefathers—would you?                                                          210

CHARLES. Every man of 'Em to the best bidder—

SIR OLIVER. What your great Uncles and Aunts?

CHARLES. Aye, and my Great grand Fathers and Grandmothers too.

SIR OLIVER. Now I give him up!—[*aside*]—what the plague have you no Bowels for your own kindred?—Odds Life—do you take me for Shylock in the Play, that you would raise Money of me, on your own Flesh and Blood?

CHARLES. Nay, my little Broker—don't be angry—what need you care, If you have your Money's worth?

SIR OLIVER. Well—I'll be the purchaser—I think I can dispose of the 220 Family—Oh I'll never forgive him—this—never!

*Enter* CARELESS.

CARELESS. Come Charles—what keeps you?

CHARLES. I can't come yet a'faith! we are going to have a Sale above—here's little Premium will buy all my Ancestors—

CARELESS. Oh burn your ancestors—

---

[1] 'A knowledge of Books . . . was formerly regarded as a proper Qualification in a Man of Fashion. . . . It will not, I presume, be regarded as any kind of Satire on the present Age, to say, that among the higher Ranks, this literary Spirit is generally vanished' (John Brown, *An Estimate of the Manners and Principles of the Times* (5th ed., 1757), pp. 42–3.

[2] Cf. Sir Jeremy's statement in Frances Sheridan's *A Journey to Bath*: 'Why the land and the Mansion house has slippd thro' our finger's boy; but thank heaven the family pictures are still extant' (Rae, p. 312).

CHARLES. No, he may do that afterwards if he pleases: Stay Careless we
want you, Egad you shall be Auctioneer. So come along with us.
CARELESS. Oh, have with you, If that's the Case—I can handle a hammer
as well as a Dice Box!
SIR OLIVER. Oh the Profligates!                                    230
CHARLES. Come Moses—you shall be appraiser if we want one, gads
Life, little Premium, you don't seem to like the business.
SIR OLIVER. Oh yes I do vastly—ha, ha, yes, yes, I think it a rare Joke to
Sell one's Family by Auction, ha! ha! Oh, the prodigal!
CHARLES. To be Sure! when a man wants money, where the plague
should he get Assistance,—If he can't make free with his own Relations.
                                                          [*Exeunt.*

END OF THE THIRD ACT


*Act 4th.   Scene 1st*

*Picture Room at* CHARLES'*s*

*Enter* CHARLES, SIR OLIVER, MOSES *and* CARELESS.


CHARLES. Walk in Gentlemen, pray walk in!—here they are, the family
of the Surfaces up to the Conquest.
SIR OLIVER. And, in my opinion a goodly Collection.
CHARLES. Aye, Aye, these are done in the true spirit of Portrait-
Painting—no Volunteer Grace, or Expression—not like the Works of
your Modern Raphael,[1] who gives you the strongest resemblance[2] yet
contrives to make your own Portrait independent of you[3]—So that you
may Sink the Original and not hurt the Picture—no—no, the merit of


[1] A cutting (in the Folger Library) from an unnamed newspaper, but dated 14 Apr.
1779, describes an Opera House masquerade, at which were present 'our modern
Raphael and his lovely companions, Sir Joshua, with his three Graces'. Sheridan also
made the comparison in *Verses to the Memory of Garrick*, lines 25–6.
[2] Cf. Edmond Malone's opinion: 'The two portraits which Sir Joshua Reynolds
has lately painted of Mr. William Windham of Norfolk and Richard Brinsley Sheridan
are so like the originals, that they seem almost alive and ready to speak to you. Painting,
in point of resemblance, can go no farther' (James Prior, *The Life of Edmond Malone*
(1860), p. 388).
[3] Sir Joshua showed thirteen pictures at the Royal Academy exhibition of 1777, and
the *Morning Chronicle*, 25 Apr. 1777, remarked of them: 'As the face of every portrait
is the speaking part of the picture, Sir Joshua is particularly happy in giving all his
figures such force of expression, that scarce a person looks at them without entering
into a kind of colloquy with the picture.'

these is the Inveterate likeness[1]—all Stiff and Aukward as the Originals
and like nothing in human Nature beside!                                    10

SIR OLIVER. Ah! we shall never see such Figures of men again.

CHARLES. No, I hope not, you See Master Premium what a domestic
Character I am—here I sit of an Evening Surrounded by my Family—
But come get to your Pulpit Mr. Auctioneer—here's an old Gouty
chair[2] of my Grandfather's—will Answer the purpose.

CARELESS. Aye—aye—this will do—but Charles I have ne'er a Hammer
and what's an Auctioneer without his Hammer?

CHARLES. Egad, that's true, What parchment have we here? [takes down
a roll] Richard Heir to Thomas—our genealogy in full! Here Careless
you shall have no Common bit of Mahogany—Here's the Family Tree   20
for you, you Rogue—this shall be your Hammer, and now you may
knock down my Ancestors with their own Pedigree.

SIR OLIVER. What an unnatural Rogue! an ex post facto Parricide!

CARELESS. Yes, yes, here's a list of your Generation indeed.—faith
Charles—this is the most Convenient thing you could have found for
the Business, for 'twill Serve not only as a Hammer, but a Catalogue into
the Bargain—but come begin—a going—a going—a going!—

CHARLES. Bravo! Careless—well here's my Great uncle Sir Richard
Raviline[3]—a Marvellous good General in his Day I assure you—He
served in all the Duke of Marlborough's Wars; and got that cut over his   30
Eye at the Battle of Malplaquet;[4] What say you Mr. Premium—look at
him—there's a Hero for you! not cut out of his Feathers, as your
Modern clipt Captains are[5]—but enveloped in Wig and Regimentals
as a General should be—what do you bid?

MOSES. Mr. Premium would have you Speak—

CHARLES. Why then he shall have him for ten Pounds and I am Sure
that's not Dear for a Staff Officer.

---

[1] Cf. Wycherley, The Plain Dealer, II: 'I find one may have a collection of all ones
acquaintances Pictures, as well at your house, as at Mr. Lely's; only the difference is,
there we find 'em much handsomer than they are, and like; here much uglier, and like'
(Complete Works, ed. M. Summers (1924), i. 123).

[2] Paraphrased in The Public Register: or Freeman's Journal, 27–29 Jan. 1778, as 'an
old easy chair', but this may still have meant one particularly adapted for sufferers of
gout, as is evident in Horace Walpole's letter to Mann, 3 Jan. 1778 (Walpole Corr., viii.
346). See for 'a gouty stool', plate 15 from Hepplewhite's Cabinet Maker and Up-
holsterer's Guide (1788), reproduced in John Gloag, Georgian Grace (1956), p. 163. Some
verses on 'The Gouty Chair, and Chimney Corner', by 'Lister Esq.', are printed in
Poetical Amusements at a Villa near Bath (2nd edn., 1776), iv. 105–11.

[3] A ravelin was a fortification with two faces at an angle to the main structure.

[4] The English and allied troops were commanded by Marlborough and Prince
Eugène at this battle, fought on 11 Sept. 1709, in the War of the Spanish Succession.

[5] Without the plumes, but (as paraphrased in the Public Register, 27–29 Jan. 1778)
'with the friseur of the modern officer'.

SIR OLIVER. Heaven deliver me! his famous uncle Richard for Ten pounds! Very well Sir—I take him at that.

CHARLES. Careless, knock down my uncle Richard—Here now is a 40 Maiden Sister of his, my Great Aunt Deborah done by Kneller thought to be in his best Manner;[1] and a very formidable Likeness—There She is you See—A Shepherdess feeding her flock—you shall have her for five pounds Ten—the Sheep are worth the Money.[2]

SIR OLIVER. Ah! poor Deborah—a woman who set such a Value on herself!—Five pound ten! She's mine.

CHARLES. Knock down my aunt Deborah! Here now are two that were a Sort of Cousins of theirs—you see Moses these Pictures were done some time ago—when Beaux wore Wigs,[3] and the Ladies wore their own Hair.                                                                      50

SIR OLIVER. Yes truly Head dresses appear to have been a little lower[4] in those Days.

CHARLES. Well take that Couple for the same.

MOSES. Tis good Bargain.

CHARLES. Careless!—This now is a Grandfather of my Mother's, a learned Judge, well known on the Western Circuit—What do you rate him at Moses?

MOSES. Four Guineas.

CHARLES. Four guineas! Gads Life, you don't bid me the Price of his Wig! Mr. Premium—you have more respect for the Woolsack—do let 60 us knock his Lordship down at fifteen.

SIR OLIVER. By all means—

CARELESS. Gone.—

CHARLES. And there are two Brothers of his William and Walter Blunt Esquires both Members of Parliament and Noted Speakers, and what's very Extraordinary, I believe this is the first time they were ever bought and Sold.

SIR OLIVER. That's very extraordinary Indeed! I'll take them at your own Price for the Honour of Parliament.

CARELESS. Well said Little Premium—I'll knock 'em down at 70 forty.

---

[1] Sir Godfrey Kneller (1646–1723). For his 'thinly painted method', see C. H. Collins-Baker, *Lely and Kneller* (1922), pp. 104–5.

[2] Cf. *The Vicar of Wakefield*: 'Sophia was to be a shepherdess, with as many sheep as the painter could put in for nothing' (*Collected Works of Oliver Goldsmith*, ed. A. Friedman (Oxford, 1966), iv. 83).

[3] Cf. Garrick's prologue to *A Trip to Scarborough*, lines 19–22.

[4] 'The female head dress had now reached the highest degree of ridicule. It was time for the stage to lay hold of such extreme folly . . .' (*Chester Chronicle*, 12 Feb. 1776). Garrick derided it when playing Sir John Brute at this date, and Foote, as Lady Pentweazle, wore a head-dress a yard wide and full of ostrich feathers.

CHARLES. Here's a Jolly Fellow—I don't know what Relation—But he was Mayor of Manchester,[1] take him at Eight pounds.

SIR OLIVER. No, no—six will do for the Mayor.

CHARLES. Come make it Guineas and I'll throw you the two Aldermen there into the Bargain.—

SIR OLIVER. They're mine.

CHARLES. Careless—knock down the Mayor and Aldermen—but Plague on't we shall be all Day—retailing in this manner, do let us deal Wholesale—what say you little Premium—give me three hundred pounds, for the Rest of the family in the Lump. 80

CARELESS. Aye—aye—that will be the best way.—

SIR OLIVER. Well, well, any thing to accommodate you, they are mine. —but there is one Portrait, which you have always passed Over—

CARELESS. What, that ill looking little Fellow over the Settee

SIR OLIVER. Yes Sir I mean that, tho' I don't think him so ill looking a little Fellow by any means.

CHARLES. What that? Oh that's my unkle Oliver, 'twas done before he went to India—

CARELESS. Your Uncle Oliver! Gad! then you'll never be friends Charles, 90 That now to me is as Stern a looking Rogue as Ever I saw—an Unforgiving Eye, and a damn'd disinheriting Countenance! an Inveterate Knave depend on't, don't you think so little Premium?

SIR OLIVER. Upon my Soul Sir, I do not; I think it is as honest a looking Face as any in the Room—dead or alive; but I suppose your Uncle Oliver goes with the rest of the Lumber

CHARLES. No hang it, I'll not part with poor Noll—The Old Fellow has been very good to me, and Egad I'll keep his Picture, while I've a Room to put it in.

SIR OLIVER. [aside] The rogue's my nephew after all!—but, sir, I 100 have Somehow taken a fancy to that Picture.

CHARLES. I'm sorry for't, for you certainly will not have it—Oons! haven't you got enough of 'Em?

SIR OLIVER. I forgive him everything! [aside]—but Sir when I take a Whim in my Head I don't Value Money—I'll give as much for that as for all the rest—

CHARLES. Don't teize me, Master Broker, I tell you I'll not part with it—And there's an End on't—

SIR OLIVER. How like his Father the Dog is! [aside] well, well, I have done; I did not perceive it before but I think I never Saw such a 110 Resemblance [aside]—well Sir—Here is a Draught for your Sum.

CHARLES. Why 'tis for Eight hundred pounds!

---

[1] The name of the town may have been varied to satisfy local prejudices. The comedy was such a success at Manchester that 'the theatre was in danger of being destroyed by the crowd who pressed for places' (*Morning Chronicle*, 19 June 1778).

SIR OLIVER. You will not let Oliver go?

CHARLES. Z——ds! no I tell you once more.

SIR OLIVER. Then never mind the Difference; we'll Ballance another
time, but give me your hand on the Bargain—you are an Honest
Fellow Charles—I beg pardon Sir for being so free,—come
Moses,—

CHARLES. Egad this is a Whimsical old Fellow—but hearkee Premium,
you'll prepare Lodgings for these Gentlemen.                           120

SIR OLIVER. Yes, Yes, I'll send for them in a Day or two—

CHARLES. But hold—do now—Send a Genteel Conveyance for them,
for I Assure you they were most of them used to Ride in their own
Carriages.

SIR OLIVER. I will, I will, for all but—Oliver—

CHARLES. Aye all, but the little honest nabob.[1]

SIR OLIVER. You're fixed on that—

CHARLES. Peremptorily.

SIR OLIVER. A Dear extravagant Rogue! Good day come Moses,—let
me hear now who dares call him Profligate!                             130

                *[Exeunt* SIR OLIVER *and* MOSES.

CARELESS. Why this is the Oddest Genius—of the Sort I ever Saw.

CHARLES. Egad he's the Prince of Brokers I think, I wonder how the
Devil Moses got acquainted with so honest a fellow—hah! here's
Rowley, do Careless; Say I'll join the Company in a Moment—

CARELESS. I will,—but don't now let that old Blockhead persuade you—to
Squander any of that Money on old Musty debts, or any such Nonsense
for tradesmen—Charles, are the most Exorbitant Fellows!—

CHARLES. Very true, and paying them is only Encouraging them.

CARELESS. Nothing else.

CHARLES. Aye—Aye—never fear.—*[Exit* CARELESS] Soh—this was an   140
Odd old Fellow Indeed! Let me See, two thirds of this is mine by
Right; five hundred and thirty pounds 'Fore Heaven, I find one's
Ancestors are more Valuable Relations than I took 'Em for!—Ladies
and Gentlemen, your most Obedient and very Grateful humble
Servant,—*[Enter* ROWLEY]—hah! old Rowley, Egad, you are Just
come in Time, to take leave of your Old Acquaintance—

ROWLEY. Yes I heard they were going—but I wonder you can have such
Spirits under so many Distresses.

CHARLES. Why there's the point,—my Distresses are so many that I
can't afford to part with my Spirits, but I shall be rich and Splenetic all  150

---

[1] A civil or military official of the East India Company, who made a fortune during
his stay in India. It is interesting to find that the word 'honest' appeared in the text
presented to Mrs. Crewe: the reputation of the 'nabobs' grew steadily worse between
1760 and 1785. For a full discussion, see James M. Holzman, *The Nabobs in England.
A Study of the Retired Anglo-Indian, 1760–85* (New York, 1926).

in good time; however I suppose you are Surprized that I am not more sorrowful at parting with so many near Relations, to be Sure 'tis very affecting—but rot 'Em you See they never move a muscle, So why should I.

ROWLEY. There's no making—you Serious a Moment.

CHARLES. Yes faith: I am so now—here my honest Rowley here get me this chang'd, and take a hundred pounds of it immediately to old Stanley—

ROWLEY. A Hundred pounds—Consider only—

CHARLES. Gad's Life don't talk about it poor Stanley's wants are 160 pressing—and if you don't make haste we shall have some one call that has a better Right to the Money—

ROWLEY. Ah! there's the point.—I never will cease Dunning you with the Old Proverb—

CHARLES. 'Be Just before you're Generous' hey!—why so I would if I could—but Justice is an Old lame hobbling Beldame—and I can't Get her to keep pace with Generosity, for the Soul of Me.[1]—

ROWLEY. Yet, Charles, believe me—one hour's reflection—

CHARLES. Aye—Aye—its all very true—but hearkee, Rowley while I have, by heaven I'll give—so Damn your economy—and now for 170 hazard . . . .                                    [*Exeunt.*

*Scene 2d: the Parlour*

*Enter* SIR OLIVER *and* MOSES.

MOSES. Well Sir I think as Sir Peter said you have seen Mr. Charles in high Glory—'tis great Pity He's so extravagant.

SIR OLIVER. True—but He wouldn't Sell my Picture—

MOSES. And loves wine and women so much—

SIR OLIVER. But He wouldn't Sell my Picture.

MOSES. And game so deep—

SIR OLIVER. But He wouldn't Sell my Picture.—O—here's Rowley!

*Enter* ROWLEY.

ROWLEY. So—Sir Oliver—I find you have made a Purchase.

SIR OLIVER. Yes—yes—Our young Rake has parted with his Ancestors like Old Tapestry.                                    10

ROWLEY. And here has he commission'd me to redeliver you Part of the purchase Money I mean tho' in your necessitous Character of old Stanley—

[1] Cf. Christopher Smart, *Jubilate Agno*, ed. W. H. Bond (1954), p. 97: 'For Tully says to be generous you must be first just, but the voice of Christ is distribute at all events.'

MOSES. Ah! there is the Pity of all! He is so damn'd charitable.

ROWLEY. And I have left a Hosier and two Tailors in the Hall—who I'm
sure won't be paid, and this hundred would Satisfy 'em!

SIR OLIVER. Well—well—I'll pay his Debts—and his Benevolences
too—but now I am no more a Broker and you shall introduce me to the
elder Brother as Old Stanley.

ROWLEY. Not yet awhile—Sir Peter I know means to call there about   20
this time.—

*Enter* TRIP.

TRIP. O Gentlemen I beg Pardon for not shewing you out—this way—
Moses a Word                                    [*Exeunt* TRIP *and* MOSES.

SIR OLIVER. There's a fellow for you—would you believe it! that
Puppy intercepted the Jew, on our coming and wanted to raise money
before he got to his master—

ROWLEY. Indeed!—

SIR OLIVER. Yes—they are now planning an annuity Business—ah!
Master Rowley in my Day Servants were content with the Follies of
their Masters when they were worn a little Thread-Bare but now they   30
have their Vices, like their Birth-Day Cloaths with the Gloss on.—

[*Exeunt.*

*Scene 3d: A Library*

SURFACE *and* SERVANT.

SURFACE. No Letter from Lady Teazle?

SERVANT. No Sir—

SURFACE. I am surprised she hasn't sent if she is prevented from
coming—? Sir Peter certainly does not suspect me—yet I wish I may
not lose the Heiress, thro' the scrape I have drawn myself in with the
wife—However Charles's imprudence and bad character are great
Points in my Favour.—                                    [*Knocking.*

SERVANT. Sir—I believe that must be Lady Teazle—

SURFACE. Hold see—whether it is or not before you go to the Door—I
have a particular Message for you if it should be my Brother—       10

SERVANT. 'Tis her Ladyship Sir, She always leaves her Chair at the
millener's in the next Street.

SURFACE. Stay—stay—draw that Skreen before the Window—that will
do—my opposite Neighbour—is a maiden Lady of so curious a
temper!—[*Servant draws the Screen and Exit*] I have a difficult Hand to
play in this Affair—Lady Teazle has lately Suspected my Views on
Maria—but She must by no means be let into that secret, at least not
'till I have her more in my Power.

*Enter* LADY TEAZLE.

LADY TEAZLE. What Sentiment in Soliloquy—have you been very impatient now?—O lud! don't pretend to look grave—I vow I couldn't come before—  20

SURFACE. O Madam Punctuality is a species of constancy, a very unfashionable quality in a Lady.

LADY TEAZLE. Upon my word you ought to pity me, do you know that Sir Peter is grown so ill-temper'd to me of Late!—and so jealous! of Charles too that's the best of the Story isn't it—?

SURFACE. I am glad my scandalous Friends keep that up—[*aside*]

LADY TEAZLE. I am sure I wish He would let Maria marry him—and then perhaps He would be convinced—don't you—Mr. Surface?

SURFACE. Indeed I do not.—[*aside*] O Certainly I do—for then my dear  30 Lady Teazle would also be convinced how wrong her suspicions were—of my having any Design on the silly Girl—[*sit*]

LADY TEAZLE. Well—well I'm inclined to believe you—But isn't it provoking to have the most ill natured Things said to one? and there's my friend Lady Sneerwell has circulated I don't know how many Scandalous Tales of me and all without any Foundation too—that's what vexes me.—

SURFACE. Aye Madam to be sure that is the Provoking circumstance—without Foundation.—yes yes—there's the mortification indeed—for when a slanderous Story is believed against one—there certainly is no  40 comfort—like the consciousness of having deserv'd it—

LADY TEAZLE. No to be sure—then I'd forgive their Malice—but to attack me who am really so innocent—and who never say an ill natured thing of anybody—that is of any Friend—! and then Sir Peter too—to have him so peevish and so suspicious—when I know the integrity of my own Heart[1]—indeed 'tis monstrous.

SURFACE. But my dear Lady Teazle 'tis your own fault if you suffer it—when a Husband entertains a groundless suspicion of his Wife, and withdraws his confidence from her—the original compact is broke and she owes it to the Honor of her sex to endeavour to outwit him.  50

LADY TEAZLE. Indeed—so that if He suspects me without cause, it follows that the best way of curing his Jealousy is to give him reason for't.

SURFACE. Undoubtedly—for your Husband should never be deceived—in you—and in that case it becomes you to be frail in compliment to his discernment.

---

[1] Cf. 'The integrity of her own heart makes her liable to be imposed on by a plausible outside; and yet the dear good woman takes a sort of pride in her sagacity' (Frances Sheridan, *Memoirs of Miss Sidney Bidulph* (Dublin (1761), i. 82).

LADY TEAZLE. To be sure what you say is very reasonable—and when the consciousness of my own Innocence—

SURFACE. Ah! my Dear—Madam there is the great mistake—'tis this very conscious Innocence that is of the greatest Prejudice to you— 60 What is it makes you negligent of Forms and careless of the world's opinion?—why the consciousness of your Innocence[1]—what makes you thoughtless in your Conduct and apt to run into a thousand little imprudences?—why the consciousness of your Innocence—what makes you impatient of Sir Peter's Temper and outrageous at his suspicions? —why the consciousness of your own Innocence—

LADY TEAZLE. Tis very true.

SURFACE. Now my dear Lady Teazle if you would but once make a trifling Faux-Pas—you can't conceive how cautious you would grow— and how ready to humour and agree with your Husband. 70

LADY TEAZLE. Do you think so—

SURFACE. O I'm sure on't—and then you would find all Scandall would cease at once—for in short your Character at Present is like a Person in a Plethora absolutely dying of too much Health.

LADY TEAZLE. So—so—then I perceive your Prescription is that I must sin in my own Defence—and part with my virtue to preserve my Reputation.—

SURFACE. Exactly so upon my credit Ma'am.

LADY TEAZLE. Well certainly this is the oddest Doctrine—and the newest Receipt for avoiding Calumny. 80

SURFACE. An infallible one—believe me—Prudence like experience must be paid for—

LADY TEAZLE. Why if my understanding were once convinced—

SURFACE. O certainly madam your understanding *should* be convinced— yes—yes—Heav'n forbid I should perswade you to do any thing you *thought* wrong—no—no—I have too much honor to desire it—

LADY TEAZLE. Don't—you think we may as well leave Honor out of the Argument?

SURFACE. Ah—the ill effects of your country education I see still remain with you. 90

LADY TEAZLE. I doubt they do indeed—and I will fairly own to you that If I could be perswaded to do wrong it would be by Sir Peter's ill-usage—sooner than your honourable Logic after all—

SURFACE. Then by this Hand which He is unworthy of—

*Enter* SERVANT.

Sdeath, you Blockhead—what do you want—

[1] 'A collection of Toasts to reform the manners of the Times' (printed in *Bath Chronicle*, 19 Dec. 1771) includes the following: 'May the consciousness of our own innocence ever afford us that pleasure which the lewd man never enjoyed, and the guilty never felt.'

SERVANT. I beg Pardon Sir but I thought you wouldn't chuse Sir Peter to come up without announcing him—?

SURFACE. Sir Peter—oons and the Devil—

LADY TEAZLE. Sir Peter! O Lud! I'm ruin'd—I'm ruin'd—

SERVANT. Sir twasn't I let him in.                                             100

LADY TEAZLE. O I'm undone—what will become of me now Mr. Logick?—O mercy He's on the Stairs—I'll get behind here—and if ever I am so imprudent again—          [*Goes behind the Screen.*

SURFACE. Give me that—Book!—

[*Sits down—*SERVANT *pretends
to adjust his Hair.*

*Enter* SIR PETER.

SIR PETER. Aye, ever improving himself!—Mr. Surface—Mr. Surface!—

SURFACE. Oh!—my Dear Sir Peter—I beg your Pardon—[*gaping and throws away the Book*][1] I have been dozing over a stupid Book! well—I am much obliged to you for this Call—you haven't been here I believe since I fitted up this Room—Books you know are the only Things I am   110 a Coxcomb in—

SIR PETER. Tis very neat indeed—well well that's proper—and you make even your screen a source of knowledge—hung I perceive with Maps—

SURFACE. O yes—I find great use in that Screen.

SIR PETER. I dare say you must—certainly—when you want to find anything in a Hurry—

SURFACE. Aye or to hide any thing in a Hurry either—(*aside*)

SIR PETER. Well I have a little private Business—

SURFACE. You needn't stay—[*to* SERVANT]                                      120

SERVANT. No, sir—                                                   [*Exit.*

SURFACE. Here's a chair—Sir Peter—I beg—

SIR PETER. Well now we are alone—there *is* a Subject—my dear—Friend —on which I wish to unburthen my Mind to you—a Point of the greatest moment to my Peace—in short—my good Friend—Lady Teazle's Conduct of late has made me extremely unhappy.

SURFACE. Indeed I'm very sorry to hear it—

SIR PETER. Yes 'tis but too plain she has not the least regard for me— but what's worse—I have pretty good Authority to suspect that she must have formed an attachment to another.                              130

---

[1] Mary Linley described the successful Bath performance of *The School for Scandal* in a letter to her sister, Mrs. Sheridan, of 14 Nov. [1777], and added, 'I particularly observed that instead of throwing the Book to the other end of the Room as Palmer does he [Dimond] very carefully pulled down the Page he was reading and gave it to his Servant w[hi]ch is certainly more consistent with his Character' (*Sheridan Correspondence*, viii. 44, in the Widener Library, Harvard University).

SURFACE. You astonish me.

SIR PETER. Yes—and between ourselves—I think I have discover'd the Person.

SURFACE. How—you alarm me exceedingly!

SIR PETER. Ah! my Dear friend I knew you would sympathize with me.—

SURFACE. Yes—believe me Sir Peter—such a discovery would hurt me just as much as it would you—

SIR PETER. I am convinced of it—ah!—it is a happiness to have a Friend whom one can trust even with one's Family Secrets—but—have you no guess who I mean?                                    140

SURFACE. I haven't the most distant Idea.—it can't be Sir Benjamin Backbite.

SIR PETER. O No—what say you to Charles?

SURFACE. My Brother—impossible!—

SIR PETER. Ah! my dear Friend—the goodness of your own Heart misleads you—you judge of others by—yourself—

SURFACE. Certainly Sir Peter—the Heart that is conscious of its own integrity is ever slow to credit another's Treachery—

SIR PETER. True but your Brother has no sentiment—you never hear him talk so.—                                    150

SURFACE. Yet I can't but think that Lady Teazle herself has too much Principle—

SIR PETER. Aye—but what's her Principle—against the flattery of a handsome—lively young Fellow—

SURFACE. That's very true—

SIR PETER. And then you know the difference of our ages makes it very improb[ab]le that she should have a great affection for me—and if she were to be frail and I were to make it Public—why the Town would only laugh at me, the foolish old Batchelor who had Married a Girl.—

SURFACE. That's true—to be sure—they *would* laugh—                                    160

SIR PETER. Laugh!—aye—and make Ballads—and Paragraphs and the Devil knows what of me—

SURFACE. No—you must never make it Public—

SIR PETER. But then again that the Nephew of my old Friend Sir Oliver should be the Person to attempt such a wrong—hurts me more nearly—

SURFACE. Aye there's the point; when Ingratitude barbs the Dart of Injury—the wound has double danger in it—

SIR PETER. Aye, I that was in a manner left his Guardian—in whose House he had been so often entertain'd—who never in my Life denied    170
him my advice—

SURFACE. O 'tis not to be credited—There may be a man capable of such Baseness to be sure—but for my Part 'till you can give me positive Proofs—I can not but doubt it. However if this should be proved on him He is no longer a Brother of mine! I disclaim kindred with him—for the Man who can break thro' the Laws of Hospitality— and attempt the wife—of his Friend deserves to be branded as the Pest of Society—

SIR PETER. What a difference there is between you—what noble sentiments!—                                                                           180

SURFACE. Yet I cannot suspect Lady Teazle's Honor—

SIR PETER. I am sure I wish to think well of her—and to remove all ground of quarrel between us—She has lately reproach'd me more than once—with having made no settlement on her—and in our last Quarrel she almost hinted that she should not break her Heart if I was Dead.— now as we seem to differ in our Ideas of Expence I have resolved she shall be her own Mistress in that Respect for the future—and if I were to die she shall find that I have not been inattentive to her Interest while living—Here my Friend are the Draughts of two Deeds which I wish to have your opinion on: by one—She will enjoy eight hundred a year  190 independent while I live—and by the other the Bulk of my Fortune after my Death—

SURFACE. This Conduct Sir Peter is indeed truly Generous!—I wish it may not corrupt my Pupil—[aside]

SIR PETER. Yes I am Determined she shall have no cause to complain— tho' I would not have her acquainted with the latter Instance of my Affection yet awhile—

SURFACE. Nor I—if I could help it—[aside]

SIR PETER. And now my Dear Friend if you please we will talk over the situation of your hopes with Maria—                                          200

SURFACE. No—no—Sir Peter—another Time if you Please—[softly]

SIR PETER. I am Sensibly chagrined at the little Progress you seem to make in her affection—

SURFACE. I beg you will not mention it—what are my Disap[p]ointments when your Happiness is in Debate! [softly] 'sdeath—I should be ruin'd every way—[aside]

SIR PETER. And tho' you are so averse to my acquainting Lady Teazle with your Passion—I am sure she's not your Enemy in the Affair—

SURFACE. Pray Sir Peter—now oblige me.—I am really too much affected by the subject we have been speaking on to bestow a thought  210 on my own concerns—The Man who is entrusted with his Friend's Distresses can never—well Sir?

*Enter* SERVANT.

SERVANT. Your Brother, Sir, is—speaking to a Gentleman in the Street— and says He knows you are within—

SURFACE. Sdeath, Blockhead—I'm not within—I'm out for the Day—

SIR PETER. Stay—hold—a thought has struck me—you shall be at home—

SURFACE. Well—well—let him up—[*Exit* SERVANT] He'll Interrupt Sir Peter—however—

SIR PETER. Now my good Friend—oblige me I entreat you—before 220 Charles comes—let me conceal myself somewhere—Then do you tax him on the Point we have been talking on—and his answers may satisfy me at once—

SURFACE. O Fie Sir Peter—would you have me join in so mean a Trick— to trepan[1] my Brother to—

SIR PETER. Nay you tell me—you are *sure* He is innocent—if so you do him the greatest service in giving him an opportunity to clear himself— and—you will set—my Heart at rest—come you shall not refuse me— here behind this Screen will be [*goes to the Screen*]—hey! what the Devil —there seems to be one list'ner here already—I'll swear I saw a 230 Petticoat.—

SURFACE. Ha! ha! ha!—well this is ridiculous enough—I'll tell you Sir Peter—tho' I hold a man of Intrigue to be a most despicable Character— yet you know it doesn't follow that one is to be an absolute Joseph[2] either.—hearkee—'tis a little French Millener—a silly Rogue that Plagues me—and having some character, on your coming she ran behind the Screen—

SIR PETER. Ah! you Rogue—but 'egad she has overheard all I have been saying of my Wife.

SURFACE. O 'twill never go any further—you may depend on't.          240

SIR PETER. No!—then—'efaith, let her hear it out.—Here's a Closet will do as well.—

SURFACE. Well go in then—

SIR PETER. Sly Rogue—sly Rogue—              [*Goes into the Closet*[3]

SURFACE. A very narrow escape indeed!—and a curious situation I'm in!—to part man and wife in this manner.

LADY TEAZLE. [*Peeping from the screen*]. Couldn't I steal off?—

SURFACE. Keep close my Angel—

SIR PETER. [*Peeping out*]. Joseph—tax him home—

SURFACE. Back—my dear Friend!                              250

LADY TEAZLE [*Peeping*]. Couldn't you Lock Sir Peter in?

SURFACE. Be still—my Life.

SIR PETER [*Peeping*]. You're sure—the little Millener won't blab?

SURFACE. In! in! my good Sir Peter—foregad—I wish I had a Key to the Door.—

---

[1] Decoy or beguile. Cf. *The Beggar's Opera*, II. xiii: 'Force or cunning | Never shall my heart trapan.'

[2] Resisting Potiphar's wife: Genesis 39: 7 seq.

[3] Cf. *A Trip to Scarborough*, IV. iii: *Exit Loveless into the Closet*.

*Enter* CHARLES.

CHARLES SURFACE. Hollo! Brother—what has been the matter? your Fellow wouldn't let me up at first—what have you had a Jew or a wench with you?

SURFACE. Neither Brother I assure you.

CHARLES SURFACE. But—what has made Sir Peter—steal off—I thought  260 He had been with you.

SURFACE. He *was* Brother—but hearing you were coming He did not chuse to stay—

CHARLES SURFACE. What was the old Gentleman afraid I wanted to borrow money of him!—

JOSEPH. No Sir—but I am Sorry—to find Charles—that you have lately given that worthy man grounds for great Uneasiness—

CHARLES SURFACE. Yes they tell me I do that to a great many worthy men—but How so Pray?

JOSEPH. To be plain with you Brother He thinks you are endeavouring—  270 to gain Lady Teazle's Affections from him.

CHARLES SURFACE. Who I—O Lud! not I upon my word. Ha! ha! ha! so the old Fellow has found out that He has got a young wife—has He? or what's worse has her Ladyship discover'd that she has an old Husband?

JOSEPH. This is—no subject to jest on Brother—He who can laugh—

CHARLES SURFACE. True Brother as you were going to say—then seriously I never had the least idea of what—you charge me with, upon my honour—

SURFACE. Well, it will give Sir Peter great satisfaction to hear this—  280 [*aloud*]

CHARLES SURFACE. To be sure I once thought the Lady seem'd to have taken a fancy to me—but upon my soul I never gave her the least encouragement.—besides, you know my Attachment to Maria—

SURFACE. But sure Brother even if Lady Teazle had betray'd the fondest partiality for you—

CHARLES SURFACE Why—lookee Joseph—I hope I shall never deliberately do a dishonourable Action—but if—a pretty woman were purposely to throw herself in my way—and that pretty woman married to a man old enough to be her Father—  290

SURFACE. Well!—

CHARLES SURFACE. —Why I believe I should be obliged to borrow a little of your Morality—that's all.—but Brother—do you know now that you surprize me Exceedingly by naming *me* with Lady—Teazle—for faith I always understood *you* were her Favourite—

SURFACE. O—for Shame Charles—this retort is Foolish

CHARLES SURFACE. Nay I swear I have seen you exchange such significant Glances—

SURFACE. Nay—nay—Sir—this is no jest—

CHARLES SURFACE. Egad—I'm serious—don't you remember—one Day when I call'd here— 300

SURFACE. Nay—prithee—Charles

CHARLES SURFACE. And found you together—

SURFACE. Zounds—Sir—I insist—

CHARLES SURFACE. And another time when your Servant—

SURFACE. Brother—Brother a word with you—gad I must stop him— [aside]

CHARLES SURFACE. Inform'd—me I say that—

SURFACE. Hush!—I beg your—Pardon but—Sir Peter has overheard all we have been saying—I knew you would clear yourself or I should not have consented— 310

CHARLES SURFACE. How Sir Peter!—where is He—?

SURFACE. Softly—there—[points to the Closet]

CHARLES SURFACE. O—'fore Heav'n I'll have him out—Sir Peter come forth—

SURFACE. No—No—

CHARLES SURFACE. I say Sir Peter—come into Court.—[pulls in Sir Peter] What—my old Guardian—what turn inquisitor and take evidence incog.—

SIR PETER. Give me your hand—Charles—I believe I have suspected you wrongfully—but you mustn't be angry with Joseph—'twas my Plan— 320

CHARLES SURFACE. Indeed!—

SIR PETER. But I acquit you.—I promise you I don't think near so ill of you as I did—what I have heard has given me great satisfaction—

CHARLES SURFACE. Egad then 'twas lucky you didn't hear any more—wasn't it Joseph? [half aside]

SIR PETER. Ah! you would have retorted on him—

CHARLES SURFACE. Aye—aye—that was a Joke—

SIR PETER. Yes—yes I know his Honor too well

CHARLES SURFACE. But you might as well have suspected him as me in this matter for all that, mightn't He Joseph? [half aside] 330

SIR PETER. Well well I believe you—

SURFACE. Would they were both well out of the Room! [aside]

*Enter* SERVANT *who Whispers* SURFACE

SIR PETER. And in future perhaps we may not be such Strangers.

SURFACE. Lady Sneerwell!—stop her by all means—[exit SERVANT] Gentlemen—I beg Pardon—I must wait on you down stairs—Here is a Person come on particular Business.—

CHARLES SURFACE. Well you can see him in another Room, Sir Peter and I haven't met a long time and I have something to say to him.—

SURFACE. They must not be left together.—I'll contrive to send Lady 340 Sneerwell away, and return directly. [*aside to him*] Sir Peter not a Word of the French milliner. [*Exit* SURFACE]

SIR PETER. O not for the world! Ah—Charles if you associated more with your Brother, one might indeed hope for your reformation—He is a man of Sentiment—well! there is nothing in the world so noble as a man of Sentiment!

CHARLES SURFACE. Pshaw—He is too moral by half—and so apprehensive of his good Name, as he calls it, that I suppose He would as soon let a Priest into his House as a Girl—

SIR PETER. No—no—come come—you wrong him—no—no Joseph is 350 no Rake but He is not such a Saint in that Respect either—I have a great mind to tell him—we should have a Laugh—[*aside*]

CHARLES SURFACE. Oh hang him! He's a very Anchorite—a young Hermit—

SIR PETER. Hearkee—you must not abuse him—He may chance to hear of it again I promise you—

CHARLES SURFACE. Why you won't tell him—

SIR PETER. No—but—this way—egad! I'll tell him!—hearkee! have you a mind to have a good Laugh at Joseph?

CHARLES SURFACE. I should like it of all things— 360

SIR PETER. Then efaith we will—I'll be quit with him for discovering me—[*aside*] He had a Girl with him when I call'd—[*Whispering*]

CHARLES SURFACE. What—Joseph! you jest—

SIR PETER. Hush!—a little—French Millener—[*whispers*] and the best of the Jest is—she's in the Room now

CHARLES SURFACE. The Devil she is—

SIR PETER. Hush—I tell you—[*points*]

CHARLES SURFACE. Behind the Screen—'slife let us unveil her—

SIR PETER. No—no! He's coming—you shan't indeed—

CHARLES SURFACE. O egad! we'll have a peep at the little Millener— 370

SIR PETER. Not for the world—Joseph—will never forgive me—

CHARLES SURFACE. I'll Stand by you—

SIR PETER. [*Strug[g]ling with* CHARLES] Oods! here he is . . .

[*Surface enters just as* CHARLES *throws down the Screen.*]

CHARLES SURFACE. Lady Teazle! by all that's wonderfull!

SIR PETER. Lady Teazle! by all that's Horrible!

CHARLES SURFACE. Sir Peter—This is one of the smartest French Milliners I ever saw!—egad you seem all to have been diverting yourselves here at Hyde and Seek—and I don't See who is out of the Secret!—Shall I beg your Ladyship—to inform me!—not a word!

Brother!—will you please to explain this matter?—what—Morality    380
Dumb too?—Sir Peter—tho' I found—you in the Dark—perhaps you
are not so now—all mute—!—well tho' I can make nothing of the Affair
I Suppose you perfectly understand one another—so I'll leave you to
yourselves—[*going*] Brother I'm Sorry to find you have given that
worthy man so much uneasiness!—Sir Peter—there's nothing in the
world so noble as a man of Sentiment!—                [*Exit* CHARLES.

[*Stand for some time looking at each other*]

SURFACE. Sir Peter—notwithstanding I confess that appearances are
against me—If you will afford me your Patience I make no doubt but
I shall explain everything to your Satisfaction.

SIR PETER. If you please—                                         390

SURFACE. The Fact is Sir—that Lady Teazle, knowing my Pretensions
to your ward Maria—I say Sir Lady Teazle—being apprehensive of the
Jealousy of your Temper—and knowing my Friendship to the Family—
She Sir I say call'd here—in order that I might explain those Preten-
sions—but on your coming—being apprehensive—as I said of your
Jealousy—she withdrew—and this you may depend on't is the whole
Truth of the Matter.

SIR PETER. A very clear account upon my word and I dare swear the
Lady will Vouch for every article of it—

LADY TEAZLE. [*Coming forward*] For not one word of it Sir Peter.    400

SIR PETER. How! don't you even think it worth while to agree in the
lie—

LADY TEAZLE. There is not one syllable of Truth in what that Gentleman has told you—

SIR PETER. I believe you upon my Soul Ma'am—

SURFACE. 'Sdeath madam will you betray me—[*aside*]

LADY TEAZLE. Good Mr. Hypocrite by your leave I will speak for
myself—

SIR PETER. Aye—let her alone Sir—you'll find she'll make out a better
story than you without Prompting.                                410

LADY TEAZLE. Hear me Sir Peter—I came hither—on no matter—
relating to your Ward and even ignorant of this Gentleman's Pretensions to her—but I came seduced by his insidious arguments, at least
to listen to his pretended Passion, if not to sacrifice your Honour to his
Baseness—

SIR PETER. Now I believe the Truth is coming indeed—

SURFACE. The Woman's mad—

LADY TEAZLE. No Sir—she has recover'd her Senses, and your own
Arts have furnish'd her with the means. Sir Peter—I do not Expect you
to credit me—but the Tenderness you express'd for me when I am sure    420
you could not think I was a witness to it, has penetrated to my Heart

and had I left the Place without the Shame of this discovery—my future
Life should have Spoke the sincerity of my Gratitude.—as for that
smooth tongue Hypocrite—who would have seduced the wife of his
too credulous Friend while he affected honourable addresses to his
ward—I behold him now in a light so truly despicable—that I shall
never again respect myself for having listen'd to him—        [*Exit*.
SURFACE. Notwithstanding all this Sir Peter—Heav'n knows—
SIR PETER. That you are a Villain!—and so I leave you to your
Conscience—                                                          430
SURFACE. You are too Rash Sir Peter—you shall hear me! the Man who
shuts out Conviction by refusing to—
SIR PETER. Oh!           [*Exeunt*, SURFACE *following and Speaking*.


END OF ACT 4TH


## Act 5th

### Scene 1st. The Library

*Enter* SURFACE *and* SERVANT.

SURFACE. Mr. Stanley! why should you think I would see him? you
must know he comes to ask something!
SERVANT. Sir—I should not have let him in but that Mr. Rowley came
to the Door with him.—
SURFACE. Pshaw!—Blockhead to Suppose that I should now be in a
Temper to receive visits from poor Relations!—well why don't you
shew the Fellow up—?
SERVANT. I will—Sir—why Sir—it was not my Fault that Sir Peter
discover'd my Lady—
SURFACE. Go—Fool—! [*Exit* SERVANT] Sure Fortune never play'd a    10
man of my Policy—such a Trick—before—my character with Sir
Peter! my Hopes with Maria!—destroy'd in a moment!—I'm in a rare
Humour to listen to other People's Distresses!—I shan't be able to
bestow even a benevolent sentiment on Stanley.—So! here—He comes
and Rowley with him—I *must* try to recover myself—and put a little
Charity into my Face however.—                                    [*Exit*.

*Enter* SIR OLIVER *and* ROWLEY.

SIR OLIVER. What! does He avoid us?—that was He—was it not?
ROWLEY. It was Sir—but I doubt you are come a little too abruptly—
his Nerves are so weak, that the sight of a poor Relation may be too
much for him—I should have gone first—to break you to him.        20

SIR OLIVER. A Plague of his Nerves—yet this is He whom Sir Peter extolls as a Man of the most Benevolent way of thinking!—

ROWLEY. As to his way of thinking—I can't pretend to decide for to do him justice He appears to have as much speculative Benevolence as any private Gentleman in the Kingdom—tho' He is seldom so sensual as to indulge himself in the Exercise of it.—

SIR OLIVER. Yet has a string of charitable Sentiments I suppose at his Fingers' ends!—

ROWLEY. Or rather at his Tongue's end Sir Oliver—for I believe there is no sentiment He has more faith in than that 'Charity begins at Home'. 30

SIR OLIVER. And his I presume is of that domestic sort which never stirs abroad at all.

ROWLEY. I doubt you'll find it so—but He's coming—I mustn't seem to interrupt you—and you know immediately—as you leave him—I come in to announce—your arrival in your real Character.—

SIR OLIVER. True—and afterwards you'll meet me at Sir Peter's.

ROWLEY. Without losing a Moment.—            [*Exit* ROWLEY.

SIR OLIVER. So—I don't like the Complaisance of his Features.

### *Re-Enter* SURFACE.

SURFACE. Sir—I beg you ten thousand Pardons—for keeping—you a moment waiting—Mr. Stanley—I presume—            40

SIR OLIVER. At your Service—

SURFACE. Sir—I beg you will do me the honor to sit down—I entreat you Sir—

SIR OLIVER. Dear Sir there's no occasion.—too civil by half!—[*aside*]

SURFACE. I have not the Pleasure of knowing you Mr. Stanley—but I am extremely happy to see you look so well—you were nearly related to my Mother—I think Mr. Stanley.

SIR OLIVER. I was Sir—so nearly that my present Poverty I fear may do discredit to her Wealthy Children—else I should not have presumed to trouble you.—            50

SURFACE. Dear Sir—there needs no Apology—He that is in Distress tho' a stranger has a right to claim kindred with the Wealthy.—I am sure I wish I was of that Class, and had it in my Power to offer you even a small relief.

SIR OLIVER. If your Unkle Sir Oliver were here—I should have a Friend.

SURFACE. I wish He were Sir with all my Heart—you should not want an advocate with him believe me Sir—

SIR OLIVER. I should not need one—my Distresses would recommend me.—but I imagined—his Bounty had enabled you to become the agent of his Charity.            60

SURFACE. My dear Sir—you were strangely misinformed. Sir Oliver is a worthy man—a very worthy sort of Man—but—avarice Mr. Stanley is the vice of age—I will tell you my good Sir—in confidence!—what—he has done for me has been a mere—nothing, tho' People I know have thought—otherwise and for my Part I never chose to contradict the Report.

SIR OLIVER. What!—has He never—transmitted—you—Bullion!—Rupees!—Pagodas![1]—

SURFACE. O Dear Sir—Nothing of the kind—no—no—a few—Presents —now and then—China—shawls—Congo[2] Tea—Avadavats[3]—and Indian Crackers—little more, believe me— 70

SIR OLIVER. Here's Gratitude for twelve thousand Pounds!—avadavats— and Indian Crackers!

SURFACE. Then my dear Sir—you have heard I doubt not of the extravagance of my Brother.—There are very few would credit what I have done for that unfortunate young man!—

SIR OLIVER. Not I for one! [aside]

SURFACE. The Sums I have lent—him!—indeed—I have been exceedingly to blame—it was an amiable Weakness!—however—I don't pretend to defend it—and now I feel it doubly culpable—since it has 80 deprived me of the Power of serving you Mr. Stanley as my Heart directs—

SIR OLIVER. Dissembler!—Then Sir—you cannot assist me?

SURFACE. At Present it grieves me to say I cannot, but whenever I have the ability you may depend upon hearing from me.

SIR OLIVER. I am extremely sorry.

SURFACE. Not more than I am believe me—to pity without the Power to relieve is still more painful than to ask and be denied—

SIR OLIVER. Kind Sir—your most obedient humble Servant.

SURFACE. You leave me deeply affected Mr. Stanley—William—be 90 ready to open the door—

SIR OLIVER. O Dear Sir—no ceremony—

SURFACE. Your very obedient—

SIR OLIVER. Sir your most obsequeous—

SURFACE. You may depend upon hearing from me—when ever I can be of service—

SIR OLIVER. Sweet Sir—you are too good—

SURFACE. In the mean time—I wish you Health and Spirits—

SIR OLIVER. Your ever grateful—and perpetual humble Servant.

SURFACE. Sir—yours as sincerely— 100

SIR OLIVER. Now I am satisfied!— [Exit.

SURFACE. [Solus] This is one bad effect of a good Character, it invites

[1] Zelida, in Kelly's *The Romance of an Hour* (1774), p. 5, is 'ballasted with rupees and pagodas': Indian coins.    [2] Chinese.

[3] Small red and black singing birds from India. Sheridan gave some to his first wife and wrote a mock elegy on the death of one of them: see Sichel, ii. 98.

applications from the unfortunate and there needs no small degree of
address to gain the reputation of Benevolence without incurring the
expence.—The silver ore of pure Charity is an expensive article in the
catalogue of a man's good Qualities—whereas the sentimental French
Plate I use instead of it, makes just as good a shew—and pays no tax.—

*Enter* ROWLEY.

ROWLEY. Mr. Surface—your Servant—I was apprehensive of inter-
rupting you—tho'—my Business demands immediate attention—as this
Note will inform you—                                                    110
SURFACE. Always Happy to see Mr. Rowley—[*reads*] how!—'Oliver—
Surface!'—my Unkle arrived!
ROWLEY. He is indeed—we have just parted—quite well—after a speedy
voyage—and impatient to embrace—his worthy Nephew—
SURFACE. I am astonish'd!—William—stop Mr. Stanley if He's not gone—
ROWLEY. O—He's out of reach—I believe.
SURFACE. Why didn't you let me know this when you came in together—?
ROWLEY. I thought you had particular—Business—but I must be gone
to inform your Brother—and appoint him here to meet his Uncle—He
will be with you in a quarter of an hour—                                120
SURFACE. So He says—well—I am Strangely overjoy'd at his coming—
never to be sure was any thing so damn'd unlucky! [*aside*]
ROWLEY. You will be delighted to see how well He looks.
SURFACE. O—I'm rejoiced to hear it—just at this time! [*aside*]
ROWLEY. I'll tell him how impatiently—you expect him—[*Exit* ROWLEY.
SURFACE. Do—do—pray—give my best duty and affection—indeed I
cannot—express the sensations I feel at the thought of seeing him!—
certainly—his coming just as this Time is the cruellest Piece of ill
Fortune—!                                                    [*Exit.*

*Scene 2d. at* SIR PETER'S

*Enter* MRS. CANDOUR—*and* MAID.

MAID. Indeed Ma'am my Lady will see nobody at Present.
MRS. CANDOUR. Did you tell her it was her Friend Mrs. Candour—
MAID. Yes Ma'am, but she begs you will excuse her—
MRS. CANDOUR. Do go again—I shall be glad to see her if it be only for
a moment—for I am sure she must be in great Distress [*Exit* MAID.
—Dear Heart—how provoking!—I'm not mistress of half the circum-
stances!—we shall have the whole affair in the news Papers with the
Names of the Parties at Length before I have dropt the story at a dozen
houses.—
*Enter* SIR BENJAMIN.

O Dear Sir Benjamin you have heard I suppose—                          10
SIR BENJAMIN. Of Lady Teazle and Mr. Surface—

MRS. CANDOUR. And Sir Peter's Discovery—

SIR BENJAMIN. O the strangest Piece of Business to be sure—

MRS. CANDOUR. Well I never was so surpris'd in my life!—I am so sorry for all Parties, indeed I am.

SIR BENJAMIN. Now I don't Pity Sir Peter at all—He was so extravagantly partial to Mr. Surface—

MRS. CANDOUR. Mr. Surface—why 'twas with Charles Lady Teazle was—detected

SIR BENJAMIN. No such thing—Mr. Surface is the gallant—                    20

MRS. CANDOUR. No—no—Charles—is the man—'twas Mr. Surface brought Sir Peter on purpose to discover them—

SIR BENJAMIN. I tell you I have it from one

MRS. CANDOUR. And I have it from one

SIR BENJAMIN. Who had it from one who had it—

MRS. CANDOUR. From one immediately—but here's Lady Sneerwell—perhaps she knows the whole affair—

*Enter* LADY SNEERWELL.

LADY SNEERWELL. So—my dear Mrs. Candour Here's a sad affair of our Friend Lady Teazle—

MRS. CANDOUR. Aye!—my Dear Friend who could have thought it.    30

LADY SNEERWELL. Well there is no trusting appearances. Tho'—indeed she was always too lively for me—

MRS. CANDOUR. To be sure her manners were a little too—free—but she was very young—

LADY SNEERWELL. And had indeed some good Qualities—

MRS. CANDOUR. So she had Indeed—but have you heard the Particulars?

LADY SNEERWELL. No—but every body says that Mr. Surface—

SIR BENJAMIN. Aye there I told—you Mr. Surface was the Man.

MRS. CANDOUR. No—no—indeed—the assignation was with Charles.

LADY SNEERWELL. With Charles!—you alarm me Mrs. Candour.    40

MRS. CANDOUR. Yes—yes—He was the Lover—Mr. Surface—do him justice—was only the Informer—

SIR BENJAMIN. Well I'll not—dispute with you Mrs. Candour—but be it which it may—I hope that Sir Peter's wound will not—

MRS. CANDOUR. Sir Peter's wound!—O Mercy! I didn't hear a Word of their Fighting—

LADY SNEERWELL. Nor I a syllable!

SIR BENJAMIN. No—what no mention of the Duel—

MRS. CANDOUR. Not a word—

SIR BENJAMIN. O Lord—yes—yes—they fought before they left the    50 Room.

LADY SNEERWELL. Pray let us hear.

MRS. CANDOUR. Aye do oblige—us with the Duel.

SIR BENJAMIN. Sir—says Sir Peter—immediately—after the Discovery—you are a most ungrateful Fellow.

MRS. CANDOUR. Aye to Charles—

SIR BENJAMIN. No—no—to Mr. Surface—a most ungrateful Fellow and old as I am Sir says He I insist on immediate satisfaction.

MRS. CANDOUR. Aye that must have been to Charles for 'tis very unlikely Mr. Surface should go to fight in his own House. 60

SIR BENJAMIN. 'Gad's Life Ma'am not at all—giving me immediate Satisfaction—on this—Madam—Lady Teazle seeing Sir Peter in such Danger—ran out of the Room in strong Hysterics—and Charles after her calling out for Hartshorn and Water! Then Madam—they began to fight with Swords—

*Enter* CRABTREE.

CRABTREE. With Pistols—Nephew—I have it from undoubted authority.—

MRS. CANDOUR. O Mr. Crabtree then it is all true—

CRABTREE. Too true indeed Ma'am and Sir Peter's Dangerously wounded— 70

SIR BENJAMIN. By a Thrust in Séconde[1]—quite thro' his left side.

CRABTREE. By a Bullet lodged in the Thorax—

MRS. CANDOUR. Mercy—on me Poor Sir Peter—

CRABTREE. Yes ma'am—tho' Charles would have avoided the matter if He could.—

MRS. CANDOUR. I knew Charles was the Person.

SIR BENJAMIN. O my Unkle I see knows nothing of the matter—

CRABTREE. But Sir Peter tax'd him with the basest ingratitude—

SIR BENJAMIN. That I told you you know.

CRABTREE. Do Nephew let me Speak—and insisted on an immediate— 80

SIR BENJAMIN. Just as I said.

CRABTREE. Odds! life! Nephew allow others to know something too—a Pair of Pistols lay on the Bureau—for Mr. Surface—it seems had come the Night before late from Salt-Hill where He had been to see the Montem[2] with a Friend who has a Son at Eaton—so unluckily the Pistols were left Charged—

SIR BENJAMIN. I heard—nothing of this—

CRABTREE. Sir Peter forced Charles to take one and They fired—it seems pretty nearly together—Charles's Shot took Place as I told you—and Sir Peter's miss'd—but what is very extraordinary the Ball struck 90

[1] A 'thrust in *seconde*' is one delivered under one's opponent's blade, and with the knuckles upwards, the wrist turned downwards.

[2] This was the procession, on Whit Tuesday, by Eton boys to Salt-hill. On the way they collected money for the senior collegers: see John Brand, *Popular Antiquities of Great Britain*, ed. W. C. Hazlitt (1870), i. 240–5.

against a little Bronze Pliny that stood over the chimney piece—grazed out of the window at a right angle—and wounded the Postman, who was just coming to the Door with a double letter from Northamptonshire—

SIR BENJAMIN. My Unkle's account is more circumstantial I must confess—but I believe mine is the true one for all that.—

LADY SNEERWELL. I am more interested in this Affair than they imagine —and must have better information.          [*Exit* LADY SNEERWELL.

SIR BENJAMIN. [*after a pause looking at each other*] Ah! Lady—Sneerwell's alarm is very easily accounted for—

CRABTREE. Yes, yes, they certainly *do* say—but that's neither here nor   100 there.

MRS. CANDOUR. But pray where is Sir Peter at present—

CRABTREE. Oh! they—brought—him home and He is now in the House tho' the Servants are order'd to deny it—

MRS. CANDOUR. I believe so—and Lady Teazle I suppose—attending him—

CRABTREE. Yes yes—I saw one of the Faculty enter just before me—

SIR BENJAMIN. Hey—who comes here—

CRABTREE. O this is He—the Physician depend on't

MRS. CANDOUR. O certainly, it must be the Physician and now we shall   110 know—

Enter SIR OLIVER.

CRABTREE. Well Doctor—what Hopes?

MRS. CANDOUR. Aye Doctor how's your Patient?

SIR BENJAMIN. Now Doctor isn't it a wound with a small sword?

CRABTREE. A Bullet lodg'd in the Thorax—for a hundred!

SIR OLIVER. Doctor!—a wound with—a small sword! and a Bullet in the Thorax! oons are you mad good People?

SIR BENJAMIN. Perhaps Sir you are not a Doctor.

SIR OLIVER. Truly I am to thank you for my Degree If I am.

CRABTREE. Only a Friend of Sir Peter's then I presume; but Sir you   120 must have heard of this Accident—

SIR OLIVER. Not a Word!

CRABTREE. Not of his being dangerously Wounded?

SIR OLIVER. The Devil he is!

SIR BENJAMIN. Run thro' the Body—

CRABTREE. Shot in the Breast—

SIR BENJAMIN. By one Mr. Surface—

CRABTREE. Aye the younger.

SIR OLIVER. Hey! what the Plague! you seem to differ Strangely in your Accounts—however you agree that Sir Peter is dangerously wounded—   130

SIR BENJAMIN. Oh, yes, we agree there—

CRABTREE. Yes, yes, I believe there can be no doubt of that.

SIR OLIVER. Then upon my Word, for a person in that Situation he is the most imprudent Man alive—For here he comes Walking as if nothing at all were the Matter.

*Enter* SIR PETER.

Odd's heart Sir Peter—you are come in good time I promise you, for we had Just given you Over.

SIR BENJAMIN. 'Egad Uncle this is the most Sudden recovery!

SIR OLIVER. Why Man what do you do out of Bed with a Small Sword thro' your Body, and a Bullet lodged in your Thorax!                    140

SIR PETER. A Small Sword and a Bullet—

SIR OLIVER. Aye these Gentlemen would have kill'd you, without Law, or Physic—and wanted to dubb me a Doctor—to make me an accomplice.

SIR PETER. Why what is all this?

SIR BENJAMIN. We rejoice Sir Peter that the Story of the Duel is not true—and are Sincerely Sorry for your other misfortunes—

SIR PETER. So So—all over the Town already—[*aside*]

CRABTREE. Tho' Sir Peter, you were certainly vastly to blame to Marry at all, at your years.

SIR PETER. Sir, what Business is that of yours?                    150

MRS. CANDOUR. Tho' indeed as Sir Peter made so good a Husband He's very much to be pitied!

SIR PETER. Plague on your Pity Ma'am, I desire none of it:

SIR BENJAMIN. However Sir Peter, you must not mind the Laughing and Jests, you will meet with on this Occasion—

SIR PETER. Sir, I desire to be Master in my own House.

CRABTREE. 'Tis no uncommon case, that's one comfort.

SIR PETER. I insist on being left to myself, without ceremony, I insist on your leaving my House directly!

MRS. CANDOUR. Well, well, we are going and depend on't we'll make the    160
best report of you we can—

SIR PETER. Leave my House—

CRABTREE. And tell how hardly you have been treated.

SIR PETER. Leave my House.

SIR BENJAMIN. And how Patiently you bear it.

SIR PETER. Fiends—Vipers!—Furies!—Oh that their own Venom would choak them—        [*Exeunt* MRS. CANDOUR, SIR BENJAMIN,
                                                        CRABTREE, *etc.*

SIR OLIVER. They are very provoking Indeed Sir Peter.

*Enter* ROWLEY.

ROWLEY. I heard high Words—what has ruffled you Sir Peter?

SIR PETER. Pshaw what Signifies asking, do I ever pass a Day without    170
my Vexations?

SIR OLIVER. Well I'm not inquisitive—I come only to tell you that I have seen both my Nephews in the Manner we proposed—

SIR PETER. A precious couple they are!

ROWLEY. Yes and Sir Oliver is convinced—that your Judgment was right Sir Peter—

SIR OLIVER. Yes, I find Joseph is indeed the Man after all—

ROWLEY. Yes as Sir Peter Says, He's a Man of Sentiment.

SIR OLIVER. And Acts up to the Sentiments he professes.

ROWLEY. It certainly is Edification to hear him talk          180

SIR OLIVER. Oh He's a Model for the young Men of the Age!—but how's this Sir Peter—you don't Join in your Friend Joseph's Praise as I Expected.

SIR PETER. Sir Oliver, we live in a damn'd wicked World, and the fewer we praise the better.

ROWLEY. What do *you* say so, Sir Peter—who were never mistaken in your Life?

SIR PETER. Pshaw—Plague on you both—I see by your sneering you have heard—the whole affair—I shall go mad among you!

ROWLEY. Then to fret you no longer Sir Peter—we are indeed acquainted   190 with it all—I met Lady Teazle coming from Mr. Surface's—so humbled that she deigned to request *me* to be her advocate with you—

SIR PETER. And does Sir Oliver know all too?

SIR OLIVER. Every circumstance!

SIR PETER. What of the—Closet—and the screen—hey

SIR OLIVER. Yes yes—and the little—French Millener—O I have—been vastly diverted with the story—ha! ha!

SIR PETER. Twas—very Pleasant—!

SIR OLIVER. I never laugh'd more in my Life—I assure you,   200 ha! ha!

SIR PETER. O vastly diverting—ha! ha!

ROWLEY. To be sure Joseph—with his Sentiments—ha! ha!

SIR PETER. Yes yes his sentiments—ha! ha!—a hypocritical Villain!

SIR OLIVER. Aye—and that Rogue Charles—to pull Sir Peter out of the Closet—ha! ha!

SIR PETER. Ha! ha! 'twas devilish entertaining to be sure—

SIR OLIVER. Ha! ha! egad Sir Peter I should like to have seen your Face when the Screen was thrown down, ha! ha!

SIR PETER. Yes yes my Face when the screen was thrown down, ha! ha!   210 O I must never Shew my head again!

SIR OLIVER. But come—come it isn't fair to laugh at you neither my old Friend—tho' upon my soul I can't help it—

SIR PETER. O pray don't—restrain your—mirth on my account—It does not hurt—me at all—I laugh at the whole affair myself—yes—yes—I think being a standing Jest for all one's acquaintances—a very happy— situation—O yes—and then of a morning to read the Paragraphs

about Mr. S—— Lady T—— and Sir P—— will—be so entertaining!—

ROWLEY. Without affectation Sir Peter you may despise the ridicule of    220
Fools—but I see Lady Teazle—going towards the next Room—I am
sure you must desire a Reconciliation as earnestly as she does—

SIR OLIVER. Perhaps my being here—prevents her coming to you—well
I'll leave honest Rowley to mediate between you.—but he must bring
you all presently to Mr. Surface's—where—I am now returning—if not
to reclaim a Libertine—at least to expose Hypocrisy—

SIR PETER. Ah!—I'll be present at your discovering yourself there with
all my heart.—tho' 'tis a vile unlucky Place for discoveries—

ROWLEY. We'll follow—                                    [exit SIR OLIVER.

SIR PETER. She is not coming here you see Rowley—                  230

ROWLEY. No but she has left the Door of that Room open you perceive.
—see She is in Tears—!

SIR PETER. Certainly a little mortification appears very becoming in a
wife—don't you think it will do her good to let her Pine a little.

ROWLEY. O this is ungenerous in you—

SIR PETER. Well I know not what to think—you remember Rowley the
Letter I found of hers—evidently intended for Charles?—

ROWLEY. A mere Forgery Sir Peter—laid in your way on Purpose—this
is one of the Points which I intend Snake shall give you conviction on—

SIR PETER. I wish I were once satisfied of that—she looks this way—    240
what a remarkably elegant Turn of the Head she has!—Rowley I'll go
to her—

ROWLEY. Certainly.

SIR PETER. Tho' when—it is known that we are reconciled People will
laugh at me ten times more!

ROWLEY. Let—them laugh—and retort their malice only by shewing
them you are happy in spite of it.

SIR PETER. Efaith so I will—and if I'm not mistaken, we may yet be
the happiest couple—in the country.

ROWLEY. Nay, Sir Peter—He who once lays aside suspicion—              250

SIR PETER. Hold my dear Rowley—if you have any Regard for me—
never let me hear you utter any thing like—a Sentiment. I have had
enough of *them* to serve me the rest of my Life.            [*Exeunt.*

*Scene the Last*

*The Library*

SURFACE *and* LADY SNEERWELL.

LADY SNEERWELL. Impossible—! will not Sir Peter immediately be
reconciled to *Charles*? and of consequence no longer oppose his union
with *Maria*?—the thought is Distraction to me!

SURFACE. Can Passion furnish a Remedy?

LADY SNEERWELL. No—nor Cunning either—O I was a Fool! an Ideot—to league with such a Blunderer!—

SURFACE. Sure Lady Sneerwell I am the greatest Sufferer—yet you see I bear the accident with Calmness.

LADY SNEERWELL. Because the Disap[p]ointment—doesn't reach your *Heart*—your interest only attached you to Maria—had you felt for her 10 —what I have for that ungrateful Libertine, neither your Temper nor Hypocrisy could prevent your shewing the sharpness of your Vexation.

SURFACE. But why should your Reproaches fall on me for this Disap[p]ointment?

LADY SNEERWELL. Are not you the cause of it?—what had you to do— to bate in your Pursuit of Maria to pervert Lady Teazle by the way?— had you not a sufficient Field for your Roguery in blinding Sir Peter and supplanting your Brother?—I hate such an avarice of Crimes—'tis an unfair monopoly and never prospers.

SURFACE. Well I admit I have—been to blame—I confess I deviated 20 from the direct Road of wrong but I don't think we're so totally defeated neither.

LADY SNEERWELL. No!

SURFACE. You tell me you have made a trial of Snake since we met—and that you Still believe him faithful to us—

LADY SNEERWELL. I do believe so—

SURFACE. And that He has undertaken should it be necessary—to swear and prove that Charles is at this Time contracted by vows and Honor to your Ladyship—which some of his former Letters to you will serve to support.— 30

LADY SNEERWELL. This indeed might have assisted—

SURFACE. Come—come it is not too late yet [*Knocking*]—but Hark! this is probably my unkle Sir Oliver—retire to that Room—we'll consult farther when He's gone.—

LADY SNEERWELL. Well!—but if He should find you out too—

SURFACE. O I have no fear of that—Sir Peter will hold his tongue for his own credit sake—and you may depend on't I shall soon Discover Sir Oliver's weak side!—

LADY SNEERWELL. I have no diffidence of your abilities—only be constant to one roguery at a time— [*Exit.* 40

SURFACE. I will—I will—so 'tis confounded—hard after such bad Fortune to be baited by one's confederate in evil.—well at all events my character is so much better than Charles's that I certainly—hey! what! —this is not Sir Oliver—but old Stanley again!—Plague on't! that He should return to teize me just now—we shall have Sir Oliver come and find him—here—and—

*Enter* SIR OLIVER.

Gad's life—Mr. Stanley—why have you come back to plague me just at
this time?—you must not stay now upon my word!

SIR OLIVER. Sir—I hear your unkle Oliver is expected here—and tho'
He has been so penurious to you I'll try what He'll do for me—                50

SURFACE. Sir 'tis—impossible for you to stay now—so I must beg—
come any other Time and I promise you you shall be assisted—

SIR OLIVER. No—Sir Oliver and I must be acquainted—

SURFACE. Zounds Sir then I insist on your quitting the—Room directly—

SIR OLIVER. Nay Sir!

SURFACE. Sir—I insist on't—here William Shew this Gentleman out.—
since you compell me Sir—not one moment—this is such insolence
                                        [*going to push him out.*

*Enter* CHARLES.

CHARLES SURFACE. Heydey! what's the matter now?—what the Devil
have you got hold of my little Broker here! Zounds—Brother don't
hurt little Premium—what's the matter—my little Fellow?                       60

SURFACE. So! He has been with you too has He?

CHARLES SURFACE. To be sure He has!—why 'tis as honest a little—
but sure Joseph, you have not been borrowing money too, have you?

SURFACE. Borrowing—no!—but Brother—you know here we—expect
Sir Oliver every—

CHARLES SURFACE. O Gad! that's true—Noll mustn't find the little
Broker here to be sure—

SURFACE. Yet Mr. Stanley insists—

CHARLES SURFACE. Stanley—why his name's Premium—

SURFACE. No—no—Stanley—                                                       70

CHARLES SURFACE. No—no—Premium—

SURFACE. Well no—matter—which but—

CHARLES SURFACE. Aye—aye Stanley or Premium 'tis the same thing
as you say—for I suppose He goes by half a hundred Names—besides
A.B.'s at the Coffee-Houses—                                        [*knock.*

SURFACE. Death—here's Sir Oliver—at the Door.—[*knocking again*]—
now I beg—Mr. Stanley—

CHARLES SURFACE. Aye and I beg Mr. Premium—

SIR OLIVER. Gentlemen—

SURFACE. Sir By Heav'n you shall go—                                          80

CHARLES SURFACE. Aye out with him certainly—

SIR OLIVER. This Violence—

SURFACE. 'Tis your own Fault—

CHARLES SURFACE. Out with him to be sure—
                                [*Both forcing* SIR OLIVER *out.*

*Enter* SIR PETER, LADY TEAZLE, MARIA, *and* ROWLEY.

SIR PETER. My old Friend Sir Oliver!—hey—what in the name of wonder!—Here are dutiful Nephews!—assault their Uncle at the first Visit—

LADY TEAZLE. Indeed Sir Oliver 'twas well we came in to rescue you—

ROWLEY. Truly it was—for I perceive Sir Oliver the character of Old Stanley was no Protection to you

SIR OLIVER. Nor of Premium—either—the necessities of the former couldn't extort a shilling from that benevolent Gentleman and now—egad!—I stood a Chance of faring worse than my Ancestors—and being knock'd down without being bid for.—

> [af[t]er a Pause—JOSEPH and CHARLES turning to each other.

SURFACE. Charles—!

CHARLES SURFACE. Joseph!

SURFACE. 'Tis now compleat!—

CHARLES SURFACE. Very.

SIR OLIVER. Sir Peter—my Friend and Rowley too—look on that elder Nephew of mine—you know what He has already received from my Bounty,—and you know also—how gladly I would have regarded half my Fortune as held in trust for him—judge then my Disap[p]oint-ment in discovering him to be destitute of Truth—Charity—and Gratitude—

SIR PETER. Sir Oliver—I should be more Surprized at this Declaration if I had not myself found him selfish—treacherous and Hypocritical—

LADY TEAZLE. And if the gentleman pleads not guilty to these—pray let him call *me* to his Character—

SIR PETER. Then I believe we need add no more—if He knows himself He will consider it as the most perfect Punishment that He is known by the world—

CHARLES SURFACE. [aside] If they talk this way to Honesty—what will they say to *me* by and bye!

SIR OLIVER. As for that Prodigal—his Brother there—

CHARLES SURFACE. [aside] Aye now comes my Turn—the damn'd Family Pictures will ruin me—

SURFACE. Sir Oliver! Unkle!—will you honor—me with a hearing?

CHARLES SURFACE. [aside] Now if Joseph would make one of his long Speeches I might recollect myself a little—

SIR OLIVER. I suppose you would undertake to justify yourself entirely.

SURFACE. I trust I could.

SIR OLIVER. Pshaw!—well Sir! and *you* [to CHARLES] could *justify* yourself too I suppose—

CHARLES SURFACE. Not that I know of Sir Oliver.—

SIR OLIVER. What little Premium—has been let too much into the secret I presume.

CHARLES SURFACE. True—Sir—but they were Family Secrets and should never be mention'd again you know.

ROWLEY. Come Sir Oliver I know you cannot Speak of Charles's Follies 130 with anger.

SIR OLIVER. Odds heart no more I can—nor with Gravity either. Sir Peter, do you know the Rogue bargain'd with me for all his Ancestors— sold me Judges and Generals by the Foot and Maiden Aunts as Cheap as broken China!

CHARLES SURFACE. To be Sure Sir Oliver I did make a little free with the Family Canvass that's the Truth on't—my Ancestors may certainly rise in Evidence against me there's no denying it—but believe me sincere when I tell you, and upon my soul I would not Say it if I was not—that if I do not appear mortified—at the exposure of my Follies— 140 it is because I feel at this moment the warmest satisfaction—in seeing you—my *liberal* Benefactor.

SIR OLIVER. Charles—I believe you—give me your hand again. The ill-looking little Fellow over the Settee has made your Peace, Sirrah!

CHARLES SURFACE. Then Sir—my Gratitude to the original is still encreased.

LADY TEAZLE. [*pointing to* MARIA] Yet I believe Sir Oliver, here is one whom Charles is still more anxious to be reconciled to.

SIR OLIVER. O I have heard of his Attachment there—and with the young Lady's Pardon if I construe right that Blush— 150

SIR PETER. Well—Child—speak your sentiments—

MARIA. Sir—I have little to say—but that I shall rejoice to hear that He is happy—for me—whatever claim I had to his Affection—I willingly resign it to one who has a better Title.

CHARLES SURFACE. How Maria!

SIR PETER. Heydey—what's the mystery now?—while He appear'd an incorrigible Rake you would give your hand to no one else and now that He's likely to reform I warrant you won't have him!—

MARIA. His own Heart—and Lady Sneerwell know the Cause.

CHARLES SURFACE. Lady Sneerwell— 160

SURFACE. Brother, it—is with great concern—I am obliged to speak on this Point but my Regard to Justice compells me.—and Lady Sneerwell's—Injuries can no longer—be concealed—      [*goes to the Door.*

*Enter* LADY SNEERWELL.

SIR PETER. Soh! another French milliner egad!—He has one in every Room in the House I suppose—

LADY SNEERWELL. Ungrateful Charles!—well may you be surprised and feel for the indelicate situation which your Perfidy has forced me into.

CHARLES SURFACE. Pray Unkle is this another Plot of yours? for as I have Life I don't understand it.                                                                170

SURFACE. I believe Sir there is but the evidence of one Person more necessary to make it extremely Clear.

SIR PETER. And that Person—I imagine is Mr. Snake—Rowley—you were perfectly—right to bring him with us—and pray let him appear.

ROWLEY. Walk in Mr. Snake—

*Enter* SNAKE.

I thought his Testimony might be wanted—however it happens unluckily that he comes to Confront Lady Sneerwell and not to support her.

LADY SNEERWELL. Villain!—treacherous to me at last!—[*aside*] speak   180
Fellow have you too conspired against me?

SNAKE. I beg your Ladyship—ten thousand Pardons, you paid me extremely Liberally for the Lie in question—but I have unfortunately been offer'd double to speak the Truth.[1]

SIR PETER. Plot and Counterplot Egad—I wish your Ladyship Joy of the Success of your Negotiation.

LADY SNEERWELL. The Torments of Shame and Disap[p]ointment on you all!—

LADY TEAZLE. Hold—Lady Sneerwell—before you go let me thank you for the trouble you and that Gentleman have taken in writing Letters   190
to me from Charles and answering them yourself—and let me also request you to make my—Respects to the Scandalous College—of which you are President—and inform them—that Lady Teazle Licentiate—begs leave to return the Diploma they granted her—as she leaves off Practice and kills Characters no longer.

LADY SNEERWELL. You too Madam—provoking—insolent!—may your Husband live these fifty years!                                                          [*Exit.*

SIR PETER. Oons what a Fury—

LADY TEAZLE. What a malicious creature it is!

SIR PETER. Hey—not for her last wish—?                                          200

LADY TEAZLE. O No—

SIR OLIVER. Well, Sir, and what have you to say now?

SURFACE. Sir, I am so confounded to find that Lady Sneerwell could be guilty of suborning Mr. Snake in this manner to impose on us all that

---

[1] Cf. T. Smollett, *The Adventures of Sir Launcelot Greaves* (1762), Ch. 24: 'Perhaps his fidelity to his employer, reinforced by the hope of many future jobs of that kind, might have been proof against the offer of fifty pounds; but double that sum was a temptation he could not resist.'

I know not what to say—however lest her Revengeful Spirit should prompt her to injure my Brother I had certainly better follow her directly—                                                                        [*Exit.*

SIR PETER. Moral to the last drop!

SIR OLIVER. Aye and marry her Joseph if you can—Oil and Vinegar egad!—you'll do very well together.—                                          210

ROWLEY. I believe we have no more occasion for Mr. Snake at Present—

SNAKE. Before I go—I beg—Pardon once for all, for whatever uneasiness I have been the humble Instrument of causing to the Parties present.

SIR PETER. Well—well you have made Atonement by a good Deed at last—

SNAKE. But I must Request of the Company that it shall never be known—

SIR PETER. Hey!—what the Plague—are you ashamed of having done a right thing once in your life?

SNAKE. Ah! Sir—consider I live by the Badness of my Character!—I         220 have nothing but my Infamy to depend on! and if it were once known that I had been betray'd into an honest Action I should lose every Friend I have in the world.

SIR OLIVER. Well—well we'll not traduce you by saying anything in your Praise never fear.                                             [*Exit* SNAKE.

SIR PETER. There's a precious Rogue—yet that Fellow is a Writer and a Critic!

LADY TEAZLE. See Sir Oliver there needs no Persuasion now to recon-cile your Nephew and Maria—              [CHARLES *and* MARIA *apart.*

SIR OLIVER. Aye—aye that's as it should—be and egad we'll have the   230 wedding tomorrow-morning.

CHARLES SURFACE. Thank you my dear Unkle.

SIR PETER. What! you rogue don't you ask the Girl's Consent first?

CHARLES SURFACE. O˙ I have done that a long time—above a minute ago—and She has look'd yes—

MARIA. For Shame—Charles—I protest Sir Peter there has not been a word—

SIR OLIVER. Well then the fewer the Better—may your love for each other never know—abatement

SIR PETER. And may you live as happily together as Lady Teazle and    240 I—intend to do.

CHARLES SURFACE. Rowley my old Friend—I am sure you congratulate me and I suspect that I owe you much.

SIR OLIVER. You do indeed Charles.

ROWLEY. If my Efforts to serve you had not succeeded you would have been in my Debt for the attempt—but deserve to be happy—and you overpay me—

SIR PETER. Aye honest Rowley always said you would Reform.

CHARLES SURFACE. Why as to Reforming Sir Peter I'll make no
    Promises—and that I take to be a proof that I intend to set about it—    250
    But Here shall be my monitor—my gentle Guide[1]—ah! can I leave the
    Virtuous path those Eyes illumine?
        Tho'—thou, dear Maid; should'st wa[i]ve thy Beauty's Sway,
        —Thou Still must Rule—because I will obey;
        An humbled Fugitive from Folly View,
        No Sanctuary near—but Love and—YOU;

                                                    [to the Audience

        You can indeed each Anxious Fear remove,
        For even Scandal dies if you approve.

                        —finis.—

[1] Cf. Faulkland's 'my future guide and monitress' in *The Rivals*, v. i: p. 66 above.

# EPILOGUE

*Written by G. Coleman, Eqr.*[1]

*Spoken by Mrs. Abington in the Character of Lady Teazle*

I who was late so volatile and gay,
Like a Trade-wind must now blow all one way,
Bend all my Cares, my Studies, and my vows,
To one old rusty weather-cock my spouse;
So wills our virtuous Bard!—the Motley Bayes[2]
Of crying Epilogues[3] and laughing Plays.

Old Bachelors, who marry smart young Wives,
Learn from our Play to regulate your lives!
Each bring his Dear to Town—all Faults upon her—
London will prove the very Source of Honour;                    10
Plung'd fairly in like a cold Bath, it serves,
When Principles relax—to brace the Nerves.
Such is my Case—and yet I might deplore
That the gay dream of dissipation's o'er;
And say, ye fair, was ever lively Wife,
Born with a genius for the highest Life
Like me, untimely blasted in her bloom,
Like me condemn'd to such a dismal doom?
Save money—when I just knew how to waste it!
Leave London—just as I began to taste it!                      20
Must I then watch the early-crowing Cock?
The melancholy Ticking of a Clock?
In the lone rustic hall for ever pounded,
With Dogs, Cats, Rats, and squalling Brats surrounded?
With humble curates can I now retire
(While good Sir Peter boozes with the Squire)
And at Back-gammon mortify my Soul,

---

[1] George Colman the elder (1732–94), manager of the Haymarket Theatre and author of *The Jealous Wife* (1761) and, with Garrick, of *The Clandestine Marriage* (1766).

[2] Cf. p. 336, n. 2, below.

[3] Colman is laughing at Sheridan's epilogue to George Ayscough's tragedy, *Semiramis* (1776).

That pants for Lu,[1] or flutters at a Vole?[2]
Seven's the Main![3]—dear sound!—that must expire,
Lost at hot-cockles[4] round a Christmas Fire!                    30
The Transient Hour of Fashion too soon spent,
'Farewell the tranquil mind, farewell Content!
Farewell the plum'd Head—the cushion'd Tete,
That takes the Cushion from its proper seat![5]
The spirit stirring Drum!—Card Drums[6] I mean—
Spadille,[7] odd Trick, Pam,[8] Basto,[9] King and Queen!
And you, ye knockers, that with Brazen Throat
The welcome Visitor's Approach denote,
Farewell!—all Quality of high Renown,
Pride, Pomp, and Circumstance of glorious Town!                   40
Farewell! your revels I partake no more,
And Lady Teazle's occupation's o'er!'[10]
—All this I told our Bard—he smil'd and said 'twas clear
I ought to play deep Tragedy next year:
Meanwhile he drew wise morals from his play,
And in these solemn Periods stalk'd away.
'Blest were the Fair, like you her Faults who stopt,
And clos'd her Follies when the Curtain dropt!
No more in vice or error to engage,
Or play the Fool at large on Life's great Stage.'                50

---

[1] Loo was a fashionable card game, played with three or five cards. In 1775 Lady Spencer recommended her daughter to satisfy herself with whist or backgammon, and not to indulge in the more expensive forms of gaming, 'quinze, lou, brag, faro' (*Georgiana* (ed. The Earl of Bessbororough), 1955, p. 24).

[2] Winning all the tricks in a deal.

[3] The main was the number (five to nine) called by the caster in hazard, before the dice were thrown. 'If seven is thrown for a Main, and four the Chance, it is two to one against the Person who throws' (*Hoyle's Games Improv'd*, rev. Thomas Jones (1778), p. 210).

[4] One of the innocent amusements enjoyed by the family in Goldsmith's *The Vicar of Wakefield* (*Collected Works*, ed. A. Friedman (Oxford, 1966), iv. 60): a blindfolded player guessed who had hit him in the back.           [5] Cf. p. 167, ll. 35–38.

[6] Card parties at private houses.           [7] The Ace of Spades in ombre and quadrille.

[8] The Knave of Clubs in loo.                        [9] The Ace of Clubs.

[10] The eleven lines, ending here, form a parody of Othello, III, iii:
                Farewell the tranquil mind; farewell content!
                Farewell the plumed troop and the big wars.

# THE CAMP

*A Musical Entertainment*

# THE

# CAMP,

A

*MUSICAL ENTERTAINMENT,*

AS PERFORMED AT THE

THEATRE ROYAL,   DRURY LANE.

BY R. B. SHERIDAN, ESQ.

𝕷𝖔𝖓𝖉𝖔𝖓:

PRINTED IN THE YEAR

M,DCC,XCV,

The title-page of the first (pirated) edition of
*The Camp*

# PROLOGUE

## *Written by Richard Tickell, Esq.*

The Stage is still the Mirror of the Day,
Where Fashion's Forms in bright Succession play;
True to its End, what Image can it yield
In Times like these, but the embattled Field?
What juster Semblance than the glittering Plains
Of village Warriors, and heroic Swains?
Invasions, Battles, now fill Rumour's Breath,
From Camps to Fleets, from Plymouth to Coxheath.
Through every Rank some pannic Terrors spread,
And each in varied Phrase express their Dread.          10
   At 'Change, no vulgar Patriot Passions fright
The firm and philosophick—Israelite:
Ask him his Hopes—' 'Tis all de shame to me!
I fix my Wishes by my Policy.
I'll do you Keppel;[1] or increase de Barters,
You will, I'll underwrite de Duke de Chartres.'[2]
*Miss Tittup*,[3] gasping from her stiff French Stays,
'Why, if these French shou'd come, we'll have French Plays:
Upon my Word, I wish these Wars wou'd cease.'
—Settling her Tucker, while she sighs for Peace.—          20
   With wilder Throbs the Glutton's Bosom beats,
Anxious and trembling, for West India Fleets,
Sir *Gobble Greenfat*[4] felt, in Pangs of Death,

---

[1] Augustus Keppel (1725-86), afterwards 1st Viscount Keppel, was Commander-in-Chief of the Fleet.

[2] Louis-Philippe-Joseph, Duc d'Orléans (1747-93), is better known as 'Philippe Egalité'. He commanded the blue squadron in the Battle of Ouessant on 27 July 1778.

[3] An arrogant woman in Garrick's farce, *Bon Ton; or, High Life Above Stairs* (1775). A line from George Colman's prologue to *Bon Ton* may have prompted Tickell's phrasing:

> The club's *bon ton. Bon ton*'s a constant trade
> Of rout, festino, ball, and masquerade:
> 'Tis plays and puppet-shews; 'tis something new;
> 'Tis losing thousands ev'ry night at Loo:
> Nature it thwarts, and contradicts all reason;
> 'Tis stiff French stays, and fruit when out of season.

[4] The epicure's delight, greenfat of turtle.

The ruling Passion taint his parting Breath:
Such in the latest as in all the past;
'O save my Turtle, Keppel!'—was his last.—
No Pang like this the Macaroni racks;
Calmly he dates the Downfall of Almack's.[1]
'As Gad's my Judge, I shall be glad to see
Our Paris Friends here, for Variety.                          30
The Clubs are poor; let them their Louis bring;
The Invasion wou'd be rather *a good Thing*.'
   Perish such Fears! What can our Arms oppose,
When Female Warriours join our martiall'd Beaus.
Fierce from the Toilet, the plum'd Bands appear;
Miss struts a Major, Ma'am a Brigadier;
A spruce *Bonduca*[2] simpers in the Rear.
Unusual Watch *her Femmes de Chambre* keep,
Militia Phantoms haunt her in her Sleep:
She starts, she wakes, she quivers, kneels, and prays,        40
'Side-saddle, my Horse! ah! lace up my Stays![3]
Soft, soft; 'twas but a Dream; my Fears are vain;
And Lady *Minikin*'s[4] herself again.'—
   Yet hold; nor let false Ridicule profane
These fair Associates of th'embattled Plain:
Victorious Wreaths their Efforts justly claim,
Whose Praise is Triumph, and whose Smiles are Fame.

---

[1] The aristocratic gaming club in Pall Mall, afterwards Brooks's.

[2] *Bonduca*, a tragedy by Beaumont and Fletcher, was revised by George Colman for performance in the summer season of 1778 at the Haymarket. It dealt with the aggressive Queen of Britain, better known as Boadicea.

[3] A distant parody of

> Give me another horse,—bind up my wounds,—
> Have mercy, Jesu!—Soft! I did but dream.—(*Richard III*, v. iii.)

[4] The heroine of Garrick's *Bon Ton*. She detests her husband and flirts with Colonel Tivy because fashion dictates her behaviour.

# DRAMATIS PERSONÆ[1]

| | |
|---|---|
| SERJEANT | Mr. Bannister |
| CORPORAL [WILLIAM] | Mr. Webster |
| O'DAUB | Mr. Moody |
| GAUGE | Mr. Parsons |
| MONSIEUR BLUARD [BOUILLARD, BOUILLE, BOULARD] | Mr. Baddeley |
| COUNTRYMEN | Mr. Wrighten, Mr. Burton, and Mr. Waldron |
| RECRUITS | Mr. Carpenter, Mr. Fawcett, Mr. Holcroft, and Mr. Chaplin |
| COMMANDER IN CHIEF AT THE CAMP | Mr. Farren |
| OFFICERS OF REGIMENTS | Mr. R. Palmer,[2] Mr. Lamash, and Mr. Kenny |
| SIR HARRY BOUQUET [PLUME, CHARLES PLUME] | Mr. Dodd |
| NELLY | Mrs. Wrighten |
| LADY SASH | Miss Farren |
| LADY PLUME | Mrs. Robinson |
| MISS GORGET [LADY GORGET] | Mrs. Cuyler |
| NANCY | Miss Walpole |
| COUNTRYWOMEN [including 'SMART GIRL' and 'MARGERY'] | Mrs. Love, Mrs. Booth, Miss Kirby, and Mrs. Bradshaw. |

[1] The cast list is taken from the *Morning Chronicle*, 16 Oct. 1778, but has been adjusted to contain the names given in the Larpent MS. and other sources. 'Sir Harry Bouquet', for example, is called 'Sir Charles Plume' in the *Morning Chronicle*; 'Sir Harry Plume' in the *Public Advertiser*, 16 Oct. 1778; 'Sir Charles Bouquet' in the *St. James's Chronicle*, 15–17 Oct. 1778; and 'Sir Henry Bouquet' in the printed version of 1803. The newspapers may have jumped to the conclusion that his surname was Plume, because Lady Plume calls him 'Brother'. For the contemporary significance of 'Bouquet', see p. 258 above, n. 2.

[2] He was painted in character for the Royal Academy exhibition of 1779: see the *London Chronicle*, 24–27 Apr. 1779.

# THE CAMP

*SCENE 1st. A Lane near the Camp*

*Country People crossing the Stage with Provisions.*

1ST MAN. Come, Deame, come, we are full late for the Subtler's[1] Market.

2ND MAN. Make haste, they are all before us.

OLD MAN. Why Robin,—why do'sn't come on?—

ROBIN. Lord Feather, why it been't my fault; the blind Colt has come down again—and there they lie, the Colt, my Mother, and the Chickens all in the Slough.—

OLD MAN. Why don't you run and help 'em you Dog?

ROBIN. I ha' help'd up the Colt, and if you please, now I'll see after the Chickens and my Mother.—                                                                                      10

OLD MAN. Out you rogue—here's neighbour Harrow has help'd her.

*Enter* MARGERY *and* COUNTRYMAN.

MARGERY. Ah! you unlucky Varlet! As sure as can be Jan, the Rogue put the Beast out of the road on purpose,—and down we came with such a Bang!

OLD MAN. Aye!—What a mercy the chickens escap'd! —but put on Margery,—put on—or the Subtlers will be all serv'd before we get to Camp. Ah! you Dog! I shall have you press'd at last.

ROBIN. Lord Feather, it been't my fault,—you know the Colt hasn't had an Eye these Eight years.

*Enter more country women and smart Girls.[2]*

1ST WOMAN. Come Madge, let's see what luck your face will have—Ah!  20
neighbour, nothing gets a good·price, like putting a good face on't, ha! ha!—

2ND WOMAN. Aye, Aye,—these soldier won't buy o' the ugly ones— There's Goody Grub sends a poor lean Wench; and her scare-crow face drives away all the Customers, tho' her Fowl are the fattest in the Market.

---

[1] Victualler. The spelling is an old form which Sheridan may have used, though 'tt' in his handwriting is commonly mistaken for 'bt'.

[2] This phrase certainly seems to have been in the prompt-book of Drury Lane Theatre, for an advertisement of a performance there, on 15 Oct. 1803, includes in the cast, 'Smart Girl: Mrs. Scott' (Drury Lane Scrapbook, Beaufoy Collection, Folger Shakespeare Library). No such words are used in the 1795 text or its derivatives.

1ST WOMAN. So! Here I see your Kinsman's Wife, Nell coming, Ah
  Deame! that Wench spoils the Market,—whenever she comes, with her
  honesty and her Nonsense; why she says she loves the Soldiers so,
  that she'd sell to them for Nothing.—                                    30
2ND WOMAN. Aye! A Churlish Jade! she'll neither cheat herself, nor
  let us cheat with Credit.—

*Enter* NELL.

NELL. So! What are you plotting there? hey now! I warrant how to take
  in the poor Soldiers, and get double price for your worst Bargains.—
1ST WOMAN. Mind your own Business Nell.—
NELL. Why now an't you asham'd to take in the honest Fellows so?—
GIRL. Lord Nell, what need you meddle?—
NELL. Indeed! Pert-face—what I suppose I don't know why you are
  disguised so.—yes, yes, the Soldiers pay for this Ribbond and Beads.
MAN. The Wench is turn'd Fool I think.—                                    40
NELL. Indeed Master Grinder! come out here, you shrivell'd sneaking
  Sot! I believe I know your Tricks too. Wer'n't you caught last week,
  soaping Nest Eggs to sell 'em for new laid ones—hey!—and didn't
  you sit in the Stocks last Saturday for Robbing the Squire's Rookery,
  to make your Pidgeon Pyes—you Rogue—hey?—
1ST WOMAN. Faith, Nell, if you go on in this way we'll inform our
  Exciseman of it, so we will.—
MAN. Aye, aye,—We'll tell Master Gauge, and I warrant he'll find some
  way to make her repent it.—
NELL. Yes, he's a pretty Protector. I'm sure I wish our Village had never  50
  seen him—why you know now, he was but a sort of a broken Attorney
  at Rochester, and bought this place[1] with his Vote, where he is both an
  Exciseman and a Smuggler at once—Just as they say Mr. Squire's
  Gamekeeper is the greatest Poacher in the Parish.
2ND WOMAN. 'Ecod there he comes—and now I believe you'll alter your
  Note Nell.
NELL. Shall I? You'll see that.
2ND WOMAN. Oh! Master Gauge!

*Enter* GAUGE.

Hey dey! what the Plague is there a civil war broke out among ye?
1ST WOMAN. Here, Master Gauge, Nell has been rating us for cheating   60
  the Soldiers.—
2ND WOMAN. Aye, and she says you encourage us in it.—
GAUGE. Encourage you in it—to be sure I do—in the way of Trade.—
MAN. Yes, yes,—in the way of Trade.

[1] Position.

GIRL. Yes, Master Gauge, and she abuses me because I go to Market
like a Christian, and says I do it to make the better Bargain—

GAUGE. Aye, and you're in the right on't—your Mother's a sensible
Woman Child—yes, yes, Dame, take plenty in your Baskets, and sell
your Ware off at the sign of your Daughter's Face.—

1ST WOMAN. So I say.—                                          70

GAUGE. Aye, Aye! Soldiers are Tasty customers, and this is the Market
where the Fair Trader will always have the best share.—

1ST WOMAN. Very true.

GAUGE. To be sure—that is the way to thrive—I hate to see an awkward
Gawky come sneaking into the Market, with her half-price Countenance, and never able to get above twice the value of her Goods.—

NELL. I have no patience.—An't you asham'd, Master Gauge—you, who
have a Post under Government, and carry his Majesty's Ink-horn, to go
to teach the Country Folks all the Court Tricks of preying on your best
Friends—Odd I wish I was on a Court Marshall against such Fellows   80
as you, who stoop to plunder a Knap-sack, and thrive by defrauding
your Defenders—You should have your deserts from the Cat o'Nine
Tails, and run the Gauntlet from Cox-heath to Wharley Common.—

GAUGE. Oons! here's a Jade—No respect to Office—stand back Neighbours—stand back—she's an arrant Scold, I'll threaten her with the
Ducking Stool.—Here you Nell, hold your Tongue you Baggage, and
here's a Pound of Smuggled Hyson in hand, and I'll owe you an India
Handkerchief.—

NELL. Here good People—here's a Bribe—You Paltry petty Fool—
here's influence and Corruption.—                              90

GAUGE. Come, Neighbours, she talks Libels, and it's illegal to listen to
her—quick, quick,—I'll prosecute the first man that hears another
word.—

NELL. There's a pretty Fellow to be in Office—But I suppose he thinks
it a part of his duty to imitate his betters.—

*SONG*

> Now coaxing, caressing,
> Now vexing, distressing,
> As fortune delights to exalt or confound.
>    Her smile or her frown
>    Sets them up, knocks them down                      100
> Turning, turning, turning, as the wheel goes round.
>
>    We see by this sample,
>    On those they would trample,
> Whom Fortune, hard fortune, has thrown to the ground;
>    To those rais'd on high,
>    Fawn, flatter and lye

Turning, turning, etc.

O fye Master Ga[u]ge,
Quit the tricks of the age,
Scorn the slaves that to fortune, false fortune are bound,          110
   Their cringes and bows,
   Protestations and vows,
Turning, turning, etc.

GAUGE *returns* [*peeping in*]

GAUGE. Let me see—is the Coast Clear? what a Termagant it is? refuse
a Bribe too! where the Devil could she learn that? Hey dey! who have
we got here? Let me see—by his Dress he should be a Smuggler or
a Subtler. As I live O'Da[u]b the Irish Painter![1] Ha! my old friend
O'Da[u]b! what brings you to Cox-heath?

*Enter* O'DAUB.

O'DAUB. Ah! My little Gauge! to be sure I'm not in luck.—I will want
an Interpreter to shew me the Views about here, and by my Soul I'll   120
force you to accept the Office.
GAUGE. Why, what's your Errant O'Daub?—
O'DAUB. Upon my conscience a very dangerous one—John the Painter's
Job[2] was a Joke to it—I'm come to take the Camp.—
GAUGE. The Devil you are.—
O'DAUB. Aye,—and to bring it away with me too.
GAUGE. Indeed!—
O'DAUB. Aye,—And here's my Military Chest—these are my Colours
you know.
GAUGE. Oh! I guess your Errand then.—                                130
O'DAUB. Faith it's a foolish one—you must know I got such Credit at
the Fete Champetre there that little Roscius recommended me to the
Managers of Drury Lane Theatre,[3] and so I am now a kind of a Deputy
Superintendent under Mr. Leatherbag[4] the great painter; that is, as
soon as he executes any thing, I design it my Jewel.
GAUGE. And what—are they going to bring the Camp on the Stage?

---

[1] 'The Irish Painter' was the name of a character (also called O'Daub), who appeared
in Burgoyne's *The Maid of the Oaks* (1774). Although he came on merely in Act I,
Sc. ii, he had forty lines to say and a song, 'Then away to Champetre', to sing. The
part was very effectively performed by Moody. The play itself celebrated the marriage
of Lord Stanley, and the 'fête champêtre' that he had given on 9 June 1774, to mark
the occasion, at The Oaks, Epsom.
[2] James Aitken (1752–77), was tried on 7 Mar. 1777 and convicted of setting fire to
the Portsmouth dockyard. See the *Gentleman's Magazine*, xlvii (1777), 121–4.
[3] The *Morning Chronicle*, 16 Oct. 1778, paraphrases this as, O'Daub, 'having gained
great applause as a painter in the *Fête Champêtre*', was recommended by David Garrick
to his successors.          [4] Philippe De Loutherbourgh (1740–1812).

O'DAUB. You have it—Cox-heath by Candle light[1] my Jewel!

GAUGE. And will that Answer?

O'DAUB. Oh to be sure it won't answer,—What! when a gentleman may
have a warm seat and see the whole Tote[2] of it for Two Thirteens,  140
and it has cost me above Three Guineas already, and I came the cheap-
est way too, by Three of us going halves in the Maidstone Diligon[3]
My Dear.

GAUGE. Well, and what do you think of the Sight?

O'DAUB. Upon my soul I don't know what to make on't,—so, I'm come
here, to be a little farther off, that I may have a clearer view of it;—I
think it only looks like my Cousin O'Doyley's great—Bleach-yard at
Antrim—Thunder and wounds! What outlandish looking Creature is
this coming here?

GAUGE. O this is Monsieur Bluard the French Subtler, who has a very  150
commodious Booth in the Front of the line—no bad Acquaintance let
me tell you, if you love Camp Bouillie and Soup Maigre.[4]


*Enter* BLUARD.

Ah! Monsieur Gauge, I am so very glad to find you, by Gar I was hunt
you all over the Camp—I have been thro' Berkshire;—Cross Suffolk,
and all over Yorkshire, and hear no word of you.

O'DAUB. Thro' Berkshire, and Suffolk, and Yorkshire!—What the Devil
does he mean?

GAUGE. Only thro' their Regiments.—

BLUARD. By Gar, I am all eat up—I have depend on you for a supply,
and there be one, two, three Brigade Dinner all order to day—besides  160
two great Alderman, with their Lady from London.

GAUGE. Oons! Monsieur Bluard, I can't help it, I have done the best
I could for you, and you must detach a Party of Waiters to forage at
Maidstone.

BLUARD. O Mon Dieu—and I have not one thing in the House.

---

[1] Cf. the prologue to F. Pilon's *The Invasion*, given at Covent Garden Theatre on
4 Nov. 1778:

> The muse in change and fashions still delighting,
> Now raves of nothing but of camps and fighting,
> Of mines, of ambuscades, and heroes slain,
> Arm'd cap-a-pie on the embattled plain
> Of Covent-Garden, or of Drury Lane.
> One night a Camp by candle light she shews.
> Next an Invasion, without wounds or blows.

[2] Sum.                                        [3] Diligence, or public stage-coach.

[4] Gruel, but 'bouillon gras' (clear soup) and 'bouillon maigre' (vegetable soup) may
be meant. Cf. also the droll acted in 1761: *The Fair Bride: or, The Unexpected Event.
With the British Tar's Triumph over Mons. Soup Maigre*: see Sybil Rosenfeld, *The
Theatre of the London Fairs in the Eighteenth Century* (Cambridge, 1960), p. 62.

O'DAUB. Oh then Master Gauge, I must look somewhere else for my Dinner.

BLUARD. O no—Monsieur.—I have ev'ry Ting ready for you in one Moment.

O'DAUB. Ha!—ha!—thank you.—But pray now if your Country- 170 men were to come, wouldn't you be puzzled a little which side to wish for?

BLUARD. Par bleu—No puzzle at all—I always wish for the strongest.

GAUGE. O! my friend Bluard is above prejudice I assure you.

BLUARD. Diable! prejudice! I love de English very well—I ver much obliged to dem—I love my Countrymen very vel and ver much obligee too—de English be beat I take a my heel and run with them—and if I can't run fast enough—by Gar I stop make de bow to Monsieur Broglio[1]—and ha my chers countrymen—I am charm to get away to you. 180

GAUGE. Well said Monsieur Bluard!

BLUARD. But I do assure you Monsieur Gauge, upon my word and Credit—indeed—I never will Desert de English—while they win—de Battle—no, no,—I have too much honour for do that—Monsieur— shall I have the honour to get you de little repast. Monsieur Gauge persuade your Friend—I must be gone—Bon jour Monsieur—no, no, Monsieur Gauge, I never vil forsake your Camp if you vin the Battle— never, never—                                      [*Exit.*

O'DAUB. Your servant Mr. Bluard—tho' faith to do him justice he seems to have forgot the fashion of his Country—for when he determines to 190 be a Rogue, he has the honesty to own it my dear.

GAUGE. O he has too much Conscience by half.

O'DAUB. But pray what connection have you with the Subtlers—you are no Victualler sure?

GAUGE. No,—but I deal with them in a variety of ways, and in a Sub- altern capacity supply the Camp with Various Articles.

O'DAUB. Indeed!

GAUGE. Aye,—But harkee—I do nothing but by *Contract.*

O'DAUB. A Contractor! What the Devil! sure you are not risen to such preferment as that?                                             200

GAUGE. No, no—Not in your first rate way[2]—no, no, mine are only Rank and file Contracts as I may say, and egad tho' they are good things, I have now and then got into a scrape with 'em too.

---

[1] Victor-Francis, duc de Broglie (1715-1804), maréchal de France.

[2] 'The only vast contracts for ordinary supplies and necessaries of life were those connected with the arming, victualling, and clothing of the Army and Navy. Cloth factors and grain merchants, ironmasters and timber dealers, pulled every possible wire to obtain Government orders . . .' (L. B. Namier, *The Structure of Politics at the Accession of George III* (2nd edn., 1965), p. 46.) Cf. N. Baker, *Government and Contractors* (1971), ch. X.

O'DAUB. As how?

GAUGE. Why you must know, sometime since, I Contracted with a certain Serjeant of Militia to furnish the Brigade with hair Powder.

O'DAUB. Hair Powder!—very well—and you sent him flour I suppose.

GAUGE. Flour! Oons! I should have got nothing by that.—no, no I went to the fountain head—I had recourse to the Chalk Pit instead of the Mill, and supply'd the Corps with a plentifull Stock of Lime.                    210

O'DAUB. With Lime! what the plague! and wasn't the Cheat found out?[1]

GAUGE. Why, we did pretty well during the fine Weather, but unluckily one day, the men being caught in a damn'd soaking Shower, our heads were *slack'd* in an instant, the Smoak ran along the line, and in less than a Week the whole Regiment were as bald as Coots.—

O'DAUB. A cross accident indeed!

GAUGE. O! a Cursed Scrape—narrowly escaped the Halbert for't—however I told my friend the Serjeant, that I had done his Men service, for they look'd like young Recruits before, and now they                    220 might pass for Veterans, for their Pates are all as smooth as an old half Crown.—

O'DAUB. You lost the Contract tho'?

GAUGE. I did.—however I got another soon after which has made me amends.—*A Shaving Contract* with a company of Granadiers.

O'DAUB. Faith I never knew you practised that Business.

GAUGE. O No! I never handled a Razor in my life, but Ignorance in the Articles agreed on is nothing in a Contract.—I shave by Deputy—had *Sam Sickle* down from London, a Dev'lish determined hand—has the swing of a Scyth[e], and will mow you a Company in the beat of a                    230 Reveillé.

O'DAUB. Upon my Conscience it's a very pretty way this of working at second hand, I wish myself could paint by Proxy.—

GAUGE. Aye,—and the best of it is this Job may lead to greater advantages; for turning my thoughts to the Subject,—I have lately with the assistance of a most ingenious Mechanick, invented an Engine, or sort of Razor Mill, by which a whole Platoon may be shaved at a time. It will save a World of Trouble—tho' I shan't make it publick, unless I can get a Patent for my Pains:—But what say you? shall we go and have a Bottle of this Frenchman's Wine, and drink his Majesty's                    240 health.

---

[1] Some satirical lines referring to Admiral Keppel's acquittal were put in later:

'On Tuesday evening, at Drury Lane Theatre, in the entertainment of The Camp, when Mr. Gage the exciseman, was relating his having sent lime for the soldiers' hair instead of flour . . . he added "but as I knew I was in the wrong, I demanded a court martial on the serjeant". The stroke was felt, and the audience marked their approbation by three loud plaudits' (*London Evening Post*, 11–13 Feb. 1779).

O'DAUB. With all my heart My Dear—and another to the two Camps if you will.

GAUGE. Which Two?—

O'DAUB. The one at Cox-heath—and the other at Drury lane to be sure my Jewel.                                                      [*Exeunt.*

*Scene near the Camp*

*Enter* COUNTRY LADS *and* RECRUITS *etc.*

1ST LAD. I tell you—I will certainly list,—I have made up my mind on't.

2ND LAD. Well, well,—I'll say no more.

1ST LAD. Besides the Camp lies so handy to me, that there mayn't be such an opportunity again.                                            250

2ND LAD. Why it does look main Jolly to be sure! 'Tis all one as a Fair I think. But if I were to List now, I think I should like hugely to belong to a Regiment of Horse, and I believe there is one of the Grandest Troops come lately; I seed two of the Officers Yesterday, mighty delicate looking Gentlemen.

1ST LAD. Aye!

2ND LAD. Yes, they are dress'd quite different from the others—their Jackets are pretty much the same—but they wear a sort of a Pettycoat as it were, with a great Hat and Feathers, and a Mortal sight of hair— I suppose they be some of your outlandish Troops, your Foreign 260 Hessians, or such like.—

1ST LAD. Like enough.—But here comes the Serjeant we're looking for; a rare Jolly Dog, and sings he does, louder than his own Drum, See how brave they March.—Oons! walking's a mighty dull way of going after all.—

*Enter* SERJEANT *and* SOLDIERS *Marching etc.*[1]

*SONG and CHORUS*

*I*

Great Cæsar once renown'd in fame
For a mighty Arm and a Laurell'd Brow
With his Veni Vidi, Vici, came
And he conquer'd the World with his
           Row dow, dow                                         270
*Chorus.* Row, dow, dow; row, dow, dow,
           And he conquer'd the world, *etc.*

[1] 'A serjeant, with his suite come on; the serjeant sings an air, and several rustics enter at the drumhead' (*Morning Chronicle*, 16 Oct. 1778).

*2*

Thus should our Vaunting Enemies come
And Winds and Waves their Course allow
In Freedom's Cause we'll beat our drum
And they'll fly all at the Sound of our row dow dow
*Chorus.* Row, dow, dow, *etc.*

*3*

Then come my Lads our Glory share
Whose honest hearts British Valor avow
At Honor's call to Camp repair                           280
And follow the Beat of my Row dow dow.
*Chorus.* Row, dow, dow, etc.

1ST LAD. There! well, can you resist now?

SERJEANT. Come my Lads, now is your time to shew your love for
your Country—If you are Lads of Spirit, you will never stay to be
scratch'd off a Church door for the Militia, or Smuggled aboard a
Man of War by a Press-Gang, when you may have the Credit of a
Volunteer, and the Bounty money too.

1ST LAD. Serjeant, I'm your man.

2ND LAD. Aye, and I too then.                             290

SERJEANT. That's my Hero! Sir, you'll be an honour to Cox-heath—
Well my Lad, what say you?

3RD LAD. I can't leave the Farm.

SERJEANT. The Farm! what, can you set yourselves to sow and plough
only for the Monsieurs to come and reap. Let your Fields be fallow
this year, and I'll insure you double Crops all your life after—here
Corporal!—Expound.—Now here's a fellow made for a Soldier!
there's a leg for a Spatterdash—with an eye[1] like the King of Prussia.—

4TH LAD. Aye, Master Serjeant,—but I hant the air, and the—

SERJEANT. Air! Oons! come to the Drill, and in a month you'll have the  300
Crest of a War Horse; why lookee there at long Ralph—he han't
been with us a Fortnight and see what a presence, there's Dignity—O
there's Nothing like the Drill for Grace—[*hits him with the Ratan*][2]

4TH LAD. Give us your hand Serjeant.

SERJEANT. Well said Captain! Corporal here—and now for a few
Questions my Lads.—

*SONG and CHORUS*
[SERJEANT]
Yet ere you're permitted to list with me
Answer me straight twice Questions three

---

[1] Described in another manuscript as a 'blood-spill eye'.
[2] 'A stick carried in the hand and used for beating someone with' (*O.E.D.*).

1ST COUNTRYMAN

No lies Master Serjeant we'll tell to you
For tho' we're poor Lads, we be honest and true.                310

SERJEANT

First can you drink well?

1ST COUNTRYMAN

Cheerly, cheerly.

SERJEANT

Each man his gallon?

1ST COUNTRYMAN

Nearly, Nearly.

SERJEANT

Love a sweet Wench too?

1ST COUNTRYMAN

Dearly, dearly.

SERJEANT

The Answer is honest, bold and fair
So drink to the King for his Soldiers you are.

SERJEANT *and* SOLDIERS (*chorus*)

The answer is honest *etc*

SERJEANT

When Bullets are whizzing around your head               320
You'll bravely march on wherever you're led?

2ND COUNTRYMAN[1]

To Death we'll rush forward without delay,
If good Master Serjeant you'll show us the way.

SERJEANT

Next can you swear well?

COUNTRYMAN

Bluffly—Bluffly.

SERJEANT

Handle a Frenchman?

COUNTRYMAN

Roughly, Roughly.

SERJEANT

Frown at a cannon?

COUNTRYMAN

Gruffly, gruffly.

---

[1] Thomas Holcroft mentions in his *Life of Thomas Holcroft*, ed. E. Colby (1925), i. 190, that he 'had no opportunity of exerting his talents till the Camp came out . . . when he endeavoured, as he expresses himself, *to make a part* of a foolish recruit, and succeeded; in consequence of which his salary was raised to thirty shillings weekly'.

SERJEANT

The Answer is honest, bold and fair,                    330
So drink to the King whose Subjects you are.

SERJEANT. Well answer'd my Lads, and you shall have your Accoutrements out of hand.

*Enter* NELL.

SERJEANT. Ha! honest Nell! how dos't my Girl?

NELL. As well as the Rogues of our Village will let me Mr. Serjeant.
—well but I'm glad to see you have had such success with your Recruiting Drum—Odds my life these honest Fellows are of the true Sort—They're worth a Regiment of Press'd men.

SERJEANT. Aye, so they are, but I have pick'd up one Lad who has been enquiring for you, and says he knew you formerly in Suffolk.—    340

NELL. Aye!—

SERJEANT. Yes.—Where's the Suffolk boy? the Rogue's always loitering behind, tho' he said he was coming here to join his Regiment[1]—Oh here he comes.

*Enter* NANCY.

NELL. Odd, it is a dainty looking youth for a Soldier.—

NANCY. Serjeant you didn't think I was lost—you know you may trust me.

SERJEANT. No, no, my Boy, I don't think you'll desert.

NELL. 'Efaith I do think I recollect his face tho'—

SERJEANT. There's the Young Woman you were enquiring for—    350

NANCY. Do then, let me stay and speak to her, I'll follow immediately.—

NELL. As sure as can be I do believe it is—

SERJEANT. Come then my Boys and let me shew you the Camp.—I shall have an eye to this Lad—Come my Lads.

*A March and Chorus*                    [*Exeunt.*

NANCY. Nelly, have you forgot me?

NELL. I don't know unless you tell me who you are—But I believe by your Laughing you are not what you seem to be, for all your Musket and Belt—

NANCY. I am not indeed!

NELL. Then Mr. Recruit can you tell me any News of a little Suffolk    360
Cousin of mine call'd Nancy Grainger?—

NANCY. The best News I can tell you of her is, that she's very happy to find you here, and kisses you with all her heart.—

NELL. My dear Nancy, I am so glad.—But hold—I must take care of

---

[1] The West Suffolk Regiment of Militia was in camp at Coxheath.

my Character.—Well, you are a brave Girl—and this is the gallantest
Freak—for I suppose you are here out of pure Love—for your King
and Country.

NANCY. Why, you wouldn't believe me if I was to tell you a lie.—So the
deuce take the Camp for robbing me of my dear William, Just as I was
to have gain'd a right, never to part with him again.                    370

### SONG

#### NANCY

When War's alarms entic'd my Willy from me
My poor Heart with grief did sigh,
Each fond remembrance brought fresh sorrow on me,
I woke ere yet the Morn was nigh,
    No other could delight him,
    Ah! why did I e'er slight him,
Coldly answering his fond tale,
    Which drove him far
    Amid the rage of war
And left silly me thus to bewail.                                        380
But I no longer tho' a maid forsaken,
    Thus will mourn like yonder Dove,
But ere the lark to-morrow shall awaken,
    I will seek my absent love.
    The Hostile Country over,
    I'll fly to seek my lover,
Scorning ev'ry threat'ning fear,
    Nor distant Shore
    Nor Cannons' roar
Shall longer keep me from my Dear.                                       390

NELL. Ha! ha!—and do you believe I don't know your Story? do you
think on *Suffolk's* coming so near Fareham, I didn't find out my old
acquaintance Will?—

NANCY. Is he well? and did he tell you how he lov'd me?

NELL. Yes, yes,—I have had the whole Story over, and he told me too,
how since his Absence your Father with a true Farmer's Conscience
wanted you to be false hearted and marry his Neighbour the rich Miller,
and I believe o' my Conscience it was my good advice that prevented
his Deserting to go to you.

NANCY. O then I needn't inform you why I gave them the Slip, or how   400
I got into this disguise—but Nell tell me, don't you think it possible
for him to procure his discharge?—[1]

---

[1] *The Public Advertiser*, 16 Oct. 1778, describes this part of the story as: 'A farmer's
daughter escapes from her Suffolk relatives (who were persuading her to a marriage of
interest) in pursuit of her lover at the camp, with a view to gaining his discharge.'

NELL. No,—but I think he would deserve to be shot if he try'd for't—

NANCY. Lord then, what shall I do?

NELL. Do!—marry him at the Drum head as soon as you can, and if he
  behaves well to you, you'll not find the Camp life so hard as you
  expect.—

### SONG

#### [NELL]

What can our wisest heads provide,
For the child we doat on dearly,
    But a merry soul and an honest heart,                    410
In a lad who loves her dearly,
      Who with kisses and chat
      And all all that,
Will sooth her late and early?
      If the truth she'll tell,
      When she knows him well,
She'll swear she loves him dearly.
Let the prude at name or sight of man,
    Pretend to rail severely;
But alack a day! unseen she'll play                    420
    With the lad who loves her dearly.
      Say old men what they will,
      'Tis a lover still
Makes day and night roll cheerly
      What makes our May
      All holiday,
But the lad we doat on dearly?

NELL. But come, as I know you have been brought up a little too tenderly
  for a Corporal's Wife, and understand some of your fine Needlework,
  and all that,—I'll tell you what I'll do for you,—There are three or Four    430
  Great Ladies who are often so kind as to take notice of me,—tho' by
  the bye they are so condescending and goodnatur'd, that you'd never
  guess 'em for Folks of fashion, and I am sure if they knew your story,
  and how you were brought up, they'd do something in your behalf,
  so I'll try to bring you to 'em.

NANCY. Dear Nell, I will be guided by you, for tho' my heart hasn't
  fail'd me yet, I shall be so afraid of being discover'd at the Camp.
  Here comes the Serjeant whose Party I join'd on the way—[*Shouldering
  her Musket*]

NELL. As I live, I can't help laughing to see how smart you handle    440
  your Arms.

NANCY. O I am Mistress of all the Exercise I assure you.

*Enter* SERJEANT.

[SERJEANT]. Why Nell, I believe you are going to run away with my
little Soldier here.—

NELL. Never fear Serjeant, he's in no danger from me.

NANCY. She thinks I have learn'd nothing since I listed. But ask the
Serjeant if I mightn't pass muster in the Lines.

SERJEANT. As handy a Lad as ever was, come, come, look at him Nell.

*The Exercise*[1]

NELL. Well done Indeed! odds me at this rate his Majesty need never
want Soldiers.                                                    450

NANCY. O then I have learn'd Something—But Courage—for my part
I shall be happy in actual Service. hey! Serjeant! in smoke and fire,
storming and wounding hey!—

*TRIO*

O the Joy when the Trumpets sound,
And the March beat around,
When the Steed tears the ground,
And shouts to the skies resound.
On glittering Arms the Sun Beams playing,
    Heighten the Soldier's Charms,
The Fife, the Spirit stirring Fife,                              460
And the roll and the Rub a Dub
    Of the distant Drum.[2]
Cry, hark: the Enemy come
To arms, to arms, the attack's begun.

## *Act 2d.*

### *Scene 1st*
### *A Grove near the Camp*[3]

*Enter* NELL, *speaking without.*

William! come speak to him another time, sure nothing could be more
lucky; however, I must obey their ladyships' instructions, and keep

---

[1] 'On the Serjeant's return, she goes through her exercise, to shew her friend Nelly
her expertness in her new profession' (*Morning Chronicle*, 16 Oct. 1778). 'Miss Walpole,
in performing the military exercise, met with great applause' (*Town and Country
Magazine*, x (1778), 544).

[2] Cf. J. Dryden, *King Arthur: or, the British Worthy* (1691), I. iii:

Come if you dare, our Trumpets sound;
Come if you dare, the Foes rebound:
We come, we come, we come, we come,
Says the double, double, double Beat of the Thund'ring Drum.

[3] This scene is not in Lapent MS. 457, and is printed from the 1795 version, which
may not be very close to the original. The setting was certainly different, for the *Morn-*

him in ignorance, that they may be present at the discovery. Poor fellow, it's almost a pity too, when one has it in one's power to make him so happy.

*Enter* WILLIAM.

WILLIAM. I am sorry Nell to make you wait, but it was an old friend.

NELL. Aye, aye, some one from Suffolk, I suppose, who has brought you news of your dear Nancy.

WILLIAM. I wish it had; it's unaccountable that I don't hear from her.

NELL. Unaccountable? not at all: I suppose she has changed her mind.    10

WILLIAM. No Nelly, that's impossible, and you would think so, had you heard how she plighted her faith to me, and vowed, notwithstanding her parents were my enemies, nothing but death should prevent our union.

NELL. O, I beg your pardon; if her father and mother indeed are against you, you need not doubt her constancy. But come, don't be melancholy, I tell you I want to have you stay somewhere near the Inn,[1] and perhaps I may bring you some intelligence of her.

WILLIAM. How! dear Nell?

NELL. Tho' Indeed I think you are very foolish to plague yourself so,    20 for even had Nancy loved you well enough to have carried your knapsack, you would have been very imprudent to have suffered her.

WILLIAM. Aye, but prudence, you know, is not a soldier's virtue. It's our business to hold life itself cheap, much more the comforts of it. Shew me a young fellow in our regiment who, if he gains the heart of a worthy girl, and [is] afraid to marry her for want of a little wealth, [and] I would have him drummed out of the regiment for discretion.

NELL. Very fine! but must not the poor girl share in all your fatigues and mishaps.

WILL. There Nell I own is the objection, but tenderness and affection    30 may soften even these; yet if my Nancy ever makes the trial, though I may not be able to prevent her from undergoing hardships, I am sure my affection will make her wonder at their being called so; I wish I could once boast that the experiment was made.

*AIR*[2]
My Nancy leaves the rural train
A camp's distress to prove,
All other ills she can sustain,
But living from her love.

---

*ing Chronicle*, 16 Oct. 1718, reported: 'The second act opens with a view of the Star Inn, on the Heath. William comes on with Nelly, who gives him hopes of seeing his beloved Nancy.'

[1] Presumably the Star Inn on Coxheath.

[2] Sung to the tune of 'Kate of Aberdeen'.

Yet, dearest, tho' your Soldier's there,
    Will not your spirits fail,                                    40
To mark the hardships you must share,
    Dear Nancy of the dale.[1]

Or should you, love, each danger scorn,
    Ah! how shall I secure,
Your health, 'mid toils which you were born
    To soothe, but not endure,

A thousand perils I must view,
    A thousand ills assail,
Nor must I tremble e'en for you,
    Dear Nancy of the dale.                                        50

### Scene 2nd[2]

#### *Enter* O'DAUB

Well to be sure this Camp is a pretty Comical Place, with their Drums
and their Fifes, and their Jigs and their Marches, and the Ladies in
their Regimentals[3]—upon my Conscience I believe they'd Form a
Troop of Cavalry if there was any hope of an Invasion.—But now I am
alone by myself, it's high time I should begin to be after taking my
Place. Well—here's Some of the Directions for it.—Now I can't think
what make[s] my hand shake so unless it is Mr. Booliard's Wine that
has got into my head—So—so—let me Study my orders a little, for
I'm not used to this Stage Business. P.S. and O.P.—who the Devil
now is to understand that?—O but here's the Explanation here, P.S.  10
—the Prompter's Side and O.P.—opposite the Prompter—I'm to mark
down the Side as it's to be on one Side or t'other. Very well—P.S.
and O.P. Somewhere here about is certainly the best Point to take it
from.

#### *Enter* SERJEANT, SOLDIERS *and* TWO COUNTRY MEN

1ST COUNTRYMAN. There! your Ships!—that's he.

2D. COUNTRYMAN. Aye, that's he sure enough, I have seen him Skulking about these two days, and if he ben't a Spy, I'll suffer hanging.

SERJEANT. He certainly must be a Spy by his drawing figures.

2D. COUNTRYMAN. Do your honors seize him, or the whole Camp may
be blown up before you're aware.                                  20

O'DAUB. Prompter's side.

SERJEANT. Hush! and we shall convict him out of his own mouth.

---

[1] Cf. Thomas Arne's song, 'Sweet Nan of the vale' (1751).

[2] The 1795 version adds, 'An open View near the Camp'.

[3] Visits were paid by a coterie of fashionable ladies, led by Georgiana, Duchess of
Devonshire. They dressed in military style.

O'DAUB. P.S.—Yet the Star and Garter[1] must certainly be P.S.[2]

SERJEANT. P.S.—What the Devil does he say?

1ST COUNTRYMAN. Treason you may Swear by our not understanding him.—

O'DAUB. Aye, and then O.P. will have the advantage.

SERJEANT. O.P.—That's the old Pretender—A Damn'd French Jacobite Spy—my Life on't!

2D. COUNTRYMAN. And P.S. Prince Steward I suppose.[3]                    30

SERJEANT. Like enough.

O'DAUB. Memorandum—the Officers' Quarters are in the Rear of the Line.

2D. COUNTRYMAN. Mark that.

O'DAUB. Nota bene—The Generals' Tents are all Houses.

1ST COUNTRYMAN. Remember.

O'DAUB. Then the Park of Artillery—O Burn the Artillery—we shall make nothing of that.

SERJEANT. There! a Villain—He'll burn the Artillery will he?

O'DAUB. Well faith this Camp is easier taken than I thought.

SERJEANT. Is it so Rogue?—But you shall find the difference. What a    40
Providential Discovery!

O'DAUB. To be sure the People must like it; and in the Course of the Season, I hope we shall Surprize his Majesty.

SERJEANT. O the Villain! Seize him directly. Fellow you're a dead man if you Stir.

CORPORAL. We seize you for a Spy.

O'DAUB. A Spy! pho, get about your Business.

SERJEANT. Bind him, and blindfold him if he resist.    [*They bind him.*

2D. COUNTRYMAN. Aye Bind him, Bind him for certain, and Search him. I warrant his Pockets are Cramm'd with Powder, Matches, and    50
Tinder Boxes.

O'DAUB. Tunder and Nouns, what do you mean?

1ST COUNTRYMAN. Hold him fast.

O'DAUB. Why here now are Ladies Coming, who know me—here's Lady Sarah Sash, Lady Plume, who were at the Fetè Champetre and will give me a character.

SERJEANT. Why Villain! your papers have prov'd you to be a Spy, and sent by the Old Pretender.

---

[1] The inn at Coxheath, shown in the previous scene and probably in this one, too.

[2] *The Critick . . . A Literary Catchpenny by R. B. Sheridan, Esquire* (London, 1780), p. 2, says 'it was from him [Thomas Sheridan] that *Young Pretender* [R.B.S.] got the joke of O.P. and P.S. that told so much in *The Camp*, last season. . . .'

[3] 'While he [O'Daub] is making laughable observations on the necessary points of perspective laid down in his instructions, as to which views as are to stand upon the stage P.S. and O.P., the serjeant and his recruits steal behind him, and misinterpret what he says, supposing that he means the Old Pretender by O.P. and the Pretender's Son by P.S.' (*Morning Chronicle*, 16 Oct. 1778.)

O'DAUB. O Lord! O Lord!

SERJEANT. Why you Dog, why didn't you say that the Camp was 60 easier taken than you thought?

2D. COUNTRYMAN. Aye—Deny that.

SERJEANT. Aye, and that you would burn the Artillery and surprize his Majesty,—So come you had better Confess who Employ'd you, before you're hang'd.

O'DAUB. Hang'd for a Spy! To be sure my Self is got into a pretty Scrape here.—I tell you Mr. Soldier or Serjeant, or what the Devil you are— that upon my Conscience and Soul I am Nothing but a poor Painter Employ'd by Monsieur de Lantherburgh.

SERJEANT. There's a Dog! Confesses himself a Foreign Emissary 70 Employ'd by Marshal Leatherbag.

2D. COUNTRYMAN. O He'll be convicted on his Tongue; you may swear 'un a Foreigner by his Lingo.

IST COUNTRYMAN. Aye, bring 'un away, I long to see un hanging.

O'DAUB. O, If I will be shot—The Devil go with the Theatre and Managers. [*Exeunt.*

*Scene 3d*

*Enter* LADY PLUME, LADY SARAH SASH, MISS GORGET *etc.*[1]

LA. PLUME. O my dear Lady Sarah indeed you were too Severe and I'm sure if Miss Gorget had been bye she'd be of my Opinion.

LA. SASH. Not in the least.

LA. PLUME. You must know She has been rallying my poor brother Sir Harry Bouquet for not being in the Militia, and so ill naturedly.

MISS GORGET. Upon my word, I think Sir Harry deserves it for he is himself perpetually ridiculing the Camp.

LA. SASH. So he is indeed, and all I said was that he look'd so French, and so finical that I thought he ran a risk of being mistaken for another Female Chevalier.[2]                                                                    10

LA. PLUME. Yet we must confess our Situation is open to a little Raillery —a few Elegancies of accommodation are certainly wanting, tho' one's Toilet is not absolutely as Sir Harry affirms spread on a Drum head.

---

[1] 'Lady Sash, Lady Plume and Lady Gorget, appear in the next scene *en militaire*, and after some laugh among themselves, Sir Charles Plume enters, who not relishing the humour of the camp, complains of the infectious manners of it having pervaded the whole county of Kent . . .' (*Morning Chronicle*, 16 Oct. 1778). The *Town and Country Magazine*, x (1778), p. 545, refers to 'Miss Gorget' and 'Sir William Plume', but *St. James's Chronicle*, 15–17 Oct. 1778, calls them 'Lady Gorget' and 'Sir Charles Bouquet'. The names given in the text above are from the Larpent MS. The version of 1795 prints 'Lady Gorget' and 'Sir Harry Bouquet'.

[2] Charles D'Éon de Beaumont (1728–1810), chevalier. He was a captain of dragoons, engaged in military and political intrigue, who afterwards adopted women's clothes.

LA. SASH. He vows there is an Eternal Confusion between our Lords'
Camp Equipage, and our dressing Apparatus—between Stores Mili-
tary and Millinery—such a description he gives—on the same Shelf
Cartri[d]ges and Cosmetics, Pouches and Patches—here Stands of
Arms, and there a file of Black Pins.[1] In one Drawer Bullet mo[u]lds
and Essence Bottles,[2] Pistol and Tweezer Cases with Battle Powder
mix'd with Mareshal.[3]                                                     20
MISS GORGET. O Malicious Exaggeration.
LA. PLUME. But pray Lady Sarah, don't renew it. See he's coming to
join us again.

*Enter* SIR HARRY BOUQUET

SIR H.B. Now Lady Sarah, I beg a Truce. Miss Gorget I am rejoyced to
meet you at this delectable Spot, where according to Lady Sarah Sash,
my sister, Lady Plume you may be amused with such eternal Variety.
LA. SASH. You see Lady Plume he perseveres.[4]
MISS GORGET. I assure you Sir Harry, I should have been against you
in your Raillery.
SIR H.B. Nay as Gad's my judge I admire the place of all things—Here  30
is all the Parade, Pomp, and Circumstance of Glorious War—Mars
in a Vis a Vis[5]—and Bellona giving a Fete Champetre.
LA. PLUME. Now but seriously Brother, what can make you Judge so
differently of the Camp from everybody else.
SIR H.B. Why then Seriously I do think it, the very worst plann'd thing
I ever beheld, for instance now the Tents are all ranged in a Strait
Line. Now Miss Gorget, can any thing be worse than a strait Line?
Isn't there a horrid uniformity in this infinite Vista of Canvas? No
Curve no break—and the Avenue of Marquees—abominable!
LA. SASH. O to be sure a Square—a Circus or a Crescent[6] would have  40
been a vastly better form.
MISS GORGET. What a pity Sir Harry wasn't Consulted!
SIR H.B. As Gad's my Judge I think so—or Brown[7]—for there is great
Capability in the Ground.

---

[1] Cf. Pope, *The Rape of the Lock* (1714), i. 137-9:

> Here Files of Pins extend their shining Rows,
> Puffs, Powders, Patches, Bibles, Billets-doux.
> Now awful Beauty puts on all its Arms.

[2] The Larpent MS. reads 'Essence Bullets', but this is probably a misreading of
Sheridan's hand. The 1795 version gives 'essence bottles'. Cf. *A Trip to Scarborough*,
III. i (p. 189, l. 88 above): 'Thou essence-bottle'.

[3] 'Marechal': scent or scented hair powder.

[4] 'A Macarony Connoisseur rallies the ladies on their Military Appearance and by
several well-turned witticisms enlivens this pleasing entertainment' (*Public Advertiser*,
16 Oct. 1778).                                        [5] See p. 187, n. 1 above.

[6] As in the designs of John Wood (1705?-54), and his son, at Bath.

[7] Lancelot Brown (1715-83), landscape gardener known as 'Capability' Brown.

LA. SASH. A Camp Cognoscente! positively Sir Harry we will have you publish a treatise on Military Virtu.

SIR H.B. Very well—But now how will you excuse this, the Officers' Tents all close to the Common Soldiers—what an Arrangement is that? Now if I might have advised, there certainly should have been one part for the Cannaille and a *West End* of the Camp for the Noblesse 50 and persons of a Certain Rank.

MISS GORGET. Very right, I hope you would have thought of proper Members for Hazard and Quinze.

LA. PLUME. To be sure with Festive Tents and Opera Pavilion.

SIR H.B. Egad the only Plan that could make the place Sufferable for a Week—well certainly the Greatest possible Defect in a General is *want of Taste.*

LA. SASH. Undoubtedly—and Conduct Discipline and humanity are no Attonement for it.

SIR H.B. None in nature. 60

LA. PLUME. But Sir Harry it is rather unlucky thàt the Military Spirit is so universal for you will hardly find any one to Side with you.

SIR H.B. Universal indeed! and the Ridicule of it is to see how this Madness has infected the whole Road—from Travelling to Maidstone.[1] The Camp jargon[2] is as Current all the Way as bad Silver. The very Postil[l]ions that drove me, talk of their Cavalry [which] refuses to charge on a Trot uphill,[3] the turnpikes seem'd converted into Redoubts, and the Dogs demand the Counter Sign from my Servants instead of their Tickets—then when I got to Maidstone I found the very Waiters had a Smattering of Tactics, for enquiring what I could have for Dinner, a 70 most drill'd Drawer reviewing his Bill of fare with the Air of a Field Marshall propos'd an advanced Party of Soup and Bouille to be follow'd by the main body of Ham and Chickens, flank'd by a Fricasee with Sallads in the intervals, and a Corps de reserve of Sweatmeats, and whipt Sillabubs to form a hollow Square in the Centre.

LA. PLUME. Ha! ha! ha! but Sir Harry I am sorry to find you have so strong a dislike to every thing that's Military—for unless you would contribute to the fortune of our little Female Recruit—

SIR H.B. Madam most willingly.—and very apropos here comes your Ladyship's Rustic Protege and has brought I see the little Soldier with 80 her, as you desired her.

*Enter* NELL *and* NANCY.

[1] This makes sense as it stands, but it is not impossible that Sheridan wrote 'Tunbridge to London'. The 1795 version prints 'Maidstone to London'.

[2] The Larpent MS. gives 'The Camp for you!' but this looks like a misreading of Sheridan's handwriting. Probably the 1795 version, 'the camp jargon', is correct.

[3] '. . . the very postboys declaring that "they won't *charge* their *cavalry* upon a *precipice*", when ordered to drive fast up hill' (*Morning Chronicle*, 16 Oct. 1785).

NELL. Here—here—Nancy—make your Court'sy or your Bow to these Ladies who have so kindly promised to protect you.

NANCY. Simple Gratitude is the only return I can make but I am sure these Ladies who have hearts to do so good natur'd a Deed, will excuse my not being able to acknowledge it as I ought.

NELL. She means and please your Ladyships that she will always acknowledge your Ladyship's Goodness to the last hour of her Life, and as in Duty bound we will pray for your Ladyship's happiness and your Ladyship's prosperity—that's [what] she means.                    90

LA. PLUME. Very well, but Nancy you are Satisfied that your Soldier should continue in his Duty?

NELL. O Yes, your Ladyship, she's quite Satisfied.

NANCY. I have seen him Madam, and I wish for Nothing now but to be enabled to continue with him in a proper Character.

NELL. Yes, your Ladyship, that's all She wishes.

SIR H.B. Upon my word a pretty little Rural Romance. I think your Ladyship should appoint her your own Aid de Camp.

LA. PLUME. Well Child we are all your Friends, and you may assure your William, you shall be no Sufferer by your Constancy.                    100

NELL. There Nancy—Say Something.

LA. SASH. But are you Sure you will be able to bear the hardships of the Situation.

NELL. O yes my Lady, She's quite Sure, and She can tell you So in a Song too.

NANCY. My heart is now so chearful, that indeed I don't know how otherwise to Comply.


### SONG[1]

The Fife and Drum sound merrily,
   A Soldier, a Soldier's the Lad for me,
   With my true Love, I soon will be,                    110
For who so kind, and true as he.

With him in every toil I'll share,
   To please him shall be all my Care.
     Each peril I'll dare,
     All hardships I'll bear
For a Soldier, a Soldier's the Lad for me.

Then if kind heaven preserve my love,
What rapturous joy shall his Nancy prove,
Swift thro' the Camp shall my footsteps bound,
To meet my William with conquest crown'd.                    120

---

[1] The Larpent MS. adds 'By Miss Walpole'.

Close to my faithful bosom prest,
Soon shall he hush his cares to rest,
Clasp'd in these arms,
Forget war's alarms,
For a Soldier, a Soldier's the lad for me.[1]

SIR H.B. Very well, and very Spirited egad—you see Ladies how your
Military example has diffused itself.

MISS GORGET. I hope we shall make a Convert of you yet Sir Harry.

LA. PLUME. Now Nancy, you must be ruled by us.

NANCY. As I live there's my dear William!                              130

LA. PLUME. Turn from him—you must.

NANCY. O, I shall discover myself—I tremble so unlike a soldier.

*Enter* NELL *with* WILLIAM.

NELL. Why I tell you, William, the ladies want to ask you some questions.

SIR HARRY. Honest corporal, here's a little recruit, son to a tenant of
mine, and, as I am told, you are an intelligent young fellow, I mean to
put him under your care.

WILLIAM. What the boy, your honour? Lord bless you sir, I shall never
be able to make any thing of him.

NANCY [*aside*]. I am sorry for that.                                  140

L. SASH. Nay corporal, he's very young.

WILLIAM. He is under-size, my lady, such a stripling is fitter for a
drummer than a rank and file.

SIR HARRY. But he's straight and well made.

NANCY. I wish I was ordered to right about.

WILLIAM. Well I'll do all in my power to oblige your ladyship. Come
youngster, turn about—ah, Nelly!—tell me, is't not she?

SIR HARRY. Why don't you march him off?

NELL. Is he undersize corporal? O, you blockhead!

NANCY. O ladies, pray excuse me!—My dear William! [*runs into his*  150
*arms.*]

NELL. They'll never be able to come to an explanation before your ladyships—Go, go and talk by yourselves. [*they retire up the stage.*]

*Enter* SERJEANT DRUM[2] *etc.*

SERJEANT. Please your Ladyship—we have taken a Sort of a Spy this
Morning—who has the assurance to deny it, tho' he Confesses he is an
Irish Painter—I have undertaken however to present this for him to
Lady Sarah Sash. [*gives a paper*]

[1] The last nine lines of the song are omitted in the Larpent MS. So, too, are lines
129–153 on this page.
[2] This is the Larpent reading, but it is probably a mistake for 'Serjeant Drill'.

SIR H.B. What appears against him.

SERJEANT. A great many Suspicious Circumstances please your honour, he has an O to his name and we took him with a Draught of the Camp in his hand.                                                                                          160

LA. SASH. Ha! ha! ha! this is ridiculous enough—'tis O'Daub the Irish painter, who diverted us some time ago, at the Fete Champetre[1]— honest Serjeant we will See your Prisoner and I fancy you may release him.

SERJEANT. He is this way, and please your Ladyship.

SIR H.B. What's to be done this way?

SERJEANT. The Line your Honour turns out and perhaps as there are Some pleasure Tents[2] pitch'd in the Front of the Line—these Ladies will condescend to hear a March and Chorus, which Some Recruits  170 are practising against his Majesty comes to the Camp.

LA. SASH. Come Sir Harry you will grow in love with a Camp Life yet.

SIR H.B. Your Ladyship will be utterly tired of it first, I'll answer for't.

LA. SASH. No No.

SIR H.B. Yes on the first bad Weather you'll give orders to Strike your Toilets, and each secure a Retreat to Tunbridge.

*THE MARCH*[3]

*Finale*

SERJEANT[4]

While the loud voice of War,
Resounds from afar,
Songs of Triumph and Duty we'll pay;
When our Monarch appears,                              180
We'll give him three Cheers,

*Chorus*[5]  With huzza, and huzza, and huzza;
May true Glory still wave her bright
banners around,
Still with Fame, Power and Freedom Old
England be crown'd.[5]—

---

[1] See p. 310, n. 1 above.

[2] 'At length they all adjourn (to a grand tent in front of the line) on the invitation of the Serjeant to see the various regiments exercised, and to hear a song intended to be sung when his Majesty reviews the camp' (*Morning Chronicle*, 16 Oct. 1778).

[3] The 1795 version prints: 'A march while the scene changes to a View of the Camp.' Cf. the *Morning Chronicle*, 16 Oct. 1778: 'the scene then draws and discovers a most striking and exact representation of the right wing with different regiments in motion, and after a variety of military manœuvres, the whole concludes with a grand song and chorus.'

[4] Omitted in the Larpent MS.

[5] Only the first stanza is given in the Larpent MS.

### WILLIAM[1]

Inspir'd by my Love all Dangers I'll prove
No Perils shall William dismay,
If Nancy but smile the reward of my Toil,

*Chorus.*   Huzza! *etc.*[2]                                              190

### NANCY[2]

Brave Sons of the Field
Whose Valor's our shield
Love and Beauty your toils shall repay,
In War's fierce alarms,
Inspir'd by those Charms,

*Chorus.*   Huzza! *etc.*[2]

### FINIS

[1] In the 1795 version, Nancy's stanza precedes William's. 'William' is omitted in the Larpent MS.
[2] Omitted in the Larpent MS.

# THE CRITIC

# THE CRITIC

## OR

### A Tragedy Rehearsed

# A Dramatic Piece

in three ACTS

*as it is performed at the*

## THEATRE ROYAL in DRURY LANE

*Richard Brinsley Sheridan Esq.*

LONDON.

Printed for T. Becket, Adelphi, Strand,

MDCCLXXXI.

The title-page of the first edition of *The Critic*

# *TO Mrs. GREVILLE.*[1]

*MADAM,*

*In requesting your permission to address the following pages to you, which as they aim themselves to be critical, require every protection and allowance that approving taste or friendly prejudice can give them, I yet ventured to mention no other motive than the gratification of private friendship and esteem. Had I suggested a hope that your implied approbation would give a sanction to their defects, your particular reserve, and dislike to the reputation of critical taste, as well as of poetical talent, would have made you refuse the protection of your name to such a purpose. However, I am not so ungrateful as now to attempt to combat this disposition in you. I shall not here presume to argue that the present state of poetry claims and expects every assistance that taste and example can afford it: nor endeavour to prove that a fastidious conceal-ment of the most elegant productions of judgment and fancy is an ill return for the possession of those endowments.—Continue to deceive yourself in the idea that you are known only to be eminently admired and regarded for the valuable qualities that attach private friendships, and the graceful talents that adorn conversation. Enough of what you have written, has stolen into full public notice to answer my purpose; and you will, perhaps, be the only person, conversant in elegant literature, who shall read this address and not perceive that by publishing your particular approbation of the following drama, I have a more interested object than to boast the true respect and regard with which*

*I have the honour to be,*

*MADAM,*

*Your very sincere,*

*And obedient humble servant,*

R. B. SHERIDAN.

[1] Frances Greville (born Macartney) was the wife of Richard Fulke Greville of Wilbury House, and mother of Sheridan's friend, Frances Crewe. Mrs. Greville was well known in literary circles for her 'Ode to Indifference'.

# PROLOGUE.

By the Honorable RICHARD FITZPATRICK[1]

THE Sister Muses, whom these realms obey,
Who o'er the Drama hold divided sway,
Sometimes, by evil counsellors, 'tis said
Like earth-born potentates have been misled:
In those gay days of wickedness and wit,
When Villiers[2] criticiz'd what Dryden writ,
The Tragick Queen, to please a tasteless crowd,
Had learn'd to bellow, rant, and roar so loud,
That frighten'd Nature, her best friend before,
The blust'ring beldam's company forswore.                      10
Her comic Sister, who had wit 'tis true,
With all her merits, had her failings too;
And would sometimes in mirthful moments use
A style too flippant for a well-bred Muse.
Then female modesty abash'd began
To seek the friendly refuge of the fan,
Awhile behind that slight entrenchment stood,
'Till driv'n from thence, she left the stage for good.
In our more pious, and far chaster times!
These sure no longer are the Muse's crimes!                    20
But some complain that, former faults to shun,
The reformation to extremes has run.
The frantick hero's wild delirium past,
Now insipidity succeeds bombast;
So slow Melpomene's cold numbers creep,
Here dullness seems her drowsy court to keep,
And we, are scarce awake, whilst you are fast asleep.
Thalia, once so ill behav'd and rude,
Reform'd; is now become an arrant prude,

---

[1] 1748–1813. He was the second son of John, 1st Earl of Upper Ossory, and was well known as soldier, wit, and friend of Fox. For Sheridan's invitation to him to see and abuse *The Critic*, see *Letters of R. B. Sheridan* (ed. C. Price, Oxford, 1966), i. 128–9.
[2] George Villiers, 2nd Duke of Buckingham (1628–87), is credited with the authorship of the burlesque, *The Rehearsal* (1671), that satirized John Dryden as 'Bayes', and laughed at heroic tragedy.

Retailing nightly to the yawning pit, 30
The purest morals, undefil'd by wit!
Our Author offers in these motley scenes,
A slight remonstrance to the Drama's queens,
Nor let the goddesses be over nice;
Free spoken subjects give the best advice.
Although not quite a novice in his trade,
His cause to night requires no common aid.
To this, a friendly, just, and pow'rful court,
I come Ambassador to beg support.
Can he undaunted, brave the critick's rage? 40
In civil broils, with brother bards engage?
Hold forth their errors to the publick eye,
Nay more, e'en News-papers themselves defy?
Say, must his single arm encounter all?
By numbers vanquish'd, e'en the brave may fall;
And though no leader should success distrust,
Whose troops are willing, and whose cause is just;
To bid such hosts of angry foes defiance,
His chief dependance must be, YOUR ALLIANCE.

# DRAMATIS PERSONÆ

| | | |
|---|---|---|
| DANGLE | Mr. Dodd. | |
| SNEER | Mr. Palmer. | |
| SIR FRETFUL PLAGIARY | Mr. Parsons. | |
| SIGNOR PASTICCIO RITORNELLO | Mr. Delpini. | 5 |
| INTERPRETER | Mr. Baddeley. | |
| UNDER PROMPTER | Mr. Phillimore. | |

AND

| | | |
|---|---|---|
| PUFF | Mr. King. | |
| MRS. DANGLE | Mrs. Hopkins. | 10 |
| ITALIAN GIRLS | { Miss Field, and the Miss Abrams. | |

### Characters of the TRAGEDY

| | | |
|---|---|---|
| LORD BURLEIGH | Mr. Moody. | |
| GOVERNOR OF TILBURY FORT | Mr. Wrighten. | 15 |
| EARL OF LEICESTER | Mr. Farren. | |
| SIR WALTER RALEIGH | Mr. Burton. | |
| SIR CHRISTOPHER HATTON | Mr. Waldron. | |
| MASTER OF THE HORSE | Mr. Kenny. | |
| BEEFEATER | Mr. Wright. | 20 |
| JUSTICE | Mr. Packer. | |
| SON | Mr. Lamash. | |
| CONSTABLE | Mr. Fawcett. | |
| THAMES | Mr. Gawdry. | |

AND                                                          25

| | | |
|---|---|---|
| DON FEROLO WHISKERANDOS | Mr. Bannister, jun. | |
| IST NIECE | Miss Collet. | |
| 2D NIECE | Miss Kirby. | |
| JUSTICE'S LADY | Mrs. Johnston. | |
| CONFIDANT | Mrs. Bradshaw. | 30 |

AND

| | | |
|---|---|---|
| TILBURINA | Miss Pope. | |

Guards, Constables, Servants, Chorus, Rivers,
Attendants, &c. &c.

1–34 DRAMATIS . . . &c. &c.] *1781*; *om. L, C*

# THE CRITIC

## ACT I

### SCENE I

MR. *and* MRS. DANGLE *at Breakfast, and reading Newspapers.*[1]

DANGLE. [*reading*] 'BRUTUS to LORD NORTH.'[2]—'Letter the second on the STATE OF THE ARMY'—Pshaw! 'To the first L— dash D of the A— dash Y.'[3]—'Genuine Extract of a Letter from ST. KITT'S.'— 'COXHEATH INTELLIGENCE.'—'It is now confidently asserted that SIR CHARLES HARDY.'[4]—Pshaw!—Nothing but about the fleet, and the nation!—and I hate all politics but theatrical politics.—Where's the MORNING CHRONICLE?

MRS. DANGLE. Yes, that's your gazette.[5]

DANGLE. So, here we have it.——'*Theatrical intelligence extraordinary,*' ——'We hear there is a new tragedy in rehearsal at Drury-Lane Theatre, 10 call'd the SPANISH ARMADA, said to be written by Mr. PUFF, a gentleman well known in the theatrical world; if we may allow ourselves to give credit to the report of the performers, who, truth to say, are in general but indifferent judges, this piece abounds with the most striking and received beauties of modern composition'—So! I am very glad my friend PUFF's tragedy is in such forwardness.—Mrs. Dangle, my dear, you will be very glad to hear that PUFF's tragedy——

MRS. DANGLE. Lord, Mr. Dangle, why will you plague me about such nonsense?—Now the plays are begun I shall have no peace.—Isn't it sufficient to make yourself ridiculous by your passion for the theatre, 20

---

[1] Cf. 'The Quidnuncs; a moral Interlude', in the *London Review*, ix (1779), 59. It begins:
  Mr. *and* Mrs. Quidnunc *are discovered sitting at a table; on which are scattered heaps of newspapers. After taking up and throwing down one after another*, Quidnunc *speaks.*
  MR. Q. Confound these barren *chronicles*, I say. Why, there's no scandal in 'em, wife, to-day.

[2] 'Brutus' was one of the pseudonyms of 'Junius' in the political controversy of 1769–72. On 6 Sept. 1779, however, 'Brutus' wrote to the editor of the *Public Advertiser*, satirizing the military discipline of the Westminster and Middlesex volunteers.

[3] John Montagu, 4th Earl of Sandwich (1718–92), first Lord of the Admiralty, and a favourite target for abuse.

[4] 1716?–1780. Commander of the Channel Fleet.

[5] William Woodfall (1746–1803) was its dramatic critic and subjected the plays that he saw to careful and dispassionate examination. The newspaper was said, in its issue of 5 Nov. 1777, to have 'the honour of taking the lead as a theatrical reviewer'.

without continually teazing me to join you? Why can't you ride your
hobby-horse without desiring to place me on a pillion behind you, Mr.
Dangle?

DANGLE. Nay, my dear, I was only going to read——

MRS. DANGLE. No, no; you will never read any thing that's worth
listening to:—you hate to hear about your country; there are letters
every day with Roman signatures, demonstrating the certainty of an
invasion, and proving that the nation is utterly undone.[1]—But you
never will read any thing to entertain one.

DANGLE. What has a woman to do with politics, Mrs. Dangle?          30

MRS. DANGLE. And what have you to do with the theatre, Mr. Dangle?
Why should you affect the character of a Critic? I have no patience with
you!—haven't you made yourself the jest of all your acquaintance by
your interference in matters where you have no business? Are not you
call'd a theatrical Quidnunc,[2] and a mock Mæcenas to second-hand
authors?

DANGLE. True; my power with the Managers is pretty notorious; but is
it no credit to have applications from all quarters for my interest?—From
lords to recommend fidlers, from ladies to get boxes, from authors to
get answers, and from actors to get engagements.                    40

MRS. DANGLE. Yes, truly; you have contrived to get a share in all the
plague and trouble of theatrical property, without the profit, or even
the credit of the abuse that attends it.

DANGLE. I am sure, Mrs. Dangle, you are no loser by it, however; YOU
have all the advantages of it:—mightn't you, last winter, have had the
reading of the new Pantomime a fortnight previous to its performance?
And doesn't Mr. Fosbrook[3] let you take places for a play before it is
advertis'd, and set you down for a Box for every new piece through the
season? And didn't my friend, Mr. Smatter, dedicate his last Farce to
you at my particular request, Mrs. Dangle?                           50

MRS. DANGLE. Yes; but wasn't the Farce damn'd, Mr. Dangle? And to
be sure it is extremely pleasant to have one's house made the motley
rendezvous of all the lackeys of literature!—The very high change of
trading authors and jobbing critics!—Yes, my drawing-room is an
absolute register-office for candidate actors, and poets without character; then to be continually alarmed with Misses and Ma'ams piping
histeric changes on JULIETS and DORINDAS, POLLYS[4] and OPHE-

---

[1] See the letters of 'Coriolanus alter', 'Scipio', 'Honestus', 'Historicus', and
'Capitilamis' in the *Public Advertiser*, 18, 23, 27, 28, 30 Sept. and 5 Oct. 1779.

[2] Gossip. See also the first note on the previous page.

[3] Thomas Fosbrook was still, officially, a numberer at Drury Lane Theatre, but must
already have been acting in the position he held for many years there—that of 'Box,
Book, and Housekeeper'.

[4] Dorinda was a character in Farquhar's *The Beaux' Stratagem*, and Polly Peachum
appeared in Gay's *The Beggar's Opera*.

LIAS; and the very furniture trembling at the probationary starts and unprovok'd rants of would-be RICHARDS and HAMLETS!—And what is worse than all, now that the Manager has monopoliz'd the Opera- 60 House,[1] haven't we the Signors and Signoras calling here, sliding their smooth semibreves, and gargling glib divisions in their outlandish throats—with foreign emissaries and French spies, for ought I know, disguised like fidlers and figure dancers!

DANGLE. Mercy! Mrs. Dangle!

MRS. DANGLE. And to employ yourself so idly at such an alarming crisis as this too—when, if you had the least spirit, you would have been at the head of one of the Westminster associations[2]—or trailing a volunteer pike in the Artillery Ground?[3]—But you—o'my conscience, I believe if the French were landed to-morrow your first enquiry 70 would be, whether they had brought a theatrical troop with them.

DANGLE. Mrs. Dangle, it does not signify—I say the stage is 'the Mirror of Nature,'[4] and the actors are 'the Abstract, and brief Chronicles of the Time:'[5]—and pray what can a man of sense study better?—Besides, you will not easily persuade me that there is no credit or importance in being at the head of a band of critics, who take upon them to decide for the whole town,[6] whose opinion and patronage all writers solicit, and whose recommendation no manager dares refuse!

MRS. DANGLE. Ridiculous!—Both managers and authors of the least merit, laugh at your pretensions.—The PUBLIC is their CRITIC— 80 without whose fair approbation they know no play can rest on the stage, and with whose applause they welcome such attacks as yours, and laugh at the malice of them, where they can't at the wit.

DANGLE. Very well, Madam—very well.

*Enter* SERVANT.

SERVANT. Mr. Sneer, Sir, to wait on you.

DANGLE. O, shew Mr. Sneer up.          *[Exit* SERVANT.

Plague on't, now we must appear loving and affectionate, or Sneer will hitch us into a story.

---

[1] Sheridan and Thomas Harris of Covent Garden Theatre had purchased the King's Theatre, but Harris had withdrawn after one season. See *Letters*, i. 116 n. 3.

[2] The volunteer militia. The Duke of Northumberland reported to the King on 1 Sept., on the recruiting, and the subscriptions raised at the Guildhall. See *Public Advertiser*, 2 Sept. 1779.

[3] Just north of Moorfields, and off Finsbury Square and Chiswell Street.

[4] Cf. Hamlet's 'mirror up to nature' (III. ii).

[5] *Hamlet*, II. ii.

[6] 'The pit is the grand court of criticism; and in the centre of it is collected that awful body, distinguished by the title of The Town. Hence are issued the irrevocable decrees; and here final sentence is pronounced on plays and players' (quoted from *The Connoisseur*, ed. Colman the Elder and Bonnell Thornton, no. 43, 20 Nov. 1754, in D. F. Smith, *The Critics in the Audience of the London Theatres from Buckingham to Sheridan* (Albuquerque, N. Mexico, 1953), p. 95).

MRS. DANGLE. With all my heart; you can't be more ridiculous than you are.                                                                                    90

DANGLE. You are enough to provoke——

*Enter* MR. SNEER.

—Hah! my dear Sneer, I am vastly glad to see you. My dear, here's Mr. Sneer.

MRS. DANGLE. Good morning to you, Sir.

DANGLE. Mrs. Dangle and I have been diverting ourselves with the papers.—Pray, Sneer, won't you go to Drury-lane theatre the first night of Puff's tragedy?

SNEER. Yes; but I suppose one shan't be able to get in, for on the first night of a new piece they always fill the house with orders to support it.[1] But here, Dangle, I have brought you two pieces, one of which you must   100 exert yourself to make the managers accept, I can tell you that, for 'tis written by a person of consequence.

DANGLE. So! Now my plagues are beginning!

SNEER. Aye, I am glad of it, for now you'll be happy. Why, my dear Dangle, it is a pleasure to see how you enjoy your volunteer fatigue, and your solicited solicitations.

DANGLE. It's a great trouble—yet, egad, it's pleasant too.—Why, sometimes of a morning, I have a dozen people call on me at breakfast time, whose faces I never saw before, nor ever desire to see again.

SNEER. That must be very pleasant indeed!                                    110

DANGLE. And not a week but I receive fifty letters, and not a line in them about any business of my own.

SNEER. An amusing correspondence!

DANGLE. [*reading*] 'Bursts into tears, and exit.' What, is this a tragedy!

SNEER. No, that's a genteel comedy, not a translation—only *taken from the French*; it is written in a stile which they have lately tried to run down; the true sentimental,[2] and nothing ridiculous in it from the beginning to the end.

---

[1] The privilege of free admission was greatly abused while Sheridan was manager of Drury Lane Theatre. At the end of Oct. 1785, Sheridan's sister-in-law, Mary Tickell, wrote that her mother 'raves about Orders that come in in Mr. Sheridan's Name every Night—She threatens to write herself about it' (Folger MS. Y. d. 35, f. 177). Cf. *Letters*, i. 140 n. 8; iii. 29–31.

[2] Cf. Richard Tickell's *The Wreath of Fashion, or, The Art of Sentimental Poetry* (1777), pp. 2–3:

> First, for true grounds of Sentimental lore,
> The scenes of modern Comedy explore;
> Dramatic Homilies! devout and sage,
> Stor'd with wise maxims, 'both for youth and age'. . . .
> But chief, let *Cumberland* thy Muse direct;
> High Priest of all the Tragic-comic sect!

MRS. DANGLE. Well, if they had kept to that, I should not have been
such an enemy to the stage, there was some edification to be got from   120
those pieces, Mr. Sneer!

SNEER. I am quite of your opinion, Mrs. Dangle; the theatre in proper
hands, might certainly be made the school of morality; but now, I am
sorry to say it, people seem to go there principally for their entertainment!'

MRS. DANGLE. It would have been more to the credit of the Managers to
have kept it in the other line.

SNEER. Undoubtedly, Madam, and hereafter perhaps to have had it
recorded, that in the midst of a luxurious and dissipated age, they
preserv'd *two* houses in the capital, where the conversation was always   130
moral at least, if not entertaining!

DANGLE. Now, egad, I think the worst alteration is in the nicety of the
audience.—No double entendre, no smart innuendo admitted; even
Vanburgh and Congreve obliged to undergo a bungling reformation!

SNEER. Yes, and our prudery in this respect is just on a par with the
artificial bashfulness of a courtezan, who encreases the blush upon her
cheek in an exact proportion to the diminution of her modesty.

DANGLE. Sneer can't even give the Public a good word!—But what have
we here?—This seems a very odd——

SNEER. O, that's a comedy, on a very new plan; replete with wit and   140
mirth, yet of a most serious moral! You see it is call'd 'THE RE-
FORMED HOUSEBREAKER;' where, by the mere force of humour,
HOUSEBREAKING is put into so ridiculous a light, that if the piece has
its proper run, I have no doubt but that bolts and bars will be entirely
useless by the end of the season.

DANGLE. Egad, this is new indeed!

SNEER. Yes; it is written by a particular friend of mine, who has discovered that the follies and foibles of society, are subjects unworthy
the notice of the Comic Muse, who should be taught to stoop only at
the greater vices and blacker crimes of humanity—gibbeting capital   150
offences in five acts, and pillorying petty larcenies in two.—In short,
his idea is to dramatize the penal laws, and make the Stage a court of
ease to the Old Bailey.

DANGLE. It is truly moral.

*Enter* SERVANT.

---

Mid darts and flames his Lover *cool[l]y* waits;
Calm as a Hero, cas'd in *Hartley's plates*;
'Till damp'd, and chill'd, by sentimental sighs,
Each stifled passion in a vapour dies.

' In an early fragment by Sheridan, quoted by Moore, i. 24–5, one of the characters
says, 'it ever was my opinion that the stage should be a place of rational entertainment;
instead of which, I am very sorry to say, most people go there for their diversion'.

Sir Fretful Plagiary, Sir.

DANGLE. Beg him to walk up.—[*Exit* SERVANT.] Now, Mrs. Dangle, Sir Fretful Plagiary is an author to your own taste.

MRS. DANGLE. I confess he is a favourite of mine, because every body else abuses him.

SNEER. —Very much to the credit of your charity, Madam, if not of your 160 judgment.

DANGLE. But, egad, he allows no merit to any author but himself, that's the truth on't—tho' he's my friend.

SNEER. Never.—He is as envious as an old maid verging on the desperation of six-and-thirty: and then the insiduous humility with which he seduces you to give a free opinion on any of his works, can be exceeded only by the petulant arrogance with which he is sure to reject your observations.[1]

DANGLE. Very true, egad—tho' he's my friend.

SNEER. Then his affected contempt of all newspaper strictures; tho', at 170 the same time, he is the sorest man alive, and shrinks like scorch'd parchment from the fiery ordeal of true criticism: yet is he so covetous of popularity, that he had rather be abused than not mentioned at all.

DANGLE. There's no denying it—tho' he is my friend.

SNEER. You have read the tragedy he has just finished, haven't you?

DANGLE. O yes; he sent it to me yesterday.

SNEER. Well, and you think it execrable, don't you?

DANGLE. Why between ourselves, egad I must own—tho' he's my friend—that it is one of the most——He's here [*Aside*]—finished and most admirable perform——                                           180

[SIR FRETFUL *without*.] Mr. Sneer with him, did you say?

*Enter* SIR FRETFUL.

Ah, my dear friend!—Egad, we were just speaking of your Tragedy.— Admirable, Sir Fretful, admirable!

SNEER. You never did any thing beyond it, Sir Fretful—never in your life.

SIR FRETFUL. You make me extremely happy;—for without a compliment, my dear Sneer, there isn't a man in the world whose judgment I value as I do yours.—And Mr. Dangle's.

MRS. DANGLE. They are only laughing at you, Sir Fretful; for it was but just now that—                                                      190

DANGLE. Mrs. Dangle!—Ah, Sir Fretful, you know Mrs. Dangle.—My friend Sneer was rallying just now—He knows how she admires you, and—

SIR FRETFUL. O Lord—I am sure Mr. Sneer has more taste and sincerity than to——A damn'd double-faced fellow!            [*Aside*.

[1] Partly at the expense of the dramatist, Richard Cumberland (1732–1811).

DANGLE. Yes, yes,—Sneer will jest—but a better humour'd——

SIR FRETFUL. O, I know——

DANGLE. He has a ready turn for ridicule—his wit costs him nothing.—

SIR FRETFUL. No, egad,—or I should wonder how he came by it. [*Aside.*

MRS. DANGLE. Because his jest is always at the expence of his friend.    200

DANGLE. But, Sir Fretful, have you sent your play to the managers yet? —or can I be of any service to you?

SIR FRETFUL. No, no, I thank you; I believe the piece had sufficient recommendation with it.—I thank you tho'.—I sent it to the manager of COVENT-GARDEN THEATRE this morning.

SNEER. I should have thought now, that it might have been cast (as the actors call it) better at DRURY-LANE.

SIR FRETFUL. O lud! no—never send a play there while I live—harkee! [*Whispers* SNEER.]

SNEER. *Writes himself!*—I know he does—[1]                          210

SIR FRETFUL. I say nothing—I take away from no man's merit—am hurt at no man's good fortune—I say nothing—But this I will say— through all my knowledge of life, I have observed—that there is not a passion so strongly rooted in the human heart as envy!

SNEER. I believe you have reason for what you say, indeed.

SIR FRETFUL. Besides—I can tell you it is not always so safe to leave a play in the hands of those who write themselves.[2]

SNEER. What, they may steal from them, hey, my dear Plagiary?

SIR FRETFUL. Steal!—to be sure they may; and, egad, serve your best thoughts as gypsies do stolen children, disfigure them to make 'em pass  220 for their own.[3]

SNEER. But your present work is a sacrifice to Melpomene, and HE, you know, never——

SIR FRETFUL. That's no security.—A dext'rous plagiarist may do any thing.—Why, Sir, for ought I know, he might take out some of the best things in my tragedy, and put them into his own comedy.

SNEER. That might be done, I dare be sworn.

---

[1] Sheridan makes a joke at his own expense.

[2] Cf. Thomas Holcroft's statement of 10 Dec. 1796: '. . . The reading of manuscripts I have found to be attended with danger. I once read two acts of a manuscript play, and was afterwards accused of having purloined one of the characters. The accusation had some semblance of truth: latent ideas floated in my mind, and there were two or three traits in the character drawn by me similar to the one I had read; though I was very unconscious of this when I wrote the character' (W. Dunlap, *A History of the American Theatre* (New York, 1832), p. 159).

[3] T. Moore, *Memoirs of . . . R. B. Sheridan* (2nd edn., 1825), i. 276, sees a resemblance to Charles Churchill's lines in *The Apology* (1761), 234–5:

> Like gypsies, least the stolen brat be known,
> Defacing first, then claiming for his own.

SIR FRETFUL. And then, if such a person gives you the least hint or assistance, he is devilish apt to take the merit of the whole.—

DANGLE. If it succeeds.                                                                  230

SIR FRETFUL. Aye,—but with regard to this piece, I think I can hit that gentleman, for I can safely swear he never read it.

SNEER. I'll tell you how you may hurt him more—

SIR FRETFUL. How?—

SNEER. Swear he wrote it.

SIR FRETFUL. Plague on't now, Sneer, I shall take it ill.—I believe you want to take away my character as an author!

SNEER. Then I am sure you ought to be very much oblig'd to me.

SIR FRETFUL. Hey!—Sir!—

DANGLE. O you know, he never means what he says.                                  240

SIR FRETFUL. Sincerely then—you do like the piece?

SNEER. Wonderfully!

SIR FRETFUL. But come now, there must be something that you think might be mended, hey?—Mr. Dangle, has nothing struck you?

DANGLE. Why faith, it is but an ungracious thing for the most part to—

SIR FRETFUL. —With most authors it is just so indeed; they are in general strangely tenacious!—But, for my part, I am never so well pleased as when a judicious critic[1] points out any defect to me; for what is the purpose of shewing a work to a friend, if you don't mean to profit by his opinion?                                                      250

SNEER. Very true.—Why then, tho' I seriously admire the piece upon the whole, yet there is one small objection; which, if you'll give me leave, I'll mention.

SIR FRETFUL. SIR, you can't oblige me more.

SNEER. I think it wants incident.

SIR FRETFUL. Good God!—you surprize me!—wants incident!—

SNEER. Yes; I own I think the incidents are too few.

SIR FRETFUL. Good God!—Believe me, Mr. Sneer, there is no person for whose judgment I have a more implicit deference.—But I protest to you, Mr. Sneer, I am only apprehensive that the incidents are too    260 crowded.—My dear Dangle, how does it strike you?

DANGLE. Really I can't agree with my friend Sneer.—I think the plot quite sufficient; and the four first acts by many degrees the best I ever read or saw in my life. If I might venture to suggest any thing, it is that the interest rather falls off in the fifth.—

SIR FRETFUL. —Rises; I believe you mean, Sir.

DANGLE. No; I don't upon my word.

SIR FRETFUL. Yes, yes, you do upon my soul—it certainly don't fall off, I assure you—No, no, it don't fall off.

[1] Sheridan quotes this phrase as 'Nothing is so pleasant as a judicious Critic who—', when inviting Fitzpatrick to see the play. Cf. *Letters*, i. 129.

DANGLE. Now, Mrs. Dangle, didn't you say it struck you in the same 270
light?

MRS. DANGLE. No, indeed, I did not—I did not see a fault in any part of
the play from the beginning to the end.

SIR FRETFUL. Upon my soul the women are the best judges after all!

MRS. DANGLE. Or if I made any objection, I am sure it was to nothing in
the piece; but that I was afraid it was, on the whole, a little too long.

SIR FRETFUL. Pray, Madam, do you speak as to duration of time; or do
you mean that the story is tediously spun out?

MRS. DANGLE. O Lud! no.—I speak only with reference to the usual
length of acting plays. 280

SIR FRETFUL. Then I am very happy—very happy indeed,—because the
play is a short play, a remarkably short play:—I should not venture to
differ with a lady on a point of taste; but, on these occasions, the watch,
you know, is the critic.

MRS. DANGLE. Then, I suppose, it must have been Mr. Dangle's
drawling manner of reading it to me.

SIR FRETFUL. O, if Mr. Dangle read it! that's quite another affair!—
But I assure you, Mrs. Dangle, the first evening you can spare me three
hours and an half, I'll undertake to read you the whole from beginning
to end, with the Prologue and Epilogue, and allow time for the music 290
between the acts.

MRS. DANGLE. I hope to see it on the stage next.

DANGLE. Well, Sir Fretful, I wish you may be able to get rid as easily of
the news-paper criticisms as you do of ours.—

SIR FRETFUL. The NEWS-PAPERS!—Sir, they are the most villainous—
licentious—abominable—infernal—Not that I ever read them—No—I
make it a rule never to look into a news-paper.

DANGLE. You are quite right—for it certainly must hurt an author of
delicate feelings to see the liberties they take.

SIR FRETFUL. No!—quite the contrary;—their abuse is, in fact, the 300
best panegyric—I like it of all things.—An author's reputation is only
in danger from their support.

SNEER. Why that's true—and that attack now on you the other day——

SIR FRETFÚL. ——What? where?

DANGLE. Aye, you mean in a paper of Thursday; it was compleatly
ill-natur'd to be sure.

SIR FRETFUL. O, so much the better.—Ha! ha! ha!—I wou'dn't have it
otherwise.

DANGLE. Certainly it is only to be laugh'd at; for—

SIR FRETFUL. —You don't happen to recollect what the fellow said, do you? 310

SNEER. Pray, Dangle—Sir Fretful seems a little anxious—

SIR FRETFUL. —O lud, no!—anxious,—not I,—not the least.—I—But
one may as well hear you know.

DANGLE.  Sneer, do *you* recollect?—Make out something.          [*Aside.*

SNEER.  I will, [*to* DANGLE.]—Yes, yes, I remember perfectly.

SIR FRETFUL.  Well, and pray now—Not that it signifies—what might the gentleman say?

SNEER.  Why, he roundly asserts that you have not the slightest invention, or original genius whatever; tho' you are the greatest traducer of all other authors living.                                                                                     320

SIR FRETFUL.  Ha! ha! ha!—very good!

SNEER.  That as to COMEDY, you have not one idea of your own, he believes, even in your common place-book[1]—where stray jokes, and pilfered witticisms are kept with as much method as the ledger of the LOST-and-STOLEN-OFFICE.

SIR FRETFUL.  —Ha! ha! ha!—very pleasant!

SNEER.  Nay, that you are so unlucky as not to have the skill even to *steal* with taste.—But that you gleen from the refuse of obscure volumes, where more judicious plagiarists have been before you; so that the body of your work is a composition of dregs and sediments—      330 like a bad tavern's worst wine.

SIR FRETFUL.  Ha! ha!

SNEER.  In your more serious efforts, he says, your bombast would be less intolerable, if the thoughts were ever suited to the expression; but the homeliness of the sentiment stares thro' the fantastic encumbrance of its fine language, like a clown in one of the new uniforms!

SIR FRETFUL.  Ha! ha!

SNEER.  That your occasional tropes and flowers suit the general coarseness of your stile, as tambour sprigs would a ground of linsey-wolsey;[2] while your imitations of Shakespeare resemble the mimicry of Falstaff's     340 Page,[3] and are about as near the standard of the original.

SIR FRETFUL.  Ha!—

SNEER.  —In short, that even the finest passages you steal are of no service to you; for the poverty of your own language prevents their assimilating; so that they lie on the surface like lumps of marl[4] on a barren moor, encumbering what it is not in their power to fertilize!—

SIR FRETFUL.  [*after great agitation.*]——Now another person would be vex'd at this.

SNEER.  Oh! but I wou'dn't have told you, only to divert you.

SIR FRETFUL.  I know it—I *am* diverted,—Ha! ha! ha!—not the least     350 invention!—Ha! ha! ha! very good!—very good!

---

[1] Cf. Buckingham's *The Rehearsal*, I. i: 'This is my book of *Drama Commonplaces*, the mother of many other plays.'

[2] Elaborate embroidery on a very ordinary fabric of wool and linen.

[3] *2 Henry IV*, II. ii. 75–7: 'Look, if the fat villain have not transformed him ape.'

[4] 'A kind of dry, soft, fossile earth, harsh to the touch; used to be cast on land, to make it more fruitful' (E. Chambers, *Cyclopædia* (5th edn., 1743), *under* 'marle').

SNEER. Yes—no genius! Ha! ha! ha!

DANGLE. A severe rogue! Ha! ha! ha! But you are quite right, Sir Fretful, never to read such nonsense.

SIR FRETFUL. To be sure—for if there is any thing to one's praise, it is a foolish vanity to be gratified at it, and if it is abuse,—why one is always sure to hear of it from one damn'd good natur'd friend or another!

*Enter* SERVANT.

Sir, there is an Italian gentleman, with a French Interpreter, and three young ladies, and a dozen musicians, who say they are sent by LADY RONDEAU and MRS. FUGE.                                            360

DANGLE. Gadso! they come by appointment. Dear Mrs. Dangle do let them know I'll see them directly.

MRS. DANGLE. You know, Mr. Dangle, I shan't understand a word they say.

DANGLE. But you hear there's an interpreter.

MRS. DANGLE. Well, I'll try to endure their complaisance till you come.
                                                            [*Exit.*

SERVANT. And Mr. PUFF, Sir, has sent word that the last rehearsal is to be this morning, and that he'll call on you presently.

DANGLE. That's true—I shall certainly be at home. [*Exit* SERVANT.] Now, Sir Fretful, if you have a mind to have justice done you in the way 370 of answer—Egad, Mr. PUFF's your man.

SIR FRETFUL. Pshaw! Sir, why should I wish to have it answered, when I tell you I am pleased at it?

DANGLE. True, I had forgot that.—But I hope you are not fretted at what Mr. Sneer——

SIR FRETFUL. —Zounds! no, Mr. Dangle, don't I tell you these things never fret me in the least.

DANGLE. Nay, I only thought——

SIR FRETFUL. —And let me tell you, Mr. Dangle, 'tis damn'd affronting in you to suppose that I am hurt, when I tell you I am not.          380

SNEER. But why so warm, Sir Fretful?

SIR FRETFUL. Gadslife! Mr. Sneer, you are as absurd as Dangle; how often must I repeat it to you, that nothing can vex me but your supposing it possible for me to mind the damn'd nonsense you have been repeating to me!—and let me tell you, if you continue to believe this, you must mean to insult me, gentlemen—and then your disrespect will affect me no more than the news-paper criticisms—and I shall treat it— with exactly the same calm indifference and philosophic contempt— and so your servant.                                        [*Exit.*

SNEER. Ha! ha! ha! Poor Sir Fretful! Now will he go and vent his 390 philosophy in anonymous abuse of all modern critics and authors—

But, Dangle, you must get your friend PUFF to take me to the rehearsal of his tragedy.

DANGLE. I'll answer for't, he'll thank you for desiring it. But come and help me to judge of this musical family; they are recommended by people of consequence, I assure you.

SNEER. I am at your disposal the whole morning—but I thought you had been a decided critic in musick, as well as in literature?

DANGLE. So I am—but I have a bad ear.—Efaith, Sneer, tho', I am afraid we were a little too severe on Sir Fretful—tho' he is my friend.  400

SNEER. Why, 'tis certain, that unnecessarily to mortify the vanity of any writer, is a cruelty which mere dulness never can deserve; but where a base and personal malignity usurps the place of literary emulation, the aggressor deserves neither quarter nor pity.

DANGLE. That's true egad!—tho' he's my friend!


## SCENE II

*A Drawing Room, Harpsichord, &c. Italian Family, French Interpreter,* MRS. DANGLE *and* SERVANTS *discovered.*

INTERPRETER. Je dis madame, ja'i l'honneur to *introduce* & de vous demander votre protection pour le Signor PASTICCIO RETORNELLO & pour sa charmante famille.

SIGNOR PASTICCIO. Ah! Vosignoria noi vi preghiamo di favoritevi colla vostra protezione.

IST DAUGHTER. Vosignoria fatevi questi grazzie.

2D DAUGHTER. Si Signora.

INTERPRETER. Madame—*me interpret.*—C'est à dire—in English— qu'ils vous prient de leur faire l'honneur—

MRS. DANGLE. —I say again, gentlemen, I don't understand a word you  10 say.

SIGNOR PASTICCIO. Questo Signore spiegheró.

INTERPRETER. Oui—*me .interpret.*—nous avons les lettres de recommendation pour Monsieur Dangle de——

MRS. DANGLE. —Upon my word, Sir, I don't understand you.

SIGNOR PASTICCIO. La CONTESSA RONDEAU e nostra padrona.

3D DAUGHTER. Si, padre, & mi LADI FUGE.

INTERPRETER. O!—*me interpret.*—Madame, ils disent—*in* English— Qu'ils ont l'honneur d'etre protegés de ces Dames.—*You understand?*

MRS. DANGLE. No, Sir,——no understand!  20

*Enter* DANGLE *and* SNEER.

INTERPRETER. Ah voici Monsieur Dangle!

ALL ITALIANS. A! Signor Dangle!

MRS. DANGLE. Mr. Dangle, here are two very civil gentlemen trying to
  make themselves understood, and I don't know which is the interpreter.
DANGLE. Ebien!

INTERPRETER. Monsieur Dangle—le grand bruit de vos talents pour
  la critique & de votre interest avec Messieurs les Directeurs a tous
  les Theatres.
SIGNOR PASTICCIO. Vosignoria siete si famoso par la vostra conos-
  censa e vostra interessa colla le Direttore da—                         30

*Speaking together.*

DANGLE. Egad I think the Interpreter is the hardest to be understood of
  the two!
SNEER. Why I thought, Dangle, you had been an admirable linguist!
DANGLE. So I am, if they would not talk so damn'd fast.
SNEER. Well I'll explain that—the less time we lose in hearing them the
  better,—for that I suppose is what they are brought here for.
                              [SNEER *speaks to* SIG. PAST.—*They sing
                              trios,*[1] *&c.* DANGLE *beating out of time.*
                              SERVANT *enters and whispers* DANGLE.
DANGLE. Shew him up.                              [*Exit* SERVANT.
  Bravo! admirable! bravissimo! admirablissimo!—Ah! Sneer! where will
  you find such as these voices in England?
SNEER. Not easily.                                                        40
DANGLE. But PUFF is coming.—Signor and little Signora's—obliga-
  tissimo!—Sposa Signora Danglena—Mrs. Dangle, shall I beg you to
  offer them some refreshments, and take their address in the next room.
                              [*Exit* MRS. DANGLE *with the* ITALIANS
                              *and* INTERPRETER *ceremoniously.*

*Re-enter* SERVANT.

  Mr. PUFF, Sir.
DANGLE. My dear PUFF!

*Enter* PUFF.

  My dear Dangle, how is it with you?
DANGLE. Mr. Sneer, give me leave to introduce Mr. PUFF to you.
PUFF. Mr. Sneer is this? Sir, he is a gentleman whom I have long panted
  for the honour of knowing—a gentleman whose critical talents and
  transcendant judgment——                                                50
SNEER. —Dear Sir——

  [1] Delpini, Miss Field, and Miss Abrams sang trios in French. The English first-lines
were 'I left my Country and my Friends' and 'A maiden blush of sweet fifteen'. But at
the first performance the two women sang an Italian duet, and joined Delpini in 'I left
my Country'.

DANGLE. Nay, don't be modest, Sneer, my friend PUFF only talks to you in the stile of his profession.

SNEER. His profession!

PUFF. Yes, Sir; I make no secret of the trade I follow—among friends and brother authors, Dangle knows I love to be frank on the subject, and to advertise myself *vivâ voce.*—I am, Sir, a Practitioner in Panegyric, or to speak more plainly—a Professor of the Art of Puffing,[1] at your service—or any body else's.

SNEER. Sir, you are very obliging!—I believe, Mr. Puff, I have often 60 admired your talents in the daily prints.

PUFF. Yes, Sir, I flatter myself I do as much business in that way as any six of the fraternity in town—Devilish hard work all the summer— Friend Dangle? never work'd harder!—But harkee,—the Winter Managers were a little sore I believe.

DANGLE. No—I believe they took it all in good part.

PUFF. Aye!—Then that must have been affectation in them, for egad, there were some of the attacks which there was no laughing at!

SNEER. Aye, the humourous ones.—But I should think Mr. Puff, that Authors would in general be able to do this sort of work for 70 themselves.

PUFF. Why yes—but in a clumsy way.—Besides, we look on that as an encroachment, and so take the opposite side.—I dare say now you conceive half the very civil paragraphs and advertisements you see, to be written by the parties concerned, or their friends?—No such thing— Nine out of ten, manufactured by me in the way of business.

SNEER. Indeed!—

PUFF. Even the Auctioneers now,—the Auctioneers I say, tho' the rogues have lately got some credit for their language—not an article of the merit their's![2]—take them out of their Pulpits, and they are as dull as 80 Catalogues.——No, Sir;—'twas I first enrich'd their style—'twas I first taught them to crowd their advertisements with panegyrical superlatives, each epithet rising above the other—like the Bidders in their own Auction-rooms! From ME they learn'd to enlay their phraseology with variegated chips of exotic metaphor: by ME too their inventive faculties were called forth.—Yes Sir, by ME they were instructed to clothe ideal walls with gratuitous fruits—to insinuate obsequious rivulets into visionary groves—to teach courteous shrubs to nod their approbation of the grateful soil! or on emergencies to raise upstart oaks, where there never had been an acorn; to create a delightful vicinage 90 without the assistance of a neighbour; or fix the temple of Hygeia in the fens of Lincolnshire!

---

[1] Sheridan was competent in this line himself. See W. Fraser Rae, *Sheridan* (1896), ii. 6 n.

[2] Robert Langford, the auctioneer, is the butt here.

DANGLE. I am sure, you have done them infinite service; for now, when a gentleman is ruined, he parts with his house with some credit.

SNEER. Service! if they had any gratitude, they would erect a statue to him, they would figure him as a presiding Mercury, the god of traffic and fiction, with a hammer in his hand instead of a caduceus.[1]—But pray, Mr. Puff, what first put you on exercising your talents in this way?

PUFF. Egad sir,—sheer necessity—the proper parent of an art so nearly allied to invention: you must know Mr. Sneer, that from the first time I tried my hand at an advertisement, my success was such, that for sometime after, I led a most extraordinary life indeed! 100

SNEER. How, pray?

PUFF. Sir, I supported myself two years entirely by my misfortunes.

SNEER. By your misfortunes!

PUFF. Yes Sir, assisted by long sickness, and other occasional disorders; and a very comfortable living I had of it.

SNEER. From sickness and misfortunes!—You practised as a Doctor, and an Attorney at once?

PUFF. No egad, both maladies and miseries were my own. 110

SNEER. Hey!—what the plague!

DANGLE. 'Tis true, efaith.

PUFF. Harkee!—By advertisements—'To the charitable and humane!'[2] and 'to those whom Providence hath blessed with affluence!'

SNEER. Oh,—I understand you.

PUFF. And in truth, I deserved what I got, for I suppose never man went thro' such a series of calamities in the same space of time!—Sir, I was five times made a bankrupt, and reduced from a state of affluence, by a train of unavoidable misfortunes! then Sir, tho' a very industrious tradesman, I was twice burnt out, and lost my little all, both times!—I 120 lived upon those fires a month.—I soon after was confined by a most excruciating disorder, and lost the use of my limbs!—That told very well, for I had the case strongly attested, and went about to collect the subscriptions myself.

DANGLE. Egad, I believe that was when you first called on me.—

---

[1] 'I perceived a tall young gentleman in a silk waistcoat, with a wing on his left heel, a garland on his head, and a caduceus in his right hand.

This is the dress in which the god appears to mortals at the theatres' (H. Fielding, *A Journey from this World to the Next* (ed. C. Rawson, 1973), p. 5.

[2] Cf. 'To the Affluent and Humane' in the *Public Advertiser*, 18 Aug. 1779: 'A Man of unblemished Character, having been a Housekeeper many Years, and carried on his Business with a Prospect of not knowing his present unhappy Situation; but through the Vicissitudes of Life, and unavoidable Misfortunes, together with the Decay of his Business, is reduced to the very lowest State of Adversity. He has a very large Family of small Children, all dependent on him for Support, and is unable to provide them with the common Necessaries of Life; it having pleased the Almighty frequently to afflict some of them with Sickness, which renders their Case extremely deplorable; they have been obliged to part with almost every Necessary for Bread . . . .'

PUFF. —In November last?—O no!—I was at that time, a close prisoner in the Marshalsea,[1] for a debt benevolently contracted to serve a friend!—I was afterwards, twice tapped for a dropsy, which declined into a very profitable consumption!—I was then reduced to—O no— then, I became a widow with six helpless children,—after having had 130 eleven husbands pressed, and being left every time eight months gone with child, and without money to get me into an hospital!

SNEER. And you bore all with patience, I make no doubt?

PUFF. Why, yes,—tho' I made some occasional attempts at felo de se; but as I did not find those *rash actions* answer, I left off killing myself very soon.—Well, Sir,—at last, what with bankruptcies, fires, gouts, dropsies, imprisonments, and other valuable calamities, having got together a pretty handsome sum, I determined to quit a business which had always gone rather against my conscience, and in a more liberal way still to indulge my talents for fiction and embellishment, thro' my 140 favourite channels of diurnal communication—and so, Sir, you have my history.

SNEER. Most obligingly communicative indeed; and your confession if published, might certainly serve the cause of true charity, by rescuing the most useful channels of appeal to benevolence from the cant of imposition.—But surely, Mr. PUFF, there is no great *mystery* in your present profession?

PUFF. Mystery! Sir, I will take upon me to say the matter was never scientifically treated, nor reduced to rule before.

SNEER. Reduced to rule? 150

PUFF. O lud, Sir! you are very ignorant, I am afraid.—Yes Sir,— PUFFING is of various sorts—the principal are, The PUFF DIRECT— the PUFF PRELIMINARY—the PUFF COLLATERAL—the PUFF COLLUSIVE, and the PUFF OBLIQUE, or PUFF by IMPLICATION.— These all assume, as circumstances require, the various forms of LETTER TO THE EDITOR—OCCASIONAL ANECDOTE—IMPARTIAL CRITIQUE—OBSERVATION from CORRESPONDENT,—or ADVER- TISEMENT FROM THE PARTY.[2]

SNEER. The puff direct, I can conceive—

PUFF. O yes, that's simple enough,—for instance—A new Comedy or 160 Farce is to be produced at one of the Theatres (though by the bye they don't bring out half what they ought to do). The author, suppose Mr. Smatter,[3] or Mr. Dapper—or any particular friend of mine—very well;

[1] The debtors' prison on the south bank of the Thames and abutting Borough High Street, that ran to London Bridge.

[2] 'A kind of parody of Touchstone's dissertation on the lye in quarrelling. . . . The only proper object which appears to have been omitted, is what are called the house paragraphs for the theatres' (*General Evening Post*, 30 Oct.–2 Nov. 1779).

[3] 'Jack Smatter' was a character (played by the youthful Garrick) in James Dance's *Pamela* (1740), an adaptation of Richardson's novel.

the day before it is to be performed, I write an account of the manner in which it was received—I have the plot from the author,—and only add—Characters strongly drawn—highly coloured—hand of a master—fund of genuine humour—mine of invention—neat dialogue—attic salt! Then for the performance—Mr. DODD was astonishingly great in the character of SIR HARRY![1] That universal and judicious actor Mr. PALMER, perhaps never appeared to more advantage than in the COLONEL;[2]—but it is not in the power of language to do justice to Mr. KING![3]—Indeed he more than merited those repeated bursts of applause which he drew from a most brilliant and judicious audience! As to the scenery—The miraculous power of Mr. DE LOUTHER-BOURG's pencil[4] are universally acknowledged!—In short, we are at a loss which to admire most,—the unrivalled genius of the author, the great attention and liberality of the managers—the wonderful abilities of the painter, or the incredible exertions of all the performers!—

SNEER. That's pretty well indeed, Sir.

PUFF. O cool—quite cool—to what I sometimes do.

SNEER. And do you think there are any who are influenced by this.

PUFF. O, lud! yes, Sir;—the number of those who go thro' the fatigue of judging for themselves is very small indeed!

SNEER. Well, Sir,—the PUFF PRELIMINARY?

PUFF. O that, Sir, does well in the form of a *Caution*.—In a matter of gallantry now—Sir FLIMSY GOSSIMER, wishes to be well with LADY FANNY FETE—He applies to me——I open trenches for him with a paragraph in the Morning Post.——It is recommended to the beautiful and accomplished Lady F four stars F dash E to be on her guard against that dangerous character, Sir F dash G; who, however pleasing and insinuating his manners may be, is certainly not remarkable for the *constancy of his attachments!*—in Italics.—Here you see, Sir FLIMSY GOSSIMER is introduced to the particular notice of Lady FANNY—who, perhaps never thought of him before—she finds herself publickly cautioned to avoid him, which naturally makes her desirous of seeing him;—the observation of their acquaintance causes a pretty kind of mutual embarrassment, this produces a sort of sympathy of interest—which, if Sir Flimsy is unable to improve effectually, he at least gains the credit of having their names mentioned together, by a particular

---

[1] The best-known 'Sir Harry' was Sir Harry Wildair in Farquhar's *The Constant Couple*, but the reference may be to Dodd as Sir Harry Bouquet in *The Camp*. He created the part of Dangle.

[2] The best-known 'Colonel' is Colonel Standard in *The Constant Couple* (taken by Palmer from 8 May 1776). A 'Colonel Promise' and a 'Sir Harry Foxchase' are to be found in Fielding's *Pasquin* (1736), but this satire had not been acted for many years.

[3] Thomas King (1730–1805) created Puff and Sir Peter at Drury Lane Theatre.

[4] Philippe de Loutherbourgh (1730–1812), painter and stage designer.

set, and in a particular way,—which nine times out of ten is the full    200
accomplishment of modern gallantry!

DANGLE. Egad, Sneer, you will be quite an adept in the business.

PUFF. Now, Sir, the PUFF COLLATERAL is much used as an appendage
to advertisements, and may take the form of anecdote.—Yesterday as
the celebrated GEORGE BON-MOT was sauntering down St. James's-
street, he met the lively Lady MARY MYRTLE, coming out of the
Park,—'Good God, LADY MARY, I'm surprised to meet you in a white
jacket,—for I expected never to have seen you, but in a full-trimmed
uniform, and a light-horseman's cap!'—'Heavens, GEORGE, where
could you have learned that?'—'Why, replied the wit, I just saw a    210
print of you, in a new publication called The CAMP MAGAZINE,
which, by the bye, is a devilish clever thing,—and is sold at No. 3, on
the right hand of the way, two doors from the printing-office, the
corner of Ivy-lane, Paternoster-row, price only one shilling!'[1]

SNEER. Very ingenious indeed!

PUFF. But the PUFF COLLUSIVE is the newest of any; for it acts in the
disguise of determined hostility.—It is much used by bold booksellers
and enterprising poets.—An indignant correspondent observes—that
the new poem called BEELZEBUB'S COTILLION, or PROSER-
PINE'S FETE CHAMPETRE, is one of the most unjustifiable perfor-    220
mances he ever read! The severity with which certain characters are
handled is quite shocking! And as there are many descriptions in it too
warmly coloured for female delicacy, the shameful avidity with which
this piece is bought by all people of fashion, is a reproach on the taste
of the times, and a disgrace to the delicacy of the age!—Here you see
the two strongest inducements are held forth;—First, that nobody
ought to read it;—and secondly, that every body buys it; on the strength
of which, the publisher boldly prints the tenth edition, before he had
sold ten of the first; and then establishes it by threatening himself with
the pillory, or absolutely indicting himself for SCAN. MAG.![2]    230

DANGLE. Ha! ha! ha!—'gad I know it is so.

PUFF. As to the PUFF OBLIQUE, or PUFF BY IMPLICATION, it is too
various and extensive to be illustrated by an instance;—it attracts in
titles, and presumes in patents; it lurks in the *limitation* of a subscription, and invites in the assurance of croud and incommodation at public
places; it delights to draw forth concealed merit, with a most disinterested assiduity; and sometimes wears a countenance of smiling censure

---

[1] '*The Morning Post* . . . is memorable for teaching advertisers how to write; and what
*Puff* says in the *Critic*, has certainly its origin from the superior style in which auctions
were advertised in *The Morning Post*, which set every body mad for high-flown,
paragraphical descriptions of trifles' (*The Musical Tour of Mr. Dibdin* (Sheffield, 1788),
pp. 428–9).

[2] Scandalum magnatum: defaming the highest in the realm.

and tender reproach.—It has a wonderful memory for Parliamentary Debates, and will often give the whole speech of a favoured member, with the most flattering accuracy.[1] But, above all, it is a great dealer in 240 reports and suppositions.—It has the earliest intelligence of intended preferments that will reflect *honor* on the *patrons*; and embryo promotions of modest gentlemen—who know nothing of the matter themselves. It can hint a ribband for implied services, in the air of a common report; and with the carelessness of a casual paragraph, suggest officers into commands—to which they have no pretension but their wishes. This, Sir, is the last principal class in the ART of PUFFING——An art which I hope you will now agree with me, is of the highest dignity—yielding a tablature of benevolence and public spirit; befriending equally trade, gallantry, criticism, and politics: the applause of genius! the register of 250 charity! the triumph of heroism! the self defence of contractors! the fame of orators!—and the gazette of ministers![2]

SNEER. Sir, I am compleatly a convert both to the importance and ingenuity of your profession; and now, Sir, there is but one thing which can possibly encrease my respect for you, and that is, your permitting me to be present this morning at the rehearsal of your new trage——

PUFF. —Hush, for heaven's sake.—*My* tragedy!—Egad, Dangle, I take this very ill—you know how apprehensive I am of being known to be the author.

DANGLE. 'Efaith I would not have told—but it's in the papers, and your 260 name at length—in the Morning Chronicle.

PUFF. Ah! those damn'd editors never can keep a secret!—Well, Mr. Sneer—no doubt you will do me great honour—I shall be infinitely happy—highly flattered——

DANGLE. I believe it must be near the time—shall we go together.

PUFF. No; It will not be yet this hour, for they are always late at that theatre: besides, I must meet you there, for I have some little matters here to send to the papers, and a few paragraphs to scribble before I go.

[*Looking at memorandums.*

—Here is 'a CONSCIENTIOUS BAKER, on the Subject of the Army Bread;' and 'a DETESTER OF VISIBLE BRICK-WORK, in favor of the 270 new invented Stucco;' both in the style of JUNIUS,[3] and promised for

---

[1] 'Looking at Messrs. Dilly's splendid edition of Lord Chesterfield's miscellaneous works, he [Johnson] laughed, and said, 'Here now are two speeches ascribed to him, both of which were written by me' (J. Boswell, *Life of Johnson*, ed. G. B. Hill; revd., L. F. Powell (Oxford, 1934), iii. 351). W. Woodfall was famous for his accurate reports.

[2] Boaden, *Kemble*, i. 67–8, sees a resemblance in manner of putting the points and in cadence of language, to Isaac Barrow's *Second Sermon on Evil Speaking* (1678), p. 44.

[3] 'Junius' is believed to have been Sir Philip Francis (1740–1818), and his letters, published in the *Public Advertiser* between 1769 and 1772, fiercely attacked George III and his ministers. Coleridge thought the letter to the King 'almost faultless in com-

to-morrow.—The Thames navigation too is at a stand.[1]—MISOMUD or ANTI-SHOAL must go to work again directly.—Here too are some political memorandums I see; aye—To take PAUL JONES,[2] and get the INDIAMEN out of the SHANNON—reinforce BYRON[3]—compel the DUTCH to—so!—I must do that in the evening papers, or reserve it for the Morning Herald, for I know that I have undertaken to-morrow, besides, to establish the unanimity of the fleet in the Public Advertiser, and to shoot CHARLES FOX[4] in the Morning Post.—So, egad, I ha'n't a moment to lose!                                                    280

DANGLE. Well!—we'll meet in the Green Room.        [*Exeunt severally.*

END OF ACT I


# ACT II

## SCENE I

### The THEATRE

*Enter* DANGLE, PUFF, *and* SNEER, *as before the Curtain.*

PUFF. No, no, Sir; what Shakespeare says of ACTORS may be better applied to the purpose of PLAYS; *they* ought to be 'the abstract and brief Chronicles of the times.' Therefore when history, and particularly the history of our own country, furnishes any thing like a case in point, to the time in which an author writes, if he knows his own interest, he will take advantage of it; so, Sir, I call my tragedy The SPANISH ARMADA; and have laid the scene before TILBURY FORT.

SNEER. A most happy thought certainly!

DANGLE. Egad it was—I told you so.—But pray now I dont understand how you have contrived to introduce any love into it.        10

PUFF. Love!—Oh nothing so easy; for it is a received point among poets, that where history gives you a good heroic out-line for a play, you may fill up with a little love at your own discretion; in doing which, nine

---

position': see *The Letters of Junius*, ed. C. W. Everard (1927), pp. lvi, 135–48. For Sheridan's interest in 'Junius', see *Letters*, i. 3–4, 6, 8; iii. 159.

    [1] Trinity House was attacked in the newspapers for not dredging the Thames adequately: see the *Public Advertiser*, 26 Oct. 1779.

    [2] John Paul Jones (1747–92), privateer, effectively menaced the shipping of Britain on behalf of the American revolutionaries.

    [3] John Byron (1723–86), circumnavigator. He commanded the West Indies fleet, 1778–9.

    [4] Charles James Fox (1749–1806), a leader of the opposition to the King, particularly in attacking naval policy.

times out of ten, you only make up a deficiency in the private history
of the times.—Now I rather think I have done this with some success.

SNEER. No scandal about Queen ELIZABETH, I hope?

PUFF. O Lud! no, no.—I only suppose the Governor of Tilbury Fort's[1]
daughter to be in love with the son of the Spanish Admiral.

SNEER. Oh, is that all?

DANGLE. Excellent, Efaith!—I see it at once.—But won't this appear    20
rather improbable?

PUFF. To be sure it will—but what the plague! a play is not to shew
occurrences that happen every day, but things just so strange, that tho'
they never *did*, they *might* happen.

SNEER. Certainly nothing is unnatural, that is not physically impossible.

PUFF. Very true—and for that matter DON FEROLO WHISKERANDOS
—for that's the lover's name, might have been over here in the train of
the Spanish Ambassador; or TILBURINA, for that is the lady's name,
might have been in love with him, from having heard his character, or
seen his picture; or from knowing that he was the last man in the world   30
she ought to be in love with—or for any other good female reason.—
However, Sir, the fact is, that tho' she is but a Knight's daughter, egad!
she is in love like any Princess!

DANGLE. Poor young lady! I feel for her already! for I can conceive how
great the conflict must be between her passion and her duty; her love
for her country, and her love for DON FEROLO WHISKERANDOS!

PUFF. O amazing!—her poor susceptible heart is swayed to and fro, by
contending passions like—

*Enter* UNDER PROMPTER.

UNDER PROMPTER. Sir, the scene is set, and every thing is ready to
begin if you please.—[2]                                                40

PUFF. 'Egad; then we'll lose no time.

UNDER PROMPTER. Tho' I believe, Sir, you will find it very short, for
all the performers have profited by the kind permission you granted
them.

PUFF. Hey! what!

UNDER PROMPTER. You know, Sir, you gave them leave to cut out or

---

[1] Built in the reign of Henry VIII to defend the mouth of the Thames. R. Brookes,
*The General Gazetteer* (8th edn., 1797), describes it as 'a regular fortification, which may
be termed the key to London'. He adds that it has 'a platform . . . on which are planted
106 guns'.

[2] 'The purpose aimed at is effected by a kind of burlesque parody, of which there
are some thousand lines extended through the greater part of two acts. These must
have been a very tedious, laborious, and disgusting task; and the effect of this kind of
ridicule is so very strong, that it soon grows tiresome and disagreeable. The public
opinion of modern tragedy is already so very low, as appears by their general desertion,
that the game is hardly worth the pursuit' (*General Evening Post*, 30 Oct.–2 Nov. 1779).

omit whatever they found heavy or unnecessary to the plot, and I must own they have taken very liberal advantage of your indulgence.

PUFF. Well, well.—They are in general very good judges; and I know I am luxuriant.—Now, Mr. HOPKINS,[1] as soon as you please.          50

UNDER PROMPTER *to the Musick*. Gentlemen, will you play a few bars of something, just to—

PUFF. Aye, that's right,—for as we have the scenes, and dresses, egad, we'll go to't, as if it was the first night's performance;—but you need not mind stopping between the acts.          [*Exit* UNDER PROMPTER.

[*Orchestra play. Then the Bell rings.*]

Soh! stand clear gentlemen.—Now you know there will be a cry of down!—down!—hats off! silence!—Then up curtain,—and let us see what our painters have done for us.


SCENE II

*The Curtain rises and discovers* TILBURY FORT

*Two Centinels asleep.*

DANGLE. Tilbury Fort!—very fine indeed!

PUFF. Now, what do you think I open with?

SNEER. Faith, I can't guess—

PUFF. A clock.—Hark!—[*clock strikes.*] I open with a clock striking, to beget an aweful attention in the audience—it also marks the time, which is four o'clock in the morning, and saves a description of the rising sun,[2] and a great deal about gilding the eastern hemisphere.

DANGLE. But pray, are the centinels to be asleep?

PUFF. Fast as watchmen.

SNEER. Isn't that odd tho' at such an alarming crisis?          10

PUFF. To be sure it is,—but smaller things must give way to a striking scene at the opening; that's a rule.—And the case is, that two great men are coming to this very spot to begin the piece; now, it is not to be supposed they would open their lips, if these fellows were watching them, so, egad, I must either have sent them off their posts, or set them asleep.

SNEER. O that accounts for it!—But tell us, who are these coming?—

---

[1] William Hopkins, prompter and copyist at Drury Lane Theatre, 1760–80.
[2] Cf. R. Cumberland, *The Battle of Hastings* (1778), III. i:

> Invention never yok'd
> A fairer courser to Apollo's car,
> When with the zephyrs and the rosy hours
> Through heav'n's bright portal he ascends the east,
> And on his beamy forehead brings the morn.

PUFF. These are they—SIR WALTER RALEIGH, and SIR CHRISTO-
PHER HATTON.—You'll know Sir CHRISTOPHER, by his turning out
his toes—famous you know for his dancing. I like to preserve all the    20
little traits of character.—Now attend.

> *Enter* SIR WALTER RALEIGH *and* SIR
> CHRISTOPHER HATTON.
> 'SIR CHRISTOPHER.
> 'True, gallant Raleigh!—

DANGLE. What, they had been talking before?[1]
PUFF. O, yes; all the way as they came along.—I beg pardon gentlemen
[*to the Actors*] but these are particular friends of mine, whose remarks
may be of great service to us.—Don't mind interrupting them whenever
any thing strikes you. [*To* SNEER *and* DANGLE.]

> 'SIR CHRISTOPHER.
> 'True, gallant Raleigh!                    30
> But O, thou champion of thy country's fame,
> There *is* a question which·I yet must ask;
> A question, which I never ask'd before—
> What mean these mighty armaments?
> This general muster? and this throng of chiefs?

SNEER. Pray, Mr. Puff, how came Sir Christopher Hatton never to ask
that question before?
PUFF. What, before the Play began? how the plague could he?
DANGLE. That's true efaith!
PUFF. But you will hear what he thinks of the matter.                    40

> 'SIR CHRISTOPHER.
> 'Alas, my noble friend, when I behold
> Yon tented plains in martial symmetry
> Array'd.——When I count o'er yon glittering lines
> Of crested warriors, where the proud steeds neigh,
> And valor-breathing trumpet's shrill appeal,
> Responsive vibrate on my listning ear;
> When virgin majesty herself I view,[2]

---

[1] Cf. Buckingham's *The Rehearsal*, II. i:
*Physician.* Sir, to conclude.
*Smith.* What, before he begins?
*Bayes.* No, Sir; you must know, they had been talking of this a pretty while without.
[2] Queen Elizabeth reviewed her soldiers at Tilbury Fort in Aug. 1588. The speech
she made then was reprinted in the *Public Advertiser*, 17 Sept. 1779.

> Like her protecting Pallas veil'd in steel,
> With graceful confidence exhort to arms!                    50
> When briefly all I hear or see bears stamp
> Of martial vigilance, and stern defence,
> I cannot but surmise.—Forgive, my friend,
> If the conjecture's rash——I cannot but
> Surmise.——The state some danger apprehends!

SNEER. A very cautious conjecture that.

PUFF. Yes, that's his character; not to give an opinion, but on secure grounds—now then.

'SIR WALTER.

> 'O, most accomplished Christopher.'——                    60

PUFF. He calls him by his christian name, to shew that they are on the most familiar terms.

'SIR WALTER.

> 'O most accomplish'd Christopher, I find
> Thy staunch sagacity still tracks the future,
> In the fresh print of the o'ertaken past.

PUFF. Figurative!

'SIR WALTER.

> 'Thy fears are just.

'SIR CHRISTOPHER.                    70

> 'But where? whence? when? and what
> The danger is——Methinks I fain would learn.

'SIR WALTER.

> 'You know, my friend, scarce two revolving suns,
> And three revolving moons, have closed their course,
> Since haughty PHILIP,[1] in despight of peace,
> With hostile hand hath struck at ENGLAND's trade.

'SIR CHRISTOPHER.

> 'I know it well.

'SIR WALTER.                    80

> 'PHILIP you know is proud, IBERIA's king!

---

[1] Philip II, King of Spain (1527–98).

'SIR CHRISTOPHER.

'He is.

'SIR WALTER.

'——His subjects in base bigotry
And Catholic oppression held,——while we
You know, the protestant persuasion hold.

'SIR CHRISTOPHER.

'We do.

'SIR WALTER.                                        90

'You know beside,——his boasted armament,
The fam'd Armada,——by the Pope baptized,
With purpose to invade these realms——

'SIR CHRISTOPHER.

'——Is sailed,
Our last advices so report.

'SIR WALTER.

'While the Iberian Admiral's chief hope,
His darling son——

'SIR CHRISTOPHER.                                  100

'——Ferolo Wiskerandos hight——

'SIR WALTER.

'The same—by chance a pris'ner hath been ta'en,
And in this fort of Tilbury——

'SIR CHRISTOPHER.

'——Is now
Confin'd,—'tis true, and oft from yon tall turrets top
I've mark'd the youthful Spaniard's haughty mien
Unconquer'd, tho' in chains!

'SIR WALTER.                                       110

'You also know——

DANGLE. —Mr. Puff, as he *knows* all this, why does Sir Walter go on
telling him?

PUFF. But the audience are not supposed to know any thing of the matter,
are they?

SNEER. True, but I think you manage ill: for there certainly appears no
reason why Sir Walter should be so communicative.

PUFF. Fore Gad now, that is one of the most ungrateful observations I
ever heard—for the less inducement he has to tell all this, the more I
think, you ought to be oblig'd to him; for I am sure you'd know nothing  120
of the matter without it.

DANGLE. That's very true, upon my word.

PUFF. But you will find he was *not* going on.

'SIR CHRISTOPHER.

'Enough, enough,—'tis plain—and I no more
Am in amazement lost!——

PUFF. Here, now you see, Sir Christopher did not in fact ask any one
question for his own information.

SNEER. No indeed:—his has been a most disinterested curiosity!

DANGLE. Really, I find, we are very much oblig'd to them both.        130

PUFF. To be sure you are. Now then for the Commander in Chief, the
EARL OF LEICESTER! who, you know, was no favourite but of the
Queen's.—We left off—'in amazement lost!'—

'SIR CHRISTOPHER.

'Am in amazement lost.——
But, see where noble Leicester comes! supreme
In honours and command.

'SIR WALTER.

'And yet methinks,
At such a time, so perilous, so fear'd,                              140
That staff might well become an abler grasp.

'SIR CHRISTOPHER.

'And so by heav'n! think I; but soft, he's here!

PUFF. Aye, they envy him.

SNEER. But who are these with him?

PUFF. O! very valiant knights; one is the Governor of the fort, the other
the master of the horse.—And now, I think you shall hear some better
language: I was obliged to be plain and intelligible in the first scene,
because there was so much matter of fact in it; but now, efaith, you have
trope, figure, and metaphor, as plenty as noun-substantives.          150

*Enter* EARL OF LEICESTER, THE GOVERNOR, *and others.*

'LEICESTER.

'How's this my friends! is't thus your new fledg'd zeal
And plumed valor moults in roosted sloth?
Why dimly glimmers that heroic flame,
Whose red'ning blaze by patriot spirit fed,
Should be the beacon of a kindling realm?
Can the quick current of a patriot heart,
Thus stagnate in a cold and weedy converse,
Or freeze in tideless inactivity?
No! rather let the fountain of your valor                            160
Spring thro' each stream of enterprize,

Each petty channel of conducive daring,
Till the full torrent of your foaming wrath
O'erwhelm the flats of sunk hostility!

PUFF. There it is,—follow'd up!

'SIR WALTER.

'No more! the fresh'ning breath of thy rebuke
Hath fill'd the swelling canvass of our souls!
And thus, tho' fate should cut the cable of      [*All take hands.*
Our topmost hopes, in friendship's closing line         170
We'll grapple with despair, and if we fall,
We'll fall in Glory's wake!

'EARL OF LEICESTER.

'There spoke Old England's genius!
Then, are we all resolv'd?

'ALL.

'We are——all resolv'd.

'EARL OF LEICESTER.

'To conquer——or be free?

'ALL.         180

'To conquer, or be free.

'EARL OF LEICESTER.

'All?

'ALL.

'All.

DANGLE. *Nem. con.* egad!
PUFF. O yes, where they *do* agree on the stage, their unanimity is
wonderful!

'EARL OF LEICESTER.

'Then, let's embrace——and now——         190

SNEER. What the plague, is he going to pray?
PUFF. Yes, hush!—in great emergencies, there is nothing like a prayer!

'EARL OF LEICESTER.

'O mighty Mars!

DANGLE. But why should he pray to *Mars*?
PUFF. Hush!

'EARL OF LEICESTER.

'If in thy homage bred,
Each point of discipline I've still observ'd;

Nor but by due promotion, and the right                          200
Of service, to the rank of Major-General
Have ris'n; assist thy votary now!

'GOVERNOR.

'Yet do not rise,——hear me!

'MASTER OF HORSE.

'And me!

'KNIGHT.

'And me!

'SIR WALTER.

'And me!                          210

'SIR CHRISTOPHER.

'And me!

PUFF. Now, pray all together.

'ALL.

'Behold thy votaries submissive beg,
That thou will deign to grant them all they ask;
Assist them to accomplish all their ends,
And sanctify whatever means they use
To gain them!

SNEER. A very orthodox quintetto!                          220
PUFF. Vastly well, gentlemen.—Is that well managed or not? Have you
such a prayer as that on the stage?
SNEER. Not exactly.

[EARL OF LEICESTER *to* PUFF.]

But, Sir, you hav'nt settled how we are to get off here.

PUFF. You could not go off kneeling, could you?[1]

[SIR WALTER *to* PUFF.]

O no, Sir! impossible!

PUFF. It would have a good effect efaith, if you could! exeunt praying!—
Yes, and would vary the established mode of springing off with a
glance at the pit.[2]

SNEER. O never mind, so as you get them off, I'll answer for it the audience          230
wont care how.

---

[1] Cf. Henry Jones, *The Earl of Essex* (1753), II. 1: *Enter Southampton | Southampton.*
(*kneeling*). Permit me, madam, to approach you thus.

[2] Cf. Garrick's 'tripping off the stage with a bridled head and an affected alertness'
(Robert Baker, *Remarks on the English Language* (2nd edn., 1779), p. xviii, quoted in
K. A. Burnim, *David Garrick, Director* (Pittsburgh, Pa., 1961), p. 55).

PUFF. Well then, repeat the last line standing, and go off the old way.

'ALL.

'And sanctify whatever means we use to gain them.  [*Exeunt.*

DANGLE. Bravo! a fine exit.

SNEER. Well, really Mr. Puff.——

PUFF. Stay a moment.——

THE CENTINELS *get up.*

'IST CENTINEL.

'All this shall to Lord Burleigh's ear.

'2D CENTINEL.                                                          240

''Tis meet it should.                     [*Exeunt* CENTINELS.

DANGLE. Hey!—why, I thought those fellows had been asleep?

PUFF. Only a pretence, there's the art of it; they were spies of Lord Burleigh's.

SNEER. —But isn't it odd, they were never taken notice of, not even by the commander in chief.

PUFF. O lud, Sir, if people who want to listen, or overhear, were not always conniv'd at in a Tragedy, there would be no carrying on any plot in the world.

DANGLE. That's certain!                                                250

PUFF. But take care, my dear Dangle, the morning gun is going to fire.
                                                    [*Cannon fires.*

DANGLE. Well, that will have a fine effect.

PUFF. I think so, and helps to realize the scene.—     [*Cannon twice.*
What the plague!—*three* morning guns!—there never is but one!—aye, this is always the way at the Theatre—give these fellows a good thing, and they never know when to have done with it. You have no more cannon to fire?

PROMPTER *from within.* No Sir.

PUFF. Now then, for soft musick.

SNEER. Pray what's that for?                                          260

PUFF. It shews that TILBURINA is coming; nothing introduces you a heroine like soft musick.—Here she comes.

DANGLE. And her confidant, I suppose?[1]

PUFF. To be sure: here they are—inconsolable to the minuet in Ariadne![2]
(*Soft musick.*)

*Enter* TILBURINA *and* CONFIDANT.

---

[1] Common in French tragedy. Cf. Ambrose Philips, *The Distressed Mother* (1719, an adaptation of Racine's *Andromaque*), IV:
   *Cephisa.* Madam, I have no will but yours. My life
             Is nothing, balanc'd with my love to you.
[2] Handel's *Ariadne in Crete* (1734).

'TILBURINA.

'Now has the whispering breath of gentle morn,
Bad Nature's voice, and Nature's beauty rise;
While orient Phœbus with unborrow'd hues,
Cloaths the wak'd loveliness which all night slept
In heav'nly drapery! Darkness is fled.                                    270
Now flowers unfold their beauties to the sun,
And blushing, kiss the beam he sends to wake them,
The strip'd carnation, and the guarded rose,
The vulgar wall flow'r, and smart gillyflower,
The polyanthus mean—the dapper daizy,
Sweet William, and sweet marjorum,——and all
The tribe of single and of double pinks![1]
Now too, the feather'd warblers tune their notes
Around, and charm the listning grove.—The lark!
The linnet! chafinch! bullfinch! goldfinch! greenfinch!                   280
——But O to me, no joy can they afford!
Nor rose, nor wall flow'r, nor smart gillyflower,
Nor polyanthus mean, nor dapper daizy,
Nor William sweet, nor marjoram——nor lark,
Linnet, nor all the finches of the grove!

PUFF. Your white handkerchief madam——
TILBURINA. I thought, Sir, I wasn't to use that 'till, 'heart rending woe.'
PUFF. O yes madam—at 'the finches of the grove,' if you please.

'TILBURINA.
              'Nor lark,                                                   290
        Linnet, nor all the finches of the grove!              [*Weeps.*

PUFF. Vastly well madam!
DANGLE. Vastly well indeed!

'TILBURINA.
'For, O too sure, heart rending woe is now
The lot of wretched Tilburina!

DANGLE. O!—'tis too much.
SNEER. Oh!——it is indeed

'CONFIDANT.
'Be comforted sweet lady——for who knows,                                  300
But Heav'n has yet some milk-white day in store.

'TILBURINA.
'Alas, my gentle Nora,
Thy tender youth, as yet hath never mourn'd

[1] Cf. Milton, *Lycidas*, ll. 139-51.

Love's fatal dart.—Else wouldst thou know, that when
The soul is sunk is comfortless despair,
It cannot taste of merryment!

DANGLE. That's certain.

'CONFIDANT.
'But see where your stern father comes;                310
It is not meet that he should find you thus.

PUFF. Hey, what the plague!—what a cut is here!—why, what is become
of the description of her first meeting with Don Whiskerandos? his
gallant behaviour in the sea fight, and the simile of the canary bird?[1]
TILBURINA. Indeed Sir, you'll find they will not be miss'd.
PUFF. Very well.—Very well!
TILBURINA. The cue ma'am if you please.

'CONFIDANT.
'It is not meet that he should find you thus.

'TILBURINA.                                320
'Thou counsel'st right, but 'tis no easy task
For barefaced grief to wear a mask of joy.

*Enter* GOVERNOR.
'How's this—in tears?——O Tilburina, shame!
Is this a time for maudling tenderness,
And Cupid's baby woes?——hast thou not heard
That haughty Spain's Pope-consecrated fleet
Advances to our shores, while England's fate,
Like a clipp'd guinea, trembles in the scale!

'TILBURINA.
'Then, is the crisis of *my* fate at hand!           330
I see the fleets approach——I see——

PUFF. Now, pray gentlemen mind.—This is one of the most useful
figures we tragedy writers have,[2] by which a hero or heroine, in consideration of their being often obliged to overlook things that *are* on
the stage, is allow'd to hear and see a number of things that are not.
SNEER. Yes—a kind of poetical second-sight!
PUFF. Yes—now then madam.

---

[1] For the current delight in similes, see 'Simon Simile' in the *Morning Chronicle*,
4 Dec. 1775: 'the first object of a song should always be a *simile*: in short a song without
a simile is like a play without a plot: the animating principle is wanting. . . .'
[2] Cf. Henry Jones, *The Earl of Essex*, I. i:
*Raleigh (to Burleigh).*          My heart exults; I see,
                    I see, my lord, our utmost wish accomplish'd!
                    I see great Cecil shine without a rival,
                    And England bless him as her guardian saint.

'TILBURINA.

'I see their decks
Are clear'd!——I see the signal made!                                    340
The line is form'd!——a cable's length asunder!
I see the frigates station'd in the rear;
And now, I hear the thunder of the guns!
I hear the victor's shouts——I also hear
The vanquish'd groan!——and now 'tis smoke——and now
I see the loose sails shiver in the wind!
I see——I see——what soon you'll see——

'GOVERNOR.

'Hold daughter! peace! this love hath turn'd thy brain:
The Spanish fleet thou *canst* not see—because                          350
——It is not yet in sight!

DANGLE. Egad tho', the governor seems to make no allowance for this
poetical figure you talk of.

PUFF. No, a plain matter-of-fact man—that's his character.

'TILBURINA.

'But will you then refuse his offer?

'GOVERNOR.

'I must—I will —I can—I ought—I do.

'TILBURINA.

'Think what a noble price.                                               360

'GOVERNOR.

'No more——you urge in vain.

'TILBURINA.

'His liberty is all he asks.

SNEER. All *who* asks Mr. Puff? Who is—

PUFF. Egad Sir, I can't tell.—Here has been such cutting and slashing, I
don't know where they have got to myself.

TILBURINA. Indeed Sir, you will find it will connect very well.

'——And your reward secure.

PUFF. O,—if they had'nt been so devilish free with their cutting here,   370
you would have found that Don Whiskerandos has been tampering for
his liberty, and has persuaded Tilburina to make this proposal to her
father—and now pray observe the conciseness with which the argument
is conducted. Egad, the *pro & con* goes as smart as hits in a fencing
match.[1] It is indeed a sort of small-sword logic, which we have borrowed
from the French.

[1] Cf. *The Rehearsal*, III. i: *Bayes*. This, Sirs, might properly enough be called a
prize of Wit; for you shall see 'em come in one upon another snip snap, hit for hit,
as fast as can be.

'TILBURINA.

'A retreat in Spain!

'GOVERNOR.

'Outlawry here!                                                    380

'TILBURINA.

'Your daughter's prayer!

'GOVERNOR.

'Your father's oath!

'TILBURINA.

'My lover!

'GOVERNOR.

'My country!

'TILBURINA.

'Tilburina!                                                         390

'GOVERNOR.

'England!

'TILBURINA.

'A title!

'GOVERNOR.

'Honor!

'TILBURINA.

'A pension!

'GOVERNOR.

'Conscience!                                                       400

'TILBURINA.

'A thousand pounds!

'GOVERNOR.

'Hah! thou hast touch'd me nearly!

PUFF. There you see——she threw in *Tilburina*, Quick, parry cart with
*England!*—Hah! thrust in teirce a title!—parried by honor.—Hah! a
pension over the arm!—put by by conscience.—Then flankonade[1] with
a thousand pounds—and a palpable hit egad!

'TILBURINA.

'Canst thou——                                                     410
Reject the *suppliant*, and the *daughter* too?

'GOVERNOR.

'No more; I wou'd not hear thee plead in vain,
The *father* softens—but the *governor*
Is fix'd!                                                    [*Exit.*

DANGLE. Aye, that antithesis of persons—is a most establish'd figure.

---

[1] The 'parry carte' and 'thrust in tierce' were fencing terms, as was the 'flanconade',
a thrust in the flank.

### 'TILBURINA.

'Tis well,——hence then fond hopes,—fond passion·hence;
Duty, behold I am all over thine——

### 'WHISKERANDOS *without*. 420
'Where is my love——my——

### 'TILBURINA.
'Ha!

### 'WHISKERANDOS *entering*.
'My beauteous enemy——

PUFF. O dear ma'am, you must start a great deal more than that;
consider you had just determined in favour of duty—when in a moment
the sound of his voice revives your passion,—overthrows your resolution, destroys your obedience.—If you don't express all that in your
start—you do nothing at all. 430
TILBURINA. Well, we'll try again!
DANGLE. Speaking from within, has always a fine effect.
SNEER. Very.

### 'WHISKERANDOS.
'My conquering Tilburina! How! is't thus
We meet? why are thy looks averse! what means
That falling tear——that frown of boding woe?
Hah! now indeed I am a prisoner!
Yes, now I feel the galling weight of these
Disgraceful chains——which, cruel Tilburina! 440
Thy doating captive gloried in before.——
But thou art false, and Whiskerandos is undone!

### 'TILBURINA.
'O no; how little dost thou know thy Tilburina!

### 'WHISKERANDOS.
'Art thou then true? Begone cares, doubts and fears,
I make you all a present to the winds;[1]
And if the winds reject you——try the waves.

PUFF. The wind you know, is the established receiver of all stolen sighs,
and cast off griefs and apprehensions. 450

[1] Henry Jones, *The Earl of Essex*, II:
*Essex*. I scorn the blaze of courts, the pomp of kings;
I give them to the winds.

'TILBURINA.

'Yet must we part?——stern duty seals our doom:
Though here I call yon conscious clouds to witness,
Could I pursue the bias of my soul,
All friends, all right of parents I'd disclaim,
And thou, my Whiskerandos, should'st be father
And mother, brother, cousin, uncle, aunt,
And friend to me!

'WHISKERANDOS.

'O matchless excellence!——and must we part?                460
Well, if——we must——we must—and in that case,
The less is said the better.

PUFF. Hey day! here's a cut!—What, are all the mutual protestations out?

TILBURINA. Now, pray Sir, don't interrupt us just here, you ruin our feelings.

PUFF. *Your* feelings!——but zounds, *my* feelings, ma'am!

SNEER. No; pray don't interrupt them.

'WHISKERANDOS.

'One last embrace.——

'TILBURINA.                 470

'Now,——farewell, for ever.

'WHISKERANDOS.

'For ever!

'TILBURINA.

'Aye, for ever.                                  [*Going*

PUFF. S'death and fury!—Gadslife! Sir! Madam! if you go out without the parting look, you might as well dance out—Here, here!

CONFIDANT. But pray Sir, how am *I* to get off here?

PUFF. *You*, pshaw! what the devil signifies how *you* get off! edge away at the top, or where you will—[*Pushes the confidant off.*] Now ma'am you      480
see—

TILBURINA. We understand you Sir.

'Aye for ever.

'BOTH.

'Ohh!——          [*Turning back and exeunt.*
[*Scene closes.*

DANGLE. O charming!

PUFF. Hey!—'tis pretty well I believe—you see I don't attempt to strike
out any thing new—but I take it I improve on the established modes.

SNEER. You do indeed.—But pray is not Queen Elizabeth to appear?

PUFF. No not once—but she is to be talked of for ever; so that egad
you'll think a hundred times that she is on the point of coming in.      490

SNEER. Hang it, I think its a pity to keep *her* in the green room all the night.

PUFF. O no, that always has a fine effect—it keeps up expectation.

DANGLE. But are we not to have a battle?

PUFF. Yes, yes, you will have a battle at last, but, egad, it's not to be by land—but by sea—and that is the only quite new thing in the piece.

DANGLE. What, Drake at the Armada, hey?

PUFF. Yes, efaith—fire ships and all—then we shall end with the procession.—Hey! that will do I think.

SNEER. No doubt on't.                                                                    500

PUFF. Come, we must not lose time—so now for the UNDER PLOT.

SNEER. What the plague, have you another plot?

PUFF. O lord, yes—ever while you live, have two plots to your tragedy.—The grand point in managing them, is only to let your under plot have as little connexion with your main plot as possible.—I flatter myself nothing can be more distinct than mine, for as in my chief plot, the characters are all great people—I have laid my under plot in low life—and as the former is to end in deep distress, I make the other end as happy as a farce.—Now Mr. Hopkins, as soon as you please.

*Enter* UNDER PROMPTER.

UNDER PROMPTER. Sir, the carpenter says it is impossible you can go to     510
the Park scene yet.

PUFF. The Park scene! No—I mean the description scene here, in the wood.

UNDER PROMPTER. Sir, the performers have cut it out.

PUFF. Cut it out!

UNDER PROMPTER. Yes Sir.

PUFF. What! the whole account of Queen Elizabeth?[1]

UNDER PROMPTER. Yes Sir.

PUFF. And the description of her horse and side-saddle?

UNDER PROMPTER. Yes Sir.                                                                 520

PUFF. So, so, this is very fine indeed! Mr. Hopkins, how the plague could you suffer this?

HOPKINS, *from within.* Sir, indeed the pruning knife—

PUFF. The pruning knife—zounds the axe! why, here has been such lopping and topping, I shan't have the bare trunk of my play left presently.—Very well, Sir—the performers must do as they please, but upon my soul, I'll print it every word.

SNEER. That I would indeed.

PUFF. Very well—Sir—then we must go on—zounds! I would not have parted with the description of the horse!—Well, Sir, go on—Sir, it was     530

---

[1] Queen Elizabeth never appears in Thomas Arne's *Eliza* (1754), and the opera also contains 'a representation of the Armada with model ships'. See Roger Fiske, *English Theatre Music in the Eighteenth Century* (1973), p. 239.

one of the finest and most laboured things—Very well, Sir, let them go on—there you had him and his accoutrements from the bit to the crupper—very well, Sir, we must go to the Park scene.

UNDER PROMPTER. Sir, there is the point, the carpenters say, that unless there is some business put in here before the drop, they shan't have time to clear away the fort, or sink Gravesend and the river.

PUFF. So! this is a pretty dilemma truly!—Gentlemen—you must excuse me, these fellows will never be ready, unless I go and look after them myself.

SNEER. O dear Sir—these little things will happen—                          540

PUFF. To cut out this scene!—but I'll print it—egad, I'll print it every word!                                                                        [*Exeunt.*

END OF ACT II

# ACT III

## SCENE I

*Before the Curtain.*

*Enter* PUFF, SNEER, *and* DANGLE.

PUFF. Well, we are ready—now then for the justices.

[*Curtain rises; Justices, Constables, &c. discovered.*

SNEER. This, I suppose, is a sort of senate scene.

PUFF. To be sure—there has not been one yet.

DANGLE. It is the under plot, isn't it?

PUFF. Yes. What, gentlemen, do you mean to go at once to the discovery scene?

JUSTICE. If you please, Sir.

PUFF. O very well—harkee, I don't chuse to say any thing more, but efaith, they have mangled my play in a most shocking manner!

DANGLE. It's a great pity!                                                  10

PUFF. Now then, Mr. Justice, if you please.

'JUSTICE.

'Are all the volunteers without?

'CONSTABLE.

'They are.
Some ten in fetters, and some twenty drunk.

'JUSTICE.

'Attends the youth, whose most opprobrious fame
And clear convicted crimes have stampt him soldier?

'CONSTABLE.                                          20

'He waits your pleasure; eager to repay
The blest reprieve that sends him to the fields
Of glory, there to raise his branded hand
In honor's cause.

'JUSTICE.

''Tis well——'tis Justice arms him!
O! may he now defend his country's laws
With half the spirit he has broke them all!
If 'tis your worship's pleasure, bid him enter.

'CONSTABLE.                                          30

'I fly, the herald of your will.          [*Exit* CONSTABLE.

PUFF. Quick, Sir!—

SNEER. But, Mr. Puff, I think not only the Justice, but the clown seems
    to talk in as high a style as the first hero among them.

PUFF. Heaven forbid they should not in a free country!—Sir, I am not
    for making slavish distinctions, and giving all the fine language to the
    upper sort of people.

DANGLE. That's very noble in you indeed.

*Enter* JUSTICE'S LADY.

PUFF. Now pray mark this scene.

'LADY.                                               40

'Forgive this interruption, good my love;
But as I just now past, a pris'ner youth
Whom rude hands hither lead, strange bodings seiz'd
My fluttering heart, and to myself I said,
An if our TOM had liv'd, he'd surely been
This stripling's height!

'JUSTICE.

'Ha! sure some powerful sympathy directs
Us both——

*Enter* SON *and* CONSTABLE.

'JUSTICE.                                            50

'What is thy name?

'SON.

'My name's TOM JENKINS[1]—*alias*, have I none—
Tho' orphan'd, and without a friend!

'JUSTICE.

'Thy parents?

---

[1] Cf. J. Home, *Douglas*, II: 'My name is Norval'.

'SON.

'My father dwelt in Rochester——and was,
As I have heard——a fishmonger——no more.

PUFF. What, Sir, do you leave out the account of your birth, parentage 60
and education?
SON. They have settled it so, Sir, here.
PUFF. Oh! oh!

'LADY.

'How loudly nature whispers to my heart!
Had he no other name?

'SON.

'I've seen a bill
Of his, sign'd *Tomkins*, creditor.

'JUSTICE. 70

'This does indeed confirm each circumstance
The gypsy told!——Prepare!

'SON.

'I do.

'JUSTICE.

'No orphan, nor without a friend art thou——
*I am thy father*,[1] *here's* thy mother, *there*
Thy uncle——this thy first cousin, and those
Are all your near relations!

'MOTHER. 80

'O ecstasy of bliss!

'SON.

'O most unlook'd for happiness!

'JUSTICE.

'O wonderful event!
[*They faint alternately in each others arms.*

PUFF. There, you see relationship, like murder, will out.

'JUSTICE.

'Now let's revive——else were this joy too much!
But come——and we'll unfold the rest within,
And thou my boy must needs want rest and food. 90

[1] Cf. R. Cumberland, *The West Indian*, v. viii:
*Stockwell.* I am your father.
*Belcour.* My father! Do I live?
*Stockwell.* I am your father.
*Belcour.* It is too much. . . .

> Hence may each orphan hope, as chance directs,
> To find a father—where he least expects! [*Exeunt.*

PUFF. What do you think of that?

DANGLE. One of the finest discovery-scenes I ever saw.—Why, this under-plot would have made a tragedy itself.

SNEER. Aye, or a comedy either.

PUFF. And keeps quite clear you see of the other.

*Enter* SCENEMEN, *taking away the Seats.*

PUFF. The scene remains, does it?

SCENEMAN. Yes, Sir.

PUFF. You are to leave one chair you know—But it is always awkward in a tragedy, to have you fellows coming in in your playhouse liveries to 100 remove things—I wish that could be managed better.—So now for my mysterious yeoman.

*Enter* A BEEFEATER.

'BEEFEATER.

'Perdition catch my soul but *I* do love thee.¹

SNEER. Haven't I heard that line before?

PUFF. No, I fancy not—Where pray?

DANGLE. Yes, I think there is something like it in Othello.

PUFF. Gad! now you put me in mind on't, I believe there is—but that's of no consequence—all that can be said is, that two people happened to 110 hit on the same thought—And Shakespeare made use of it first, that's all.

SNEER. Very true.

PUFF. Now, Sir, your soliloquy—but speak more to the pit, if you please —the soliloquy always to the pit—that's a rule.²

'BEEFEATER.

'Tho' hopeless love finds comfort in despair,
It never can endure a rival's bliss!
But soft——I am observ'd. [*Exit* BEEFEATER.

DANGLE. That's a very short soliloquy.

PUFF. Yes—but it would have been a great deal longer if he had not been 120 observed.

---

¹ *Othello*, III. iii.
² 'Their ridiculous practice of approaching the pit with an arch leer of familiarity and communicating to their good friends, the company, every sentiment they have been intrusted with by their poor cully, the author' (Aaron Hill and William Popple, *The Prompter* (1734–6; repr. New York, 1966, ed. W. W. Appleton and K. A. Burnim), p. 116).

SNEER. A most sentimental[1] Beefeater that, Mr. Puff.

PUFF. Hark'ee—I would not have you be too sure that he *is* a Beefeater.

SNEER. What! a hero in disguise?

PUFF. No matter—I only give you a hint—But now for my principal character—Here he comes—LORD BURLEIGH in person! Pray, gentlemen, step this way—softly—I only hope the Lord High Treasurer is perfect—if he is but perfect!

*Enter* BURLEIGH, *goes slowly to a chair and sits.*

SNEER. Mr. Puff!

PUFF. Hush!—vastly well, Sir! vastly well! a most interesting gravity!    130

DANGLE. What, isn't he to speak at all?

PUFF. Egad, I thought you'd ask me that—yes it is a very likely thing—that a Minister in his situation, with the whole affairs of the nation on his head, should have time to talk!—but hush! or you'll put him out.

SNEER. Put him out! how the plague can that be, if he's not going to say any thing?[2]

PUFF. There's a reason!—why, his part is to *think*, and how the plague! do you imagine he can *think* if you keep talking?

DANGLE. That's very true upon my word!

[BURLEIGH *comes forward, shakes his head and exit.*

SNEER. He is very perfect indeed—Now, pray what did he mean by that?    140

PUFF. You don't take it?

SNEER. No; I don't upon my soul.

PUFF. Why, by that shake of the head, he gave you to understand that even tho' they had more justice in their cause and wisdom in their measures—yet, if there was not a greater spirit shown on the part of the people—the country would at last fall a sacrifice to the hostile ambition of the Spanish monarchy.

SNEER. The devil!—did he mean all that by shaking his head?

PUFF. Every word of it—If he shook his head as I taught him.

DANGLE. Ah! there certainly is a vast deal to be done on the stage by    150 dumb shew, and expression of face, and a judicious author knows how much he may trust to it.

SNEER. O, here are some of our old acquaintance.

*Enter* HATTON *and* RALEIGH

'SIR CHRISTOPHER.

'*My* niece, and *your* niece too!

By heav'n! there's witchcraft in't——He could not else

Have gain'd their hearts——But see where they approach;

Some horrid purpose low'ring on their brows!

---

[1] Sententious.

[2] Cf. Buckingham, *The Rehearsal*, v. i: *Johnson*. . . . if I were in your place I would make 'em go out again without ever speaking one word.

'SIR WALTER.

'Let us withdraw and mark them.                    [*They withdraw.*  160

SNEER.  What is all this?

PUFF.  Ah! here has been more pruning!—but the fact is, these two
young ladies are also in love with Don Whiskerandos.—Now, gentlemen, this scene goes entirely for what we call SITUATION and STAGE
EFFECT, by which the greatest applause may be obtained, without the
assistance of language, sentiment or character: pray mark!

*Enter the* TWO NIECES.

'1ST NIECE.

'Ellena here!
She is his scorn as much as I—that is
Some comfort still.                                                170

PUFF.  O dear madam, you are not to say that to her face!—*aside*, ma'am,
*aside*.—The whole scene is to be *aside*.

'1ST NIECE.

'She is his scorn as much as I—that is
Some comfort still!                                    [*Aside.*

'2D NIECE.

'I know he prizes not Pollina's love,
But Tilburina lords it o'er his heart.                 [*Aside.*

'1ST NIECE.

'But see the proud destroyer of my peace.                      180
Revenge is all the good I've left.                     [*Aside.*

'2D NIECE.

'He comes, the false disturber of my quiet.
Now vengeance do thy worst——                           [*Aside.*

*Enter* WHISKERANDOS

'O hateful liberty—if thus in vain
I seek my Tilburina!

'BOTH NIECES.

'And ever shalt!

'SIR CHRISTOPHER AND SIR WALTER *come forward.*

'Hold! we will avenge you.                                     190

'WHISKERANDOS.

'Hold *you*——or see your nieces bleed!

[*The two nieces draw their two daggers to strike* WHISKERANDOS, *the
two Uncles at the instant with their two swords drawn, catch their two
nieces' arms, and turn the points of their swords to* WHISKERANDOS, *who
immediately draws two daggers, and holds them to the two nieces' bosoms.*

PUFF.  There's situation for you!—there's an heroic group!—You see the
ladies can't stab Whiskerandos—he durst not strike them for fear of their

uncles—the uncles durst not kill him, because of their nieces—I have
them all at a dead lock!—for every one of them is afraid to let go first.
SNEER. Why, then they must stand there for ever.
PUFF. So they would, if I hadn't a very fine contrivance for't—Now
  mind——

*Enter* BEEFEATER *with his Halberd.*

                'In the Queen's name I charge you[1] all to drop                    200
                Your swords and daggers!

                                    [*They drop their swords and daggers.*

SNEER. That is a contrivance indeed.
PUFF. Aye—in the Queen's name.

                    'SIR CHRISTOPHER.

          'Come niece!

                    'SIR WALTER.

          'Come niece!                              [*Exeunt with the two nieces.*

                    'WHISKERANDOS.

          'What's he, who bids us thus renounce our guard?

                    'BEEFEATER.                                                    210

          'Thou must do more, renounce thy love!

                    'WHISKERANDOS.

          'Thou liest——base Beefeater!

                    'BEEFEATER.

                          'Ha! Hell! the lie!
          By heav'n thou'st rous'd the lion in my heart!
          Off yeoman's habit!—base disguise!—off! off!

                [*Discovers himself, by throwing off his upper dress,
                        and appearing in a very fine waistcoat.*

          Am I a Beefeater now?
          Or beams my crest as terrible as when
          In Biscay's Bay I took thy captive sloop.                                220

PUFF. There, egad! he comes out to be the very Captain of the privateer
  who had taken Whiskerandos prisoner—and was himself an old lover of
  Tilburina's.[2]

---

[1] Henry Jones, *The Earl of Essex*, I:
*Queen.* We charge you on your duty and allegiance,
        To stop this vile proceeding.
[2] Cf. John Home, *Douglas*, IV:
*Norval.* Returning homewards by Messina's port,
                Loaded with wealth and honours bravely won,
                A rude and boist'rous captain of the sea
                Fastened a quarrel on him. Fierce they fought:
                The stranger fell, and with his dying breath
                Declared his name and lineage. 'Mighty God!'
                The soldier cried, 'My brother! Oh my brother!'

DANGLE. Admirably manag'd indeed.
PUFF. Now, stand out of their way.

'WHISKERANDOS.

'I thank thee fortune! that hast thus bestow'd
A weapon to chastise this insolent.    [*Takes up one of the swords.*

'BEEFEATER.

'I take thy challenge, Spaniard, and I thank          230
Thee Fortune too!—                    [*Takes up the other sword.*

DANGLE. That's excellently contrived!—it seems as if the two uncles had
left their swords on purpose for them.
PUFF. No, egad, they could not help leaving them.

'WHISKERANDOS.

'Vengeance and Tilburina!

'BEEFEATER.

'Exactly so——
[*They fight—and after the usual number
of wounds given,* WHISKERANDOS *falls.*

'WHISKERANDOS.

'O cursed parry!——that last thrust in tierce          240
Was fatal——Captain, thou hast fenced well!
And Whiskerandos quits this bustling scene
For all eter——

'BEEFEATER.

'—nity—He would have added, but stern death
Cut short his being, and the noun at once![1]

PUFF. O, my dear Sir, you are too slow, now mind me.—Sir, shall I
trouble you to die again?

'WHISKERANDOS.

'And Whiskerandos quits this bustling scene          250
For all eter——

'BEEFEATER.

'——nity—He would have added——

PUFF. No, Sir—that's not it—once more if you please—
WHISKERANDOS. I wish, Sir—you would practise this without me——
I can't stay dying here all night.

---

[1] Cf. Henry Brooke, *Gustavus Vasa, the Deliverer of his Country* (1739), III. ii:
          Tell him—for once, that I have fought like him,
          And wou'd like him have—
          Conquer'd—he shou'd have said—but there, O there,
          Death sto—pt him short.

PUFF. Very well, we'll go over it by and bye——I must humour these gentlemen!                                                    [*Exit* WHISKERANDOS.

'BEEFEATER.

'Farewell——brave Spaniard! and when next——                   260

PUFF. Dear Sir, you needn't speak that speech as the body has walked off.

BEEFEATER. That's true, Sir—then I'll join the fleet.

PUFF. If you please.                                     [*Exit* BEEFEATER.
   Now, who comes on?

*Enter* GOVERNOR, *with his hair properly disordered.*

'GOVERNOR.

'A hemisphere of evil planets reign!
And every planet sheds contagious phrensy!
My Spanish prisoner is slain! my daughter,
Meeting the dead corse borne along——has gone
Distract!                           [*A loud flourish of trumpets.*  270

      But hark! I am summon'd to the fort,
Perhaps the fleets have met! amazing crisis!
O Tilburina! from thy aged father's beard
Thou'st pluck'd the few brown hairs which time had left!
                                        [*Exit* GOVERNOR.

SNEER. Poor gentleman!

PUFF. Yes—and no one to blame but his daughter!

DANGLE. And the planets——

PUFF. True.—Now enter Tilburina!—

SNEER. Egad, the business comes on quick here.

PUFF. Yes, Sir—now she comes in stark mad in white satin.        280

SNEER. Why in white satin?

PUFF. O Lord, Sir—when a heroine goes mad, she always goes into white satin—don't she, Dangle?

DANGLE. Always—it's a rule.

PUFF. Yes—here it is—[*looking at the book.*] 'Enter Tilburina stark mad in white satin, and her confidant stark mad in white linen.'

*Enter* TILBURINA *and* CONFIDANT *mad, according to custom.*

SNEER. But what the deuce, is the confidant to be mad too?

PUFF. To be sure she is, the confidant is always to do whatever her mistress does; weep when she weeps, smile when she smiles, go mad when she goes mad.——Now madam confidant—but—keep your  290 madness in the back ground, if you please.

'TILBURINA.

'The wind whistles——the moon rises——see
They have kill'd my squirrel in his cage![1]
Is this a grasshopper!——Ha! no, it is my
Whiskerandos——you shall not keep him——
I know you have him in your pocket——
An oyster may be cross'd in love!——Who says
A whale's a bird?—Ha! did you call, my love?
——He's here! He's there!——He's every where!        300
Ah me! He's no where!'                    [*Exit* TILBURINA.

PUFF. There, do you ever desire to see any body madder than that?

SNEER. Never while I live!

PUFF. You observed how she mangled the metre?

DANGLE. Yes—egad, it was the first thing made me suspect she was out of her senses.

SNEER. And pray what becomes of her?

PUFF. She is gone to throw herself into the sea to be sure—and that brings us at once to the scene of action, and so to my catastrophe—my sea-fight, I mean.        310

SNEER. What, you bring that in at last?

PUFF. Yes—yes—you know my play is *called* the *Spanish Armada*, otherwise, egad, I have no occasion for the battle at all.—Now then for my magnificence![2]—my battle!—my noise!—and my procession!—You are all ready?

PROMPTER *within*. Yes, Sir.

PUFF. Is the Thames drest?

*Enter* THAMES *with two Attendants.*

THAMES. Here I am, Sir.

PUFF. Very well indeed—See, gentlemen, there's a river for you!—This is blending a little of the masque with my tragedy—a new fancy you        320
know—and very useful in my case; for as there *must be* a *procession*, I suppose Thames and all his tributary rivers to compliment Britannia with a fete in honor of the victory.

SNEER. But pray, who are these gentlemen in green with him.

PUFF. Those?—those are his banks.

---

[1] Cf. R. Steele, *The Funeral*, v. iii: *Enter Widow in deep Mourning, with a dead Squirrel on her Arm. . . .*
    *Widow.* Poor Harmless Animal—Pretty ev'n in Death:
.        .        .        .
        But chearfully didst bear thy little Chain.
[2] Cf. Buckingham, *The Rehearsal*, v. i:
    *Bayes.* I'll shew you the greatest Scene that ever England saw: I mean not for words, for those I do not value; but for state, shew, and magnificence.

SNEER. His banks?

PUFF. Yes, one crown'd with alders and the other with a villa!—you take
the allusions?—but hey! what the plague! you have got both your
banks on one side—Here Sir, come round—Ever while you live,
Thames, go between your banks. (*Bell rings*.)[1] —There, soh! now for't!  330
—Stand aside my dear friends!—away Thames!

[*Exit* THAMES *between his banks.*

[*Flourish of drums——trumpets——cannon, &c. &c. Scene changes to the
sea——the fleets engage——the musick plays 'Britons strike home.'[2]—
Spanish fleet destroyed by fire-ships, &c.—English fleet advances—musick
plays 'Rule Britannia.'—The procession of all the English rivers and their
tributaries with their emblems, &c. begins with Handels water musick—
ends with a chorus, to the march in Judas Maccabæus.[3]—During this scene,
Puff directs and applauds every thing——then*

PUFF. Well, pretty well—but not quite perfect—so ladies and gentlemen,
if you please, we'll rehearse this piece again to-morrow.

CURTAIN DROPS

FINIS

---

[1] So that music would begin or a curtain fall.

[2] Britons strike home, revenge your country's wrongs,
Fight and record yourselves in Druids' songs.

From *Bonduca* (1696), adapted by G. Powell[?] from Beaumont and Fletcher's play
of the same name, and set by Henry Purcell.

[3] Handel's oratorio *Judas Maccabeus* was first performed in London at Covent
Garden on 1 Apr. 1747.

# PIZARRO

# PIZARRO;

### A
## TRAGEDY,

### IN FIVE ACTS;

#### AS PERFORMED AT THE THEATRE ROYAL IN

### 𝔇𝔯𝔲𝔯𝔶-𝔏𝔞𝔫𝔢:

#### TAKEN FROM THE GERMAN DRAMA OF

## KOTZEBUE;

### AND

## ADAPTED TO THE ENGLISH STAGE

### BY
## RICHARD BRINSLEY SHERIDAN.

---

### London:

#### PRINTED FOR JAMES RIDGWAY, YORK STREET,
#### ST. JAMES'S SQUARE.

#### 1799.

#### Price 2s. 6d.

*A superior Edition, on fine wove Paper, hot-pressed, Price 5s.*

The title-page of the first edition of
*Pizarro*

# ADVERTISEMENT

As the two translations[1] which have been published of Kotzebue's 'SPANIARDS IN PERU' have, I understand, been very generally read, the Public are in possession of all the materials necessary to form a judgment on the merits and defects of the Play performed at Drury Lane Theatre.

[1] By Anne Plumptre and Thomas Dutton.

# DEDICATION[1]

To Her, whose approbation of this Drama, and whose peculiar delight in the applause it has received from the Public, have been to *me* the highest gratification its success has produced—I dedicate this Play.

RICHARD BRINSLEY SHERIDAN.

[1] To his second wife, though *The Oracle*, 5 July 1799, reported that 'A good deal of wit is sported on Mr. Sheridan's Dedication of his Play; some say it is inscribed to the Queen, others to Mrs. Sheridan, others to Mrs. Siddons, and why not—Mrs. Jordan? Perhaps the fact is, that it is dedicated to no *earthly power*, but to *Melpomene*, who has rendered no small assistance on the occasion.'

# PROLOGUE

WRITTEN BY RICHARD BRINSLEY SHERIDAN, ESQ.

SPOKEN BY MR. KING.

CHILL'D by rude gales, while yet reluctant May
Withholds the beauties of the vernal day;
As some fond maid, whom matron frowns reprove,
Suspends the smile her heart devotes to love;
The season's pleasures too delay their hour,
And winter revels with protracted power:
Then blame not, Critics, if, thus late, we bring
A Winter Drama—but reproach—the spring.
What prudent Cit dares yet the season trust,
Bask in his whisky, and enjoy the dust?                    10
Hors'd in Cheapside, scarce yet the gayer spark
Achieves the Sunday triumph of the Park;
Scarce yet you see him, dreading to be late,
Scour the New Road, and dash thro' Grosvenor-gate:—
Anxious—yet timorous too!—his steed to show,
The hack Bucephalus of Rotten-row.
Careless he seems, yet, vigilantly sly,
Woos the stray glance of Ladies passing by,
While his off heel, insidiously aside,
Provokes the caper which he seems to chide.[1]             20
Scarce rural Kensington due honour gains;
The vulgar verdure of her walk remains!
Where white-rob'd misses amble two by two,
Nodding to booted beaux—'How'do, how'do?'
With gen'rous questions that no answer wait,
'How vastly full! A'n't you come vastly late?
'I'n't it quite charming? When do you leave town?
'A'n't you quite tir'd? Pray can we set you down?'
These suburb pleasures of a London May,
Imperfect yet, we hail the cold delay;                     30
Should our Play please—and you're indulgent ever—
Be your decree—''Tis better late than never.'

---

[1] Samuel Rogers said, 'Sheridan was a great artist: what could be more happy in expression than the last of these lines? You may see it illustrated in the Park every Sunday' (*Recollections of the Table Talk of Samuel Rogers* (1856), p. 68).

# DRAMATIS PERSONÆ

ATALIBA, *King of Quito*,      Mr. Powell.
ROLLA,   ⎱ *Commanders of*    ⎧ Mr. Kemble.
ALONZO, ⎰   *his Army*,      ⎨ Mr. C. Kemble.
CORA, *Alonzo's Wife*,      Mrs. Jordan.
PIZARRO, *Leader of the*
    *Spaniards*,      Mr. Barrymore.
ELVIRA, *Pizarro's Mistress*,    Mrs. Siddons.
ALMAGRO,      Mr. Caulfield.
GONZALO,  ⎱    ⎧ Mr. Wentworth.
DAVILLA,   ⎬ *Pizarro's*   ⎨ Mr. Trueman.
GOMEZ,    ⎰ *Associates*,    ⎩ Mr. Surmont.
VALVERDE, *Pizarro's*
    *Secretary*,      Mr. R. Palmer.
LAS-CASAS, *a Spanish*
    *Ecclesiastic*,      Mr. Aickin.
*An old blind Man*,      Mr. Cory.
OROZEMBO, *an old Cacique*,    Mr. Dowton.
A BOY,      MASTER Chatterley.
A CENTINEL,      Mr. Holland.
ATTENDANT,      Mr. Maddocks.
PERUVIAN OFFICER,      Mr. Archer.
SOLDIERS, MESS. FISHER, EVANS, CHIPPENDALE, WEBB, *&c.*

*The Vocal Parts by*

MESSRS. KELLY, SEDGWICK, DIGNUM, DANBY, *&c.*—
MRS. CROUCH, MISS DE CAMP, MISS STEPHENS,
MISS LEAK, MISS DUFOUR, *&c.*

# PIZARRO

## ACT I

### SCENE I

*A magnificent Pavilion near* PIZARRO's *Tent—a View of the Spanish Camp in the back Ground.*—[1] ELVIRA *is discovered sleeping under a canopy on one side of the Pavilion—*VALVERDE *enters, gazes on* ELVIRA, *kneels, and attempts to kiss her hand;* ELVIRA, *awakened, rises and looks at him with indignation.*

ELV. Audacious! Whence is thy privilege to interrupt the few moments of repose my harassed mind can snatch amid the tumults of this noisy camp? Shall I inform your master of this presumptuous treachery? shall I disclose thee to Pizarro? Hey!

VAL. I am his servant, it is true—trusted by him— and I know him well; and therefore 'tis I ask, by what magic could Pizarro gain your heart, by what fatality still holds he your affection?

ELV. Hold! thou trusty SECRETARY![2]

VAL. Ignobly born! in mind and manners rude, ferocious, and unpolished, though cool and crafty if occasion need—in youth audacious—ill his 10 first manhood—a licensed pirate—treating men as brutes, the world as booty; yet now the Spanish hero is he styled—the first of Spanish conquerors! and for a warrior so accomplished, 'tis fit Elvira should leave her noble family, her fame, her home, to share the dangers, humours, and the crimes of such a lover as Pizarro!

ELV. What! Valverde moralizing! But grant I am in error, what is my incentive? Passion, infatuation, call it as you will; but what attaches *thee* to this despised, unworthy leader?—Base lucre is thy object,

---

[1] The Spanish conquest of Peru was not a new subject for the theatre. As far back as 1658, Davenant had published *The Cruelty of the Spaniards in Peru. Exprest by Instrumentall and Vocall Musick, and by Art of Perspective in Scenes.* In Sheridan's day, *The World,* 17 Apr. 1790, advertised a performance at Sadler's Wells of 'An entire new piece consisting of Song, Dance, and Recitative, aided by Picturesque Scenery, Machinery, etc., and called THE INCAS OF PERU; *or,* THE CHILDREN OF THE SUN'.

[2] 'As the Inca drew near the Spanish quarters, father Vincent Valverde, chaplain to the expedition, advanced with a crucifix in one hand, and a breviary in the other, and in a long discourse explained to him the doctrine of the creation . . .' (W. Robertson, *The History of America* (5th edn., 1788), iii. 34).

mean fraud thy means. Could you gain me, you only hope to win a
higher interest in Pizarro—I know you.                                          20

VAL. On my soul, you wrong me; what else my faults, I have none towards you: but indulge the scorn and levity of your nature; do it while
yet the time permits; the gloomy hour, I fear, too soon approaches.

ELV. Valverde, a prophet too!

VAL. Hear me, Elvira—Shame from his late defeat, and burning wishes
for revenge, again have brought Pizarro to Peru; but trust me, he
over-rates his strength, nor measures well the foe. Encamped in a
strange country, where terror cannot force, nor corruption buy a single
friend, what have we to hope? The army murmuring at increasing
hardships, while Pizarro decorates with gaudy spoil the gay pavilion of  30
his luxury! each day diminishes our force.

ELV. But are you not the heirs of those that fall?

VAL. Are gain and plunder then our only purpose? Is this Elvira's
heroism?

ELV. No, so save me Heaven! I abhor the motive, means, and end of
your pursuits; but I will trust none of you:—in your whole army
there is not one of you that has a heart, or speaks ingenuously—aged
Las-Casas, and he alone, excepted.

VAL. He! an enthusiast in the opposite and worse extreme!

ELV. Oh! had I earlier known that virtuous man, how different might  40
my lot have been!

VAL. I will grant, Pizarro could not then so easily have duped you;
forgive me, but at that event I still must wonder.

ELV. Hear me, Valverde.—When first my virgin fancy waked to love,
Pizarro was my country's idol. Self-taught, self-raised, and self-
supported, he became a hero; and I was formed to be won by glory
and renown. 'Tis known that when he left Panama in a slight vessel,
his force was not an hundred men. Arrived in the island of Gallo,
with his sword he drew a line upon the sands, and said, 'Pass those
who fear to die or conquer with their leader.' Thirteen alone remained,  50
and at the head of these the warrior stood his ground. Even at the
moment when my ears first caught this tale, my heart exclaimed,
'Pizarro is its lord!' What since I have perceived, or thought, or felt!
you must have more worth to win the knowledge of.

VAL. I press no further; still assured that while Alonzo de Molina, our
General's former friend and pupil, leads the enemy, Pizarro never
more will be a conqueror. [*Trumpets without.*]

ELV. Silence! I hear him coming; look not perplexed.—How mystery
and fraud confound the countenance! Quick, put on an honest face,
if thou canst.                                                                 60

PIZARRO. [*Speaking without*]. Chain and secure him; I will examine him
myself.

PIZARRO *enters.*

(VALVERDE *bows*—ELVIRA *laughs.*)

PIZ. Why dost thou smile, Elvira?

ELV. To laugh or weep without a reason, is one of the few privileges we women have.

PIZ. Elvira, I will know the cause, I am resolved!

ELV. I am glad of that, because I love resolution, and am resolved not to tell you. Now my resolution, I take it, is the better of the two, because it depends upon myself, and yours does not.

PIZ. Psha! trifler!                                                    70

VAL. Elvira was laughing at my apprehensions that——

PIZ. Apprehensions!

VAL. Yes—that Alonzo's skill and genius should so have disciplined and informed the enemy, as to——

PIZ. Alonzo! the traitor! How I once loved that man! His noble mother entrusted him, a boy, to my protection. At my table did he feast—in my tent did he repose. I had marked his early genius, and the valorous spirit that grew with it. Often I had talked to him of our first adventures —what storms we struggled with—what perils we surmounted. When landed with a slender host upon an unknown land—then, when I told  80 how famine and fatigue, discord and toil, day by day, did thin our ranks; amid close-pressing enemies, how still undaunted I endured and dared—maintained my purpose and my power in despite of growling mutiny or bold revolt, till with my faithful few remaining I became at last victorious!—When, I say, of these things I spoke, the youth, Alonzo, with tears of wonder and delight, would throw him on my neck, and swear, his soul's ambition owned no other leader.

VAL. What could subdue attachment so begun?

PIZ. Las-Casas—he it was, with fascinating craft and canting precepts of humanity, raised in Alonzo's mind a new enthusiasm, which forced  90 him, as the stripling termed it, to forego his country's claims for those of human nature.

VAL. Yes, the traitor left you, joined the Peruvians, and became thy enemy and Spain's.

PIZ. But first with weariless remonstrance he sued to win me from my purpose, and untwine the sword from my determined grasp. Much he spoke of right, of justice and humanity, calling the Peruvians our innocent and unoffending brethren.

VAL. They!—Obdurate heathens!—They our brethren!

PIZ. But when he found that the soft folly of the pleading tears he dropt  100 upon my bosom fell on marble, he flew and joined the foe: then, profiting by the lessons he had gain'd in wrong'd Pizarro's school, the youth so disciplined and led his new allies, that soon he forc'd me—

Ha! I burn with shame and fury while I own it! in base retreat and foul discomfiture to quit the shore.

VAL. But the hour of revenge is come.

PIZ. It is; I am returned—my force is strengthened, and the audacious Boy shall soon know that Pizarro lives, and has—a grateful recollection of the thanks he owes him.

VAL. 'Tis doubted whether still Alonzo lives.     110

PIZ. 'Tis certain that he does; one of his armour-bearers is just made prisoner: twelve thousand is their force, as he reports, led by Alonzo and Peruvian Rolla. This day they make a solemn sacrifice on their ungodly altars. We must profit by their security, and attack them unprepared—the sacrificers shall become the victims.

ELV. [*Aside.*] Wretched innocents! And their own blood shall bedew their altars!

PIZ. Right! [*Trumpets without.*] Elvira, retire!

ELV. Why should I retire?

PIZ. Because men are to meet here, and on manly business.     120

ELV. O, men! men! ungrateful and perverse! O, woman! still affectionate though wrong'd! The Beings to whose eyes you turn for animation, hope, and rapture, through the days of mirth and revelry; and on whose bosoms in the hour of sore calamity you seek for rest and consolation; THEM, when the pompous follies of your mean ambition are the question, you treat as playthings or as slaves!—I shall not retire.[1]

PIZ. Remain then—and, if thou canst, be silent.

ELV. They only babble who practise not reflection. I shall think—and thought is silence.

PIZ. Ha!—there's somewhat in her manner lately—     130
[PIZARRO *looks sternly and suspiciously towards* ELVIRA, *who meets him with a commanding and unaltered eye.*]

*Enter* LAS-CASAS, ALMAGRO, GONZALO, DAVILLA, *Officers and Soldiers.
—Trumpets without.*

LAS-C. Pizarro, we attend your summons.

PIZ. Welcome, venerable father—my friends, most welcome. Friends and fellow-soldiers, at length the hour is arrived, which to Pizarro's hopes presents the full reward of our undaunted enterprise and long-enduring toils. Confident in security, this day the foe devotes to solemn sacrifice: if with bold surprise we strike on their solemnity—trust to your leader's word—we shall not fail.

ALM. Too long inactive have we been mouldering on the coast—our stores exhausted, and our soldiers murmuring—Battle! Battle!—then death to the arm'd, and chains for the defenceless.     140

[1] 'Elvira, who appeared a few minutes before, the enfeebled slave of her passion, assumes a dignity and resolution, which even shook the tyrant for a moment.' (*The Oracle*, 25 May 1799.)

DAV. Death to the whole Peruvian race!

LAS-C. Merciful Heaven!

ALM. Yes, General, the attack, and instantly! Then shall Alonzo, basking
at his ease, soon cease to scoff our suffering and scorn our force.

LAS-C. Alonzo!—scorn and presumption are not in his nature.

ALM. 'Tis fit Las-Casas should defend his pupil.

PIZ. Speak not of the traitor—or hear his name but as the bloody summons to assault and vengeance. It appears we are agreed?

ALM. *and* DAV. We are.

GON. All!—Battle! Battle!                                              150

LAS-C. Is then the dreadful measure of your cruelty not yet compleat?—
Battle!—gracious Heaven! Against whom?—Against a King, in whose
mild bosom your atrocious injuries even yet have not excited hate! but
who, insulted or victorious, still sues for peace. Against a People who
never wronged the living Being their Creator formed: a People, who,
children of innocence received you as cherish'd guests with eager
hospitality and confiding kindness. Generously and freely did they
share with you their comforts, their treasures, and their homes: you
repaid them by fraud, oppression, and dishonour. These eyes have
witnessed all I speak—as Gods you were received; as Fiends have you  160
acted.[1]

PIZ. Las-Casas!

LAS-C. Pizarro, hear me!—Hear me, chieftains!—And thou, All-powerful! whose thunders can shiver into sand the adamantine rock—whose
lightnings can pierce to the core of the rived and quaking earth—
Oh! let thy power give effect to thy servant's words, as thy spirit gives
courage to his will! Do not, I implore you, Chieftains—Countrymen—
Do not, I implore you, renew the foul barbarities which your insatiate
avarice has inflicted on this wretched, unoffending race!—But hush,
my sighs—fall not, drops of useless sorrow!—heart-breaking anguish,  170
choke not my utterance—All I entreat is, send me once more to those
you *call* your enemies—Oh! let me be the messenger of penitence from
you, I shall return with blessings and with peace from them.—Elvira,
you weep!—Alas! and does this dreadful crisis move no heart but
thine?

ALM. Because there are no women here but she and thou.

PIZ. Close this idle war of words: time flies, and our opportunity will
be lost. Chieftains, are ye for instant battle?

ALL. We are.

---

[1] 'The speech of this good old Priest is one of the finest and most impressive in the
whole Piece . . .' (*The Oracle*, 25 May 1799). Harvard MS. fms Thr 5 reads: 'What a
dreadful reflexion! a Battle—against whom? against a King, that a few days ago offered
peace—against a nation, that in innocence, and with purity worship their Creator in
their accustomed way and manner.'

LAS-C. Oh, men of blood!—[*Kneels.*] God! thou hast anointed me thy 180
servant—not to curse, but to bless my countrymen: yet now my blessing on their force were blasphemy against thy goodness.—[*Rises*]. No!
I curse your purpose, homicides! I curse the bond of blood by which
you are united. May fell division, infamy, and rout, defeat your pro-
jects and rebuke your hopes! On you, and on your children, be the
peril of the innocent blood which shall be shed this day! I leave you,
and for ever! No longer shall these aged eyes be feared by the horrors
they have witnessed. In caves, in forests, will I hide myself; with
Tigers and with savage beasts will I commune: and when at length
we meet again before the bless'd tribunal of that Deity, whose mild 190
doctrines and whose mercies ye have this day renounced, then shall
YOU feel the agony and grief of soul which tear the bosom of your
accuser now! [*Going.*]

ELV. Las-Casas! Oh! take me with thee, Las-Casas.

LAS-C. Stay! lost, abused lady! I alone am useless here. Perhaps thy
loveliness may persuade to pity, where reason and religion plead in
vain. Oh! save thy innocent fellow-creatures if thou canst: then shall
thy frailty be redeemed, and thou wilt share the mercy thou bestowest.

[*Exit.*

PIZ. How, Elvira! wouldst thou leave me?

ELV. I am bewildered, grown terrified!—Your inhumanity—and that 200
good Las-Casas—oh! he appeared to me just now something more
than heavenly: and you! ye all looked worse than earthly.

PIZ. Compassion sometimes becomes a beauty.

ELV. Humanity always becomes a conqueror.

ALM. Well! Heaven be praised, we are rid of the old moralist.

GON. I hope he'll join his preaching pupil, Alonzo.

PIZ. Now to prepare our muster and our march. At mid-day is the hour
of the sacrifice. Consulting with our guides, the route of your divisions
shall be given to each commander. If we surprise, we conquer; and if
we conquer, the gates of Quito will be open to us.                     210

ALM. And Pizarro then be monarch of Peru.

PIZ. Not so fast—ambition for a time must take counsel from discretion.
Ataliba still must hold the shadow of a sceptre in his hand—Pizarro
still appear dependant upon Spain: while the pledge of future peace,
his daughter's hand, secures the proud succession to the crown I
seek.

ALM. This is best. In Pizarro's plans observe the statesman's wisdom
guides the warrior's valour.

VAL. [*Aside to* ELVIRA.] You mark, Elvira?

ELV. O, yes—this is best—this is excellent.                           220

PIZ. You seem offended. Elvira still retains my heart. Think—a sceptre
waves me on.

ELV. Offended?—No!—Thou know'st thy glory is my idol; and this will be most glorious, most just and honourable.

PIZ. What mean you?

ELV. Oh! nothing—mere woman's prattle—a jealous whim, perhaps: but let it not impede the royal hero's course.—[*Trumpets without.*] The call of arms invites you—Away! away! you, his brave, his worthy fellow-warriors.

PIZ. And go you not with me?                                    230

ELV. Undoubtedly! I needs must be the first to hail the future monarch of Peru.

*Enter* GOMEZ.

ALM. How, Gomez! what bring'st thou?

GOM. On yonder hill among the palm trees we have surprised an old cacique; escape by flight he could not, and we seized him and his attendant unresisting; yet his lips breathe nought but bitterness and scorn.

PIZ. Drag him before us.

[GOMEZ *leaves the tent, and returns conducting* OROZEMBO *and* ATTENDANT, *in chains, guarded.*

What art thou, stranger?

ORO. First tell me which among you is the captain of this band of robbers. 240

PIZ. Ha!

ALM. Madman!—Tear out his tongue, or else——

ORO. Thou'lt hear some truth.

DAV. [*Shewing his poniard.*] Shall I not plunge this into his heart?

ORO. [*To* PIZ.] Does your army boast many such heroes as this?

PIZ. Audacious!—This insolence has sealed thy doom. Die thou shalt, grey-headed ruffian. But first confess what thou knowest.

ORO. I know that which thou hast just assured me of—that I shall die.

PIZ. Less audacity perhaps might have preserved thy life.

ORO. My life is as a withered tree—it is not worth preserving.       250

PIZ. Hear me, old man. Even now we march against the Peruvian army. We know there is a secret path that leads to your strong-hold among the rocks: guide us to that, and name thy reward. If wealth be thy wish—

ORO. Ha! ha! ha! ha!

PIZ. Dost thou despise my offer?

ORO. Thee and thy offer!—Wealth!—I have the wealth of two dear gallant sons—I have stored in heaven the riches which repay good actions here—and still my chiefest treasure do I bear about me.

PIZ. What is that? Inform me.                                     260

ORO. I will; for it never can be thine—the treasure of a pure unsullied conscience.

PIZ. I believe there is no other Peruvian who dares speak as thou dost.

ORO. Would I could believe there is no other Spaniard who dares act as thou dost!

GON. [*Aside.*] Obdurate Pagan!—How numerous is your army?

ORO. Count the leaves of yonder forest.

ALM. Which is the weakest part of your camp?

ORO. It has no weak part—on every side 'tis fortified by justice.

PIZ. Where have you concealed your wives and your children? 270

ORO. In the hearts of their husbands and their fathers.

PIZ. Know'st thou Alonzo?

ORO. Know him!—Alonzo!—Know him!—Our nation's benefactor!—The guardian angel of Peru!

PIZ. By what has he merited that title?

ORO. By not resembling thee.

ALM. Who is this Rolla, joined with Alonzo in command?

ORO. I will answer that; for I love to hear and to repeat the hero's name. Rolla, the kinsman of the King, is the idol of our army; in war a tiger, chased by the hunter's spear; in peace as gentle as the unweaned lamb. 280 CORA was once betrothed to him; but finding she preferred Alonzo, he resigned his claim, and, I fear, his peace, to friendship and to CORA's happiness: yet still he loves her with a pure and holy fire.

PIZ. Romantic savage!—I shall meet this Rolla soon.

ORO. Thou hadst better not! The terrors of his noble eye would strike thee dead.

DAV. Silence, or tremble!

ORO. Beardless robber! I never yet have trembled before God—why should I tremble before man?—Why before thee, thou less than man!

DAV. Another word, audacious heathen, and I strike! 290

ORO. Strike, Christian! Then boast among thy fellows—I too have murdered a Peruvian!

DAV. Hell and vengeance seize thee! [*Stabs him.*]

PIZ. Hold!

DAV. Couldst thou longer have endured his insults?

PIZ. And therefore should he die untortured?

ORO. True! Observe, young man—your unthinking rashness has saved me from the rack; and you yourself have lost the opportunity of a useful lesson; you might have seen with what cruelty vengeance would have inflicted torments, and with what patience virtue would have borne them. 300

ELV. [*Supporting* OROZEMBO's *head upon her bosom.*] Oh! ye are monsters all. Look up, thou martyr'd innocent—look up once more, and bless me ere thou diest. God! how I pity thee!

ORO. Pity me!—Me! so near my happiness! Bless thee, lady!—Spaniards—Heaven turn your hearts, and pardon you as I do. [OROZEMBO *is borne off dying.*]

PIZ. Away!—Davilla! If thus rash a second time—

DAV. Forgive the hasty indignation which—

PIZ. No more—unbind that trembling wretch—let him depart; 'tis
well he should report the mercy which we show to insolent defiance.—    310
—Hark!—our troops are moving.

ATTENDANT. [*On passing* ELVIRA.] If through your gentle means my
master's poor remains might be preserved from insult—

ELV. I understand you.

ATT. His sons may yet thank your charity, if not avenge their father's
fate.                                                                    [*Exit.*

PIZ. What says the slave?

ELV. A parting word to thank you for your mercy.

PIZ. Our guard and guides approach. [*Soldiers march through the tents.*]
Follow me, friends—each shall have his post assigned, and ere Peruvia's  320
God shall sink beneath the main, the Spanish banner, bathed in blood,
shall float above the walls of vanquish'd Quito.             [*Exeunt.*

*Manent* ELVIRA *and* VALVERDE.

VAL. Is it now presumption that my hopes gain strength with the increasing horrors which I see appal Elvira's soul?

ELV. I am mad with terror and remorse! Would I could fly these dreadful scenes!

VAL. Might not Valverde's true attachment be thy refuge?

ELV. What wouldst thou do to save or to avenge me?

VAL. I dare do all thy injuries may demand—a word—and he lies bleed-    330
ing at your feet.

ELV. Perhaps we will speak again of this. Now leave me.

[*Exit* VALVERDE.

ELV. [*Alone.*] No! not this revenge—no! not this instrument. Fie, Elvira!
even for a moment to counsel with this unworthy traitor!—Can a
wretch, false to a confiding master, be true to any pledge of love or
honour?—Pizarro will abandon me—yes; me—who, for his sake, have
sacrificed—Oh, God!—What have I not sacrificed for him; yet, curb-
ing the avenging pride that swells this bosom, I still will further try
him. Oh, men! ye who, wearied by the fond fidelity of virtuous love,
seek in the wanton's flattery a new delight, oh, ye may insult and leave  340
the hearts to which your faith was pledged, and, stifling self-reproach,
may fear no other peril; because such hearts, howe'er you injure and
desert them, have yet the proud retreat of an unspotted fame—of
unreproaching conscience. But beware the desperate libertine who
forsakes the creature whom his arts have first deprived of all natural
protection—of all self-consolation! What has he left her!—Despair
and vengeance!                                                        [*Exit.*

END OF THE FIRST ACT

# ACT II

## SCENE I

*A Bank surrounded by a wild Wood, and Rocks.*—CORA, *sitting on the root of a tree, is playing with her Child.*—ALONZO *looks over them with delight and chearfulness.*

CORA. Now confess, does he resemble thee, or not?

AL. Indeed he is liker thee—thy rosy softness, thy smiling gentleness.

CORA. But his auburn hair, the colour of his eyes, Alonzo—O! my lord's image, and my heart's adored! [*Pressing the Child to her bosom.*]

AL. The little daring urchin robs me, I doubt, of some portion of thy love, my Cora. At least he shares caresses, which till his birth were only mine.

CORA. Oh no, Alonzo! a mother's love for her dear babe is not a stealth, or taken from the father's store; it is a new delight that turns with quicken'd gratitude to HIM, the author of her augmented bliss.                   10

AL. Could Cora think me serious?

CORA. I am sure he will speak soon: then will be the last of the three holydays allowed by Nature's sanction to the fond anxious mother's heart.

AL. What are those three?

CORA. The ecstacy of his birth I pass; that in part is selfish: but when first the white blossoms of his teeth appear, breaking the crimson buds that did incase them; that is a day of joy: next, when from his father's arms he runs without support, and clings, laughing and delighted, to his mother's knee; that is the mother's heart's next holyday: and sweeter   20 still the third, whene'er his little stammering tongue shall utter the grateful sound of, Father, Mother!—O! that is the dearest joy of all!

AL. Beloved Cora!

CORA. Oh! my Alonzo! daily, hourly, do I pour thanks to Heaven for the dear blessing I possess in him and thee.

AL. To Heaven and Rolla.

CORA. Yes, to Heaven and Rolla: and art thou not grateful to them too, Alonzo? art thou not happy?

AL. Can Cora ask that question?

CORA. Why then of late so restless on thy couch? Why to my waking   30 watching ear so often does the stillness of the night betray thy struggling sighs?

AL. Must not I fight against my country, against my brethren?

CORA. Do they not seek our destruction, and are not all men brethren?

AL. Should they prove victorious?

CORA. I will fly, and meet thee in the mountains.

AL. Fly, with thy infant, Cora?

CORA. What! think you a mother, when she runs from danger, can feel the weight of her child?

AL. Cora, my beloved, do you wish to set my heart at rest? 40

CORA. Oh yes! yes! yes!

AL. Hasten then now to the concealment in the mountains; there dwells your father, and there all our matrons and virgins, and our warriors' offspring, are allotted to await the issue of the war. Cora will not alone resist her husband's, her sisters', and her monarch's wish.

CORA. Alonzo, I cannot leave you: Oh! how in every moment's absence would my fancy paint you, wounded, alone, abandon'd! No, no, I cannot leave you.

AL. Rolla will be with me.

CORA. Yes, while the battle rages, and where it rages most, brave Rolla 50 will be found. He may revenge, but cannot save thee. To follow danger, he will leave even theé. But I have sworn never to forsake thee but with life. Dear, dear Alonzo! can you wish that I should break my vow?

AL. Then be it so. Oh! excellence in all that's great and lovely, in courage, gentleness, and truth; my pride, my content, my all! Can there on this earth be fools who seek for happiness, and pass by love in the pursuit?

CORA. Alonzo, I cannot thank you: silence is the gratitude of true affection: who seeks to follow it by sound will miss the track. [*Shout without*.] Does the King approach? 60

AL. No, 'tis the General placing the guard that will surround the temple during the sacrifice. 'Tis Rolla comes, the first and best of heroes. [*Trumpets sound*.]

### ROLLA.

ROL. [*as entering*.] Then place them on the hill fronting the Spanish camp. [*Enters*.]

CORA. Rolla! my friend, my brother!

AL. Rolla! my friend, my benefactor! how can our lives repay the obligations which we owe you?

ROL. Pass them in peace and bliss.—Let Rolla witness it, he is overpaid.

CORA. Look on this child—He is the life-blood of my heart; but if ever he loves or reveres thee less than his own father, his mother's hate fall 70 on him!

ROL. Oh, no more!—What sacrifice have I made to merit gratitude? The object of my love was Cora's happiness.—I see her happy.—Is not my object gain'd, and am I not rewarded? Now, Cora, listen to a friend's advice. You must away; you must seek the sacred caverns, the unprofan'd recess, whither, after this day's sacrifice, our matrons, and e'en the Virgins of the Sun, retire.

CORA. Not secure with Alonzo and with thee, Rolla?

ROL.. We have heard Pizarro's plan is to surprise us.—Thy presence,
Cora, cannot aid, but may impede our efforts.                          80

CORA. Impede!

ROL. Yes, yes. Thou know'st how tenderly we love thee; we, thy husband
and thy friend. Art thou near us? our thoughts, our valour—vengeance
will not be our own.—No advantage will be pursued that leads us from
the spot where thou art placed; no succour will be given but for thy
protection. The faithful lover dares not be all himself amid the war,
until he knows that the beloved of his soul is absent from the peril of
the fight.

AL. Thanks to my friend! 'tis this I would have urged.

CORA. This timid excess of love, producing fear instead of valour, flatters,  90
but does not convince me: the wife is incredulous.

ROL. And is the mother unbelieving too?

CORA. No more—Do with me as you please. My friend, my husband!
place me where you will.

AL. My adored! we thank you both. [*March without.*] Hark! the King
approaches to the sacrifice. You, Rolla, spoke of rumours of surprise.—
A servant of mine, I hear, is missing; whether surprised or treacherous,
I know not.

ROL. It matters not. We are every where prepared. Come, Cora, upon
the altar 'mid the rocks thou'lt implore a blessing on our cause. The  100
pious supplication of the trembling wife, and mother's heart, rises
to the throne of mercy, the most resistless prayer of human homage.

[*Exeunt.*

## SCENE II

*The Temple of the Sun: it represents the magnificence of Peruvian
idolatry: in the centre is the altar.—A solemn march.*[1]*—The Warriors
and King enter on one side of the Temple.—*ROLLA, ALONZO, *and*
CORA, *on the other.*

ATA. Welcome, Alonzo! [*To* ROLLA.] Kinsman, thy hand.—[*To* CORA.]
Bless'd be the object of the happy mother's love.

CORA. May the sun bless the father of his people![2]

ATA. In the welfare of his children lives the happiness of their King.
Friends, what is the temper of our soldiers?

[1] 'Grand March in the Temple of the Sun [by] Kelly': see *The Music of Pizarro*,
pp. 1–2.

[2] 'To those *Children of the Sun*, for that was the appellation bestowed upon all the
offspring of the first Inca, the people looked up with the reverence due to beings of a
superior order. They were deemed to be under the immediate protection of the deity
from whom they issued' (W. Robertson, *The History of America* (5th edn., 1788),
iii. 204).

ROL. Such as becomes the cause which they support; their cry is, Victory
or death! our King! our Country! and our God!

ATA. Thou, Rolla, in the hour of peril, hast been wont to animate the
spirit of their leaders, ere we proceed to consecrate the banners which
thy valour knows so well to guard.                                                              10

ROL. Yet never was the hour of peril near, when to inspire them words
were so little needed. My brave associates—partners of my toil, my
feelings and my fame!—can Rolla's words add vigour to the virtuous
energies which inspire your hearts?——No—YOU have judged as I
have, the foulness of the crafty plea by which these bold invaders
would delude you—Your generous spirit has compared as mine has,
the motives, which, in a war like this, can animate *their* minds, and
OURS.—THEY, by a strange frenzy driven, fight for power, for plunder,
and extended rule—WE, for our country, our altars, and our homes.—
THEY follow an Adventurer whom they fear—and obey a power which   20
they hate—WE serve a Monarch whom we love—a God whom we
adore.—Whene'er they move in anger, desolation tracks their progress!
—Where'er they pause in amity, affliction mourns their friendship!—
They boast, they come but to improve our state, enlarge our thoughts,
and free us from the yoke of error!—Yes—THEY will give enlightened
freedom to *our* minds, who are themselves the slaves of passion, avarice,
and pride.—They offer us their protection—Yes, such protection as
vultures give to lambs—covering and devouring them!—They call on
us to barter all of good we have inherited and proved, for the desperate
chance of something better which they promise.—Be our plain answer   30
this: The throne WE honour is the PEOPLE'S CHOICE—the laws we
reverence are our brave Fathers' legacy—the faith we follow teaches
us to live in bonds of charity with all mankind, and die with hope of
bliss beyond the grave. Tell your invaders this, and tell them too, we
seek no change; and, least of all, such change as they would bring us.
                                                    [*Trumpets sound.*

ATA. [*Embracing* ROLLA.] Now, holy friends, ever mindful of these
sacred truths, begin the sacrifice. [*A solemn Procession commences from
the recess of the Temple above the Altar—The Priests and Virgins of the
Sun arrange themselves on either side—The High-Priest approaches the
Altar, and the solemnity begins—The Invocation of the High-Priest*[1] *is*

---

[1] The procession was accompanied by a march by Gluck. See Kelly, *The Music of
Pizarro*, pp. 3–11, for this, and for the invocation, made up of 'Solo and Semi-Chorus':

[*High-Priest*: Mr. Sedgwick]

Oh pow'r Supreme! in mercy smile
With favor on thy Servants' toil!
Our hearts from guileful passions free
Which here we render unto thee!

*followed by the Chorusses of the Priests and Virgins—Fire from above
lights upon the Altar.—The whole assembly rise, and join in the Thanksgiving.]* Our offering is accepted.—Now to arms, my friends, prepare
for battle.

*Enter* ORANO.

ORA. The enemy!                                                        40

ATA. How near?

ORA. From the hill's brow, e'en now as I o'er-looked their force, suddenly
I perceived the whole in motion: with eager haste they march towards
our deserted camp, as if apprised of this most solemn sacrifice.

ROL. They must be met before they reach it.

ATA. And you, my daughters, with your dear children, away to the
appointed place of safety.

CORA. Oh, Alonzo! [*Embracing him.*]

AL. We shall meet again.

CORA. Bless us once more, ere you leave us.                            50

AL. Heaven protect and bless thee, my beloved; and thee, my innocent!

ATA. Haste, haste!—each moment is precious!

CORA. Farewell, Alonzo! Remember thy life is mine.

ROL. Not one farewell to Rolla?

CORA. [*Giving him her hand.*] Farewell! The God of war be with you:
but, bring me back Alonzo.                          [*Exit with the Child.*

ATA. [*Draws his sword.*] Now, my brethren, my sons, my friends, I know
your valour.—Should ill success assail us, be despair the last feeling
of your hearts.—If successful, let mercy be the first.[1] Alonzo, to you

[*Priests and Virgins*]
[Kelly, Dignum, Mrs. Crouch, Miss Decamp, Stephens, Dufour, Leak]

> Oh pow'r supreme! in mercy smile
> With favor on thy Servants' toil!
> Our hearts from guileful passions free
> Which here we render unto thee.

[*Chorus of Priests and Virgins*: by Sacchini]

> Thou Parent Light but deign to hear
>    The voices of our feeble choir;
> And this, our sacrifice of fear,
>    Consume with thine own hallowed fire!

[*Thanksgiving*]

> Give praise, give praise, the God has heard,
> Our God most awfully rever'd!
> The altar his own flames enwreath'd!
> Then be the conquering sword unsheath'd,
> And victory sit on Rolla's brow,
> Our foes to crush—to overthrow!

[1] 'This patriotic address, which was greatly applauded, was concluded with a chorus;
at the end of which the Peruvians filed off the stage, led by Rolla, who told them, "that

I give to defend the narrow passage of the mountains. On the right of 60
the wood be Rolla's station. For me, strait forwards will I march to
meet them, and fight until I see my people saved, or they behold their
Monarch fall. Be the word of battle—God! and our native land.
[*A march.*]¹                                                    [*Exeunt.*

## SCENE III

*The Wood between the Temple and the Camp.*

*Enter* ROLLA *and* ALONZO.

ROL. Here, my friend, we separate—soon, I trust, to meet again in
triumph.

AL. Or perhaps we part to meet no more. Rolla, a moment's pause;
we are yet before our army's strength; one earnest word at parting.

ROL. There is in language now no word but battle.

AL. Yes, one word more—Cora!

ROL. Cora! Speak!

AL. The next hour brings us—

ROL. Death or victory!

AL. It may be victory to one—death to the other.                    10

ROL. Or both may fall.

AL. If so, my wife and child I bequeath to the protection of Heaven and
my King. But should I only fall, Rolla, be thou my heir.

ROL. How?

AL. Be Cora thy wife—be thou a father to my child.

ROL. Rouse thee, Alonzo! Banish these timid fancies.

AL. Rolla! I have tried in vain, and cannot fly from the foreboding which
oppresses me: thou know'st it will not shake me in the fight: but give
me your promise.

ROL. If it be Cora's will—Yes—I promise—[*Gives his hand.*]        20

AL. Tell her it was my last wish! and bear to her and to my son, my last
blessing.

ROL. I will.—Now then to our posts, and let our swords speak for us.
[*They draw their swords.*]

AL. For the King and Cora!

ROL. For Cora and the King!     [*Exeunt different ways. Alarms without.*

---

in case of a defeat, despair should be the last quality that should fill their bosoms; and
in case of victory, mercy should be the first!" A blind man next appeared' (*The Oracle*,
25 May 1799). If the report is correct, the text of the first night differed from the printed
version at this point, and immediately afterwards.

¹ Kelly, *The Music of Pizarro*, p. 12: by Thomas Shaw, conductor of the band.

## SCENE IV

*A View of the Peruvian Camp, with a distant View of a Peruvian
Village. Trees growing from a rocky Eminence on one Side. Alarms
continue.*

### Enter an OLD BLIND MAN *and a* BOY.

O. MAN. Have none returned to the camp?

BOY. One messenger alone. From the temple they all march'd to meet
the foe.

O. MAN. Hark! I hear the din of battle. O! had I still retain'd my sight,
I might now have grasp'd a sword, and died a soldier's death! Are we
quite alone?

BOY. Yes!—I hope my father will be safe!

O. MAN. He will do his duty. I am more anxious for thee, my child.

BOY. I can stay with you, dear grandfather.

O. MAN. But should the enemy come, they will drag thee from me, my    10
boy.

BOY. Impossible, grandfather! for they will see at once that you are old
and blind, and cannot do without me.

O. MAN. Poor child! you little know the hearts of these inhuman men.—
[*Discharge of cannon heard.*] Hark! the noise is near—I hear the dreadful
roaring of the fiery engines of these cruel strangers.—[*Shouts at a
distance.*] At every shout, with involuntary haste I clench my hand,
and fancy still it grasps a sword! Alas! I can only serve my country
by my prayers. Heaven preserve the Inca and his gallant soldiers!

BOY. O father! there are soldiers running—                               20

O. MAN. Spaniards, boy?

BOY. No, Peruvians!

O. MAN. How! and flying from the field!—It cannot be.

### Enter two Peruvian SOLDIERS.

O speak to them, boy!—Whence come you? How goes the battle?

SOL. We may not stop; we are sent for the reserve behind the hill. The
day's against us.                                    [*Exeunt* SOLDIERS.

O. MAN. Quick, then, quick!

BOY. I see the points of lances glittering in the light.

O. MAN. Those are Peruvians. Do they bend this way?

### Enter a Peruvian SOLDIER.

BOY. Soldier, speak to my blind father.                                  30

SOL. I'm sent to tell the helpless father to retreat among the rocks:
all will be lost, I fear. The King is wounded.

O. MAN. Quick, boy! Lead me to the hill, where thou may'st view the plain. [*Alarms.*]

*Enter* ATALIBA, *wounded, with* ORANO, OFFICERS, *and* SOLDIERS.

ATA. My wound is bound; believe me, the hurt is nothing: I may return to the fight.

ORA. Pardon your servant; but the allotted priest who attends the sacred banner has pronounced that the Inca's blood once shed, no blessing can await the day until he leave the field.

ATA. Hard restraint! O! my poor brave soldiers!—Hard that I may no 10 longer be a witness of their valour. But haste you; return to your comrades: I will not keep one soldier from his post. Go, and avenge your fallen brethren. [*Exeunt* ORANO, OFFICERS, *and* SOLDIERS.] I will not repine; my own fate is the last anxiety of my heart. It is for you, my people, that I feel and fear.

OLD MAN *and* BOY *advance.*

O. MAN. Did I not hear the voice of an unfortunate?—Who is it complains thus?

ATA. One almost by hope forsaken.

O. MAN. Is the King alive?

ATA. The King still lives.                                        20

O. MAN. Then thou art not forsaken! Ataliba protects the meanest of his subjects.

ATA. And who shall protect Ataliba?

O. MAN. The immortal Powers, that protect the just. The virtues of our Monarch alike secure to him the affection of his people and the benign regard of Heaven.

ATA. How impious, had I murmured! How wondrous, thou supreme Disposer, are thy acts! Even in this moment, which I had thought the bitterest trial of mortal suffering, thou hast infused the sweetest sensation of my life—it is the assurance of my people's love.     30

BOY. [*Turning forward.*] O, father!—Stranger, see those hideous men that rush upon us yonder!

ATA. Ha! Spaniards!—And I—Ataliba—ill-fated fugitive, without a sword even to try the ransom of a monarch.life.

*Enter* DAVILLA, ALMAGRO, *and Spanish* SOLDIERS.

DAV. 'Tis he—our hopes are answered—I know him well—it is the King!

ALM. Away! Follow with your royal prize. Avoid those Peruvians, though in flight. This way we may regain our line.

[*Exeunt* DAVILLA, ALMAGRO, *and* SOLDIERS, *with* ATALIBA *prisoner.*

O. MAN. The King! Wretched old man, that could not see his gracious
form!—Boy, would thou hadst led me to the reach of those ruffians' 40
swords!

BOY. Father! all our countrymen are flying here for refuge.

O. MAN. No—to the rescue of their King—they never will desert him.
[*Alarms without.*]

*Enter Peruvian* OFFICERS *and* SOLDIERS, *flying across
the stage;* ORANO *following.*

ORA. Hold, I charge you! Rolla calls you.

OFFICER. We cannot combat with their dreadful engines.

*Enter* ROLLA.

ROL. Hold, recreants! cowards!—What, fear ye death, and fear not
shame? By my soul's fury, I cleave to the earth the first of you that
stirs, or plunge your dastard swords into your leader's heart, that he
no more may witness your disgrace. Where is the King?

ORA. From this old man and boy I learn that the detachment of the 50
enemy which you observed so suddenly to quit the field, have succeeded
in surprising him; they are yet in sight.

ROL. And bear the Inca off a prisoner?—Hear this, ye base, disloyal
rout! Look there! The dust you see hangs on the bloody Spaniards'
track, dragging with ruffian taunts your King, your father!—Ataliba
in bondage. Now fly, and seek your own vile safety, if you can.

O. MAN. Bless the voice of Rolla—and bless the stroke I once lamented,
but which now spares these extinguished eyes the shame of seeing the
pale trembling wretches who dare not follow Rolla though to save their
King!　　　　　　　　　　　　　　　　　　　　　　　　　　　　　　　　　60

ROL. Shrink ye from the thunder of the foe—and fall ye not at this rebuke? Oh! had ye each but one drop of the loyal blood which gushes
to waste through the brave heart of this sightless veteran! Eternal shame
pursue you, if you desert me now!—But do—alone I go—alone—to
die with glory by my monarch's side!

SOLDIERS. Rolla! we'll follow thee. [*Trumpets sound;* ROLLA *rushes out,
followed by* ORANO, OFFICERS, *and* SOLDIERS.]

O. MAN. O godlike Rolla!—And thou sun, send from thy clouds avenging lightning to his aid!—Haste, my boy; ascend some height, and
tell to my impatient terror what thou seest.

BOY. I can climb this rock, and the tree above. [*Ascends a rock, and from* 70
*thence into the tree.*] O—now I see them—now—yes—and the Spaniards
turning by the steep.

O. MAN. Rolla follows them?

BOY. He does—he does—he moves like an arrow!—now he waves his arm
to our soldiers—[*Report of cannon heard.*] Now there is fire and smoke.

O. MAN. Yes, *fire* is the weapon of those fiends.

BOY. The wind blows off the smoke: they are all mixed together.

O. MAN. Seest thou the King?

BOY. Yes—Rolla is near him! His sword sheds fire as he strikes!

O. MAN. Bless thee, Rolla! Spare not the monsters. 80

BOY. Father! father! the Spaniards fly!—O—now I see the King embracing Rolla. [*Waving his cap for joy. Shouts of victory, flourish of trumpets, &c.*]

O. MAN. [*Falls on his knees.*] Fountain of life! how can my exhausted breath bear to thee thanks for this one moment of my life! My boy, come down, and let me kiss thee—My strength is gone! [*The* BOY *having run to the* OLD MAN.]

BOY. Let me help you, father—You tremble so——

O. MAN. 'Tis with transport, boy! [BOY *leads the* OLD MAN *off.*

*Shouts, Flourish, &c.*

*Enter* ATALIBA, ROLLA, *and Peruvian* OFFICERS *and* SOLDIERS.

ATA. In the name of my people, the saviour of whose sovereign you have this day been, accept this emblem of his gratitude. [*Giving* ROLLA *his sun of diamonds.*] The tear that falls upon it may for a moment dim 90 its lustre, yet does it not impair the value of the gift.

ROL. It was the hand of Heaven, not mine, that saved my King.

*Enter* ORANO, *and* SOLDIERS.

ROL. Now, soldier, from Alonzo?

ORA. Alonzo's genius soon repaired the panic which early broke our ranks; but I fear we have to mourn Alonzo's loss; his eager spirit urged him too far in the pursuit!

ATA. How! Alonzo slain?

1ST SOL. I saw him fall.

2D SOL. Trust me I beheld him up again and fighting—he was then surrounded and disarmed. 100

ATA. O! victory, dearly purchased!

ROL. O Cora! Who shall tell thee this?

ATA. Rolla, our friend is lost—our native country saved! Our private sorrows must yield to the public claim for triumph. Now go we to fulfil the first, the most sacred duty which belongs to victory—to dry the widowed and the orphaned tear of those whose brave protectors have perished in their country's case.

[*Triumphant march, and exeunt.*

END OF THE SECOND ACT

# ACT III

## SCENE I

*A wild Retreat among stupendous Rocks.*—CORA *and her Child, with other Wives and Children of the Peruvian Warriors, are scattered about the scene in groups.*—*They sing alternately, Stanzas expressive of their situation, with a* CHORUS, *in which all join.*[1]

1ST PERUVIAN WOMAN. Zuluga, seest thou nothing yet?

ZUL. Yes, two Peruvian soldiers, one on the hill; the other entering the thicket in the vale.

2D PER. WOMAN. One more has pass'd.—He comes—but pale and terrified.

CORA. My heart will start from my bosom.

*Enter a Peruvian* SOLDIER, *panting for breath.*

WOM. Well! joy or death?

SOLD. The battle is against us. The King is wounded, and a prisoner.

WOM. Despair and misery!

CORA. [*In a faint voice.*] And Alonzo?                                    10

SOLD. I have not seen him.

1ST WOM. Oh! whither must we fly?

2D WOM. Deeper into the forest.

CORA. I shall not move.

ANOTHER PERUVIAN SOLDIER, [*without.*] Victory! victory!

*He enters hastily.*

Rejoice! Rejoice! We are victorious!

WOM. [*Springing up.*] Welcome! welcome! thou messenger of joy: but the King!

SOLD. He leads the brave warriors, who approach.

[*The triumphant march of the army is heard at a distance.*—*The Women and Children join in a strain expressive of anxiety and exultation.*—*The Warriors enter singing the Song of Victory, in which all*

---

[1] Kelly, *The Music of Pizarro*, pp. 13–16, reads: 'Glee sung by Mrs. Crouch, Miss Decamp, Stephens, Dufour, and Leak [by Kelly].

> Fly away, fly away, fly away time,
> Nor be the Anxious hour delay'd.
> Fly away, fly away, fly away time,
> That soothes the heart by grief dismay'd.
> Should gastley Death Appear in view
> We can dare it.
> With friends we love So brave and true
> We will share it.
> Fly away, fly away, fly away time, etc.'

*join.*[1]*—The King and* ROLLA *follow, and are met with rapturous and affectionate respect.* CORA, *during this scene, with her Child in her arms, runs through the ranks searching and inquiring for* ALONZO.]

ATA. Thanks, thanks, my children! I am well: believe it; the blood once 20 stopp'd, my wound was nothing. [CORA *at length approaches* ROLLA, *who appears to have been mournfully avoiding her.*] Where is Alonzo?
                    [ROLLA *turns away in silence.*

CORA. [*Falling at the King's feet.*] Give me my husband, give this child his father.

ATA. I grieve that Alonzo is not here.

CORA. Hop'd you to find him?

ATA. Most anxiously.

CORA. Ataliba! is he not dead?

ATA. No! the Gods will have heard our prayers.

CORA. Is he not dead, Ataliba? 30

ATA. He lives—in my heart.

CORA. Oh King! torture me not thus! speak out, is this child fatherless?

ATA. Dearest Cora! do not thus dash aside the little hope that still remains.

CORA. The little hope! yet still there *is* hope! Speak to me, Rolla: *you* are the *friend of truth.*

ROL. Alonzo has not been found.

CORA. Not found! What mean you? will not *you*, Rolla, tell me truth? Oh! let me not hear the thunder rolling at a distance; let the bolt fall and crush my brain at once.—Say not that he is not found: say at 40 once that he is dead.

ROL. Then should I say false.

CORA. *False!* Blessings on thee for that word! But snatch me from this terrible suspense. Lift up thy little hands, my child; perhaps thy ignorance may plead better than thy mother's agony.

ROL. Alonzo is taken prisoner.

CORA. Prisoner! and by the Spaniards? Pizarro's prisoner? Then is he dead.

ATA. Hope better—the richest ransom which our realm can yield, a herald shall this instant bear. 50

---

[1] Kelly, *The Music of Pizarro*, pp. 17–20, reads: 'Distant military march and chorus of Peruvians [by Kelly].

[*Warriors.*] Victory now has made us free;
            We haste, we haste, our friends to see!

[*Women.*] Hush! hush! don't you hear?
            Some footsteps near
            A distant march assails the Ear;—
            Hark! louder still from yonder Hill
            Encreasing sounds with terror fill—'
[Sung simultaneously.]

PER. WOM. Oh! for Alonzo's ransom—our gold, our gems!—all! all!—
Here, dear Cora,—here! here!

[*The Peruvian Women eagerly tear off all their ornaments, and run
and take them from their children, to offer them to* CORA.]

ATA. Yes, for Alonzo's ransom they would give all!—I thank thee, Father,
who hast given me such hearts to rule over!

CORA. Now one boon more, beloved monarch. Let me go with the
herald.

ATA. Remember, Cora, thou art not a wife only, but a mother too:
hazard not your own honour, and the safety of your infant. Among
these barbarians the sight of thy youth, thy loveliness, and innocence,
would but rivet faster your Alonzo's chains, and rack his heart with 60
added fears for thee.—Wait, Cora, the return of the herald.

CORA. Teach me how to live till then.

ATA. Now we go to offer to the Gods, thanks for our victory, and prayers
for our Alonzo's safety.          [*March and procession. Exeunt omnes.*

## SCENE II

### *The Wood.*

#### *Enter* CORA *and child.*

CORA. Mild innocence, what will become of thee?

#### *Enter* ROLLA.

ROL. Cora, I attend thy summons at th' appointed spot.

CORA. Oh my child, my boy!—hast thou still a father?

ROL. Cora, can thy child be fatherless, while Rolla lives?

CORA. Will he not soon want a mother too?—For canst thou think I
will survive Alonzo's loss?

ROL. Yes! for his child's sake.—Yes, as thou didst love Alonzo, Cora,
listen to Alonzo's friend.

CORA. You bid me listen to the world.—Who was not Alonzo's friend?

ROL. His parting words——                                          10

CORA. His parting words! [*Wildly.*] Oh, speak!

ROL. Consign'd to me two precious trusts—his blessing to his son, and
a last request to thee.

CORA. His *last* request! his *last*!—Oh, name it!

ROL. If I fall, said he—(and sad forebodings shook him while he spoke)—
promise to take my Cora for thy wife; be thou a father to my child.—
I pledged my word to him, and we parted.—Observe me, Cora, I
repeat this only, as my faith to do so was given to Alonzo—for myself,
I neither cherish claim [n]or hope.

CORA. Ha! does my reason fail me, or what is this horrid light that presses 20 on my brain? Oh, Alonzo! It may be thou hast fallen a victim to thy own guileless heart—hadst thou been silent, hadst thou not made a fatal legacy of these wretched charms——

ROL. Cora! what hateful suspicion has possessed thy mind?

CORA. Yes, yes, 'tis clear—his spirit was ensnar'd; he was led to the fatal spot, where mortal valour could not front a host of murderers—He fell—in vain did he exclaim for help to Rolla. At a distance you look'd on and smil'd—You could have saved him—could—but did not.

ROL. Oh, glorious sun! can I have deserved this? Cora, rather bid me strike this sword into my heart. 30

CORA. No! live! live for love! for that love thou seekest; whose blossoms are to shoot from the bleeding grave of thy betray'd and slaughter'd friend!—But thou hast borne to me the *last words* of my *Alonzo!* Now hear *mine*—Sooner shall this boy draw poison from this tortured breast— —sooner would I link me to the pallid corse of the meanest wretch that perish'd with Alonzo, than he call Rolla father—than I call Rolla husband!

ROL. Yet call me what I am—thy friend, thy protector!

CORA. [*Distractedly.*] Away! I have no protector but my God!—With this child in my arms will I hasten to the field of slaughter—There 40 with these hands will I turn up to the light every mangled body— seeking, howe'er by death disfigur'd, the sweet smile of my Alonzo:— with fearful cries I will shriek out his name till my veins snap! If the smallest spark of life remains, he will know the voice of his Cora, open for a moment his unshrouded eyes, and bless me with a last look: But if we find him not—Oh! then, my boy, we will to the Spanish camp— that look of thine will win me passage through a thousand swords— They too are men.—Is there a heart that could drive back the wife that seeks her bleeding husband; or the innocent babe that cries for his imprison'd father? No, no, my child, every where we shall be safe.— 50 A wretched mother bearing a poor orphan in her arms, has Nature's passport through the world. Yes, yes, my son, we'll go and seek thy father. [*Exit with the Child.*

ROL. [*After a pause of agitation.*] Could I have merited one breath of thy reproaches, Cora, I should be the wretch—I think I was not formed to be.—HER safety must be my present purpose—then to convince her she has wronged me! [*Exit.*

# SCENE III.

## PIZARRO'S *Tent.*

PIZARRO, *traversing the scene in gloomy and furious agitation.*

Well, capricious idol, Fortune, be my ruin thy work and boast. To myself I will still be true.—Yet ere I fall, grant me thy smile to prosper in one act of vengeance, and be that smile Alonzo's death.

*Enter* ELVIRA.

Who's there? who dares intrude? Why does my guard neglect their duty?

ELV. Your guard did what they could—but they knew their duty better than to enforce authority, when I refused obedience.

PIZ. And what is it you desire?

ELV. To see how a hero bears misfortune. Thou, Pizarro, art not now collected—not thyself.                                                                                                   10

PIZ. Wouldst thou I should rejoice that the spears of the enemy, led by accurs'd Alonzo, have pierced the bravest hearts of my followers?

ELV. No!—I would have thee cold and dark as the night that follows the departed storm; still and sullen as the awful pause that precedes Nature's convulsion: yet I would have thee feel assured that a new morning shall arise, when the warrior's spirit shall stalk forth—nor fear the future, nor lament the past.

PIZ. Woman! Elvira!—Why had not all my men hearts like thine?

ELV. Then would thy brows have this day worn the crown of Quito.

PIZ. Oh! hope fails me while that scourge of my life and fame, Alonzo,       20
leads the enemy.

ELV. Pizarro, I am come to probe the hero farther: not now his courage, but his magnanimity—Alonzo is your prisoner.

PIZ. How!

ELV. 'Tis certain; Valverde saw him even now dragged in chains within your camp. I chose to bring you the intelligence myself.

PIZ. Bless thee, Elvira, for the news!—Alonzo in my power!—then I am the conqueror—the victory is MINE!

ELV. Pizarro, this is savage and unmanly triumph. Believe me, you raise impatience in my mind to see the man whose valour, and whose genius,       30
awe Pizarro; whose misfortunes are Pizarro's triumph; whose bondage is Pizarro's safety.

PIZ. Guard!—[*Enter Guard.*]—Drag here the Spanish prisoner, Alonzo!
—Quick bring the traitor here.                                                   [*Exit Guard.*

ELV. What shall be his fate?

PIZ. Death! death! in lingering torments! protracted to the last stretch that burning vengeance can devise, and fainting life sustain.

ELV. Shame on thee! Wilt thou have it said that the Peruvians found Pizarro could not conquer till Alonzo felt that he could murder?

PIZ. Be it said—I care not. His fate is sealed.                                    40

ELV. Follow then thy will: but mark me; if basely thou dost shed the blood of this brave youth, Elvira's lost to thee for ever.

PIZ. Why this interest for a stranger? What is Alonzo's fate to thee?

ELV. His fate!—nothing!—thy glory, every thing!—Think'st thou I
could love thee stript of fame, of honour, and a just renown?—Know
me better.

PIZ. Thou shouldst have known ME better. Thou shouldst have known,
that, once provoked to hate, I am for ever fixed in vengeance.—
[ALONZO *is brought in, in chains, guarded.* ELVIRA *observes him with
attention and admiration.*]—Welcome, welcome, Don Alonzo de Molina;   50
'tis long since we have met: thy mended looks should speak a life of
rural indolence. How is it that amid the toils and cares of war thou
dost preserve the healthful bloom of careless ease? Tell me thy secret.

AL. Thou wilt not profit by it. Whate'er the toils or cares of war, peace
still is *here*. [*Putting his hand to his heart.*]

PIZ. Sarcastic boy!

ELV. Thou art answered rightly. Why sport with the unfortunate?

PIZ. And thou art wedded too, I hear; aye, and the father of a lovely
boy—the heir, no doubt, of all his father's loyalty; of all his mother's
faith.                                                                 60

AL. The heir, I trust, of all his father's scorn of fraud, oppression, and
hypocrisy—the heir, I hope, of all his mother's virtue, gentleness, and
truth—the heir, I am sure, to all Pizarro's hate.

PIZ. Really! Now do I feel for this poor orphan; for fatherless to-morrow's
sun shall see that child. Alonzo, thy hours are numbered.

ELV. Pizarro—no!

PIZ. Hence—or dread my anger.

ELV. I will not hence; nor do I dread thy anger.

AL. Generous loveliness! spare thy unavailing pity. Seek not to thwart
the tiger with his prey beneath his fangs.                             70

PIZ. Audacious rebel! Thou renegado from thy monarch and thy God!

AL. 'Tis false.

PIZ. Art thou not, tell me, a deserter from thy country's legions—and,
with vile heathens leagued, hast thou not warred against thy native
land?.

AL. No! Deserter I am none! I was not born among robbers! pirates!
murderers!—When those legions, lured by the abhorred lust of gold,
and by thy foul ambition urged, forgot the honour of Castilians, and
forsook the duties of humanity, THEY deserted ME. I have not warred
against my native land, but against those who have usurped its power.   80
The banners of my country, when first I followed arms beneath them,
were Justice, Faith, and Mercy. If these are beaten down and trampled
under foot—I have no country, nor exists the power entitled to reproach
me with revolt.

PIZ. The power to judge and punish thee at least exists.

AL. Where are my judges?

PIZ. Thou wouldst appeal to the war council?

AL. If the good Las-Casas have yet a seat there, yes; if not, I appeal to Heaven!

PIZ. And to impose upon the folly of Las-Casas, what would be the 90 excuses of thy treason?

ELV. The folly of Las-Casas!—Such, doubtless, his mild precepts seem to thy hard-hearted wisdom!—O! would I might have lived as I will die, a sharer in the follies of Las-Casas!

AL. To him I should not need to urge the foul barbarities which drove me from your side; but I would gently lead him by the hand through all the lovely fields of Quito; there, in many a spot where late was barrenness and waste, I would show him how now the opening blossom, blade, or perfumed bud, sweet bashful pledges of delicious harvest, wasting their incense to the ripening sun, give chearful promise to the 100 hope of industry. This, I would say, is my work! Next I should tell how hurtful customs, and superstitions strange and sullen, would often scatter and dismay the credulous minds of these deluded innocents; and then would I point out to him where now, in clustered villages, they live like brethren, social and confiding, while through the burning day Content sits basking on the cheek of Toil, till laughing Pastime leads them to the hour of rest—this too is mine!—And prouder yet— at that still pause between exertion and repose, belonging not to pastime, labour, or to rest, but unto Him who sanctions and ordains them all, I would show him many an eye, and many a hand, by gentle- 110 ness from error won, raised in pure devotion to the true and only God!— this too I could tell him is Alonzo's work!—Then would Las-Casas clasp me in his aged arms; from his uplifted eyes a tear of gracious thankful- ness would fall upon my head, and that one blessed drop would be to me at once *this* world's best proof, that I had acted rightly *here*, and surest hope of my Creator's mercy and reward *hereafter*.

ELV. Happy, virtuous Alonzo! And thou, Pizarro, wouldst appal with fear of death a man who thinks and acts as he does!

PIZ. Daring, obstinate enthusiast! But know the pious blessing of thy preceptor's tears does not await thee here: he has fled like thee—like 120 thee, no doubt, to join the foes of Spain. The perilous trial of the next reward you hope, is nearer than perhaps you've thought; for, by my country's wrongs, and by mine own, tomorrow's sun shall see thy death.

ELV. Hold!—Pizarro—hear me!—If not always *justly*, at least act always *greatly*. Name not thy country's wrongs—'tis plain they have no share in thy resentment. Thy fury 'gainst this youth is private hate, and deadly personal revenge; if this be so—and even now thy detected conscience in that look avows it—profane not the name of justice or thy country's cause, but let him arm, and bid him to the field on equal 13. terms.

PIZ. Officious advocate for treason—peace!—Bear him hence—he knows his sentence.

AL. Thy revenge is eager, and I'm thankful for it—to me thy haste is mercy. For thee, sweet pleader in misfortune's cause, accept my parting thanks. This camp is not thy proper sphere. Wert thou among yon *savages*, as they are called, thou'dst find companions more congenial to thy heart.

PIZ. Yes; she shall bear the tidings of thy death to Cora.

AL. Inhuman man! that pang at least might have been spared me; but 140 thy malice shall not shake my constancy. I go to death—many shall bless, and none will curse my memory. Thou still wilt live, and still wilt be—Pizarro.                [*Exit, guarded.*

ELV. Now by the indignant scorn that burns upon my cheek, my soul is shamed and sickened at the meanness of thy vengeance.

PIZ. What has thy romantic folly aimed at? He is mine enemy, and in my power.

ELV. He is in your power, and therefore is no more an enemy. Pizarro, I demand not of thee virtue—I ask not from thee nobleness of mind— I require only just dealing to the fame thou hast acquired; be not the 150 assassin of thine own renown. How often have you sworn that the sacrifice which thy wondrous valour's high report had won you from subdued Elvira, was the proudest triumph of your fame? Thou knowest I bear a mind not cast in the common mould—not formed for tame sequestered love—content 'mid household cares to prattle to an idle offspring, and wait the dull delight of an obscure lover's kindness—no! my heart was framed to look up with awe and homage to the object it adored; my ears to own no music but the thrilling records of his praise; my lips to scorn all babbling but the tales of his achievements; my brain to turn giddy with delight, reading the applauding 160 tributes of his monarch's and his country's gratitude; my every faculty to throb with transport, while I heard the shouts of acclamation which announced the coming of my hero; my whole soul to love him with devotion! with enthusiasm! to see no other object—to own no other tie—but to make HIM my WORLD! Thus to love is at least no common weakness.—Pizarro!—was not such my love for thee?

PIZ. It *was*, Elvira!

ELV. Then do not make me hateful to myself, by tearing off the mask at once—baring the hideous imposture that has undone me!—Do not an act which, howe'er thy present power may gloss it to the world, 170 will make thee hateful to all future ages—accursed and scorned by posterity.

PIZ. And should posterity applaud my deeds, think'st thou my mouldering bones would rattle then with transport in my tomb?—This is renown for visionary Boys to dream of—I understand it not. The fame I value

shall uplift my living estimation—o'erbear with popular support the
envy of my foes—advance my purposes, and aid my power.

ELV. Each word thou speakest—each moment that I hear thee—dispels
the fatal mist through which I've judged thee. Thou man of mighty
name, but little soul, I see thou wert not born to feel what genuine 180
fame and glory are—yes, prefer the flattery of thy own fleeting day to
the bright circle of a deathless name—yes, prefer to stare upon the
grain of sand on which you trample, to musing on the starred canopy
above thee. Fame, the sovereign deity of proud ambition, is not to be
worshipped so: who seeks alone for living homage, stands a mean
canvasser in her temple's porch, wooing promiscuously from the fickle
breath of every wretch that passes, the brittle tribute of his praise.
He dares not approach the sacred altar—no noble sacrifice of his is
placed there, nor ever shall his worship'd image, fix'd above, claim for
his memory a glorious immortality.                                      190

PIZ. Elvira, leave me.

ELV. Pizarro, you no longer love me.

PIZ. It is not so, Elvira. But what might I not suspect—this wondrous
interest for a stranger!—Take back thy reproach.

ELV. No, Pizarro; as yet I am not lost to you—one string still remains,
and binds me to your fate. Do not, I conjure you—do not for thine
own sake, tear it asunder—shed not Alonzo's blood!

PIZ. My resolution's fixed.

ELV. Even though that moment lost you Elvira for ever?

PIZ. Even so.                                                          200

ELV. Pizarro, if not to honour, if not to humanity, yet listen to affection;
bear some memory of the sacrifices I have made for thy sake. Have
I not for thee quitted my parents, my friends, my fame, my native land?
When escaping, did I not risk in rushing to thy arms to bury myself
in the bosom of the deep? Have I not shared all thy perils, heavy
storms at sea, and frightful 'scapes on shore? Even on this dreadful
day, amid the rout of battle, who remained firm and constant at
Pizarro's side? Who presented her bosom as his shield to the assailing
foe?

PIZ. 'Tis truly spoken all. In love thou art thy sex's miracle—in war 210
the soldier's pattern—and therefore my whole heart and half my
acquisitions are thy right.

ELV. Convince me I possess the first—I exchange all title to the latter,
for—mercy to Alonzo.

PIZ. No more!—Had I intended to prolong his doom, each word thou
utterest now would hasten on his fate.

ELV. Alonzo then at morn will die?

PIZ. Think'st thou yon sun will set?—As surely at his rising shall
Alonzo die.

ELV. Then be it done—the string is crack'd—sundered for ever.—But  220
mark me—thou hast heretofore had cause, 'tis true, to doubt my resolution, howe'er offended—but mark me now—the lips which, cold and
jeering, barbing revenge with rancorous mockery, can insult a fallen
enemy, shall never more receive the pledge of love: the arm unshaken
by its bloody purpose, shall assign to needless torture the victim who
avows his heart, never more shall press the hand of faith!—Pizarro,
scorn not my words—beware you slight them not!—I feel how noble
are the motives which now animate my thoughts—who *could* not feel
as I do, I condemn—who, feeling so, yet *would* not act as I SHALL, I
despise!                                                                  230

PIZ. [*After a pause, looking at her with an affected smile of contempt.*] I
have heard thee, Elvira, and know well the *noble* motives which inspire
thee—fit advocate in virtue's cause!—Believe me, I pity thy tender
feelings for the youth Alonzo!—He dies at sun-rise!            [*Exit.*

ELV. 'Tis well! 'tis just I should be humbled—I had forgot myself, and
in the cause of innocence assumed the tone of virtue. 'Twas fit I should
be rebuked—and by Pizarro. Fall, fall, ye few reluctant drops of weakness—the last these eyes shall ever shed. How a woman can love
Pizarro, thou hast known too well—how she can hate, thou hast yet
to learn. Yes, thou undaunted! Thou, whom yet no mortal hazard has  240
appalled! Thou, who on Panama's brow didst make alliance with the
raving elements, that tore the silence of that horrid night—when thou
didst follow, as thy pioneer, the crashing thunder's drift, and stalking
o'er the trembling earth, didst plant thy banner by the red volcano's
mouth! Thou, who when battling on the sea, and thy brave ship was
blown to splinters, wast seen—as thou didst bestride a fragment of
the smoking wreck—to wave thy glittering sword above thy head—
as thou wouldst defy the world in that extremity!—Come, fearless
man—now meet the last and fellest peril of thy life—meet! and survive
—an injured woman's fury, if thou canst.                  [*Exit.* 250


END OF THE THIRD ACT[1]


[1] Kelly, *The Music of Pizarro*, pp. 21–4, adds words for a chorus by Cherubini,
sung by the priests at sacrifice:

> To thee be praise
> O Glorious Sun,
> Beneath whose beams
> The field was won!
> Raise high the voice,
> With shouts rejoice.

R. C. Rhodes, *The Plays and Poems of . . . Sheridan* (Oxford, 1928), iii. 59, prints this as
Scene iv, and says that it appears in the editions (1823) of Dolby and of Hughes.

# ACT IV

## SCENE I

*A Dungeon in the Rock, near the Spanish Camp.*—ALONZO *in Chains.*—
*A* CENTINEL *walking near the Entrance.*

ALONZO. For the last time, I have beheld the shadow'd ocean close
upon the light.—For the last time, thro' my cleft dungeon's roof,
I now behold the quivering lustre of the stars.—For the last time, O
sun! (and soon the hour) I shall behold thy rising, and thy level beams
melting the pale mists of morn to glittering dewdrops.—Then comes
my death, and in the morning of my day, I fall, which—No, Alonzo,
date not the life which thou hast run, by the mean reck'ning of the hours
and days, which thou hast breath'd: A life spent worthily should be
measured by a nobler line—by deeds—not years—Then woud'st thou
murmur not—but bless the Providence, which in so short a span, made 10
THEE the instrument of wide and spreading blessings, to the helpless
and oppress'd!—Tho' sinking in decrepid age—HE prematurely falls,
whose memory records no benefit conferred by him on man: They
only have lived long, who have lived virtuously.

*Enter a* SOLDIER—*shews the* CENTINEL *a Passport, who withdraws.*

ALONZO. What bear you there?
SOL. These refreshments I was order'd to leave in your dungeon.
AL. By whom order'd?
SOL. By the lady Elvira; she will be here herself before the dawn.
AL. Bear back to her my humblest thanks; and take thou the refresh-
ments, friend—I need them not.                                         20
SOL. I have served under you, Don Alonzo.—Pardon my saying, that
my heart pities you.                                          [*Exit.*
AL. In Pizarro's camp, to pity the unfortunate, no doubt requires forgive-
ness.—[*Looking out*] Surely, even now, thin streaks of glimmering light
steal on the darkness of the East.—If so, my life is but one hour more.—
I will not watch the coming dawn; but in the darkness of my cell, my
last prayer to thee, Power Supreme! shall be for my wife and child!—
Grant them to dwell in innocence and peace; grant health and purity
of mind—all else is worthless. [*Enters the Cavern.*]
CEN. Who's there? answer quickly! who's there?                         30
ROL. A Friar, come to visit your prisoner.

ROLLA *enters, disguised as a Monk.*

ROL. Inform me, friend—Is not Alonzo, the Spanish prisoner, confined
in this dungeon?

CEN. He is.

ROL. I must speak with him.

CEN. You must not.

ROL. He is my friend.

CEN. Not if he were your brother.

ROL. What is to be his fate?

CEN. He dies at sun-rise.                40

ROL. Ha!—then I am come in time.

CEN. Just—to witness his death.

ROL. Soldier—I must speak with him.

CEN. Back,—back.—It is impossible!—

ROL. I do entreat you, but for one moment!

CEN. You entreat in vain—my orders are most strict.

ROL. Even now, I saw a messenger go hence.

CEN. He brought a pass, which we are all accustomed to obey.

ROL. Look on this wedge of massive gold—look on these precious gems.
—In thy own land they will be wealth for thee and thine, beyond thy  50
hope or wish. Take them—they are thine.—Let me but pass one minute
with Alonzo.

CEN. Away!—woud'st thou corrupt me?—Me!—an old Castilian!—I
know my duty better.

ROL. Soldier!—hast thou a wife?

CEN. I have.

ROL. Hast thou children?

CEN. Four—honest, lively boys.

ROL. Where did'st thou leave them?

CEN. In my native village—even in the cot where myself was born.    60

ROL. Do'st thou love thy children and thy wife?

CEN. Do I love them! God knows my heart,—I do.

ROL. Soldier! imagine thou wer't doom'd to die a cruel death in this
strange land—What would be thy last request?

CEN. That some of my comrades should carry my dying blessing to my
wife and children.

ROL. Oh! but if that comrade was at thy prison gate—and should there
be told——thy fellow soldier dies at sun-rise,—yet thou shalt not for
a moment see him—nor shalt thou bear his dying blessing to his poor
children or his wretched wife,—what would'st thou think of him, who  70
thus cou'd drive thy comrade from the door?

CEN. How!

ROL. Alonzo has a wife and child—I am come but to receive for *her*, and
for her *babe*, the last blessing of my friend.

CEN. Go in.—[*Retires.*]

ROL. Oh! holy Nature! thou do'st never plead in vain—There is not, of
our earth, a creature bearing form, and life, human or savage—native

of the forest wild, or giddy air—around whose parent bosom, THOU hast not a cord entwined of power to tie them to their offspring's claims, and at thy will to draw them back to thee. On iron pennons borne—the 80 blood-stain'd vulture, cleaves the storm—yet, is the plumage closest to her heart, soft as the Cygnet's down, and o'er her unshell'd brood, the murmuring ring-dove sits not more gently!—Yes—now he is beyond the porch, barring the outer gate! Alonzo!—Alonzo!—my friend! Ha!—in gentle sleep!—Alonzo—rise!

AL. How!—Is my hour elaps'd?—Well, [*returning from the recess,*] I am ready.

ROL. Alonzo,—know me.

AL. What voice is that?

ROL. 'Tis Rolla's. 90

AL. Rolla!—my friend!—[*Embraces him.*] Heavens! how could'st thou pass the guard? Did this habit——

ROL. There is not a moment to be lost in words;—this disguise I tore from the dead body of a Friar, as I pass'd our field of battle—it has gain'd me entrance to thy dungeon—now take it thou, and fly.

AL. And Rolla——

ROL. Will remain here in thy place.

AL. And die for me!—No!—Rather eternal tortures rack me.

ROL. I shall not die, Alonzo.—It is *thy* life Pizarro seeks, not Rolla's— and from my prison soon will thy arm deliver me;—or, should it be 100 otherwise—I am as a blighted Plantain standing alone amid the sandy desart—Nothing seeks or lives beneath my shelter—Thou art a husband, and a father—The being of a lovely wife and helpless infant hang upon thy life—Go!—Go!—Alonzo!—Go—to save—not thyself—but Cora, and thy child!—

AL. Urge me not thus, my friend—I had prepar'd to die in peace.

ROL. To die in peace!—devoting her you've sworn to live for,—to madness, misery, and death!—For, be assured—the state I left her in forbids all hope, but from thy quick return.

AL. Oh! God! 110

ROL. If thou art yet irresolute, Alonzo—now heed me well.—I think thou hast not known that Rolla ever pledg'd his word, and shrunk from its fulfilment.—And, by the heart of truth I swear, if thou art proudly obstinate to deny thy friend the transport of preserving Cora's life, in thee,—no power that sways the will of man shall stir me hence;— and thou'lt but have the desperate triumph, of seeing Rolla perish by thy side,—with the assur'd conviction, that Cora, and thy child, are lost for ever.

AL. Oh! Rolla!—you distract me!

ROL. A moment's further pause, and all is lost—The dawn approaches 120 —Fear not for me—I will treat with Pizarro as for surrender and submission;—I shall gain time, doubt not—while thou, with a chosen band, passing the secret way, may'st at night return—release thy friend, and bear him back in triumph.—Yes—hasten—dear Alonzo!— Even now I hear the frantic Cora call thee!—Haste!—Haste!—Haste!

AL. Rolla, I fear your friendship drives me from honour, and from right.

ROL. Did Rolla ever counsel dishonour to his friend?

AL. Oh! my preserver!—[*Embracing him.*]

ROL. I feel thy warm tears dropping on my cheek—Go!—I am rewarded —[*Throws the Friar's garment over* ALONZO.]—There!—conceal thy face; and that they may not clank, hold fast thy chains—Now—God be with thee! 130

AL. At night we meet again.—Then,—so aid me Heaven! I return to save—or—perish with thee! [*Exit.*

ROL. [*alone.*] He has pass'd the outer porch—He is safe!—He will soon embrace his wife and child!—Now, Cora, did'st thou not wrong me? This is the first time throughout my life I ever deceived man—Forgive me, God of truth! if I am wrong—Alonzo flatters himself that we shall meet again—Yes—There! [*lifting his hands to heaven*] assuredly, we shall meet again:—there possess in peace, the joys of everlasting love, and friendship—on earth, imperfect, and embitter'd.—I will retire, lest the guard return before Alonzo may have pass'd their lines. 140

[*Retires into the Recess.*

*Enter* ELVIRA.

ELV. No—not Pizarro's brutal taunts—not the glowing admiration which I feel for this noble youth, shall raise an interest in my harrass'd bosom which honour would not sanction. If he reject the vengeance my heart has sworn against the tyrant, whose death alone can save this land— yet, shall the delight be mine to restore him to his Cora's arms, to his dear child, and to the unoffending people, whom his virtues guide, and valour guards.—Alonzo, come forth!

*Enter* ROLLA.

Ha!—who art thou?—Where is Alonzo? 150

ROL. Alonzo's fled.

ELV. Fled!

ROL. Yes—and he must not be pursued—Pardon this roughness, [*seizing her hand*]—but a moment's precious to Alonzo's flight.

ELV. What if I call the guard?

ROL. Do so—Alonzo still gains time.

ELV. What if thus I free myself? [*Shews a dagger.*]

ROL. Strike it to my heart—Still, with the convulsive grasp of death, I'll hold thee fast.

ELV. Release me—I give my faith, I neither will alarm the guard, nor   160
cause pursuit.

ROL. At once, I trust thy word—A feeling boldness in those eyes assures
me that thy soul is noble.

ELV. What is thy name? Speak freely—By my order the guard is remov'd
beyond the outer porch.

ROL. My name is Rolla.

ELV. The Peruvian Leader?

ROL. I was so yesterday—To-day, the Spaniard's captive.

ELV. And friendship for Alonzo, moved thee to this act?

ROL. Alonzo is my friend—I am prepared to die for him. Yet is the   170
cause a motive stronger far than friendship.

ELV. One only passion else could urge such generous rashness.

ROL. And that is——

ELV. Love?

ROL. True!

ELV. Gallant!—ingenuous Rolla!—Know that my purpose here was
thine; and were I to save thy friend——

ROL. How!—a woman bless'd with gentleness and courage, and yet not
Cora!

ELV. Does Rolla think so meanly of all female hearts?                180

ROL. Not so—you are worse and better than we are!

ELV. Were I to save thee, Rolla, from the tyrant's vengeance—restore
thee to thy native land—and thy native land to peace—would'st thou
not rank Elvira with the good?

ROL. To judge the action, I must know the means.

ELV. Take this dagger.

ROL. How to be used!

ELV. I will conduct thee to the tent where fell Pizarro sleeps—The
scourge of innocence—the terror of thy race—the fiend, that desolates
thy afflicted country.                                               190

ROL. Have you not been injur'd by Pizarro?

ELV. Deeply as scorn and insult can infuse their deadly venom.

ROL. And you ask that I shall murder him in his sleep!

ELV. Would he not have murder'd Alonzo in his chains? He that sleeps,
and he that's bound, are equally defenceless. Hear me, Rolla—so may
I prosper in this perilous act as searching my full heart, I have put by
all rancorous motive of private vengeance there, and feel that I advance
to my dread purpose in the cause of human nature, and at the call of
sacred justice.

ROL. The God of Justice sanctifies no evil as a step towards good. Great   200
actions cannot be achieved by wicked means.

ELV. Then, Peruvian! since thou do'st feel so coldly for thy country's
wrongs, this hand, tho' it revolt my soul, shall strike the blow.

ROL. Then is thy destruction certain, and for Peru thou perishest!—
Give me the dagger!

ELV. Now follow me;—but first—and dreadful is the hard necessity—
you must strike down the guard.

ROL. The soldier who was on duty here?

ELV. Yes, him—else, seeing thee, the alarm will be instant.

ROL. And I must stab that soldier as I pass?—Take back thy dagger.    210

ELV. Rolla!

ROL. That soldier, mark me, is a man.—All are not men that bear the
human form. He refus'd my prayers—refus'd my gold—denying to
admit me—till his own feelings brib'd him.—For my nations' safety,
I would not harm that man!

ELV. Then he must with us—I will answer for his safety.

ROL. Be that plainly understood between us:—for, whate'er betide our
enterprize, I will not risk a hair of that man's head, to save my heart-
strings from consuming fire.                              [*Exeunt.*

## SCENE II

*The inside of* PIZARRO's *Tent.—*PIZARRO *on a Couch, in disturbed sleep.*

PIZ. [*in his sleep.*] No mercy, traitor.—Now at his heart!—Stand off
there, you—Let me see him bleed!—Ha! ha! ha!—Let me hear that
groan again.

### *Enter* ROLLA *and* ELVIRA.

ELV. There!—Now, lose not a moment.

ROL. You must leave me now.—This scene of blood fits not a woman's
presence.

ELV. But a moment's pause may—

ROL. Go!—Retire to your own tent—and return not here—I will come
to you—Be thou not known in this business, I implore you!

ELV. I will withdraw the guard that waits.          [*Exit* ELVIRA.    10

RQL. Now have I in my power the accurs'd destroyer of my country's
peace: yet tranquilly he rests.—God!—can this man sleep?

PIZ. [*in his sleep.*] Away! away!—Hideous fiends!—Tear not my bosom
thus!

ROL. No:—I was in error—the balm of sweet repose he never more can
know.—Look here, ambition's fools!—Ye, by whose inhuman pride,
the bleeding sacrifice of nations is held as nothing—behold the rest
of the guilty!—He is at my mercy—and one blow!—No!—my heart
and hand refuse the act: Rolla cannot be an assassin!—Yet Elvira must
be saved! [*Approaches the Couch.*] Pizarro! awake!—                20

PIZ. [*Starts up.*] Who?—Guard!—

ROL. Speak not—another word is thy death—Call not for aid!—this arm
will be swifter than thy guard.

PIZ. Who art thou? and what is thy will?

ROL. I am thine enemy! Peruvian Rolla!—Thy death is not my will, or I could have slain thee sleeping.

PIZ. Speak, what else?

ROL. Now thou art at my mercy—answer me! Did a Peruvian ever yet wrong or injure thee, or any of thy nation? Didst thou, or any of thy nation, ever yet shew mercy to a Peruvian in your power? Now shalt 30 thou feel—and if thou hast a heart, thou'lt feel it keenly!—a Peruvian's vengeance! [*Drops the dagger at his feet*] There!

PIZ. Is it possible! [*Walks aside confounded.*]

ROL. Can Pizarro be surprised at this? I thought Forgiveness of Injuries had been the Christian's precept—Thou seest, at least, it is the Peruvian's practice.

PIZ. Rolla—thou hast indeed surpris'd—subdued me. [*Walks again aside as in irresolute thought.*]

*Re-enter* ELVIRA, [*not seeing* PIZARRO].

ELV. Is it done? Is he dead? [*Sees* PIZARRO] How!—still living! Then I am lost! And for you, wretched Peruvians! mercy is no more!—Oh! Rolla! treacherous, or cowardly?— 40

PIZ. How can it be, that—

ROL. Away Elvira speaks she knows not what! Leave me [*to* ELVIRA] I conjure you, with Pizarro.

ELV. How!—Rolla, do'st thou think I shall retract—or that I meanly will deny, that in thy hand *I* plac'd a poignard to be plung'd into that tyrant's heart? No:—my sole regret is, that I trusted to thy weakness, and did not strike the blow myself.—Too soon thou'lt learn that mercy to that man is direct cruelty to all thy race!

PIZ. Guard! quick! a guard, to seize this frantic woman.

ELV. Yes, a guard! I call them too! And soon I know they'll lead me to 50 my death. But think not, Pizarro, the fury of thy flashing eyes shall awe me for a moment!—Nor think that woman's anger, or the feelings of an injur'd heart, prompted me to this design—No! Had I been only influenced so—this failing, shame and remorse would weigh me down. But tho' defeated and destroyed, as now I am, such is the greatness of the cause that urged me, I shall perish, glorying in the attempt, and my last breath of life shall speak the proud avowal of my purpose— to have rescued millions of innocents from the blood-thirsty tyranny of ONE—by ridding the insulted world of THEE.

ROL. Had the act been noble as the motive—Rolla would not have shrunk 60 from its performance.

*Enter* GUARDS.

PIZ. Seize this discover'd fiend, who sought to kill your Leader.

ELV. Touch me not, at the peril of your souls;—I am your prisoner, and
will follow you.—But thou, their triumphant Leader, shalt hear me.
Yet, first—for thee, Rolla, accept my forgiveness: even had I been the
victim of thy nobleness of heart, I should have admir'd thee for it—
But 'twas myself provok'd my doom—Thou would'st have shielded
me.—Let not thy contempt follow me to the grave. Didst thou but know
the spell-like arts, by which this hypocrite first undermin'd the virtue
of a guileless heart! how, even in the pious sanctuary wherein I dwelt,   70
by corruption and by fraud, he practis'd upon those in whom I most
confided—'till my distemper'd fancy led me, step by step, into the
abyss of guilt——

PIZ. Why am I not obey'd?—Tear her hence!

ELV. 'Tis past—but didst thou know my story, Rolla, thou would'st
pity me.

ROL. From my soul I do pity thee!

PIZ. Villains! drag her to the dungeon!—prepare the torture instantly.

ELV. Soldiers—but a moment more—'Tis to applaud your General—
It is to tell the astonished world, that, for once, Pizarro's sentence is an   80
act of justice: Yes, rack me with the sharpest tortures that ever agoniz'd
the human frame; it will be justice. Yes—bid the minions of thy fury—
wrench forth the sinews of those arms that have caress'd, and——even
have defended thee! Bid them pour burning metal into the bleeding
cases of these eyes, that so oft—oh, God!—have hung with love and
homage on thy looks—then approach me bound on the abhorred
wheel—there glut thy savage eyes with the convulsive spasms of that
dishonour'd bosom, which was once thy pillow!—Yet, will I bear it all;
for it will be justice, all! And when thou shalt bid them tear me to my
death, hoping that thy unshrinking ears may at last be feasted with the   90
music of my cries, I will not utter one shriek or groan—but to the last
gasp, my body's patience shall deride thy vengeance, as my soul defies
thy power.

PIZ. [*Endeavouring to conceal his agitation.*] Hear'st thou the wretch whose
hands were even now prepared for murder?

ROL. Yes! And if her accusation's false, thou wilt not shrink from hearing
her: if true, thy barbarity cannot make *her* suffer the pangs thy conscience will inflict on *thee*.

ELV. And now, farewell, world!—Rolla, farewell!—Farewell, thou condemn'd of Heaven! [*to* PIZARRO;]—for repentance and remorse, I   100
know, will never touch thy heart.—We shall meet again.—Ha! be it
thy horror here, to know that we shall meet hereafter! And when thy
parting hour approaches—hark to the knell, whose dreadful beat will
strike to thy despairing soul. Then, will vibrate on thy ear the curses of
the cloister'd saint from whom you stole me. Then, the last shrieks
which burst from my mother's breaking heart, as she died, appealing

to her God against the seducer of her child! Then the blood-stifled groan of my murder'd brother—murdered by thee, fell monster!—seeking atonement for his sister's ruin'd honour.—I hear them now! To me, the recollection's madness!—At such an hour,—what will it be to thee? 110

PIZ. A moment's more delay, and at the peril of your lives——

ELV. I have spoken—and the last mortal frailty of my heart is past.—And now, with an undaunted spirit, and unshaken firmness, I go to meet my destiny. That I could not *live* nobly, has been PIZARRO'S ACT. That I will *die* nobly, shall be my OWN.          [*Exit, guarded.*

PIZ. Rolla, I would not thou, a warrior, valiant and renown'd, should'st credit the vile tales of this frantic woman. The cause of all this fury—O! a wanton passion for the rebel youth Alonzo, now my prisoner.

ROL. Alonzo is not now thy prisoner.          120

PIZ. How!

ROL. I came to rescue him—to deceive his guard—I have succeeded;—*I* remain thy prisoner.

PIZ. Alonzo fled!—Is then the vengeance dearest to my heart never to be gratified?

ROL. Dismiss such passions from thy heart; then thou'lt consult it's peace.

PIZ. I can face all enemies that dare confront me—I cannot war against my nature.

ROL. Then, Pizarro, ask not to be deem'd a hero—To triumph o'er our- 130 selves, is the only conquest, where fortune makes no claim. In battle, chance may snatch the laurel from thee, or chance may place it on thy brow—but in a contest with yourself, be resolute, and the virtuous impulse must be the victor.

PIZ. Peruvian! thou shalt not find me to *thee* ungrateful, or ungenerous—Return to your countrymen—You are at liberty.

ROL. Thou do'st act in this, as honour, and as duty, bid thee.

PIZ. I cannot but admire thee, Rolla; I wou'd we might be friends.

ROL. Farewell.—Pity Elvira!—Become the friend of virtue—and thou wilt be mine.          [*Exit.* 140

PIZ. Ambition! tell me what is the phantom I have follow'd? where is the one delight which it has made my own? My fame is the mark of envy—my love the dupe of treachery—my glory eclips'd by the boy I taught—my revenge defeated and rebuked by the rude honour of a savage foe—before whose native dignity of soul I have sunk confounded and subdued! I would I cou'd retrace my steps—I cannot—Would I could evade my own reflections!—No!—thought and memory are my Hell.          [*Exit.*

END OF THE FOURTH ACT

# ACT V

## SCENE I

*A thick Forest—In the background, a Hut almost covered by Boughs of Trees—A dreadful Storm, with Thunder and Lightning.*—CORA *has covered her Child on a Bed of Leaves and Moss—Her whole appearance is wild and distracted.*

CORA. O nature! thou hast not the strength of love. My anxious spirit is untired in its march; my wearied, shivering frame, sinks under it. And, for thee, my boy—when faint beneath thy lovely burthen, could I refuse to give thy slumbers that poor bed of rest! O my child! were I assured thy father breathes no more, how quickly would I lay me down by thy dear side—but down—down for ever. [*Thunder and lightning.*] I ask thee not, unpitying storm! to abate thy rage, in mercy to poor Cora's misery; nor while thy thunders spare his slumbers will I disturb my sleeping cherub. Though Heaven knows I wish to hear the voice of life, and feel that life is near me. But I will endure all while  10 what I have of reason holds.

### SONG.[1]

Yes, yes, be merciless, thou Tempest dire;
  Unaw'd, unshelter'd, I thy fury brave:
I'll bare my bosom to thy forked fire,
  Let it but guide me to ALONZO's grave!

O'er his pale corse then while thy lightnings glare,
I'll press his clay-cold lips, and perish there.

But thou wilt wake again, my boy,
Again thou'lt rise to life and joy,
  Thy father never!——                              20
Thy laughing eyes will meet the light,
Unconscious that eternal night
  Veils his for ever.

On yon green bed of moss there lies my child,
  Oh! safer lies from these chill'd arms apart;
He sleeps, sweet lamb! nor heeds the tempest wild,
  Oh! sweeter sleeps, than near this breaking heart.

Alas! my babe, if thou would'st peaceful rest,
Thy cradle must not be thy mother's breast.

---

[1] See Kelly, *The Music of Pizarro*, pp. 25–8. It was by Kelly himself to words by Sheridan. Kelly prints 'kiss' for 'press' (l. 17); 'But' for 'Yet' (l. 30).

Yet, thou wilt wake again, my boy,                                          30
Again thou'lt rise to life and joy,
   Thy father never!——
Thy laughing eyes will meet the light,
Unconscious that eternal night
   Veils his for ever.                           [*Thunder and lightning.*]

CORA. Still, still, implacable! unfeeling elements! yet still dost thou
sleep, my smiling innocent! O, death! when wilt thou grant to this
babe's mother such repose? Sure I may shield thee better from the
storm; my veil may——
   *While she is wrapping her mantle and her veil over him,* ALONZO's *voice*
   *is heard at a great distance.*
AL. Cora!                                                                   40
CORA. Hah!!! [*rises.*]
AL. [*again*] Cora!
CORA. O, my heart! Sweet Heaven deceive me not!—Is it not Alonzo's
voice?
AL. [*nearer*] Cora!
CORA. It is—it is Alonzo!
AL. [*nearer still*] Cora! my beloved!——
CORA. Alonzo!—Here!—here!—Alonzo!                            [*Runs out.*

### Enter two *Spanish* SOLDIERS.

1ST SOL. I tell you we are near our out-posts, and the word we heard
just now was the countersign.                                               50
2D SOL. Well, in our escape from the enemy, to have discover'd their
secret passage thro' the rocks, will prove a lucky chance to us—Pizarro
will reward us.
1ST SOL. This way—The sun, though clouded, is on our left. [*Perceives
the child.*] What have we here?—A child!—as I'm a soldier.
2D SOL. 'Tis a sweet little babe. Now would it be a great charity to take
this infant from its pagan mother's power.
1ST SOL. It would so—I have one at home shall play with it.—Come
along.                                                        [*Takes the child.*
                                         [*Exeunt.*

### Re-enter CORA *with* ALONZO.

CORA. [*speaking without*] This way, dear Alonzo. Now am I right—there   60
—there—under that tree. Was it possible the instinct of mother's heart
could mistake the spot! Now will you look at him as he sleeps, or shall
I bring him waking with his full blue laughing eyes to welcome you at
once—Yes—yes.—Stand thou there—I'll snatch him from his rosy
slumber, blushing like the perfum'd morn.

*She runs up to the spot, and, finding only the mantle and veil, which she tears from the ground, and the child gone, [shrieks] and stands in speechless agony.*

AL. [*running to her*] Cora!—my heart's beloved!

CORA. He is gone!

AL. Eternal God!

CORA. He is gone!—my child! my child!

AL. Where did you leave him?                                          70

CORA. [*Dashing herself on the spot.*] Here!

AL. Be calm, beloved Cora—he has wak'd, and crept to a little distance— we shall find him—Are you assured this was the spot you left him in?

CORA. Did not these hands make that bed, and shelter for him?—and is not this the veil that covered him?

AL. Here is a hut yet unobserved.

CORA. Ha! yes, yes! there lives the savage that has rob'd me of my child— [*Beats at the door, exclaiming*] Give me back my child—restore to me my boy!

*Enter* LAS CASAS *from the Hut.*

LAS C. Who calls me from my wretched solitude?                        80

CORA. Give me back my child! [*Goes into the hut, and calls*] Fernando!

AL. Almighty powers! do my eyes deceive me! Las Casas!!!

LAS C. Alonzo,—my belov'd young friend!

AL. My rever'd instructor. [*Embracing.*]

CORA. [*Return'd.*] Will you embrace this man before he restores my boy?

AL. Alas, my friend—in what a moment of misery do we meet!

CORA. Yet his look is goodness and humanity.—Good old man, have compassion on a wretched mother—and I will be your servant while I live.—But do not, for pity's sake—do not say, you have him not— do not say, you have not seen him.                    [*Runs into the Wood.*]  90

LAS C. What can this mean?

AL. She is my wife.—Just rescued from the Spaniards' prison, I learn'd she had fled to this wild forest—Hearing my voice, she left the child, and flew to meet me—he was left sleeping under yonder tree.

LAS C. How! did you leave him?—[CORA *returns.*]

CORA. O, you are right!—right!—unnatural mother, that I was—I left my child—I forsook my innocent——but I will fly to the earth's brink, but I will find him. [*Runs out.*]

AL. Forgive me, Las Casas, I must follow her: for at night, I attempt brave Rolla's rescue.                                               100

LAS C. I will not leave thee, Alonzo—you must try to lead her to the right—that way lies your camp—Wait not my infirm steps,—I follow thee, my friend.                                          [*Exeunt.*

## SCENE II

*The Out-Post of the Spanish Camp.—The back ground wild and rocky, with a Torrent falling down the Precipice, over which a Bridge is formed by a fell'd Tree.* [*Trumpets sound without.*

ALMAGRO. [*Without.*] Bear him along—his story must be false. [*Entering.*]

ROLLA [*in Chains*] brought in by SOLDIERS.

ROL. False!—Rolla, utter falsehood!—I would I had thee in a desert with thy troop around thee;—and I, but with my sword in this unshackled hand!—[*Trumpets without.*]

ALM. Is it to be credited that Rolla, the renown'd Peruvian hero—shou'd be detected like a spy, skulking thro' our camp?

ROL. Skulking!

ALM. But answer to the General—he is here.

*Enter* PIZARRO.

PIZ. What do I see! Rolla!

ROL. O! to thy surprise, no doubt.                                                        10

PIZ. And bound too!

ROL. So fast, thou need'st not fear approaching me.

ALM. The guards surpris'd him, passing our out-post.

PIZ. Release him instantly.—Believe me, I regret this insult.

ROL. You feel then as you ought.

PIZ. Nor can I brook to see a warrior of Rolla's fame disarm'd—Accept this, tho' it has been thy enemy's. [*Gives a sword.*] The Spaniards know the courtesy that's due to valour.

ROL. And the Peruvian, how to forget offence.

PIZ. May not Rolla and Pizarro cease to be foes?                                20

ROL. When the sea divides us; yes!—May I now depart?

PIZ. Freely.

ROL. And shall I not again be intercepted?

PIZ. No!—let the word be given that Rolla passes freely.

*Enter* DAVILLA *and* SOLDIERS, *with the* CHILD.

DAV. Here are two soldiers, captived yesterday, who have escap'd from the Peruvian hold,—and by the secret way we have so long endeavoured to discover.

PIZ. Silence,—imprudent!—Seest thou not—? [*pointing to* ROLLA.]

DAV. In their way, they found a Peruvian child, who seems——

PIZ. What is the imp to me?—Bid them toss it into the sea.        30

ROL. Gracious heaven! it is Alonzo's child!—give it to me.

PIZ. Ha! Alonzo's child!—Welcome, thou pretty hostage.—Now Alonzo is again my prisoner!

ROL. Thou wilt not keep the infant from its mother?

PIZ. Will I not!—What, when I shall meet Alonzo in the heat of the victorious fight—think'st thou I shall not have a check upon the valour of his heart, when he is reminded that a word of mine is this child's death?

ROL. I do not understand you.

PIZ. My vengeance has a long arrear of hate to settle with Alonzo!—and 40 this pledge may help to settle the account.

ROL. Man! Man!—Art thou a man?—Could'st thou hurt that innocent? —By Heaven! it's smiling in thy face.

PIZ. Tell me, does it resemble Cora?

ROL. Pizarro! thou hast set my heart on fire—If thou do'st harm that child—think not his blood will sink into the barren sand—No!—faithful to the eager hope that now trembles in this indignant heart—'twill rise to the common God of nature and humanity, and cry aloud for vengeance on its accurs'd destroyer's head.

PIZ. Be that peril mine. 50

ROL. [*Throwing himself at his feet*] Behold me at thy feet—Me, Rolla!— Me, the preserver of thy life!—Me, that have never yet bent or bow'd before created man!—In humble agony I sue to you—prostrate I implore you—but spare that child, and I will be your slave.

PIZ. Rolla! still art thou free to go—this boy remains with me.

ROL. Then was this sword Heaven's gift, not thine! [*Seizes the* CHILD]— Who moves one step to follow me, dies upon the spot.

[*Exit, with the* CHILD.

PIZ. Pursue him instantly—but spare his life. [*Exeunt* ALMAGRO *and* SOLDIERS.] With what fury he defends himself!—Ha!—he fells them to the ground—and now—— 60

*Enter* ALMAGRO.

ALM. Three of your brave soldiers are already victims to your command to spare this madman's life; and if he once gains the thicket——

PIZ. Spare him no longer. [*Exit* ALMAGRO.] Their guns must reach him—he'll yet escape—holloa to those horse—the Peruvian sees them—and now he turns among the rocks—then is his retreat cut off.

[ROLLA *crosses the wooden bridge over the cataract, pursued by the* SOLDIERS—*they fire at him—a shot strikes him*—PIZARRO *exclaims*——

PIZ. Now! quick! quick! seize the child!—

[ROLLA *tears from the rock the tree which supports the bridge, and retreats by the back ground, bearing off the child.*]

*Re-enter* ALMAGRO.

ALM. By Hell! he has escaped!—and with the child unhurt.

DAV. No—he bears his death with him—Believe me, I saw him struck upon the side.

PIZ. But the child is sav'd—Alonzo's child! Oh! the furies of disappointed  70
vengeance!

ALM. Away with the revenge of words—let us to deeds—Forget not we
have acquired the knowledge of the secret pass, which thro' the rocky
cavern's gloom brings you at once to the strong hold, where are lodg'd
their women, and their treasures.

PIZ. Right, Almagro! Swift as thy thought draw forth a daring and a
chosen band—I will not wait for numbers.—Stay, Almagro! Valverde
is informed Elvira dies to-day?

VAL. He is—and one request alone she——

PIZ. I'll hear of none.                                                  80

VAL. The boon is small—'tis but for the noviciate habit which you first
beheld her in—she wishes not to suffer in the gaudy trappings, which
remind her of her shame.

PIZ. Well, do as thou wilt—but tell Valverde, that at our return, as his
life shall answer it, to let me hear that she is dead.

[*Exeunt, severally.*

## SCENE III

### ATALIBA's *Tent.*

#### Enter ATALIBA, *follow'd by* CORA *and* ALONZO.

CORA. Oh! Avoid me not, Ataliba! To whom, but to her King, is the
wretched mother to address her griefs?—The Gods refuse to hear my
prayers! Did not my Alonzo fight for *you*?—and will not my sweet
boy, if thou'lt but restore him to me, one day fight thy battles too?

AL. Oh! my suffering love—my poor heart-broken Cora!—you but
wound our Sovereign's feeling soul, and not relieve thy own.

CORA. Is he our Sovereign, and has he not the power to give me back
my child?

ATA. When I reward desert, or can relieve my people, I feel what is the
real glory of a King—when I hear them suffer, and cannot aid them,  10
I mourn the impotence of all mortal power. [*Voices behind*] Rolla!
Rolla! Rolla!

#### Enter ROLLA, *bleeding, with the* CHILD, *follow'd by Peruvian* SOLDIERS.

ROL. Thy child! [*Gives the* CHILD *into* CORA's *arms, and falls.*]

CORA. Oh God!—there's blood upon him!

ROL. 'Tis my blood, Cora!

AL. Rolla, thou diest!

ROL. For thee, and Cora—[*Dies.*]

*Enter* ORANO.

ORANO. Treachery has revealed our asylum in the rocks. Even now the foe assails the peaceful band retired for protection there.

AL. Lose not a moment!—Swords be quick!—Your wives and children 20 cry to you—Bear our lov'd hero's body in the van—'Twill raise the fury of our men to madness.—Now, fell Pizarro! the death of one of us is near!—Away! Be the word of assault, Revenge and Rolla—[*Exeunt.*
[*Charge.*

## SCENE IV

*A romantic part of the Recess among the Rocks*—[Alarms] *Women are seen flying, pursued by the Spanish Soldiers,—The Peruvian Soldiers drive the Spaniards back from the Field.—The Fight is continued on the Heights.*

*Enter* PIZARRO, ALMAGRO, VALVERDE, *and Spanish* SOLDIERS.

PIZ. Well!—if surrounded, we must perish in the centre of them—Where do Rolla and Alonzo hide their heads?

*Enter* ALONZO, ORANO, *and Peruvians.*

AL. Alonzo answers thee, and Alonzo's sword shall speak for Rolla.

PIZ. Thou know'st the advantage of thy numbers.—Thou dar'st not singly face Pizarro.

AL. Peruvians, stir not a man!—Be this contest only our's.

PIZ. Spaniards!—observe ye the same.          [*Charge.*
*They fight.* ALONZO'S *shield is broken, and he is beat down.*

PIZ. Now, traitor, to thy heart!
*At this moment* ELVIRA *enters, habited as when* PIZARRO *first beheld her.—*PIZARRO, *appalled, staggers back.—*ALONZO *renews the Fight, and slays him.*          [*Loud shouts from the Peruvians.*

ATALIBA *enters, and embraces* ALONZO.

ATA. My brave Alonzo!

ALM. Alonzo, we submit.—Spare us! we will embark, and leave the 10 coast.

VAL. Elvira will confess I sav'd her life; she has sav'd thine.

AL. Fear not. You are safe. [*Spaniards lay down their arms.*]

ELV. Valverde speaks the truth;—nor could he think to meet me here.— An awful impulse which my soul could not resist, impell'd me hither.

AL. Noble Elvira! my preserver! How can I speak what I, Ataliba, and his rescued country, owe to thee? If amid this grateful nation thou would'st remain——

ELV. Alonzo, no!—the destination of my future life is fix'd. Humbled
in penitence, I will endeavour to atone the guilty errors, which, how-   20
ever mask'd by shallow cheerfulness, have long consum'd my secret
heart—When, by my sufferings purified, and penitence sincere, my
soul shall dare address the Throne of Mercy in behalf of others,—for
thee, Alonzo—for thy Cora, and thy child,—for thee, thou virtuous
Monarch, and the innocent race you reign over, shall Elvira's prayers
address the God of Nature.—Valverde, you have preserved my life.
Cherish humanity—avoid the foul examples thou hast view'd.—
Spaniards returning to your native home, assure your rulers, they
mistake the road to glory, or to power.—Tell them, that the pursuits
of avarice, conquest, and ambition, never yet made a people happy, or   30
a nation great.—[*Casts a look of agony on the dead body of* PIZARRO *as
she passes, and exit.*]                              [*Flourish of Trumpets.*

VALVERDE, ALMAGRO, *and Spanish* SOLDIERS, *exeunt, bearing off*
PIZARRO'S *Body.—On a signal from* ALONZO, *flourish of Music.*

AL. Ataliba! think not I wish to check the voice of triumph—when
I entreat we first may pay the tribute due to our lov'd Rolla's memory.

*A solemn March*[1]—*Procession of Peruvian Soldiers, bearing* ROLLA'S
*Body on a Bier, surrounded by Military Trophies. The Priests and
Priestesses attending chaunt a Dirge*[2] *over the Bier.*—ALONZO *and*
CORA *kneel on either side of it, and kiss* ROLLA'S *hands in silent agony—
In the looks of the King, and of all present, the Triumph of the Day is
lost, in mourning for the fallen Hero.* [*The Curtain slowly descends.*

----

[1] See Kelly, *The Music of Pizarro*, p. 29, 'Dead March'. No composer is named.

[2] Kelly, *The Music of Pizarro*, p. 30, reads: 'Sung by Mrs. Crouch, Miss Decamp,
Miss Dufour, Miss Leak, Miss Menage:

> Let the tears of gratitude and woe
> For the brave Rolla ever flow!'

It was by Kelly himself.

# EPILOGUE

WRITTEN BY THE HON. WILLIAM LAMB

SPOKEN BY MRS. JORDAN

ERE yet Suspense has still'd its throbbing fear,
Or Melancholy wip'd the grateful tear,
While e'en the miseries of a sinking State,
A Monarch's danger, and a Nation's fate,
Command not now your eyes with grief to flow,
Lost in a trembling Mother's nearer woe;
What moral lay shall Poetry rehearse,
Or how shall Elocution pour the verse
So sweetly, that its music shall repay
The lov'd illusion, which it drives away?                    10
Mine is the task, to rigid custom due,
To me ungrateful, as 'tis harsh to you,
To mar the work the tragic scene has wrought,
To rouse the mind that broods in pensive thought,
To scare Reflection, which, in absent dreams,
Still lingers musing on the recent themes;
Attention, ere with contemplation tir'd,
To turn from all that pleas'd, from all that fir'd;
To weaken lessons strongly now imprest,
And chill the interest glowing in the breast—             20
Mine is the task; and be it mine to spare
The souls that pant, the griefs they see, to share;
Let me with no unhallow'd jest deride
The sigh, that sweet Compassion owns with pride—
The sigh of Comfort, to Affliction dear,
That Kindness heaves, and Virtue loves to hear.
E'en gay THALIA will not now refuse
This gentle homage to her Sister-Muse.
    O ye, who listen to the plaintive strain,
With strange enjoyment, and with rapturous pain,          30
Who erst have felt the *Stranger*'s[1] lone despair,
And *Haller*'s settled, sad, remorseful care,

---

[1] Kotzebue's *Menschenhass und Reue* (1788), translated as *The Stranger* by Benjamin
Thompson, and adapted for performance at Drury Lane Theatre in 1798 by Sheridan.

Does *Rolla*'s pure affection less excite
The inexpressive anguish of delight?
Do *Cora*'s fears, which beat without control,
With less solicitude engross the soul?
Ah, no! your minds with kindred zeal approve
Maternal feeling, and heroic love.
You must approve; where Man exists below,
In temperate climes, or 'midst drear wastes of snow,          40
Or where the solar fires incessant flame,
Thy laws, all-powerful Nature, are the same:
Vainly the Sophist boasts, he can explain
The causes of thy universal reign—
More vainly would his cold presumptuous art
Disprove thy general empire o'er the heart:
A voice proclaims thee, that we must believe,
A voice, that surely speaks not to deceive;
That voice poor *Cora* heard, and closely prest
Her darling infant to her fearful breast;                     50
Distracted dar'd the bloody field to tread,
And sought *Alonzo* through the heaps of dead,
Eager to catch the music of his breath,
Though faltering in the agonies of death,
To touch his lips, though pale and cold, once more,
And clasp his bosom, though it stream'd with gore;
That voice too *Rolla* heard, and, greatly brave,
His *Cora*'s dearest treasure died to save,
Gave to the hopeless Parent's arms her child,
Beheld her transports, and expiring smil'd.                   60
That voice ye hear—Oh! be its will obey'd!
'Tis Valour's impulse and 'tis Virtue's aid—
It prompts to all Benevolence admires,
To all that heav'nly Piety inspires,
To all that Praise repeats through lengthen'd years,
That Honour sanctifies, and Time reveres.

THE END